ETHICS
AND THE
LEGAL
PROFESSION

ETHICS
AND THE
LEGAL
PROFESSION

EDITED BY MICHAEL DAVIS
AND FREDERICK A. ELLISTON

PROMETHEUS BOOKS
700 East Amherst Street, Buffalo, New York 14215

Published 1986 by Prometheus Books
700 East Amherst Street, Buffalo, New York 14215

Library of Congress Catalog Card Number: 86-61919
ISBN 0-87975-331-5

Printed in the United States of America

Acknowledgments

Dr. Michael Davis would like to thank the students and faculty of the Backus Law School of Case Western Reserve University for giving him the chance to learn about legal ethics by teaching "Professional Responsibility" during the 1974-1975 academic year; the lawyers of Cleveland for providing, out of their experience, many of the harder problems included here; his undergraduate research assistants at Illinois State University—Joe Polan, Sandra Rassler, Lisa Romero, and Bob Epperson—for helping with the bibliography by reading and commenting on much of the current legal ethics literature; and Louis Lombardi for useful advice on a much larger collection of readings used to teach an experimental undergraduate course in legal ethics at Illinois State University during 1981-1983, when Dr. Davis could find no text appropriate for undergraduates.

Dr. Frederick Elliston would like to thank Jane van Schaik for her counsel, both legal and nonlegal; Terrence O'Neill for his vigorous and conscientious bibliographic assistance at the Albany Law School; the indefatigable librarians at the Schenectady Public Library; Karen McLaughlin, who is the best sixteen-year-old word processor he knows; Dr. Mark Frankel, the director of the Center for the Study of Ethics in the Professions, at the Illinois Institute of Technology; and the center's staff, Philip MacFarland and Randy Tomaszewski.

Contents

Introduction

The Reemergence of Legal Ethics

This volume is predicated on the principle that ethics is neither an incidental adjunct to the curriculum, nor merely a way for lawyers to stay out of trouble. Rather, ethics is treated as central to the practice of law and so, to the understanding of that practice. But what is ethics, professional ethics in particular, and what is its place in the practice of law?

Legal ethics has a strong and venerable history in America, dating back to Judge Sharwood's essay in the mid-nineteenth century. In our own time it has reemerged as the result of a number of developments.

The Watergate scandal made the public aware of the questionable practices of notable lawyers. In its wake, the American Bar Association, beginning in 1974, mandated that law schools: ". . . provide and require for all student candidates for a professional degree, receive instruction in the duties and responsibilities of the legal profession."[1] A 1977 survey by the Association of American Law Schools found that the most popular approach to teaching professional responsibility is a required course, usually entitled "professional responsibility" or "legal ethics." In most of these, the *Model Rules of Professional Conduct* is the primary text, but frequently it is supplemented with case materials."[2]

Lawyers themselves have become increasingly concerned about their esteem— or, more precisely, the lack of it—in the public's eyes. A 1977 Gallup poll on the honesty of lawyers found that only twenty-six percent of the sample rated lawyers' standards as high or very high, while twenty-seven percent rated their standards as low or very low.[3] Members of the Virginia Bar, surveyed in 1978, believed that one out of every five lawyers frequently failed to perform satisfactory work for his or her clients.[4] The legal profession has come under attack from within and without by such notables as Ralph Nader, Monroe Freedman, and Chief Justice Warren Burger.[5] Today there is a growing consensus about the need for some measure of reform but it lacks a political, procedural, or philosophical base.

A third impetus for change has come from the ranks of philosophers. Trained in conceptual analysis and moral reasoning, they are intent on applying their expertise to the problems professionals face in diverse fields like medicine, engineering, computer science, policing, and law.

As a result of these political, professional, and philosophical forces, legal ethics is a growing but disjointed field. Concern about the professional conduct of lawyers has erupted periodically; it generates commissions, studies, and publications but eventually fades away. In the midst of these vicissitudes, can anything of permanent value be achieved?

ETHICS AND THE PRACTICE OF LAW[6]

More precisely, what can ethics contribute to the professional life of lawyers that is of enduring worth? The legal profession is ambivalent in its answer to this question. Sometimes ethics is treated as a necessary evil to be endured in law school, but put aside as one starts to practice law. At other times ethics is invoked to buttress the image of lawyers and to prove to the public that they are more than "hired guns."

The Rise of Professional Ethics

Over the past two decades there has been a revolution in philosophy, one having several dimensions—new courses, new texts, new professional societies, new research projects and new journals. In many philosophy departments courses are now offered that were unthinkable twenty years ago. Topics like civil disobedience, ecology, sports, death, drug use, victimless crimes, and human sexuality[7] are regularly covered. Specialized courses are offered to professional schools and programs including law, medicine, business, engineering, architecture, computer science, nursing, social work, journalism, and public health. Centers and institutes have been created at over a dozen universities to integrate these curricular offerings, to provide student internships and interdisciplinary degrees, and conduct major research projects. A great many books have been published on social and political issues such as feminism, euthanasia, homicide, animal rights, energy, immigration policy, parenting, the population explosion, affirmative action, criminal justice administration, and war.[8] New societies have been formed in the past two decades on law, ethics, social philosophy, sports, professional ethics, sex, and business.[9] In addition, journals have appeared during the past few years to promote this work.[10]

These developments reflect a growing awareness among philosophers that their theoretical reflections need to be tested against the realities of everyday life. The professions in turn have come to recognize that the many questions they confront go beyond their technical expertise and require clear articulation of ethical and social values as well as philosophical principles.

What is professional ethics and what can it hope to accomplish? In simple terms, it is the philosophical study of the moral problems that arise within a profession. In more theoretical terms, it is the articulation of a set of ethical principles that enable one to conceptualize and address these problems in a systematic and comprehensive fashion.

One can approach the professions in two ways. The first uses *case studies,* which outline the conduct of professionals and seek to understand and appraise the values and principles embedded in it. Are these consistent with each other? Do they advance the expressed goals and purposes of the particular profession? Are they the kinds of principles that a reasonable and objective person would choose?

The second approach takes standard ethical principles and seeks to *apply* them to professional conduct. If it is wrong in general for people to lie, then it is wrong for a physician to lie to dying patients about their illnesses. Or one can take standard moral prescriptions, such as respect for the autonomy of persons, and infer a moral injunction for physicians to secure the consent of patients before operating. Whether one begins with positive or negative moral imperatives, the logic is the same: to start with familiar moral rules and apply them to the actions and practices of professionals.

This metaphor of *applying* philosophy to a profession—as one might apply a bandaid to a cut—has seldom proved as straightforward as it might seem. Questions arise at both ends: What is one applying and to what does it get applied? It would certainly be convenient if one integrated and comprehensive set of principles, an ethical theory, existed that "fit" all the professions uniformly: then one would only need to take this theory and "apply" it by using each profession to instantiate its generalizations. Doing applied philosophy would then be comparable to doing engineering. Much as the engineer adapts the theoretical principles of physics, chemistry, and biology to solve practical problems, the applied philosopher would use the concepts and principles of ethical theories to solve professional problems. As in engineering, some "modifications" would be made to accommodate the realities of our everyday world. Unfortunately, no single ethical theory exists that resolves all or even most professional dilemmas in any satisfactory way. Even medical ethics, which has the longest history, has yet to see a well-received or widely-accepted theoretical account of what doctors should do. Indeed, philosophers disagree whether it is even possible to articulate a comprehensive theory of professional ethics.[11]

What Is a Profession?

Even if one assumes a comprehensive theory is possible, it is not altogether clear what the theory is supposed to apply to. In other words, exactly what is a profession? Most agree that doctors and lawyers are professionals, and many acknowledge that university faculty, engineers, accountants, and dentists are as well. But there is less agreement on social workers, nurses, politicians, police officers, and soldiers. A description of the term *profession* is needed.

Generally speaking, a profession is characterized by four traits: a specialized body of knowledge, a commitment to the social good, the ability to regulate itself, and high social status. These can be illustrated by looking at three professions.

Lawyers, engineers, and doctors all have *special skills* that enable them to do for us what we cannot readily do for ourselves. Engineers can build safe bridges, durable houses, and economical buildings. Doctors can cure us when we become sick and they help us avoid illness when we are well. Lawyers arrange our legal affairs, help us exercise and protect our rights, and defend these rights against violations. It is the unique ability to accomplish these objectives that distinguishes the three groups as professionals.

The knowledge professions have is their power, and our trust in them is based upon their commitment to use this power for the *social good*. All professionals have an implicit or explicit code of conduct committing them to use their special skills for the welfare of others. Lack of this commitment has prompted some to exclude business people *per se* from the ranks of the professions and to include judges and other public officials almost automatically.

Professions enjoy a significant measure of autonomy, protected by mechanism for *self-regulation*. Because professionals have an expertise that the average person lacks, the latter hesitates to pass judgment on the former. Peer review therefore is relied upon to assure proper standards and qualifications for membership, disqualification, and expulsion.

Because of their knowledge, power, social commitment, and autonomy, professions are typically held in high regard. It is desirable to be a member of such an elite group, and its members are *esteemed* and respected by others in the community.

Given these four characteristics of a profession, we can understand why engineering is a profession and plumbing is not. Plumbers are not held in as much esteem, their work is not as intellectually complex, and they do not have the same autonomy that engineers have in licensing their members. In terms of these traits, we can also understand why doctors feel that socialized medicine is a threat to their status as a profession. To the extent that the government sets a pay scale for different medical services and determines the conditions of employment, doctors lose their autonomy. They become less like professionals and more like employees of the state.

Ethics and Professionalism

What is the relationship between ethics and professionalism? According to the radical thesis, to be a professional requires professional ethics; a failure to master the skills of professional ethics signals one's failure to be a professional. To defend this claim requires showing that what professional ethics achieves is essential to the conduct of professionals.

What can ethics do, what good is it? The recent series by the Hastings Center on the Teaching of Ethics in Higher Education serves as a useful point of departure for answering this question.[12] According to its authors, the teaching of ethics can have several different goals. At the most modest level, it can serve to *raise one's moral consciousness*. Sensitizing people to the language of morals makes them aware of a moral point of view quite different from prudential aesthetic, epistemological, or political ones. To ask what is morally right or wrong is not to ask what is in my interests or those of my group. Nor is it to ask about the beauty of actions or the evidence to support truth claims. Ethics has to do with right and wrong action; teaching ethics makes people aware that they act upon moral decisions for which they are accountable. Such moral self-consciousness is the first step to self-knowledge and a necessary condition for the responsible behavior we demand of all professionals.

Closely related to this first objective is a second: *values clarification.* After one realizes that good-bad or right-wrong can be used in a moral sense, one can begin to discover what that moral meaning is. To say that someone is a good man or that he did the right thing is to refer to a set of virtues that we esteem and a set principles of justice we acknowledge. One cannot be a good doctor or a good lawyer for long if one does not know what goodness is.

Moral terms are used to advance moral claims, which are backed by reasons. A third task in teaching ethics is to provide tools for *the analysis of moral arguments.* Here the general principles of formal and informal logic come into play, as do fundamental principles on which moral judgments and social institutions rest. Doctors must know what health is, engineers must know what safety is, and lawyers must know what justice is if each of these professions is to fulfil its social role.

A full defense of particular moral judgments or principles requires a complete ethical theory that integrates them in a coherent and consistent fashion. Such a theory would provide a clear understanding of the difference between ethical and nonethical disputes, the meaning of the moral terms involved, and the strength of the arguments offered. Most important, it would allow us to resolve these disputes, and proclaim one position the most defensible or correct one. As a fourth and final goal, teaching ethics may serve to *provide solutions* to moral problems and teach these solutions as moral lessons. Each profession needs these solutions. A doctor cannot forgo deciding whether or not to operate on a patient. Similarly, a lawyer cannot avoid deciding whether or not to accept a client. Moral choices are inevitable and more defensible if based on clearly stated principles, cogent arguments, and well-articulated values. If these are the four purposes of teaching ethics, what do they have to do with lawyering?

PROFESSIONAL ETHICS FOR LAWYERS

Moral Consciousness Raising and Professionalism

In the exercise of one's professional expertise, factual judgments and value judgments are inextricably bound together. Professionals are called upon to make difficult judgments in which their technical competence and moral values are interwoven. For example, heart transplants are modern miracles of medical technology. What the appropriate procedures and techniques are for performing such operations can best be answered by surgeons, not sages. Yet *whether* to perform them is not just a technical question about the effectiveness of surgical techniques, but a moral question about the rights of patients, the importance of personal autonomy, and the conflicting rights of others competing for scarce health care dollars. Questions about the appropriate distribution of limited medical resources go beyond the technical expertise of doctors and health care practitioners and require the balancing of competing moral rights according to clearly articulated principles of distributive justice.

Similarly, philosophical concepts and principles underlie the entire field of law. Just as medicine requires a careful understanding of the nature of health, law requires a careful understanding of the nature of justice. One cannot achieve justice, except inadvertently and sporadically, unless one knows what justice is. Much like the doctor, who uses techniques for securing health, the lawyer has techniques for securing justice. The law possesses a powerful set of tools for approximating justice in an imperfect society In so doing, lawyers like other professionals must be careful to distinguish between the technical questions their training equips them to ask and the ethical questions that inevitably accompany them. Every experienced lawyer has paused at one time or another to reflect on what to do in a morally ambiguous situation.

The moral hazards of lawyering cannot be overcome simply by the application of technique. They raise questions about the moral weight of economic hardships, moral merit, the obligation to tell the truth and the moral imperative not to exploit the ill- or uninformed. As a guide through these moral mazes, lawyers have devised a Code or Model Rules. But these are statements of professional standards, not moral principles. They cannot function as the final arbiter of right and wrong inasmuch as they are one group's imperfect effort, at a particular time and place, to articulate standards of conduct. Their provisions change according to emerging insights into what justice requires, along with economic, ideological, and political developments in both the legal profession and society at large.

Values Clarification and Professionalism

The contrast between ethical and technical judgments, though critical, is not always easy to discern. Some terms like "justice," "guilty," or "good" slide almost imperceptibly back and fourth between the two. Only through a careful examination of the context can one determine which sense is operative. The study of ethics can help professionals draw this distinction more sharply. It can help them become clearer about the meaning of moral discourse and conflicting values in the workplace. Two examples will illustrate this contrast.

The criminal justice system serves different purposes. It has a punitive function: to mete out to offenders their "just deserts." It has a protective function: to keep society safe from dangerous offenders. It also has a rehabilitative function: to teach criminals to mend their ways. These objectives can easily conflict: the habitual pickpocket, having served his time, still poses a threat to society, yet he ought to be released. The punitive environment of prison compromises the trust and confidence necessary for effective therapy. One of the tasks of philosophy is to sort out these value conflicts, thereby facilitating the work of the professional, who would otherwise lack an integrated and coherent approach.

These conflicting principles of justice, though somewhat lofty and abstract, nevertheless impinge on the conduct of lawyers. Consider the following hypothetical in which you are attorney for the defense.

> In a private talk the county prosecutor, Fred Grim, offers to reduce the charges against your client, Vinnie Krule, from rape (which carries a six-to-thirty-year sentence) to gross sexual imposition (six months to five years) provided your client is willing to return a guilty plea. Further, he will recommend probation. But Grim is seriously mistaken in his belief that your client is a first offender who deserves this break. In fact, he is a real masher with two rape charges and an armed robbery conviction against him in another state. What should you, as his defense counsel, do?

If rehabilitation were the primary concern, probation is unlikely to succeed unless stringent conditions are attached. If retribution were the issue, then Krule has gotten off far too lightly for the offense he actually committed, though he may be getting the sentence his offense deserves on Grim's erroneous understanding of it. If the concern is one of specific deterrence, you, as his defense counsel, should reject the plea bargain: if anything it is likely to encourage Krule to future misconduct on the grounds that he can easily get away with it. And if general deterrence and protecting society are the goals, then the punishment may be appropriate to deter the offender Grim has in mind, but it will not deter people like Krule.

Of course, the problems of doing justice in an imperfect society have been compounded by questions of the moral responsibility of lawyers to ensure that decisions are made on the basis of facts. We cannot always do justice, given imperfect knowledge and fallible people. Here lawyers, like other professionals, must deal with conflicting obligations to their clients, to their colleagues, and to the system of which they are a part.

All professionals, to one degree or another, experience such conflicting obligations. One of these dilemmas has become familiar under the rubric "whistleblowing." Upon learning of intended wrongdoing by a client, the lawyer has to make a decison whether to report it or not. Due weight must be given to one's allegiance to the client, to the code of professional conduct, and to the public. Such decisions require delicate judgment, which is an integral part of professional life. Individually, they serve to define the kind of professional one is, and collectively the kind of profession one serves.

Moral Reasoning and Professionalism

When professionals confront a moral dilemma, they confront a series of arguments. The resolution of the dilemma requires a decision about which arguments are good and which are bad. Philosophers, as logicians, can appraise these arguments against the canons of consistency, coherence, validity, and soundness. They can point out fallacies in reasoning that easily lead one astray, explain what makes an argument valid and what makes it sound, and identify invalid and unsound arguments according to their logical form. Philosophers can dispel some disputes as verbal—merely differences in the use of terms. And they can locate the ground on which the battle must ultimately be waged—the basic value judgments on which the others depend.

By bringing a measure of rationality into disputes within the professions, moral philosophers keep professionals from being led astray by spurious reasoning. In so doing these professionals have not necessarily been led to the truth, but they have at least been checked from falling into irrationality, nonsense, and error.

Professionalism and Moral Truth

One of the tasks of the professional is to seek the social good. It follows from this that one cannot be a professional unless one has some sense of what the social good is. Accordingly, one's very status as a professional requires that one possess this moral truth. But it requires more, for each profession seeks the social good in a different form, according to its particular expertise: doctors seek it in the form of health; engineers in the form of safe, efficient buildings; and lawyers seek it in the form of justice. Each profession must know its own form of the social good. Without such knowledge professionals cannot perform their social roles.

Moral considerations also function as constraints on the means that can be used to achieve the social good, especially since good ends can be subverted by illegitimate means. Doctors who lie to patients run the risk of undermining the trust on which successful treatment depends. Engineers who fail to blow the whistle on a faulty brake design call into question their commitment to public safety. Likewise, lawyers who conceal evidence that would incriminate innocent clients use bad means to achieve a good end, and in so doing jeopardize their standing as agents of the court. Similarly, if they let stand the perjured testimony of innocent clients, they condone in the name of justice that which is *prima facie* immoral. Morality thus imposes restrictions not only on the ends that are sought, but on the ways that we pursue them.

Whether or not one accepts these examples, it is clear that some restrictions are to be imposed on the means that lawyers can use in the pursuit of justice. Accordingly, some conception of moral truth is required for lawyers to fulfil their social role. To give up moral restrictions is to invite a no-holds-barred war in which lawyers can do whatever works to get justice for their clients. Such unregulated and unmitigated legal warfare would threaten the very existence of law as a profession.

ETHICS AND THE LEGAL PROFESSION

This book explores the ethics of lawyering in a new way by establishing a dialogue between philosophers and legal scholars on central issues in the current practice of law. Thus, we begin with the notion of law as a profession: its historic context, ethical problems concerning entry into the profession, and questions about its regulation.

Part 2 turns to a critique of the legal profession. How is the role of the lawyer conceptualized, and how should the limits of lawyers' responsibility be demarcated? In America these questions are answered in terms of the adversary system of justice, which provides the framework in which ethical questions can be asked and answered. Accordingly, Part 3 examines this framework.

Part 4 initiates a shift in scope away from general questions and toward specific issues in ethics, both pure and applied. It deals with conflict of interest—what it is and how it can be resolved. Is the lawyer's primary allegiance to the client, the courts, the profession, or the public?

Part 5 raises the familiar problem of what to do when someone lies, or is about to lie. Client perjury has been a touchstone of debate within the legal profession, and has shaped the image of the lawyer within the eyes of the public as perhaps no other practice has ever done.

Distributive justice is the topic of Part 6. The issue has been much debated within the medical profession, with dramatic decisions about who among several candidates should get the one and only kidney dialysis machine. Its analogue within the legal profession has only begun to be addressed: How are legal services distributed in our country and is our system adequate and fair?

It is impossible to treat the full range of ethical problems that arise in the practice of law.[13] Because excellent materials are readily available on topics like plea-bargaining, we have not included them. Nor have we dealt with such important concerns as prosecutorial discretion, advertising and specialized practices like public interest law. Instead, we sought the most salient issues for which there were engaging and informative materials available.

At the end of each part, hypothetical cases have been provided to facilitate classroom discussion. We have also appended a list of further references to assist students with assignments, or to help them explore a given issue in more depth.

We hope that this book will encourage philosophers to test the principles and prescriptions of ethical theories against the realities of professional life. We hope that it will aid and abet the legal profession in its own examination of the values and principles that underlie the practice of law and the place of lawyers in contemporary American society. We hope students, both professional and undergraduate, will find much to engage them.

Michael Davis
Chicago, Illinois

Frederick Elliston
Honolulu, Hawaii

NOTES

1. *ABA Approval of Law Schools—ABA Standards and Rules of Procedure,* Section 302(a)(iii)(1979).

2. Michael J. Kelly, *Legal Ethics and Legal Education* (Hastings-on-the-Hudson, N.Y: Hastings Center, 1980), p. 68.

3. Gallup. "Honesty and Ethical Standards," *The Gallup Poll: Public Opinion 1972–1977,* pp. 1196-1197.

4. *Washington Star* (August 28, 1978).

5. See Ralph Nader and Mark Green, *Verdict on Lawyers* (New York: Thomas Y. Crowell, 1976); Monroe Freedman, "Professional Responsibility of the Criminal Defense Lawyer: The Three Hardest Questions," *Michigan Law Review* 64 (1966):1469-1484 and reprinted in this volume, pp. 000-000; and Warren E. Burger, "The Role of the Law School in the Teaching of Legal Ethics," *Cleveland State Law Review* 29 (1980):377-395.

6. An earlier version of this material was presented to the Professional Responsibility Committee of the Chicago Bar Association, Young Lawyers' Section, and revised for publication in the *Loyola University of Chicago Law Journal* 16 (Spring 1985):401-419. We are grateful for their kind permission to reprint it.

7. See Hugh Wilder, "Starter Kit in Philosophy of Love and Sexuality" (New York: Helvetia Press, 1981) for syllabi of courses by philosophers on human sexuality.

8. See Jane English, Frederick Elliston, and Mary Vetterling Braggin, eds., *Feminism and Philosophy* (Totowa, N.J.: Littlefield Adams, 1977); John A. Behnke and Sissela Bok, eds., *The Dilemmas of Euthanasia* (New York: Doubleday, 1975) for an early but still useful collection; Philip E. Devine, *The Ethics of Homicide* (Ithaca, N.Y.: Cornell University Press, 1978) for one effort to examine the general practice of killing; Peter Singer and Tom Regan, eds., *Animal Rights and Human Obligations,* (Englewood Cliffs, N.J: Prentice-Hall, 1976); Douglas MacLean and Peter G. Brown, eds., *Energy and the Future,* (Totowa, N.J.: Littlefield Adams, 1983); Peter G. Brown and Henry Shue, eds., *The Border that Joins: Mexican Immigrants and U.S. Responsibility* (Totowa, N.J.: Littlefield Adams, 1983); Jeffrey Blustein, *Parents and Children: The Ethics of the Family* (New York: Oxford University Press, 1983); Michael Bayles, ed., *Ethics and Population* (Cambridge, Mass.: Schenckman, 1976); Robert Fullinwider, *The Reverse Discrimination Controversy* (Totowa, N.J.: Littlefield Adams, 1980); Frederick Elliston and Norman Bowie, eds., *Ethics, Public Policy and Criminal Justice,* (Cambridge, Mass.: Oelgeschlager, Gunn and Hain, 1982); Michael Waltzer, *Just and Unjust Wars,* (New York: Basic Books, 1977).

9. More specifically, these include the American Section of the International Association for the Philosophy of Law and Social Philosophy (AMINTAPHIL), the American Society for Value Inquiry (1970), the Association for the Philosophy of the Unconscious (1971), Colloquium for Social Philosophy (1972), and the Philosophical Society for the Study of Sport (1972). More recently one can list the Society for Women in Philosophy (1977), the Society for the Study of Professional Ethics (1978), and the Society for Business Ethics (1980).

10. These include the following: *Business and Professional Ethics, The Journal of Business Ethics, Environmental Ethics, Criminal Justice Ethics, The Westminster Review,* two journals called *Applied Philosophy* (one published in England) and most recently *Agriculture Ethics.* These are in addition to the *Hastings Center Report* on bioethics, *Philosophy and Medicine,* various newsletters on the philosophy of law and philosophy of medicine, and IIT's *Perspectives on the Professions.*

11. See Alan Goldman's *The Moral Foundations of Professional Ethics* (Totowa, N.J.: Littlefield Adams, 1980).

12. See *The Teachings of Ethics in Higher Education: A Report by the Hastings Center* (Hastings-on-Hudson, N.Y.: The Hastings Center, 1980).

13. For a comprehensive listing of materials, see Frederick Elliston and Jane van Schaick *Legal Ethics: An Annotated Bibliography and Resource Guide* (Littleton, Colo.: Fred Rothman, 1984).

Part I

The Profession of Law

Introduction

Legal ethics is concerned with how a community should have its legal business done (assuming lawyers do it) and how this important activity should be conducted. Thus, broadly speaking, legal ethics is as much a part of political philosophy (i.e., the study of the proper role of social institutions) as of ethics. The title of this book is *Ethics and the Legal Profession,* however, and not *Legal Ethics.* Including "profession" in the title stresses its centrality to the ethics of lawyering. Legal ethics is professional ethics. Indeed, among lawyers "professional responsibility" is just another name for legal ethics.

"Ethics" here has its familiar use. As "moral philosophy," that is, the study of the norms that should guide the conduct of rational agents, ethics is concerned with what makes acts right or wrong, good or bad, virtuous or vicious, and with the reasons properly offered to justify conduct. Ethics makes explicit our understanding of norms, opening them to criticism and revision. Although ethics cannot make people good, it can help people to see better what the good is.

Legal ethics assumes no more knowledge of *ethics* than one may reasonably expect of any educated person. Unfortunately, the knowledge of an ordinary educated person is nevertheless not enough to understand legal ethics. Even if legal ethics is no more than the application of ordinary norms of conduct to lawyering (and even this is controversial), ordinary persons could not apply these norms without more knowledge of lawyering than they are likely to have. One cannot understand, for example, why lawyers consider "commingling of funds" to be a serious breach of legal ethics until one understands the importance they attach to avoiding even the appearance of wrongdoing. (What, after all, is wrong with putting your client's money in an account with yours if you have no intention of embezzling it?) The fact that lawyers think themselves to be members of a "profession" influences the way they think about what they do. Because few nonlawyers have a sense for how much history, organization, and controversy rustle beneath the surface when lawyers talk of *their* "profession," the study of legal ethics must begin with what lawyers mean when they describe themselves as a profession.

PROFESSIONS AND PROFESSIONALISM

When lawyers describe law as a profession, they mean in part to associate it with such vocations as medicine, the ministry, and engineering, and to distinguish it from others—for example, carpentry, selling shoes, or speculation. *Profession* is a term of respect, as are *professional* and *professionalism,* but the respect they show is not the same. Professionalism is the style of a professional, usually cool and effective. To describe someone as a "professional" (or a "pro") is to say that he exhibits the competence one would expect of a member of a profession. Though "professional" in "professional sports" now denotes only that athletes earn their living by playing sports, it still suggests a relatively high competence (that is, more than one would expect of an "amateur"). The contrast between the respect invited by "professional" and by "profession" is therefore great. A profession is not just a group of professionals, however competent. Football is not a profession even for professional players, and so we hear nothing of "football ethics." ("Good sportsmanship" is no equivalent, since that virtue is at least as appropriate to amateurs as it is to professionals. To be a member of a profession seems somehow better than being a mere professional. What then is a profession? What makes being a member of a profession so good? And why is law a profession?

According to the lawyers' conception, a certain number of persons constitute a profession if, and only if, (1) they are all engaged in the same learned art, (2) that engagement is more or less full-time, (3) the art itself is helpful to others in some important way, (4) the persons so engaged form an organization governing how they practice their art, and (5) the governance so imposed is primarily for the public good rather than for the good of those so organized. This definition is complex. Let us look at its main points again.

The members of a profession must practice an "art." Unskilled workers cannot, according to this definition, form a profession because what they practice is not an "art," that is, an activity requiring long training to develop even minimal competence. Carpentry or football, though certainly an art, is, however, not the right sort of art to be a profession. The art must be "learned," that is, one depending heavily on books. Though one can be a carpenter or football player without being able to read, one cannot be a doctor, a minister, or an engineer.

But even "book learning" is not enough to make an art a profession. The art must be one that a person can practice more or less full-time, otherwise the art could only have amateur practitioners. (A lawyer who works only part-time is often said to be partially retired from the profession.) The art must also be helpful to others in an important way. Thus, medicine can be a profession because it cures the sick. In contrast, solving crossword puzzles, though a learned art and one a few may practice full-time, cannot be a profession. It is "just a game."

Those engaged in a learned art must, according to this conception, be organized as well. Without organization, practitioners of even the most learned and helpful art would not be a profession but simply so many individuals practicing the same art. The organization need not be self-governing. The Anglican ministry is no less a profession because the Church of England is organized as part of the state apparatus. But even a self-governing organization of practitioners of the most learned and helpful art might be no more than a trade association or union. Indeed, some professions (for example, teaching) seem to have both professional organizations and unions.

To practice a profession is, it is often said, not to pursue a "mere money-making calling." To organize as a profession is to undertake more than serving oneself. There must, in addition (or instead), be a commitment to the good of others—clients, patients, parishioners, or the like—even when carrying out that commitment does not benefit those who practice the art. The members of some professions must, for example, be ready to help those who cannot afford to pay. A lawyer who, though working full-time, never accepted payment, would be no less a member of the profession than one who usually exacted high fees. To organize as a profession is to impose upon the members a discipline they would not otherwise be subject to. Professional organizations may maintain such discipline by informal peer pressure; by promulgating an express "code of ethics"; by limiting who may join the organization; and by censuring, suspending, or expelling members whose conduct is "unprofessional." To be a member of a profession is to declare oneself to be someone of whom more than ordinary good conduct may properly be expected.

LAW AS A PROFESSION

Is law a profession under this definition? Certainly, it is now. Law is a learned art; its members must have an advanced degree and pass a difficult competency examination. Lawyers spend much of their time providing an important service to others: The typical client would be helpless to defend himself in a criminal case, to collect damages for a serious injury, or even to prepare a complicated will. Lawyers have organized themselves into national, state, county, and city associations. Among the purposes of such associations are maintaining the integrity and competence of lawyers, making legal counsel available to all who need it, and improving the legal system.

Though law is now a profession in this strict sense, it has not always been one, nor will it necessarily always remain one. David R. Papke's history of lawyering in the United States reports two periods in which law was not a profession (as well as two when it was). The history of legal practitioners may be read as a series of experiments with the provision of legal services.

The early colonial period was an experiment in amateur lawyering. Lawyers were few. Most were unskilled "pettifoggers," which sometimes led to the practice of law being banned outright. More often the practice of law was so regulated that making a living at the bar was almost impossible. But during the later colonial period, groups similar to the modern bar associations appeared in commercial centers such as Boston, New York, and Philadelphia. This was America's first experiment with a profession of law.

The American Revolution brought on a long period of decline in the profession of law. Lawyers became increasingly important but bar organizations almost disappeared. Lawyers were subject to no special discipline but that provided by the formal supervision of courts (which usually was quite lax) and the informal judgment of peers or the market. Some states abolished all educational requirements for admission to practice. Law was just one business among many. Only after the Civil War did this process reverse. The reemergence of an organized bar was contemporaneous with the rise of trade associations, unions, and giant corporations. But, unlike these, the declared purpose of the bar associations was public service rather than the advantage of their members.

Though Papke seems to take a jaundiced view of much that the bar associations accomplished, does the definition of "profession" itself suggest another? Might these associations have been trying to do nothing more unobjectionable than create a profession of law?

Papke's history provides a natural orientation to the contemporary problems of legal ethics. Of special importance is the conflict between (what we may call) "client-centered" conceptions of professional responsibility (associated by Papke with Sharswood's famous code) and "justice-centered" conceptions (associated with Geneva's code of ethics). Under a client-centered conception, a lawyer is an "agent" whose public service is primarily (or even exclusively) helping clients do what they want within the bounds of the law. Lawyers serve the public by serving clients. On the other hand, under a justice-centered conception, the lawyer's public service is to help clients get justice. The profession bars lawyers from appearing in unjust causes. They are to serve the public by serving justice. They are "officers of the court." Papke suggests that the client-centered conception has won a complete victory over the justice-centered conception. But do the American Bar Association's new *Model Rules of Professional Conduct* confirm this? Consider, for example, the requirement of "candor toward a tribunal" found in Rule 3.3

Frederick Elliston's paper is concerned with admission to the bar. Non-lawyers are usually surprised to learn that one cannot be admitted to the practice of law without passing a test for "character and fitness." There seems to be something quaint (if not positively Victorian) about would-be lawyers having to present letters from the dean of their law school, a member of the bar, and others attesting to their good character and their fitness to practice law. More surprising perhaps is that would-be lawyers must also provide all addresses of places they have lived or worked, information about their parents, spouses, children, and other relatives, and access to their credit records, academic records, and so on. But most surprising may be the gravity with which the bar seems to take the question of character and fitness. There may be a special committee to meet with each prospective lawyer, to question her, and then to make a recommendation. Though the work of such committees often seems *pro forma,* it is not. An applicant who is discovered to have cheated on a college examination may, for example, be denied admission to the bar if the committee cannot be convinced that the candidate has reformed. Character and fitness committees seem to be especially hard on offenses that suggest to other lawyers that the would-be lawyer may not be trustworthy.

Elliston's paper covers almost every aspect of the character and fitness test. His criticism raises sobering doubts about even the possibility of such tests. What is good moral character? How can we tell whether someone's character is good? What is fitness to practice law (apart from possessing knowledge sufficient to pass the bar exam)? How is a committee of lawyers to tell whether such "fitness" exists? Elliston also suggests alternatives. Why not treat past wrongdoing not as a sign of bad character justifying flat (and permanent) rejection but as a crime to be punished by a certain period of nonadmission? Perhaps the profession should give up the character and fitness test altogether as a requirement for admission and instead substitute a regular "moral audit" after admission? Elliston even wonders whether we really want lawyers to be moral.

Marks and Cathcart pick up the discussion of discipline where Elliston leaves off. They are concerned with what the bar does to ensure good character and fitness *after* admission to practice. Their essay offers considerable information about the organization of the bar, but their theme is the need for large reforms.

Marks and Cathcart divide questions of discipline into those concerned with "performance" and those concerned with "conduct." Performance is measured by standards of competence. Here there is no question of fault: Either one is capable of doing the job or one is not. An attorney would, for example, be suspended from practice on performance grounds if suspended because he was drunk so often he could not perform as an attorney should. Such a suspension would not be punishment for drunkenness, but merely a means of protecting clients from the lawyer's inability to work. "Conduct" violations, on the other hand, presuppose fault. That an attorney had no knowledge of wrongdoing *would* be relevant to the attorney's fitness to practice.

Marks and Cathcart also argue that bar grievance committees (the bodies responsible for hearing complaints against attorneys) tend to concern themselves with conduct rather than performance, and to be confused about whether they are supposed to protect the public, safeguard the good name of the profession, or punish wrongdoing. The criminal law model seems to dominate and, for Marks and Cathcart, that is unfortunate, especially since so few attorneys suffer severe discipline. They seem to think many more attorneys should be disbarred or suspended than in fact are. What criteria should one use to decide how much discipline is to be expected? Does one, for example, compare the rate of disciplinary action in law with that in other professions (in which case lawyer discipline comes out looking rather tough)? Or does one compare it with similar rates in the criminal law? Or what? But, assuming Marks and Cathcart are right about the failings of today's system of professional discipline, what follows with respect to Elliston's proposal to abolish the character and fitness test in favor of stricter supervision?

DILEMMA FOR THE ETHICS COMMITTEE

In addition to the committees already mentioned, many bar associations have an "ethics committee," the purpose of which is to answer questions about the professional responsibilities of lawyers. The following letter poses the sort of question an ethics committee might be asked. How would you answer it now? As you read the essays in this and subsequent sections, consider this letter again and see whether your answer has changed (that is, whether your knowledge of the legal *profession* has affected your sense of what it is right to do as a lawyer). You might also want to consult the ABA's *Model Rules of Professional Conduct.*

Dear Ethics Committee:

I am in a partnership with L. L is a good negotiator, but sharp in his practices. Last week we had a client who owed $1000 for furniture to a local store. The store was threatening to put our client, a working woman in her mid-thirties, into collection. The furniture had been lost in a fire a month after delivery. The store had not insured the loan, and our client had not been insured against loss by fire. She did not want her credit ruined, needed every cent she could earn to replace what she had lost in the fire, and could not pay $1000. She had savings of $400. She wanted to settle with the store. When she had personally inquired about settling, she had been told no. (She had not even been given a chance to suggest an amount.)

Our fee for arranging the settlement was $100. L negotiated the settlement in this way: He asked the client to bring her remaining $300 in savings in small bills. He put $100 of the $300 into his own wallet (having removed all other money). He then accompanied the client to the credit office of the store, met with the credit manager, and explained the situation: the fire, inability to pay in full, and the wish to settle. There was the usual probing and parrying, but when the credit manager asked "How much?" L asked the client to produce her money. He then said, "This is all she has now, $200." The credit manager hesitated, the amount apparently too small for him. L then said, "Look, I think you ought to show some compassion under the circumstances." The credit manager still hesitated. L continued: "Look," reaching for his wallet, "I'll even add to her money out of my own pocket," opening his wallet and throwing the $100 onto the table. The credit manager counted the money, thought for a moment, and then agreed to settle.

Did L act unethically? If so, do I have an obligation to report him to the Grievance Committee? Do I have an obligation to do something else instead?

Sincerely, etc.

David R. Papke

The Legal Profession and Its Ethical Responsibilities: A History

While one might study certain areas of law by focusing only on contemporary doctrine, the study of the legal profession's ethics can profit greatly from a historical perspective. As the American nation evolved from traditional communities into a complex, bureaucratic society, the legal profession itself developed different social practices and self-impressions. In the context of this evolution, the profession gradually began to direct its attention to the conduct of American lawyers. In each period, the central and often inherently contradictory questions of an attorney's ethical responsibility toward clients, social groups, and the society in general took on new meanings and received new answers. These changes set the stage for the difficult and sometimes disillusioning issues of professional ethics, which have emerged in the final decades of the twentieth century.

THE COLONIAL BAR'S STRUGGLE FOR SOCIAL ACCEPTANCE

The American colonies, operating independently of one another with different principles and goals, constituted a varied patchwork; from New England to the Carolina plantations, colonial legal practice was precarious and lacking in uniformity. For a century following the founding of the first colonies, traditional elites dominated the largely agrarian social structures: for the most part, these dominant groups refused to sanction legal practice. Few in number, poorly trained, and unorganized as a profession, lawyers practiced in communities where the value of their work was suspect. Was the practice of law ethical? Not until the last half of the eighteenth century did the colonies answer this question in the affirmative. Only then, with social acceptance contributing to professional confidence and autonomy, could lawyers begin dealing with the more specific questions pertinent to their professional responsibilities.

Definitive histories of the assorted colonial legal professions remain to be written, but modern scholars have collected intriguing information concerning the practice of law in two socially and ideologically different colonies—Virginia

29

and Massachusetts. In Virginia, the founders were proud Englishmen, but they were not determined to bring all of England's trappings to the New World. The founders adopted English Common Law as the general basis for jurisprudence, but their 1606 charter urged a civil justice that resembled the English Chancery, geared to "naturall right and equity" rather than "the niceness and lettre of the lawe."[1] Once the colony was established, a landed gentry supplied the most prominent citizens, judges, and legislators. This planter class believed that the law should support rather than threaten the social structure, which they directed and controlled. From the perspective of this Virginia elite, an independent legal profession seemed a factious, fracturing nuisance.

Seventeenth-century Virginia legislation regarding the practice of law illustrates how ominous the legal profession seemed to men who attempted to maintain a stratified farming community.[2] Most pointedly, a 1645 act of the Virginia House of Burgesses ordered all attorneys practicing for a fee to be expelled from office. The act proved awkward and difficult to enforce, but after briefly tempering its terms, the legislature decreed again in 1656 that no one could accept reward or profit for pleading a case in the courts or for giving legal advice. In keeping with the dominant economy of the period, the penalty for violating this act was five thousand pounds of tobacco. Throughout the late seventeenth century, Virginia leaders perceived lawyers as troublesome encouragers of needless legal suits, as men more interested in fees than in the good of their community.

Royal nullification of anti-lawyer legislation during this period was partly responsible for Virginia's reluctant acceptance of the roughly forty lawyers practicing in the colony. Yet this step was cautious, and well into the eighteenth century, Virginia attempted to restrict legal practice to "gentlemen" who were likely to have a particular perspective on the social role of attorneys. With appropriate preparatory education, gentlemen could study at the English Inns of Court, the sanctioned form of legal education. With ties to the planter elite, they could honestly take the colony's professional oath to foment neither strife nor lawsuits. As men of financial means, the gentry could still prosper even though the colony's courts set lawyers' fees at low levels. Most importantly, gentlemen lawyers were likely to appreciate and respect Virignia's stratified social structure.

In the Massachusetts Bay Colony, Puritan magistrates and ministers rather than a landed gentry led early efforts to suppress lawyers. The colony's courts recognized English law, but the Scriptures were also made a part of their jurisprudential framework. This natural law, the word of God, was crucial for Puritan courts. Surely one did not need a legal education to comprehend it; indeed, too much legal education might prevent one from seeing clearly the everlasting meaning of God's divine words. More generally, the dominant ministry's utopian community, a "City on the Hill," theoretically precluded the sort of disagreement conducive to legal work. In a predominantly agrarian community united by faith, the early Puritan ministry questioned the usefulness of lawyers.[3]

Given the power of a Puritan jurisprudence and world view in the Massachusetts Bay Colony's social life, it should come as no surprise that the colony's earliest lawyers encountered difficulties practicing.[4] None of the sixty-five male founders actively practiced law, although John Winthrop and Emanuel Downing had studied at the Inns of Court and had practiced law prior to their immigration.[5] Thomas Morton, perhaps the first practicing lawyer in the colony, claimed to have studied at the distinguished Clifford's Inn, but critics alleged that he was a mere Chancery pettifogger. After exhausting Puritan tolerance with his Maypole, secular songs, and commercial trade with the Indians—just the type of conduct one might expect from a lawyer—Morton found himself rudely expelled from the colony.[6] Morton was followed at the bar by Thomas Lechford, a gentleman of Clifford's Inn, who practiced in Boston in 1637 and 1638. In 1639, after Lechford had sought to influence a jury out of court, Puritan magistrates reprimanded and temporarily disbarred him. At the time, Lechford acknowledged that "he had overshot himselfe, and was sorry for it," but in 1642, after his return to England, he asserted more grumpily that New England Puritans did not respect the Common Law or the lawyers who understood it.[7] In addition to the individual cases of Morton and Lechford, the Massachusetts Bay Colony completely banned the practice of law by professional pleaders during several periods of social unrest.[8]

Puritan hostility toward lawyers continued but by the end of the seventeenth century the colony had implicitly acknowledged the legitimacy of its legal profession. In 1689, in fact, Edward Randolph, secretary to Governor Andros, wrote to England requesting "two, or three honest attorneys, (if any such thing in nature),"[9] and the new royal charter of 1691 also led to an expanded role for lawyers. Yet this acknowledgment of lawyers' legitimacy hardly gave the profession full reign. As was the case in early-eighteenth-century Virginia, courts determined who was eligible to take the lawyers' oath, how much lawyers could charge, and how they could practice. Lawyer Daniel Ela, for example, was ordered whipped late in the seventeenth century for charging what the courts considered excessive fees.[10]

The controlling opinion concerning lawyers in early-eighteenth-century Massachusetts can be gauged by considering a 1710 address of Cotton Mather. One of the most prominent ministers in Puritan New England, Mather addressed lawyers as a group, beginning with assurances that he found them to be liberally educated gentlemen and scholars. As such, Mather continued, lawyers had the responsibility to "shun all those indirect ways of making haste to be rich, in which a man cannot be innocent." Mather urged attorneys to keep a Court of Chancery always in their breasts and to "abhor . . . to appear in a dirty cause." A learned man, accustomed to respect, Mather conceived of colonial society as communal and unified. Lawyers, he thought, should not approach their work as experts for hire but rather as men devoted to fairness and justice. By being loyal to truth rather than victory, by thinking of the social community rather than individual clients, lawyers could respect the God who looked over the affairs of men.[11]

It was not until the mid-eighteenth century that the legal profession in Massachusetts, Virginia, and the rest of the colonies began to achieve the professional security that is taken for granted today. In rural areas the profession remained small. As late as 1760, Massachusetts' counties in what is now Maine had only four lawyers.[12] Even lawyers in the cities lacked complete occupational differentiation; they provided clerical, copying, and bookkeeping services as well as legal advice. But in general, by 1750, lawyers were sufficiently numerous and distinct as legal workers to feel confident of their social activities. In addition, planter and ministerial elites had lost their firm grip on colonial affairs, and particularly in the larger settlements a more commercial economy began to emerge. Although merchants, like the landed gentry and Puritan ministers before them, were not always enamored of the legal profession, they were forced to turn more and more frequently to lawyers as commerce expanded. The growth of towns brought with it the first glimmerings of a diversified society and an individualistic world view; social security for lawyers inevitably accompanied these developments.

As the history of Massachusetts illustrates, security enabled lawyers to elaborate their professional identity.[13] In the words of John Adams, himself a member of the bar, lawyers in mid-eighteenth-century Massachusetts had begun to "swarm and multiply."[14] In 1758, Boston lawyers formed the Suffolk County Bar Association, and ten years later lawyers in nearby Essex County also organized. A professional subculture began to flower in rituals, reading groups, and folklore. As social units increased, along with the development of shared perspectives and presumptions, lawyers were, more than ever before, a self-conscious professional group.

In the context of these developments, attorneys began addressing matters of professional qualifications, conduct, and ethics. In particular, the Suffolk County Bar Association drafted formal apprenticeship and training requirements and appointed committees to examine would-be lawyers. Members of the Massachusetts associations also agreed not to enter, argue or assist in actions brought by self-trained practitioners. In Essex County, the bar association introduced a minimum fee schedule for its members. Prior to the American Revolution, Massachusetts bar associations were voluntary; they could not enforce their rules on all practitioners, but association admission requirements and fee schedules were steps in that direction.

The Revolutionary War reversed the growth of the organized bar, but the political prominence of lawyers during the conflict indicated how far the profession had come since the founding of the colonies. Strong ties and loyalties to the English government led one-quarter of the profession to return to England when the war began. But on the patriots' side, revolutionary leaders such as John Adams, William Byrd, Thomas Lee, Patrick Henry, and Thomas Jefferson were lawyers. When fifty-six delegates signed the Declaration of Independence, twenty-five were lawyers, and thirty-one of the fifty-five members of the Constitutional Convention were also lawyers. Indeed, several of the core documents of the Revolution demonstrated the legal training of their authors. Made bold by their new security and respectability, by the late 1700s, lawyers were prepared to comment not only on the ethics of their legal practice but also on that of Revolution and nationhood.

ANTEBELLUM PROFESSIONALISM AND THE PRIMACY OF
RESPONSIBILITIES TO THE CLIENT

During the years that separated the American Revolution and the Civil War, the practice of law grew as rapidly as America's cities and its entrepreneurial economy. Often embodying the initiative and enterprise of their period, lawyers scurried to make their fortunes. The profession's formal organization remained rudimentary, but changes in society and in the social roles of attorneys brought a new conception of the profession. In particular, a new ethical presumption appeared, one that would remain a central feature of the profession's thinking for more than a century.

The legal profession's development during the early nineteenth century was not always in step with other sectors of the rapidly changing society. Throughout the period, popular hostility toward lawyers was prevalent in American life. To some extent, this hostility reflected unique concerns. At the turn of the century, for example, animosity toward British Common Law, hopes for a utopian republic, and the work of lawyers as postwar debt collectors fueled a truly rabid dislike for the practice of law. Boston merchant Benjamin Austin, writing as "Honestus," called for the abolition of the profession, while other critics demanded a small profession paid by the state and a greater reliance on lay arbiters.[15] This early-nineteenth-century hostility toward lawyers also assumed a more general character, for lawyers were doing the type of work that was certain to displease assorted clients, litigants, and observers.[16]

While popular commentators continued to rail against pettifoggery, lawyers, according to an 1818 *Niles Register,* became "as plentiful as blackberries."[17] In the rural South and West, a few attorneys became sophisticated practitioners, but most depended far more on the speed of a good horse than on Lord Blackstone. Whether riding circuit or stationed in a clapboard office, frontier lawyers primarily did criminal, probate, collection, and land transfer work.[18] In the East, where cities were growing rapidly, some lawyers provided low-skilled legal services comparable to those supplied by their rural brethren, while others won the confidence of larger commercial interests.[19] Daniel Webster, the dignified lawyer-politician who could bring tears to the eyes of Supreme Court justices with pleas on behalf of beloved Dartmouth College, represented the advance group of commercial capitalism during his years of greatest prominence.[20] When the French political observer Alexis De Tocqueville surveyed the American republic in the 1830s, the elite eastern bar rather than the scrambling generalists inspired his belief that the profession could effectively bridle democratic excesses.[21]

While a diversified American legal profession thrived in the entrepreneurial frenzy of early-nineteenth-century America, it achieved only limited organization. Private and university-based law schools of the antebellum period trained hundreds of lawyers, but the majority of these practitioners learned their calling through informal office apprenticeships. John Livingston's American Legal Association became a nationwide legal referral service, but bar associations, lawyers' clubs, and "moots" atrophied. The profession's eastern elite commanded fees that were ten or fifteen times higher than general practitioners, but attempts to follow the English model of a formally established and graded profession ended in failure. For certain traditional historians, the overall picture of professional organization during the period was one of tragic disintegration. One historian has described the early-nineteenth-century legal profession as "an undifferentiated mass."[22] Most recent scholarly work has tempered these appraisals, but it nevertheless remains clear that in the early years the legal profession did not constitute a cohesive guild.[23]

Given the unstructured state of the profession, its limited role in self-management during this period was hardly surprising. In general, legislatures and courts rather than the profession made decisions regarding legal training requirements and admissions to the bar. In keeping with the growing demand for legal services and a belief in social mobility, state legislatures required less and less preparation for the practice of law. Apprenticeship periods were shortened and, in a few cases, they were completely abolished. Judges, themselves increasingly subject to popular election, did little to hinder men who sought admission to their courts. Court-administered entrance examinations were perfunctory at best. Would-be lawyers passed routinely, and admission to one court enabled a lawyer to practice before other courts in the same state, and before the courts of other states as well.

State codes regarding professional conduct provided a framework for lawyers' discipline, but the codes were short and vague. Sometimes, as in the case of a Tennessee code that threatened to disbar any lawyer who gambled, the codes reflected specialized concerns. But more commonly, the codes stressed lawyers' punctuality and merely prohibited unauthorized holding of client funds and the buying up of notes and confused land titles. With imprecise standards of practice and with lawyers and their clients frequently on the move, courts only rarely initiated formal disciplinary procedings.[24]

Even though legislatures and courts rather than the profession dealt formally with questions of legal ethics, individual lawyers still offered their opinions regarding ethical issues. Lawyers' statements were often reactions to the allegations that the profession consisted of usurers and sharpers, snakes and sharks. J. F. Jackson, one of the many lawyers who contributed to *The Knickerbocker,* argued that the popular attack on lawyers represented a "vulgar and mistaken notion" and "the bitter feelings of an ignorant rabble." In Jackson's opinion, the profession of the advocate could be "consistent with perfect integrity."[25] More generally, the comments made by lawyers with respect to legal ethics were part of their changing view of social life and professionalism. As the Civil War approached, lawyers, like many other Americans, abandoned visions of a unified, Christian community and endorsed instead an open society of action and mobility. Lawyers increasingly understood themselves not as benevolent practitioners serving the community but rather as businessmen with specialized knowledge.

The presumptions of legal ethics also changed, as lawyers began to discuss their relative responsibilities to the society and to the individual client. For centuries, as the words of Cotton Mather illustrated, the lawyer's larger responsibility to the society and its values had been primary. This presumption constrained lawyers from representing criminal defendants whom they knew to be guilty, or civil clients whose causes they considered unjust. In the antebellum periods, however, lawyers began to assert that the morality of human conduct was difficult to appraise and that justice was impossible unless defendants and clients were fully represented. As early as the 1830s, some lawyers argued that the profession's primary ethical responsibility was loyalty to the will of clients. Editors of *The Law Reporter* posited a "somber truth": "the more mercenary our profession is, the more it will deserve respect." Influential Philadelphia lawyer, judge, and law teacher George Sharswood, about whom more remains to be said, told his colleagues and students that professional morality was entirely compatible with arguing any and every case.[26]

THE BAR ASSOCIATION MOVEMENT AND THE CODIFICATION OF LAWYERS' ETHICS

The Civil War acutely convulsed American society, but after several years of postwar adjustment, the country and its legal profession resumed the transformation that had begun in the antebellum years. Industrial capital accumulated, particularly in the steel and farm equipment industries, and with the help of federal subsidies, railroads crisscrossed the continent. National markets developed for commodities and labor, and as bloody strikes suggested, industrial laborers sometimes tried to organize unions. Cities burgeoned, with several in the Midwest surpassing in size some of the great cities of the East. The legal profession grew from 22,000 practitioners in 1850 to 60,000 in 1880, and 114,000 in 1900.[27]

The actual practice of law between 1865 and 1915 was more diverse and stratified than ever before. In less settled areas, small-town lawyers had a great variety of clients. Courtroom criminal work remained a staple, as did debt collection, but particularly on the Great Plains and in the West, rural lawyers also turned to land speculation and money brokerage for their livelihood.[28] In the larger cities, the bar differentiated in ways that belied notions of a profession of equals. On the bottom rung were thousands of solo practitioners doing probate, criminal, and personal injury work for low rates. Like Attorney

Charles Guiteau, the assassin of President Garfield, these solo practitioners often jumped from city to city hoping to catch a break.[29] In the final years of the century, Irish, Jewish, Italian, and Polish immigrants entered this professional sector and constituted the so-called "ethnic bar." Looking down on them from more lucrative perches were legal specialists: the in-house lawyers of railroads and insurance companies, the first generation of Wall Street corporate lawyers, and firms of criminal law specialists, such as New York's notorious Howe & Hummel.[30] While intra-professional stratification had begun during the antebellum period, the profession's divisions grew more rigid and permanent as the nation's economy became more complex.

After fading away during the middle of the century, bar associations reappeared and lent the profession increased organizational stability. Some of the bar associations counted reform among their chief goals, as in the case of the Association of the Bar of New York City, which was founded in 1870 by prominent lawyers concerned about the self-interested behavior of the city's ethnic machine.[31] Others were primarily interested in professional contacts and restricting competition. These various associations came eventually to be affiliated with the American Bar Association (ABA).

Founded in 1878, the ABA held annual meetings in Saratoga and offered membership only to well-established practitioners.[32] Country lawyers could rise to prominence in the bar associations of rural states, but in general urban lawyers, with the resources and types of practices that could facilitate conventioneering and organized bar work, were the leaders of the bar associations. Influential in state legislatures and courts, bar associations of the late nineteenth century successfully championed written comprehensive bar examinations and state boards of bar examiners. Through these mechanisms and others bar associations hoped to control the practice of law.

New developments in the training of lawyers meshed with the emergence of elite bar associations. In 1870 only one-quarter of the men entering the profession were law school graduates, but by 1910 the proportion had jumped to two-thirds.[33] State legislatures did not require law degrees for admisison to the profession, but as lawyers festoned their office walls with diplomas, the public came to expect them. Small private law schools, offering part-time instruction and night classes, were a haven for upwardly mobile men who often held full-time jobs while earning law degrees.[34] State schools, such as the University of Wisconsin, envisioned themselves as university-based, teaching law offices and sent their graduates to all sectors of the profession.[35] Elite eastern law schools, most notably Harvard under Dean Christopher Columbus Langdell, hired full-time faculty, raised admission standards, pioneered the case method, and sent their graduates to prestigious law firms.[36] Particularly intriguing was the insistence of professors at prestigious schools that law could be scientific. Oliver Wendell Holmes and other legal theorists questioned this argument, but in adopting the pretentions of scientific inquiry, elite law schools echoed the ideological assumptions of the profession's upper crust. Secure in a sense of themselves as objective scientists, graduates of the schools could ignore the social and political implications of their jobs in large law firms.

The pronouncements of the elite bar associations and law schools commingled with the "new judicialism" or "creative conservatism," which one scholar has found prevalent in late-nineteenth-century America. In national politics, this new attitude became prominent in the 1890s when, after the populist conventions and Homestead and Pullman strikes, government leaders called for a national policy more supportive of industrialists and owners of capital.[37] In professional circles, the new attitude included demands for improved professional ethics and greater surveillance of lawyers' conduct. During the last decade of the century, twenty state bar associations adopted formal codes of professional responsibility, sometimes appending curious canons from the Swiss Canton of Geneva. In addition, George R. Peck, president of the American Bar Association, appointed a committee to consider a nationwide code of ethics. The committee included prominent lawyers such as Francis L. Stetson of New York and Henry St. George Tucker of Virginia and judges Alton P. Parker and Thomas Goode Jones; in 1906 it reported that the adoption of a code of ethics was advisable. In 1908 the association accepted the committee's draft of the Canons of Professional Ethics, a step hailed by the majority of state bar associations.[38]

If lawyers had taken this step during the early colonial years or during the antebellum period, it would have provoked protests from those enamored, respectively, with visions of communal unity or open-ended individual enterprise. But in the context of early-twentieth-century America, the legal profession's new boldness regarding the management of its own affairs hardly seemed out of place. As the fluid, entrepreneurial economy of the early nineteenth century gave way to an integrated, industrial economy, many organized groups with shared occupational and social perspectives garnered control over their particular sectors. The legal profession was but one group that assumed responsibility for its affairs.[39]

Since the adoption of the Canons of Professional Ethics constitutes an important bench mark in lawyers' ethics, students should carefully consider their inspiration, dimensions, and normative thrust. It was not a modern time-motion study or progressive tract that most inspired the codifiers of ethics; rather, it was a slim 1854 volume titled *An Essay on Professional Ethics*. George Sharswood, the author of the volume, was a graduate of the University of Pennsylvania who read law in the Philadelphia office of Joseph Ingersoll, at one time American Minister to Great Britain. After his clerkship, Sharswood became a prominent lawyer and judge. In 1850, at a time when elite Philadelphia lawyers still controlled admission to the local bar through mandatory clerkships in their offices, Sharswood accepted appointment as the head of the University of Pennsylvania's new law department. His lectures to students formed the basis of *An Essay on Professional Ethics*.[40]

For today's reader, Sharswood's volume seems old-fashioned and even stuffy. The author's vision of the profession was august, stressing the dignity and importance of lawyers and casting them as God's helpmates in earthly society. Lawyers, he felt, should never be speculators or higglers, men imbued with a commerical lust; they should be men with prudence, restraint, and a taste for fine literature. They should avoid pertness or flippancy before the court and disdain tricking their professional brethren. Pleasing one's brethren, Sharswood admitted, might cause hardship for the beginning lawyer, but "Sooner or later, the real public—the business men of the community, who have important lawsuits, and are valuable clients—endorse the estimate of a man entertained by his associates of the Bar."[41]

While Sharswood acknowledged that lawyers had responsibilities not only to clients but also to courts, other lawyers, and society, he insisted that the attorney's primary responsibility was to the client. Devoting most of his volume to this concern, Sharswood argued that the lawyer was not responsible for the social utility of the cause he represented. If the lawyer began judging cases on his own, he would be usurping the powers of judge and jury who, more so than lawyers, carried a responsibility to the public at large.

How consoling Sharswood's notions must have been to elite lawyers at the turn of the century! A lawyers' code could sanction fierce loyalty to individual clients and in the process contribute to fairness. Lost in the shuffle was a realistic appraisal of the specialization and stratification of the legal profession. The lawyers' code, which expanded on Sharswood's text, endorsed loyalty to the client while at the same time making it difficult to provide full representation to certain classes of clients.

According to the drafters of the Canons of Professional Ethics, those lawyers most likely to represent clients improperly were solo metropolitan practitioners serving working-class people. Occupying the lowest rung in the profession's hierarchy, these lawyers went largely unrepresented on bar association committees. To the chagrin of these lawyers, the newly approved Canons most severely affected their practice. One canon prohibited lawyers from publicly claiming a specialty. It hardly affected members of large firms with well-known corporate specialties, but it did hinder the solo practitioner who specialized in criminal or negligence work. Another canon prohibiting advertising had little impact on the prominent lawyer whose membership in professional clubs and participation in the management of charities, universities, and hospitals kept his name before the public. It did restrict practitioners whose working-class clients did not know if they had a legal claim or, for that matter, what to make of a dignified business card, the only sanctioned form of advertising. Still another canon prohibiting solicitation restricted the personal injury lawyer, the much demeaned "ambulance chaser," who alerted the injured to their rights and offered to represent them. The canons, it seems, would have different meanings for lawyers with differing clienteles.[42]

Only the canon pertaining to contingency fees provoked manifest disagreement in bar association circles. Sharswood had argued that the use of contingency fees tended "to corrupt and degrade the character of the profession,"[43] and most elite lawyers agreed with him. Yet, a growing number of work-and transportation-related accidents had made such fees an increasingly common arrangement between lawyers and injured clients. Certain mercenary practitioners used contingency fees to promote lawsuits and reap unduly large payments, but such fees also enabled some injured workers and travelers to pursue otherwise unaffordable legal actions.

Although contingency fees had been deemed "beyond legal controversy" by the Supreme Court in 1877,[44] the framers of the proposed canon concerning such fees cast them as immoral and urged close court supervision of their utilization. Some lawyers protested, noting both the canon's impact on solo practitioners who depended on contingency fees and also the general undesirability of any court control of fees. In the end, the framers of the canons left the matter to state jurisdictions, a stance respectful of states' rights and peculiarities among local bar associations. Some state bars in turn adopted a provision more stringent than even the original American Bar Association proposal.[45]

The dispute over the contingency fee canon hardly impeded the adoption of the whole code, and by the beginning of World War I, three-quarters of all state bar associations adopted the canons. As organizations with selected memberships, state bar associations had no power to enact legislation for all lawyers within the state, but state legislatures commonly welcomed the profession's new articulation of purpose and ethics. In most states, a complaint regarding a lawyer's misconduct was heard first by a bar association committee whose members made a preliminary finding after referring to the Canons, a finding that could then be appealed to a court. Both bar association committees and courts were aided by advisory opinions of the American Bar Association Committee on Professional Ethics and Grievances, which was established shortly after the original drafting of the canons.[46]

By the time President Wilson reluctantly led the United States into war, the profession had achieved virtually complete self-direction in ethical matters. In particular, primary control of the profession's ethics had passed from the legislatures and courts to bar associations and elite sections of the profession. Inspired by nostalgic pronouncements and sure of the rectitude of their own practices, the elite sectors endorsed the antebellum assumption that the legal profession's primary ethical responsibility was to represent fully the individual client. The elite sectors then elaborated this assumption in ways detrimental to the practices of ethnic solo practitioners. Expanded by bar committees, the canons would guide professional conduct for the next fifty years.

TWENTIETH-CENTURY CHALLENGES TO ETHICAL STANDARDS

Between World War I and the Vietnam War, American bureaucracies grew rapidly, and while old beliefs in individual enterprise lived on, a new ideology emphasizing efficiency and expertise emerged. The development of the American legal profession during the same years paralleled American social structure and values, but as critics recognized the problems of white-collar society, they also noted the failures of the legal profession. In the 1960s, critics alleged that the profession grossly underserved important groups of Americans. In the early 1970s, they wondered if the profession's normal practices might not leave its members particularly prone to immorality. Both in the 1960s and later, conservative defenders of the profession responded to the critics, but by the time the tainted Nixon Administration left Washington, the profession faced an avalanche of questions regarding the sources and implications of its ethics.

The most striking social change in the twentieth-century legal profession was bureaucratization. Private law firms with dozens and even hundreds of lawyers spread not only from Wall Street to midtown Manhattan, but also from New York to every other large city. Any corporation worth its stock market citation boasted an in-house legal staff, and even local companies brought salaried lawyers on board. In the public sphere, prosecutorial and public defense staffs expanded, and commissions, agencies, and departments on the state and federal level employed thousands of lawyers in both political and civil service positions. In the context of this large-scale bureaucratization of legal practice, the attorney's most typical work shifted from courtroom pleading to drafting, negotiating, and counseling. Roughly one-half of the nation's lawyers continued to practice on their own or in two- and three-person firms, but the rapid growth, economic power, and professional prestige of bureaucratic legal practices made the solo practitioner seem a marginal member of the legal fraternity.

Until roughly twenty years ago interpreters and enforcers of the canons, most of whom had ties to bureaucratic legal practices, encountered little difficulty directing the profession. Notions of efficiency, good management, and expertise buoyed the canons, but in general these rules of conduct maintained most of their 1908 language and form. Admirality specialists garnered a special dispensation from restrictions on specialty designations, but if Henry St. George Tucker, Alton Parker, or any of the framers could have reviewed the canons in the immediate post-World War II decades, they would have recognized their work. They also would have observed that the canons continued to have their greatest impact on solo practitioners representing working-class clients. The great majority of lawyers appearing before bar disciplinary committees had advertised or solicited legal work in ways that elite lawyers considered improper.[47]

With the canons palatable for burgeoning legal bureaucracies and suitable for controlling commercially rambunctious solo practitioners, the profession's ethics and professional responsibility committees turned from the conduct of its members to their qualifications. As a special American Bar Association committee chaired by Elihu Root asserted, something should be done to "purify the stream at its source."[48] In the 1920s, bar associations supported more stringent admission standards for the profession. The associations pressured state legislatures to require two or three years of college for applicants to the bar and to add character and fitness examinations to the traditional bar examinations. The state legislatures, where lawyers had become the largest occupational group, were at first slow to act, but when the Depression left many lawyers at short ends, pressure for more stringent admission standards mounted. By 1940, most states had adopted the bar association proposals.[49]

During the same twenty-year period, the American Bar Association and the Association of American Law Schools also promoted improvements in legal education. Although some states still allowed would-be lawyers to study law in office apprenticeships, legal education outside of law school had almost disappeared. Among the law schools, meanwhile, the hierarchy that had emerged in the late nineteenth century hardened, in large part due to the American Bar Association and the Association of American Law Schools' new practice of accrediting law schools. Accreditation standards, which stressed professor-student ratios and library size, greatly favored three-year full-time law schools with university affiliations. University law schools seemed to bar association and education leaders to be ideal institutions for the education of twentieth-century lawyers. State legislatures, prodded by state bars and universities, gradually accepted the accreditation standards and made graduation from an accredited law school a prerequisite for taking the state bar examination.[50] Only in California did the unaccredited law schools continue to prosper; the states's so-called "Lincoln laws" allowed graduates of unaccredited law schools to take state bar examinations.[51]

Law school enrollments soared after World War II. The profession's stream had been "purified at its source" as almost all beginning lawyers counted both college and three-year law degrees to their credit. Bar examinations grew more comprehensive, customarily including standardized multistate sections, and character and fitness examinations often enabled bar examiners to exclude the morally unfit. The Canons of Professional Ethics, buoyed by hundreds of opinions rendered by the American Bar Association Committee on Professional Ethics and Grievances, functioned as a guide to legal conduct. Institutions which taught and spoke for the profession's ethics were socially and ideologically synchronized with twentieth-century American social change.

But if the synchronization seemed perfect, contradictions within the profession and within the society as a whole soon jarred the gears. Aggressive professional self-criticism, which had begun with the left-leaning National Lawyers' Guild during the 1930s, revived in the 1960s. Civil rights lawyers traveled south to fight for racial equality, and in the process they attacked the profession for its failure to represent blacks. The decade's counterculture spawned legal communes in Cambridge, New York, and San Francisco. The legal workers in the communes and radical lawyers such as William Kunstler and Charles Garry argued that the profession as a whole was too greatly concerned with making money. Closer to the mainstream but still critical of the profession, "public interest" lawyers led and inspired by Ralph Nader sought to prevent federal agencies from giving large corporations preferential treatment. Large corporate entities had an abundance of forceful lawyers, but who, the public interest lawyers asked, represented American consumers?

In general, critics of the profession had little power in bar association committees, and indeed, William Kunstler and other radical lawyers found themselves before bar disciplinary panels.[52] Yet, critics of the profession did prove persuasive outside of the profession. In particular, Robert F. Kennedy, Sargent Shriver, and other members of the Kennedy and Johnson administrations championed a drive for federally funded legal services for the poor. Once established in the Office of Economic Opportunity, the legal services program grew in a few years to over 2,000 lawyers. Its legal staff not only represented individual indigent clients but also vigorously spoke out in the courts and before administrative panels on behalf of all the poor. The program, participants agreed, could begin correcting the legal profession's long-standing failure to serve the poor.[53]

If the initial success of the legal services program indicated the reformers' power, the program's fate illustrated that more traditional forces within the profession were ready for a fight. Local lawyers, some fearing a loss of business to storefront lawyers, argued that the latter's class actions disregarded the profession's primary responsibility to individuals. County bar associations, consisting primarily of local solo practitioners, agreed, as did Spiro Agnew. A former solo practitioner himself, the vice-president claimed in the *American Bar Association Journal* that storefront lawyers were stirring up litigation.[54] Leaders of the American Bar Association, although publicly supporting legal services, remained skeptical of the new legal institution's impact on professional norms and authority. Behind the scenes, the association urged restrictions on the program's size and power.[55]

Responsive to these arguments, members of Congress and the Nixon Administration worked to reshape the program. First, federal legal service lawyers lost the power to represent criminal defendants, and in 1973 the whole program itself was moved from the supportive environment of the federal antipoverty agency to the confines of a newly constituted corporation. With a charter prohibiting legal work in politically sensitive areas and with an appointed board of directors, the National Legal Services Corporation had much in common with other modern bureaucracies.[56]

Meanwhile, bar associations were feebly attempting to reset the profession's ethical controls. Several state bar associations began requiring lawyers to enroll in classes concerning recent developments in the law. The responsible lawyer, they argued, kept abreast of legal change. Other associations loosened their restrictions on specialty designations, asserting that the public would be better served if it could locate legal specialists.[57] Most importantly, the American Bar Association in 1969 replaced the Canons of Professional Ethics with the new Code of Professional Responsibility.

Unlike the outdated canons, the code articulated the profession's responsibility to make legal services available to all Americans; it also specified "ethical considerations" for all lawyers. The framers of the Code balked, however, at sanctioning group legal services by salaried attorneys, and restricted lawyers' advertising to "reputable" law lists approved by the American Bar Association.[58] Despite large-scale bureaucratization in the profession and mounting evidence that many Americans were underserved, the framers of the code reasserted the responsibility of individual lawyers to individual clients. Established ethical presumptions died hard.

The new code briefly quieted controversy regarding the profession's ethical responsibilities, but an unforeseen development again brought the controversy into the open. As the ugly saga of Watergate played on the country's television screens during 1973 and 1974, most of the major perjurers and obstructors of justice turned out to be lawyers. For some commentators, the crimes of the Nixon Administration lawyers, the attorney general, the vice-president and even the president himself seemed merely acute misconduct. But in some bar associations and lay circles, observers wondered if modern legal practice might invite a fundamental abandonment of morality.

Particularly troubling was the fact that the Nixon lawyers had worked in the type of bureaucratic setting that dominated the profession. Like their brethren in other private and public bureaucracies, the Nixon lawyers were primarily advisers and negotiators rather than courtroom pleaders. They believed in efficiency, good management, and expertise. Yet the work settings, practices, and professional codes of the Watergate participants had apparently not translated into ethical conduct. What were the foundations of a workable code of legal ethics? What were the modern lawyer's ethical responsibilities?

THE CONTEMPORARY DILEMMA OF PROFESSIONAL ETHICS

In the years since Watergate, the debate concerning professional ethics has continued in bar association and law school forums and in the courts. On one level, the debate reflects the bar's concern that public confidence in the profession is at a twentieth-century ebb. Some bar leaders fear that if public confidence is not restored through a new emphasis on professional ethics, attempts to restrict the profession's long-standing autonomy might be forthcoming. On another, more altruistic level, the debate reflects professional awareness that the dynamic nature of both the profession and society in general demands new standards for professional ethics. Important questions remain unformulated, but at the core of the debate is the problem of properly balancing one's responsibilities toward the client with those toward society.

A great deal of the contemporary debate concerns the recasting of codes of lawyers' ethics, and the American Bar Association's Commission on Evaluation of Professional Standards, formed in 1977, has stood at the center of this controversy. Chaired by Robert J. Kutak, the head of a multi-city law firm, the commission spent three years studying lawyers' ethics before, in 1980, offering to the American Bar Association a draft of the new Model Rules of Professional Conduct. Association members in turn debated the rules for three more years before approving a revised version in the summer of 1983. In the course of the six-year struggle one displeased lawyers' organization, The National Association of Criminal Defense Lawyers, urged that the rules be tabled. Another, The American Trial Lawyers' Association, offered an alternative code. In the words of one commentator, "The controversy over the rules poses the most serious threat to the unity of the American legal profession since the beginning of the bar association movement in the 1870s."[59]

What made the Model Rules so controversial? Media coverage stressed debates during the final stages of the approval process concerning a lawyer's responsibility to disclose a client's on-going illegal activities, but earlier the controversy involved the more fundamental question of the lawyer's responsibilities to the client and to society. Original drafts of the rules did not assume that contemporary society was integrated or communal—the contradictory social relations of modern life precluded such nostalgia. The drafts recognized the fact that bureaucratization and specialization of contemporary practice often isolated lawyers from larger social issues and perspectives. More pointedly, early drafts of the rules required lawyers to serve charities, public service groups, and the poor and to report annually the manner in which they had served the public.[60]

Proposals of this sort prompted hostile reactions from commentators who believed that the rules dangerously underestimated the social value of traditional loyalty to specific clients. In a symposium in the *Connecticut Bar Journal,* only one of several symposia that have appeared in print, one author charged the Kutak Commission with embracing an "essentially totalitarian view." Referring to the assumption that became dominant in the early nineteenth century well before the complexly interlocking modern society was in place, the author insisted, "Our duty to the legal system is, in the last analysis, our duty to the clients whom we represent."[61] Another symposium participant suggested that the corporate lawyers who dominated the Kutak Commission were unaccustomed to articulating a reasoned basis for loyalty to the client. They, as a result, took "the public relations route of seeking to appease their attackers by change where change was not necessary or desirable, but would look better."[62]

While bar associations have taken conflicting positions concerning the new codes, the associations' positions regarding ethical instruction in law schools is unambiguous. In 1974, recognizing that public confidence in the profession had been shaken by the Watergate affair, the American Bar Association launched a review of law school courses concerning legal ethics, professional responsibility, and the legal profession. These courses, the association concluded, needed strengthening. In particular, the association decreed that any law school seeking accreditation must provide ethical instruction covering "the history, goals, structure, and responsibilities of the legal profession and its members."[63] In the minds of association leaders, this curricular requirement—the first in the history of law school accreditation—explicitly commits the organized bar to the ethical socialization of its members.

The jury remains out as to whether the accreditation requirement has improved the ethical conduct of men and women entering the profession, but the requirement has clearly stimulated interest in professional ethics. During the last five years law professors have published hundreds of articles, conducted dozens of symposia, and generated innumerable packets of teaching materials concerning professional ethics. In the words of one commentator, "Professional responsibility is at long last assuming its rightful place in both legal thought and education, as the most important and intellectually stimulating subject in the curriculum."[64]

Student response to the increased law school emphasis on professional responsibility has been quite different. An American Bar Foundation study reveals that regardless of the contemporary law school's new emphasis on professional responsibility, students often look upon courses in the area as relatively unimportant. In a survey conducted at seven law schools, fifty-four percent of those currently enrolled in courses on professional responsibility or ethics indicated that other students were "not very" or "not at all" concerned with the subject. In contrast, ninety-four percent of the respondents felt fellow students were "concerned about making money." Ronald Pipkin, the scholar who has carefully studied these survey results, suggests that they indicate a "latent curriculum." Law students, with a certain degree of institutional encouragement, often rank their courses by considering doctrinal reliability, classroom procedures, and teaching success. Courses in professional responsibility—resting on a new and shifting doctrinal base, often approached without the traditional socratic method, and taught by inexperienced faculty members—customarily rank near the bottom of the students' curricular hierarchy. If teaching ethics in law school is to produce better, more ethically sensitive lawyers, Pipkin concludes, it must incorporate new, perhaps radically different methods that can counter disrespect for the subject in the latent curriculum.[65]

The most promising development in the teaching of professional responsibility involves the utilization of law school clinical programs. These programs gained a foothold in the late-1960s as law students demanded greater "relevance" in their education, but in the post-Watergate period schools have increasingly used clinical programs to teach professional responsibility. This approach remains in a developmental stage, but the early results are encouraging. In the context of clinical activities, memorization of shifting codes gives way to exposure to the ethical problems in the actual practice of law. Often clinical instruction emphasizing issues of professional responsibility leads students to reflect not only on lawyers' ethics but also on general moral assumptions. In addition, students in a clinical program for needy clients confront questions of the ethics of the whole system—its goals, its accomplishments, and its failures. More so than standard classroom instruction, clinical education has the potential to create young lawyers with a heightened sense of the ethical dimensions of legal work.[66]

The federal courts have in recent years also contributed to the resolution of debates regarding standards for legal conduct. In 1975, for example, the Supreme Court held that Virginia Bar Association fee schedules for title examination work affected interstate commerce. Since these schedules were not advisory but rather supported by bar disciplinary procedures, they constituted a violation of the Sherman Antitrust Act.[67] In 1977, in a case arising in Arizona, the Supreme Court held that bar association restrictions on advertising were not binding on a legal clinic whose advertisements listed fees for certain services. The clinic's advertising fell within the scope of First Amendment protection.[68] As these opinions and others indicate, the organized bar's fear that certain institutions might limit the profession's control of professional practices is well founded. Should the bar fail to pursue its reexamination and restructuring of professional standards, the courts seem willing to protect what they perceive to be the public interest.

The contemporary disputes in bar associations, law schools, and courts concerning professional ethics constitute an exciting but unfinished stage in the history of the American bar's effort to articulate its responsibilities. In the colonial period lawyers frequently collided with traditional social elites anxious to preserve social cohension and fearful of the way representation of individual clients could fracture the community. Only at the end of the colonial period did society conclude that the practice of law was in itself ethical. In the nineteenth century, fears lingered that lawyers would so vigorously represent clients that society as a whole would be harmed. But in the context of a blossoming entrepreneurial economy, bar leaders were persuaded that the lawyer's primary ethical responsibility should be the full representation of the individual client. This ethical premise remained dominant in the profession throughout the nineteenth century and, as current debates over lawyers' codes of responsibility indicate, the premise still has its advocates. Given the growth, differentiation, and bureaucratization of the profession in the twentieth century, new questions have arisen regarding the way social groups as opposed to individual clients are either over-or underrepresented. For some, the time seems at hand to reemphasize the lawyer's larger social responsibilities.

What are the ethical presumptions that might resolve the contradictions in the varied practices of lawyers? What are the modern lawyer's responsibilities? Answers are elusive, but an awareness of the bar's development and its handling of ethical questions over time helps illuminate contemporary dilemmas. If one understands the way in which the past has turned into the present, the difficult task of understanding and shaping professional ethics may begin.

NOTES

1. Quoted in Charles Warren, *A History of the American Bar* (Boston: Little, Brown, 1911), p. 40.

2. For discussions of the legal profession in colonial Virginia, see Anton-Hermann Chroust, *The Rise of the Legal Profession in America* (Norman: University of Oklahoma Press, 1965), I, pp. 262-263; Warren, op. cit., pp. 39–48.

3. For an excellent study of the interplay of tradition and design in early Massachusetts law, see George L. Haskins, *Law and Authority in Early Massachusetts* (New York: Macmillan, 1960).

4. For discussions of the legal profession in early Massachusetts, see Chroust, I, op. cit., pp. 55-108 and Warren, op. cit., pp. 59-89.

5. Winthrop had served during the 1620s as common attorney at the Royal Court of Wards and Liveries, and during this period the corruption he observed contributed to his disillusionment with English law. Edmund S. Morgan, *The Puritan Dilemma* (Boston: Little, Brown, 1958), pp. 22-44.

6. Chroust, I, op. cit., p. 72; Warren, op. cit., pp. 67-68.

7. Edwin Powers, *Crime and Punishment in Early Massachusetts, 1620-1692* (Boston: Beacon Press, 1966), pp. 435-437.

8. Gerard W. Gawalt, *The Promise of Power: The Emergence of the Legal Profession in Massachusetts, 1760-1840* (Westport: Greenwood Press, 1979), p. 8.

9. Warren, op. cit., p. 73.

10. Powers, op. cit., p. 438.

11. Cotton Mather, "Officials and Lawyers," in *Bonifacius, An Essay upon the Good* (1710; Cambridge, Mass.: Belknap Press, 1966), pp. 120-131.

12. Gawalt, op. cit., p. 25.

13. For a discussion of the legal profession in pre-War Massachusetts, see Gawalt, op. cit., p. 36-80.

14. John Adams, *Diary and Autobiography of John Adams*, ed. L. H. Butterfield (New York: Atheneum, 1964), I (1755-1770), p. 316.

15. For discussions of hostility toward lawyers during the 1790s, see Chroust, II, op. cit., pp. 281-283 and Warren, op. cit., pp. 211-239.

16. Maxwell Bloomfield, *American Lawyers in a Changing Society, 1776-1876* (Cambridge, Mass.: Harvard University Press, 1976), pp. 32-58.

17. Quoted in Warren, op. cit., p. 301. The Massachusetts bar grew from only 71 practitioners in 1776 to 493 in 1810. Gawalt, op. cit., p. 118.

18. For discussions of early-nineteenth-century frontier lawyers, see Elizabeth G. Brown, "The Bar on a Frontier: Wayne County, 1796-1836," *American Journal of Legal History* 14 (1970):136-156; Daniel H. Calhoun, "Branding Iron and Retrospect: Lawyers in the Cumberland River Country," in *Professional Lives in America: Structure and Aspiration, 1750-1850* (Cambridge, Mass.: Harvard University Press, 1965), pp. 59-87; Chroust, II, op. cit., pp. 92-128; Lawrence Friedman, *A History of American Law* (New York: Simon and Schuster, 1973), pp. 265-275.

19. Morton Horwitz, *The Transformation of American Law, 1780-1860* (Cambridge, Mass.: Harvard University Press, 1977), pp. 140-160.

20. R. Kent Newmeyer, "Daniel Webster as Tocqueville's Lawyer: The Dartmouth College Case Again," *American Journal of Legal History* 11 (1967):127-147.

21. Alexis de Tocqueville, *Democracy in America*, trans. Henry Reeve (New York: Schocken Books, 1961), I, pp. 321, 328.

22. Friedman, op. cit., p. 276.

23. For traditional interpretations stressing the decline of the early-nineteenth-century bar, see Chroust, II; Warren; and Roscoe Pound, *The Lawyer from Antiquity to Modern Times with Particular Reference to the Development of Bar Associations in the United States* (St. Paul, Minn.: West, 1953). For challenges to these interpretations, see Bloomfield, Brown, and Gawalt.

24. For a state by state review of early-nineteenth-century legislation regarding lawyers, see Chroust, II, op. cit., pp. 224-280.

25. J. F. Jackson, "Is the Profession of the Advocate Consistent with Perfect Integrity?" *The Knickerbocker*, 28 (1846):377-383.

26. These lawyers' opinions regarding their ethical responsibilities are collected by Perry Miller in *The Life of the Mind in America* (New York: Harcourt, Brace & World, 1965), pp. 203-205. Miller was at work on the volume at the time of his death, and the volume lacks citations for quoted material.

27. Friedman, op. cit., p. 549.

28. Ibid., pp. 557–560.

29. For a sketch of Charles Guiteau's legal career, see Charles E. Rosenberg, *The Trial of the Assassin Guiteau* (Chicago: University of Chicago Press, 1968), pp. 27–31.

30. For discussions of late-nineteenth-century in-house counsel, Wall Street lawyers and criminal law specialists, see, respectively, Morton Keller, *The Life Insurance Enterprise, 1885–1910* (Cambridge, Mass.: Belknap, 1963); Robert T. Swaine, *The Cravath Firm and Its Predecessors, 1819–1948* (New York: private printing, 1946), I (1819–1906); and Richard Rovere, *The Magnificent Shysters; The True and Scandalous History of Howe & Hummel* (New York: Grosset and Dunlop, 1947).

31. Friedman, op. cit., pp. 561–562.

32. Ibid., p. 563.

33. Jerold S. Auerbach, *Unequal Justice: Lawyers and Social Changes in Modern America* (New York: Oxford University Press, 1976), p. 94.

34. Robert Stevens, "Two Cheers for 1870: The American Law School," *Perspectives in American History* 5 (1971):428–430.

35. William R. Johnson, *Schooled Lawyers: A Study in the Clash of Professional Cultures* (New York: New York University Press, 1978).

36. Auerbach, op. cit., pp. 74–102; Stevens, op. cit., pp. 424–441.

37. Arnold M. Paul, *Conservative Crisis and the Rule of Law: Attitudes of the Bar and Bench, 1887–1895* (Ithaca: Cornell University Press, 1960).

38. Henry S. Drinker, *Legal Ethics* (New York: Columbia University Press, 1953), pp. 23–26.

39. For provocative discussions of professionalization in late-nineteenth-century America, see Burton J. Bledstein, *The Culture of Professionalism: The Middle Class and the Development of Higher Education in America* (New York: W. W. Norton, 1976); Corinne Gilb, *Hidden Hierarchies: The Professions and Government* (New York: Harper & Row, 1966); and Magali Sarfatti Larson, *The Rise of Professionalism: A Sociological Analysis* (Berkeley: University of California Press, 1977).

40. Gary B. Nash, "The Philadelphia Bench and Bar," *Comparative Studies in Society and History* 7 (1965):207–208.

41. George Sharswood, *An Essay on Professional Ethics* (1854; Philadelphia: T. & J. W. Johnson, 1907), p. 75.

42. Auerbach, op. cit., pp. 41–52; Drinker, op. cit., pp. 215–224.

43. Sharswood, op. cit., p. 159.

44. Stanton v. Embry, 93 U.S. 548 (1877).

45. Auerbach, op. cit., p. 47.

46. Drinker, op. cit., pp. 30–41.

47. Jerome E. Carlin, *Lawyers' Ethics: A Survey of the New York City Bar* (New York: Russell Sage Foundation, 1966).

48. Quoted in Auerbach, op. cit., p. 113.

49. Stevens, op. cit., pp. 501–504.

50. Ibid., pp. 464, 494, 501–504.

51. David R. Papke, "The Last Gasp of the Unaccredited Law Schools," *Juris Doctor* 3 (1973):30–37.

52. Auerbach, op. cit., pp. 289–292.

53. Ibid., pp. 269–275.

54. Spiro T. Agnew, "What's Wrong with the Legal Services Program," *American Bar Association Journal* 58 (1972):930–932; William R. Klaus, "Legal Services Programs: Reply to Vice-President Agnew," *American Bar Association Journal* 58 (1972):1178–1181.

55. Auerbach, op. cit., pp. 271–272.

56. Abortion, school desegregation, and the draft were three areas in which legal services lawyers were prohibited from working. Auerbach, op. cit., pp. 272–280.

57. Jerome A. Hochberg, "The Drive to Specialization," in *Verdicts on Lawyers,* ed. Ralph Nader and Mark Green (New York: Thomas Y. Crowell, 1976), pp. 118–128.

58. Auerbach, op. cit., pp. 285–288.

5p. Edward J. Imwinkelried, "A Sociological Approach to Legal Ethics," *American University Law Review* 30 (1981):350.

60. Some lawyers actually felt this requirement was too weak and unsuccessfully urged that lawyers be required to contribute a fixed number of hours to public service. Robert J. Kutak, "Coming: The New Modern Rules of Professional Conduct," *American Bar Association Journal* 66 (1980):49.

61. Theodore I. Koskoff, "Proposed New Code of Professional Responsibility: 1984 Is Now!" *Connecticut Bar Journal* 54 (1980):263.

62. Ralph Gregory Elliot, "The Proposed Model Rules of Professional Conduct: Invention Not Mothered by Necessity?" *Connecticut Bar Journal* 54 (1980):269.

63. American Bar Association, *Approval of Law Schools: American Bar Association Standards and Rules of Procedure, as Amended—1977* (Chicago: American Bar Association, 1977).

64. Stuart C. Goldberg, "1977 National Survey on Current Methods of Teaching Professional Responsibility in American Law Schools," in Stuart C. Goldberg, ed., *Pre-Conference Materials: 1977 National Conference on Teaching Professional Responsibility* (Detroit: University of Detroit School of Law, 1977), p. xiii.

65. Ronald M. Pipkin, "Law School Instruction in Professional Responsibility: A Curricular Paradox," *American Bar Foundation Research Journal* (1979), pp. 247–273.

66. Gilda M. Tuoni, "Teaching Ethical Considerations in the Clinical Setting: Professional, Personal and Systemic," *University of Colorado Law Review* 52 (1981).

67. Goldfarb v. Virginia State Bar, 421 U.S. 773 (1975).

68. Bates v. State Bar of Arizona, 433 U.S. 350 (1977).

Frederick A. Elliston

The Ethics of Ethics Tests for Lawyers

CONTROLLING THE PROFESSIONS

According to sociologists, one of the distinguishing characteristics of professionals is their possession of "dangerous knowledge." A doctor has the means to cure you or kill you. A nuclear scientist can light a city or build a bomb that levels it. A mechanical engineer can build a bridge to transport you or a prison to trap you. As Sir Francis Bacon remarked, knowledge is power; in the case of professionals, their specialized knowledge gives them power over our lives.

For this reason society is rightly concerned that the power of professionals be used properly. It requires not only that they be competent in order to reduce the probability of accidents, but that some mechanisms be in place to ensure that their power will not be abused.

In the case of lawyers, two mechanisms exist for regulating their conduct: a fitness test, whereby a candidate who is otherwise competent to practice law can be denied admission to the bar; and disciplinary proceedings, through which a lawyer who has already been admitted to the bar can be disbarred.

The power to set standards for admission to the bar resides in the courts and in the state legislatures, who in turn have delegated it to a board or committee of bar examiners. Though the decisions of bar examiners are not final, they are rarely overturned.

Despite variations in the specific standards and provisions, across states, one requirement remains constant: the candidate must demonstrate that he or she has "good moral character." In effect, to be admitted to the bar a lawyer must pass an ethics test.

As a profession law is not unique in testing candidates for ethics. The National Board of Medical Examiners and the American Board of Internal Medicine have introduced ethics questions into their examinations.[1] Most of the discussions of ethics tests for lawyers have been written by lawyers and legal scholars. Their questions focus on whether ethics tests violate provisions of the constitution, particularly First Amendment rights to freedom of speech and privacy.[2] But my purpose is to examine these character and fitness tests from

---

This essay was originally published as "Character and Fitness Tests: An Ethical Perspective," *The Bar Examiner* vol. 51, no. 3 (August 1982):8-16.

what Kurt Baier terms "the moral point of view."[3] Are ethics tests themselves ethical? Is there any good reason to believe that they violate the moral rights of candidates?

MORALITY, MORALS, AND MORES

What is a "good moral character"? Unless this question can be answered clearly and convincingly, the very basis for moral fitness tests is undermined. In one sense the question is easy—too easy—for almost everyone has a conception of what a good person is. The problem, to put it succinctly, is not that we have no answer, but that we have too many. Whose morality, or whose conception of morality, should prevail? Supreme Court Justice Hugo Black broached just such a question when he characterized this "unusually ambiguous" term, "easily adapted to fit personal views and predilections," as a potentially "dangerous instrument for arbitrary and discriminatory denial of the right to practice law."[4]

The Enforcement of Morals

When a board of bar examiners interviews a candidate, are they testing that person's morals against morality itself, someone else's morals, or the mores of the community? According to one member of a fitness board, the test "is applying contemporary community standards of morality and character to those who seek to practice law."[5] But there are difficulties in appealing to community mores, or what Lord Patrick Devlin refers to as positive or public morality,[6] as H. L. A. Hart[7] and Devlin's other critics[8] have argued persuasively.

First, any appeal to the morality of the community presupposes that the community is one group with one coherent set of values that remain relatively constant over time. However, if the community is made up of several different groups—ethnic, economic, and political—then this assumption is overly simplistic. On a pluralistic model of society, there is no single set of values to use as a standard. The Fitness Board Members, then, must choose one group and elevate its morality to a privileged status. But what is the moral justification for the selection of this group? Certainly there can be various historical and political explanations for the preeminence of white, middle-class male values. But any appeal to that group's morality as a basis for its special treatment would beg the question. Furthermore, circularity cannot be avoided by appealing to a principle of morality beyond that of the group. If we were to do so, then that very principle, rather than the group's morality, would function as the ultimate source of moral justification. The community mores, whether they agree or disagree with these objective principles, will be of no account.

Second, the values of individuals, groups, and communities shift over time, and these shifts generate inequities when Fitness Boards appeal to community mores. The various discussions of homosexual applicants or those who cohabitate illustrate this problem.

In the past, many communities regarded homosexuality as unnatural and perverted.[9] Understandably, Fitness Boards, whose decisions are based on community mores, excluded applicants who were practicing homosexuals. In doing so they were simply reflecting the moral values operative in their community at the time. And insofar as their actions were supposed to be based on community mores, they were right.

But sexual mores change, and many communities today regard private homosexual acts as permissible conduct, provided they are restricted to informed consenting adults. Such changes in community mores generate a moral paradox. On the one hand, if the community was mistaken in its earlier belief that homosexuality was wrong, then it was equally mistaken in denying applicants admission to the bar because they were homosexuals. If, on the other hand, the community was not mistaken at that time, then it must be mistaken now. Either way, some applicants for admission to the bar will be treated unfairly.

Third, the current procedures for applying community standards generates moral anomalies similar to the moral paradox just described. In practice they take state lines as the boundaries of the community. Consequently, an applicant can be rejected from the bar in Virginia because of cohabitation but admitted in Georgia. But if cohabitation is indeed sufficiently serious to justify disqualification, as the Virginia Bar believes, then the admission practice in Georgia is wrong. If cohabitation is not sufficiently serious to justify disqualification, as the Georgia Bar believes, then the practice in Virginia is wrong. In either case some candidates for admission to the bar will be wronged. Such moral mistakes are inevitable if admission practices are based on the moral beliefs of communities that do not agree.

The fourth and final objection can be elicited by an analogy. Suppose we substitute interracial marriage for cohabitation and, in addition, change the time frame to the period when blacks were considered inferior. Under these conditions, a black candidate would be denied admission to the bar; even though from a moral point of view such a denial is blatantly wrong because it betrays an obvious racist bias. But if one is appealing to the morality of the community, and the community is sexist or racist, then one's admission practices are racist or sexist.

Though community mores may serve as a point of departure, they cannot as such serve as a final court of appeal without perpetuating injustices. Before making the community's moral beliefs the basis for law or legal practice, we must subject them to careful scrutiny. Fundamental principles of ethics and social justice must be invoked to appraise shifting conventional values. It is not the communty's moral beliefs, but the logical force of the arguments used to sustain them, that should shape the legal profession's policy. Failure to appreciate this distinction between the beliefs and their rationale can easily lead to the enthronement of social baises and shared prejudices.

A Factual Challenge

Do Fitness Boards in fact apply community standards? One survey suggests that they do not: "Bar Examiners and the general, though informed public, while responding with identical criteria, arrived at recommendations that were uniformly opposed."[10] When we look at the actual decisions of Fitness Boards, we find that the board members from the legal profession do not always agree with the public's evaluation of some candidates. In view of this discrepancy, the ideology that claims a preeminence of community standards is suspect.

Moreover, if Fitness Boards were serious in their intention to apply community standards, they would need to conduct systematic surveys to discover just what the community's standards are. But such surveys could place them in the difficult situation of having to decide what to do when their own evaluations are at odds with that of the public. Wisely, Fitness Boards forego community surveys.

One solution is to substitute the Board's decisions for the community's morality, which is thereby relegated to a secondary status. Indeed, this is the solution of many boards. This substitution is typical in the life of any organization: though initially deriving its authority from without, it can all too easily become a power unto itself.

One consequence of this displacement of authority is illustrated by the Board's response to lack of candor from applicants who fail to disclose fully all the information the Board requested. Withholding information threatens the operation of the Board, and is therefore taken seriously by its members. Lack of candor is itself a serious transgression—indeed sometimes more serious than the wrong-doing the applicant sought to conceal. Candidates are rejected for failure to provide information that, upon disclosure, would not have been a bar to admission. For example, refusal to answer a question about one's membership in a communist party has been grounds for dismissal, despite pleas that such a question violates the applicant's constitutional rights. Such Board actions are more a reflection of operational need than principles of justice.

ALTERNATIVE IDEOLOGIES

The Purpose of the Test

Perhaps we can get a firmer grip on the question "Whose morality should prevail?" if we consider the purposes of moral fitness tests. Their ostensible purpose has already been identified: to protect the public. Given this purpose, the public's morality should prevail, rather than that of the legal profession.

But ethics tests serve a less visible but equally important second purpose: to protect the public image of the legal profession. Members of the bar want to be held in esteem by the community, a particularly urgent demand after the high involvement of lawyers in the Watergate scandal. Accordingly, prospective new members must exhibit high standards of personal conduct. Do such standards reflect principles of fairness, or the social aspirations of lawyers? Even putting aside questions of effectiveness, one can ask: Do these standards visit the sins of their predecessors on the next generation of lawyers?

To these two purposes—protecting the public and protecting the public image of lawyers—I would add two others. First, ethics tests are designed to protect prospective clients. Since businessmen with financial problems would not want to compound them by hiring an unscrupulous attorney who had been convicted of embezzlement, candidates for the bar who have been convicted of such a crime are disqualified. More generally, disqualifying applicants with felony convictions protects clients. But disqualification is not the only means of protection. Such applicants could be restricted in the kind of practice they could undertake—e.g., prohibiting them from practicing corporate law, handling bankruptcy cases, or being hired to process real estate closings. Admittedly it would be difficult to monitor compliance, but the machinery might be no more complicated than that set up for fitness tests. Or, one could require that the lawyer reveal his past crimes to prospective clients who are then free to determine for themselves the attorney's fitness to represent them. Some clients might believe that an embezzler is just the kind of shrewd lawyer they want!

The disqualification of a schizophrenic applicant is an example of the fourth purpose—to protect the applicant. If the stress of a courtroom situation may induce a schizophrenic attack, then disqualifying such an applicant averts it. Disqualification on this basis is obviously paternalistic: the Board is implicitly asserting that it knows better than the applicants what is in their best interests and how to achieve it. As an empirical thesis, such a paternalistic presumption is problematic. Boards know comparatively little about applicants, much less what is in their best interest. As an ideological thesis, paternalism is a crude tool for shaping adult behavior, especially compared to alternatives like educating, advising, and counselling.

But again, one can ask if disqualification is the fairest or most effective way to protect candidates. If the candidate has no intention of becoming a courtroom lawyer, disqualification is unnecessary. If he or she does have this inspiration, disqualification is extreme: the candidate could be admitted with the stipulation (or recommendation) that he or she select a less stressful type of practice.

The general point I am trying to make with these examples is that denying someone access to his or her chosen profession is a severe action that should not be undertaken unless equally effective, less drastic, and more equitable means can not be found. Moreover, since preventing people from pursuing their careers is blatanty harmful, the burden of proof is on those who defend such a measure. It will be difficult to provide this proof until the alternatives have been much more fully explored.

An Immodest Proposal

What are the alternatives? There are many, a few of which I have mentioned in passing. Greater disclosure of the attorney's background would allow a client to make an informed choice about the kind of lawyer he or she wants. More restrictions on the attorney's choice of practice may help protect both the lawyer and the client. I would like to suggest an ethical audit as one of the most promising alternatives.

Some businesses, in order to accommodate the demand for greater social accountability, have undertaken a social audit. One member of their senior management team has the task of appraising the company's contribution to the community. In so doing, the manager has an opportunity to take stock of what the company has done, both the good and the bad, as a measure of its contribution to and its status in the community.

Private law firms could undertake a similar ethical audit to determine how well their senior and junior partners are measuring up to their social responsibilities. They could undertake their own assessment of the extent to which the standards of the Code of Professional Conduct are being met. Lawyers in small private practices could be randomly subject to an ethical audit. Such an investigation, carried out by the State Bar Ethics Committee, would be comparable to an income tax audit: it would serve to determine how well lawyers are fulfilling their professional responsibilities. The virtue of making such audits random is that they would serve as a deterrent to questionable conduct and provide each lawyer with an incentive to meet all minimal disciplinary standards.

If the legal profession seriously believes that lawyers should be honest and truthful, it could ask a random sample of recent clients whether their attorneys ever displayed a lack of candor in professional dealings with them, whether important information was ever withheld or if the clients were misled in any way. The clients' assessment of their lawyers' moral characters, filtered through an informed and critical committee of peers, would provide a more significant and reliable measure of the moral status of practicing lawyers than preadmission interviews or tests. Of course, complaints from clients, like complaints from patients, do not always indicate that something is wrong. But they are a starting point for a profession trying to regulate itself, and could prove to be an effective way to maintain high standards of professional responsibility.

Rehabilitation

Suppose the candidate fails the moral fitness test. Must he or she be excluded from the practice of law forever? In an effort to treat candidates more humanely, boards are increasingly willing to answer in the negative. Over time, rejected candidates may mend their ways and therefore deserve reconsideration. As their rationale, Fitness Boards have invoked a rehabilitative ideology. Though they are doing the right thing, they are doing so for the wrong reason.

Until recently, this rehabilitative ideology permeated penal policy. But over the past decade it has been widely discredited by criminologists. It is ironic to find such a view creeping into the legal profession after its failure to achieve widespread support in the courts and prisons. There are several problems with it.

First, the track record of rehabilitative programs in prisons raises serious doubts that anything works. They are largely ineffective because people cannot be forced to mend their ways. When it is a matter of a person's character or way of life, there is little that others can do to force change. If prisoners cannot be forced to change their ways when they are almost totally in the power of those who are euphemistically called "correctional authorities," then it is highly unlikely that prospective lawyers will be forced to change their ways by threatening to deny them access to their chosen career.

Second, it is almost impossible to tell when a person is rehabilitated. Correctional personnel are able to monitor an individual's behavior twenty-four hours a day, seven days a week for months on end. And yet, as the discouraging statistics on recidivism prove, mistakes are frequently made. How, then, is a Fitness Board, having far less information and time with which to base its decision, to determine when a person has been rehabilitated? The task is more than difficult, it is next to impossible.

Boards correctly realize that the lack of a subsequent similar offense on an individual's record over a fixed period of time does not mean that another such offense will not be committed. Perhaps the opportunity never presented itself. Since the Board cannot distinguish between lack of opportunity and lack of desire, it cannot distinguish between the rehabilitated and the "deprived."

One solution for the Fitness Board is to follow the courts and corrections in abandoning the principle of rehabilitation in favor of a principle of "just deserts."[11] Guided by this principle the Board could delay consideration of an application for a period of time proportional to the seriousness of the offense. If an embezzlement conviction makes a person unfit to practice law, then defer reconsideration for a fixed period of time (say, equal to the minimum sentence for embezzlement). This deferral would constitute a fair penalty, and when the time had been "served" the individual could reapply. There would be no question of whether the person was rehabilitated, but there would be a question of whether any offenses had been committed in the interim. If so, these would be the basis for a further deferral, again proportional to the seriousness of the new offense.

THE MENTAL HEALTH ISSUE

In addition to moral fitness, Boards are charged with the responsibility of assessing an applicant's mental health. The question of whether an applicant is emotionally and psychologically fit to practice law is, at one level, a straightforward empirical one, to be answered by mental health specialists. Yet difficult problems of confidentiality and equity underly this question.[12]

How might a Board of Bar Examiners learn that an applicant is emotionally unstable? There are three sources from whom such information can be obtained: a professional counsellor, the applicant, or someone who knows the applicant's situation. Yet there are moral hurdles in using any one of these sources.

The Psychiatrist's New Code of Conduct

Consider first professional psychiatrists or psychologists. Insofar as they offer a professional judgment, it falls under their own professional code of ethics. Typically, under such codes, a judgment about a patient's mental condition should not be made public except in extreme cases such as an immediate threat to someone's life. Whatever threats a candidate for the bar may pose to the public, the "danger" is not usually immediate. Accordingly, the psychiatrist's disclosure often violates a professional commitment of confidentiality. For this reason, it would be morally unjustifiable and wrong for lawyers to request such information.

The request from lawyers to psychiatrists for information about patients is ironic: lawyers are themselves strictly enjoined by their own code of ethics to safeguard the confidences—indeed the secrets—of their own clients. They cannot secure privileged information from psychiatrists, psychologists, and therapists without at the same time violating a principle of their own profession. Consistency in the application of principles governing disclosures precludes lawyers from asking other professionals to provide information when they are forbidden to do so themselves. Both the disclosure and the request for the disclosure are morally proscribed by a principle of confidentiality in professional ethics.

Self Disclosure

Is it right to require applicants to disclose this information themselves? Several cases have challenged this request on the grounds that it violates constitutional guarantees against intrusion into one's personal and most intimate self. The relevant moral principle is that of the right to privacy. Everyone has a right not to be required to reveal information about their innermost life. As a corollary they also have a moral right not to be forced to reveal information that would harm them. This moral right underlies the Fifth Amendment guarantee against self-incrimination. The legal parallel is telling: requiring applicants to furnish information about their past, information that may be used to deny them admission to the bar, is like requiring witnesses to testify against themselves. In both legal and moral contexts, such intrusions have been properly condemned. Moreover, a troublesome irony is that the applicants most willing to admit personal problems are often less disturbed than those who refuse to acknowledge them.

Other Sources of Information

Another source of information is third parties who are knowledgeable about the applicant's mental condition. Typically they would come by such knowledge as the result of the applicant's decision to seek help from them—e.g., support groups, counsellors, or friends. The problem with using this source of information is ably identified by Dr. Kaslow's question: What about the applicant who never sought such help and for whom consequently no such source of information is available?[13] These people, who may be more emotionally unstable, would be admitted to the bar. Their willingness to seek help is an important first step on the road to mental health. Yet, to disqualify persons who take this step while admitting those who do not is surely wrongheaded, and it would be a weak defense of such a policy simply to say that nothing can be done about those who do not seek help. If we are to be fair, we must abandon a procedure that discriminates against those who seek help and in favor of those who do not.

I have tried to show that the conventional avenues for obtaining information about mental or psychological fitness are blocked. If I have succeeded, then we should drop any effort to test the mental health of applicants to the bar. Some may fear that the result would be to diminish the stature of the bar by admitting "crazies." I doubt such fears are warranted. The teaching profession does not screen applicants for mental fitness and yet universities are not populated by academics with mental disorders. The main reason for this is not hard to find: a doctoral program is so demanding that those who are mentally unfit are unlikely to complete it. Similarly, the law school program is sufficiently demanding that those who are emotionally unstable are unlikely to see it through. Until the data can be generated to demonstrate that the sanity of lawyers is a serious problem, I would not fear the consequence of abandoning mental health screening.

GOOD LAWYERS AND GOOD PEOPLE

Underlying moral fitness tests is the assumption that to be a good lawyer one must be a morally good person. I shall call this the principle of identity for it identifies a good lawyer with a good person. From this principle it follows logically that if one is not a morally good person, one will not be a good lawyer. On the basis of this inference the various boards of bar examiners disqualify individuals who are not morally good people.

What makes someone a morally good person, and how does one decide? Does a homosexual orientation, membership in a communist organization, political dissent,[14] a declaration of bankruptcy to avoid paying student loans,[15] a series of convictions for drunk driving or for brewing beer[16] constitute ample grounds for disqualification as a morally good person, and hence justify exclusion from the legal profession? All these questions are beside the point, however, if it is not necessary to be a morally good person in order to be a good lawyer. If indeed it is sometimes a hindrance, then moral fitness tests are pointless. I believe that the identity principle is false, and in its place I shall offer two others. The first is that a good lawyer sometimes does otherwise immoral actions for good ends. The second is that a good lawyer is amoral, i.e., simply the instrument of the client's will.

A Philosophical Challenge

The work of Allan Goldman provides a theoretical challenge to the simplistic view that standard moral principles "apply" uniformly across all professions.[17] He argues that moral principles must be worked out within the context of a professional role and he goes on to distinguish two types. A professional role is strongly differentiated if it requires unique and distinctive moral principles different from those of morality generally. A role is weakly differentiated if the general moral principles are qualified by the institutional context but not violated. In the case of the former, actions which would otherwise be wrong could, for a certain profession, be permissible or obligatory.

For example, it is ordinarily wrong to shoot people except in self defense. But the police regularly shoot offenders who pose no threat to the officer's life in order to prevent their escape and to apprehend them. Similarly, in order to uphold the rule of law, judges must defer to legal precedent when it violates their own moral sensibilities or challenges those of the community at large. The role of these criminal justice officials is, according to Goldman, strongly differentiated.

What these two examples show, along with the arguments Goldman develops to defend them, is that one cannot without further ado move from general moral principles to an evaluation of the conduct of professionals. The relation between ethics and the professions is more complicated—and must be worked out for each profession. Until it has been worked out, moral fitness tests are a problematic and perhaps unwarranted procedure.

Challenges from the Profession

The recent literature on the professional responsibilities of lawyers attempts to work out a professional ethic for lawyers. In so doing many legal scholars have challenged the assumption that a good lawyer is a good person. Perhaps the most famous (or infamous) example of this is Monroe Freedman.[18] In a groundbreaking article, he argued that lawyers must put clients on the stand even when it is known that there is intent to commit perjury. By ordinary moral standards it is wrong to lie or to help others lie. Yet Freedman's lawyers would permit it and perhaps through their silence facilitate the client's lying.

Similarly, it is ordinarily wrong to prevent others from discovering the truth. Yet in the celebrated Garrow case, the lawyer, who knew where the two bodies were buried and deliberately did not tell, has been defended by writers and exonerated by the New York State Bar.[19]

Ordinarily it is wrong to harm innocent people. But if a defense attorney can discredit a truthful rape victim's testimony, because she is emotionally distraught, the Code of Professional Conduct would allow such cross examination.

These examples can be multiplied, qualified, and questioned. But the fact that actions ordinarily judged wrong are defended by legal scholars challenges the testing of candidates for their adherence to ordinary moral principles.

The Roots of the Paradox

No doubt many would like to dismiss these examples as aberrations, exceptions to the rule that good lawyers are good people. But I do not think they are. The roots of lawyers' moral obligations are planted in their duty to represent client interests zealously within the limits of the law. However one quibbles over the qualification "zealously," the point remains that the primary constraint on the actions of attorneys is the law and not morality—certainly not their own morality, the community's morality, or any general or ordinary morality, except insofar as these have been enacted into law.

If an action is legal and will help a client, then a lawyer is obliged to so act. If the action is legal and immoral but will nonetheless help a client, then a lawyer is still enjoined or at least allowed to do it. Lawyers are agents of and advocates for client interests; they are bound to pursue these interests, and morality plays no role.

In helping a client do something legal but wrong, the action of lawyers can be judged in two ways. First we might say that it is wrong to help others to do wrong, i.e., the sins of the client are to be visited on the lawyer. Alternatively, we can treat lawyers as mere tools of their clients: their actions are not so much immoral as amoral. On this second interpretation the moral neutrality of lawyers is stressed; they are treated not as persons but as things.

But whether the lawyers are regarded as occasionally immoral or basically amoral, a paradox arises at the heart of the legal profession today. When it is a matter of entry, prospective lawyers are required to be morally good persons. Yet once admitted, they are required to be immoral, if not amoral. It is inconsistent and self-defeating to test people for qualities they must have to be admitted to a profession if they are subsequently required to abjure those same qualities in order to function within it.

I have painted this paradox in bold strokes in order to emphasize the contrast. One can propose various measures to mediate the conflict between these opposing demands. The most common means proposed is to give lawyers the option of withdrawing when the actions of clients violate personal moral codes. But this provision displaces the problem without solving it. As long as everyone is entitled to representation, some lawyers will need to assist persons in legal but immoral acts. There are only two solutions if the system is to be made consistent: the first is to drop the demand that prospective lawyers be moral persons;

the second is to deny individuals the opportunity to use the law to achieve immoral ends. The first entails the abolition of moral fitness tests. The second calls for far-reaching reforms in law as it is currently practiced.

NOTES

1. See the symposium "Ethics Tests for Medical Boards: The State of the Question," *The Hastings Center Report* 13 (June 1983):20-33.

2. See the section of the bibliography at the back of this volume for helpful further readings.

3. Kurt Baier, *The Moral Point of View* (New York: Random House, 1965).

4. Konigsburg v State Bar, 353 U.S. 252, 263 (1957).

5. Lawrence B. Custer. "Georgia's Board to Determine Fitness of Bar Applicants," *The Bar Examiner* 51 (August 1982):17-21.

6. Lord Patrick Devlin. *The Enforcement of Morals* (New York: Oxford University Press, 1965), chapter 1.

7. See H. L. A. Hart's *Law Liberty and Morality* (Stanford, Calif.: Stanford University Press, 1963).

8. Excepts from Lord Devlin's essay and the responses of several critics are gathered together in Richard Wasserstrom's useful little collection *Morality and the Law* (Belmont, Calif.: Wadsworth Publishing Co., 1971).

9. Ibid., p. 3.

10. Ms. Susan Robinson.

11. For an early and popular discussion of this philosophy as applied to sentencing, see Andrew Von Hirsch's *Doing Justice* (New York: Hill and Wang, 1976). Richard D. Singer offers a more scholarly appraisal of the retributivist philosophy in his *Just Deserts* (Cambridge, Mass.: Ballinger Publishers, 1979).

12. Florence W. Kaslow. "Moral, Emotional and Physical Fitness for the Bar: Pondering (seeming) Imponderables," *The Bar Examiner* 51 (August 1982):38-48.

13. Ibid.

14. See Donald Weckstein's "Recent Developments in the Character and Fitness Qualifications for the Practice of Law: The Law School Role; the Political Dissident," *The Bar Examiner* 40 (January 1971):17-24.

15. The case is the Florida Board of Bar Examiners re G. W. L., 364 So. 2d 164 (Fla. 1978). For a discussion of it, see Michael D. White's "Good Moral Character and Admission to the Bar: A Constitutionally Invalid Standard?" *Cincinnati Law Review* 48 (1979):876.

16. An attorney was disbarred for three years simply because he brewed beer. See Barton v. USDC Nebraska, 19 F 2d 722 (1927).

17. See Allan Goldman's *The Moral Foundations of Professional Ethics* (Totowa, N.J.: Littlefield Adams, 1978).

18. See Monroe Freedman, "Professional Responsibility of the Criminal Defense Lawyer: The Three Hardest Questions." *Michigan Law Review* 64 (1966):1469-1484. See this volume, pp. 328-339.

19. See Frank H. Armani, "The Obligation of Confidentiality," *Juris* (March 1975):3-5 and Jeffrey F. Chamberlain, "Legal Ethics: Confidentiality and the Case of Garrow's Lawyers," *Buffalo Law Review* 25 (1975):211-239.

F. Raymond Marks and Darlene Cathcart

Discipline Within the Legal Profession

The practice of law is recognized by most people in the community and by the state to be a "profession."[1] Lawyers think of themselves and speak of themselves as belonging to a profession. Moreover, the organized bar addresses itself to professional aspects of the common calling. Yet, in a crucial element of true professional identity—the meaningful regulation of its own members—the organized bar is seriously deficient.

Formally, the legal profession asserts exclusive authority to determine who is competent to practice law and who in the course of practice is subject to reprimand, suspension, or disbarment.[2] At the present time the courts and the organized bar are the only formal forums where *any* review of the professional conduct and performance of lawyers occurs.[3] The principle of self-regulation continues to be asserted despite public uneasiness about the ethical conduct of lawyers,[4] despite uneasiness from inside and outside the profession about defining and maintaining standards of competence for the many varieties of legal work, and despite an apparent gap between the ideal and the reality of self-regulation.

Previous studies of self-regulation within the legal profession have viewed the subject from two main perspectives. They have attempted to understand either why lawyers deviate from ethical and professional standards[5] or why existing practices and procedures of disciplinary agencies fail to control adequately even egregious departures from community and professional standards.[6]

Both of these approaches are too narrow. By focusing on the way things are and the way things have been done, they relate to issues of misconduct alone. These studies, as well as the disciplinary agencies we examined, fail to recognize that two tasks are involved in the process of self-regulation: the task of monitoring conduct and the task of maintaining the quality of performance. In our judgment, an approach is needed that not only takes into account the way the disciplinary agencies go about their tasks, but also attempts to understand why the agencies have defined their tasks as narrowly as they have. We need to relate

From *University of Illinois Law Forum* (1974):193-236. Copyright 1974 by the Board of Trustees of the University of Illinois. Reprinted by permission of the publisher.

the disciplinary function to expectations—both professional and public—arising from the professional status of lawyers and the fact that they are licensed. What is needed is a functional definition of professional self-regulation that embraces assurances of both integrity and competence among practicing lawyers.[7]

What expectations regarding professionalism arise from the fact of licensing? The rationale for licensing rests on an assumption that the public will be protected against both unethical conduct and substandard performance. This rationale is reflected in *Dent v. West Virginia,* in which the United States Supreme Court said:

> The power of the State to provide for the general welfare of its people authorizes it to prescribe all such regulations as, in its judgment, will secure or tend to secure them against the consequences of *ignorance* and *incapacity* as well as deception and *fraud.* As one means to this end it has been the practice of different States . . . to exact in many pursuits a certain degree of skill and learning upon which the community may confidently rely. . . .[8]

The licensing rationale is, at least theoretically, carried out by bench and bar supervision of legal education and admission. But all semblance of following the licensing rationale disappears once the license has been issued. This omission seems to turn on a presumption that the initial screening did all that is necessary, or desirable, or practicable, or possible, with respect to competence. While this presumption ignores the need for the perpetual updating and refinement of knowledge that characterizes modern law practice, it may reflect another reality, the inability to define and measure criteria against which competence can be assessed. Furthermore, a formal mechanism for peer review of lawyer performance is lacking. Whether one could be created raises the same question at a different level. In any event, rather than engage a review of performance, something else has been the goal of the disciplinary agencies; their proceedings have related solely to conduct. Existing disciplinary processes have tended to imitate the criminal justice system rather than to regulate the legal profession. Language of wrongdoing and deviance rule the approach.

This article examines the existing approaches to self-regulation within the legal profession with an attempt to understand some of the reasons, not heretofore suggested, for what appears to be an endemic inability on the part of the organized profession to regulate its own members. In order to arrive at an overview of the disciplinary process, the article is based on interviews with bar executives, bar counsel, and disciplinary personnel in seventeen jurisdictions, and a review of the current literature about the disciplinary process.

To arrive at a functional definition of discipline and self-regulation, we need to understand the kinds of matters presently brought and not brought to the attention of the disciplinary agencies, the kinds of matters to which the disciplinary agencies respond and the kinds to which they do not respond, and whom—what constituencies—the disciplinary agencies perceive themselves as representing. Like the American Bar Association Special Committee on Evaluation of Disciplinary Enforcement (the Clark Committee), our focus is on the disciplinary agencies. But unlike the Clark Committee, we are more interested in the roles and relationships of those agencies and in their sense of accountability than we are in their procedures. The procedures of the disciplinary agencies are of interest to us, of course, but mainly as an explanation of the ways in which these agencies account to the involved lawyers, the bar, the courts, the complainants, and the public. In the end it may be that some mechanisms of self-regulation other than disciplinary agencies exist or are needed.

To accomplish our objectives, we will first examine the standards of performance, in theory and practice, of the legal profession. We will then discuss the current process of receiving and acting on complaints against lawyers. Following that discussion we will assess several analytic models for the treatment of complaints and the apparent discrepancy between the inputs and outputs of the present disciplinary process. Finally we will present an overview of professional self-regulation, including what we perceive to be changes necessary for effective professional review, as well as the consequences of the present disciplinary approach.

Before beginning our task, however, several concepts, which can be troublesome if not carefully delineated, should be clarified. Performance and conduct must be distinguished. Performance is how skill is applied for the execution or completion of a task. It is devoid of any moral conduct or standards and assumes a standard of and thus some agreement about, measurement. Conduct, in contrast, relates to the behavior of lawyers. It assumes both community and professional standards; hence agreement about norms exists, whether they be criminal laws or professional ethics.

The terms neglect, negligence, and competence have also been troublesome. The lines of demarcation are not clear. Some will insist that a lawyer is always competent, but sometimes neglectful. Others will say that neglect in some instances, or at least when it is repeated, is evidence of incompetence. For our purposes, competence is a general term that implies the possession of a skill. It also implies a measurable standard. At the level of performance, however, the term competence picks up an active connotation; it is the appropriate application of skill to the performance and the completion of particular tasks. Negligence is the failure to perform a task in accordance with the standard applied, whereas neglect is a part of negligence and is the failure to perform in a timely fashion. Significantly, the terms overlap; a substandard performance may be the result of an inability to perform or it may be the result of an instance of omission or commission in a particular matter. In other words, competent lawyers can perform incompetently.[9]

STANDARDS OF PERFORMANCE—THEORY AND PRACTICE

Perhaps the best way to understand the present status of professional self-regulation is to observe the difference between enunciated standards of performance and conduct—the Code of Professional Responsibility—and the reality of disciplinary enforcement. The contrast between the profession's aspirations and its actual performance is striking. To fully perceive this contrast, we shall examine the Code to see (1) how it defines the realm of work to be regulated, (2) what constitutes adequate performance, and (3) who shall have the final authority of review. But before we look at these specific features of the Code, a brief overview of past and present standards of self-regulation is beneficial.

The codes of professional responsibility and conduct, which were promulgated by the ABA, historically have been key guidelines for the bar as a whole. The state and local bar associations, the legislatures, and the courts have for the most part adopted and enacted the earlier Canons of Professional Ethics (1908) and the recent Code of Professional Responsibility (1970) as proffered by the ABA. The old Canons of Professional Ethics, adopted in 1908, were based principally on a code of ethics adopted in 1887 by the Alabama Bar Association. Between 1887 and 1970, the profession's guidelines were not substantially revised. The original Canons of Professional Ethics contained thirty-two canons which barely touched on the public responsibilities of either the profession or the individual lawyer. No statement or guideline concerned the central issue of competence.[10]

The new Code, at least in general terms, addresses both public responsibility and competence. Moreover, the format of the new Code is significantly different. The Code contains nine canons that are general statements of axiomatic norms.[11] Following each canon are "ethical considerations" (EC), which, in the language of the preliminary statement of the Code, are "aspirational." In addition, the ethical considerations are followed by "disciplinary rules" (DR), which are "mandatory." The disciplinary rules supply the operating force of the Code, for they spell out duties of the lawyer. In short, the present Code is intended to be "an inspirational guide to the members of the profession" and "a basis for disciplinary action when the conduct of a lawyer falls below the required minimum standards stated in the Disciplinary Rules.[12]

Definition of Work

Only those elements of the Code dealing specifically with unauthorized practice of law deal *directly* with a definition of legal work. The ethical considerations conclude that a definition is impossible given the historical development of law and instead rely upon an almost mystical elevation of professional "judgment." Ethical Consideration 3-5 states, in part:

> Functionally, the practice of law relates to the rendition of services for others which call for the professional judgment of a lawyer. The essence of the professional judgment of the lawyer is his educated ability to relate the general body and philosophy of law to a specific legal problem of a client; and thus, the public interest will be better served if only lawyers are permitted to act in matters involving professional judgment. Where this professional judgment is not in-

volved, non-lawyers . . . may engage in occupations that require a special knowledge of the law in certain areas. But the services of a lawyer are essential in the public interest whenever the exercise of professional legal judgment is required.

The wording of EC 3-5 shows a trend common to most professions in the United States: they can no longer provide functional definitions of or for themselves. The Code admits that all sorts of people can do the work that lawyers usually do, and can do it without an expensive legal education."[13] Lawyers themselves are left with the vague area of "judgment." They provide general counsel, represent clients in court, and take responsibility for the work of nonlawyers. In law as in many other areas of American life, the large corporate and bureaucratic models of organization and work definition seem to be the trend. These models also seem to provide the most economically efficient way to organize one's work in an overspecialized economy: lawyers do general counseling and formal representation, while nonlawyers handle much of the paper and leg work. For example, in a formal opinion, the ABA Committee on Professional Ethics said:

> A lawyer can employ lay secretaries, lay investigators, lay detectives, lay researchers, accountants, lay scriveners, nonlawyer draftsmen or nonlawyer researchers. In fact, he may employ nonlawyers to do any task for him except counsel clients about law matters, engage directly in the practice of law . . . or appear in formal proceedings . . . .[14]

Of course, not all lawyers practice in large units. Indeed, sole practitioners make up the largest single category of lawyers in the United States. Lawyers who do not practice in large firms must often compete for clients with lay draftsmen, accountants, and others who offer the same services, either alone or working for the large firms. The point is that lawyers are engaged in vastly different types of work situations within the profession, each with its particular pressure and temptations. Any code which assumes a community of professional interest is unrealistic.

What does this mean for the question of discipline or supervision? Simply, no definitions currently exist of the work to be supervised and regulated. The Code treats the lawyer population as those with common training who are in the licensed status group, even though they do work that cannot be neatly defined and categorized.[15]

The intractable difficulty of defining what is meant by the practice of law is, of course, paralleled by the difficulty of defining what is meant by the competent practice of law. Certainly it means, among other things, doing a competent job of drafting, research, and presentation. But the skill of applying judgment is also central. And this last attribute is difficult to pinpoint, particularly when applied to the multitude of practice situations.

The Question of Competent Performance

Canon 6 provides the theoretical underpinnings for the regulation of competence by declaring that "a lawyer should represent a client competently." Developing a definition and measure of competent performance is obviously critical to the principle of ongoing review of the quality of legal services and to the process of responding to complaints about attorney neglect. Thus a review of the pertinent disciplinary rules is necessary. Of most interest are DR 6-101, DR 1-102, and DR 1-103. DR 6-101 states:

Failing to Act Competently.

(A) A lawyer shall not:
　(1) Handle a legal matter which he knows or should know that he is not competent to handle, without associating with him a lawyer who is competent to handle it.
　(2) Handle a legal matter without preparation adequate in the circumstances.
　(3) Neglect a legal matter entrusted to him.

DR 6-101 is a new start, but because it lacks a meaningful frame of reference in the Code, in the general literature of the profession, or in professional tradition, its application is made difficult from the outset. DR 6-101 goes to the heart of performance expectancies: a lawyer should be competent for the task he undertakes, he should be prepared, and he should always do what he undertakes to do. Surprisingly, a similar norm was not stated in the Canons of Professional Ethics. Indeed, the closest statement was Canon 21, which provided that it "is the duty of the lawyer not only to his client but also to the Courts and to the public to be punctual in attendance, and to be concise and direct in the trial and disposition of causes."

It is clear that the Wright Committee—the ABA Special Committee on Evaluation of Ethical Standards—saw the need for a new point of departure. It is equally clear that the Committee did not nurture the new point of departure by providing either a new environment, in the form of a no-fault system for reviewing performance, or a proper parentage, in the form of professionally recognized performance criteria. DR 6-101 needs a system of recognized specialization and it needs as well an independent system of review and recertification tied in to that review. Unfortunately, it has neither. Accordingly, while DR 6-101 augurs well for the future, in the short run it fails to eliminate the discrepancy between performance issues and conduct issues in the disciplinary process.

DR 1-102 deals with misconduct. It provides:

Misconduct.

(A) A lawyer shall not:
   (1) Violate a Disciplinary Rule.
   (2) Circumvent a Discipinary Rule through actions of another.
   (3) Engage in illegal conduct involving moral turpitude.
   (4) Engage in conduct involving dishonesty, fraud, deceit, or mis-representation.
   (5) Engage in conduct that is prejudicial to the administration of justice.
   (6) Engage in any other conduct that adversely reflects on his fitness to practice law.

DR 1-103 then provides:

Disclosure of Information to Authorities.

(A) A lawyer possessing unprivileged knowledge of a violation of DR 1-102 [which relates to misconduct] shall report such knowledge to a tribunal or other authority empowered to investigate or act upon such violation.
(B) A lawyer possessing unprivileged knowledge or evidence concerning another lawyer or a judge shall reveal fully such knowledge or evidence upon proper request of a tribunal or other authority empowered to investigate or act upon the conduct of lawyers or judges.

It is here, in the relationship between DR 1-102 and 1-103, that one of the major defects of the present disciplinary process appears most clearly and its greatest potential for ultimate expansion emerges. Lawyers and judges have a duty to report violations of the disciplinary rules, including violations of the rule that requires competence and preparation in the performance of services.[16] Lawyers and judges, in other words, are putative complainants and have an ethical duty to complain under the Code. Any mature system of professional self-regulation would necessarily include this process, even if it were not an exclusive approach to professional review. If a system relies almost solely on complaints, as the present disciplinary system does, the existence of professional complainants is important. In fact, however, lawyers and judges do not regularly report known breaches of disciplinary rules. While there is little opportunity for others to observe what goes on in lawyers' offices, that cannot explain the absence of complaints by lawyers and judges. After all, services involving negotiations or litigation are carried on in a veritable fish bowl before judges and other lawyers.

In other studies we have often heard judges complain of both the general incompetence and the lack of preparation of lawyers who appear before them. One state supreme court chief justice told us that only one out of five lawyers who appeared before his court was sufficiently prepared to assist the court in determining the issues presented. We heard, during the course of our interviews in this and other projects, depressingly similar assessments from both trial and appellate judges. Even allowing for some exaggeration, these statements indicate the present dissatisfaction with the general level of legal competence. The fact remains, however, that judges do not generally complain to disciplinary bodies about observed substandard performance. Nor do adverse or cooperating counsel complain. Important, and presumably qualified, inputs into a system of professional review are perhaps stifled from the outset by the harsh penalties, the lack of criteria, and the emphasis on fault.

When we view the Code as a whole and recognize that lawyers and judges do not complain about substandard performance of other lawyers, the importance of what clients complain about becomes even greater. So, too, does the response to client complaints. The Code seems to invite complaints about performance. If client complaints cannot adequately raise performance issues, then independent audit of performance is needed.

A system of professional self-regulation, to be adequate, must reach beyond reliance on client complaints; it must supplement client complaints with professional review of performance. Performance standards, as distinct from conduct standards, need to be applied in a no-fault context; there must be adequate opportunities to review lawyer performance, and there must be refined criteria on which to base continuing judgments about competence. Moreover, the profession must want to regulate performance standards; it must be able to face the possibilities and realities of incompetence among those already holding the license.

Formal and Informal Accountability

The Code fully embraces the notion that lawyers are accountable to the profession as a whole. The courts and the organized bar are viewed as the exclusive agents of regulation and discipline. The preamble to the Code recognizes this view by stating, in essence, that the attorney's desire for the respect and confidence of the profession and society provides the incentive to strive for high ethical conduct.[17] This perception is consistent with the persistent notion that the bar is the guardian of the public interest and knows best how to handle its own members. Indeed, the assumption is made repeatedly that no agency outside the profession is competent to handle the question of discipline or regulation. Yet, as the Clark Committee has indicated, as this article suggests, and as most lawyers themselves recognize, the bar has almost no ongoing regulation of attorney performance or competence. Even its disciplinary machinery for dealing with misconduct is seriously defective.[18]

Some professional review, already at work within the legal profession, incorporates elements not found in a formal disciplinary approach. In fact, the most extensive review of lawyer performance is informal and unsystematic and is not carried on in the name of the profession or in the name of the public generally. Formal review, on the other hand, is systematic but minimal. Some occurs as a result of judicial review of performance in attorney malpractice cases. Formal judicial review is also possible in cases in which an indigent defendant in a criminal case has been afforded the assistance of a public defender or an appointed counsel, because the Sixth and Fourteenth Amendments assure these defendants the right to competent counsel. The indigent criminal defenses provide a more extensive base for judicial review of lawyer performance than do the less frequent malpractice cases. Moreover, with the recent Supreme Court decision in *Argersinger v. Hamlin*,[19] which extends the right to counsel to state misdemeanor cases, the basis for this kind of judicial review of performance should become even more extensive.

A lawyer's performance is reviewed informally whenever he performs his services in front of his fellow lawyers (or judges) and in front of others, be they adversaries, cooperators, neutral participants, or mere onlookers. The full meaning of any informal review depends ultimately on the sanctions or rewards available from those viewing the lawyer. To some extent a lawyer seeks approval from his fellow lawyers if for no other reason than to validate or revalidate his own self-image, his professional status.

Professional reputation is a general reward that can be earned or frustrated by the way the lawyer behaves in front of his fellow lawyers. Moreover, the reward of reputation usually has an important economic aspect. Other lawyers are not only an important source of direct referrals but also, by crediting or discrediting a lawyer, are a crucial element of general community reputation. Professional reputation may be based more on friendship and social and professional accommodation than on assessments of skill. But if a lawyer performs poorly before other lawyers, they probably would hesitate to refer any business to him. In addition, their negative observation will probably be exchanged with other members of the bar. Of course, only extremely poor performances ensure that effect. Although an average or a mediocre job will be noted by an adversary, a cooperating counsel, or a judge, it probably will not be noted by onlookers or discussed among lawyers. The informal control of professional reputation among other lawyers varies, of course, from community to community. As a general proposition, it is a function of the size and cohesion of the local bar: the smaller the bar, the more frequent the opportunities for observation and the more effective the informal sanctions.

Professional behavior, particularly behavior affecting other members of the bar, is more important to professional reputation than quality of performance or even misconduct and thus is more susceptible to informal control. This notion is especially true of behavior that Jerome Carlin has classified as offenses against the bar.[20] Informal controls are important when the offenses are minor, such as attempting to take technical advantage of another lawyer or failing to accommodate another lawyer on the resetting of a court date. The direct consequences of nonaccommodation are both a withdrawal of trust by the lawyers involved and a negative reputation.

But what about major deviations in conduct, such as stealing, bribery, and misrepresentation? And what about gross incompetence and neglect? Are there meaningful informal controls beyond the limited and uncertain sanction of harm to professional reputation? The answers are not clear. The effectiveness of informal controls depends on professional relationship and meaningful opportunity to observe the application of skill. We doubt that members of the general bar have opportunities either to assess or to control the performance of a lawyer with whom they do not regularly associate. In larger units, however, supervising lawyers and law partners can both observe and apply direct economic sanctions as a result of their observations. Thus the law office, particularly the large law office, performs some of the functions that the hospital performs for the medical profession. Short of taking action directly relating to the lawyer's or doctor's license, those in a law office and in a hospital can evaluate, assign, advance, demote, and even terminate employment or association. The law office may not now have mechanisms as formidable as a hospital's death committee, surgery committee, or pathology committee.[21] But in large law offices, particularly where the young lawyer is concerned, there are mechanisms for training, supervision, review, assignment, and, in extreme cases, severance of relationship.[22] Moreover, the large law office recognizes what the profession does not yet formally recognize—areas of specialization. By the process of case assignment, even informal assignment, an attempt is made to meet the guidelines of DR 6-101. Supervision and observation are limited, however. Because of the private nature of preparation, even when a lawyer participates with a group he is not under constant observation.

Another element of informal control relates to an issue to be discussed below: informal two-party disposition by disciplinary agencies of complaints against lawyers.[23] The felt presence of the disciplinary agency affects settlements between the attorney and the complainant and thereby exerts an informal control over lawyer behavior. Thus, to the extent that the lawyer involved feels the disciplinary presence, even if there is a two-party settlement, the element of informal control is operating.

Finally, the marketplace will always operate as an element of informal control. Professional good will depends on general community reputation and, closely related thereto, reputation among the buyers of legal services. Potential clients will credit the tales of dissatisfied clients even if grievance committees do not. Dissatisfied clients, whether sophisticated or not, can harm reputation; thus there will always be some market check on the nature of services rendered. Just how much remains uncertain.

COMPLAINTS AGAINST LAWYERS

The process of receiving and acting on complaints—or the failure to act on them—is the chief way that the legal profession now formally approaches the post-admission task of self-regulation. For all intents and purposes it is the exclusive approach. Investigations of lawyer behavior almost never occur without specific complaint. Occasionally an investigation is undertaken on the basis of an adverse item about a lawyer in a newspaper that comes to the attention of the bar through a clipping service.[24] Even less frequently a disciplinary agency will undertake an investigation into the whole pattern of a particular type of lawyer behavior that at the moment is creating public pressure. But we did not find any systematic or regularized process of peer review of either lawyer conduct or performance.[25] Those isolated investigations into patterns of behavior that came to our attention were related to lawyer misconduct and not to lawyer performance. They concerned issues such as "ambulance chasing," advertising, and courtroom conduct.[26] Isolated investigations aside, however, the process of peer review within the legal profession starts, and frequently ends, with a complaint.

Thus the nature of complaints made against lawyers is crucial. So, too, are questions about who complains and who does not complain. Lawyers rarely complain to disciplinary agencies about other lawyers. Judges, too, are reluctant to complain to disciplinary agencies about either lawyer performance or lawyer conduct.[27] Instead, clients most frequently supply the regulatory inputs. We do not suggest that all dissatisfied clients complain. We do, however, suggest that operationally most complainants are dissatisfied clients.

What the disciplinary agencies do about the complaints they receive is crucial to understanding the nature of existing regulation. We are interested in more than simple dispositions, however. Thus, to fully comprehend the role of the disciplinary agency, we will look closely at client complaints, not only to examine the subject matter of the complaint, but also to see what type of client complains about his legal services. We will then review the various ways the disciplinary agencies react to the complaint. Finally we will discuss the question of client credibility, directing particular attention to what we believe to be the source of the agencies' general attitude of insensitivity. But first, to present some preliminary understanding of disciplinary procedures, we will describe a typical disciplinary process.

Typical Disciplinary Procedures

In practically all jurisdictions, complaints about lawyers are directed either to state grievance boards or to local or state bar associations. Records are seldom well kept.[28] Most of the work is voluntary; there is no staff paid to handle disciplinary problems. We were informed in some states that a complaint is frequently informally disposed of at intake screening without any investigation.[29] Beyond intake, disciplinary agencies have a broad range of options: they can dismiss the complaint, investigate, introduce informal arbitration for minor complaints, privately admonish, or recommend formal proceedings against a lawyer. Formal charges are usually heard first by disciplinary panels. In serious cases, usually in which suspension or disbarment is sought, a court must either rule on the attorney's conduct and exonerate him, or subject him to public censure, suspension, or disbarment.[30]

While the degree of centralization, procedural rigor, and availabiity of staff varies among jurisdictions, several general observations can be made.

1. *The process is controlled by members of the bar.* The legal profession has zealously resisted lay or even legislative intervention in the disciplinary process. Nonetheless, the legislatures in some states have developed considerable authority over the rules of discipline. But for the most part bar associations have successfully resisted the inclusion of lay members on disciplinary panels.[31]

2. *The emphasis is on procedural informality and discipline by "conscience of peers."* The private bar has seemed unable or unwilling to define and exercise its full supervisory potential, particularly when judging a colleague's competence.

3. *The process is essentially decentralized.* Most disciplinary work is done locally, either by screening out complaints, holding initial hearings, or performing an informal arbiter role for minor complaints. In some states, such as Texas, the process never gets beyond local levels, whether within the bar or in the district courts. As the Clark Committee said:

> We have found that in many states the disciplinary jurisdiction is so decentralized that members of a local legal community are required to discipline each other. As a result, the disciplinary agencies in these areas are reluctant to proceed against prominent lawyers. They fail to submit even serious caes to the court having disciplinary jurisdiction, and the local court, when a case is submitted to it, is reluctant to impose substantial discipline.[32]

4. *The process stresses secrecy.* The expressed policy of the bar is to keep hearings secret in order to protect the "unjustly accused lawyer." Unless there is a decision against the lawyer, the particulars of the case ordinarily remain secret. Even after an adverse decision, the fact of discipline and the reasons for the discipline generally are not publicized.[33] In most states more than half the disbarments are by consent, and in those cases the full records are never made public. For example, no records have been preserved in more than one-third of the cases adjudicated in the Appellate Division of the First Department in New York from 1929 to 1963.

Client Complaints

We have seen few client complaints.[34] Our view of complaints is, therefore, based mainly on published and unpublished reports of disciplinary agencies and interviews with persons involved in the disciplinary process, namely, bar and grievance board executives, bar counsel, volunteer members of the disciplinary panels, and judges. Although interviewees were both cooperative and helpful, we were struck by the generalities they used in describing what particular agencies (or courts) do. We found an established litany about the discipline function and disciplinary proceedings. All will say the legal profession's disciplinary processes are generally poor; few will admit their own deficiencies. Moreover, most say that they perform better than others; and few, if any, will break away from established ways of discussing the subject. We also found that very little statistical data had been compiled. Even when reports were available, the differing styles of enumerating and reporting did not allow for valid comparisons.

The widespread lack of records on complaints is largely attributable to the techniques used in the early screening process. Even agencies that attempt to keep accurate records often do not include the complaints which are "straightened out" with a phone call or letter, reasoning that the calls are merely "inquiries,"[35] and that the record of complaints should include only complaints formally filed. The attitudes toward complainants held by disciplinary agency personnel screening complaints appeared to affect the decision whether to treat a communication as an inquiry or as a complaint.[36]

When asked to state the greatest single cause of complaints, most interviewees specified a breakdown in communications between lawyer and client.[37] They often described the typical case as one in which a low- to middle-income client with little or no previous contact with lawyers had a "misunderstanding" with his attorney. If the "misunderstanding" or "breakdown in communications" is seen to be attributable to the lawyer rather than the client, the agency may chide the offender for breach of etiquette and lack of business acumen. In general, however, interviewees did not view a lawyer's failure to communicate with his client as raising an issue of substandard performance. Refusal to communicate was seen much more often as a public relations rather than as a discipline problem.[38] For example, a report of the Chicago Bar Association stated:

> Probably the most common complaint is brought to the Committee by unhappy people who say that numerous calls and letters to their lawyer evoke no response. They do not seem to be able to break through the shield of what to them appears as indifference and neglect. Obviously, the harm done to the individual lawyer and the lawyer group as a whole is considerable. Thus, ordinary common sense and reasonable business procedures would dictate the wisdom of keeping the client abreast of all action taken. This would go a long way in creating and maintaining a good relationship with the client and ultimately a better relationship with the public generally.[39]

The report also suggested an explanation for the problem of client complaints. It attributed many complaints to "losers" who vent their rage and frustration on their lawyer. The report, describing some of the docket, stated:

> 1. There is the complaint by the convict who would have us believe that he had been deprived of his freedom solely because of the incompetence of his attorney. The convict states that he could have done a better job of defending himself than his attorney. The attorney will patiently search his files and submit a detailed explanation revealing painstaking preparation and a spirited defense of a hopelessly guilty client.

2. The field of matrimonial law is a fertile source of complaints because many litigants in such cases are suffering from anxiety and depression. Here again, either or both parties consider themselves losers and pour all of their frustrations into a bitter attack on their own attorney, opposing counsel, or both.

3. If a business deal goes sour, or if the client does not profit in a transaction as he had hoped, a complaint may be filed charging that the attorney is responsible.[40]

The Chicago Bar Association report expressed more willingness to undertake disciplinary action for possible criminal violations or soliciting. The report continued:

4. There has been a great deal of discussion as to the timing of disciplinary proceedings when a lawyer has been charged with or convicted of a crime. It has been the practice to wait until the conviction has become final and appellate rights exhausted. This year the Committee has determined that it will attempt to proceed when the conviction has become final in the trial court and not wait for appellate review.

5. Disposition of client's funds is another source of complaint. Usually, the answer is a failure to render a complete accounting. Sometimes endorsing clients' names on checks without any clear authority to do so or commingling funds is exposed.

6. The continuing problem of solicitation will be reexamined in depth during the next year. We are confident that increasing emphasis will be placed on minimizing this breach of professional conduct.[41]

The Association of the Bar of the City of New York, which handles the disciplinary functions in the First Department of New York State,[42] publishes the most detailed (and probably the most accurate) classification of complaints.[43] For the year ending April 30, 1970, the report of the Association's Grievance Committee gave the distribution of complaints shown in Table I. Of the 966 complaints in the First Department which, in the judgment of the intake screeners, stated a prima facie allegation that came within the jurisdiction of the disciplinary agency, 524 (54.6 per cent) involved "neglect." Other jurisdictions studied show similarly high percentages of prima facie complaints of neglect.[44]

TABLE I

CLASSIFICATION OF COMPLAINTS, ASSOCIATION OF THE BAR OF THE
CITY OF NEW YORK, YEAR ENDING APRIL 30, 1970

1. Offenses Against Clients
   a. Conversion   32
   b. Overreaching   36
   c. Neglect   524
   d. Misinforming   16
   e. Conflict of interest 13
   f. Fraud   12
   g. Other   80   713

2. Direct Offenses Against Colleagues
    a. Personal relationships   4
    b. Agreements   13
    c. By-passing other attorney   10
    d. Other   4   31
3. Indirect Offenses Against Colleagues
    a. Solicitation   7
    b. Advertising   7   14
4. Direct Offenses Against the Administration of Justice
    a. Improper influence   8
    b. Other   7   15
5. Indirect Offenses Against the Administration of Justice
    a. Fraudulent representation   12
    b. False swearing   7
    c. Actions in bad faith—abuse of process   41
    d. Violations of Court Rules   2
    e. Concealing of evidence   1
    f. Other   26   89
6. Other Professional Misconduct
    a. Derelictions   18
    b. Lack of cooperation   7
    c. Other   16   41
7. Non-Professional Misconduct
    a. Financial irresponsibility   19
    b. Fraud   11
    c. Other   38   68
8A Crime
    a. Larceny   6
    b. Forgery   1
    c. Perjury   2
    d. Bribery   5
    e. Income tax evasion, failure to file   3
    f. Other   4   21
8B Minor Offenses
    a. Miscellaneous (disorderly conduct, violation of
       Administrative Code, etc.)   4   4
SUBTOTAL, CATEGORIES 1 TO 8B   996
9. Complaints Against Attorneys Outside
   Committee's Jurisdiction   315   315
10. Complaints Which Set Forth No Unethical Behavior
    a. Advice—Requests for legal advice or assistance   164
    b. Minor fee disputes   174
    c. Minor disagreements in personal business transactions   51
    d. Minor disagreements not attributable to misconduct   181
    e. Other   148   720
TOTAL ALL CATEGORIES   2,031

Source: Committee on Grievances, the Association of the Bar of the City of New York, Annual Report 1969-1970.

Fee disagreements constitute another major grievance. But as a general rule, fee disputes fall outside disciplinary agency jurisdiction.[45] When a fee dispute raises issues of fraud or overreaching, however, the disciplinary agency may have jurisdiction (see Table I, Categories 1b and 1f). One bar counsel even suggested that if one could consider as "fee disputes" all complaints in which the client felt "short-changed," fee disputes would account for 75 per cent of his docket. This system of classification would, of course, include what others have called "neglect": a lawyer accepts money and fails to act promptly or even fails to act at all.

Disciplinary Action on Complaints

In the year ending April 30, 1970, 1,716 complaints were filed in the First Department of New York against attorneys within its jurisdiction. The Grievance Committee determined that 996 of the complaints set forth prima facie cases of misconduct. After investigation, 144 resulted in letters of admonition. In addition, three attorneys admitted their guilt and were permitted to surrender their licenses against any right to be reinstated automatically. Only 41 lawyers, some of whom faced multiple charges, were brought before the hearing committee on formal charges representing 66 complaints. The results of these hearings were:[46]

Prosecution in the courts recommended	19
Formally admonished	15
Dismissed	5
Pending	2
	41

Thus, in one of the best administered discipline systems, 213 complaints, or about 12 percent of all complaints, resulted in admonition, resignation, or recommendation of suspension or disbarment. Considerably less than 1 per cent of the 30,000 lawyers in the First Department were disciplined in any way.

As shown in Table II, during 1969-70 even fewer California attorneys were the subjects of disciplinary proceedings. Of 3,407 complaints initiated, only 810 (about 24 per cent) were considered by a preliminary investigatory committee. Moreover, only slightly more than 1 per cent of those 3,407 complaints resulted in private or public reprimands or recommendations of suspension or disbarment. Thus only 37 of California's 30,672 attorneys (about 0.1 per cent) were disciplined or recommended to be disciplined.

TABLE II

DISPOSITION OF COMPLAINTS IN CALIFORNIA 1969-1970

Disposition of 3,407 Complaints and Inquiries	Number	As Per Cent of Complaints $N = 3183$	As Per Cent of Complaints Investigated $N = 810$
Inquiries not filed*	224		
Complaints	3183		
Dismissed without consideration by preliminary investigating committee	2370	74.5%	
Considered by preliminary investigating committee	810	25.5%	
Dismissed without notice to show cause	697	21.9%	86.0%
Resulted in notice to show cause	113	3.6%	14.0%
Dismissed without review by disciplinary board	56	1.5%	6.9%
Reviewed by disciplinary board	57	1.5%	7.0%
Dismissed by disciplinary board	20	0.7%	2.5%
Acted on by disciplinary board	37	1.2%	4.6%
Private reprimands	7	0.2%	0.9%
Public reprimands	9	0.3%	1.1%
Recommendation of suspension	13	0.4%	0.6%
Recommendation of disbarment	8	0.2%	0.9%

* As a result of reading the California Bar Association's jurisdictional statement or talking with investigator.

Source: Compiled from various California sources by project staff.

In Wisconsin about 14 per cent of all complaints reach a formal preliminary hearing stage; 8 per cent of all complaints result in action (either private admonition or reference to the state board) by the local grievance committee. Only 2.8 per cent of all complaints resulted in public disciplinary sanctions, and nearly one-half of those were public reprimands.[47] Similar percentages were found wherever statistics were available.[48] The relatively low figures for disciplinary action can be partially explained in several ways. The most favorable explanation, much advanced by the bar, is that very few lawyers are involved in serious violations of ethical and professional standards. Another explanation is the underreporting of violations and informal dispositions without a complaint to a disciplinary agency. A third explanation relates solely to dispositions and involves the quality of the disciplinary agency's handling of its complaint docket; large numbers of complaints that arguably have merit are considered unrelated to ethical standards by those responsible for intake screening. The preceding figures that interested us most, those concerning the disposition of complaints actually received, perhaps reflect this last explanation.

Given the small percentage of complaints resulting in discipline, what types of cases lead to suspension or disbarment? Remember that a large proportion of client complaints center on neglect and fee disputes. But fee disputes and cases of neglect or other negligence rarely result in either suspension or disbarment. Indeed, few of the less stringent sanctions are even applied to these types of complaints.

Most agencies do not treat neglect or other negligence as within their jurisdiction, unless it is gross negligence. If a neglect or negligence case is taken, it may be treated as a "breakdown of communication" that can be handled by a phone call or letter to the attorney asking him to explain the situation to the client. Even in the jurisdictions that do handle negligence complaints, complainants may be viewed as "probably mistaken" because "the client doesn't really understand what he wants."

While some jurisdictions will arbitrate fee disputes, none generally consider fee disputes to be matters that deserve the attention of grievance committees. This attitude might be acceptable if all the complaints lumped into the fee dispute category were squabbles over the amount of the fee. But a variety of situations give rise to a fee dispute. The following types of complaints illustrate these differences.

1. The fee is excessive.
2. An attorney demands that the wife pay his fees after assuring her that the husband would be required to pay them.
3. An attorney who has been discharged refuses to give the client the file until his fee is paid.
4. An attorney has agreed to perform services for a certain amount and then submits a bill for a substantially higher amount.
5. An attorney for a plaintiff in a divorce action refuses to proceed to trial unless his fee is paid in full.[49]

Arguably, these situations involve varying degrees of professional irresponsibility. All seem capable of regulation, however, by a professional body charged with self-discipline. Yet disciplinary agencies in most jursidictions have not become involved in fee disputes. They believe that such complaints are outside their jurisdiction unless the fee is so exorbitant that it amounts to overreaching. Attempts to justify this position stress the difficulty in assessing the worth of an individual lawyer's services and the problems inherent in applying objective criteria to intangible value judgments.[50] The ABA supported this nonregulatory position in a 1968 formal ethics opinion:

> An attorney has the right to contract for any fee he chooses so long as it is not excessive . . . and this Committee is not concerned with the amount of such fees unless so excessive as to constitute a misappropriation of the client's funds. . . .[51]

In sum, most disciplinary agencies decline to take jurisdiction in the types of cases with which most complainants are concerned—neglect, other negligence, and fee disputes. They devote a large amount of their time to screening out these complaints and to an informal handling of those complaints they classify as a "misunderstanding" or "lack of communication." A diversionary process is involved: rather than formal acceptance of jurisdiction and official recognition of the problems of competence, neglect, other negligence, and fee disputes, informal adjustment is relied on. We call this process a diversion because, as we shall see, a disciplinary agency that treats complaints against lawyers as merely raising a two-party dispute is refusing regulatory jurisdiction. This proposition is still true even when the agency attempts to bring the parties together.

When we look at the types of cases that reach the formal hearing stage and that may result in serious discipline, generally we find the list dominated by conversion, bribery, fraud, conviction of a felony, income tax evasion, and solicitation. The largest number of discipline adjudications and those that receive the severest sanctions involve conversion; yet this is the least frequent type of complaint. One must keep in mind that conversion is usually covered by the criminal law under theft and embezzlement provisions and by a wide range of civil remedies. What specific function (or utility), then, do bar procedures and sanctions have when applied to conduct already covered by the criminal and civil law? In particular, this issue must be differentiated from regulation of performance and conduct that violate professional standards but fall short of being violations of the criminal code.

We found difficulties not only with the types of complaints that the disciplinary agencies handled or refused to handle, but also with the agencies' relationship with the complainants. In general, the agencies we interviewed did not appear much concerned with the manner in which the client-as-complainant is treated. When the agency simply acts as arbiter, without asserting jurisdiction, the client has the satisfaction of knowing that the disciplinary agency has relayed his complaint to the lawyer. Paradoxically, however, when jurisdiction is asserted—when the complaint leads to investigation or a formal hearing—the client is often forgotten. If the investigator concludes there is insufficient evidence to pursue the matter, our sources lead us to believe that the client is seldom informed of the action or, if informed, denied an explanation of the results. When formal charges are brought against the lawyer, in many jurisdictions the client may never know of the hearing unless he is called as witness;[52] and even if he is called to testify there is no provision for automatically notifying him of the outcome. Ironically, some disciplinary agencies, while confronted with a large number of complaints alleging neglect and failure to communicate, seem to be blind to their own treatment of a client.[53] The irony points up, perhaps, considerable confusion about to whom the agencies are accountable.[54]

In contrast to the usual approaches to fee complaints, Minnesota recently proposed a method of handling fee disputes that involves notions of overall professional accountability to clients even when disciplinary jurisdiction is not asserted or accepted. Beyond simply offering mediation or binding arbitration, as many states do, Minnesota proposes that when the client is willing to arbitrate but the lawyer is not, a panel appointed by the bar association will hold a hearing to determine the fair fee for the services rendered in the matter. The panel will then offer expert tesitmony *against* the lawyer in court if the dispute reaches a civil suit by providing testimony about the profession's specific view of a reasonable fee in the disputed matter. While the main impact of this measure is expected to be the leverage that will be exerted on lawyers to agree to binding arbitration, new departures in the task of professional self-regulation are inherent in the Minnesota proposal.[55]

First, the Minnesota proposal accepts the notion of accountability to clients, even in such difficult areas as the fair value of a lawyer's services—in marked contrast to the 1968 ABA opinion of fees previously mentioned. Second, the proposal contemplates that the profession, as such, would be taking a public position adverse to a lawyer involved in a dispute. Third, underlying the proposal is the perception that true regulation entails something more than the possible application of extreme sanctions in cases of breaches of professional or community responsibility. The ultimate impact of the Minnesota proposal might be to induce lawyers to be more circumspect about their billing practices in the first instance.

If the Minnesota proposal works in the one great area of nonaccepted jurisdiction—fee disputes—it could also work in other areas such as neglect, negligence, and incompetence. As with fair value of services, criteria relating to tasks and performance are involved. The profession could stand ready publicly to specify objective standards for lawyers' tasks or more particularly to offer assistance to the courts in instances in which malpractice suits have been brought against lawyers. While the extension of the Minnesota proposal into the area of competence and performance standards presents more complex problems than the issue of reasonable fees, the possibilities are exciting. First, the extension would necessarily involve the profession in a long overdue dialogue on definitions of lawyer tasks, on standards of performance, on specialization, and on the myth of lawyer omnicompetence. But more important, it would involve the profession in a system of regulation that relied on something other than such ultimate punishments as disbarment or suspension or such illusory sanctions as admonition and censure.

Credibility of Client Complaints

What credibility do clients have with the screening agent or the disciplinary agency when they complain about lawyer performance as distinguished from lawyer misconduct? How much credence is given the client's view of the abilities or inabilities of his lawyer or his view of the failure or success of the lawyer-client relationship? Our study indicates usually very little. The client's view seems to be rejected out of hand and an independent, professional standard is applied. When there is no time for investigation, this lack of credibility is determinative of the result. But when there is time to investigate, the complaint leads to a de novo investigation. The client's view, even when no factual dispute exists, has little effect on the outcome.

The issue of client credibility turns on what the disciplinary agencies view as an ideal lawyer-client relationship. If the relationship were viewed as a cooperative relationship, with the client as a participant, then the client could also be seen to have a meaningful power of direction and a meaningful sense of when his expectations have been frustrated.[56] But the more prevalent view of the lawyer-client relationship is authoritarian, with a client passive and incapable of understanding either the decisions to be made or the work to be done by the lawyer. Accordingly, one can easily understand why client complaints about lawyer performance tend to receive little credibility.

Both the authoritarian view of the lawyer-client relationship and the discounting of client complaints about lawyer performance can be rationalized. Nonlawyers are not supposed to be able to understand what lawyers do. If they do understand, the very basis of professionalism and self-regulation is threatened because understanding of lawyers implies the threat of outside regulation. That is, if no mystique of lawyering exists, "reasonable man" standards could be applied to the work of lawyers, even by outsiders.[57] Thus, only to the extent that the client is viewed as mystified by the work of lawyers does the prestige of the license remain intact. This pressure on disciplinary agencies causes them to discount client complaints about lawyer performance and to substitute their own standards for those of the client.

During our study, we found that the degree of discounting often depended upon the subject matter of the client complaint. For example, complaints about embezzlement or conversion of client funds and of sexual intimacy with a client are given a high degree of credibility. Even complaints of a breach of professional ethics, which is serious but short of a crime, are also given a high degree of credibility. These cases concerning breach of professional ethics raise factual questions of professional standards as distinct from, or at least independent of, community standards. Yet the dialogue about these professional standards is not as guarded as when performance standards are involved. The client is often privy to the dialogue, and his view about such matters as disloyalty is considered. Conduct complaints do not involve a professional mystique; in the arena of behavior and conduct the disciplinary agencies are not faced with confusing standards and constituencies. The agencies do not have to guard the inner sanctum of the profession. They can adopt the view of the public once deviance from community or professional norms is perceived.[58]

Complaints about lawyer conduct present material from which conceptions of professional honesty and professional pride can be refined. In the handling of conduct complaints, more than an independent professional standard is involved; both professional and general community standards of conduct are involved. While some of the departures from conduct standards can be handled by informal means, the more serious breaches of professional and community standards involve the profession in a pattern closely paralleling the criminal justice system. In any event, a professional association can deal more easily with matters of deviance from norms of conduct than it can deal with matters of performance. Once a lawyer is seen as deviating from expected standards of behavior, he can be labeled an "outsider," or at least treated as one.[59] That stigma does two things: (1) it helps the profession assert or reassert the norm by defining the kind of behavior expected from "insiders," and (2) it allows the profession to apply sanctions.

ANALYTIC MODELS OF TREATMENT OF COMPLAINANTS

We have seen a variety of responses that disciplinary agencies make to complainants and a variety of ways that the complainant is treated after a formal proceeding has been instituted against a lawyer. But as yet we have not analytically examined the relationships between the client-complainant, the attorney, and the disciplinary agency. For purposes of our study, we can divide disciplinary approaches into two-party and three-party models.[60]

Two- and Three-Party Models

The two-party model reflects a view that a complaint states a private cause of action held by the client-complainant against a lawyer. The action is a private dispute brought to the professional disciplinary agency for mediation or, conceivably, for judgment, not for an application of the profession's independent standards. The two-party model, a civil dispute model, is relatively simple.

The three-party model is more complex. The complaint triggers a response from an interested party distinct from the client and lawyer involved. The interested party may be the profession acting for itself against a member or at least determining for itself whether it should act. Or it may be the profession assuming the role of representative of the public at large. In either event a third party is involved. But whether the third party is seen as the profession itself or as the public at large is critical. When the third party is the profession itself, the three-party model is likely to resemble the criminal justice system. When the third party is seen as the public, the resemblance to a criminal justice system continues, but the possibilities of a regulatory, noncriminal approach are increased.

Some generalizations can be made from our initial observation of both the two-party and three-party models. The two-party or civil dispute model occurs most frequently in jurisdictions in which the court or the organized bar—whichever has assumed direct responsibility for the initial screening of complaints—does not have a professional staff at its disposal.[61] Under these circumstances, the screener of complaints, whether a volunteer lawyer or a bar executive, is usually forced to a series of rapid and informal dispositions. The screener may often deal with complaints by suggesting one or another of the following: (a) "Why don't the two of you get together and work this out?" Or (b) (to the lawyer) "Why don't you make some kind of settlement with your client?" Or (c) (to the client) "We can't do anything, but you can sue your lawyer if you wish."

A fourth option is less frequently used: (d) "We can refer the matter to a committee to see if something can be worked out. You understand, we have no formal position, but we will be happy to help you get some resolution of this matter." The final option brings in a third party to assist in the resolution. But, although a committee is frequently used as arbitrator in fee disputes, it is rarely used when the issue is lawyer competence or lawyer neglect or other negligence. In these latter instances, the screener of the complaints attempts to bring the parties together. The two-party model, though, has elements of a three-party model if the lawyer involved feels that despite the outcome of a given complaint, someone, for example, the bar association, is looking over his shoulder or recording the number of complaints against him.[62] The third party is a regulator, however, only to the extent that the lawyer believes he is being monitored.

The two-party model has the formal appearance of "settling" the client's dispute with his lawyer, while in actuality it lends itself to refusal of jurisdiction and diversion of the complaint through rapid, summary, and informal disposition. For instance, complaints with merit can usually be separated from those without merit only after an investigation is made, but most complaints are disposed of without investigation.[63] Those complaints disposed of informally or by suggesting civil damage actions are never actually docketed before the disciplinary agencies. Unfortunately, disciplinary personnel do not appear aware of the presumptions in favor of the lawyer that accrue as a result of a rapid, summary disposition of complaints.

Even for those agencies using a two-party approach for performance complaints, a three-party approach is inherent in the treatment of conduct complaints. Not only does the client-complainant have greater credibility in conduct cases, but third-party interests—professional or public—emerge. The role of the disciplinary screening agent changes. He is no longer a mediator but a representative of broader interests seeking to determine whether formal disciplinary charges should be brought. In this respect he is like a prosecutor.

In the three-party model, disciplinary agencies assume at the outset that more is at stake than simply a dissatisfied client or a breakdown of one lawyer-client relationship. Disciplinary agencies that assert jurisdiction over performance complaints at least formally acknowledge the possibility of interests transcending the immediate lawyer-client relationship. Pursuit of a neglect or negligence complaint by the disciplinary agency implicitly recognizes that the interest of the public requires the examination. That the inquiry is limited to the single complaint may mean, however, that there is a limited view of the public as a constituency.

When disciplinary agencies do not entertain complaints concerning performance or fee disputes, their responses resemble the two-party model; they suggest arbitration or mediation. This result may seem to be a contradiction, but it is not. To dispose of a large part of its caseload, an agency using a three-party model will use a two-party approach for those matters that it does not consider serious. In this respect the disciplinary agency is like the public prosecutor, who often uses his judgment or discretion to produce similar results in the criminal justice system. For example, a prosecutor's fraud and complaint department will often bring the complainant and the accused party together in an effort to settle the matter short of formal process. A similar diversionary process is at work in the field of professional discipline, even though the reasons for it may not always be the same.

More important, however, when a disciplinary agency with a three-party approach resorts to diversion, the result differs considerably from the two-party model's diversion of complaints. Broader interests are always present, always inferred. Notwithstanding efforts at two-party resolution, those agencies using a three-party approach will probably watch and record complaints. Three-party disciplinary agencies maintain better records, observe the cumulative effect of complaints against specific lawyers, and develop an independent assessment of where and when to investigate.

Agencies using a three-party approach tend to be those with a professional staff. This result is by no means accidental. A professional staff plays distinctly different roles and has distinctly different perspectives than agencies without professional staff. The presence of professional staff in a disciplinary agency increases the probability that the staff will perceive its constituency as broader than the agency, or even broader than the bar. This constituency more readily resembles *the public* but in reality is more likely the staff itself as the representative of community values. Thus the staff validates both its role and its function. Surely this is the genesis of the three-party model.

For those agencies with professional staff that accept jurisdiction over both conduct and performance complaint, there is a tendency to approach both in the same way: an issue is presented that cannot be reconciled simply between the client and the lawyer involved. While in theory these agencies should approach conduct complaints on a no-fault basis, particularly since they entertain jurisdiction over performance, they have, in fact, relied largely on the fault notion. This reliance is caused by the tendency of full-time professionals to adopt a "we-they" perspective, which allows them to interject their particular moral outlook. In this respect also, disciplinary professionals are like prosecutors. Even when their agencies theoretically deal with performance standards, the disciplinary professionals are unable to resist the lofty perspective of the "we-they" approach.

An agency with a professional staff that does not assert jurisdiction over performance complaints appears to be even more purely prosecutorial than agencies that do accept performance complaints. Refusal of jurisdiction over performance complaints relieves the agency of the necessity of diverting complaints and reinforces the professional's staff view that dealing with deviance from community and professional standards of conduct is their particular métier.[64] Again, however, the way that these particular agencies refuse jurisdiction over performance complaints is worth noting. They do observe the settlement of the dispute, and even if the sole remedy for the client is in court, the presence of the professional staff has a regulatory effect.

In summary, our study of disciplinary agency models has revealed not only two- and three-party approaches but also formal and informal dispositions. The formal dispositions occur more frequently in the three-party model and also more frequently resemble formal criminal justice dispositions. The informal dispositions resemble civil law dispositions, with some room for the professional staff of disciplinary agencies to act as regulatory overseers, even though they are not actively engaged in the dispositions.

The Guild Model

We have said little about the relationship between the disciplinary agencies and the lawyer against whom a complaint is lodged. The discounting of client complaints about performance implies that certain presumptions favor the lawyer. But more is involved than simply discounting clients' viewpoints. For example, we found that disciplinary agencies presume that lawyers who have passed the bar examination, even years ago, and who have been exposed to the original character and fitness screening, are entitled to the benefit of any doubt. Indeed, the disciplinary agencies treat the license as a vested right. Even those agencies that entertain negligence complaints, thereby necessarily accepting the abstract notion that a lawyer may be capable of rendering inadequate service, lean toward a presumption that, in reality, all lawyers are competent. Even if the reality of this statement is not accepted within the legal profession, at least between the profession and the outside world omnicompetence is treated as a reality.

Overlaid on both the two- and three-party models, then, is a guild model. The guild model has an all-lawyer constituency. So far as that model applies, until a strong showing is made that a lawyer is not entitled to protection, he receives protection from the disciplinary agency. His fall from grace is usually signaled by a finding of "wrongdoing" or "misconduct." Thus the guild approach puts the emphasis on conduct rather than performance. Further, the guild approach is enlisted as readily for offenses against the profession, such as unfair competition, advertising, or taking technical advantage, as it is for offenses against the public. As we shall see, the guild approach fosters the conversion of performance inputs into conduct outputs.

THE MISMATCH BETWEEN INPUTS AND OUTPUTS

We have seen that clients complain chiefly about matters touching on performance while the agencies to which they complain concern themselves almost exclusively with misconduct. A mismatch is apparent. What is even more apparent is the inability or unwillingness of the profession to deal adequately with the issue of competence. Even when a disciplinary agency accepts jurisdiction over a complaint about performance, the investigation is more apt to result in a search for moral deviance or fault than for substandard practice of law. In this regard, regulatory agencies within the legal profession tend to follow the pattern of the criminal justice system of society in general: lawyers are neither decertified nor limited in their future performance unless they have offended basic community standards, *i.e.,* unless they have committed crimes or been seriously unethical in a generally understood sense.

The divergence between inputs that center on performance and outputs that emphasize misconduct and moral deviance is striking. It is our thesis that this divergence is no accident. The inputs are client complaints which are primarily concerned with performance-matters of competence, diligence, and applied skill. But the inputs are discounted because disciplinary agencies, and perhaps the profession as a whole, believes clients are unable to discern the proper or meaningful elements of the practice of law. Thus the outputs tend to presume that the complaints may raise only issues of lawyer misconduct or moral deviance. But if it is admitted that a client is capable of perceiving at least prima facie shoddy performance, then the bar must admit that the practice of law may not be as occult as the professional mystique suggests. If client complaints continue to be discounted, however, and if we continue to license attorneys as competent to practice law,[65] it would seem that an independent mechanism for reviewing performance must be provided. On the other hand, the bar could flatly refuse to accept jurisdiction over complaints alleging substandard performance or it could treat such complaints as raising issues of fault and deviance rather than issues of competence. At present, the bar generally takes the latter approach.

Circular reasoning is used to justify the present concept of self-regulation: self-regulation has not historically involved issues of performance and competence and therefore existing institutions have been geared to deal with other problems. Because existing disciplinary agencies are geared to deal with other problems, competence and performance are not issues that fall within the realm of professional self-regulation. The circularity involves defining the nature of self-regulation in historical and institutional terms and not in functional terms.

The professionals in the disciplinary agencies insist that they are unable to deal with issues of competence. They argue that they have inadequate staff even to fulfill their "primary" disciplinary functions, that the notion of competence is an issue distinct from neglect or other negligence, and that the issues are unmanageable because no criteria for proper performance exist. The first of these arguments has considerable merit; professional disciplinary agency staffs are indeed pushed to their limits, and the agencies without professional staffs are unable to cope with even the glaring cases of professional misconduct and misbehavior. This understaffing does not mean, however, that the profession shall not deal with issues of competence. It simply means that additional resources will have to be made available.

The assertion that dealing with misbehavior is the primary function of the existing disciplinary agencies may also have some merit. If the argument runs to what these agencies now do or are equipped to do, it is likely that issues of performance are beyond their scope and that it would be a mistake for them to attempt to mix functions or dilute their present function. It does not necessarily follow, however, that the process of dealing with deviance and fault is or should be either the total or the primary self-regulation effort of the profession. Nor does it follow that issues of competence should be handled by the same agencies that now handle complaints or at least by these agencies as presently constituted.

The assertion that competence and neglect or other negligence are separate issues is more complex; it, too, has merit. The terms competence and neglect overlap,[66] a substandard performance may be the result of an inability to perform or it may be the result of an instance of omission or commission in a particular matter. In other words, competent lawyers can indeed perform incompetently.

The disciplinary agency professionals contend that most client complaints about substandard lawyer performance, at least those remaining after the "crank" complaints and complaints resulting from "failure of communication" have been weeded out, involve "misconduct" and "wrongdoing." That is, some aspect of fault is inevitably singled out as the reason for substandard performance. We suggest that this approach is the result of a presumption of competence made by the disciplinary agents about their fellow lawyers. It is an approach validated by the absence of meaningful definitions of lawyering. Regardless of its source, however, the fault approach of the disciplinary agencies most certainly results in presumptions of license holder competence. Unless the client's view is given greater credence and triggers broader inquiry or unless independent inputs, review, and standards are applied, the disciplinary agencies will continue to view performance issues in a context of fault or ignore them altogether and concentrate on issues of conduct and behavior.

The tension between disciplinary inputs and outputs is not caused solely by the twin factors of reliance on complaints as the primary occasions for self-regulation and confusion about the nature of self-regulation. Confusion about constituencies is also a contributing factor. Uncertainty on the part of disciplinary agencies regarding whom they are representing is bound to affect and distort disciplinary outcomes. It is unclear whether disciplinary agencies are expected to represent the accusing party, the public, the lawyer involved, or the profession.

The language of the current disciplinary approach reveals an underlying schizophrenia. It reveals that there are indeed conflicting constituencies. The agencies that receive and act on complaints are most frequently called "Grievance Committees." The complaints themselves are generally called "grievances." Hence, the style of the inputs seems to be hospitable to the function of professional review, to the licensing rationale that presumes the profession will regulate its members in order to protect the public. The term "grievance" can be viewed as client-centered. It describes both the process and the forum where it is expected that clients will air their complaints against lawyers. The language describing the process after the complaint is received, including the negative dispositions, takes on a wholly different tone. At this stage, there is a search for "misconduct." The outcome turns on decisions about whether the lawyer involved should be "disciplined," or "deserves to be disciplined." Indeed, the generic terms that the profession applies to the entire process are "discipline" and "disciplinary." These are not client-centered terms, nor are they regulatory terms. They describe a profession-centered concern about deviance. Somewhere between inputs and outputs the language changes appear to signal formal changes in constituencies—from client and public to lawyer and profession. While it is arguable that there is no real change in constituencies, that the input language merely reflects a desire to appear hospitable to public complaint, we believe that more than appearance is involved, that those who manage the inputs really want to respond to the clients, but the outcomes turn more crucially on a process described by the terminating language, "discipline." In other words, the profession is unintentionally and unconsciously misleading itself and the public. The discipline process commits the profession to a split between appearance and reality.

One of the central themes in this article can thus be stated: when we consider the disciplinary process as a whole we are looking at the ways that the legal profession gives the appearance of self-regulation without in fact engaging in the act of self-regulation. There is a subtle conversion of complaints about lawyer performance into a search for misconduct, moral guilt, and deviance. Performance standards tend to be abandoned in the process. The legal profession, in the way that it relates more to its members than to the public about discipline, looks more like a guild than like a licensed and regulated profession. This particular posture toward the disciplinary function produces several paradoxes.

The major paradox rests on the fact that the legal profession is by definition a profession concerned with the administration of justice. Another profession concerned with the administration of justice is the judiciary, which draws most, if not all of its members, from the legal profession. And still another profession concerned with the rulemaking function—the legislature—draws generously from the ranks of the legal profession. The paradox is that the legal profession operates the rulemaking and conflict-resolving functions for society in ways quite dissimilar to the ways that it approaches the problems of self-regulation and self-governance.

The legal profession, in common with other associations, makes its own rules of membership and promulgates its own standards of conduct. Unlike other associations, however, when the conduct of its members impinges upon the rights or expectations of others, the legal profession seeks to decide the issues without external regulation or outside participation. The rules for the governance of the legal profession cover disparate relationships and situations. They cover standards for relationships between lawyers, between lawyers and clients, and between the lawyer and his community. Yet the procedures for the application of the rules are strikingly similar in each instance. The charges (or issues) are investigated by lawyers and heard by lawyers. There is no outside participation in most jurisdictions. Such a procedure can work when strictly professional breaches of conduct are involved. But when community expectations and client expectations are involved, the exclusion of "outsiders" from the entire disciplinary process is difficult to justify.

Another interesting paradox involves the legal profession's strong bias in favor of the common law jury and the underlying notion that inexpert panelists can approach complex clusters of facts, receive complex instructions on complex issues of law, and arrive at just, meaningful, fair, or at least acceptable results. The layman, however, is deemed to lack this capacity when contemplating, complaining of, or judging lawyer performance, and to some degree when complaining of or judging lawyer conduct.

A third paradox relates to clarity and application of rules. A vague rule is like no rule at all. Hence rules that start off vague are known by the legal profession to require either legislative revision or judicial or administrative gloss to make them workable. Under this principle, standards for performance grounded on a "reasonable man" standard have been converted to workability in many areas. A notable example is in the field of negligence. Yet when the legal profession in its self-regulatory function contemplates the central issue of competence, it frequently hedges the issue by declaring that no workable criteria for performance can be developed—that the issues are unmanageable. In Georgia, for example, the supreme court adopted the new Code of Professional Responsibility without DR 6-101 which subjects lawyers to discipline for accepting employment in matters beyond either their competence or their capacity for preparation. The elimination of DR 6-101 was explained to us on grounds that it involved "vague and unworkable" standards.[67]

Similar explanations of the unworkability of performance standards were offered to us in the course of our interviews as the reason for not facing the issue of lawyer competence. In short, for its own regulation, the legal profession pleads initial vagueness without making an attempt at either judicial development or legislative revision—without making an attempt to evolve "reasonable lawyer" standards. Even though DR 6-101 could serve as a basis for subsequent development of the criteria for competence, many of our disciplinary agency respondents appeared to reject it out of hand. Yet when a client sues a lawyer for malpractice, the courts by necessity have had to try to develop a reasonable lawyer standard. Although the standard is not well developed, at least the courts have been willing to attempt to develop a standard. When, however, the profession seemingly represents the complainant or the public in a disciplinary hearing, it has avoided the same attempt at developing a reasonable lawyer standard.

What the foregoing paradoxes point up, particularly by their accumulation, is that there are probably several pressures at work which convert performance inputs into conduct or deviance outputs in the operation of the legal profession's disciplinary function. In performing its central functions for society the legal profession operates on a wholly different basis than it does when it attempts the function of self-regulation. What we have is a system of self-regulation tied into a fault or deviance notion that appears to be antithetical to licensing and regulation for the protection of the public.

PROFESSIONAL REVIEW: WHAT SHOULD IT INCLUDE?

The overall effect of the legal profession's self-regulation bears a remarkable resemblance to the criminal justice system. Like criminal justice, the profession regulates wrongdoing but not competence. The punishment of wrongdoing does give the appearance of an attempt at self-regulation. It gives professional review a patina of visibility, and visibiity is a key issue. In dealing with licensed occupations the public expects a degree of regulation, even though it may recognize that the regulation will never be thorough. When the public deals with professions, however, the expectancy of regulation is somewhat higher. The profession must at least respond to this expectancy that the profession police itself. This demand of the public then lends force to the search for wayward members. Even if the task of reviewing performance were accomplished, the results of that review would be less dramatic and less responsive to public demand than suspension or disbarment because of wrongdoing.

Although the criminal justice model acts to satisfy public demand for self-regulation, we are not suggesting that the public has been well served by the apparent levels of disciplinary enforcement. Indeed, the public demand has not been met despite strenuous efforts in some jurisdictions to meet the perceived needs. Much of the current discussion within the legal profession—notably the Clark Committee Report—has indicated awareness of public disappointment and resulting distrust of the deficiencies of disciplinary enforcement. Increased levels of enforcement would be a conscious attempt to demonstrate to the public that something is being done. But this attempt at visibility reinforces both the fault notion and the resemblance to criminal procedure. Thus the desire to be visible is one of the pressures that convert performance inputs into conduct inputs.

Some members of the legal profession have been attempting to formulate not only workable performance standards but also a disciplinary process that enforces those standards. The recently adopted Code of Professional Responsibility reflects such an attempt. DR 6-101 allows penalties to be assessed for substandard performance,[68] although its history indicates that some who opted for its inclusion in the Code thought it both premature and unworkable. The adoption of DR 6-101 preceded any formalization of specialty boards; the profession has not even been able to formulate a definition of competence in the areas of specialization.[69] Thus DR 6-101 seems wishful, at best. For the profession as a whole, the idea of reviewing and regulating performance is not yet favored. The profession prefers a review apparatus that will deal with moral deviance alone.

Changes Necessary for Effective Professional Review

Even if the legal profession wanted a system of performance review and regulation, there are serious questions about its feasibility without major changes in professional alignment. Sincere and competent disciplinary professionals who have expressed their intentions to review performance are frustrated from the start. First, the passive posture of waiting for complaints results in a highly distorted selection of matters to review. Second, the disciplinary professionals working with the complaint process fall into the language of fault and its attendant outlook. Third, even avoiding the first two traps, the disciplinary professionals are not the ultimate decisionmakers. The professionals are more concerned with performance standards than are the volunteer panels that make the decisions and recommendations in disciplinary matters beyond the preliminary screening stage. In addition, grievance committees, disciplinary boards, and courts are more lenient than the disciplinary professionals regarding substandard lawyer performance.[70] The receptiveness of these tribunals to cases dealing with performance standards is bound to have an effect on intake and screening decisions.

Formal tribunals, the fault notion, and the severity of punishment may be the critical barriers to effective, ongoing professional review. The interplay between formality and punishment emphasizes the importance of the procedure. Discipline is viewed in this context as a one-time matter rather than an ongoing review designed to protect the public. The severity of punishments—dealing ultimately with the right of livelihood—has forced the disciplinarians into a search for misconduct and wrongdoing, when these are the least relevant standards to apply to performance. Recent moves to add formal censure and formal private reprimand to the options available to the deciders, a move suggested by the Clark Commission, are steps in the right direction; they broaden the base of disciplinary enforcement. These moves do not, however, convert the process to one of self-regulation, because the less severe penalties of censure and reprimand still remain rooted in the language and outlook of fault.

What is needed is to remove the fault notion from the process of professional self-regulation. This would be a recognition that the profession really calls upon the lawyer to do three basic things: (1) obey the laws of the community, (2) adhere to the rules of conduct of the profession, and (3) practice law competently. Fault notions may be crucial to the enforcement of the first two, but they are irrelevant or, worse, counterproductive to a system that seeks assurances of at least minimally acceptable levels of performance. A clear separation of the issues of conduct and performance is needed. Such a separation would allow for innovation and fresh approaches to the problems of regulating performance.

Another built-in problem facing the legal disciplinarians is the nature of the license; presently, it is perpetual and general. Under these circumstances remedies available for dealing with substandard performance are limited. The requirement of specialty examinations as a condition for handling certain matters cannot be expected. Nor can other requirements be regularly imposed as conditions of recertification. The perpetual nature of the license, therefore, reinforces the fault bias of self-regulation. Punishment is the only remedy available when the practices of a holder of a perpetual license are questioned.

Conflicting Policies in Disciplinary Proceedings

The present approach to discipline in the profession leads to several conflicting policies. The focus for considering these policies is whether professional interests are served. The first of these conflicting policies is whether disciplinary proceedings should be open or confidential. As disciplinary proceedings are now handled, a cloak of secrecy usually remains until the very last stage when punishment is meted out by the highest court in the jurisdiction. The confidentiality of proceedings conceals the filing of complaints, all preliminary investigations, preliminary hearings, some formal hearings, and even some adverse results. Confidentiality is defended in terms of protecting the lawyer involved against adverse publicity which might result from groundless charges. This confidentiality of disciplinary proceedings is in sharp contrast to the way that criminal charges for society-at-large are handled.

All stages of a disciplinary proceeding should be disclosed because confidentiality is incompatible with the profession's need to publicize at least its formal efforts at self-regulation, and because the nature of the proceedings (except for the confidentiality) more closely resembles a criminal trial than an informal regulatory hearing. The origins of secrecy in disciplinary proceedings are remote; perhaps they are rooted in a guild outlook. Secrecy, however, does not serve the broader professional interests. Further, there is a question whether secrecy of proceedings, at least after preliminary screenings, is consistent with the licensing rationale, which requires accountability to the public.[71]

Recently, the State of Michigan made all formal proceedings (after charges are filed by the State Bar Grievance Board) open to the public.[72] The facts pertaining to complaints and investigations prior to formal hearings, however, remain confidential. One would have to evaluate the quality of recent complaints in Michigan to determine if the publicity about proceedings has produced a different type of response.

Whether disciplinary proceedings should have professional or lay review is a second area of conflicting policies. A principal question for consideration is: Does the exclusion of lay participation on reviewing tribunals serve professional interests? To the extent that the issues being considered resemble those in the criminal justice system, exclusion of nonprofessionals is gratuitous. Nonprofessionals are in as good a position as professionals to apply general community standards of conduct. Under these circumstances, exclusion of nonprofessionals from reviewing positions is hardly merited; instead, the exclusion appears created to protect the lawyers involved. When the matters under consideration involve issues of criminal justice, the exclusion of nonprofessionals runs contrary to the needs of the profession to account to the public and make its efforts at self-regulation more visible.[73] To the extent that the matters being considered by the disciplinary tribunal relate to lawyer performance—the opposite of a criminal trial—the exclusion of nonprofessionals may be more benign; exclusion is a means of avoiding the difficulties surrounding performance criteria, and of avoiding the ultimate question whether performance can be effectively regulated.

If performance review were separated from conduct hearings, a strong argument could be made in favor of the exclusion of nonlawyers from the review process for the former. The argument becomes even stronger if the process of review is tied in with recertification. When, however, specific instances of performance are reviewed in response to complaints, the strength of the argument in favor of excluding lay members diminishes. Indeed, the presence of nonlawyers on the reviewing board can lead to implicit pressures on the lawyer members to articulate their criteria for performance in plain everyday language.[74]

Consequences of the Present Disciplinary Approach

The present disciplinary approach fosters a belief on the part of the public that incompetent lawyers are weeded out and that lawyers who remain certified are competent. It is not certain how prevalent the belief is and whether the public really relies on the implied certification of lawyers who continue to be licensed. Whether or not the public does rely, the implication of self-regulation without the reality of self-regulation has unfortunate consequences. If members of the public rely on certification and are then faced with the dismal reality of incompetence, the consequence will be lost prestige to the profession. If in fact the public does not rely on the bar's certification and supervision processes, then the meaning of the license has already been eroded.

What is the cost to lawyers? We found little evidence that lawyers generally have the feeling that either their performance or their conduct is being systematically reviewed. For lawyers, the cost of the present disciplinary practice is twofold. Without a sense of being reviewed, attorneys may adopt indifferent attitudes toward the profession's standard of conduct.[75] Moreover, in the performance area, independent of moral or ethical bending, the same slothfulness may also appear. The second effect may be just as serious. One of the good elements of professionalism dies when there is no systematized review; lawyers fail to internalize a sense of excellence, a sense of service, and a sense of integrity.

The present disciplinary system is, at best, a randomized and partial replication of the criminal justice system. It lends itself nicely to the issues of moral fitness and deviance. But it does not easily or usually apply to issues of performance. There are side benefits to the present system, of course. By asking "Should a lawyer convicted of income tax evasion be permitted to continue to practice law?" the organized bar can move easily—even unwittingly—into concern with questions about mental instability, social outlook and conduct, and independent of performance, the assessment of criteria that give rise to public confidence. Under the present system we have ways of dealing with alcoholism and mental illness but not stupidity, laziness, or overevaluation of skill. The present disciplinary system is strongly based on a conception of who ought to be an outsider and who ought to be an insider. It is an ironic twist of equity; the system pays more attention to the actor than the performance.

CONCLUSION

If self-regulation is going to be addressed to the issue of assuring the profession and the public that current license holders are both competent and morally reliable, either the fault core of the present disciplinary process must be removed, or performance must be dealt with separately. Even when the profession addresses conduct, when the fault or deviance is unavoidable, the style of regulation can depend on the question that is being asked. "Is X a good practice risk?" is a far different question from "Has X offended us?" If the first question is being asked, a disciplinary agency can review a complaint by determining how the lawyer is handling other clients and matters other than the one that may be the subject of the complaint. This is not generally done. Yet the central issue of assurance about future practice risks is not reached unless some such review is undertaken.

When the issue is performance, the notion of fault is even more strange, if what is sought is assurance about future performance. We have suggested that reliance on the complaint system strains the way that issues of competence are approached; this reliance forces the issue of performance into the fault mold. The issue of punishment or nonpunishment becomes more important than the issue of assurance about future levels of performance. Like the response to a single-conduct complaint, the response to a single-performance complaint improperly focuses on fault rather than on questions about continuing certification.[76] For self-regulation to be relevant to issues of certification, the profession must create opportunities to review performance and not simply occasions for accusation. It may be that both the perpetual nature of the law license and the sense that a vested right arises from it frustrate the impulses or destroy the opportunities for no-fault review. If this is the case, some thought should be given to short-term licenses or no licenses at all.

Another crucial problem facing the profession's self-regulation system is the absence of workable criteria for judging performance. The licensing structure is pertinent here, too. The law license is a generalist license. Yet claims are made that the skills are specialized. If the profession remains formally organized along generalist lines, it is possible that any scheme of review of performance is doomed to failure.

It is conceivable that the profession could not regulate itself even if it tried.

It is also possible that the administrative apparatus required to review performance may be more costly—both in terms of money and in terms of loss of freedom and prestige—than the social utility of monitoring the quality of lawyer services. If either proves to be the case, then assuredly the license itself should be dropped so that the marketplace will become the sole and ultimate judge of competing skills. As things now stand the license and its implications, unaccompanied by the reality of self-regulation, interfere with the free flow of services, information, and exchanges in the market.

NOTES

1. J. Ben-David, Professions and Professionalization 1, 1970 (unpublished monograph at the University of Chicago Department of Sociology), suggests that a "profession is an occupational category, not a theoretical concept."

A "profession" is distinguished from other occupations, even other licensed occupations, by the following characteristics: (1) a skill acquired through higher education and specialized training as a prerequisite to entry; (2) monopoly rights over the performance of certain functions; (3) control of admission; and (4) assertion of formal and informal authority of the professional community over at least minimum standards of professional conduct and perhaps performance. The legal profession fits this model reasonably well, although it has failed, for the most part, to exercise authority over the ways that its members perform their services and conduct themselves. This failure it shares with other professions, few of which go very far in controlling performance or competence. *Id.* at pp. 1-2.

2. See, *e.g., In re* Day, 181 Ill. 73, 54 N.E. 646 (1899); *In re* Integration of Nebraska State Bar Association, 133 Neb. 283, 275 N.W. 265 (1937); *Ex parte* Splane, 123 Pa. 527, 16 A. 481 (1899); *In re* Davies, 93 Pa. 116 (1880); *In re* Cannon, 206 Wis. 374, 240 N.W. 441 (1932). See generally ABA Special Committee on Evaluation of Disciplinary Enforcement, *Problems and Recommendations in Disciplinary Enforcement* 1-9 (final draft 1970) [hereinafter cited as *Clark Committee Report*]

Cf. Dent v. West Virginia, 129 U.S. 114 (1888) (upholding constitutionality of West Virginia statute requiring certification of the medical profession). Many occupations and callings are both licensed and regulated by the state. It is the so-called professions which lay claim to, and are generally granted, the right to regulate their own members. The degree of self-regulation versus state regulation varies. In no other profession is the prerogative of self-regulation claimed with as vigorous assertion of natural right as it is in the legal profession. Of course self-regulation in the legal profession means in large part supervision by the judiciary.

3. Lawyers who violate the society's criminal laws are subject to court jurisdiction but *qua* individuals, not lawyers.

4. A few years ago, perhaps as a result of public outcry over open and notorious corruption within the bar, a bill was introduced in the Michigan Legislature calling for external (lay) control of the regulation of the bar. But through the efforts of the state bar association and the state supreme court, a compromise was arrived at providing for a professional board of review—the Michigan State Bar Grievance Board—appointed by and reporting directly to the state supreme court, with two of the seven members to be laymen. See *Rules Concerning the State Bar of Michigan, Rule 16.* Minnesota has recently added a lay minority to its professional review body. *Minnesota Rules of Professional Responsibility, Rule 3.*

5. This perspective is typified by J. Carlin, *Lawyers' Ethics* (1966). See also J. Handler, *The Lawyer and His Community* (1967).

6. This perspective was the thrust of the recent *Clark Committee Report.* The *Clark Com-*

mittee Report was preceded by the *Report of the Special Committee of the American Bar Foundation on Canons of Ethics* (1958). Both reports found existing disciplinary practices to be seriously inadequate. The *Clark Committee Report* observed, at p. 1: "After three years of studying lawyer discipline throughout this country, this Committee must report the existence of a scandalous situation that requires the immediate attention of the profession. With few exceptions, the prevailing attitude of lawyers toward disciplinary enforcement ranges from apathy to outright hostility. Disciplinary action is practically nonexistent in many jurisdictions; practices and procedures are antiquated; many disciplinary agencies have little power to take effective steps against malefactors."

7. The issues of training and admission to the bar raise similar problems. Indeed, a study of the disciplinary function may itself raise the basic question whether lawyers should be licensed in the first place unless provision is made for continuing regulation. These collateral issues, however, are beyond the scope of this article, which assumes, pragmatically, that licensing will continue despite its shortcomings.

8. 129 U.S. 114, 122 (1888) (emphasis added). See also Note, "Entrance and Disciplinary Requirements for Occupational Licenses in California," *Stanford Law Review* 14 (1962):533

9. One further element confounds our definitinal problems. The competent rendering of legal services is partly a function of the number and kinds of matters that clients offer to lawyers and partly a function of the number and kinds of legal matters that lawyers undertake at any given time. The lawyer never works on client problems until he has made an intake decision.

At first glance the lawyer's failure to relate his intake decisions realistically to his skills or available sources (including both the assistance of others and his available time) may appear to rest on a fault notion; he may be negligent in accepting more work than he can do properly. But this situation need not be seen in that manner. It is capable of being viewed in terms of a lawyer's maturity; *i.e.,* how realistic is the lawyer's view of himself in relation to the outside world. In one sense this article examines the realism, or lack of realism, of the organized bar's view of lawyers. Thus, when we discuss a lawyer's intake decision, we are discussing the same process from the viewpoint of the actor. One need not—perhaps should not—discuss the reality of self-views in terms of fault.

10. Canons 33 to 47 were added over the years from 1928 to 1937; they also do not deal with the public responsibilities of the lawyer.

11. The nine Canons are:

Canon 1. A Lawyer Should Assist in Maintaining the Integrity and Competence of the Legal Profession.

Canon 2. A Lawyer Should Assist the Legal Profession in Fulfilling Its Duty to Make Legal Counsel Available

Canon 3. A Lawyer Should Assist in Preventing the Unauthorized Practice of Law

Canon 4. A Lawyer Should Preserve the Confidence and Secrets of a Client

Canon 5. A Lawyer Should Exercise Independent Professional Judgment on Behalf of a Client

Canon 6. A Lawyer Should Represent a Client Competently

Canon 7. A Lawyer Should Represent a Client Zealously Within the Bounds of the Law

Canon 8. A Lawyer Should Assist in Improving the Legal System

Canon 9. A Lawyer Should Avoid Even the Appearance of Professional Impropriety

The first three canons deal with the attorney's relationship to the profession. The next four deal with the attorney's relationship to the client. The last two deal with the public life of attorneys. Perhaps a more appropriate title for the Code would be the Code of Professional Responsibilities.

12. *ABA Code of Professional Responsibility,* "Preliminary Statement"(1970).

13. Not every layman, of course, is likely to achieve the embarrassing success (to the legal profession) of Charles Ross, a "natural-born lawyer." See Kirp, "The Consequence of Credentialism," *Christian Science Monitor* (September 14, 1972) at p. 20, col. 1:

Several weeks ago, federal marshals arrested Charles Ross, a 36-year-old heroin addict who, posing as an attorney, had represented five fellow addicts in state and federal court. What was ironically galling to the government was that, as the Unted States magistrate observed, "he battled 1,000 percent before the bar," regularly besting the Brooklyn District Attorney's office.

Charles Ross' crime, in the words of the indictment, was that he had "impersonated an attorney." Mr. Ross was doing a lawyer's job—and, by all accounts, doing it better and more cheaply than many lawyers—without the requisite credentials. A six-month correspondence course, and 15 years of semilegal work, were all the training Ross had. That is insufficient even to allow a person to take the bar examination.

14. *ABA Committee on Professional Ethics Opinions,* No. 316 (1967).

15. In this connection we should note other consequences resulting from the absence of a definition of work and skill. The main one is the dilemma facing the would-be client when he goes to select a lawyer. The same dilemma faces the lawyer hiring or rating other lawyers. Indeed, Martindale-Hubbell, Inc., which publishes a directory of American lawyers and provides ratings of lawyers based on information given by other lawyers (peer review?), states: "No arbitrary rule for determining legal ability has been formulated. The ratings are based upon the standard of ability for the place or area in which the lawyer practices. Age, practical experience, nature and length of practice and other relevant qualifications are to be considered." Enclosure entitled *Confidential Rating Explanation* sent to attorneys in January 1972 for rating courses on file at the American Bar Foundation, Chicago.

16. The argument supporting the duty proceeds: (1) Violations of disciplinary rules are defined as misconduct under DR 1-102; (2) DR 6-101 provides that lawyers shall not take cases in which they are not competent, or handle a matter for which they have not adequately prepared in advance; (3) DR 1-103 provides that lawyers (and judges are lawyers, too) shall report violations of DR 1-102 and, therefore, shall report violations of DR 6-101, as well.

17. The Code of Professional Responsibility points the way to the aspiring and provides standards by which to judge the transgressor. Each lawyer must find within his own conscience the touchstone against which to test the extent to which his actions should rise above minimum standards. But in the last analysis it is the desire for the respect and confidence of the members of his profession and of the society which he serves that should provide to a lawyer the incentive for the highest possible degree of ethical conduct. The possible loss of that respect and confidence is the ultimate sanction. So long as its practitioners are guided by these principles, the law will continue to be a noble profession. This is its greatness and its strength, which permit no compromise. *ABA Code of Professional Responsibility,* "Preamble" (1970).

18. The *Clark Committee Report* found that even when suspension or disbarment occurred, the result took too long; the lawyer practiced in the interim between judgment and appeal; there was no systematic exchange of information that could in the interim protect clients, other than the complainant, or the general public; and no systematic search was made for other instances of wrongdoings by the "guilty" lawyer. *Clark Committee Report* 1-8. The *Clark Committee Report* has stimulated a good deal of action within the bar to improve at least discipline for misconduct. The aggregate effect, however, will not be clear for some time yet.

19. 407 U.S. 25 (1972).

20. Carlin's exact terminology was "offenses against colleagues." J. Carlin, *Lawyers' Ethics* 153 (1966).

21. Committees, styled in these or similar names, are universally found in hospitals. They review medical procedures used prior to death to see if there was fault, neglect, or even bad judgment. A doctor's standing in the hospital frequently is affected by adverse decisions.

22. The medical profession relies heavily on hospital control. Derbyshire, "What Should the Profession Do About the Incompetent Physician?" *Journal of the American Medical Association* 194 (1965):1287, 1288, notes that only seven state medical societies had disciplined doctors for "incompetence"; the societies had indicated that hospitals should handle such problems before formal review by medical societies is needed.

23. The two parties are the complainant and the lawyer. In the three-party model the agency is involved. See text accompanying notes 60-65 *infra.*

24. See *Clark Committee Report* 63 for one state bar counsel's description of the usefulness of a clipping service.

25. Recently Wisconsin adopted a review of lawyers' handling of client funds through a spot check, a practice that amounted to an audit of lawyers. This approach was thought to be a desirable way to deal with the Wisconsin bar's contingent liability under the trust accounts statute. See *Wisconsin Statutes Annotated* § 256.293 (1971). It was pointed out to us, however, that the deterrent threat, not the actuality of audit, was the principal control sought. The intent of the announced policy would stimulate introspection on the part of lawyers about handling client funds. Interview with Wisconsin bar counsel, on file at the American Bar Foundation, Chicago.

The Law Society of Upper Canada goes one step further and actually audits lawyers' accounts. Each lawyer is audited once every 2 years. The audits are unannounced: on a given morning chartered public accountants appear at the office of every lawyer in a town or a selected section of a city. The auditors look at and copy everything in sight. They may look not only at the files but at appointment books and miscellaneous notes as well. The refusal of access to any available information is an offense subject to discipline. Interviews by American Bar Foundation personnel of the Law Society of Upper Canada.

26. In one jurisdiction in 1971, lawyers armed with tape measures actually measured the lettering on law office doors and windows. Based upon this example, one can fairly assume that the impetus for self-initiated investigations arises chiefly from the profession's concern about its status and the image it projects to the outside world.

27. A wide gap exists between the exercise of contempt power and professional review. While some judges may deal with courtroom breaches of the Canons by holding a lawyer in contempt, few seem willing to attack the problem of poor representation by subjecting a lawyer to systematic review of competence. Judicial criticism of a lawyer's performance in open court, however, is not unknown.

28. Our observations confirm the observations of the Clark Committee in this respect. See *Clark Committee Report* 77.

29. In California, complainants are given the following informal memorandum:

This memorandum is given to you so that you will know some things about the State Bar and what it can do and cannot do when it considers a complaint against an attorney. . . .

. . . It cannot, for example, investigate the competence with which an attorney handled your case, or the results obtained, because these matters are generally not within the limited jurisdiction of the State Bar.

State Bar Association of California Informal Memorandum, on file at the American Bar Foundation, Chicago.

30. A distinction must be drawn between informal and public censure. Informal censure (private admonition) frequently can be done by the disciplinary agency without court approval. The fact of admonition is generally kept confidential, being released only by the involved attorney or in the event of subsequent action.

31. Even the reform-minded Clark Committee refused to entertain the notion that persons other than lawyers, or agencies outside professsonal associations or courts, ought to be included in some stage of the discipline process. See *Clark Committee Report* 46-47.

32. *Clark Committee Report* 5.

33. The lack of publicity may reflect disinterest of the media rather than policy of the disciplinary agencies. Unless the case has some particularly dramatic overtones, it may not be perceived as "news."

34. The confidentiality of records kept us from our desired preliminary view of the actual complaints. Some states have since made them available. Any in-depth analysis would require access to all complaints, all proceedings, and all records in the jurisdictions studied.

35. Interview with Wisconsin bar counsel, on file at the American Bar Association, Chicago.

36. The attitudes we observed toward complainants ranged from respect to unconcealed contempt.

37. A study of complaints against both barristers and solicitors in Great Britain arrived at a similar characterization of the bulk of client complaints: a high proportion allege negligence, and a high proportion of these and other complaints are explained as a "failure to communicate." *Justice* (British Section of International Commission of Jurists), *Complaints Against Lawyers* 12 (1970).

38. The picture is not entirely bleak, however. In an interview, one bar counsel described the issues of communications and accountability in jurisdictional terms: "The lawyer accepting a case treats a trust relationship. He has a duty to account to his client about the progress of the matter he is handling." Interview with Norman Faulkner, Chief Counsel, State Bar of Florida, Tallahassee, Fla., October 28, 1971, on file at the American Bar Foundation, Chicago.

39. *Chicago Bar Association Annual Reports Submitted by Committees in the Association Year 1969-70,* at p. 22.

40. *Id.* at p. 23.

41. *Id.*

42. Approximately 30,000 of the state's 50,000 lawyers are in the First Department, New York *Legal Directory, 1972-73* (1972).

43. The Association classifies complaints in a manner first used by J. Carlin, *supra* note 5, at p. 154.

44. In Minnesota, for example, about 50% of the complaints concerned neglect. Both New York and Minnesota will act on simple neglect. In states which will act only in cases of gross neglect, the percentage of cases involving neglect may appear to be smaller. For example, in a study involving a middle-sized Midwestern city, only 23% of the cases that reached the Hearing Division involved neglect. J. Handler, *supra* note 5, at p. 79. In the latter states many simple neglect cases probably are screened out informally. Furthermore, knowledge that a state will not act on simple neglect cases might have a circular effect and ultimately discourage people from even contacting the committee concerning these cases. As a result, persons so discouraged would not even enter into the committee's intake statistics.

45. See, e.g., the 174 minor fee disputes, which according to the Association of the Bar of the City of New York, "set forth no unethical behavior." Table 1, Category 10.

46. Committee on Grievances, the Association of the Bar of the City of New York, *Annual Report 1969-1970.*

47. Interview with Wisconsin bar counsel, on file at the American Bar Foundation, Chicago.

48. In Georgia, for example, which lacks a paid staff for the grievance committee, only 2% of the complaints reach the formal hearing stage. In contrast, we found that in states having paid staff, an average of 10 to 15% of the complaints reach the formal hearing stage.

49. *Bench & Bar of Minnesota* 28 (December, 1971):15.

50. The absence of criteria for defining legal work is cited as a reason why the profession cannot deal with the issues of competence. Yet the fee problem is certainly related to the competence problem—payment for what?

51. ABA Committee on Professional Ethics, *Opinions,* No. 320 (1968) (citations omitted).

52. When a complainant is called as a witness he may be so intimidated that he regrets having started the action.

53. See *Justice, supra* note 37, at p. 11.

54. Beyond this confusion as to agency accountability lies, in our view, an even more basic question about lawyer loyalty and accountability to the client.

55. Interview with R. B. Reavill, Administrative Director of Professional Responsibility, the Minnesota bar, on file at the American Bar Foundation, Chicago. See also *Bench of Bar of Minnesota* 28 (May-June, 1972):11-12.

56. The cooperative versus the authoritarian model of lawyer-client relationships was suggested in D. Rosenthal, Client Participation in Professional Decison-Making: The Lawyer-Client Relationship in Personal Injury Cases, 1970 (unpublished Ph.D. dissertation in Yale University

Library). See also Comment, "Restructuring Informed Consent: Legal Therapy for the Doctor-Patient Relationship," *Yale Law Journal* 79 (1970):1533, in which a similar thesis is applied to the doctor-patient relationship. The ultimate concern is the amount of control over his life and affairs a patient or client loses or is asked to surrender when he seeks and receives assistance from a doctor or a lawyer.

57. If we consider this threat in the context of a jury trial, we see that "expert" witness (lawyers) could be called upon to explain to jurors, in everyday parlance, standards for specific tasks or relationships in the same way that explanations are made to clients. The outside regulators need not be lay clients and lay jurors only; they could also be lay members of regulatory or disciplinary agencies.

58. See Goode, "Community Within a Community: The Professions," *American Sociological Review* 22 (1957):194. See Florida Bar v. Heft, 213 So. 2d 422 (Fla. 1968).

59. See H. Becker, *The Outsiders* (1963).

60. The distinction was suggested by John Bonomi, Chief Counsel, Association of the Bar of the City of New York, a member of this project's advisory committee.

61. The mere fact that bar personnel handle complaints does not indicate that there is professional staff. A bar secretary or bar executive acting as a screener of complaints would not be "professional staff." A bar counsel is one step toward a professional staff. The reality of counsel as professional staff, however, depends on the nondisciplinary duties assigned to him and the kinds of investigative and legal assistance at his disposal.

62. Sadly, those disciplinary functionaries without professional staff rarely record complaints once they are disposed of, and almost never place the matter in a lawyer's file. Few even keep a central file for all lawyers in the jurisdiction.

63. See Table II and note 48 *supra.*

64. If the legal profession were to undertake an extensive system of reviewing performance, a second agency might be needed. Existing disciplinary agencies may not be the proper models for approaching the problem of competence.

65. One could view the present state of affairs as proclaiming, "We can't define lawyering, but we know it should be licensed."

66. For this article's definition of competence and negligence see text accompanying note 10 *supra.*

At first glance the lawyer's failure to relate his intake decisions realistically to his skills or available resources (including both the assistance of others and his available time) may appear to rest on a fault notion, *i.e.,* negligence in accepting more work than he can do properly. But this situation need not be seen in that manner. It is capable of being viewed in terms of a lawyer's maturity, *i.e.,* how realistic is the lawyer's view of himself in relation to the outside world. In one sense we are talking in this article about the realism or lack of realism of the corporate or organized bar's view of lawyers. When we talk of a lawyer's intake decision, we are talking of the same process from the viewpoint of the actor. One need not—perhaps should not—talk about the reality of self-views in terms of fault.

67. Interview with Mallory Atkinson, Georgia bar counsel, Macon, Ga., June 16, 1971, on file at the American Bar Foundation, Chicago.

68. Disciplinary Rule 6-101 is an assertion that performance standards and competence are viable issues. But the absence of machinery to effect review of competence and reliance on client complaints without such machinery indicates ambivalence about the desirability of applying performance standards.

69. An American Bar Foundation project under the direction of Barlow F. Christensen is currently studying the tasks and roles of lawyers in an attempt to arrive at functional definitions of the terms "lawyer," "lawyers," and "[modifier] lawyer"—such as "labor lawyer" or "appellate lawyer."

70. Again we must consider the effect of mixing two approaches—review of performance and punishment of misconduct—in a single tribunal.

71. Separating review of performance from proceedings concerning alleged wrongdoing can also lead to simpler analysis of the confidentiality issue. Review of performance would not be a "trial" or a "proceeding" and reputation need not be threatened in instances of review. The remainder of the docket then could be seen to be directly analogous to criminal trials.

72. Newspapers are notified of hearings which will be held in their locale. Originally, the Michigan State Bar Grievance Board gave the name of the lawyer involved in their press releases. Now they simply give the date, time, and place of the hearing, leaving it to the press to attend in order to obtain the name.

73. *Justice, supra* note 37, at pp. 8, 14, 16, discusses lay participation in professional review. As in note 4 *supra,* Michigan and Minnesota have nonlawyers on their state grievance boards. Of nine members Michigan has two nonlawyers and Minnesota has three of eighteen.

74. In an interview, October 7, 1971, Lansing, Michigan, John Murray, journalist, a member of the Michigan State Bar Grievance Board and formerly its chairman, said that lay participants had to rely on the lawyer members for direction. In this respect lay members of disciplinary tribunals are like jurors; they take their instructions from the experts—the judge or the professional members. Yet their presence alone has the effect of making the experts articulate what they might not if the lay members were not present.

75. See J. Carlin, *Lawyers' Ethics* (1966), 175-176.

76. When there are single complaints, perhaps the profession (for the disposition of the complaint) should urge lawsuits against lawyers, with the profession appearing "for the court" as a propounder of the expected standards.

PROBLEMS

SLICK SLIPS UP

You are the attorney for Breed D. Fastbucks, who died only yesterday along with his wife. He is survived by two nasty children and by his sister and her family. Fastbucks, Jr., has brought you all of his father's legal papers, including a will.

Fastbucks's estate is now worth at least $500,000, but the will under which it is to be administered was drawn up in 1970 at a cost of $10 and, it seems, the document is not worth even that. The will was drafted by Lawton Slick, then a hungry attorney fresh out of law school who has since achieved fame as a criminal defense lawyer. Fastbucks never bothered to get a new will made because, as he so often put it, "I haven't changed how I want my money distributed after I die, so why should I pay you $1,000 to do the work I already paid another lawyer $10 to do?" He never even let you see the will.

Fastbucks was a good businessman, but sometimes he was too frugal for his own good. The will he left is a good example of what can happen when one is too frugal. The intent of the will is clear. The money is to go to the poor children of Fastbucks's sister. His own children, who are well-to-do in their own right, will receive nothing. Unfortunately, the will is irretrievably flawed in a way that most first-year law students would recognize and every competent attorney should be on guard against. Slick violated the rule against perpetuities. Thus, for all practical purposes, Fastbucks has died without a will. His children will inherit everything.

You roll back into your chair and think of Slick's expensive suits, his Mercedes, and his eighteen-room house in the country. You also think of his brilliant courtroom tactics, his eloquence, his reputation for doing all he can for the people he defends. When all of this is set against the $10 will laying on your desk, you conclude that Slick either did not know enough to draft a will or he did not spend the time required to do it right. The $10 fee suggests that Slick was cutting corners, a cut-rate job for a cut-rate price. But you cannot be sure. Anyway, that was years ago. The will tells you nothing about Slick now.

You wonder: Did Slick do something unethical when he drafted that will? Should he be disciplined for it now so many years after the fact? Do you have a professional obligation to say anything to him about what he has done; to ask him whether he wrote any other wills; to ask whether he wants to make some compensation to the children of Fastbucks's sister? Do you have a professional obligation to report Slick to the grievance committee of your local bar association? You are reasonably sure that, if you do nothing, the local probate judge will also do nothing. Fastbucks's sister is not likely to seek legal assistance, much less to file a grievance or pursue a malpractice action. What should you do? Although you have met Slick at social functions, you and he are not friends.

FALSE ANSWER IN GOOD CAUSE

Your client is a poor old widow who lives in a house for which she has long since paid the mortgage. She has $900 in outstanding debts, due to repairs made on her roof approximately one year ago. A finance company is now seeking payment of the debt. The repair work was done satisfactorily, and the price, although a little high, is not unreasonable.

She paid $400 in advance and $50 per month for four months, but inflation and various unexpected medical bills have rendered her unable to continue the payments. Faced with the choice of meeting basic needs or not making the monthly payments, she stopped making payments. The finance company, after sending letters for six months, is now seeking a judgment against her, with the forced sale of her house as a possibility.

The ailing widow does not expect to live much longer, and would like to spend her remaining years in the house her husband left her. She can afford no more than $50 for legal help.

After reviewing the facts, you see no grounds for resisting payment (and no hope of working out a compromise with the finance company). But, given the congestion of the courts, you could delay any action against the widow for up to eighteen months, simply by filing a general denial. This move might force the finance company to give up trying to collect, since the debt is not sufficiently large to make it economical for the creditor to pursue further action. There is one "technical" hitch, however. While filing a denial solely for the purpose of delay is "common," it is contrary to court rules of procedure (and you must file a form along with the denial affirming that the arguments made are in "good faith"). Should you file the denial or just tell the widow there is nothing you can do?

THIS FEE MEANS "NO"

Bob Blackard, a regular client, has been sued for $22,000. He admits to owing the plaintiff, a box company, $16,000. Blackard contends that the plaintiff treated him poorly, first billing him for more boxes than he received and, when Blackard refused to pay, notifying other suppliers of his refusal.

Blackard is not a particularly agreeable fellow. He refused to pay anything toward the debt because he felt that the company should have taken his word about the number of boxes delivered rather than asking for documentation. He also refused to negotiate with the box company for the same reason. Blackard is willing to pay the $16,000 "eventually" but he wants to make the plaintiff "sweat" for the money. He wants you to delay the litigation as long as possible.

The court backlog would provide an automatic delay of almost a year, even if you did nothing but file a denial. The fact that the plaintiff notified other suppliers offers some ground for a counterclaim, which allows for additional delay. The counterclaim is not strong, however, since there were only two other suppliers, the brother-in-law and an uncle of the owner of the box company, and communication between them might well have been as innocent as it was natural.

Basically, Blackard wants you to delay for the sake of delay. It is purely fortuitous that you can make good-faith arguments in support of the denial that would be filed on his behalf. You can't bring yourself to take the case, but you don't want to lose Blackard as a client. Should you offer to do what he asks but at a fee that is so high he will not want to proceed? Or should you do something else?

Suggested Readings

For other works on historical issues raised here, see Bibliography, Part 1A, especially Pound (1953), for a survey of diverse forms the profession of law has taken in Western culture, and Hurst (1953) or Warren (1966) for a history of lawyering in America, including some discussion of legal ethics. For other works on issues of moral fitness or discipline, see Part 1B or 1C, especially Eschete (1984), Brown (1980), Comment (1979), Finman (1981), Gray (1982), Davis (1986), and Soble (1978).

Part II

The Moral Critique of Professionalism

Introduction

THE NATURE AND NEED FOR A MORAL CRITIQUE

A "critique" is a judicious separating out and weighing, a judgment defended by careful analysis of a subject. A critique may be favorable or unfavorable, but it must be searching. A *moral* critique is based on ethical considerations. Professionalism, as noted in the preceding chapter, is a style characteristic of members of a profession. The three essays in this chapter are concerned, then, with making a searching judgment, based on considerations of the style characteristic of members of the legal profession.

Why is such a critique necessary? Having been introduced to the profession of law in chapter 1, we are likely to want to move immediately into discussion of particular problems of legal ethics. That move may be premature. There may be an ethical problem about joining the profession at all and, if there is, there may be no problems of professional ethics. No profession is morally permissible by virtue of merely existing. Professions are defined, in part, by the good they aim at and the learning required to practice them, not at all by the moral permissibility of their *means*. Therefore, it is easy to imagine professions entrance into which would not be morally permissible. For example, even if torturing were as learned an occupation as medicine (and as dedicated to the public good), it seems unlikely that a good person could wish to become a good torturer. Questions of "torturer's ethics" (e.g., "Should one *ever* torture someone to death?" or "Is it permissible to torture a child under fourteen if the information likely to be gained will prevent the assassination of an important public official?") sound like grim jokes, not subjects of serious moral concern. The public service torturers perform cannot make what they do morally permissible. To enter such a profession would be morally bad. Discussion of legal ethics thus presupposes not only that law is a profession but that it is a morally permissible one; in other words, that moral critique has turned out favorably.

In chapter 1 a distinction was made between two terms, *profession* (a certain kind of organization) and *professionalism* (a certain style of practice). Attention will now be given to revealing some of the importance of that distinction. The topic for discussion is a moral critique of legal professionalism rather than of the profession itself. All three selections take for granted the possibility that law can be practiced as a profession in a morally permissible way. Though two of the three essays suggest "deprofessionalizing" law to some degree, there is no suggestion that society should return to the amateur lawyering of the early colonial period, or even to the unorganized bar of the period between the Revolution and the Civil War. The concern is only a certain *style* of lawyering. To "deprofessionalize" lawyering means to reduce lawyers' *professionalism,* especially the detachment with which lawyers look upon the morally important consequences of what they do for their clients.

Richard Wasserstrom considers two objections to the style in which law is now practiced: *first,* that the lawyer-client relationship renders the lawyer at best the amoral tool of the client ("a hired gun," so to speak); and *second,* that the lawyer also seems required to treat the client in an impersonal and paternalistic way. Wasserstrom finds a good deal of truth in each objection and explains both as arising from the lawyer's "role-differentiated behavior." The roles we play seem to alter enormously the kinds of actions we presume to be required or allowable. For example, ordinarily we suppose that parents are allowed, if not indeed required, to prefer the interests of their own children to those of others. The burden of proof, Wasserstrom thinks, should fall upon those who favor role-differentiated behavior. Absent some special reason, the moral point of view requires, for example, that the needs of all children receive equal consideration. Wasserstrom claims that, to be justified in preferring one's own children to those of someone else, one must have some reason beyond the simple fact of biological or social relationship.

Role-differentiated behavior leads to a simplified moral universe in which certain sorts of concerns (for example, the welfare of other children) lose importance. For criminal defense work, Wasserstrom admits that such simplification may be justified. A defense attorney may be acting morally even if, in a jurisdiction where this is still legally possible, he helps a rapist go free by requiring the victim to undergo psychiatric examination and then using the results to impugn her testimony. That is so in part because there is a useful division of labor between the defense attorney and the prosecutor in our "adversary system." But, for Wasserstrom, more important is the accused's need in a desperate hour. What Wasserstrom objects to is extension of the style of criminal lawyering beyond the conditions that make it necessary or at least useful. The adversary system seems to place far too much confidence in legal institutions. The system also seems to encourage character traits (such as "aggressiveness") that are notably undesirable, to conceive the lawyer's role as "play acting," and so to introduce into the center of the lawyer's life traits likely to make him a bad person. For most sorts of lawyering, Wasserstrom is inclined to urge "less professionalism" than more.

Role-differentiation, Wasserstrom argues, makes the relation between lawyer and client morally undesirable. Because lawyering is a learned art, the client is ordinarily not the lawyer's equal in the relation. The client hires the lawyer but thereafter must more or less let the lawyer control what is done. The lawyer needs the client's consent at every step in a case, but the client's consent will in general be a function of how the lawyer explains the options. The exercise of such power over an individual is both personally satisfying and morally dangerous. The lawyer's dominance tends to reduce the client to a mere object of his lawyer's solicitude. The lawyer comes to see relations with other lawyers as the focus of his professional life. His client becomes a mere "case." Wasserstrom suggests a number of ways to reduce such morally objectionable inequality, for example, simplyfing legal language and procedures. He seems to recognize, however, that much of the inequality is a byproduct of the good that comes from having a profession of law, and he is not willing to give that up.

Charles Fried offers a more favorable judgment of the lawyer's role. He contends that a good person can be a good lawyer even as the role of lawyer is now constituted. Like Wasserstrom, Fried begins with the role of parent—but with a difference. No reasonable morality, Fried argues, could ask us to look upon ourselves as a mere resource to benefit others. We are free, within certain bounds, to bestow our energies as we wish. Thus, a person needs no special reason to put his own child through college rather than someone else's, even though someone else's may be more deserving in every way. The parent's biological or social relationship with the child is reason enough. Morality does, of course, set bounds on such partiality. I may not kill another child to save my own.

There are, Fried thinks, many relationships permitting such special preference. Friendship, like parenthood, is one, but friendship rather than parenthood seems to be the most apt analogy here. The lawyer is "a special purpose friend," someone who will make the client's legal interests his own. Just as there is nothing wrong with showing special preference for the interests of a friend, so, too, there is nothing wrong with a lawyer showing special preference for the legal interests of his client.

This leaves Fried with the question of whether it is morally permissible to become anyone's legal friend. His answer seems to be that it is, within the bounds set by relatively just laws. Helping someone with a legal problem is, for Fried, always to perform a morally worthy function. A lawyer cannot be faulted for bestowing his services on the rich rather than on the poor because even the rich need a legal friend (and the lawyer should not be treated like a scarce resource to be dispatched where needed most). He should be free to do good where he will. A lawyer also cannot be faulted for helping the guilty go free, defeating a just debt by pleading the statute of limitations, or otherwise helping a client to work the levers of the law that he cannot work for himself. Giving such help does for a client what he would do for himseslf had he the legal knowledge. The lawyer thus contributes to the client's moral autonomy, and that is certainly good to do.

Much of Fried's essay is devoted to showing that the analogies between friendship and the lawyer-client relationship are more important than the disanalogies. But the paper concludes by trying to give rough definition to the limits of what a lawyer as legal friend may do for a client. Fried's "moral universe" turns out not to be all that simple. The means that a lawyer uses cannot, according to Fried, be immoral. Lying, stealing, degrading, inflicting pain, and the like are "personal relations" governed by ordinary moral constraints. Pleading the statute of limitations is, in contrast, an "institutional relation" not subject to ordinary moral restraints. The lawyer may plead the statute of limitations to defeat a just debt, but may not lie, steal, or deceive for any client.

Gerald Postema accepts most of Fried's argument but draws Wasserstrom's conclusion from it. For Postema, Fried's argument misses certain important features of moral life. For instance, Fried expresssly allows lawyers to detach themselves from moral concern about the ends their clients seek. Lawyers may not use immoral means, but they may pursue any legal end so long as the means are moral. The lawyer simply helps the client pull levers. According to Postema, this view of lawyering cuts the lawyer off from the values that structure moral choice, makes him insensitive to moral costs, and deprives him of the power to recognize his client as a moral person. Because Fried's lawyer is supposed to be morally neutral with regard to the client's ends, the lawyer canot *as lawyer* confront the client as a moral agent. That would be "unprofessional." The client would, it seems, be entitled to say, "I hired your legal training, not your moral judgment." The lawyer becomes a "moral prostitute."

Postema contends that the lawyer should act, in this respect at least, like an ordinary friend. Ordinary friends do judge each other's ends and act accordingly. The problem is not professionalization as such (that is, organization as a learned art), but "professionalism" (that is, moral neutrality). Calls for "deprofessionalization" ignore (according to Postema) the significant value professional roles produce by their division of moral and social labor. What is needed, Postema thinks, is a restructuring of the lawyer's role that will hold him responsible for what he says and does on behalf of a client. Postema expressly rejects Fried's distinction between "personal" and "institutional" injuries. Some acts can be characterized by doing both, and no important moral principle should rest on arbitrary distinctions between equally appropriate characterizations of an act. Unlike Wasserstrom, Postema does not make an exception for the defense attorney in a criminal case. Is Postema then recommending that lawyers not defend the guilty, or that the defense should be much more limited than it is now?

As you read the essays in this section, consider what each author would say about accepting the following case (and what each might advise you to say *to* the client if you decided to decline it):

George Thomas has provided you with two successful and lucrative personal injury suits. In each case, the injury he sustained was one of a sort most people would have shrugged off. George, however, is someone who likes to stand on his rights and get everything the law gives. He is, in short, instinctively litigious.

Today George has come to you with another case. As with the others, he is legally right in a way likely to make some money for both of you.

George bought a used car from Happy Sam's on the installment plan. The price was, by George's own admission, fair; and, in your opinion, more than fair. The interest rate was a little lower than the prevailing rate.

George nevertheless has a case. He reads the financial section of the morning newspaper religiously. Several days ago he read about the truth-in-lending law. Upon examining his contract with Sam (who finances his own cars), George determined that Sam had not filled in the contract properly. He had left several lines blank, thus committing a clear but technical violation of the law. (Though the purpose of the law is to assure that borrowers are not tricked into signing unfair loan agreements, the law itself does not require that one demonstrate an intention to trick, because such intention is usually hard to prove and the requirement made earlier legislation ineffective.) Under the law, George is entitled to both double the interest charge and the cost of suing. Suing Sam would be easy, lawful, and profitable for both you and your client.

But, Sam is an old man, running a small used-car lot without the usual deceit and thievery. He did not harm George. You therefore wonder whether it would be morally permissible to use the technicalities of the law in this way? Or should you instead tell George to forget this one? Should you just refuse to take the case and send George elsewhere? Or do you have a professional obligation to proceed with the suit?

Richard Wasserstrom

Lawyers as Professionals:
Some Moral Issues

In this paper I examine two moral criticisms of lawyers which, if well-founded, are fundamental. Neither is new but each appears to apply with particular force today. Both tend to be made by those not in the mainstream of the legal profession and to be rejected by those who are in it. Both in some sense concern the lawyer-client relationship.

The first criticism centers around the lawyer's stance toward the world at large. The accusation is that the lawyer-client relationship renders the lawyer at best systematically amoral and at worst more than occasionally immoral in his or her dealings with the rest of mankind.

The second criticism focuses upon the relationship between the lawyer and the client. Here the charge is that it is the lawyer-client relationship which is morally objectionable because it is a relationship in which the lawyer dominates and in which the lawyer typically, and perhaps inevitably, treats the client in both an impersonal and a paternalistic fashion.

To a considerable degree these two criticisms of lawyers derive, I believe, form the fact that the lawyer is a professional. And to the extent to which this is the case, the more generic problems I will be exploring are those of professionalism generally. But in some respects, the lawyer's situation is different from that of other professionals. The lawyer is vulnerable to some moral criticism that does not as readily or as easily attach to any other professional. And this, too, is an issue that I shall be examining.[1]

Although I am undecided about the ultimate merits of either criticism, I am convinced that each is deserving of careful articulation and assessment, and that each contains insights that deserve more acknowledgment than they often receive. My ambition is, therefore, more to exhibit the relevant considerations and to stimulate additional reflection, than it is to provide any very definite conclusions.

From "Lawyers as Professionals: Some Moral Issues," *Human Rights Quarterly* vol. 5, no. 1 (1975):105-128. Reprinted by permission of Johns Hopkins University Press and the author.

I

As I have indicated, the first issue I propose to examine concerns the ways the professional-client relationship affects the professional's stance toward the world at large. The primary question that is presented is whether there is adequate justification for the kind of moral universe that comes to be inhabited by the lawyer as he or she goes through professional life. For at best the lawyer's world is a simplified moral world; often it is an amoral one; and more than occasionally, perhaps, an overtly immoral one.

To many persons, Watergate was simply a recent and dramatic illustration of this fact. When John Dean testified before the Select Senate Committee inquiring into the Watergate affair in the Spring of 1973, he was asked about one of the documents that he had provided to the Committee. The document was a piece of paper which contained a list of a number of the persons who had been involved in the cover-up. Next to a number of the names an asterisk appeared. What, Dean was asked, was the meaning of the asterisk? Did it signify membership in some further conspiracy? Did it mark off those who were decision makers from those who were not? There did not seem to be any obvious pattern: Ehrlichman was starred, but Haldeman was not; Mitchell was starred, but Magruder was not. Oh, Dean answered, the asterisk really didn't mean anything. One day when he had been looking at the list of participants, he had been struck by the fact that so many of them were lawyers. So, he marked the name of each lawyer with an asterisk to see just how many there were. He had wondered, he told the Committee, when he saw that so many were attorneys, whether that had had anything to do with it; whether there was some reason why lawyers might have been more inclined than other persons to have been so willing to do the things that were done in respect to Watergate and the cover-up. But he had not pursued the matter; he had merely mused about it one afternoon.

It is, I think, at least a plausible hypothesis that the predominance of lawyers was not accidental—that the fact that they were lawyers made it easier rather than harder for them both to look at things the way they did and to do the things that were done. The theory that I want to examine in support of this hypothesis connects this activity with a feature of the lawyer's professionalism.

As I have already noted, one central feature of the professions in general and of law in particular is that there is a special, complicated relationship between the professional, and the client or patient. For each of the parties in this relationship, but especially for the professional, the behavior that is involved is to a very significant degree, what I call, role-differentiated behavior. And this is significant because it is the nature of role-differentiated behavior that it often makes it both appropriate and desirable for the person in a particular role to put to one side considerations of various sorts—and especially various moral considerations—that would otherwise be relevant if not decisive. Some illustrations will help to make clear what I mean both by role-differentiated behavior and by the way role-differentiated behavior often alters, if not eliminates, the significance of those moral considerations that would obtain, were it not for the presence of the role.

Being a parent is, in probably every human culture, to be involved in role-differentiated behavior. In our own culture, and once again in most, if not all, human cultures, as a parent one is entitled, if not obligated, to prefer the interests of one's own children over those of children generally. That is to say, it is regarded as appropriate for a parent to allocate excessive goods to his or her own children, even though other children may have substantially more pressing and genuine needs for these same items. If one were trying to decide what the right way was to distribute assets among a group of children all of whom were strangers to oneself, the relevant moral considerations would be very different from those that would be thought to obtain once one's own children were in the picture. In the role of a parent, the claims of other children vis-à-vis one's own are, if not rendered morally irrelevant, certainly rendered less morally significant. In short, the role-differentiated character of the situation alters the relevant moral point of view enormously.

A similar situation is presented by the case of the scientist. For a number of years there has been debate and controversy within the scientific community over the question of whether scientists should participate in the development and elaboration of atomic theory, especially as those theoretical advances could then be translated into development of atomic weapons that would become a part of the arsenal of existing nation states. The dominant view, although it was not the unanimous one, in the scientific community was that the role of the scientist was to expand the limits of human knowledge. Atomic power was a force which had previously not been utilizable by human beings. The job of the scientist was, among other things, to develop ways and means by which that could now be done. And it was simply not part of one's role as a scientist to forego inquiry, or divert one's scientific explorations because of the fact that the fruits of the investigation could be or would be put to improper, immoral, or even catastrophic uses. The moral issues concerning whether and when to develop and use nuclear weapons were to be decided by others; by citizens and statesmen; they were not the concern of the scientist *qua* scientist.

In both of these cases it is, of course, conceivable that plausible and even thoroughly convincing arguments exist for the desirability of the role-differentiated behavior and its attendant neglect of what would otherwise be morally relevant considerations. Nonetheless, it is, I believe, also the case that the burden of proof, so to speak, is always upon the proponent of the desirability of this kind of role-differentiated behavior. For in the absence of special reasons why parents ought to prefer the interests of their children over those of children in general, the moral point of view surely requires that the claims and needs of all children receive equal consideration. But we take the rightness of parental preference so for granted, that we often neglect, I think, the fact that it is anything but self-evidently morally appropriate. My own view, for example, is that careful reflection shows that the *degree* of parental preference systematically encouraged in our own culture is far too extensive to be morally justified.

All of this is significant just because to be a professional is to be enmeshed in role-differentiated behavior of precisely this sort. One's role as a doctor, psychiatrist, or lawyer, alters one's moral universe in a fashion analogous to that described above. Of special significance here is the fact that the professional *qua* professional has a client or patient whose interests must be represented, attended to, or looked after by the professional. And that means that the role of the professional (like that of the parent) is to prefer in a variety of ways the interests of the client or patient over those of individuals generally.

Consider, more specifically, the role-differentiated behavior of the lawyer. Conventional wisdom has it that where the attorney-client relationship exists, the point of view of the attorney is properly different—and appreciably so— from that which would be appropriate in the absence of the attorney-client relationship. For where the attorney-client relationship exists, it is often appropriate and many times even obligatory for the attorney to do things that, all other things being equal, an ordinary person need not, and should not do. What is characteristic of this role of a lawyer is the lawyer's required indifference to a wide variety of ends and consequences that in other contexts would be of undeniable moral significance. Once a lawyer represents a client, the lawyer has a duty to make his or her expertise fully available in the realization of the end sought by the client, irrespective, for the most part, of the moral worth to which the end will be put or the character of the client who seeks to utilize it. Provided that the end sought is not illegal, the lawyer is, in essence, an amoral technician whose peculiar skills and knowledge in respect to the law are available to those with whom the relationship of client is established. The question, as I have indicated, is whether this particular and pervasive feature of professionalism is itself justifiable. At a minimum, I do not think any of the typical, simple answers will suffice.

One such answer focuses upon and generalizes from the criminal defense lawyer. For what is probably the most familiar aspect of this role-differentiated character of the lawyer's activity is that of the defense of a client charged with a crime. The received view within the profession (and to a lesser degree within the society at large) is that having once agreed to represent the client, the lawyer is under an obligation to do his or her best to defend that person at trial, irrespective, for instance, even of the lawyer's belief in the client's innocence. There are limits, of course, to what constitutes a defense: a lawyer cannot bribe or intimidate witnesses to increase the likelihood of securing an acquittal. And there are legitimate questions, in close cases, about how those limits are to be delineated. But, however these matters get resolved, it is at least clear that it is thought both appropriate and obligatory for the attorney to put on as vigorous and persuasive a defense of a client believed to be guilty as would have been mounted by the lawyer thoroughly convinced of the client's innocence. I suspect that many persons find this an attractive and admirable feature of the life of a legal professional. I know that often I do. The justifications are varied and, as I shall argue below, probably convincing.

But part of the difficulty is that the irrelevance of the guilt or innocence of an accused client by no means exhausts the altered perspective of the lawyer's conscience, even in criminal cases. For in the course of defending an accused, an attorney may have, as a part of his or her duty of representation, the obligation to invoke procedures and practices which are themselves morally objectionable and of which the lawyer in other contexts might thoroughly disapprove. And these situations, I think, are somewhat less comfortable to confront. For example, in California, the case law permits a defendant in a rape case to secure in some circumstances an order from the court requiring the complaining witness, that is the rape victim, to submit to a psychiatric examination before trial.[2] For no other crime is such a pretrial remedy available. In no other case can the victim of a crime be required to undergo psychiatric examination at the request of the defendant on the ground that the results of the examination may help the defendant prove that the offense did not take place. I think such a rule is wrong and is reflective of the sexist bias of the law in respect to rape. I certainly do not think it right that rape victims should be singled out by the law for this kind of pretrial treatment, and I am skeptical about the morality of any involuntary psychiatric examination of witnesses. Nonetheless, it appears to be part of the role-differentiated obligation of a lawyer for a defendant charged with rape to seek to take advantage of this particular rule of law—irrespective of the independent moral view he or she may have of the rightness or wrongness of such a rule.

Nor, it is important to point out, is this peculiar, strikingly amoral behavior limited to the lawyer involved with the workings of the criminal law. Most clients come to lawyers to get the lawyers to help them do things that they could not easily do without the assistance provided by the lawyer's special competence. They wish, for instance, to dispose of their property in a certain way at death. They wish to contract for the purchase or sale of a house or a business. They wish to set up a corporation which will manufacture and market a new product. They wish to minimize their income taxes. And so on. In each case, they need the assistance of the professional, the lawyer, for he or she alone has the special skill which will make it possible for the client to achieve the desired result.

And in each case, the role-differentiated character of the lawyer's way of being tends to render irrelevant what could otherwise be morally relevant considerations. Suppose that a client desires to make a will disinheriting her children because they opposed the war in Vietnam. Should the lawyer refuse to draft the will because the lawyer thinks this is a bad reason to disinherit one's children? Suppose a client can avoid the payment of taxes through a loophole only available to a few wealthy taxpayers. Should the lawyer refuse to tell the client of a loophole because the lawyer thinks it an unfair advantage for the rich? Suppose a client wants to start a corporation that will manufacture, distribute and promote a harmful but not illegal substance, *e.g.,* cigarettes. Should the lawyer refuse to prepare the articles of incorporation for the corporation? In each case, the accepted view within the profession is that these matters are just of no concern to the lawyer *qua* lawyer. The lawyer need not of course agree to represent the client (and that is equally true for the unpopular client accused of a heinous crime), but there is nothing wrong with representing a client whose aims and purposes are quite immoral. And having agreed to do so, the lawyer is required to provide the best possible assistance, without regard to his or her disapproval of the objective that is sought.

The lesson, on this view, is clear. The job of the lawyer, so the argument typically concludes, is not to approve or disapprove of the character of his or her client, the cause for which the client seeks the lawyer's assistance, or the avenues provided by the law to achieve that which the client wants to accomplish. The lawyer's task is, instead, to provide that competence which the client lacks and the lawyer, as professional, possesses. In this way, the lawyer as professional comes to inhabit a simplified universe which is strikingly amoral— which regards as morally irrelevant any number of factors which nonprofessional citizens might take to be important, if not decisive, in their everyday lives. And the difficulty I have with all of this is that the arguments for such a way of life seem to be not quite so convincing to me as they do to many lawyers. I am, that is, at best uncertain that it is a good thing for lawyers to be so professional—for them to embrace so completely this role-differentiated way of approaching matters.

More specifically, if it is correct that this is the perspective of lawyers in particular and professionals in general, is it right that this should be their perspective? Is it right that the lawyer should be able so easily to put to one side otherwise difficult problems with the answer: but these are not and cannot be my concern as a lawyer? What do we gain and what do we lose from having a social universe in which there are professionals, such as lawyers, who, as such, inhabit a universe of the sort I have been trying to describe?

One difficulty in even thinking about all of this is that lawyers may not be very objective or detached in their attempts to work the problem through. For one feature of this simplified, intellectual world is that it is often a very comfortable one to inhabit.

To be sure, on occasion, a lawyer may find it uncomfortable to represent an extremely unpopular client. On occasion, too, a lawyer may feel ill at ease invoking a rule of law or practice which he or she thinks to be an unfair or undesirable one. Nonetheless, for most lawyers most of the time, pursuing the interests of one's clients is an attractive and satisfying way to live in part just because the moral world of the lawyer is a simpler, less complicated, and less ambiguous world than the moral world of ordinary life. There is, I think, something quite seductive about being able to turn aside so many ostensibly difficult moral dilemmas and decisions with the reply: but that is not my concern; my job as a lawyer is not to judge the rights and wrong of the client or the cause; it is to defend as best I can my client's interests. For the ethical problems that can arise within this constricted point of view are, to say the least, typically neither momentous nor terribly vexing. Role-differentiated behavior is enticing and reassuring precisely because it does constrain and delimit an otherwise often intractable and confusing moral world.

But there is, of course, also an argument which seeks to demonstrate that it is good and not merely comfortable for lawyers to behave this way.

It is good, so the argument goes, that the lawyer's behavior and concomitant point of view are role-differentiated because the lawyer *qua* lawyer participates in a complex institution which functions well only if the individuals adhere to their institutional role.

For example, when there is a conflict between individuals, or between the state and an individual, there is a well-established institutional mechanism by which to get that dispute resolved. That mechanism is the trial in which each side is represented by a lawyer whose job it is both to present his or her client's case in the most attractive, forceful light and to seek to expose the weaknesses and defects in the case of the opponent.

When an individual is charged with having committed a crime, the trial is the mechanism by which we determine in our society whether or not the person is in fact guilty. Just imagine what would happen if lawyers were to refuse, for instance, to represent persons whom they thought to be guilty. In a case where the guilt of a person seemed clear, it might turn out that some individuals would be deprived completely of the opportunity to have the system determine whether or not they are in fact guilty. The private judgment of individual lawyers would in effect be substituted for the public, institutional judgment of the judge and jury. The amorality of lawyers helps to guarantee that every criminal defendant will have his or her day in court.

In addition, of course, appearances can be deceiving. Persons who appear before trial to be clearly guilty do sometimes turn out to be innocent. Even persons who confess their guilt to their attorney occasionally turn out to have lied or to have been mistaken. The adversary system, so this argument continues, is simply a better method than any other that has been established by which to determine the legally relevant facts in any given case. It is certainly a better method than the exercise of private judgment by any particular individual. And the adversary system only works if each party to the controversy has a lawyer, a person whose institutional role is to argue, plead and present the merits of his or her case and the demerits of the opponent's. Thus if the adversary system is to work, it is necessary that there be lawyers who will play their appropriate, professional, institutional role of representative of the client's cause.

Nor is the amorality of the institutional role of the lawyer restricted to the defense of those accused of crimes. As was indicated earlier, when the lawyer functions in his most usual role, he or she functions as a counselor, as a professional whose task it is to help people realize those objectives and ends that the law permits them to obtain and which cannot be obtained without the attorney's special competence in the law. The attorney may think it wrong to disinherit one's children because of their views about the Vietnam war, but here the attorney's complaint is really with the laws of inheritance and not with his or her client. The attorney may think the tax provision an unfair, unjustifiable loophole, but once more the complaint is really with the Internal Revenue Code and not with the client who seeks to take advantage of it. And these matters, too, lie beyond the ambit of the lawyer's moral point of view as institutional counselor and facilitator. If lawyers were to substitute their own private views of what ought to be legally permissible and impermissible for those of the legislature, this would constitute a surreptitious and undesirable shift from a democracy to an oligarchy of lawyers. For given the fact that lawyers are needed to effectuate the wishes of clients, the lawyer ought to make his or her skills available to those who seek them without regard for the particular objectives of the client.

Now, all of this certainly makes some sense. These arguments are neither specious nor without force. Nonetheless, it seems to me that one dilemma which emerges is that if this line of argument is sound, it also appears to follow that the behavior of the lawyers involved in Watergate was simply another less happy illustration of lawyers playing their accustomed institutional role. If we are to approve on institutional grounds of the lawyer's zealous defense of the apparently guilty client and the lawyer's effective assistance of the immoral cheat, does it not follow that we must also approve of the Watergate lawyer's zealous defense of the interests of Richard Nixon?

As I have indicated, I do not think there is any easy answer to this question. For I am not, let me hasten to make clear, talking about the easy cases—about the behavior of the lawyers that was manifestly illegal. For someone quite properly might reply that it was no more appropriate for the lawyer who worked in the White House to obstruct justice or otherwise violate the criminal law than it would be for a criminal defense lawyer to shoot the prosecution witness to prevent adverse testimony or bribe a defense witness in order to procure favorable testimony. What I am interested in is all of the Watergate behavior engaged in by the Watergate lawyers that was not illegal, but that was, nonetheless, behavior of which we quite properly disapprove. I mean lying to the public; dissembling; stonewalling; tape-recording conversations; playing dirty tricks. Were not these just effective lawyer-like activities pursued by lawyers who viewed Richard Nixon as they would a client and who sought, therefore, the advancement and protection of his interests—personal and political?

It might immediately be responded that the analogy is not apt. For the lawyers who were involved in Watergate were hardly participants in an adversary proceeding. They were certainly not participants in that institutional setting, litigation, in which the amorality of the lawyer makes the most sense. It might even be objected that the amorality of the lawyer *qua counselor* is clearly distinguishable from the behavior of the Watergate lawyers. Nixon as President was not a client; they, as officials in the executive branch, were functioning as governmental officials and not as lawyers at all.

While not wholly convinced by a response such as the above, I am prepared to accept it because the issue at hand seems to me to be a deeper one. Even if the involvement of so many lawyers in Watergate was adventitious (or, if not adventitious, explicable in terms of some more benign explanation) there still seems to me to be costs, if not problems, with the amorality of the lawyer that derives from his or her role-differentiated professionalism.

As I indicated earlier, I do believe that the amoral behavior of the *criminal* defense lawyer is justifiable. But I think that jurisdiction depends at least as much upon the special needs of an accused as upon any more general defense of a lawyer's role-differentiated behavior. As a matter of fact I think it likely that many persons such as myself have been misled by the special features of the criminal case. Because a deprivation of liberty is so serious, because the prosecutorial resources of the state are so vast, and because, perhaps, of a serious skepticism about the rightness of punishment even where wrongdoing has occurred, it is easy to accept the view that it makes sense to charge the defense counsel with the job of making the best possible case for the accused—without regard, so to speak, for the merits. This coupled with the fact that it is an adversarial proceeding succeeds, I think, in justifying the amorality of the criminal defense counsel. But this does not, however, justify a comparable perspective on the part of lawyers generally. Once we leave the peculiar situation of the criminal defense lawyer, I think it quite likely that the role-differentiated amorality of the lawyer is almost certainly excessive and at times inappropriate. That is to say, this special case to one side, I am inclined to think that we might all be better served if lawyers were to see themselves less as subject to role-differentiated behavior and more as subject to the demands of the moral point of view. In this sense it may be that we need a good deal less rather than more professionalism in our society generally and among lawyers in particular.

Moreover, even if I am wrong about all this, four things do seem to me to be true and important.

First, all of the arguments that support the role-differentiated amorality of the lawyer on institutional grounds can succeed only if the enormous degree of trust and confidence in the institutions themselves is itself justified. If the institutions work well and fairly, there may be good sense to deferring important moral concerns and criticisms to another time and place, to the level of institutional criticism and assessment. But the less certain we are entitled to be of either the rightness or the self-corrective nature of the larger institutions of which the professional is a part, the less apparent it is that we should encourage the professional to avoid direct engagement with the moral issues as they arise. And we are, today, I believe, certainly entitled to be quite skeptical both of the fairness and of the capacity for self-correction of our larger institutional mechanisms, including the legal system. To the degree to which the institutional rules and practices are unjust, unwise or undesirable, to that same degree is the case for the role-differentiated behavior of the lawyer weakened if not destroyed.

Second, it is clear that there are definite character traits that the professional such as the lawyer must take on if the system is to work. What is less clear is that they are admirable ones. Even if the role-differentiated amorality of the professional lawyer is justified by the virtues of the adversary system, this also means that the lawyer *qua* lawyer will be encouraged to be competitive rather than cooperative; aggressive rather than accommodating; ruthless rather than compassionate; and pragmatic rather than principled. This is, I think, part of the logic of the role-differentiated behavior of lawyers in particular, and to a lesser degree of professionals in general. It is surely neither accidental nor unimportant that these are the same character traits that are emphasized and valued by the capitalist ethic—and on precisely analogous grounds. Because the ideals of professionalism and capitalism are the dominant ones within our culture, it is harder than most of us suspect even to take seriously the suggestion that radically different styles of living, kinds of occupational outlooks, and types of social institutions might be possible, let alone preferable.

Third, there is a special feature of the role-differentiated behavior of the lawyer that distinguishes it from the comparable behavior of other professionals. What I have in mind can be brought out through the following question: Why is it that it seems far less plausible to talk critically about the amorality of the doctor, for instance, who treats all patients irrespective of their moral character than it does to talk critically about the comparable amorality of the lawyer? Why is it that it seems so obviously sensible, simple, and right for the doctor's behavior to be narrowly and rigidly role-differentiated, *i.e.,* just to try to cure those who are ill? And why is it that at the very least it seems so complicated, uncertain, and troublesome to decide whether it is right for the lawyer's behavior to be similarly role-differentiated?

The answer, I think, is twofold. To begin with (and this I think is the less interesting point), it is, so to speak, intrinsically good to try to cure disease, but in no comparable way is it intrinsically good to try to win every lawsuit or help every client realize his or her objective. In addition (and this I take to be the truly interesting point), the lawyer's behavior is different in kind from the doctor's. The lawyer—and especially the lawyer as advocate—directly says and affirms things. The lawyer makes the case for the client. He or she tries to explain, persuade, and convince others that the client's cause should prevail. The lawyer lives with and within a dilemma that is not shared by other professionals. If the lawyer actually believes everything he or she asserts on behalf of the client, then it appears to be proper to regard the lawyer as in fact embracing and endorsing the points of view that he or she articulates. If the lawyer does not in fact believe what is urged by way of argument, if the lawyer is only playing a role, then it appears to be proper to tax the lawyer with hypocrisy and insincerity. To be sure, actors in a play take on roles and say things that the characters, not the actors believe. But we know it is a play and that they are actors. The law courts are not, however, theaters, and the lawyers both talk about justice and they genuinely seek to persuade. The fact that the lawyer's words, thoughts, and convictions are, apparently, for sale and at the service of the client helps us, I think, to understand the peculiar hostility which is more than occasionally uniquely directed by lay persons toward lawyers. The verbal, role-differentiated behavior of the lawyer *qua* advocate puts the lawyer's integrity into question in a way that distinguishes the lawyer from the other professionals.[3]

Fourth, and related closely to the three points just discussed, even if on balance the role-differentiated character of the lawyer's way of thinking and acting is ultimately deemed to be justifiable within the system on systemic instrumental grounds, it still remains the case that we do pay a social price for that way of thought and action. For to become and to be a professional, such as a lawyer, is to incorporate within oneself ways of behaving and ways of thinking that shape the whole person. It is especially hard, if not impossible, because of the nature of the professions, for one's professional way of thinking not to dominate one's entire adult life. Thus, even if the lawyers who were involved in Watergate were not, strictly speaking, then and there functioning as lawyers, their behavior ws, I believe, the likely if not inevitable consequence of their legal acculturation. Having been taught to embrace and practice the lawyer's institutional role, it was natural, if not unavoidable, that they would continue to play that role even when they were somewhat removed from the specific institutional milieu in which that way of thinking and acting is arguably fitting and appropriate. The nature of the professions—the lengthy educational preparation, the prestige and economic rewards, and the concomitant enhanced sense of self—makes the role of professional a difficult one to shed even in those obvious situations in which that role is neither required nor approriate. In important respects, one's professional role becomes and is one's dominant role, so that for many persons at least they become their professional being. This is at a minimum a heavy price to pay for the professions as we know them in our culture, and especially so for lawyers. Whether it is an inevitable price is, I think, an open question, largely because the problem has not begun to be fully perceived as such by the professionals in general, the legal profession in particular, or by the educational institutions that train professionals.

II

The role-differentiated behavior of the professional also lies at the heart of the second of the two moral issues I want to discuss, namely, the character of the interpersonal relationship that exists between the lawyer and the client. As I indicated at the outset, the charge that I want to examine here is that the relationship between the lawyer and the client is typically, if not inevitably, a morally defective one in which the client is not treated with the respect and dignity that he or she deserves.

There is the suggestion of paradox here. The discussion so far has concentrated upon defects that flow from what might be regarded as the lawyer's excessive preoccupation with and concern for the client. How then can it also be the case that the lawyer qua professional can at the same time be taxed with promoting and maintaining a relationship of dominance and indifference vis-à-vis his or her client? The paradox is apparent, not real. Not only are the two accusations compatible; the problem of the interpersonal relationship between the lawyer and the client is itself another feature or manifestation of the underlying issue just examined—the role-differentiated life of the professional. For the lawyer can both be overly concerned with the interest of the client and at the same time fail to view the client as a whole person, entitled to be treated in certain ways.

One way to begin to explore the problem is to see that one pervasive, and I think necessary, feature of the relationship between any professional and the client or patient is that it is in some sense a relationship of inequality. This relationship of inequality is intrinsic to the existence of professionalism. For the professional is, in some respects at least, always in a position of dominance vis-à-vis the client, and the client in a position of dependence vis-à-vis the professional. To be sure, the client can often decide whether or not to enter into a relationship with a professional. And often, too, the client has the power to decide whether to terminate the relationship. But the significant thing I want to focus upon is that while the relationship exists, there are important aspects in which the relationship cannot be a relationship between equals and must be one in which it is the professional who is in control. As I have said, I believe this is a necessary and not merely a familiar characteristic of the relationship between professionals and those they serve. Its existence is brought about by the following features.

To begin with, there is the fact that one characteristic of professions is that the professional is the possessor of expert knowledge of a sort not readily or easily attainable by members of the community at large. Hence, in the most straightforward of all senses the client, typically, is dependent upon the professional's skill or knowledge because the client does not possess the same knowledge.

Moreover, virtually every profession has its own technical language, a private terminology which can only be fully understood by the members of the profession. The presence of such a language plays the dual role of creating and affirming the membership of the professionals within the profession and of preventing the client from fully discussing or understanding his or her concerns in the language of the profession.

These circumstances, together with others, produce the added consequence that the client is in a poor position effectively to evaluate how well or badly the profession performs. In the professions, the professional does not look primarily to the client to evaluate the professional's work. The assessment of ongoing professional competence is something that is largely a matter of self-assessment conducted by the practicing professional. Where external assessment does occur, it is carried out not by clients or patients but by other members of the profession, themselves. It is significant, and surely surprising to the outsider, to discover to what degree the professions are self-regulating. They control who shall be admitted to the professions and they determine (typically only if there has been a serious complaint) whether the members of the profession are performing in a minimally satisfactory way. This leads professionals to have a powerful motive to be far more concerned with the way they are viewed by their colleagues than with the way they are viewed by their clients. This means, too, that clients will necessarily lack the power to make effective evaluations and criticisms of the way the professional is responding to the client's needs.

In addition, because the matters for which professional assistance is sought usually involve things of great personal concern to the client, it is the received wisdom within the professions that the client lacks the perspective necessary to pursue in a satisfactory way his or her own best interests, and that the client requires a detached, disinterested representative to look after his or her interests. That is to say, even if the client had the same knowledge or competence that the professional had, the client would be thought to lack the objectivity required to utilize that competency effectively on his or her own behalf.

Finally, as I have indicated, to be a professional is to have been acculturated in a certain way. It is to have satisfactorily passed through a lengthy and allegedly difficult period of study and training. It is to have done something hard. Something that not everyone can do. Almost all professions encourage this way of viewing oneself; as having joined an elect group by virtue of hard work and mastery of the mysteries of the profession. In addition, the society at large treats members of a profession as members of an elite by paying them more than most people for the work they do with their heads rather than their hands, and by according them a substantial amount of social prestige and power by virtue of their membership in a profession. It is hard, I think, if not impossible, for a person to emerge from professional training and participate in a profession without the belief that he or she is a special kind of person, both different from and somewhat better than those nonprofessional members of the social order. It is equally hard for the other members of society not to hold an analogous view of the professionals. And these beliefs surely contribute, too, to the dominant role played by a professional in any professional-client relationship.

If the foregoing analysis is correct, then one question that is raised is whether it is a proper and serious criticism of the professions that the relationship between the professional and the client is an inherently unequal one in this sense.

One possible response would be to reject the view that all relationships of inequality (in this sense of inequality) are in fact undesirable. Such a response might claim, for example, that there is nothing at all wrong with inequality in relationships as long as the inequality is consensually imposed. Or, it may be argued, this kind of inequality is wholly unobjectionable because it is fitting, desired, or necessary in the circumstances. And, finally, it may be urged, whatever undesirability does attach to relationships by virtue of their lack of equality is outweighed by the benefits of role-differentiated relationships.

Another possible response would be to maintain that all human relationships of inequality (again in this sense of inequality) are for that reason alone objectionable on moral grounds—any time two or more persons are in a relationship in which power is not shared equally, the relationship is on that ground appropriately to be condemned. This criticism would solve the problem by abolishing the professions.

A third possible response, and the one that I want to consider in some detail, is a more sophisticated variant of the second response. It might begin by conceding, at least for purposes of argument, that some inequality may be inevitable in any professional-client relationship. It might concede, too, that a measure of this kind of inequality may even on occasion be desirable. But it sees the relationship between the professional and the client as typically flawed in a more fundamental way, as involving far more than the kind of relatively benign inequality delineated above. This criticism focuses upon the fact that the professional often, if not systematically, interacts with the client in both a manipulative and a paternalistic fashion. The point is not that the professional is merely dominant within the relationship. Rather, it is that from the professional's point of view the client is seen and responded to more like an object than a human being, and more like a child than an adult. The professional does not, in short, treat the client like a person; the professional does not accord the client the respect that he or she deserves. And these, it is claimed, are without question genuine moral defects in any meaningful human relationship. They are, moreover, defects that are capable of being eradicated once their cause is perceived and corrective action taken. The solution, so the argument goes, is to "deprofessionalize" the professions; not do away with the professions entirely, but weaken or eliminate those features of professionalism that produce these kinds of defective, interpersonal relationships.

To decide whether this would be a good idea we must understand better what the proposal is and how the revisions might proceed. Because thinking somewhat along these lines has occurred in professions other than the law, *e.g.,* psychiatry, a brief look at what has been proposed there may help us to understand better what might be claimed in respect to the law.

I have in mind, for example, the view in psychiatry that begins by challenging the dominant conception of the patient as someone who is sick and in particular need of the professional, the psychiatrist, who is well. Such a conception, it is claimed, is often inadequate and often mistaken. Indeed, many cases of mental illness are not that at all; they are merely cases of different, but rational behavior. The alleged mental illness of the patient is a kind of myth, encouraged, if not created, by the professionals to assure and enhance their ability to function as professionals. So, on this view, one thing that must occur is that the accepted professional concepts of mental illness and health must be revised.[4]

In addition, the language of psychiatry and mental illness is, it is claimed, needlessly technical and often vacuous. It serves no very useful communicative purpose, but its existence does of course help to maintain the distinctive status and power of the psychiatric profession. What is called for here is a simpler, far less technical language that permits more direct communication between the patient and the therapist.

Finally, and most significantly, the program calls for a concomitant re-placement of the highly role-differentiated relationship between the therapist and the patient by a substantially less differentiated relationship of wholeness of interaction and equality. There should not, for instance, be mental hospitals in which the patients are clearly identified and distinguished from the staff and the professionals. Instead, therapeutic communities should be established in which all of the individuals in the community come to see themselves both as able to help the other members of the community and as able to be helped by them. In such a community, the distinctions between the professionals and the patients will be relatively minor and uninteresting. In such a community the relationship among the individuals, be they patients or professionals, will be capable of being more personal, intimate and complete—more undifferentiated by the accident of prior training or status.

Now, if this is a plausible proposal to make, it is possible that it is because of reasons connected with therapy rather than with the professions generally. But I do not think this is so. The general analysis and point of view is potentially generic; and certainly capable, I think, of being taken seriously in respect to the law as well as in respect to psychiatry, medicine, and education. If the critique is extravagant even when applied to psychiatry, as I think it is, I am more im-pressed by the truths to be extracted from it than I am by the exaggerations to be rejected. For I do think that professionals generally and lawyers in particular do, typically enter into relationships with clients that are morally objectionable in virtue of the paternalistic and impersonal fashion in which the client is viewed and treated.

Thus it is, for example, fairly easy to see how a number of the features already delineated conspire to depersonalize the client in the eyes of the lawyer *qua* professional. To begin with, the lawyer's conception of self as a person with special competencies in a certain area naturally leads him or her to see the client in a partial way. The lawyer *qua* professional is, of necessity, only centrally interested in that part of the client that lies within his or her special competency. And this leads any professional including the lawyer to respond to the client as an object—as a thing to be altered, corrected, or otherwise assisted by the professional rather than as a person. At best the client is viewed from the perspective of the professional not as a whole person but as a segment or aspect of a person—an interesting kidney problem, a routine marijuana possession case, or another adolescent with an identity crisis.[5]

Then, too, the fact already noted that the professions tend to have and to develop their own special languages has a lot to do with the depersonalization of the client. And this certainly holds for the lawyers. For the lawyer can and does talk to other lawyers but not to the client in the language of the profession. What is more, the lawyer goes out of his or her way to do so. It is satisfying. It is the exercise of power. Because the ability to communicate is one of the things that distinguishes persons from objects, the inability of the client to communicate with the lawyer in the lawyer's own tongue surely helps to make the client less a person in the lawyer's eyes—and perhaps even in the eyes of the client.

The forces that operate to make the relationship a paternalistic one seem to me to be at least as powerful. If one is a member of a collection of individuals who have in common the fact that their intellectuals are highly trained, it is very easy to believe that one knows more than most people. If one is a member of a collection of individuals who are accorded high prestige by the society at large, it is equally easy to believe that one is better and knows better than most people. If there is, in fact, an area in which one does know things that the client doesn't know, it is extremely easy to believe that one knows generally what is best for the client. All this, too, surely holds for lawyers.

In addition there is the fact, also already noted, that the client often establishes a relationship with the lawyer because the client has a serious problem or concern which has rendered the client weak and vulnerable. This, too, surely increases the disposition to respond toward the client in a patronizing, paternalistic fashion. The client of necessity confers substantial power over his or her wellbeing upon the lawyer. Invested with all of this power both by the individual and the society, the lawyer *qua* professional responds to the client as though the client were an individual who needed to be looked after and controlled, and to have decisions made for him or her by the lawyer, with as little interference from the client as possible.

Now one can, I think, respond to the foregoing in a variety of ways. One could, to begin with, insist that the paternalistic and impersonal ways of behaving are the aberrant rather than the usual characteristics of the lawyer-client relationship. One could, therefore, argue that a minor adjustment in better legal education aimed at sensitizing prospective lawyers to the possibility of these abuses is all that is required to prevent them. Or, one could, to take the same tack described earlier, regard these features of the lawyer-client relationship as endemic but not as especially serious. One might have a view that, at least in moderation, relationships having these features are a reasonable price to pay (if it is a price at all) for the very appreciable benefits of professionalism. The impersonality of a surgeon, for example, may make it easier rather than harder for him or for her to do a good job of operating successfully on a patient. The impersonality of a lawyer may make it easier rather than harder for him or for her to do a good job at representing a client. The paternalism of lawyers may be justified by the fact that they do in fact know better—at least within many areas of common concern to the parties involved—what is best for the client. And, it might even be claimed, clients want to be treated in this way.

But if these answers do not satisfy, if one believes that these are typical, if not systemic, features of the professional character of the lawyer-client relationship, and if one believes, as well, that these are morally objectionable features of that or any other relationship among persons, it does look as though one way to proceed is to "deprofessionalize" the law—to weaken, if not excise, those features of legal professionalism that tend to produce these kinds of interpersonal relationships.

The issue seems to me difficult just because I do think that there are important and distinctive competencies that are at the heart of the legal profession. If there were not, the solution would be simple. If there were no such competencies—if, that is, lawyers didn't really help people any more than (so it is sometimes claimed) therapists do—then no significant social goods would be furthered by the maintenance of the legal profession. But, as I have said, my own view is that there are special competencies and that they are valuable. This makes it harder to determine what to preserve and what to shed. The question, as I see it, is how to weaken the bad consequences of the role-differentiated lawyer-client relationship without destroying the good that lawyers do.

Without developing the claim at all adequately in terms of scope or detail, I want finally to suggest the direction this might take. Desirable change could be brought about in part by a sustained effort to simplify legal language and to make the legal processes less mysterious and more directly available to lay persons. The way the law works now, it is very hard for lay persons either to understand it or to evaluate or solve legal problems more on their own. But it is not at all clear that substantial revisions could not occur along these lines. Divorce, probate, and personal injury are only three fairly obvious areas where the lawyers' economic self-interest says a good deal more about resistance to change and simplification than does a consideration on the merits.

The more fundamental changes, though, would, I think, have to await an explicit effort to alter the ways in which lawyers are educated and acculturated to view themselves, their clients, and the relationships that ought to exist between them. It is, I believe, indicative of the state of legal education and of the profession that there has been to date extremely little self-conscious concern even with the possibility that these dimensions of the attorney-client relationship are worth examining—to say nothing of being capable of alteration. That awareness is, surely, the prerequisite to any serious assessment of the moral character of the attorney-client relationship as a relationship among adult human beings.

I do not know whether the typical lawyer-client relationship is as I have described it; nor do I know to what degree role-differentiation is the cause; nor do I even know very precisely what "deprofessionalization" would be like or whether it would on the whole be good or bad. I am convinced, however, that this, too, is a topic worth taking seriously and worth attending to more systematically than has been the case to date.

NOTES

1. Because of the significance for my analysis of the closely related concepts of a profession and a professional, it will be helpful to indicate at the outset what I take to be the central features of a profession.

But first there is an ambiguity that must be noted so that it can be dismissed. There is one sense of "professional" and hence of "profession" with which I am not concerned. That is the sense in which there are in our culture, professional athletes, professional actors, and professional beauticians. In this sense, a person who possesses sufficient skill to engage in an activity for money and who elects to do so is a professional rather than, say, an amateur or a volunteer. This is, as I have said, not the sense of "profession" in which I am interested.

I am interested, instead, in the characteristics of professions such as law, or medicine. There are, I think, at least six that are worth noting.

(1) The professions require a substantial period of formal education—at least as much if not more than that required by any other occupation.

(2) The professions require the comprehension of a substantial amount of theoretical knowledge and the utilization of a substantial amount of intellectual ability. Neither manual nor creative ability is typically demanded. This is one thing that distinguishes the professions both from highly skilled crafts—like glassblowing—and from the arts.

(3) The professions are both an economic monopoly and largely self-regulating. Not only is the practice of the profession restricted to those who are certified as possessing the requisite competencies, but the questions of what competencies are required and who possesses them are questions that are left to the members of the profession to decide for themselves.

(4) The professions are clearly among the occupations that possess the greatest social prestige in the society. They also typically provide a degree of material affluence substantially greater than that enjoyed by most working persons.

(5) The professions are almost always involved with matters which from time to time are among the greatest personal concerns that humans have: physical health, psychic well-being, liberty, and the like. As a result, persons who seek the services of a professional are often in a state of appreciable concern, if not vulnerability, when they do so.

(6) The professions almost always involve at their core a significant interpersonal relationship between the professional, on the one hand, and the person who is thought to require the professional's services: the patient or the client.

2. Ballard v. Superior Court, 64 Cal. 2d 159, 410 P.2d 838, 49 Cal. Rptr. 302 (1966).

3. I owe this insight, which I think is an important and seldom appreciated one, to my colleague, Leon Letwin.

4. On this, and the points that follow, I am thinking in particular of the writings of Thomas Szasz, *e.g.,* T. S. Szasz, *The Myth of Mental Illness* (1974), and of R. D. Laing, *e.g.,* R. D. Laing & A. Esterson, *Sanity, Madness and the Family* (1964).

5. This and other features are delineated from a somewhat different perspective in an essay by Erving Goffman. See *The Medical Model and Mental Hospitalization: Some Notes on the Vicissitudes of the Tinkering Trades* in E. Goffman, *Asylums* (1961), especially Parts V and VI of the essay.

Charles Fried

The Lawyer as Friend

Can a good lawyer be a good person? The question troubles lawyers and law students alike. They are troubled by the demands of loyalty to one's client and by the fact that one can win approval as a good, maybe even great, lawyer even though that loyalty is engrossed by overprivileged or positively distasteful clients. How, they ask, is such loyalty compatible with that devotion to the common good characteristic of high moral principles? And whatever their views of the common good, they are troubled because the willingness of lawyers to help their clients use the law to the prejudice of the weak or the innocent seems morally corrupt. The lawyer is conventionally seen as a professional devoted to his client's interests and as authorized, if not in fact required, to do some things (though not anything) for that client which he would not do for himself.[1] In this essay I consider the compatibility between this traditional conception of the lawyer's role and the ideal of moral purity—the ideal that one's life should be lived in fulfillment of the most demanding moral principles, and not just barely within the law. So I shall not be particularly concerned with the precise limits imposed on the lawyer's conduct by positive rules of law and by the American Bar Association's *Code of Professional Responsibility*[2] except as these provide a background. I assume that the lawyer observes these scrupulously. My inquiry is one of morals: Does the lawyer whose conduct and choices are governed only by the traditional conception of the lawyer's role, which these positive rules reflect, lead a professional life worthy of moral approbation, worthy of respect—ours and his own?

THE CHALLENGE TO THE TRADITIONAL CONCEPTION

The Two Criticisms

Two frequent criticisms of the traditional conception of the lawyer's role attack both its ends and its means. First, it is said that the ideal of professional loyalty

From *Yale Law Review*, 85 (1975): 1060–1069. Copyright © 1975 by Charles Fried. Reprinted by permission of the author, The Yale Law Journal Company, and Fred B. Rothman & Company.

to one's client permits, even demands, an allocation of the lawyer's time, passion, and resources in ways that are not always maximally conducive to the greatest good of the greatest number.[3] Interestingly, this criticism is leveled increasingly against doctors[4] as well as lawyers. Both professions affirm the principle that the professional's primary loyalty is to his client,[5] his patient. A "good" lawyer will lavish energy and resources on his existing client, even if it can be shown that others could derive greater benefit from them. The professional ideal authorizes a care for the client and the patient which exceeds what the efficient distribution of a scarce social resource (the professional's time) would dictate.

That same professional ideal has little or nothing to say about the initial choice of clients or patients. Certainly it is laudable if the doctor and lawyer choose their clients among the poorest or sickest or most dramatically threatened, but the professional ideal does not require this kind of choice in any systematic way—the choice of client remains largely a matter of fortuity or arbitrary choice. But once the client has been chosen, the professional ideal requires primary loyalty to the client whatever his need or situation. Critics contend that it is wasteful and immoral that some of the finest talent in the legal profession is devoted to the intricacies of, say, corporate finance or elaborate estate plans, while important public and private needs for legal services go unmet. The immorality of this waste is seen to be compounded when the clients who are the beneficiaries of this lavish attention use it to avoid their obligations in justice (if not in law) to society and to perpetuate their (legal) domination of the very groups whose greater needs these lawyers should be meeting.[6]

The second criticism applies particularly to the lawyer. It addresses not the misallocation of scarce resources, which the lawyer's exclusive concern with his client's interests permits, but the means which this loyalty appears to authorize, tactics which procure advantages for the client at the direct expense of some identified opposing party. Examples are discrediting a nervous but probably truthful complaining witness[7] or taking advantage of the need or ignorance of an adversary in a negotiation. This second criticism is, of course, related to the first, but there is a difference. The first criticism focuses on a social harm: the waste of scarce resources implicit in a doctor caring for the hearts of the sedentary managerial classes or a lawyer tending to the estates and marital difficulties of the rich. The professional is accused of failing to confer benefits wisely and efficiently. By the second criticism the lawyer is accused not of failing to benefit the appropriate, though usually unidentified, persons, but of harming his identified adversary.[8]

Examples

Consider a number of cases which illustrate the first criticism: A doctor is said to owe a duty of loyalty to his patient, but how is he to react if doing his very best for his patient would deplete the resources of the patient's family, as in the case of a severely deformed baby who can only be kept alive through extraordinarily expensive means? Should a doctor prescribe every test of distinct but marginal utility for every patient on public assistance, even if he knows that in the aggregate such a policy will put the medical care system under intolerable burdens?[9] Should he subject his patients to prudent testing of new remedies because he knows that only in this way can medicine make the strides that it has in the past?[10]

These problems are analogous to problems which are faced by the lawyer. The lawyer who advises a client how to avoid the effects of a tax or a form of regulation, though it is a fair tax or a regulation in the public interest, is facing the same dilemma and resolving it in favor of his client. So does the public defender who accedes to his client's demands and takes a "losing" case to trial, thereby wasting court time and depleting the limited resources of his organization. We tolerate and indeed may applaud the decision of a lawyer who vigorously defends a criminal whom he believes to be guilty and dangerous.[11] And I for one think that a lawyer who arranges the estate of a disagreeable dowager or represents one of the parties in a bitter matrimonial dispute must be as assiduous and single-minded in fulfilling his obligation to that client as the lawyer who is defending the civil liberties case of the century.

Illustrative of the second criticism (doing things which are offensive to a particular person) are familiar situations such as the following: In a negotiation it becomes clear to the lawyer for the seller that the buyer and his lawyer mistakenly believe that somebody else has already offered a handsome price for the property. The buyer asks the seller if this is true, and the seller's lawyer hears his client give an ambiguous but clearly encouraging response.[12] Another classic case is the interposition of a technical defense, such as the running of the statute of limitations to defeat a debt that the client admits he owes.[13]

There is another class of cases which does not so ambiguously involve the lawyer's furthering of his client's interests at the direct expense of some equally identified, concrete individual, but where furthering those interests does require the lawyer to do things which are personally offensive to him. The conventional paradigms in the casuistic literature deal with criminal defense lawyers who are asked improper questions by the trial judge ("Your client doesn't have a criminal record, does he?" or "Your client hasn't offered to plead guilty to a lesser offense, has he?"), a truthful answer to which would be damningly prejudicial to the client, but which the lawyer cannot even refuse to answer without running the risk of creating the same prejudice. There are those who say that the lawyer must lie in defense of his client's interests even though lying is personally and professionally offensive to him.[14] The defense lawyer who cross-examines a complaining rape victim (whom he knows to be telling the truth) about her chastity or lack thereof in order to discredit her accusing testimony faces a similar moral difficulty. In some respects these cases might be taken to illustrate both principal criticisms of the traditional conception. On the one hand, there is harm to society in making the choice to favor the client's interests: a dangerous criminal may escape punishment or an appropriately heavy sentence. On the other hand, this social harm is accomplished by means of acting toward another human being—the judge, the complaining witness—in ways that seem demeaning and dishonorable.

THE LAWYER AS FRIEND

The Thesis

In this essay I will consider the moral status of the traditional conception of the professional. The two criticisms of this traditional conception, if left unanswered, will not put the lawyer in jail, but they will leave him without a moral basis for his acts. The real question is whether, in the face of these two criticisms, a decent and morally sensitive person can conduct himself according to the traditional conception of professional loyalty and still believe that what he is doing is morally worthwhile.

It might be said that anyone whose conscience is so tender that he cannot fulfill the prescribed obligations of a professional should not undertake those obligations. He should not allow his moral scruples to operate as a trap for those who are told by the law that they may expect something more. But of course this suggestion merely pushes the inquiry back a step. We must ask, then, not how a decent lawyer may behave, but whether a decent, ethical person can ever be a lawyer. Are the assurances implicit in assuming the role of lawyer such that an honorable person would not give them and thus would not enter the profession? And, indeed, this is a general point about an argument from obligation:[15] It may be that the internal logic of a particular obligation demands certain forms of conduct (*e.g.,* honor among thieves), but the question remains whether it is just and moral to contract such obligations.

I will argue in this essay that it is not only legally but also morally right that a lawyer adopt as his dominant purpose the furthering of his client's interests— that it is right that a professional put the interests of his client above some idea, however valid, of the collective interest. I maintain that the traditional conception of the professional role expresses a morally valid conception of human conduct and human relationships, that one who acts according to that conception is to that extent a good person. Indeed, it is my view that, far from being a mere creature of positive law, the traditional conception is so far mandated by moral right that any advanced legal system which did not sanction this conception would be unjust.

The general problem raised by the two criticisms is this: How can it be that it is not only permissible, but indeed morally right, to favor the interests of a particular person in a way which we can be fairly sure is either harmful to another particular individual or not maximally conducive to the welfare of society as a whole?[16]

The resolution of this problem is aided, I think, if set in a larger perspective.

Charles Curtis made the perspicacious remark that a lawyer may be privileged to lie for his client in a way that one might lie to save one's friends or close relatives.[17] I do not want to underwrite the notion that it is justifiable to lie even in those situations, but there is a great deal to the point that in those relations— friendship, kinship—we recognize an authorization to take the interests of particular concrete persons more seriously and to give them priority over the interests of the wider collectivity. One who provides an expensive education for his own children surely cannot be blamed because he does not use these resources to alleviate famine or to save lives in some distant land. Nor does he blame himself. Indeed, our intuition that an individual is authorized to prefer identified persons standing close to him over the abstract interests of humanity finds its sharpest expression in our sense that an individual is entitled to act with something less than impartiality to that person who stands closest to him—the person that he is. There is such a thing as selfishness to be sure, yet no reasonable morality asks us to look upon ourselves as merely plausible candidates for the distribution of the attention and resources which we command, plausible candidates whose entitlement to our own concern is no greater in principle than that of the other human being. Such a doctrine may seem edifying, but on reflection it strikes us as merely fanatical.

This suggests an interesting way to look at the situation of the lawyer. As a professional person one has a special care for the interests of those accepted as clients, just as his friends, his family, and he himself have a very general claim to his special concern. But I concede this does no more than widen the problem. It merely shows that in claiming this authorization to have a special care for my clients I am doing something which I do in other contexts as well.

The Utilitarian Explanation

I consider first an argument to account for fidelity to role, for obligation, made most elaborately by the classical utilitarians, Mill[18] and Sidgwick.[19] They argued that our propensity to prefer the interests of those who are close to us is in fact perfectly reasonable because we are more likely to be able to benefit those people. Thus, if everyone is mainly concerned with those closest to him, the distribution of social energies will be most efficient and the greatest good of the greatest number will be achieved. The idea is that the efforts I expend for my friend or my relative are more likely to be effective because I am more likely to know what needs to be done. I am more likely to be sure that the good I intend is in fact accomplished. One might say that there is less overhead, fewer administrative costs, in benefiting those nearest to us. I would not want to ridicule this argument, but it does not seem to me to go far enough. Because if that were the sole basis for the preference, then it would be my duty to determine whether my efforts might not be more efficiently spent on the collectivity, on the distant, anonymous beneficiary. But it is just my point that *this* is an inquiry we are not required, indeed sometimes not even authorized, to make. When we decide to care for our children, to assure our own comforts, to fulfill our obligations to our clients or patients, we do not do so as a result of a cost-benefit inquiry which takes into account the ease of producing a good result for our friends and relations.

Might it not be said, however, that the best means of favoring the abstract collectivity is in certain cases not to try to favor it directly but to concentrate on those to whom one has a special relation? This does not involve tricking oneself, but only recognizing the limitations of what an individual can do and know. But that, it seems to me, is just Mill's and Sidgwick's argument all over again. There is no trickery involved, but this is still a kind of deliberate limitation of our moral horizon which leaves us uncomfortable. Do I know in a particular case whether sticking to the narrow definition of my role will *in that case* further the good of all? If I know that it will not further the general good, then why am I acting as the role demands? Is it to avoid setting a bad example? But for whom? I need not tell others—whether I tell or not could enter into my calculation. For myself then? But that begs the question, since if short-circuiting the role-definition of my obligation and going straight for the general good is the best thing to do in that case, then the example I set myself is not a bad example, but a good example. In short, I do not see how one can at the same time admit that the general good is one's only moral standard, while steadfastly hewing to obligations to friends, family, and clients. What we must look for is an argument which shows that giving some degree of special consideration to myself, my friends, my clients is not merely instrumentally justified (as the utilitarians would argue) but to some degree intrinsically so.[20]

I think such an argument can be made. Instead of speaking the language of maximization of value over all of humanity, it will speak the language of rights. The stubborn ethical datum affirming such a preference grows out of the profoundest springs of morality: the concepts of personality, identity, and liberty.

Self, Friendship, and Justice

Consider for a moment the picture of the human person that would emerge if the utilitarian claim were in fact correct. It would mean that in all my choices I must consider the well-being of all humanity—actual and potential—as the range of my concern. Moreover, every actual or potential human being is absolutely equal in his claims upon me. Indeed, I myself am to myself only as one of this innumerable multitude. And that is the clue to what is wrong with the utilitarian vision. Before there is morality there must be the person. We must attain and maintain in our morality a concept of personality such that it makes sense to posit choosing, valuing entities—free, moral beings. But the picture of the moral universe in which my own interests disappear and are merged into the interests of the totality of humanity is incompatible with that,[21] because one wishes to develop a conception of a responsible, valuable, and valuing agent, and such an agent must first of all be dear to himself. It is from the kernel in individuality that the other things we value radiate. The Gospel says we must love our neighbor as ourselves, and this implies that any concern for others which is a *human* concern must presuppose a concern for ourselves.[22] The human concern which we then show others is a concern which first of all recognizes the concrete individuality of that other person just as we recognize our own.

It might be objected that the picture I sketch does not show that each individual, in order to maintain the integral sense of himself as an individual, is justified in attributing a greater value to his most essential interests than he ascribes to the most essential interests of all other persons. Should not the individual generalize and attribute in equal degree to all persons the value which he naturally attributes to himself? I agree with those who hold that in the essence of morality for reason to push us beyond inclination to the fair conclusion of our premises.[23] It *is* a fair conclusion that as my experience as a judging, valuing, choosing entity is crucial to me, I must also conclude that for other persons their own lives and desires are the center of their universes. If morality is transcendent, it must somehow transcend particularity to take account of this general fact. I do not wish to deny this. On the contrary, my claim is that the kind of perference which an individual gives himself and concrete others is a preference which he would in exactly this universalizing spirit allow others to exhibit as well. It is not that I callously overlook the claim of the abstract individual, but, indeed, I would understand and approve were I myself to be prejudiced because some person to whom I stood in a similar situation of abstraction preferred his own concrete dimensions.

Finally, the concreteness which is the starting point of my own moral sensibility, the sense of myself, is not just a historical, biographical fact. It continues to enter into and condition my moral judgments because the effects which I can produce upon people who are close to me are qualitatively different from those produced upon abstract, unknown persons. My own concreteness is important not only because it establishess a basis for understanding what I and what all other human beings might be, but because in engaging that aspect of myself with the concrete aspects of others, I realize special values for both of us. Quite simply, the individualized relations of love and friendship (and perhaps also their opposites, hatred and enmity) have a different, more intense aspect than do the cooler, more abstract relations of love and service to humanity in general. The impulse I describe, therefore, is not in any sense a selfish impulse. But it does begin with the sense of self as a concrete entity. Those who object to my thesis by saying that we must generalize it are not wholly wrong; they merely exaggerate. Truly, I must be ready to generalize outward all the way. That is what justice consists of. But justice is not all of morality; there remains a circle of intensity which, through its emphasis on the particular and the concrete, continues to reflect what I have identified as the source of all sense of value—our sense of self.

Therefore, it is not only consonant with, but also required by, an ethics for human beings that one be entitled first of all to reserve an area of concern for oneself and then to move out freely from that area if one wishes to lavish that concern on others to whom one stands in concrete, personal relations. Similarly, a person is entitled to enjoy this extra measure of care from those who choose to bestow it upon him without having to justify this grace as either just or efficient. We may choose the individuals to whom we will stand in this special relation, or they may be thrust upon us, as in family ties. Perhaps we recognize family ties because, after all, there often has been an element of choice, but also because— by some kind of atavism or superstition—we identify with those who share a part of our biological natures.

In explicating the lawyer's relation to his client, my analogy shall be to friendship, where the freedom to choose and to be chosen expresses our freedom to hold something of ourselves in reserve, in reserve even from the universalizing claims of morality. These personal ties and the claims they engender may be all-consuming, as with a close friend or family member, or they may be limited, special-purpose claims, as in the case of the client or patient.[24] The special-purpose claim is one in which the beneficiary, the client, is entitled to all the special consideration *within* the limits of the relationship which we accord to a friend or a loved one. It is not that the claims of the client are less intense or demanding; they are only more limited in their scope. After all, the ordinary concept of friendship provides only an analogy, and it is to the development of that analogy that I turn.

Special-Purpose Friends

How does a professional fit into the concept of personal relations at all? He is, I have suggested, a limited-purpose friend. A lawyer is a friend in regard to the legal system. He is someone who enters into a personal relation with you—not an abstract relation as under the concept of justice. That means that, like a friend, he acts in your interests, not his own; or rather he adopts your interests as his own. I would call this the classic definition of friendship. To be sure, the lawyer's range of concern is sharply limited. But within that limited domain the intensity of identification with the client's interests is the same. It is not the specialized focus of the relationship which may make the metaphor inapposite, but the way in which the relation of legal friendship comes about and the one-sided nature of the ensuing "friendship." But I do insist upon the analogy, for in overcoming the arguments that the analogy is false, I think the true moral foundations of the lawyer's special role are illuminated and the utilitarian objections to the traditional conception of that role are overthrown.

The Professional Role as Socially Defined
The Content of the Relation

The claims that are made on the doctor or lawyer are made within a social context and are defined, at least in part, by social expectations. Most strikingly, in talking about friendship the focus of the inquiry is quite naturally upon the free gift of the donor; yet in professional relationships it is the recipient's need for medical or legal aid which defines the relationship. So the source of the relationship seems to be located at the other end, that of the recipient. To put this disquiet another way, we might ask how recognizing the special claims of friendship in any way compels society to allow the doctor or the lawyer to define his role on the analogy of those claims. Why are these people not like other social actors designated to purvey certain, perhaps necessary, goods? Would we say that one's grocer, tailor, or landlord should be viewed as a limited-purpose friend? Special considerations must be brought forward for doctors and lawyers.[25]

A special argument is at hand in both cases. The doctor does not minister just to any need, but to health. He helps maintain the very integrity which is the concrete substratum of individuality. To be sure, so does a grocer or landlord. But illness wears a special guise: it appears as a critical assault on one's person. The needs to which the doctor ministers usually are implicated in crises going to one's concreteness and individuality, and therefore what one looks for is a kind of ministration which is particularly concrete, personal, and individualized. Thus, it is not difficult to see why I claim that a doctor is a friend, though a special-purpose friend, the purpose being defined by the special needs of illness and crisis to which he tends.

But what, then, of the lawyer? Friendship and kinship are natural relations existing within, but not defined by, complex social institutions. Illness, too, is more a natural than social phenomenon. The response here requires an additional step. True, the special situations—legal relations or disputes—in which the lawyer acts as a limited-purpose friend are themselves a product of social institutions. But it does not follow that the role of the lawyer, which is created to help us deal with these social institutions, is defined by and is wholly at the mercy of the social good. We need only concede that at the very least the law must leave us a measure of autonomy, whether or not it is in the social interest to do so. Individuals have rights over and against the collectivity.[26] The moral capital arising out of individuals' concrete situations is one way of expressing that structure of rights of individuals that the law must also create and support the specific role of legal friend. For the social nexus—the web of perhaps entirely just institutions—has become so complex that without the assistance of an expert adviser an ordinary layman cannot exercise that autonomy which the system must allow him. Without such an adviser, the law would impose constraints on the lay citizen (unequally at that) which it is not entitled to impose explicitly. Thus, the need which the lawyer serves in his special-purpose friendship may not be, as in the case of the doctor, natural, pre-social. Yet it is a need which has a moral grounding analogous to the need which the physician serves: the need to maintain one's integrity as a person. When I say the lawyer is his client's legal friend, I mean the lawyer makes his client's interests his own insofar as this is necessary to preserve and foster the client's autonomy within the law. This argument does not require us to assume that the law is hostile to the client's rights. All we need to assume is that even a system of law which is perfectly sensitive to personal rights would not work fairly unless the client could claim a professional's assistance in realizing that autonomy which the law recognizes.

The Asymmetry of Motive and Duty
The Form of the Relation

The institutional origin of the lawyer-client relationship is not its only characteristic which suggests that the analogy to natural friendship is vulnerable. In natural friendship the ideal relation is reciprocal; in legal friendship it is not. The lawyer is said to be the client's friend insofar as he is devoted to his client's interests, but it is no part of the ideal that the client should have any reciprocal devotion to the interests of his lawyer. Furthermore, I have argued that our right to be a friend to whomever we choose is a product of our individual autonomy. But in legal friendship the emphasis has been on the autonomy of the client, and it is the client who chooses the lawyer;[27] yet it is the lawyer who acts as a friend in the relation. And as a final contrast to natural friendship, the usual motive for agreeing or refusing to provide legal services is money. Indeed, when we speak of the lawyer's right to represent whomever he wishes, we are usually defending his moral title to represent whoever pays.

But recall that the concept of legal friendship was introduced to answer the argument that the lawyer is morally reprehensible to the extent that he lavishes undue concern on some particular person. The concept of friendship explains how it can be that a particular person may rightfully receive more than his share of care from another: he can receive that care if he receives it as an act of friendship. Although in natural friendship I emphasized the freedom to bestow, surely, that freedom must imply a freedom to receive that extra measure of care. And it is the right of the client to receive such an extra measure of care (without regard, that is, to considerations of efficiency or fairness) as much as the lawyer's right to give it, that I have been trying to explicate. Thus, the fact that the care in legal friendship systematically runs all the way does not impair the argument.

Yet the unease persists. Is it that while I have shown that the lawyer has a right to help the "unworthy" client, I have not shown that whenever the lawyer exercises this right he does something which is morally worthy, entitling him to self-respect? I may have shown that the law is obliged to allow the "unworthy" client to help seek legal help and the lawyer to give it. But have I also shown that every lawyer who avails himself of this legal right (his and the client's legal right) performs a *morally worthy* function? Can a good lawyer be a good person?

The lawyer acts morally because he helps to preserve and express the autonomy of his client vis-à-vis the legal system. It is not just that the lawyer helps his client accomplish a particular lawful purpose. Pornography may be legal, but it hardly follows that I perform a morally worthy function if I lend money or artistic talent to help the pornographer flourish in the exercise of this right.

What is special about legal counsel is that whatever else may stop the pornographer's enterprise, he should not be stopped because he mistakenly believes there is a legal impediment. There is no wrong if a venture fails for lack of talent or lack of money—no one's rights have been violated. But rights *are* violated if, through ignorance or misinformation about the law, an individual refrains from pursuing a wholly lawful purpose. Therefore, to assist others in understanding and realizing their legal rights is always morally worthy. Moreover, the legal system, by instituting the role of the legal friend, not only assures what it in justice must—the due liberty of each citizen before the law—but does it by creating an institution which exemplifies, at least in a unilateral sense, the ideal of personal relations of trust and personal care which (as in natural friendship) are good in themselves.

Perhaps the unease has another source. The lawyer does work for pay. Is there not something odd about analogizing the lawyer's role to friendship when in fact his so-called friendship must usually be bought? If the lawyer is a public purveyor of goods, is not the lawyer-client relationship like that underlying any commercial transaction? My answer is no. The lawyer and doctor have obligations to the client or patient beyond those of other economic agents. A grocer may refuse to give food to a customer when it becomes apparent that the customer does not have the money to pay for it. But the lawyer and doctor may not refuse to give additional care to an individual who cannot pay for it if withdrawal of their services would prejudice that individual.[28] Their duty to the client or patient to whom they have made an initial commitment transcends the conventional quid pro quo of the marketplace. It is undeniable that money is usually what cements the lawyer-client relationship. But the content of the relation is determined by the client's needs, just as friendship is a response to another's needs. It is not determined, as are simple economic relationships, by the mere coincidence of a willingness to sell and a willingness to buy. So the fact that the lawyer works for pay does not seriously undermine the friendship analogy.

Institutional Clients

Another possible objection to my analysis concerns the lawyer in government or the lawyer for a corporation. My model posits a duty of exclusive concern (within the Law) for the interests of the client. This might be said to be inappropriate in the corporate area because larger economic power entails larger social obligations, and because the idea of friendship, even legal friendship, seems peculiarly far-fetched in such an impersonal context. After all, corporations and other institutions, unlike persons, are creatures of the state. Thus, the pursuit of their interests would seem to be especially subject to the claims of the public good. But corporations and other institutions are only formal arrangements of real persons pursuing their real existence. If the law allows real persons to pursue their interests in these complex forms, then why are they not entitled to loyal legal assistance, "legal friendship," in this exercise of their autonomy just as much as if they pursued their interests in simple arrangements and associations?

The real problem in these cases is that the definition of the client is complicated and elusive. The fundamental concepts remain the same, but we must answer a question which so far we could treat as straight-forward: Who is the client? It is the corporation. But because the corporation is an institutional entity, institutional considerations enter into both the definition of the entity to whom the loyalty is owed and the substance of that loyalty. This is dramatically so in the case of a government lawyer, since his client might be thought to be the government of the United States, or the people of the United States, mediated by an intricate political and institutional framework. So it is said that a United States attorney is interested (unlike any ordinary lawyer) not only in winning his case but also in seeing that "justice is done," because his client's interests are served only if justice is done. Since more and more lawyers have only institutional clients, the introduction of institutional concerns into the definition of the representational obligation is virtually pervasive. From this some would conclude that my argument is inappropriate or at least anachronistic. I insist that my analogy is the correct one, that it is applicable to the institutional client, but that it must be combined in a complicated though wholly coherent way with other arguments about who one's client is and how that client's interests are to be identified.

THE TWO CRITICISMS AND THE FRIENDSHIP ANALOGY

The Choice of Clients: The Question of Distribution

It is time to apply the concept of legal friendship to the first of the two criticisms with which this essay began: that the lawyer's ethic of loyalty to his client and his willingness to pick clients for any and every reason (usually, however, for money) result in a maldistribution of a scarce resource, the aid of counsel. It is this criticism which the lawyer shares with the doctor. The preceding sections demonstrated at least this much: that legal counsel—like medical care—must be considered a good, and that he who provides it does a useful thing. But this first criticism in no way questions that conclusion. On the contrary, precisely because medical care and legal counsel are benefits to those who receive them, the critic blames the individual doctor or lawyer for not bestowing his skills in the way which best meets the social need. The notion of legal friendship helps us respond to his criticism.

The lawyer-client relation is a personal relation, and legal counsel is a personal service. This explains directly why, *once the relation has been contracted,* considerations of efficiency or fair distribution cannot be allowed to weaken it. The relation itself is not a creature of social expediency (though social circumstances provide the occasion for it); it is the creature of moral right, and therefore expediency may not compromise the nature of the relation. This is true in medicine because the human need creates a relation of dependence which it would be a betrayal to compromise. In the lawyer-client relation, the argument is more complex but supports the same conclusion. The relation must exist in order to realize the client's rights against society, to preserve that measure of autonomy which social regulation must allow the individual. But to allow social considerations—even social regulations—to limit and compromise what by hypothesis is an entailment of the original grant of right to the individual is to take away with the left hand what was given with the right. Once the relation has been taken up, it is the client's needs which hold the reins—legally and morally.

If I have a client with legal needs, then neither another person with greater needs nor a court should be able to compel or morally oblige me to compromise my care for those needs. To hold differently would apply the concept of battlefield emergency care *(triage)* to the area of regular legal service. But doctors do not operate that way and neither should lawyers. For it is just the point about emergencies and wars that they create special, brutal, and depersonalized relations which civilization, by its very essence, must keep from becoming the general rule of social life.[29]

So much for the integrity of the relation once it has taken hold. But what of the initial choice of client? Must we not give some thought to efficiency and relative need at least at the outset, and does this not run counter to the picture of purely discretionary choice implicit in the notion of friendship? The question is difficult, but before considering its difficulties we should note that the preceding argumentation has surely limited its impact. We can now affirm that whatever the answer to this question, the individual lawyer does a morally worthy thing whomever he serves and, moreover, is bound to follow through once he has begun to serve. In this he is like the doctor. So if there is fault here it is a limited fault. What would be required for a lawyer to immunze himself more fully from criticism that he is unjust in his allocation of care? Each lawyer would have to consider at the outset of his career and during that career where the greatest need for his particular legal talents lies. He would then have to allocate himself to that area of greatest need. Surely there is nothing wrong in doing this (so long as loyalty to relations already undertaken is not compromised); but is a lawyer morally at fault if he does not lead his life in this way? It is at this point too that the metaphor of friendship and the concept of self as developed above suggest the response. But this time they will be viewed from another perspective—the lawyer's as opposed to the client's rights and liberties.

Must the lawyer expend his efforts where they will do the most good, rather than where they will draw the largest fee, provide the most excitement, prove most flattering to his vanity, whatever? Why must he? If the answer is that he must because it will produce the most good then we are saying to the lawyer that he is merely a scarce resource. But a person is not a resource. He is not bound to lead his life as if he were managing a business on behalf of an impersonal body of stockholders called human society. It is this monstrous conception against which I argued earlier. Justice is not all; we are entitled to reserve a portion of our concern and bestow it where we will. We may bestow it entirely at our discretion as in the case of friendship, or we may bestow it at what I would call "constrained discretion" in the choice and exerciseof a profession. That every exercise of the profession is morally worthwhile is already a great deal to the lawyer's credit. Just as the principle of liberty leaves one morally free to choose a profession according to inclination, so within the profession it leaves one free to organize his life according to inclination. The lawyer's liberty—moral liberty—to take up what kind of practice he chooses and to take up or decline what clients he will is an aspect of the moral liberty of self to enter into personal relations freely.

I would not carry this idea through to the bitter end. It has always been accepted, for instance, that a court may appoint an available lawyer to represent a criminal defendant who cannot otherwise find counsel. Indeed, I would be happy to acknowledge the existence of some moral duty to represent any client whose needs fit one's particular capacities and who cannot otherwise find counsel. This is not a large qualification to the general liberty I proclaim. The obligation is, and must remain, exceptional; it cannot become a kind of general conscription of the particular lawyer involved. And the obligation cannot compromise duties to existing clients. Furthermore, I would argue that this kind of representaiton should always be compensated—the duty to the client who cannot afford representation is initially a duty of society, not of the individual lawyer. I go this far for a number of reasons. If the representation is properly compensated, then the very need to appoint a lawyer will be exceptional, an anomaly arising in one of two ways: a fortuitous perturbation in the law of supply and demand or a general, if not concerted, professional boycott of this particular client. If the first is the reason, then the lifetime imposition on any one lawyer will be slight indeed. If it is the second, then the assertion of a duty, oddly enough, serves to express and strengthen the principle of the lawyer's independence. For the moral position of the lawyer rests on the claim that he takes up his client's interests irrespective of their merits.[30] By accepting from time to time the duty to represent the undesirable, he affirms this independence.

But surely I must admit that the need for legal representation far exceeds what such an unstructured, largely individualistic system could supply. Are there not vast numbers of needy people with a variety of legal problems who will never seek us out, but must be sought out? And what of the general responsibility that just laws be passed and justly administered? These are the obligations which the traditional conception of the lawyer, with his overriding loyalty to the paying client, is thought to leave unmet. At this point I yield no further. If the lawyer is really to be impressed to serve these admitted social needs, then his independence and discretion disappear, and he does indeed become a public resource cut up and disposed of by the public's needs. There would be no justice to such a conception. If there are really not enough lawyers to care for the needs of the poor, then it is grossly unfair to conscript the legal profession to fill those needs. If the obligaiton is one of justice, it is an obligation of society as a whole. It is cheap and hypocritical for society to be unwilling to pay the necessary lawyers from the tax revenues of all, and then to claim that individual lawyers are morally at fault for not choosing to work for free. In fact, as provision of legal services has come to be seen as necessary to ensure justice, society has indeed hired lawyers in an effort to meet that need.

Finally, I agree that the lawyer has a moral obligation to work for the establishment of just institutions generally, but entirely the wrong kind of conclusions have been drawn from this. Some of the more ecstatic critics have put forward the lawyer as some kind of anointed priest of justice—a high priest whose cleaving to the traditional conception of the lawyer's role opens him to the charge of apostasy.[31] But this is wrong. In a democratic society, justice has no anointed priests. Every citizen has the same duty to work for the establishment of just institutions,[32] and the lawyer has no special moral responsibilities in that regard. To be sure, the lawyer like any citizen must use all his knowledge and talent to fulfill that general duty of citizenship, and this may mean that there are special perspectives and opportunities for him.[33]

The Choice of Means

More difficult problems are posed by the conflict between the interests of the client and the interests of some other concrete and specified person to whom the client stands in opposition. How does my friendship analogy help to resolve the conflict which a lawyer must feel if his client asks him to lie, to oppress, or to conceal—to do something which is either illegal or felt by the lawyer to be immoral?

Staying Within the Law

I have defined the lawyer as a client's legal friend, as the person whose role it is to insure the client's autonomy within the law. Although I have indicated that the exercise of that autonomy is not always consonant with the public interest, it does not at all follow that the exercise of that autonomy, therefore, must also violate the law. If the legal system is itself sensitive to moral claims, sensitive to the rights of individuals, it must at times allow that autonomy to be exercised in ways that do not further the public interest. Thus, the principle that the lawyer must scrupulously contain his assistance and advocacy within the dictates of the law seems to me perfectly consistent with my view of the lawyer as the client's friend, who maintains the client's interests even against the interests of society.

To be sure, there may have been and may still be situations where the law grossly violates what morality defines as individual rights; and there have been lawyers who have stood ready to defy such laws in order to further their client's rights—the rights which the law should, but did not, recognize. Whatever might be said about these cases, the lawyer's conduct in them travels outside the bounds of legal friendship and becomes political friendship, political agitation, or friendship *tout court*. But that is not the case I am examining. The moral claims which a client has on his lawyer can be fully exhausted though that lawyer contains his advocacy strictly within the limits of the law.

A critic who fails to see the importance of the lawyer's moral status in assisting the autonomy of his client may also be inclined to complain that the constraints of the law restrain his advocacy of truly just causes too much. Such a critic has things wrong at both ends. Just as it is false to argue that the lawyer is morally reprehensible if he furthers the interests of some clients and not others or some purposes and not others, so it is false to assume that the lawyer fails to have the proper zeal if he does for his client only what the law allows. The distinction between the role of the lawyer as a personal adviser and that of the lawyer as a citizen and member of the community should be quite clear. It is by controlling what the law is and by varying the interests that clients may lawfully pursue that social policy should be effectuated; it is not by deforming the role of the lawyer as the client's legal friend and asking him to curb his advocacy in that relationship.

This explains why in a reasonably just system which properly commands the lawyer's loyalty, he must confine his advocacy to what the rules of advocacy permit. He may not counsel his client to commit a crime, nor to destroy evidence, nor to perjure himself on the witness stand. Of course, here as elsewhere there will be borderline problems. It may not be a crime to lie to the judge who has asked the improper and prejudicial question of the defense attorney, but the implicit or quasi-official rules defining the limits of the lawyer's advocacy may nonetheless forbid this. Nothing in my model should discourage the lawyer from observing such limits scrupulously.

A very difficult question would arise if the law imposed upon the lawyer an obligation first to seek and then to betray his client's trust, an obligation to do that which seems outrageous and unjust. I do not mean to say that the resolution of this question would be easy, but my analysis at least clearly locates the area in which a resolution should be sought. For such laws, if they are to be opposed, ought to be opposed as are other unjust laws, and not because the lawyer is in general entitled to travel outside the constraints of the law in protecting his client's interests. Maybe in such a dilemma a conscientious lawyer would keep his client's confidence as would a priest or a natural friend, but if conscientiousness requires this, it requires it as an act of disobedience and resistance to an unjust law, rather than as a necessary entailment of some extreme view of the lawyer's general role.

Immoral Means

I come to what seems to me one of the most difficult dilemmas of the lawyer's role. It is illustrated by the lawyer who is asked to press the unfair claim, to humiliate a witness, to participate in a distasteful or dishonorable scheme. I am assuming that in none of these situations does the lawyer do anything which is illegal or which violates the ethical canons of his profession; the dilemma arises if he acts in a way which seems to him personally dishonorable, but there are no sanctions—legal or professional—which he need fear.

This set of issues is difficult because it calls on the same principles which provide the justification for the lawyer's or the friend's exertions on behalf of the person with whom he maintains a personal relation. Only now the personal relation is one not of benefit but of harm. In meeting the first criticism, I was able to insist on the right of the lawyer as friend to give this extra weight to the interests of his client when the only competing claims were the general claims of the abstract collectivity. But here we have a specific victim as well as a specific beneficiary. The relation to the person whom we deceive or abuse is just as concrete and human, just as personal, as to the friend whom we help.

It is not open to us to justify this kind of harm by claiming that personal relations must be chosen, not thrust upon us. Personal relations are indeed typically chosen. If mere proximity could place on us the obligations of friendship, then there would soon be nothing left of our freedom to bestow an extra measure of care over and above what humanity can justly claim. But there is a personal relation when we inflict intentional harm; the fact that it is intentional reaches out and particularizes the victim. "Who is my neighbor?" is a legitimate question when affirmative aid is in question; it is quite out of order in respect to the injunction "Do not harm your neighbor." Lying, stealing, degrading, inflicting pain and injury are personal relations too. They are not like failing to benefit, and for that reason they are laid under a correspondingly stricter regime than abstract harms to the collectivity.[34] If I claim respect for my own concrete particularity, I must accord that respect to others. Therefore, what pinches here is the fact that the lawyer's personal engagement with the client is urging him to do that to his adversary which the very principles of personal engagement urge that he not do to anyone.

It is not wrong but somewhat lame to argue that the lawyer like the client has autonomy. From this argument it follows that the lawyer who is asked to do something personally distasteful or immoral (though perfectly legal) should be free either to decline to enter into the relationship of "legal friendship" or to terminate it.[35] And if the client can find a lawyer to do the morally nasty but legally permissible thing for him, then all is well—the complexities of the law have not succeeded in thwarting an exercise of autonomy which the law was not entitled to thwart. So long as the first lawyer is reasonably convinced that another lawyer can be found, I cannot see why he is less free to decline the morally repugnant case than he is the boring or poorly paid case. True, but lame, for one wants to know not whether one *may* refuse to do the dirty deed, but whether one is morally *bound* to refuse—bound to refuse even if he is the last lawyer in town and no one else will bail him out of his moral conundrum.

If personal integrity lies at the foundation of the lawyer's right to treat his client as a friend, then surely consideration for personal integrity—his own and others'—must limit what he can do in friendship. Consideration for personal integrity forbids me to lie, cheat, or humiliate, whether in my own interests or those of a friend, so surely they prohibit such conduct on behalf of a client, one's legal friend. This is the general truth, but it must be made more particular if it is to do service here. For there is an opposing consideration. Remember, the lawyer's special kind of friendship is occasioned by the right of the client to exercise his full measure of autonomy within the law. This suggests that one must not transfer uncritically the whole range of personal moral scruples into the arena of legal friendship. After all, not only would I not lie or steal for myself or my friends, I probably also would not pursue socially noxious schemes, foreclose on widows or orphans, or assist in the avoidance of just punishment. So we must be careful lest the whole argument unravel on us at this point.

Balance and structure are restored if we distinguish between kinds of moral scruples. Think of the soldier. If he is a citizen of a just state, where foreign policy decisions are made in a democratic way, he may well believe that it is not up to him to question whether the war he fights is a just war. But he is personally bound not to fire dum-dum bullets, not to inflict intentional injury on civilians, and not to abuse prisoners. These are personal wrongs, wrongs done by his person to the person of the victim.[36] So also, the lawyer must distinguish between wrongs that a reasonably just legal system permits to be worked by its rules and wrongs which the lawyer personally commits. I do not offer this as a rule which is tight enough to resolve all borderline questions of judgment. We must recognize that the border is precisely the place of friction between competing moral principles. Indeed, it is unreasonable to expect moral arguments to dispense wholly with the need for prudence and judgment.

Consider the difference between humiliating a witness or lying to the judge on one hand, and, on the other hand asserting the statute of limitations or the lack of a written memorandum to defeat what you know to be a just claim against your client. In the latter case, if an injustice is worked, it is worked because the legal system not only permits it, but also defines the terms and modes of operation. Legal institutions have created the occasion for your act. What you do is not personal; it is a formal, legally-defined act. But the moral quality of lying or abuse contains both without and within the context of the law. Therefore, my general notion is that a lawyer is morally entitled to act in this formal, representative way even if the result is an injustice, because the legal system which authorizes both the justice (*e.g.,* the result following the plea of the statute of limitations) and the formal gesture for working it insulates him from personal moral responsibility. I would distinguish between the lawyer's own wrong and the wrong of the system used to advantage by the client.

The clearest case is a lawyer who calls to the attention of the court a controlling legal precedent or statute which establishes his client's position even though that position is an unjust one. (I assume throughout, however, that this unjust law is part of a generally just and decent system. I am not considering at all the moral dilemmas of a lawyer in Nazi Germany or Soviet Russia.) Why are we inclined to absolve him of personal moral responsibility for the result he accomplishes? I assert it is because the wrong is wholly institutional, it is a wrong which does not exist and has no meaning outside the legal framework. The only thing preventing the client from doing this for himself is his lack of knowledge of the law or his lack of authority to operate the levers of the law in official proceedings. It is to supply that lack of knowledge or of formal capacity that the lawyer is in general authorized to act, and the levers he pulls are all legal levers.

Now contrast this to the lawyer who lies to an opposing party in a negotiation. I assume that (except in extreme cases akin to self-defense) an important lie with harmful consequences is an offense to the victim's integrity as a rational moral being, and thus the liar affirms a principle which denigrates is own moral status.[37] Every speech set invites belief, and so every lie is a betrayal. However, may a lawyer lie in his representative capacity? It is precisely my point that a man cannot lie just in his representative capacity; it is like stabbing someone in the back "just" in a representative capacity. The injury and betrayal are not worked by the legal process, but by an act which is generally harmful quite apart from the legal context in which it occurs.

There is an important class of cases which might be termed "lying in a representative capacity." An example is the lawyer presenting to the court a statement by another that he knows to be a lie, as when he puts a perjurious client defendant on the stand. There is dispute as to whether and when the positive law of professional responsibility permits this,[38] but clearly in such instances it is not the lawyer who is lying. He is like a letter carrier who delivers the falsehood. Whether he is free to do that is more a matter of legal than personal ethics.

A test that might make the distinction I offer more palpable is this: How would it be if it were known in advance that lawyers would balk at the practice under consideration? Would it not be intolerable if it were known that lawyers would not plead the defense of the Statute of Frauds or of the statute of limitations? And would it not be quite all right if it were known in advance that you cannot get a lawyer to lie for you, though he may perhaps put you on the stand to lie in your own defense?

A more difficult case to locate in the moral landscape is abusive and demeaning cross-examination of a complaining witness. Presumably, positive law and the canons of ethics restrict this type of conduct, but enforcement may be lax or interpretation by a trial judge permissive. So the question arises: What is the lawyer *morally* to do? Here agian I urge the distinction between exposing a witness to the skepticism and scrutiny envisaged by the law and engaging in a personal attack on the witness. The latter is a harm which the lawyer happens to inflict in court, but it is a harm quite apart from the institutional legal context. It is perhaps just a matter of style or tone, but the crucial point is that the probing must not imply that the lawyer believes the witness is unworthy of respect.

The lawyer is not morally entitled, therefore, to engage his own person in doing personal harm to another, though he may exploit the system for his client even if the system consequently works injustice. He may, but must he? This is the final issue to confront. Since he may, he may also need not if there is anyone else who will do it. Only if there is no one else does the agony become acute. If there is an obligation in that case, it is an institutional obligation that has devolved upon him to take up a case, to make arguments when it is morally permissible but personally repugnant to him to do so. Once again, the iniquity is moral, for if the law enjoins an obligation against conscience, a lawyer, like any conscientious person, must refuse and pay the price.

The obligation of an available lawyer to accept appointment to defend an accused is clear. Any moral scruples about the proposition that no man should be accused and punished without counsel are not morally well-founded. The proposition is intended to enhance the autonomy of individuals within the law. But if you are the last lawyer in town, is there a moral obligation to help the finance company foreclose on the widow's refrigerator? If the client pursues the foreclosure in order to establish a legal right of some significance, I do not flinch from the conclusion that the lawyer is bound to urge this right. So also if the finance company cannot foreclose because of an ideological boycott by the local bar. But if all the other lawyers happen to be on vacation and the case means no more to the finance company than the resale value of one more used refrigerator, common sense says the lawyer can say no. One should be able to distinguish between establishing a legal right and being a cog in a routine, repetitive business operation, part of which just happens to play itself out in court.

CONCLUSION

I do not imagine that what I have said provides an algorithm for resolving some of these perennial difficulties. Rather, what I am proposing is a general way of looking at the problem, a way of understanding not so much the difficult borderline cases as the central and clear ones, in the hope that the principles we can there discern will illuminate our necessarily approximate and prudential quest for resolution on the borderline. The notion of the lawyer as the client's legal friend, whatever its limitations and difficulties, does account for a kind of callousness toward society and exclusivity in the service of the client which otherwise seem quite mysterious. It justifies a kind of scheming which we would deplore on the part of a lay person dealing with another lay person—even if he were acting on behalf of a friend.

But these special indulgences apply only as a lawyer assists his client in his legal business. I do not owe my client my political assistance. I do not have to espouse his cause when I act as a citizen. Indeed, it is one of the most repellent features of the American legal profession—one against which the barrister-solicitor split has to some extent guarded the English profession—that many lawyers really feel that they are totally bought by their clients, that they must identify with their clients' interests far beyond the special purpose of advising them and operating the legal system for them. The defendants' antitrust lawyer or defendants' food and drug lawyer who writes articles, gives speeches, and pontificates generally about the evils of regulation may believe these things, but too often he does so because it is good for business or because he thinks that such conduct is what good representation requires.[39] In general, I think it deplorable that lawyers have specialized not only in terms of subject matter—that may or may not be a good thing—but in terms of plaintiffs or defendants, in terms of the position that they represent.[40]

There is a related point which cuts very much in the opposite direction. It is no part of my thesis that the *client* is not morally bound to avoid lying to the court, to pay a just debt even though it is barred by the statute of limitations, to treat an opposite party in a negotiation with humanity and consideration for his needs and vulnerability, or to help the effectuation of policies aimed at the common good. Further, it is no part of my argument to hold that a lawyer must assume that the client is not a decent, moral person, has no desire to fulfill his moral obligations, and is asking only what is the minimum that he must do to stay within the law. On the contrary, to assume this about anyone is itself a form of immorality because it is a form of disrespect between persons. Thus in very many situations a lawyer will be advising a client who wants to effectuate his purposes within the law, to be sure, but who also wants to behave as a decent, moral person. It would be absurd to contend that the lawyer must abstain from giving advice that takes account of the client's moral duties and his presumed desire to fulfill them. Indeed, in these situations the lawyer experiences the very special satisfaction of assisting the client not only to realize his autonomy within the law, but also to realize his status as a moral being. I want to make very clear that my conception of the lawyer's role in no way disentitles the lawyer from experiencing this satisfaction. Rather, it has been my purpose to explicate the less obvious point that there is a vocation and a satisfaction even in helping Shylock obtain his pound of flesh or in bringing about the acquittal of a guilty man.[41]

Finally, I would like to return to the charge that the morality of role and personal relationship I offer here is almost certain to lead to the diversion of legal services from areas of greatest need. It is just my point, of course, that when we fulfill the office of friend—legal, medical, or friend *tout court*—we do right, and thus it would be a great wrong to place us under a general regime of always doing what will "do the most good." What I affirm, therefore, is the moral liberty of a lawyer to make his life out of what personal scraps and shards of motivation his inclination and character suggest: idealism, greed, curiosity, love of luxury, love of travel, a need for adventure or repose; only so long as these lead him to give wise and faithful counsel. It is the task of the social system as a whole, and of all its citizens, to work for the conditions under which everyone will benefit in fair measure from the performance of doctors, lawyers, teachers, and musicians. But I would not see the integrity of these roles under-mined in order that the millennium might come sooner. After all, it may never come, and then what would we be left with?

NOTES

1. See, e.g., J. Auerbach, *Unequal Justice* (1976); M. Green, *The Other Government* (1975). Lord Broughman stated the traditional view of the lawyer's role during his defense of Queen Caroline.

> An advocate, in the discharge of his duty, knows but one person in all the world, and that person is his client. To save that client by all means and expedients, and at all hazards and costs to other persons, and, among them, to himself, is his first and only duty, and in performing his duty he must not regard the alarm, the torments, the destruction which he may bring upon others. Separating the duty of a patriot from that of an advocate, he must go on reckless of consequences, though it should be his unhappy fate to involve his country in confusion.

Trial of Queen Caroline 8 (J. Nightingale ed. 1821). A sharply contrasting view was held by law professors at the University of Havana who said that "the first job of a revolutionary lawyer is not to argue that his client is innocent, but rather to determine if his client is guilty and, if so, to seek the sanction which will best rehabilitate him." Berman, "The Cuban Popular Tribunals," *Columbia Law Review* 69 (1969):1317,1341. And a Bulgarian attorney has been quoted as saying, "'In a Socialist state there is no division of duty between the judge, prosecutor and defense counsel . . . the defense must assist the prosecution to find the objective truth in a case.'" J. Kaplan, *Criminal Justice: Introductory Cases and Materials* (1973), pp. 264-265.

2. The American Bar Association approved a Revised *Code of Professional Responsibility* in 1969. In part that revision was a response to the criticism that the legal profession, by failing to make legal services more widely available, had not met its public responsibilities. J. Auerbach, *supra* note 1, at pp. 285-286. See also Preface, *ABA Code of Professional Responsibility*.

3. See M. Green, *Supra* note 1, at pp. 268-269, 285-289.

4. See V. Fuchs, *Who Shall Live?* (1974), p. 60; Havighurst & Blumstein, "Coping With Quality/Cost Trade-Offs in Medical Care: The Role of PSROs," *Northwestern University Law Review* 70 (1975):6, 25-28. But see Fried, "Equality and Rights in Medical Care," *Hastings Center Reports* 6 (1976):29, 33-34.

5. See *ABA Code of Professional Responsibility* Canon 7.

6. For a description of the growth of such criticisms, see J. Auerbach, *supra* note 1, at pp. 275-288.

7. For a defense of an attorney's use of such tactics, see M. Freedman, *Lawyers' Ethics in an Adversary System* (1975), pp. 43-49. See also Curtis, "The Ethics of Advocacy," *Stanford Law Review* 4 (1951):3.

8. The point really carries further than the distinction between benefit and harm. In the former case, though some particular person may have benefited had the distribution been efficient, it does not seem correct to say that for that reason this person had a right to the benefit which he was denied, or that this person was wronged by not receiving the benefit. Individuals do not acquire rights under policies which are dictated purely by considerations of efficiency. See gen-erally Dworkin, "Hard Cases," *Harvard Law Review* 88 (1975):1057, 1058-1078.

Professor Anscombe makes the following suggestive argument:

If saving the life of one patient requires a massive dose of a drug that could be divided up and used to save five other people, not one of those five can claim that he has been wronged, that the smaller dose of the drug was owed to him.

Yet all can reproach me if I gave it to none. It was there, ready to supply human need, and human need was not supplied. So any one of them can say, you ought to have used it to help us who needed it; and so all are wronged. But if it was used for someone, as much as he needed it to keep him alive, no one has any ground for accusing me of having wronged *himself.*—Why, just because he was one of five who could have been saved, is he wronged in not being saved, if someone is supplied with it who needed it? What is *his* claim, except the claim that what was needed go to him rather than be wasted? But it was not wasted. So he was not wronged. So who was wronged? And if no one was wronged, what injury did I do?

. . .

I did not mean that "because they are more" isn't a good reason for helping these and not that one, or these rather than those. It is a perfectly intelligible reason. But it doesn't follow from that that a man acts badly if he doesn't make it his reason. He acts badly if human need for what is in his power to give doesn't work in him as a reason. He acts badly if he chooses to rescue rich people rather than poor ones, having ill regard for the poor ones because they are poor. But he doesn't act badly if he uses his resources to save X, or X, Y and Z, *for no bad reason,* and is not affected by the consideration that he could save a larger number of people. For, once more: who can say he is wronged? And if no one is wronged, how does the rescuer commit any wrong?

Anscombe, "Who Is Wronged?" *Oxford Review* 5 (1967):16, 16-17 (emphasis in original).

9. See generally V. Fuchs, *supra* note 4, at pp. 94-95; Fried "Rights and Health Care—Beyond Equity and Efficiency," *New England Journal of Medicine* 293 (1975):241, 244.

10. For a discussion of this dilemma, see A. Cochrane, *Effectiveness and Efficiency* (1972); C. Fried, *Medical Experimentation: Personal Integrity and Social Policy* (1974).

11. See M. Freedman, *supra* note 7, at pp. 43-49.

12. DR 7-102(A) (5) of the *Code of Professional Responsibility* states that a lawyer shall not knowingly make a false statement of law or fact in his representation of a client. The issue is how to apply this admonition in the context of negotiation, where deception is commonplace. See M. Meltsner & P. Schrag, *Public Interest Advocacy: Materials for Clinical Legal Education* (1974), pp. 231-239

13. For a striking example, see Zabella v. Pakel, 242 F.2d 452 (7th Cir. 1957), where the debtor asserting the technical defenses was a savings and loan association president, and the creditor was a man who had worked for him as a carpenter and had lent him money in earlier, less fortunate days.

14. Although Charles Curtis explicitly denounces lying to the court, his observation that the propriety of lying might depend on whether the question is asked "by someone who has a right to ask it" at least implies a possible qualification in the case of improper questioning by the court. Curtis, *supra* note 7, at pp. 7-9. Monroe Freedman does not specifically address this problem, but his argument that an attorney's duty to safeguard the attorney-client privilege requires the attorney to introduce his client's perjurious testimony would seem to extend to this situation. M. Freedman, *supra* note 7, at pp. 27-41. Cf. *ABA Committee on Professional Ethics,* Opinions No. 287 (1967) (if attorney for defendant learns of previous criminal record through his communications with his client, he has no duty to correct misapprehension on part of court that client has no record).

15. That one assumes obligations to persons which cannot always be overridden by the benefits which would accure from aiding some third person is a standard objection to utilitarianism. See, e.g. W. Ross, *The Right and the Good* (1930), pp. 17-19.

16. I have discussed this problem elsewhere. C. Fried, *An Anatomy of Values* (1970); pp. 207-236 C. Fried, *supra* note 10, at pp. 132-137. Cf. Schelling, *The Life You Save May Be Your Own,* in *Problems in Public Expenditure Analysis* (S. Chase ed. 1968) pp. 127, 129-130, (also discussing our greater concern for known, as opposed to unknown, individuals).

17. Curtis, *supra* note 7, at p. 8. Analogizing the lawyer to a friend raises a range of problems upon which I shall not touch. These have to do with the lawyer's benevolent and sometimes not so benevolent tyranny over and imposition on his client, seemingly authorized by the claim to be acting in the client's interests. Domineering paternalism is not a normal characteristic of friendship. This point is due to Jay Katz.

18. Mill, *Utilitarianism,* in *The Philosophy of John Stuart Mill* (M. Cohen ed. 1961) pp. 321, 342-344.

19. H. Sidgwick, *The Methods of Ethics* (7th ed. 1907) pp. 252.

20. See generally D. Lyons, *Forms and Limits of Utilitarianism* (1965); J. Smart and B. Williams. *Utilitarianism: For and Against* (1973); Harrod, "Utilitarianism Revised," *Mind* 45 (1936):137; Mabbott, "Punishment," *Mind* 48 (1936):152.

21. See generally C. Fried, *An Anatomy of Values,* pp. 203-206; Rawls, "The Independence of Moral Theory," American-Philosophical Association 48 (1975):17-20, (Kantian theory as compared to utilitarianism, takes seriously basic moral fact of primacy of notion of individual personality).

22. . . . It is written (Lev. xix. 18, Matth. xxii. 39); *Thou shalt love thy neighbor* (Lev. *loc. cit.,-friend) as thyself.* Whence it seems to follow that man's love for himself is the model of his love for another. But the model exceeds the copy. Therefore, out of charity, a man ought to love himself more than his neighbor.

. . .

We must, therefore, say that, even as regards the affection we ought to love one neighbor more than another. The reason is that, since the principle of love is God, and the person who loves, it must needs be that the affection of love increases in proportion to the nearness to one or the other of those principles.

. . .

. . . As stated above . . . we ought out of charity to love those who are more closely united to us more, both because our love for them is more intense, and because there are more reasons to loving them. . . .

Accordingly we must say that friendship among blood relations is based upon their connection by natural origin, the friendship of fellow-citizens on their civic fellowship, and the friendship of those who are fighting side by side on the comradeship of battle. Wherefore in matters pertaining to nature we should love our kidred most, in matters concerning relations between citizens, we should prefer our fellow-citizens, and on the battlefield our fellow-soldiers. . .

. . .

If however we compare union with union, it is evident that the union arising from natural origin is prior to, and more stable than, all others, because it is something affecting the very substance, whereas other unions supervene and may cease altogether.

II Thomas Aquinas, *Summa Theologica* 1297-13-1 (Fathers of the English Dominican province trans. 1947).

23. See G. Warnock, *The Object of Morality* (1971), pp. 79-80; Nagel, Book Review, *Yale Law Journal* 85 (1975):136, 140.

24. This argument is, of course, just a fragment which must be fitted into a larger theory. This larger theory would have to explain, among other things, what the precise contents of the various personal roles might be and how conflict between personal roles are to be resolved. My later discussion of permissible and impermissible tactics in legal representation deals with this conflict in one context. A complete theory would also have to spell out the relation between personal roles and duties to the larger collectivity. These latter duties to man in the abstract as opposed to concrete persons are the subject of principles of justice. I have no doubt that such abstract duties exist and that they can be very demanding. Roughly, I would adopt something like the principles put forward in J. Rawls, *A Theory of Justice* (1971), pp, 54-117. I would require, however, that these principles of justice leave sufficient scope for the free definition and inviolability of personal relations—to a greater extent perhaps than Rawls allows. These systematic

concerns are the subject of a larger work from which the present essay is drawn. The relation of principles of justice to other aspects of right and wrong is a principal concern of that larger work.

25. This question might be more troubling in a socialist system in which the profit motive is theoretically subordinated to the service of the general good. But my argument is that the needs for which lawyers and doctors provide are significantly different in kind from those met by other economic agents. Therefore, my argument about doctors and lawyers should be general enough to apply in either a free enteprise or a socialist system.

26. For a recent forceful statement of this conception of rights, see Dworkin, "Taking Rights Seriously," in *Is Law Dead?* (E. Rostow ed. 1971), p. 168. See generally Dworkin, "The Original Position," *University of Chicago Law Review* 40 (1973):500, 522-528.

27. The lawyer is generally free to decline to serve for any or no reason. But even that freedom is qualified; there will be times when there may be a duty to serve, as when a court appoints the lawyer to serve or when his declining may leave a person unrepresented. See pp. 1078-1089, 1086-1087 *infra*.

28. See *ABA Committee on Professional Ethics*, Opinions 56 (1967) (Informal Opinion No. 334); *ABA Code of Professional Responsibility* EC 2-31, 2-32. Compare *id*. Dr 2-110 (C) (1) (f) with *id*. DR 2-11- (A) (2).

29. Fried, *supra* note 9, at p. 245.

30. Carried further, this argument would hold that, as to clients who are within his area of competence, are able to pay his fee, and create no conflict with existing clients, a doctor or lawyer is perfectly justified in taking whoever happens to be next in the queue in his waiting room. Places in the queue may be determined by luck, the price system, or even some bureaucratic method of assignment. The doctor or lawyer does no wrong if he chooses not to concern himself with how the queue was formed. For a more detailed discussion of the moral significance of queuing, see C. Fried, *supra* note 10, at pp. 132-137.

31. See, e.g., M. Green, *supra* note 1, at pp. 268-272.

32. See J. Rawls, *supra* note 24, at pp. 333-391.

33. See *ABA Code of Professional Responsibility* Canon 8.

34. This point is discussed in detail in Fried, "Right and Wrong: Preliminary Considerations," *Journal of Legal Studies* 5 (June, 1976). The notion that abstention from harming particular persons is a special kind of duty is expressed in Ross's concept of nonmaleficence. See W. Ross, *supra* 15, at pp. 21-22.

35. DR 2-110(B) (1) of the *Code of Professional Responsibility* makes withdrawal *mandatory* if the attorney "knows or it is obvious that his client is bringing the legal action, conducting the defense, or asserting a position in the litigation, or is otherwise having steps taken for him, merely for the purpose of harassing or maliciously injuring any person." DR 2-110(C) (1) (c) and (1) (d) *permit* a lawyer to seek withdrawal if the client either "(i)nsists that the lawyer pursue a course of conduct that is illegal or that is prohibited under the Disciplinary Rules" or "(b)y other conduct renders it unreasonably difficult for the lawyer to carry out his employment effectively." For an argument that an attorney should make his own moral judgments about whether and how to represent clients, see M. Green, *supra* note 1, at pp. 268-289. See also J. Auerbach, *supra* note 1, at pp. 279-282.

36. See Nagel, "War and Massacre," *Philosophy & Public Affairs* 1 (1972):123, 133-134, 136; Fried, *supra* note 34.

37. Here I follow Augustine, "Lying," in *Treatises on Various Subjects* (R. Deferrari ed. 1952), and I. Kant, the *Metaphysical Principles of Virtue* (J. Ellington trans. 1964), pp. 90-93.

38. Compare M. Freedman, *supra* note 7, at pp. 27-41 with Noonan, "The Purposes of Advocacy and the Limits of Confidentiality" *Michigan Law Review* 64 (1966):64.

39. The implications of this idea are particularly important for the so-called Washington lawyer (wherever he might be) who is hired to represent his client before agencies and legislatures contemplating new law. This may put us on one of the borderlines I do not pretend to resolve definitely, yet I think we can get an idea of how to think about these cases too. To the extent that such representation involves participation in a formal proceeding in which laws or regulations are

drafted and technical competence is required, the task is *closer* to the traditional task of the lawyer as I have sketched it, and the legal friend concept is more appropriate. To the extent that the representation involves (wholly lawful) deployment of political pressures, inducements, and considerations, it is closer to being political action, and thus to requiring the kind of overriding concern for the common good that should motivate all political actors. Certainly it is absurd that a man should seek to be insulated from moral judgments of his accomplishments as a political string-puller or publicist by the defense that he was only doing it for money.

40. In England barristers are regularly hired by the government in all manner of litigation, thereby accomplishing the many-sidedness I call for here. See Q. Johnstone and D. Hopson, *Lawyers and Their Work* (1967), pp. 374-375. Why should this not be done in the United States? Perhaps there is fear that this might simply become the occasion for a suspect form of patronage.

41. This point is due to Albert Sacks and Richard Stewart.

Gerald J. Postema

Moral Responsibility in Professional Ethics

Lawyers, like other professionals, acknowledge gravely that they shoulder special responsibilities, and believe that they should conform to "higher" ethical standards than laypersons.[1] Yet, lawyers also claim special warrant for engaging in some activities which, were they performed by others, would be likely to draw moral censure.[2] Skeptical of this claim to special license, Macaulay asked "[w]hether it be right that a man should, with a wig on his head, and a band around his neck, do for a guinea what, without these appendages, he would think it wicked and infamous to do for an empire."[3] This conflict may trouble the layperson, but for the lawyer who must come to grips with his professional responsibilities it is especially problematic.

Montaigne offered one solution, the complete separation of personal and professional lives. "There's no reason why a lawyer . . . should not recognize the knavery of his vocation," he insisted. "An honest man is not responsible for the vices or the stupidity of his calling."[4] The key to maintaining both professional and personal integrity in the face of professionally required "knavery" was, Montaigne thought, scrupulously to keep the two personalities apart: "I have been able to concern myself with public affairs without moving the length of my nail from myself. . . . The mayor and Montaigne have always been two people, clearly separated."[5]

Montaigne's solution is tempting. Maintaining a hermetically sealed professional personality promises to minimize internal conflicts, to shift responsibility for professional "knavery" to broader institutional shoulders, and to enable a person to act consistently within each role he assumes. But for this strategy to succeed, the underlying values and concerns of important professional roles, and the characteristic activities they require, must themselves be easily segregated and compartmentalized. However, since there is good reason to doubt they can be easily segregated, Montaigne's strategy risks a dangerous simplification of moral reality. Furthermore, in compartmentalizing moral responses one blocks the cross-fertilization of moral experience necessary for personal and profes-

From Gerald J. Postema, "Moral Responsibility in Professional Ethics," 55 N.Y.U.L. Rev. 63 (1980). Reprinted by permission of the publisher.

sional growth. This article considers whether it is possible to follow Montaigne's suggestion and to separate one's private and professional personalities without jeopardizing one's ability to engage in professional activities in a morally and professionally responsible way. The central issue I address is not whether there is sufficient justification of or a distinct professional code for lawyers, but whether, given the need for such a code, it is possible to preserve one's sense of responsibility. I argue that such preservation is not possible when a professional must adopt Montaigne's strategy in order to function well in his professional role. I contend that a sense of responsibility and sound practical judgment depend not only on the quality of one's professional training, but also on one's ability to draw on the resources of a broader moral experience. This, in turn, requires that one seek to achieve a fully integrated moral personality. Because this is not possible under the present conception of the laywer's role, as exemplified in the *Code of Professional Responsibility,* that conception must be abandoned, to be replaced by a conception that better allows the lawyer to bring his full moral sensibilities to play in his professional role.

MORAL DISTANCE AND THE PERSPECTIVE OF THE RESPONSIBLE PERSON

It is not uncommon for lawyers to face dilemmas caused by the clash of important principles implicit within the professional code. A good example of this is the problem posed for a criminal defense lawyer by a client who announces a firm intention to perjure himself at trial.[6] Here, the deeply embedded principle of confidentiality[7] conflicts sharply with the equally important duty of candor before the court.[8]

But this is not the sort of clash Montaigne had in mind. Indeed, similar moral quandaries and conflicts are common outside of professional contexts. Rather, Montaigne draws attention to the conflict between principles of professional ethics and concerns of private morality. The requirements of professional ethics can sometimes move some distance from the concerns of private or ordinary morality, a phenomenon we might call *moral distance.* The range of practical considerations which alone are relevant to a proper ethical decision in a professional role is the *moral universe* of that role.[9] For many professional roles the moral universe of the role is considerably narrower than that of ordinary morality, and, when the two overlap, they often assign different weights to the same set of considerations. This often gives rise to conflicts, as the following cases illustrate.

The first example involves the duty of the criminal defense attorney to maintain client confidentiality. In the course of preparing a defense for a criminal trial in Lake Pleasant, New York, the client told his attorneys that he was responsible for three other murders unrelated to the pending case. The lawyers visited the location where one of the bodies had been hidden and confirmed the client's story. Nevertheless, they maintained silence for six months and refrained from disclosing the whereabouts of the body to the authorities or to the family one of the victims, which had sought their help in locating the missing victim.[10] The duty of confidentiality, which here protects the client against self-incrimination, clearly forbade disclosure in this case,[11] even though the attorneys' personal inclinations were to disclose.

The second example, illustrated by the case of *Zabella v. Pakel*,[12] concerns the lawyer's use of legally available defenses to circumvent enforcement of his client's moral obligations. At the time of suit, defendant Pakel was president and manager of the Chicago Savings and Loan Association. In earlier and less fortunate circumstances, he had borrowed heavily from his employee, Zabella. Pakel gave a note for the borrowed sums, but, before the debt was paid, he declared bankruptcy, Zabella sued Pakel in 1954, contending that the defendant had made a subsequent promise to pay the outstanding debt. Under Illinois law, a new promise is sufficient to block the defense of discharge in bankruptcy, but because Pakel's promise was not in writing the defendant was able successfully to assert the statute of limitations as a defense. Despite the moral obligation of the affluent Pakel to repay the old debt, the statute of limitations blocked legal enforcement.[13] Many lawyers would argue that for Pakel's lawyer to have failed to assert the statute of limitations defense would have been a gross violation of his professional responsibility.[14] Yet from the point of view of ordinary morality, the lawyer was implicated in the moral wrong done by his client. Professionally upright activities advancing the client's morally questionable, though legally sound, schemes, are paradigmatic of the knavery to which Montaigne referred.

If we admit that some distance is likely to separate private and public morality, then several additional questions come to mind. How are these moralities related? How are conflicts between them to be resolved? Do they share a common foundation which could provide elements for resolution of the conflicts? One might seek a casuistry for a broad range of dilemmas that are likely to arise (which could then perhaps be taught to those preparing to enter the profession). Alternatively, one might seek some general account of the relationship between the principles governing each morality from which one could derive solutions to particular problems as they arise. The present approach to legal ethics, as embodied in the Code, largely utilizes the first strategy; philosophers tend to be partial to the second. Both can be useful, yet they both represent an approach to the problems posed by moral distance which is inadequate in important ways.

The first problem with these strategies is that they are only of limited usefulness in practice. Casuistry gives us solutions to isolated problems, but no strategy for resolving new problems. The systematic strategy is also not likely to help us in situations in which we experience the most puzzlement, since the moral dilemma facing a lawyer generally cannot be reduced to a single perspective. Our personal and professional concerns do not have the collective uniformity necessary for the construction of a general scheme of principles and priority rules. On the contrary, our concerns are characterized by a complexity and a variety which resist reduction to a uniform scale.[15] As Thomas Nagel has argued, we are subject to moral and other motivational claims of very different kinds, because we are able to view the world from a variety of perspectives, each presenting a different set of claims. Nagel maintains that conflicts between perspectives

> [c]annot . . . be resolved by subsuming either of the points of view under the other, or both under a third. Nor can we simply abandon any of them. There is no reason why we should. The capacity to view the world simultaneously from the point of view of one's relations to others, from the point of view of one's life extended through time, from the point of view of everyone at once, and finally from the detached viewpoint often described as the view *sub specie aeternitatis* is one of the marks of humanity. This complex capacity is an obstacle to simplification.[16]

Are we left without any rational means for resolving this conflict? Nagel rightly resists this skeptical response.[17] The conflict Nagel describes shows only that it may be futile to search for a general reductive method or a clear set of priority rules to structure our basic concerns. There is always likely to be a significant gap between general practical theory and actual decision and practice.

In Aristotle's view, this gap is bridged by the faculty of *practical judgment*[18]—what he called practical wisdom.[19] Our ability to resolve conflicts on a rational basis often outstrips our ability to enunciate general principles. In doing so, we exercise judgment. Judgment is neither a matter of simply applying general rules to particular cases nor a matter of mere intuition. It is a complex faculty, difficult to characterize, in which general principles or values and the particularities of the case both play important roles. The principles or values provide a framework within which to work and a target at which to aim. But they do not determine decisions. Instead, we rely on our judgment to achieve a coherence among the conflicting values which is sensitive to the particular circumstances. Judgment thus involves the ability to take a comprehensive view of the values and concerns at stake, based on one's experience and knowledge of the world. And this involves awareness of the full range of shared experience, beliefs, relations, and expectations within which these values and concerns have significance.

In professional contexts there is much need for practical judgment in this Aristotelian sense. Judgment, however, is both a disposition—a trait of character—and a skill which must be learned and continually exercised. It is important, then, if we are seriously to consider matters of moral responsibility in professional contexts, that we pay attention to the conditions of development of this disposition and the exercise of this skill.

The second difficulty with the current approach to questions raised by the conflict between private and professional moralities is that it rests on a mistaken view of moral judgment and moral experience. Practical moral reasoning is wrongly viewed as strictly analogous to theoretical reasoning, the central objective of which is to arrive at correct answers to specific problems. This view of moral reasoning and experience is too narrow, for moral reasoning is not so singularly outcome-determinative. Our evaluations of ourselves and our actions depend not only on getting our moral sums right, but also on having the appropriate attitudes and reactions to the moral situation in which we act. Let me illustrate.[20]

Consider the truck driver who, through no fault of his own, hits and seriously injures a child. It may be correct to say that, since he drove with care and could not have avoided hitting the child, the driver is guilty of no wrong and thus is not blameworthy. However, consider the accident and the driver's involvement in it from his point of view. There is a very important difference between the driver's likely reaction and that of an uninvolved spectator. Both may feel and express regret, but the nature and behavioral expression of this regret will be quite different. The driver's direct, personal (albeit unintentional) involvement in the accident alters the structure of the moral situation and the driver's attitude toward it. The difference in the emotional responses of the driver and the spectator will be reflected in the way these feelings are expressed. The driver may attempt to make restitution in the hope that he can repair the injury he caused. The spectator may offer help, or contribute money for hospital bills, or even visit the child, but these actions would be understood (by him and by us) as expressions of pity, kindly concern, or perhaps generosity. From the driver, these same actions would be intended and understood as expressions of a special form of regret. Suppose, however, that the driver takes the attitude of the uninvolved spectator, perhaps expressing detached regret, but feeling no need to make restitution. He can rightly argue that he was not to be blamed for the accident, that he had done no wrong. In doing so, he could perhaps be rightly said to have gotten his moral sums right. But in asserting this defense quite sincerely and too quickly, he would reveal a defect of character—a defect much deeper and more serious than a lack of generosity. Morality seems to require not only that one be able to apply moral principles properly to one's own or another's conduct, but also that one be able to appreciate the moral costs of one's actions, perhaps even when those actions are unintentional. By "moral costs" I mean those features of one's action and its consequences touching on important concerns, interests, and needs of others that, in the absence of special justification, would provide substantial if not conclusive moral reasons against performing it."[21]

Similarly, in cases in which obligations to other persons are correctly judged to be overridden by weightier moral duties, with the result that some injury is done, it is not enough for one to work out the correct course of action and pursue it. It is also important that one appreciate the moral costs of that course of action. This appreciation will be expressed in a genuine reluctance to bring about the injury, and a sense of the accompanying loss or sacrifice. It may even call for concrete acts of reparation: explaining and attempting to justify the action of the person injured, or making up the loss or injury to some extent. This is one way in which the moral status of the principle of right which was violated is acknowledged, and the moral relations between the parties affirmed and, when necessary, repaired.

Moral sentiments are an essential part of the moral life. The guilt or remorse one feels after mistreating a person is not merely a personal sanction one imposes on oneself after judging the action to have been wrong: it is the natural and most appropriate expression of this judgment. Similarly, the outrage we feel at injustice done to another and the resentment we feel at wrong done to ourselves are not just the emotional coloring of detached moral judgments, but the way in which we experience and express these judgments. Thus, morality is not merely a matter of getting things right—as in solving a puzzle or learning to speak grammatically—but a matter of relating to people in a special and specifically human way.

It must be admitted that these elements of practical wisdom and moral sentiment are not needed to understand the proper performance of duties in *some* professional or occupatinal roles. We need spend little time worrying about whether our understanding of the duties of bank clerks or auto mechanics properly allows for these elements. A person's moral faculties are not extensively engaged in the characteristic activities of these roles. In contrast, the characteristic activities of the lawyer's role demand a much greater involvement of the moral faculties.

For these reasons, we must approach the problems of professional ethics from a perspective that recognizes the importance of practical judgment and moral sentiment. The notion of professional responsibility should take on a different and broader meaning. The primary concern is not with the definition, structuring, and delimitation of a lawyer's professional *responsibilities* (his official concerns and duties), nor with those situations in which the lawyer is to be held professionally *responsible (i.e.,* liable to blame or sanction). Rather, the concern is with responsibility as a virtue or trait of character.[22] The focus, then, is on the notion of a *responsible* person—or perhaps better, on the notion of a person's *sense of responsibility.* My concern in the rest of this essay is to explore the ways in which institutional structures and public expectations, as well as the personal attitudes and self-conceptions of professionals, affect the development of this sense of responsibility.

MORAL DISTANCE AND THE CALL FOR "DEPROFESSIONALIZATION"

Before we proceed with the argument, however, we must consider briefly a more radical solution to the problems posed by the phenomenon of moral distance. It is sometimes argued that the dissonance between the dictates of professional and private morality is *itself* a symptom of a deep social and moral problem. The solution, it is claimed, lies in a "deprofessionalization" of professional roles[23] that would reduce all professional responsibilities to species of private morality.

This view holds that it either is or should be the case that the duties and responsibilities of a professional are no different from those of any lay person facing a similar moral problem.

This approach to professional responsibility makes two serious mistakes. First, it rests on a mistaken objection to what we might call the "exclusionary character" of professional morality.[24] We have already seen that the moral universe of a professional role characteristically is narrower than that of ordinary morality. But since the moral universe defines the range of considerations that a role agent may take into account in choosing a course of action, it is possible that otherwise relevant considerations may be effectively excluded from the agent's deliberation. Thus, cases may arise in which an agent is required by his role to act without considering the full range of moral reasons before him; rather, he must consider only those moral reasons within his particular moral universe. Critics argue that this is both irrational and morally suspect since it denies the role agent his essential autonomy.

But it is not difficult to show that there is nothing inherently irrational or morally objectionable in this exclusionary character of professional morality. Some examples should make this clear. Suppose I have a tendency to spend my paycheck frivolously, with the result that my monthly bills pile up unpaid. To avoid this dangerous situation I adopt the policy of paying bills first and spending on pleasure only what is left over. I know that in the absence of this personal policy, I am liable to be moved by immediate desires to postpone paying my regular bills. Suppose that after adopting this policy I come to believe, at the end of a very tiring month, that I deserve a weekend holiday, although I know I can afford it only if I postpone payment on several bills. I decide, however, by appealing to my policy, to pay the bills. In this case, the policy operates not as an additional factor to consider along with the good the holiday would do for me and for the difficulty I will face if my bills are not paid, but as an exclusionary factor. Indeed, it may be true that this month no particular harm would come from my postponing payment of the bills. The policy, however, instructs me not to consider other factors, it excludes them from consideration and provides a reason for not acting on the balance of reasons in this case. Of course, the exclusionary policy must itself be supported by sufficient reasons, but they need not apply directly to the particular case. Similarly, the moral appropriateness of exclusionary reasons is evident in any standard case of promising. Suppose I promise to drive you across town to your doctor's appointment tomorrow. In this case, considerations of cost and inconvenience which otherwise might be sufficient to persuade me not to take the trip are excluded—the exclusion is not absolute. In neither of these cases, then, am I subject to a charge of irrationality or moral irresponsibility.

Second, the call for deprofessionalization fails to appreciate the important social value of professional roles having this exclusionary character. We design social institutions to perform important tasks and to meet social needs or serve important social values. To carry out these tasks we design specific roles within the institutional framework and entrust them with responsibility over a particular range of social concerns. The domain of practical concerns determined by the basic tasks of the role is the oral universe of that role. Thus, social and professional roles represent an important division of social and moral labor. And carefully defined boundaries of concern and responsibility are needed for the efficient and successful achievement of important social goals served by the division of labor.

Thus, there is nothing objectionable in general, nor anything unique, about the phenomenon of distance between private and public morality. Critical attention must be turned, rather, to the way in which the moral universe of a given role is defined and structured, and the effect this has on the professional's ability to act responsibly in the moral universe so defined.

RESPONSIBLE ACTION UNDER THE STANDARD CONCEPTION

The central problem I am concerned with is whether, given the fact of moral distance, it is possible to retain and act out of a mature sense of responsibility in a professional role. In this section, I argue that because of particular social and psychological features of professional roles, the pressures and tensions of acting and deliberating within such roles pose a serious threat to responsible professional behavior. In addition, I hope to show that the atrophy of the professional's sense of general moral responsibility is a serious and costly matter. If this argument is correct, we have discovered an important reason for radically rethinking the standard conception of the lawyer's role.[25] This standard conception[26] is marked by two central ideals:

(i) *Partisanship:* the lawyer's sole allegiance is to the client; the lawyer is the partisan of the client. *Within,* but all the way *up to,* the limits of the law, the lawyer is committed to the aggressive and single-minded pursuit of the client's objectives.

(ii) *Neutrality:* once he has accepted the client's case, the lawyer must represent the client, or pursue the client's objectives, regardless of the lawyer's opinion of the client's character and reputation, and the moral merits of the client's objectives. On this conception, the lawyer need not consider, nor may he be held responsible for, the consequences of his professional activities as long as he stays within the law and acts in pursuit of the client's legitimate aims.[27] Thus, the proper range of the lawyer's concern—the boundaries of the lawyer's "moral universe"—is defined by two parameters: the law and the client's interests and objectives. These factors are the exclusive points of reference for professional deliberation and practical judgment. I contend that, far from encouraging the development and preservation of a mature sense of responsibility, the standard conception tends seriously to undermine it. To show why this is so I must sketch briefly what might be called "the problem of responsibility."

The problem is suggested in a rather grand way by Sartre in a familiar argument from his early existentialist period.[28] Sartre insisted that to take role moralities seriously is to fail to take responsibility for oneself and one's actions. The essential property of human consciousness, according to Sartre, is its absolute freedom—the capacity to define oneself in action independently of one's role or roles. Roles, however, come "ready-made," packaged by society. When acting in a role, one simply acts as others expect one to act. Simply to identify with one's role is to ignore the fact that one is free to choose not to act in this way. In Sartre's view, it is therefore essential that one be capable of walking away from one's role. Furthermore, although it is psychologically possible to identify deeply with one's role, doing so is, in Sartre's view, morally unthinkable and a form of bad faith. Identification is a strategy for evading one's freedom and, consequently, one's responsibility for one who is and what one does. By taking shelter in the role, the individual places the responsibility for all of his acts at the door of the institutional author of the role.[29]

Sartre's problem arises from the fact that in addition to moral distance, there is a second dimension—psychological distance—characteristic of the experience of persons who assume professional roles. Echoing Sartre, Goffman notes that

> in performing a role the individual must see to it that the impressions of him that are conveyed in the situation are compatible with role-appropriate personal qualities effectively imputed to him: a judge is supposed to be deliberate and sober; a pilot, in a cockpit, to be cool. . . . These personal qualities, effectively imputed and effectively claimed, combine with a position's title, where there is one, to provide a basis of *self-image* for the incumbent and a basis for the image [others will have of his role]. A self, then, virtually awaits the individual entering a position . . . .[30]

Psychological distance is especially characteristic of professional roles. As Goffman seeks to show in his essay, one can identify with, or distance oneself in varying degrees from, this available self-image. The more closely one identifies with one's role, the more one's sense of self is likely to be shaped by the defining features of the role.[31] At one extreme, maximal identification is characterized by an unquestioning acceptance of the duties and responsibilities of one's role. For the person who maximally identifies with his role, the response "because I am a lawyer," or more generally "because that's my job," suffices as a complete answer to the question "why do that?" One minimally identifies, on the other hand, when one conforms only to avoid the external consequences of failing to do so, in no way internalizing the role or its basic principles. Several possible intermediate states separate these extremes.[32]

Thus, in addition to the dimension of moral distance between private and professional morality there is the dimension of psychological distance between oneself, or one's moral personality, and one's role. Furthermore, these two dimensions are interrelated: the extent to which one identifies with one's role is a function not only of one's moral personality but also of the moral distance between role morality and one's private morality. The opposite influence is also possible. Acting and deliberating within the special moral universe of any role that involves a large investment of one's moral faculties will tend to shape one's moral personality and, thus, one's inclination to identify with the role. The problem of responsibility lies in the fact that as the moral distance between private and professional moralities increases, the temptation to adopt one or the other extreme strategy of identification also increases; one either increasingly identifies with the role or seeks resolutely to detach oneself from it. Under either extreme, however, one's practical judgment and sense of responsibility are cut off from their sources in ordinary moral experience. Yeats warned that "once one makes a thing subject to reason, as distinguished from impulse, one plays with it, even if it is a very serious thing."[33] We might say, paraphrasing Yeats, that the artificial reason of professional morality, which rests on claims of specialized knowledge and specialized analytical technique, and which is removed from the rich resources of moral sentiment and shared moral experience in the community, tempts the professional to distort even the most serious of moral questions.

The problem of responsibility is especially troubling for the legal profession. The risk of severing professional judgment from its moral and psychological sources is particularly strong in a profession that serves a system of institutionalized justice.[34] As a result, the problem of developing a sense of personal responsibility is critical for the legal profession. First, the factors inducing maximal psychological identification are strong.[35] Publicly dedicated to serving socially valued institutions, the lawyer occupies a key role in society, enjoying considerable social status. His claim to specialized knowledge and skill puts the lawyer in a position of power relative to his client. These facts, in addition to the important intrinsic satisfaction of exercising his special skills, encourage a high degree of role identification. As a result, principles of professional responsibility, originally justified on functional grounds, take on independent value and significance for lawyers. Professional integrity becomes a mark, often the most significant mark, of personal integrity.

Second, the characteristic activities of lawyering often require the lawyer to act in the place of the client, and thus require the direct involvement of the lawyer's moral faculties—*i.e.,* his capacities to deliberate, reason, argue, and act in the public arena. All professionals, and many persons in service-oriented occupations, do things for a client that the client is unable or unwilling to do for himself. But, unlike the lawyer, the physician or auto mechanic acts only to provide services for the client. The lawyer also acts as the client's *agent*. Although an individual may employ a physician or mechanic to operate on his body or his automobile, the work of these professionals is in no sense attributable to the patient or customer. When the lawyer acts to secure the client's interests, however, he often acts, speaks, and argues in the place of the client. He enters into relationships with others in the name of the client. When he argues in his client's behalf, he often presents his client's arguments; when he acts he is often said to be "exercising his client's rights." And what he does is typically attributable to the client.[36] Thus, at the invitation of the client, the lawyer becomes an extension of the legal, and to an extent the moral, personality of the client.

Since the lawyer often acts as an extension of the legal and moral personality of the client, the lawyer is under great temptation to refuse to accept responsibility for his professional actions and their consequences. Moreover, except when his beliefs coincide with those of his client, he lives with a recurring dilemma: he must engage in activities, make arguments, and present positions which he himself does not endorse or embrace. The lawyer's integrity is put into question by the mere exercise of the duties of his profession.[37]

To preserve his integrity, the lawyer must carefully distance himself from his activities. Publicly, he may sharply distinguish statements or arguments he makes for the client and statements on which he stakes his professional honor.[38] The danger in this strategy is that a curious two-stage distancing may result. First, the lawyer distances himself from the argument: it is not his argument, but that of his client. His job is to construct the arguments; the task of evaluating and believing them is left to others. Second, after detaching himself from the argument, he is increasingly tempted to identify with this stance of detachment. What first offers itself as a device for distancing oneself from personally unacceptable positions becomes a defining feature of one's professional self-concept. This, in turn, encourages an uncritical, uncommitted state of mind, or worse, a deep moral skepticism. When such detachment is defined as a professional ideal, as it is by the standard conception, the lawyer is even more apt to adopt these attitudes.

The foregoing tensions and pressures have sources deep in the nature of the lawyer's characteristic activities. To eradicate them entirely would be to eliminate much of what is distinctive and socially valuable in these activities. Nevertheless, these tensions can be eased, and the most destructive tendencies avoided, if lawyers have a framework within which they can obtain an integrated view of their activities both within the role and outside it. The framework must provide the resources for responsible resolution of the conflicts that inevitably arise. The standard conception of the lawyer's role, however, fails notably on this score. Clearly, the standard conception calls for a sharp separation of private and professional morality in which, to quote Bellow and Kettleson, "the lawyer is asked to do 'as a professional' what he or she would not do 'as a person.'"[39] The conception requires a public endorsement, as well as private adoption, of the extreme strategy of detachment. The good lawyer is one who is capable of drawing a tight circle around himself and his client, allowing no other considerations to interfere with his zealous and scrupulously loyal pursuit of the client's objectives. The good lawyer leaves behind his own family, religious, political, and moral concerns, and devotes himself entirely to the client.[40] But since professional integrity is often taken to be the most important mark of personal integrity, a very likely result is often that a successful lawyer is one who can strictly identify with this professional strategy of detachment. That is, the standard conception both directly and indirectly *encourages* adoption of one or the other of the extreme strategies of identification. But, as we have seen, both strategies have in common the unwanted consequence that practical deliberation, judgment, and action *within* the role are effectively cut off from ordinary moral beliefs, attitudes, feelings, and relationships—resources on which responsible judgment and action depend. This consequence is very costly in both personal and social terms.

Consider first the personal costs the lawyer must pay to act in this detached manner. The maximal strategy yields a severe impoverishment of moral experience. The lawyer's moral experience is sharply constrained by the boundaries of the moral universe of the role. But the minimal strategy involves perhaps even higher personal costs. Since the characteristic activities of the lawyer require a large investment of his moral faculties, the lawyer must reconcile himself to a kind of moral prostitution. In a large portion of his daily experience, in which he is acting regularly in the moral arena, he is alienated from his own moral feelings and attitudes and indeed from his moral personality as a whole. Moreover, in light of the strong pressures for role identification, it is not unlikely that the explicit and conscious adoption of the minimal identification strategy involves a substantial element of self-deception.

The social costs of cutting off professional deliberation and action from their sources in ordinary moral experience are even more troubling. First, cut off from sound moral judgment, the lawyer's ability to do his job well—to determine the applicable law and effectively advise his clients—is likely to be seriously affected.[41] Both positivist and natural law theorists agree that moral arguments have an important place in the determination of much of modern law.[42] But the lawyer who must detach professional judgment from his own moral judgment is deprived of the resources from which arguments regarding his client's legal rights and duties can be fashioned. In effect, the ideal of neutrality and detachment wars against its companion ideal of zealous pursuit of client interests.

Second, the lawyer's practical judgment, in the Aristotelian sense, is rendered ineffective and unreliable.[43] In section I, I argued that, because human values are diverse and complex, one is sometimes thrown back on the faculty of practical judgment to resolve moral dilemmas.[44] This is as true within the professional context as outside of it. To cut off professional decisionmaking from the values and concerns which structure the moral situation, thereby blocking appeal to a more comprehensive point of view from which to weigh the validity of role morality, is to risk undermining practical judgment entirely.[45]

Third, and most importantly, when professional action is estranged from ordinary moral experience, the lawyer's sensitivity to the moral costs in both ordinary and extraordinary situations tends to atrophy. The ideal of neutrality permits, indeed requires, that the lawyer regard his professional activities and their consequences from the point of view of the uninvolved spectator. One may abstractly regret that the injury is done, but this regret is analogous to the regret one feels as a spectator to the traffic accident mentioned in an earlier example;[46] one is in no way personally implicated. The responses likely from a mature sense of the present Code. This has troubling consequences; without a proper appreciation of moral costs of one's actions one cannot make effective use of the faculty of practical judgment. In fact, a proper perspective of the moral costs of one's action has both intrinsic and instrumental value. The instrumental value lies in the added safeguard that important moral dilemmas will receive appropriate reflection. As Bernard Williams argued, "only those who are [by practice] reluctant or disinclined to do the morally disagreeable when it is really necessary have much chance of not doing it when it is not necessary. . . . [A] habit of reluctance is an essential obstacle against the happy acceptance of the intolerance."[47]

But this appreciation is also important for its own sake. To experience sincere reluctance to feel the need to make restitution, to seek the other's pardon—these simply are appropriate responses to the actual feature of the moral situation. In this way, the status and integrity of important moral principles are maintained in compromising circumstances, and the moral relations between persons are respected or restored.

Finally, the moral detachment of the lawyer adversely affects the quality of the lawyer-client relationship. Unable to draw from the responses and relations of ordinary experience, the lawyer is capable of relating to the client only as a client. He puts his moral faculties of reason, argument, and persuasion wholly at the service of the client, but simultaneously disengages his moral personality. He views himself not as a moral actor but as a legal technician. In addition, he is barred from recognizing the client's moral personality. The moral responsibilities of the client are simply of no interest to him. Thus, paradoxically, the combination of partisanship and neutrality jeopardizes client autonomy and mutual respect (two publicly stated objectives of the standard conception), and yields instead a curious kind of *impersonal* relationship.

It is especially striking, then, that Charles Fried, the most sophisticated defender of these central ideals of the standard conception, should describe the lawyer as a "special purpose" friend.[48] Indeed, it is the contrast between the standard conception of the lawyer-client relationship and the characteristics of a relationship between friends which, on reflection, is likely to make the deepest impression. The impersonalization and moral detachment characteristic of the lawyer's role under the standard conception are not found in relations between friends. Loyalty to one's friend does not call for disengagement of one's moral personality. When in nonprofessional contexts we enter special relationships and undertake special obligations which create duties of loyalty or special concern, these special considerations must nevertheless be integrated into a coherent picture of the moral life as a whole. Often we must view our moral world from more than one perspective simultaneously.[49] As Goffman points out, roles are often structured with the recognition that persons occupying the role fill other roles which are also important to them. Room is left for the agent to integrate his responsibilities from each role into a more or less coherent scheme encompassing his entire moral life.[50]

But it is precisely this integrated conception of the moral personality that is unavailable to the professional who adopts either the minimal or the maximal identification strategy. Either the moral personality is entirely fragmented or compartmentalized, or it is shrunk to fit the moral universe defined by the role. Neither result is desirable.

TOWARD AN ALTERNATIVE CONCEPTION: THE RECOURSE ROLE

The unavoidable social costs of the standard conception of professional legal behavior argue strongly for a radical rethinking of the lawyer's role. One alternative is a "deprofessionalization" of legal practice so as to eliminate the distance between private and professional morality. Deprofessionalization, however, would involve a radical restructuring of the entire legal system, reducing the complexity of the law as it currently exists so that individuals could exercise their rights without the assistance of highly specialized legal technicians. But, setting aside obvious questions of feasibility, to discredit this proposal we need only recall that deprofessionalization ignores the significant social value in a division of moral and social labor produced by the variety of public and professional roles.

A second, more plausible alternative is to recognize the unavoidable discontinuities in the moral landscape and to bridge them with a unified conception of moral personality. Achieving any sort of bridge, however, requires that lawyers significantly alter the way they view their own activities. Each lawyer must have a conception of the role that allows him to serve the important functions of that role in the legal and political system while integrating his own sense of moral responsibility into the role itself. Such a conception must improve upon the current one by allowing a broader scope for engaged moral judgment in day-to-day professional activities while encouraging a keener sense of personal responsibility for the consequences of these activities.[51]

The task of forging a concrete alternative conception is a formidable one. To begin, however, it may be useful to contrast two conceptions of social roles: the fixed role and the recourse role.[52] In a fixed role, the professional perceives the defining characteristics of the role—its basic rules, duties, and responsibilities—as entirely predetermined. The characteristics may be altered gradually through social evolution or more quickly by profession-wide regulatory legislation, but as far as the individual practitioner is concerned, the moral universe of his role is an objective fact, to be reckoned with, but not for him to alter.[53] Sartre, proponents of the standard conception, and advocates of deprofessionalization all rest their positions on the assumption that the defining features of each role remain fixed. But this assumption fits only some social roles. A bank clerk, for example, must follow set routines; little judgment is required, and he has no authority to set aside the rules under which he acts or alter these rules to fit new occasions.[54] This is not troubling because the sorts of situations one is likely to face in such a job lend themselves to routine treatment.

In contrast, in a recourse role, one's duties and responsibilities are not fixed, but may expand or contract depending on the institutional objectives the role is designed to serve.[55] The recourse role requires the agent not only to act according to what he perceives to be the explicit duties of the role in a narrow sense, but also to carry out those duties in keeping with the functional objectives of the role.[56] The agent can meet these requirements only if he possesses a comprehensive and integrated concept of his activities both within and outside the role. Role morality, then, within a recourse role is not properly served by maximal identification with one's role. Nor can the role agent minimally identify with his role so as to abandon or disengage his personal morality or basic sense of responsibility. Indeed, responsible professional judgment will rely heavily on a sense of responsibility.

If we perceive the role of the lawyer in our legal system as a recourse role, a viable solution to the problem of responsibility may be available. A recourse role conception forces the lawyer to recognize that the exercise of his role duties must fully engage his rational and critical powers, and his sense of moral responsibility as well. Although not intended to obliterate the moral distance between professional and private moralities, a recourse role conception bridges that gap by integrating to a significant degree the moral responsibility of the individual with the performance of role responsibilities. Most significantly, this conception prevents the lawyer from escaping responsibility by relying on his status as an agent of the client or an instrument of the system. He cannot consider himself simply a legal technician, since his role essentially involves the exercise of his *engaged* moral judgment.

OBJECTIONS AND REPLIES

Two initial objections to the recourse role conception should be addressed: (1) that it is paternalistic,[57] and (2) that it is unnecessary, since the standard conception adequately allows for the exercise of individual moral judgment by permitting the attorney to decide whether to accept or withdraw from representation.[58]

Both these objections are mistaken. Paternalism involves interfering with the actions of others or, in subtler cases, making judgments for others, for their own good. Engaging a lawyer's moral judgment in the day-to-day practice of law in no way entails paternalism—and will involve paternalism only if the lawyer himself holds strongly paternalistic moral views. There is an important distinction between evaluating alternatives in terms of the client's long-range good and making decisions without the client's consent (or against his will), on the one hand, and exercising one's moral judgment regarding those alternatives, on the other. The recourse role conception is not paternalistic even in the very broad sense that the lawyer is encouraged to make the client's moral decisions for him. The moral judgments that the lawyer makes are made on his own behalf; he does not make the client's decisions. Indeed, it is an advantage of my proposal, in contrast to the standard conception, that it enables both lawyer and client to recognize and respect the moral status of the other. The lawyer-client relationship should not be any more paternalistic than a relationship between friends.

As to the second objection, it may be admitted that the *Code of Professional Responsibility* does provide some room for the individual lawyer to exercise moral judgment in the acceptance and withdrawal from representation. But the scope allowed for such judgment is limited, and the motivation skewed. The Code mandates refusal to accept employment only when the client clearly intends to bring an action "merely for the purpose of harassing or maliciously injuring any person,"[59] or seeks to bring an action for which no reasonable legal argument can be made.[60]

The lawyer may refuse to accept employment when his personal feelings are sufficiently intense as to diminish his ability effectively to represent the client,[61] although the Code permits such refusal only in fairly compelling circumstances.[62] Once the lawyer has undertaken to represent the client, however, permissive withdrawal is allowed only in a few restricted circumstances,[63] none of which includes the conscience of the lawyer. Permissive withdrawal for what might be termed "moral reasons" is condoned only when the client insists upon presenting a claim or defense for which no reasonable legal justification can be advanced,[64] or when the client insists upon an illegal course of action.[65] Withdrawal for moral reasons is required only when the lawyer knows that the client is conducting the litigation solely to harass.[66]

Thus, in cases in which the Code permits the lawyer to refuse employment, the rationale seems to be that a lawyer who has scruples about the client's proposed legal action is not likely to be able adequately to serve his client.[67] And such scruples generally are not permitted at all once the attorney agrees to represent a client.[68] This point of view encourages the lawyer to steel himself against such scruples and to view them as strictly personal feelings which have no place in professional behavior—a kind of unbecoming moral squeamishness. It is hard to dismiss the thought that this reaction is at bottom morally cynical.

Charles Fried raises a more sophisticated objection to the conception of the lawyer's role developed above. On this point, he insists that the law must respect the autonomy and rights of individual citizens. According to Fried, one way we respect individual rights is through the creation of specific rules and institutions to protect them. But when the legal system is so complex that the ordinary person is unable to exercise his rights without an expert advisor, the interjection of a lawyer's moral judgment might prevent the individual from exercising fully these lawful rights. In this way, "the law . . . would impose constraints on the lay citizen [implicitly] . . . which it is not entitled to impose explicitly."[69] Thus,

Fried argues, although no rights are violated when a pornography venture fails because a person refuses on moral grounds to lend it funds, rights are violated when "through ignorance or misinformation about the law [because of an attorney's moral judgment] an individual refrains from pursuing a wholly lawful purpose."[70]

The problem with this argument is that while we might agree that individual autonomy and rights should be respected, we might still deny that it is the lawyer's moral as well as role duty to assist his client in any lawful exercise of his legal rights. Fried's mistake is to confuse *moral* rights with *legal* rights. He fails to distinguish the rights and sphere of autonomy defined by *morality* from the rights and area of free action defined by law. The area of legally permitted behavior need not coincide with that circumscribed as a matter of individual moral right. A lack of fit betweeen legal and moral rights is most obvious when legal rights appear unjust or otherwise morally objectionable. But lack of fit may occur even when the legal system is morally ideal. For various reasons the law paints the canvas of legal relations, regulations, and rights with broad strokes. Many forms of social behavior otherwise harmful or morally objectionable are left unproscribed in light of the moral or social costs of enforcement.

Fried complains that if the services of the lawyer were restricted, the law would, in effect, implicitly impose constraints that it is not entitled to impose explicitly.[71] But this is not the case in the instances I am considering. For reasons of administrative efficiency, a particular restriction may not be imposed, but it does follow that the lawmaker is not *entitled*—because it would violate someone's rights—to impose such a restriction.

Not all rights, powers, or permissions defined by the law protect moral rights. Fried's argument has force only for those legal rights that protect important individual moral rights and fundamental political liberties. It does not necessarily hold for other legal rights. My argument is not that the exercise of these legal rights is never justified. I merely contend that it is not always morally right for the individual to exercise these rights, and that it may, in particular instances, be wrong for a lawyer to help him. Thus, it is a matter of *moral argument* whether in particular cases it is appropriate for the lawyer to assist in what may be considered a morally questionable exercise of clear legal rights.

However, Fried seems to qualify his commitment to the standard conception of the lawyer's role. He rejects the contention advanced by proponents of the standard conception, that whatever is legally permissible for a lawyer is morally permissible as well.[72] He has no trouble with a lawyer who assists his client in exercising his legal rights when only the collective good or abstract interests are adversely affected.[73] But Fried is troubled by those activities of a lawyer that cause harm to specific persons known to the lawyer and client, such as the adverse witness who may be abused by the defense lawyer. To resolve this tension, he distinguishes between personal wrongs (wrongs *personally* committed by the lawyer in the course of his professional activities) and institutional wrongs (wrongs worked by the rules of the legal system).[74] However, in the absence of some independent principle by which to distinguish between personal and institutional wrongs, Fried seriously begs the very question at issue. The question can be rephrased: for what harms or wrongs done to specific individuals other than the client is the lawyer personally responsible, and what harms or wrongs must be laid at the door of the system itself?

Fried does suggest one answer, which turns on whether the description of the harmful action in question essentially refers to law or legal institutions. This principle can be illustrated by the difference between (a) abusing a witness in court and (b) exploiting unfairly the defense of the statue of limitations. In the second case, the harmful action is formally denied by the procedural rules of the legal system itself. Thus, legal institutions created the occasion for the action and are essential to the definition of the action itself. There is, for example, no action fitting the description "asserting the defense of the statute of limitations" outside a specific legal context, just as there is no action fitting the description "hitting a home run" outside the context of baseball. So, says Fried, the action is not personal, it is institutional—an action of the system, not of the individual lawyers.[75] In contrast, the act of abusing the witness is a personal act of the lawyer. Although it occurs in a legal context, it is an action that can be done both within and outside that context. There is nothing essentially institutional about it. Thus, Fried concludes, "[t]he lawyer is not morally entitled . . . to engage his own person in doing personal harm to another, though he may exploit the system for his client even if the system consequently works injustice."[76]

Fried's distinction between personal and institutional wrongs is open to criticism on two grounds. First, it relies too heavily on chosen characterizations. Consider, for example, a situation in which the lawyer is seeking to obtain custody of the children for the husband, his client, in a divorce proceeding. The lawyer knows that the wife has been conducting an adulterous affair for some time and that, under the law of the jurisdiction, this would disqualify her from obtaining custody. He also knows that the wife would be humiliated by having details of the affair brought out in open court. If he chooses to advance his client's interests and raise the issue of adultery, is he merely raising a point of law (an institutional action) or is he doing a personal wrong to the wife? The first characterization would pass Fried's test; the second might not. No important moral principle should rest on arbitrary distinctions between equally appropriate characterizations of the actions.

Second, there is the more fundamental problem of an individual's absolving himself of moral responsibility by shifting guilt to institutional shoulders. How can an action done within an institutional setting be morally appropriate, perhaps even morally required, when it is *wrong?* Fried suggests that responsibility shifts because the action is the action of the system—the institution—and not of the individual lawyer. Fried's reasoning seems to rest on the assumption that "if an action is essentially institutional then the good or bad consequences of the action are not attributable to the agent, but only to the institution." But, while it is important, for purposes of correction, to trace "institutional wrongs" back to the source, it does not follow that only the system may be blamed, or that the only possible action is to seek institutional reform. It is a mistake to insist that either the system is to blame or the individual agent is to blame. It is possible that moral criticism of both is appropriate. To rest blame with just one or the other suggests that when the system is to blame, there is nothing the individual can do about it but work to change the system, or the offending part of it. But that is not true: one can also avoid exploiting the defects of the law to the injury of others.

The lawyer must recognize that the institution acts only through the voluntary activities of the lawyer and client. The lawyer is not the instrument of the institution; rather the institution is the instrument of the client and the client engages the lawyer to make use of the instrument.

It is far more desirable to recognize at the outset that the lawyer, as well as the client, bears at least some responsibility for harms done by both "institutional" and "personal" actions. The question, then, is whether in particular cases there is a moral justification for the harms done. Whether there is or is not will be determined by the substantive moral considerations relevant in the case. And it is these substantive moral considerations that the moral lawyer must take into account in making his decision.

NOTES

1. "Lawyers, as guardians of the law, play a vital role in the preservation of society. The fulfillment of this role requires an understanding by lawyers of their relationship with and function in our legal system. A consequent obligation of lawyers is to maintain the highest standards of ethical conduct." ABA, *Model Code of Professional Responsibility,* Preamble, at p. 1 (1980) [hereinafter Code](footnote omitted).

2. For examples, see text accompanying notes 10-14 *infra.*

3. T. Macaulay, Lord Bacon, in 2 *Critical and Historical Essays* (F. Montague ed. 1903), pp. 121, 152.

4. Quoted in Curtis, "The Ethics of Advocacy," *Stanford Law Review* 4(1951):3, 20.

5. Id.

6. See M. Freedman, *Lawyers' Ethics in an Adversary System* (1975), pp. 27-42.

7. See Code, *supra* note 1, Canon 4, especially EC 4-1, EC 4-5, DR 4-101(A), DR 4-101(B), DR 4-101(C)(3).

8. See *id.* Canon 7, especially EC 7-27, DR 7-102(A)(4), (5), DR 7-102(B)(1). Also see ABA Project on Standards Relating to the Prosecution Function and the Defense Function § 7.7 (Approved Draft 1971).

9. I borrow this term from Wasserstrom, "Lawyers as Profesisonals: Some Moral Issues," *Human Rights Quarterly* 5 (1975):2-8.

10. People v. Belge, 83 Misc. 2d 186, 372 N.Y.S.2d 798 (Onondaga County Ct.), aff'd mem., 50 A.D. 2d 1088, 376 N.Y.S.2d 771 (1975), aff'd per curiam, 41 N.Y.2d 60, 359 N.E.2d 377, 390 N.Y.S. 2d 867 (1976).

11. See Code, *supra* note 1, EC 4-1, EC 4-4. Also see Callan & David, "Professional Responsibility and the Duty of Confidentiality: Disclosure of Client Misconduct in an Adversary System," *Rutgers Law Review* 29 (1976):332. The prosecution argued that failure to report the deaths amounted to a criminal violation of the New York State Public Health Law, 83 Misc. 2d at p. 187, 372 N.Y.S.2d at p. 799, which would render disclosure *permissible* under DR 4-101(C)(2).

On more general moral grounds, however, it is hard to imagine that the ends served by the Health Code could outweigh the demands of confidentiality, if consideration of the much more significant injury to the families of the murdered women could not.

12. 242 F.2d 452 (7th Cir. 1957), cited in Fried, "The Lawyer as Friend: The Moral Foundations of the Lawyer-Client Relation," *Yale Law Journal* 85 (1976): 132, 154 n. 13.

13. The *Zabella* court reasoned that "[o]f course, the jury was justified in thinking that defendant who then was in a position of some affluence and was the Chief Executive Officer of the Chicago Savings and Loan Association should feel obligated to pay an honest debt to his old friend, employee and countryman. Nevertheless, we are obliged to follow the law of Illinois." 242 F.2d at 455.

14. See Code, *supra* note 1, EC 7-1, DR 7-101(A)(1).

15. Perhaps one of the most serious general objections to Utilitarianism is that, although it professes to give full respect to all sources of value, it creates its simple normative structure by reducing all such values to a single dimension. The net effect is that either it distorts radically the world of human concerns, or it limits its scope to that range of values to which its simplifying assumptions are most natural. See generally S. Hampshire, *Two Theories of Morality* (1977), pp. 25-26; R. Unger, *Knowledge and Politics* (1975), pp. 86-88.

16. Nagel, "The Fragmentation of Value," in *Mortal Questions* (1979), p. 134. See also S. Hampshire, *supra* note 15.

17. See Nagel, *supra* note 16, at p. 135.

18. See generally Aristotle, *Nicomachean Ethics,* bk. VI (H. Rackham trans. 1962).

19. See S. Hampshire, *supra* note 16, at pp. 28-39; Nagel, *supra* note 16, at p. 135. See also Hampshire, "Public and Private Morality," in *Public and Private Morality* (S. Hampshire ed. 1978), pp. 29-33.

20. I borrow this example, for an entirely different purpose, from Williams, "Moral Luck," *Proceedings of the Aristotelian Society* 50 (Supp. 1976): 115, 124.

21. One aspect of the failure of professionals in law to appreciate the moral costs of their actions is captured by G. K. Chesterton:

> [T]he horrible thing about all legal officials, even the best, about all judges, magistrates, barristers, detectives, and policemen, is not that they are wicked (some of them are good), not that they are stupid (several of them are quite intelligent), it is simply that they have got used to it.
>
> Strictly they do not see the prisoner in the dock; all they see is the usual man in the usual place. They do not see the awful court of judgment; they only see their own workshop.

Chesterton, "The Twelve Men," in *Tremendous Trifles* (1955), pp. 57-58.

22. See Haydon, "On Being Responsible," *Philosophical Quarterly* 28 (1978):46, 46-57.

23. This appears to be the approach suggested by Wasserstrom. See Wasserstrom, *supra* note 9 at p. 12.

24. A useful formal discussion of exclusionary reasons can be found in J. Raz, *Practical Reasons and Norms* (1975), pp. 35-48.

25. By "conceptions of the lawyer's role," I do not mean some abstract model of a laywer's professional behavior. Rather I have in mind the more or less complex pattern of beliefs and attitudes which tend to structure a person's practical judgment and his view of his actions and relations to others, *i.e.,* his view of himself in the role. Although there is a personal or idiosyncratic element in any person's conception, nevertheless, because the role of lawyer is largely socially defined, significant public or shared elements are also involved. I shall concentrate on these latter elements, keeping in mind that they are shared elements in an individual's conception of himself in the role.

26. Although my argument has general implications for the evaluation of conceptions of many professional roles, I shall restrict my attention here to what I shall call the standard conception of the lawyer's role.

27. Samuel Johnson is often quoted with approval in support of this idea: "[A] lawyer has no business with the justice or injustice of the cause which he undertakes, unless his client asks his

opinion, and then he is bound to give it honestly. The justice or injustice of the cause is to be decided by the Judge.'" Boswell's Journal of a Tour to the Hebrides, August 15, 1773, at 14 (F. Pottee & C. Bennett eds. 1936) (quoted in M. Freedman, *supra* note 6, at 151).

28. J.-P. Sartre, *Existentialism and Humanism* (P. Mairet trans. 1948).

29. See generally *id.* at pp. 45-58.

30. E. Goffman, *Encounters* (1961), pp. 87-88.

31. Consider, for example, the epitaph on a Scottish gravestone: "'Here lies Tammas Jones, who was born a man and died a grocer.'" D. Emmet, *Rules, Roles and Relations* (1966) (quoting W. Sperry, *The Ethical Basis of Medical Practice* [1951], p. 41).

32. I am indebted to Bernard Williams' lectures at the Institute on Law and Ethics sponsored by the Council for Philosophical Studies in 1977 for the remarks at this point.

33. Curtis, *supra* note 4, at p. 22 (1951) (quoting R. Ellman, Yeats [1949], p. 178).

34. See Bellow & Kettleson, "The Mirror of Public Interest Ethics: Problems and Paradoxes," in *Professional Responsibility: A Guide for Attorneys* (1978), pp. 219, 257-258:

> At the root of the dilemma is a professional ethic that requires a sharp separation between personal and professional morality. The lawyer is asked to do "as a professional" what he or she would not do "as a person"; to subordinate personal qualms about results in particular cases to the general rule of law and the bar's role within it. There is much to be said for such a combination of responsibility and neutrality, if the "law job" is to be performed. But it may be that over time, such a division between the personal and the professional will atrophy those qualities of moral sensitivity and awareness upon which all ethical behavior depends.

35. See Elkins, "The Legal Persona: An Essay on the Professional Mask," *Virginia Law Review* 64 (1978): 735, 749, which argues that the pressure upon lawyers to identify with their role comes from a number of pervasive factors, including linguistic factors, specialized modes of reasoning, and even characteristic clothing styles.

36. As a result, serious questions arise when the lawyer acts negligently or irresponsibly. Is the client, thereby, committed to the consequences of such actions, of which he may not have been aware or did not approve? In general, the client is committed, failure of counsel to appear or respond may result in a default judgment as effectively as if the client never retained counsel in the first place. See Mazor, "Power and Responsibility in the Attorney-Client Relation," *Stanford Law Review* 20 (1968): 1121-23, 1124 and n. 24.

37. Wasserstrom, *supra* note 9, at p. 14.

38. See generally Simon, "The Ideology Of Advocacy: Procedural Justice and Professional Ethics," *Wisconsin Law Review* (1978):30, 96; Code, *supra* note 1. DR 7-106 (C) (4) (attorneys prohibited from expressing personal opinions regarding, *inter alia*, the justness of a cause).

39. See note 34 *supra*.

40. Cf. A. Neier, *Defending My Enemy* (1979) (belief in the higher value of the legal system *qua* system necessitates defending persons and causes antithetical to the lawyer's own beliefs).

41. This point was suggested to me by Philippe Nonet.

42. See generally R. Dworkin, *Taking Rights Seriously,* (1977), ch. 4; H.L.A. Hart, *The Concept of Law* (1961), pp. 199, 205-207; D. Richards, *The Moral Criticism of Law* (1977), pp. 31-36.

43. See text accompanying note 33 *supra*.

44. See text accompanying notes 15-19 *supra*.

45. This may explain, in part, the attitude of "ethical minimalism" among lawyers which many, both within and outside the profession, deplore. This minimalism is an understandable reaction, in light of the fact that there are few fixed and settled rules in the Code and the lawyer is effectively cut off from the resources to resolve the indeterminacies unavoidably left by the Code.

46. See p. 162 *supra*.

47. Williams, "Politics and Moral Character," in *Private and Public Morality* (S. Hampshire ed. 1978), p. 64. Milgram's well-known experiments underscore the commonplace that the more we are able to distance ourselves (often literally) from the consequences of our actions, the more we able able to inflict pain and suffering on others without moral qualms. See generally S. Milgram, *Obedience to Authority: An Experimental View* (1974), pp. 32-43.

48. Fried, *supra* note 12, at p. 154.

49. Tammas Jones, see note 31 *supra,* was not just a grocer; he was also, *inter alia,* a father, husband, friend, and neighbor. It was possible for him to relate to his family, customers, neighbors, and friends, not as a role-agent, but as a person, because it could have been recognized that his moral personality penetrated through his activities in his roles, and that these roles did not exhaust that personality.

50. E. Goffman, *supra* note 30, at p. 142.

51. David Hoffman, a nineteenth-century legal educator in Maryland, offered a conception of lawyering in which the lawyer's sense of responsibiilty was central. 2 D. Hoffman, *A Course of Legal Study* (2d ed. 1836) (I am indebted to Michael Kelly for this reference.). Hoffman wrote: "My client's conscience, and my own, are distinct entities; and though my vocation may sometimes justify my maintaining as facts, or principles, in doubtful cases, what may be neither one nor the other, I shall ever claim the privilege of solely judging to what extent to go." *Id.* at p. 755. Furthermore, he insisted that:

> Should my client be disposed to insist on captious requisitions, or frivolous and vexatious defences, they shall be neither enforced nor countenanced by me. . . . If, after duly examining a case, I am persuaded that my client's claim or defence . . . cannot, or rather ought not, to be sustained, I will promptly advise him to abandon it. To press it further in such a case, with the hope of gleaning some advantage by an extorted compromise, would be lending myself to a dishonourable use of legal means, in order to gain a *portion* of that, the *whole* of which I have reason to believe would be denied to him both by law and justice.

Id. at p. 754.

52. S. Kadish & M. Kadish, *Discretion to Disobey* (1973), pp. 31-36.

53. See *id.* at pp. 33-34.

54. *Id.*

55. *Id.* at p. 35.

56. *Id.* at pp. 35-36.

57. See Fried, *supra* note 12, at p. 155 n. 17.

58. See Freedman, "Personal Responsibility in a Professional System," *Catholic University Law Review* 27 (1978): 191, 193-195.

59. Code, *supra* note 1, DR 2-109(A)(1).

60. *Id.* DR 2-109(A)(2).

61. *Id.* EC 2-30.

62. *Id.* EC 2-26.

63. See *id.* DR 2-110(C).

64. *Id.* DR 2-110(C)(1)(a). Withdrawal is permitted for a number of reasons, all unrelated to the present argument. These include, among others, failure by the client to pay fees, DR 2-110(C)(1)(f), and inability to work effectively with co-counsel, DR 2-110(c)(3).

65. *Id.* DR 2-110(C)(1)(b), (c).

66. *Id.* DR 2-110(B)(1). Withdrawal is mandated for a variety of morally neutral reasons, such as a conflict of interest with another client whom the lawyer is representing, DR 2-110(B)(2); see DR 5-105, or the lawyer's ill health, DR 2-110(B)(3).

67. *Id.* EC 2-30.

68. The Code *does* allow permissive withdrawal, however, if the client insists that the lawyer engage in conduct that is contrary to the lawyer's advice and judgment *and the matter is not before a tribunal. Id.* DR 2-110(C)(1)(e).

69. Fried. *supra* note 12, at p. 140.

70. *Id.* at p. 142.

71. *Id.* at p. 140.

72. *Id.* at pp. 147-151.

73. *Id.* at pp. 149-151.

74. *Id.*

75. *Id.* at pp. 149-150.

76. *Id.* at pp. 150-151.

PROBLEMS

A CLIENT WHOM A LIE MIGHT HELP

You have represented Bonji Bosso for many years—indeed, until two years ago when he was duly and legally committed to a mental hospital as a person of unsound mind. You attended the competency hearing at his request and did what you could for him there. You have no doubt about his incompetency or about the propriety of his commitment and retention. But Bosso does. In fact, he believes himself to be wholly competent and therefore illegally restrained. He frequently writes begging you to do something to get him out of the mental hospital. These letters leave you with no doubt that Bosso is not ready to get out.

A few weeks ago, one of the hospital's psychologists called you to ask whether you could tell Bosso that you are working on his release. The psychologist thought that such a statement on your part might have a soothing effect on him and so make treating him easier and more likely to succeed. Since that call, you have also received calls from some members of Bosso's family urging you to do as the psychologist asked. You can think of no good-faith argument for Bosso's release. Should you agree to humor your former client?

NEGOTIATING WITH THE PROSECUTOR.

You are sitting in the office of Fred Grim, county prosecutor. Under discussion is the case of Vinnie Krule, your client by court appointment. Krule is charged with one count of rape (six to thirty years upon conviction, with no chance of probation). You and Grim are the only ones in the room. After examining the file on his desk, Grim says: "Since your client has, as I read here, no previous criminal record, I'm willing to knock the charge down to the lesser included offense of gross sexual imposition, in return for a guilty plea. I am also prepared to recommend probation. I wouldn't do this if your client weren't a first offender. Frankly, in person he looks to me like a real masher. Is the deal okay with you?"

Gross sexual imposition means a sentence of between six months and five years, some or all of which could be served on probation. Fred has a reputation as a good prosecutor and a decent man. It is well known that he does not make a charge unless he believes he can convict. He is also known to avoid rape prosecutions except in cases of repeat offenders.

On the other hand, your client is, as Fred suggests, a *real masher*. Besides a rape conviction, his criminal record includes two rape charges (later dropped), a conviction for armed robbery, and two convictions for aggravated assault. You know this because your client admitted the rape charges and the armed robbery conviction to you, and because you thereafter verified his admissions at the Hall of Records, discovering the rape and aggravated assault convictions at the same time.

180

You know Fred only professionally, seeing him a couple times a year to plea bargain for someone like Krule. You have a general practice that seldom includes a criminal case. You know the judge will use the same file Grim has on his desk. You suppose some clerk pulled the wrong record.

What would you do? What should you do?

CRAZY JANE TAKES THE STAND

You don't usually do criminal cases. But one day you receive a call from Judge Vernolli: Your name has reached the top of the bar list, he said, and would you handle a case? You agree, having been told by the partners in your firm that the best way for a young associate to get trial experience is to serve on the bar panel, taking those cases which legal aid for some reason cannot.

Your client is one Crazy Jane Fish, accused of assault with a deadly weapon. The person allegedly assaulted is a bartender about twice her size; the weapon appears to have been a beer bottle. The assault took place in a nearly empty tavern early one Saturday morning. The only witness may well have been drunk.

The first time you talk to Crazy Jane, you ask her why she is called *Crazy* Jane. She says, "Because I'm crazy, don't you know."

Jane refuses to plea bargain, even though, as you have already told her, you probably can get her a short probation in return for a plea of simple assault. But you're happy with her refusal, since you took the case for the trial practice. Nevertheless, you carefully explain the risks of trial. She responds that it's okay to take the risks because she is innocent. You again explain, adding that, if the facts are as she claims them to be, she is guilty of assault *at least* and, if the prosecutor can convince the judge of that, she will be found guilty of assault and perhaps of assault with a deadly weapon. She again says it's okay, adding that "the assault was justified."

Jane probably did commit an assault, though not assault with a *deadly* weapon. From all you know, the prosecutor will have trouble getting a conviction even on the simple assault. Crazy Jane is, after all, half the size of the man she assaulted, she succeeded in doing him no visible harm, and there is only one witness against her (in addition to the bartender) and he is probably unreliable.

The only thing that could convict Crazy Jane is her taking the stand and telling her side of the story. Her reason for wanting to do it does not concern the merits of the case. "I want the judge to know what I did and why. I don't care if I go to jail. The bartender made fun of my religion. He deserved to have his lousy face bashed in. And I would have done it too, if I hadn't slipped. I want everybody to know that."

Should you prevent her from taking the stand? If so, how? If not, should you continue as her attorney? After all, she seems to want to use the court for nonlegal purposes.

Suggested Readings

For other works on issues raised here, see Bibliography, Part 2, especially Frankena (1963), Sartorius (1975), or Harman (1977) for general introductions to ethics; Bayles (1981) or Goldman (1980) for introductions to professional ethics; and Luban (1981), Shaffer (1979), Schwartz (1978), and Wolf (1984) for discussions of professionalism in law.

Part III

The Adversary System

Introduction

THREE SENSES OF "ADVERSARY SYSTEM"

Lawyers sometimes do for their clients what they would not do for anyone else: for example, ask humiliating questions in front of a crowded courtroom, evict a poor widow from her home of fifty years, or fail to reveal that a corporation is poisoning the local drinking water. Lawyers often justify (or, at least, excuse) such acts by pointing to their professional role in the "adversary system." The critique of professionalism has already suggested that the adversary system might be much of what makes lawyering in the United States more troubling morally than, say, teaching or medicine. Wasserstrom and Postema are both concerned that the adversary system tends to generate an amoral view of life. Fried does not deny such a tendency, arguing only that a good person could be a good lawyer. Even Fried leaves open the question whether we might be better off under some other system. In this section, we will look into that open question.

What is the "adversary system"? The term has at least three senses, which are not always clearly distinguished. In one sense, an adversary system is any system of trial that recognizes opposing parties ("adverse interests"). No legal system is completely adversary in this sense. Even under Anglo-American law, some legal proceedings (for example, adoption or name changing) do not have adverse parties. But some systems are less adversary than ours. In most civil law countries, for example, contracts are regularly drawn up and signed before an impartial notary without the intervention of partisan lawyers. In Bulgaria and Cuba even criminal proceedings seem to be nonadversary. While the accused may have an attorney, the attorney is not there to fight the state. The client's interests are supposed to be the same as the state's, that is, to determine whether he is guilty and, if he is, to determine what it would be best for society (and him) to do. The defense attorney is there—much as attorneys in our own juvenile courts used to be—to present what the client knows.

In another sense of "adversary system," the term is contrasted with "inquisitorial." The common law form of trial is adversarial (or "accusatorial"); the civil law form, "inquisitorial." An adversary system is (in this sense) defined by a division of functions *at trial* rather than (as in the previous sense) by an opposition of interests. Under an adversary system the judge is relatively passive, while the attorneys before him are relatively active. The judge does not make an independent investigation, has little to say about which witnesses are called or

185

what they will be asked, and may even depend upon the opposing attorneys to raise relevant points of law, to brief legal points so raised, and to help draft an opinion. Under an inquisitorial system, on the other hand, the judge is relatively active. He (or, more commonly, one of a panel) will make a preliminary investigation of the case, prepare a file to put into evidence, decide who will be called as witnesses, and do most of the questioning. The parties' attorneys can, of course, advise on such matters; and, from time to time, counsel may ask a question or two helpful to their side. But their role, though adverse, is quite secondary until all the evidence has been presented. Each attorney ("advocate") is then permitted to argue his client's position. Under the inquisitorial system, lawyers tend to be only interpreters of evidence (and law), not (as under the adversary system) presenters as well. There are, of course, no pure inquisitorial or adversarial systems, but systems do seem to be very much one or the other. Even among democratic countries, the inquisitorial system is more common than the adversarial.

"Adversary system" may also be used in a third sense to refer to a certain *style* of lawyering. Lawyers act as if all persons but their client were potential (or actual) adverse litigants and all questions of law or justice should be left to be decided by trial. There is (as in the second sense) a division of labor, but this division is not confined to the courtroom. In this third sense, the adversary system is a complete form of professional life. An attorney in a civil law country may adopt the adversary style as easily as any attorney in a common law country. The procedures at trial do not make it much more or less reasonable to leave certain questions to be decided by trial.

This third sense of "adversary system" is also independent of the first. A lawyer might, for example, think of trial as a cooperative attempt to determine what justice requires and yet still suppose other legal relations between persons to be adversarial (in our third sense). "If I have gotten too much for my client," the lawyer may reason, "it will come out at trial and justice will be done. It's not my concern now. My concern is to get all I can for my client."

The first selection in this section, a report of the Joint Conference on Professional Responsibility, is an example of the importance the idea of profession has for lawyers' discussions of legal ethics. In this official ABA document, Lon L. Fuller and John D. Randall agree that the "adversary system" represents "the chief obstacle" to lay people, law students, and even lawyers understanding the lawyer's professional responsibilities. They therefore undertake a defense of the system that will (they hope) make sense of what lawyers do. Their defense is not intended to show merely that what lawyers do is legal and useful to their clients. Instead, Fuller and Randall try to show that what lawyers do (within the adversary system) is a *public* service. In the courtroom, lawyers serve justice by serving their clients; outside, they serve their clients by serving justice.

Fuller and Randall seem not to see the ambiguity of "adversary system."

Their concern is to dispel the charge that a lawyer is "nothing but a hired brain and voice" (and so, not the member of a profession at all). This charge is older than the common law, older even than the legal profession. Thus, twenty-three hundred years ago, Socrates was already describing the lawyer (or, at least, the sort of person who goes to court a lot) much as Wasserstrom and Postema did in the last section:

> He is always in a hurry; . . . and there is his adversary standing over him, enforcing his rights; the affidavit, which in their phraseology is termed the brief, is recited; and from this he must not deviate. He is a servant before his master, who is seated, and has the cause in his hands; . . . . The consequence has been, that he has become keen and shrewd; he has learned how to flatter his master in word and indulge him in deed; but his soul is small and unrighteous. His slavish condition has deprived him of growth and uprightness and independence; dangers and fears, which were too much for his truth and honesty, came upon him in early years, when the tenderness of youth was unequal to them, and has driven him into crooked ways; from the first he has practiced deception and retaliation, and has become stunted and warped. And so he has passed out of youth into manhood, having no soundness in him; and is now, as he thinks, a master of wisdom. Such is the lawyer, Theodorus. (*Theaetetus* III: 172-173)

Though the charge of being a hired brain and voice ("a servant") is quite old, Fuller and Randall unaccountably take their problem to be defending the practice of law within the adversary system understood in our second sense, that is, as trial before a relatively passive judge. Their defense is provocative. The role of partisan advocate is, they argue, not a regrettable necessity but an indispensble part of the larger ordering of affairs. It is their claim that attempts to dispense with the distinct roles traditionally implied in adjudication under the common law have generally "failed." The truth, it is thought, is most likely to come from the clash of partisans before an impartial judge who has not had to invest himself in preparing the case. The partisan advocate's zeal in his client's cause promotes a wise and informed decision in the best way possible. That zeal should not, of course, extend to making "muddy the headwaters of decision." For Fuller and Randall "zeal" does not include lying, fabricating evidence, or misstating the law. Does "zeal" include failing to reveal adverse facts or law, asking "leading questions," or humiliating a witness? They do not say.

The benefits of partisan advocacy appear, according to Fuller and Randall, only in the special environment of "open court." Elsewhere lawyers need not (and indeed should not) behave as partisan advocates. The same lawyer who should be zealous in his defense of a guilty client should not participate as legal adviser in conduct that is immoral, unfair, or of doubtful legality. He should instead be at pains to preserve sufficient detachment from his client's interests to remain capable of sound and objective appraisal of the propriety of what the client proposes to do. Indeed, even in open court, not all lawyers are equaly free to engage in partisan advocacy. The public prosecutor should not, Fuller and

Randall say, take as his guide the standards of an attorney appearing on behalf of an individual. The prosecutor must recall that he occupies a dual role: being obligated, on the one hand, to furnish the adversary element essential for informed decision and, on the other, to see that impartial justice is done.

Fuller and Randall thus seem to defend only a limited version of the adversary system (even in our second sense of that term). The adversary style (our third sense) is justified only in the courtroom and then only for an advocate acting for a private party. That limit seems odd given the advantages Fuller and Randall find in partisan advocacy. If the adversary trial is the best means for getting at the truth, why should the prosecutor not leave impartial justice to the judge instead of preempting the judge's role? Why should a lawyer not always resolve all reasonable doubts in favor of his client (when it is in the client's interest to do so) even when he is advising? Why should he not leave the courts to decide what is legal or just?

Edmund Byrne is also primarily interested in the "adversary system" in the second sense (though he now and then also makes criticism of the adversarial style in our third sense). His catalogue of the ills of the adversary system in the United States today is a sobering counter to the praise Fuller and Randall offer. Byrne argues that few cases are actually heard before an impartial judge. Most cases, both civil and criminal, are settled outside of court by negotiation between the parties. Most criminal cases are plea-bargained, a judge having only a formal part in accepting the plea. Civil cases are often settled by arbitration when ordinary negotiation fails. The adversary system is almost too cumbersome to use. What it contributes to justice is an apparent arbitrariness that makes all parties prefer to escape trial if they can. The power of attorneys to shape the evidence, raise points of law, and control the flow of information to the judge has made many a trial into a joust between private attorneys rather than a public search for truth. The delays possible under the adversary system have produced cases lasting for a generation. The adversary system itself, not the alternatives, seems to Byrne to be a failure. It is hard to believe that he is talking about the same system Fuller and Randall are.

Perhaps he is not. Simon shifts the focus of discussion in a way that might explain such a possibility. Simon is concerned with the "ideology of advocacy." In this context, an ideology is a system of belief largely independent of experience. Ideology provides rationalization for what we do, not (good) reasons. A particular ideology is more likely to be useful than true. So, to describe a set of beliefs as an ideology is already to call its truth into question.

For Simon, the ideology of advocacy is primarily a defense of the adversary system in our third sense, a certain style of lawyering, the lawyer's "explicit refusal to be bound by personal and social norms which he considers binding on [nonlawyers]." We thus return to the question of professionalism, which was taken up in the preceding chapter. Simon identifies three different defenses of the adversarial style, each one relying upon what seems to be a different theory of law.

One defense, that of the "positivist," understands law to consist of whatever commands or rules happen to issue from those having authority to issue them. Laws that are vague or incomplete are to be filled in by the courts. For a positivist, a person's legal rights are just what he can get the lawgiver, whether legislator or judge, to say they are. A lawyer cannot know what his client's legal rights are until there has been a final authoritative ruling on the question. So, a lawyer who refuses to use all his skill on behalf of his client has simply weakened his client's case.

The second defense, that of the "purposivist," understands the law as an expression of certain common human purposes, an organic part of everyday life rather than the arbitrary injunctions of some outside authority. The purposivist can tell whether her client is seeking legal justice. She may nevertheless properly do all she legally can to achieve the client's ends, however unjust. She may do so because her *function* is to present his side, not to act as "judge and jury." If lawyer, judge, and jury each perform their assigned function, the system will be able to achieve its purpose, which is justice. Simon gives Fuller and Randall as examples of purposivists.

The third defense Simon identifies, the "ritualist," understands legal procedure as having not justice but people's ability to express themselves *through* legal acts as its end. The process *is* the purpose for "ritualists." The lawyer is a play-actor rather than someone who really does something. As a lawyer, he can do no wrong because his acts are all legal acts and as such are like "actions" in a play, satisfying but (ordinarily) not what they seem. Simon identifies Fried as a "ritualist."

Each of these three defenses tries to analyze the lawyer's role so that it serves the client's autonomy, responsibility, or dignity. Such an analysis, if successful, would provide a justification for anything lawyers do within their role. But, for Simon, each defense ends up a mere ideology because each flies in the face of experience. The adversary style necessarily (and systematically) fails to serve the client's autonomy, responsibility, and dignity. Simon therefore suggests substituting "nonprofessional advocacy" for the adversarial style. Like Wasserstrom and Postema, Simon is not suggesting that we do away with the profession of law (or with the adversary system in our second or first sense). He is suggesting only that we do away with the lawyer's "professionalism," her supposed moral insulation from the ends she pursues for her client.

SOLVING THE PROBLEM BY CHANGING THE RULES

In 1974, Marvin Frankel, then a federal judge, named as the chief fault of the "adversary system" the failure of partisan advocates to cooperate in the search for truth. He proposed to cure that fault by adding the following provision to the *Code of Professional Responsibility:*

(1) In his representation of a client, unless prevented from doing so by a privilege reasonably believed to apply, a lawyer shall:

   (a) Report to the court and opposing counsel the existence of relevant evidence or witnesses where the lawyer does not intend to offer such evidence or witnesses.

   (b) Prevent, or when prevention has proved unsuccessful, report to the court and opposing counsel the making of any untrue statement by client or witness or any omission to state a material fact necessary in order to make statements made, in the light of the circumstances under which they were made, not misleading.

   (c) Question witnesses with a purpose and design to elicit the whole truth, including particularly supplementary and qualifying matters that render evidence already given more accurate, intelligible, or fair than it otherwise would be.

(2) In the construction and application of the rules in subdivision (1), a lawyer shall be held to possess knowledge he actually has or, in the exercise of reasonable diligence, should have.[1]

Would adopting Frankel's proposal improve our legal system? If so, how? Would you recommend any other changes?

NOTE

1. Marvin E. Frankel, "The Search for Truth: An Umpireal View," *University of Pennsylvania Law Review* 123 (1975):1032-1059, p. 1059.

Lon L. Fuller and John D. Randall

Professional Responsibility:
Report of the Joint Conference

The Joint Conference on Professional Responsibility was established in 1952 by the American Bar Association and the Association of American Law Schools. At the first meeting of the Conference the general problem discussed was that of bringing home to the law student, the lawyer and the public an understanding of the nature of the lawyer's professional responsibilities. All present considered that the chief obstacle to the success of this undertaking lay in "the adversary system." Those who had attempted to arrange conferences on professional ethics between lawyers, on the one side, and philosophers and theologians, on the other, observed that communcation broke down at this point. Similarly, those who had attempted to teach ethical principles to law students found that the students were uneasy about the adversary system, some thinking of it as an unwholesome compromise with the combativeness of human nature, others vaguely approving of it but disturbed by their inability to articulate its proper limits. Finally, it was observed that the legal profession is itself generally not very philosophic about this issue. Confronted by the layman's charge that he is nothing but a hired brain and voice, the lawyer often finds it difficult to convey an insight into the value of the adversary system or an understanding of the tacit restraints with which it is infused.

Accordingly, it was decided that the first need was for a reasoned statement of the lawyer's responsibilities, set in the context of the adversary system. The statement printed below is intended to meet that need. It is not expected that all lawyers will agree with every detail of the statement, particularly in matters of emphasis. It was considered, however, that the statement would largely fail of its purpose if it were confined to generalities too broad to elicit dissent, but, by the same token, too broad to sharpen insight or to stimulate useful discussion.

The Conference would welcome proposals as to ways in which its statement may be put to use. It would also be grateful for suggestions of further steps that

From *American Bar Association Journal,* 44 (December 1958):1159-1218. Reprinted in edited form with permission from the *ABA Journal.*

may be taken to convey to students, laymen and lawyers a better understanding of the role played by the profession and of the restraints inherent in that role.

LON L. FULLER
JOHN D. RANDALL
Co-Chairmen of the Joint
Conference on Professional
Responsibility

I

A profession to be worthy of the name must inculcate in its members a strong sense of the special obligations that attach to their calling. One who undertakes the practice of a profession cannot rest content with the faithful discharge of duties assigned to him by others. His work must find its direction within a larger frame. All that he does must evidence a dedication, not merely to a specific assignment, but to the enduring ideals of his vocation. Only such a dedication will enable him to reconcile fidelity to those he serves with an equal fidelity to an office that must at all times rise above the involvements of immediate interest.

The legal profession has its traditional standards of conduct, its codified Canons of Ethics. The lawyer must know and respect these rules established for the conduct of his professional life. At the same time he must realize that a letter-bound observance of the Canons is not equivalent to the practice of professional responsibility.

A true sense of professional responsibility must derive from an understanding of the reasons that lie back of specific restraints, such as those embodied in the Canons. The grounds for the lawyer's peculiar obligations are to be found in the nature of his calling. The lawyer who seeks a clear understanding of his duties will be led to reflect on the special services his profession renders to society and the services it might render if its full capacities were realized. When the lawyer fully understands the nature of his office, he will then discern what restraints are necessary to keep that office wholesome and effective.

Under the conditions of modern practice it is peculiarly necessary that the lawyer should understand, not merely the established standards of professional conduct, but the reasons underlying these standards. Today the lawyer plays a changing and increasingly varied role. In many developing fields the precise contribution of the legal profession is as yet undefined. In these areas the lawyer who determines what his own contribution shall be is at the same time helping to shape the future role of the profession itself. In the duties that the lawyer must now undertake, the inherited traditions of the Bar often yield but an indirect guidance. Principles of conduct applicable to appearance in open court do not, for example, resolve the issues confronting the lawyer who must assume the delicate task of mediating among opposing interests. Where the lawyer's work is of sufficient public concern to become newsworthy, his audience is today often vastly expanded, while at the same time the issues in controversy are less readily understood than formerly. While performance under public scrutiny may at times reinforce the sense of professional obligation, it may also create grave temptations to unprofessional conduct.

For all these reasons the lawyer stands today in special need of a clear understanding of his obligations and of the vital connection between those obligations and the role his profession plays in society.

II

In modern society the legal profession may be said to perform three major services. The most obvious of these relates to the lawyer's role as advocate and counselor. The second has to do with the lawyer as one who designs a framework that will give form and direction to collaborative effort. His third service runs not to particular clients, but to the public as a whole.

The Lawyer's Service in the Administration and Development of the Law

The Lawyer's Role as Advocate in Open Court

The lawyer appearing as an advocate before a tribunal presents, as persuasively as he can, the facts and the law of the case as seen from the standpoint of his client's interest. It is essential that both the lawyer and the public understand clearly the nature of the role thus discharged. Such an understanding is required not only to appreciate the need for an adversary presentation of issues, but also in order to perceive truly the limits partisan advocacy must impose on itself if it is to remain wholesome and useful.

In a very real sense it may be said that the integrity of the adjudicative process itself depends upon the participation of the advocate. This becomes apparent when we contemplate the nature of the task assumed by any arbiter who attempts to decide a dispute without the aid of partisan advocacy.

Such an arbiter must undertake, not only the role of judge, but that of representative for both of the litigants. Each of these roles must be played to the full without being muted by qualifications derived from the others. When he is developing for each side the most effective statement of its case, the arbiter must put aside his neutrality and permit himself to be moved by a sympathetic identification sufficiently intense to draw from his mind all that it is capable of giving—in analysis, patience, and creative power. When he resumes his neutral position, he must be able to view with distrust the fruits of this identification and be ready to reject the products of his own best mental efforts. The difficulties of this undertaking are obvious. If it is true that a man in his time must play many parts, it is scarcely given to him to play them all at once.

It is small wonder, then, that failure generally attends the attempt to dispense with the distinct roles traditionally implied in adjudication. What generally occurs in practice is that at some early point a familiar pattern will seem to emerge from the evidence; an accustomed label is waiting for the case and, without awaiting further proofs, this label is promptly assigned to it. It is a mistake to suppose that this premature cataloguing must necessarily result from impatience, prejudice or mental sloth. Often it proceeds from a very understandable desire to bring the hearing into some order and coherence, for without some tentative theory of the case there is no standard of relevance by which testimony may be measured. But what starts as a preliminary diagnosis designed to direct the inquiry tends, quickly and imperceptibly, to become a fixed conclusion, as all that confirms the diagnosis makes a strong imprint on the mind while all that runs counter to it is received with diverted attention.

An adversary presentation seems the only effective means for combatting this natural human tendency to judge too swiftly in terms of the familiar that which is not yet fully known. The arguments of counsel hold the case, as it were, in suspension between two opposing interpretations of it. While the proper classification of the case is thus kept unresolved, there is time to explore all of its peculiarities and nuances.

These are the contributions made by partisan advocacy during the public hearing of the cause. When we take into account the preparations that must precede the hearing, the essential quality of the advocate's contribution becomes even more apparent. Preceding the hearing, inquiries must be instituted to determine what facts can be proved or seem sufficiently established to warrant a formal test of their truth during the hearing. There must also be a preliminary analysis of the issues, so that the hearing may have form and direction. These preparatory measures are indispensable whether or not the parties involved in the controversy are represented by advocates.

Where that representation is present there is an obvious advantage in the fact that the area of dispute may be greatly reduced by an exchange of written pleadings or by stipulations of counsel. Without the participatin of someone who can act responsibly for each of the parties, this essential narrowing of the issues becomes impossible. But here again the true significance of partisan advocacy lies deeper, touching once more the integrity of the adjudicative process itself. It is only through the advocate's participation that the hearing may remain in fact what it purports to be in theory: a public trial of the facts and issues. Each advocate comes to the hearing prepared to present his proofs and arguments, knowing at the same time that his arguments may fail to persuade and that his proofs may be rejected as inadequate. It is a part of his role to absorb these possible disappointments. The deciding tribunal, on the other hand, comes to the hearing uncommitted. It has not represented to the public that any fact can be proved, that any argument is sound, or that any particular way of stating a litigant's case is the most effective expression of its merits.

The matter assumes a very different aspect when the deciding tribunal is compelled to take into its own hands the preparations that must precede the public hearing. In such a case the tribunal cannot truly be said to come to the hearing uncommitted, for it has itself appointed the channels along which the public inquiry is to run. If an unexpected turn in the testimony reveals a miscalculation in the design of these channels, there is no advocate to absorb the blame. The deciding tribunal is under a strong temptation to keep the hearing moving within the boundaries originally set for it. The result may be that the hearing loses its character as an open trial of the facts and issues, and becomes instead a ritual designed to provide public confirmation for what the tribunal considers it has already established in private. When this occurs adjudication acquires the taint affecting all institutions that become subject to manipulation, presenting one aspect to the public, another to knowing participants.

These, then, are the reasons for believing that partisan advocacy plays a vital and essential role in one of the most fundamental procedures of a democratic society. But if we were to put all of these detailed considerations on one side, we should still be confronted by the fact that, in whatever form adjudication may appear, the experienced judge or arbitrator desires and actively seeks to obtain an adversary presentation of the issues. Only when he has had the benefit of intelligent and vigorous advocacy on both sides can he feel fully confident of his decision.

Viewed in this light, the role of the lawyer as a partisan advocate appears not as a regrettable necessity, but as an indispensable part of a larger ordering of affairs. The institution of advocacy is not a concession to the frailties of human nature, but an expression of human insight in the design of a social framework within which man's capacity for impartial judgment can attain its fullest realization.

When advocacy is thus viewed, it becomes clear by what principle limits must be set to partisanship. The advocate plays his role well when zeal for his client's cause promotes a wise and informed decision of the case. He plays his role badly, and trespasses against the obligations of professional responsibility, when his desire to win leads him to muddy the headwaters of decision, when, instead of lending a needed perspective to the controversy, he distorts and obscures its true nature.

The Lawyer's Role as Counselor

Vital as is the lawyer's role in adjudication, it should not be thought that it is only as an advocate pleading in open court that he contributes to the administration of the law. The most effective realization of the law's aims often takes place in the attorney's office, where litigation is forestalled by anticipating its outcome, where the lawyer's quiet counsel takes the place of public force. Contrary to popular belief, the compliance with the law thus brought about is not generally lip-serving and narrow, for by reminding him of its long-run costs the lawyer often deters his client from a course of conduct technically permissible under existing law, though inconsistent with its underlying spirit and purpose.

Although the lawyer serves the administration of justice indispensably both as advocate and as office counselor, the demands imposed on him by these two roles must be sharply distinguished. The man who has been called into court to answer for his own actions is entitled to a fair hearing. Partisan advocacy plays its essential part in such a hearing, and the lawyer pleading his client's case may properly present it in the most favorable light. A similar resolution of doubts in one direction becomes inappropriate when the lawyer acts as counselor. The reasons that justify and even require partisan advocacy in the trial of a cause do not grant any license to the lawyer to participate as legal adviser in a line of conduct that is immoral, unfair, or of doubtful legality. In saving himself from this unworthy involvement, the lawyer cannot be guided solely by an unreflective inner sense of good faith; he must be at pains to preserve a sufficient detachment from his client's interests so that he remains capable of a sound and objective appraisal of the propriety of what his client proposes to do.

The Lawyer as One Who Designs the Framework of Collaborative Effort

In our society the great bulk of human relations are set, not by governmental decree, but by the voluntary action of the affected parties. Men come together to collaborate and to arrange their relations in many ways: by forming corporations, partnerships, labor unions, clubs and churches; by concluding contracts and leases; by entering a hundred other large and small transactions by which their rights and duties toward one another are defined.

Successful voluntary collaboration usually requires for its guidance something equivalent to a formal charter, defining the terms of the collaboration, anticipating and forfending against possible disputes, and generally providing a framework for the parties' future dealings. In our society the natural architect of this framework is the lawyer.

This is obvious where the transactions or relationship proposed must be fitted into existing law, either to insure legal enforcement or in order not to trespass against legal prohibitions. But the lawyer is also apt to be called upon to draft the bylaws of a social club or the terms of an agreement known to be unenforceable because cancelable by either party at any time. In these cases the lawyer functions, not as an expert in the rules of an existing government, but as one who brings into existence a government for the regulation of the parties' own relations. The skill thus exercised is essentially the same as that involved in drafting constitutions and international treaties. The fruits of this skill enter in large measure into the drafting of ordinary legal documents, though this fact is obscured by the mistaken notion that the lawyer's only concern in such cases is with possible future litigation, it being forgotten that an important part of his task is to design a framework of collaboration that will function in such a way that litigation will not arise.

As the examples just given have suggested, in devising charters of collaborative effort the lawyer often acts where all of the affected parties are present as participants. But the lawyer also performs a similar function in situations where this is not so, as, for example, in planning estates and drafting wills. Here the instrument defining the terms of collaboration may affect persons not present and often not born. Yet here, too, the good lawyer does not serve merely as a legal conduit for his client's desires, but as a wise counselor, experienced in the art of devising arrangements that will put in workable order the entangled affairs and interests of human beings.

The Lawyer's Opportunities and Obligations of Public Service

Private Practice as a Form of Public Service

There is a sense in which the lawyer must keep his obligations of public service distinct from the involvements of his private practice. This line of separation is aptly illustrated by an incident in the life of Thomas Talfourd. As a barrister Talfourd had successfully represented a father in a suit over the custody of a child. Judgment for Talfourd's client was based on his superior legal right, though the court recognized in the case at bar that the mother had a stronger moral claim to custody than the father. Having thus encountered in the course of his practice an injustice in the law as then applied by the courts, Talfourd later as a member of Parliament secured the enactment of a statute that would make impossible a repetition of the result his own advocacy had helped to bring about. Here the line is clearly drawn between the obligation of the advocate and the obligation of the public servant.

Yet in another case, Talfourd's devotion to public service grew out of his own enlightened view of his role as an advocate. It is impossible to imagine a lawyer who was narrow, crafty, quibbling or ungenerous in his private practice having the conception of public responsibility displayed by Talfourd. A sure sense of the broader obligations of the legal profession must have its roots in the lawyer's own practice. His public service must begin at home.

Private practice is a form of public service when it is conducted with an appreciation of, and a respect for, the larger framework of government of which it forms a part, including under the term government those voluntary forms of self-regulation already discussed in this statement. It is within this larger framework that the lawyer must seek the answer to what he must do, the limits of what he may do.

Thus, partisan advocacy is a form of public service so long as it aids the process of adjudication; it ceases to be when it hinders that process, when it misleads, distorts and obfuscates, when it renders the task of the deciding tribunal not easier, but more difficult. Judges are inevitably the mirrors of the Bar practicing before them; they can with difficulty rise above the sources on which they must depend in reaching their decision. The primary responsibility for preserving adjudication as a meaningful and useful social institution rests ultimately with the practicing legal profession.

Where the lawyer serves as negotiator and draftsman, he advances the public interest when he facilitates the processes of voluntary self-government; he works against the public interest when he obstructs the channels of collaborative effort, when he seeks petty advantages to the detriment of the larger processes in which he participates.

Private legal practice, properly pursued, is, then, itself a public service. This reflection should not induce a sense of complacency in the lawyer, nor lead him to disparage those forms of public service that fall outside the normal practice of law. On the contrary, a proper sense of the significance of his role as the representative of private clients will almost inevitably lead the lawyer into broader fields of public service.

The Lawyer as a Guardian of Due Process

The lawyer's highest loyalty is at the same time the most intangible. It is a loyalty that runs, not to persons, but to procedures and institutions. The lawyer's role imposes on him a trusteeship for the integrity of those fundamental processes of government and self-government upon which the successful functioning of our society depends.

All institutions, however sound in purpose, present temptations to interested exploitation, to abusive short cuts, to corroding misinterpretations. The forms of democracy may be observed while means are found to circumvent inconvenient consequences resulting from a compliance with those forms. A lawyer recreant to his responsibilities can so disrupt the hearing of a cause as to undermine those rational foundations without which an adversary proceeding loses its meaning and its justification. Everywhere democratic and constitutional government is tragically dependent on voluntary and understanding cooperation in the maintenance of its fundamental processes and forms.

It is the lawyer's duty to preserve and advance this indispensable cooperation by keeping alive the willingness to engage in it and by imparting the understanding necessary to give it direction and effectiveness. This is a duty that attaches not only to his private practice, but to his relations with the public. In this matter he is not entitled to take public opinion as a datum by which to orient and justify his actions. He has an affirmative duty to help shape the growth and development of public attitudes toward fair procedures and due process.

Without this essential leadership, there is an inevitable tendency for practice to drift downward to the level of those who have the least understanding of the issues at stake, whose experience of life has not taught them the vital importance of preserving just and proper forms of procedure. It is chiefly for the lawyer that the term "due process" takes on tangible meaning, for whom it indicates what is allowable and what is not, who realizes what a ruinous cost is incurred when its demands are disregarded. For the lawyer the insidious danger contained in the notion that "the end justifies the means" is not a matter of abstract philosophic conviction, but of direct professional experience. If the lawyer fails to do his part in educating the public to these dangers, he fails in one of his highest duties.

Making Legal Services Available to All

If there is any fundamental proposition of government on which all would agree, it is that one of the highest goals of society must be to achieve and maintain equality before the law. Yet this ideal remains an empty form of words unless the legal profession is ready to provide adequate representation for those unable to pay the usual fees.

At present this representation is being supplied in some measure through the spontaneous generosity of individual lawyers, through legal aid societies, and—increasingly—through the organized efforts of the Bar. If those who stand in need of this service know of its availability, and their need is in fact adequately met, the precise mechanism by which this service is provided becomes of secondary importance. It is of great importance, however, that both the impulse to render this service, and the plan for making that impulse effective, should arise within the legal profession itself.

The moral position of the advocate is here at stake. Partisan advocacy finds its justification in the contribution it makes to a sound and informed disposition of controversies. Where this contribution is lacking, the partisan position permitted to the advocate loses its reason for being. The legal profession has, therefore, a clear moral obligation to see to it that those already handicapped do not suffer the cumulative disadvantage of being without proper legal representation, for it is obvious that adjudication can neither be effective nor fair where only one side is represented by counsel.

In discharging this obligation, the legal profession can help to bring about a better understanding of the role of the advocate in our system of government. Popular misconceptions of the advocate's function disappear when the lawyer pleads without a fee, and the true value of his service to society is immediately perceived. The insight thus obtained by the public promotes a deeper understanding of the work of the legal profession as a whole.

The obligation to provide legal services for those actually caught up in litigation carries with it the obligation to make preventive legal advice accessible to all. It is among those unaccustomed to business affairs and fearful of the ways of the law that such advice is often most needed. If it is not received in time, the most valiant and skillful representation in court may come too late.

The Representation of Unpopular Causes

One of the highest services the lawyer can render to society is to appear in court on behalf of clients whose causes are in disfavor with the general public.

Under our system of government the process of adjudication is surrounded by safeguards evolved from centuries of experience. These safeguards are not designed merely to lend formality and decorum to the trial of causes. They are predicated on the assumption that to secure for any controversy a truly informed and dispassionate decision is a difficult thing, requiring for its achievement a special summoning and organization of human effort and the adoption of measures to exclude the biases and prejudgments that have free play outside the courtroom. All of this goes for naught if the man with an unpopular cause is unable to find a competent lawyer courageous enough to represent him. His chance to have his day in court loses much of its meaning if his case is handicapped from the outset by the very kind of prejudgment our rules of evidence and procedure are intended to prevent.

Where a cause is in disfavor because of a misunderstanding by the public, the service of the lawyer representing it is obvious, since he helps to remove an obloquy unjustly attaching to his client's position. But the lawyer renders an equally important, though less readily understood, service where the unfavorable public opinion of the client's cause is in fact justified. It is essential for a sound and wholesome development of public opinion that the disfavored cause have its full day in court, which includes, of necessity, representation by competent counsel. Where this does not occur, a fear arises that perhaps more might have been said for the losing side and suspicion is cast on the decision reached. Thus, confidence in the fundamental processes of government is diminished.

The extent to which the individual lawyer should feel himself bound to undertake the representation of unpopular causes must remain a matter for individual conscience. The legal profession as a whole, however, has a clear moral obligation to represent the client whose cause is in popular disfavor, the organized Bar can not only discharge an obligation incumbent on it, but at the same time relieve the individual lawyer of the stigma that might otherwise unjustly attach to his appearance on behalf of such a cause. If the courage and the initiative of the individual lawyer make this step unnecessary, the legal profession should in any event strive to promote and maintain a moral atmosphere in which he may render this service without ruinous cost to himself. No member of the Bar should indulge in public criticism of another lawyer because he has undertaken the representation of causes in general disfavor. Every member of the profession should, on the contrary, do what he can to promote a public understanding of the service rendered by the advocate in such situations.

The Lawyer and Legal Reform

There are few great figures in the history of the Bar who have not concerned themselves with the reform and improvement of the law. The special obligation of the profession with respect to legal reform rests on considerations too obvious to require enumeration. Certainly it is the lawyer who has both the best chance to know when the law is working badly and the special competence to put it in order.

When the lawyer fails to interest himself in the improvement of the law, the reason does not ordinarily lie in a lack of perception. It lies rather in a desire to retain the comfortable fit of accustomed ways, in a distaste for stirring up controversy within the profession, or perhaps in a hope that if enough time is allowed to pass, the need for change will become so obvious that no special effort will be required to accomplish it.

The lawyer tempted by repose should recall the heavy costs paid by his profession when needed legal reform has to be accomplished through the initiative of public-spirited laymen. Where change must be thrust from without upon an unwilling Bar, the public's least flattering picture of the lawyer seems confirmed. The lawyer concerned for the standing of his profession will, therefore, interest himself actively in the improvement of the law. In doing so he will not only help to maintain confidence in the Bar, but will have the satisfaction of meeting a responsibility inhering in the nature of his calling.

The Lawyer as Citizen

Law should be so practiced that the lawyer remains free to make up his own mind how he will vote, what causes he will support, what economic and political philosophy he will espouse. It is one of the glories of the profession that it admits of this freedom. Distinguished examples can be cited of lawyers whose views were at variance from those of their clients, lawyers whose skill and wisdom made them valued advisers to those who had little sympathy with their views as citizens.

Broad issues of social policy can and should, therefore, be approached by the lawyer without the encumbrance of any special obligation derived from his profession. To this proposition there is, perhaps, one important qualification. Every calling owes to the public a duty of leadership in those matters where its training and experience give it a special competence and insight. The practice of his profession brings the lawyer in daily touch with a problem that is at best imperfectly understood by the general public. This is, broadly speaking, the problem of implementation as it arises in human affairs. Where an objective has been selected as desirable, it is generally the lawyer who is called upon to design the framework that will put human relations in such an order that the objective will be achieved. For that reason it is likely to be the lawyer who best understands the difficulties encountered in this task.

A dangerous unreal atmosphere surrounds much public discussion of economic and political issues. The electorate is addressed in terms implying that it has only to decide which among proffered objectives it considers most attractive. Little attention is paid to the question of the procedures and institutional arrangements which these objectives will require for their realization. Yet the lawyer knows that the most difficult problems are usually first encountered in giving workable legal form to an objective which all may consider desirable in itself. Not uncommonly at this stage the original objective must be modified, redefined, or even abandoned as not being attainable without undue cost.

Out of his professional experience the lawyer can draw the insight needed to improve public discussion of political and economic issues. Whether he considers himself a conservative or a liberal, the lawyer should do what he can to rescue that discussion from a world of unreality in which it is assumed that ends can be selected without any consideration of means. Obviously if he is to be effective in this respect, the lawyer cannot permit himself to become indifferent and uninformed concerning public issues.

Special Obligations Attaching to Particular Positions Held by the Lawyer

No general statement of the responsibilities of the legal profession can encompass all the situations in which the lawyer may be placed. Each position held by him makes its own peculiar demands. These demands the lawyer must clarify for himself in the light of the particular role in which he serves.

Two positions of public trust require special attention. The first of these is the office of public prosecutor. The manner in which the duties of this office are discharged is of prime importance, not only because the powers it confers are so readily subject to abuse, but also because in the public mind the whole administration of justice tends to be symbolized by its most dramatic branch, the criminal law.

The public prosecutor cannot take as a guide for the conduct of his office the standards of an attorney appearing on behalf of an individual client. The freedom elsewhere wisely granted to partisan advocacy must be severely curtailed if the prosecutor's duties are to be properly discharged. The public prosecutor must recall that he occupies a dual role, being obligated, on the one hand, to furnish that adversary element essential to the informed decision of any controversy, but being possessed, on the other, of important governmental powers that are pledged to the accomplishment of one objective only, that of impartial justice. Where the prosecutor is recreant to the trust implicit in his office, he undermines confidence, not only in his profession, but in government and the very ideal of justice itself.

Special fiduciary obligations are also incumbent on the lawyer who becomes a representative in the legislative branch of government, especially where he continues his private practice after assuming public office. Such a lawyer must be able to envisage the moral disaster that may result from a confusion of his role as legislator and his role as the representative of private clients. The fact that one in this position is sometimes faced with delicate issues difficult of resolution should not cause the lawyer to forget that a failure to face honestly and courageously the moral issues presented by his position may forfeit his integrity both as lawyer and as legislator and pervert the very meaning of representative government.

Mention of special positions of public trust should not be taken to imply that delicate moral issues are not confronted even in the course of the most humble private practice. The lawyer deciding whether to undertake a case must be able to judge objectively whether he is capable of handling it and whether he can assume its burdens without prejudice to previous commitments. In apportioning his time among cases already undertaken the lawyer must guard against the temptation to neglect clients whose needs are real but whose cases promise little financial reward. Even in meeting such everyday problems, good conscience must be fortified by reflection and a capacity to foresee the less immediate consequences of any contemplated course of action.

III

To meet the highest demands of professional responsibility the lawyer must not only have a clear understanding of his duties, but must also possess the resolution necessary to carry into effect what his intellect tells him ought to be done.

For understanding is not of itself enough. Understanding may enable the lawyer to see the goal toward which he should strive, but it will not furnish the motive power that will impel him toward it. For this the lawyer requires a sense of attachment to something larger than himself.

For some this will be attainable only through religious faith. For others it may come from a feeling of identification with the legal profession and its great leaders of the past. Still others, looking to the future, may find it in the thought that they are applying their professional skills to help bring about a better life for all men.

These are problems each lawyer must solve in his own way. But in solving them he will remember, with Whitehead, that moral education cannot be complete without the habitual vision of greatness. And he will recall the concluding words of a famous essay by Holmes:

> Happiness, I am sure from having known many successful men, cannot be won simply by being counsel for great corporations and having an income of fifty thousand dollars. An intellect great enough to win the prize needs other foods besides success. The remoter and more general aspects of the law are those which give it universal interest. It is through them that you not only become a great master in your calling, but connect your subject with the universe and catch an echo of the infinite, a glimpse of its unfathomable process, a hint of the universal law.

Edmund Byrne

The Adversary System: Who Needs It?

According to common folklore, what is most characteristic of the American legal system is its reliance on the so-called adversary system. This, the legend goes, is as it should be. For there are two sides to every question, so the best way to get to an answer is by arguing each side before an impartial and, insofar as possible, enlightened arbiter of fact and law. This model applies strictly, of course, only to cases that go to litigation. It is generally recognized that the vast majority of cases never do, because they are withdrawn, dismissed, settled out of court, submitted to arbitration, plea-bargained, discovered to death, or on occasion just plain lost in the shuffle of crowded court calenders. Nonetheless, the legend continues, even these alternative dispositions are made possible precisely because of the burdensome threat of courtroom battle. In a word, we are asked to believe that in our society justice, like success, is a byproduct of the very same competitiveness that is supposed to underly our capitalist approach to economic well-being.

If indeed we are required to reach justice by way of competition, then the justice we achieve is not likely to be any more "equal" than are the competitors who participate in the process. But sociobiology will have its say, and Rawls and others will try to explain why what often seems patently unfair turns out to be contractually fair after all. We have prenatally agreed to do combat in the courts, and any second thoughts at this late date must be understood as requiring no more than minor adjustments. The system itself must be saved, because it is all that stands between us and the jungle.

All this folklore notwithstanding, the system does not seem to be working. Or, if it is working, it does so in spite of and not because of any virtue inherent in trial by confrontation. One is not likely any more to hear someone assert, as did evidence authority John H. Wigmore in 1923, that the adversary system is "the greatest legal engine ever invented for the discovery of truth."[1] The best one is likely to hear these days is the sort of backhanded compliment to the inevitable that Geoffrey C. Hazard, Jr., recently put into print:

> If it is possible that the adversary system can work satisfactorily, and necessary that it must do so because no other system of adjudication is likely to be any better, it remains true that the system in its present form is pretty sick.[2]

In Wigmore's day such a negative assessment would have bordered on treason. But today it is hardly disputed as to the complaint itself. What is disputed is the gravity of the complaint. Some would contend that current difficulties with the adversary system are primarily procedural and can be solved by one or more modifications. Others are convinced that the system itself is the source of the difficulties, either because it is wrongly applied to some kinds of cases or because it is structurally flawed in its original design. I tend toward the latter view, but will propound it only after first considering the more favored theory of incidental or procedural inadequacies.

What is said to be only incidentally flawed is, as is well known, a system in which the parties, through their attorneys, investigate the facts, frame the legal issues, and present the evidence to what is thought to be an impartial tribunal that then arrives at a decision.[3] Thus, our system is set apart from the court-conducted "inquisitorial" system that prevails in countries committed to the civil law tradition. This latter, which has its counterpart in our administrative agencies, is seldom proposed as a viable alternative because of our heritage of distrust for government controlled adjudication.

It is this same heritage of distrust, otherwise known as a love for freedom, that causes us to worry about the process whereby our *judges* are selected and about the products of such selection.[4] Of course, the assessment of a judge's qualifications can easily be influenced by the outcome of one's case. Such partisan bias is somewhat neutralized by the recognition that the comparatively low salaries paid to judges tends to select out those whose brilliance is better rewarded in private practice. But not even brilliance can guarantee the sort of omnicompetence that random case assignment requires. Thus, Judge David Bazelon, who had become something of an expert on mental illness law, wrote in his decision on an auto pollution case:

> I do not know enough about dynamometer extrapolations, deterioration factor adjustments and the like to decide whether or not the government's approach was statistically valid.[5]

Similarly, the federal judge assigned to the AT&T antitrust case, one of the most important such cases in our nation's history, is considered marginal at best; and John Sirica of Watergate fame is not often thought of as a particularly outstanding judge. The groundbreaking Century City case involving patent claims, to be considered later, was decided by a judge unfamiliar with patent law. It is not likely that mismatches of this sort can be eliminated simply by upgrading judicial salaries, unless in fact it is possible after all to buy wisdom without tainting it in the very transaction.

A second incidental flaw is found in the process of *jury selection.* In the case of a jury, our ideal of impartial adjudication requires the screening out of anyone who has any familiarity either with the subject matter of the case or with legal procedures as such. Ignorance is deemed a virtue not only at the outset of a trial but throughout, as jurors are systematicaly prohibited from availing themselves of even the more ordinary means of recording what has been presented before them as evidence. Thus it can happen, as in *Trans America Computer Corporation v. IBM,* that after listening to technical details for seven long months, the jury wound up evenly divided on a verdict. Proposals to abolish the jury entirely face seemingly insurmountable constitutional obstacles, but the constitution is no longer held to require either twelve members or unanimity. More to the point would be a switch to the English practice whereby cases involving technical matters draw their jurors from among persons most knowledgeable about the subject matter. An alternative and perhaps better solution to the problem of ignorance, be it that of judge or jury, is ABA President Leonard S. Janovsky's recommendation that special masters be employed in complex cases, as is being done in California in litigation before a judge.[6]

Chief Justice Warren Burger has been pointing to a third incidental flaw in the adversary system, namely, the inadequate skills of the litigating *attorneys.* As witness to the recent rash of proposals for more "trial advocacy" instruction in the law schools, this particular scapegoat could be rather easily chased off into the desert. If, on the other hand, attorneys are, as often as not, just the sort of rascals that their post-Watergate image would suggest, then it would seem to be the height of folly to hone their technical skills without at the same time encouraging a more publicly responsible professional ethic.[7] Of late, of course, there has been movement on the ethical front; but all of this will come to nought if the Vince Lombardi philosophy that winning is everything continues to provide the criterion for sorting out good lawyers from bad.

A fourth incidental flaw might even be traced to *court reporters and clerks,* whose inability to process paperwork beyond the limits of human possibility ties them to the complaint that slow justice is no justice. Few would advocate anything as simplistic as five finger exercises to remedy this problem. But the technological fix being suggested by the ABA's Action Commission to Reduce Court Costs and Delay, i.e., computer-assisted transcription ("C.A.T."), may actually be as promising as the merchants of the system like to claim.[8] Gadgetry by itself, however, does not respond to the finding by the National Center for State Courts that "the comity that exists between lawyers and judges in a jurisdiction can be the single most powerful cause of cost to the client and delay in the work of the courts."[9]

The problem of delay and delay-generated cost is somewhat paradoxical in view of a fifth flaw incidental to the adversary system, namely, the mounting litigiousness of the American people together with an ever-mounting list of hurts for which legal remedies are provided.[10] This ongoing expansion of the repertoire of causes of action represents *prima facie* an expansion of people's rights before the law. But in the absence of adequate staff and mechanisms for processing complaints, as in the case of the Equal Employment Opportunity Commission (EEOC) and other agencies charged with enforcing affirmative action legislation, such a right may be worth little more than a ticket on a lottery. Nor is this situation likely to improve under policies espoused by the present administration.

So there are indeed flaws in the adversary system that can be traced to inadequacies or at least limitations in the human beings who participate in one capacity or another in that system. Lurking behind the foregoing analysis, however, is a most serious suggestion that these qualitative problems are in fact quantitative in origin. The system, so this argument would run, was simply not designed to handle the volume of cases that is now winding up in court. From the time of its origins in English law, our system controlled the numbers through a variety of technical devices, most notably such threshold questions as jurisdiction, standing, and proper statement of a cause of action. As determined by stringent rules regarding the form of pleadings, the latter was an excellent device for keeping "careless" (read: poorly represented) folks off a court's docket. But since the demise of formal pleading and the rise of statutory causes of action, court dockets grow ever more voluminous in spite of such restrictions as minimum damage claimed.[11]

In the federal system, for example, there are only about four hundred judges for every six hundred cases and every one thousand attorneys that come before the federal bench. Ninety-one percent of all federal cases are never heard, at least indirectly because of court congestion. State courts similarly "streamline" their dockets by prematurely terminating "weak" (read: more difficult?) cases, thereby rationing justice.[12] Appellate judges may also control their case loads by routinely upholding whatever decision has been reached at the trial level or by avoiding mandatory jurisdiction insofar as possible.[13]

Nor is this problem of docket clogging made any the less severe by relying on administrative agencies. Backlog at EEOC is a case in point. Consider also the problem at the Social Security Administration in recent years. Largely because of unemployment and disability claims, this agency was hearing two hundred thousand cases a year by 1979. About half of these were successful; and of the unsuccessful ones ten thousand appeals led to thirty-five hundred second hearings. In the face of this kind of volume administrative law judges were told, according to Jack Anderson, to dispose of twenty-six cases per month. To meet this quota they tended to approve weak cases just to avoid having to hear them again after appeal, and to rule against good, i.e., time consuming, cases. The end result was an overall increase in payments, expected (prior to Mr. Reagan's election) to reach twenty-seven billion dollars just for disability cases by 1985.[14]

What to do about docket clogging? A number of experiments have been tried, and these are well worth discussing; but their results to date are mixed at best. The development of small claims courts, or some variation thereof, is well known and needs no elaboration here. Also pertinent in this regard are the so-called Neighborhood Justice Centers, which were started experimentally by then Attorney-General Griffin Bell in Atlanta, Kansas City, and Los Angeles, and then given statutory status when Jimmy Carter signed into law the Dispute Resolution Act of 1980. Better known, of course, is the Legal Services Corporation, whose state affiliates have attempted to stretch the national budget of three hundred twenty-one million dollars (FY 1981) through lobbying and class action suits.[15] These tactics are likely to be prohibited under legislation now pending before Congress; and the Legal Services Corporation will continue, if at all, with substantially less funding than before. Aside from the obvious impact of such retrenchment on poor people's right to redress of grievances, it is difficult to assess just how it will affect court clogging. For, a little appreciated side effect of legal services office is its function as screener of poor people's complaints, the vast majority of which never reach a courtroom. It is unlikely, however, that the legal profession will fill the gap very noticeably with *pro bono* service.[16]

Also viewed as an anti-clogging device is court-ordered pre-trial arbitration of cases involving comparatively low damages. Eight states have authorized this approach for cases involving seventy-five hundred dollars or less. Since July 1979, California superior courts have been required to shift cases involving less than fifteen thousand dollars to arbitration. Local courts may do so at their option, as may the plaintiff in a case at any court level. The arbitrator's award may be appealed, but appellant pays both court costs and arbitrator's fees if the trial does not result in a better outcome. In the first year of the program, some twenty-four thousand cases were processed by arbitration, but these were the small-value damage suits usually settled anyway. Besides, additional delays have resulted from a shortage of arbitrators. This problem may soon be alleviated by the appearance of a number of independent organizations offering arbitration services; and Los Angeles County, anticipating statutory authorization, has raised its ceiling for arbitration cases to twenty-five thousand dollars.

A timely response to such mandated statutory arbitration is Carl Person's "free-enterprise court system."[18] What Person offers is a "National Private Court" that, he claims, will complete a case within three months through use of low cost, specialized judges, selected from a panel of over one hundred, who will function essentially as arbitrators and will be paid an hourly "judicial fee." So as to interface with the court system in case of appeal, Person's NPC would follow federal rules of procedure, provide a written decision giving facts and conclusions, and appellate briefs based on the entire record.

Another, and to some extent overlapping, quantitative problem is the monetary cost of litigation. This factor, sometimes in combination with concern about clogging, has led to various experiments aimed at disposing of cases with little or no litigation.

One such appeal is the so-called summary jury trial, devised by Thomas D. Lambros, a U.S. district court judge in Cleveland. Each side is allowed one hour for an opening statement, a summary of evidence, and a closing statement before a six-member jury, which renders its nonbinding decision at once. The parties then have two weeks to think about the decision. In thirty-three of thirty-seven cases submitted to such a "mini-trial," settlement was arrived at without a full trial.[19]

The Lambros approach, which involves the court directly in the process of trying to divert litigants from going to court, is comparable to a variety of experiments begun two years ago in California to foster settlement through court-monitored pre-trial conferences. These settlement conferences, according to an early report by a participating judge, are aimed at resolving "the crisis of impossible caseloads in our courts."[20] In San Diego the Superior Court declared a week-long "trial holiday," put judges on conference panels, and achieved settlement of seventy percent of its one hundred fifteen cases. Comparable results were reported in San Bernadino and Riverside County. In the Superior Court of Los Angeles fifty percent of cases assigned to either voluntary or mandatory pre-trial conference were settled.[21]

As compared to the foregoing, the already famous Century City experiment arose, also in California, not in response to court congestion but to the high cost of litigation. This approach, which involves what amounts to tripartite arbitration was developed to resolve a patent case after "more than two years of increasingly rancorous pretrial maneuvering and outlay of more than $500,000 [by] each [side], most of it spent on lawyers."[22] What this approach involved, according to one participant, was an alternative to arbitration and negotiation, called a "mini-trial."[23] The mini-trial was carried out in July 1977, before a neutral adviser and one executive from each company involved (TRW Inc. and Telecredit Inc.), with nine lawyers and six technical experts participating. The result, according to Ronald A. Katz, originator of the mini-trial, was a savings of a million dollars in lawyers' fees and a resolution of the controversy acceptable to both parties without being subjected to what Katz calls "the Russian-roulette quality of the federal system" in patent cases.[24] Much has been written about this experiment, but nothing that is more significant than Katz's own statement of its purpose: "We have to remove lawyers from their pugilistic environment and bring in the problem-solving abilities of businessmen."[25] Byard G. Nilsson, on the other hand, who participated as co-counsel for plaintiff, sees the mini-trial as needing just the right amount of pugilism:

> A powerful psychological consequence of the mini-trial results from the adverse proceeding before the neutral adviser. Within critical limits, expressions of adversity are creative in developing an atmosphere that is conducive to settlement. Some expression of adversity is therapeutic both in relieving the source and impacting the target, but if it exceeds the critical limit, the rapport for settlement will be destroyed and the slugfest of full-scale litigation will resume. Participation in a mini-trial invites careful planning that will create an atmosphere of settlement.[26]

Nilsson notwithstanding, psychology has been giving way in corporate circles to an even greater need to economize, and mini-trial purveyors are responding to the opportunity. To encourage adoption by others of the mini-trial approach, Katz's Center for Public Resources (CPR) has published a manual on how to avoid lawsuits as a way of cutting costs.[27] So attractive is this new corporate interest in cutting legal costs that many companies are bringing all but the most specialized legal work in-house. Consultants, including none other than Ralph Nader, are offering to show them just how to do so.[28]

What these various anti-clogging and/or cost-cutting maneuvers call to our attention is the incontrovertible fact that our courts are not able to handle all the cases that are or could be brought to them. By identifying the problem, however, as an incidental (qualitative or quantitative) limitation they disregard the very real possibility that the adversary system itself is ill-designed for some kinds of cases, even in the best of circumstances. This criticism of the system has been made with regard to cases involving intercorporate (especially patent) matters, consumer complaints, employee grievances, and family law, especially divorce.

The Century City mini-trial was developed precisely to bypass a judge who was not able to deal with the complexities of a patent dispute. And problems no less severe tend to arise in intercorporate battle over contracts, unfair competition, and antitrust law. Sherman antitrust cases, for example, must be heard and decided by one judge, who typically has to work through multitudinous documents on his way to a just decision. No wonder, then, that decisions in these cases are hard to come by. The federal case against IBM, for example, has been going in its more recent version since 1969. (An earlier case started in 1952 produced a consent decree in 1956.) The judge who came on the case in 1972 took over while carrying three hundred other cases. He had some twenty-seven million documents to assess with the help of three law clerks. The total cost of the case was estimated to have gone beyond one hundred million dollars by 1976. A similar case against AT&T made even less progress since it was begun in 1972, in large part because the phone company spent two million dollars a year in legal fees while working elsewhere for more congenial legislation.[29]

At the other end of the economic spectrum (usually) are consumer complaints. But these, too, are unlikely candidates for full-fledged litigation, not only from the viewpoint of a cost-benefit analysis but because of psychological and public relations considerations. Various alternative models have been developed in this area, including the small claims court. But perhaps the most interesting approach is the use of optional arbitration in Washington state to handle complaints such as that against Glenn W. Turner's "Dare To Be Great" Company (filed 1971). The simplified procedure includes presentation of the case, questions from parties and from the arbitrator, closing statements, and the arbitrator's award within 10 days. Under this procedure, cases come up within 60.5 days from the date of filing (compared to one year in the Superior Court of King County, Washington) and are completed on average in 1.5 hours. The award is final except on a showing of corruption, fraud, misconduct or gross partiality.[30] Nationwide, a comparable arbitration service is available through most of the offices of the Better Business Bureau and has also been built into consent decrees by the Federal Trade Commission.[31]

Arbitration is also being used as a more appropriate way of arriving at a separation agreement in divorce cases. This is as it should be, according to Stephen Gillers, because it is too costly "in terms of money, time, and human pain" to apply to such matters "adversarial skills that are fundamentally inconsistent with empathic ones. . . ." "Rather than solving the problem [of resolving family dissolution issues]", he goes on, "legal adversariness contributes to it."[32]

"Adversariness can't be totally omitted from the resolution process," Gillers acknowledges, "but it can be changed, eased, and directed constructively."[33] This is being done through a new instrumentality known as a family dissolution unit, which consists of the two separating spouses, one lawyer, one therapist, and two laypersons (a man and a woman). The unit meets two to three times a week for from four to six weeks, with a view to arriving at a majority agreement, provision being made for breaking ties. Activation of the unit may be (1) mandatory but nonbinding, (2) discretionary on the part of either the parties or the trial judge, or (3) voluntary but binding absent substantial injustice. The latter would be most likely to succeed because it presupposes well disposed divorcing spouses.

In labor relations, as is well known, arbitration has long been recognized as the preferred method of resolving workplace disputes, especially with regard to settling upon or interpreting the terms of a bargained contract.[34]

But perhaps the extreme example of a type of case that is ill-suited to full-scale litigation is the case of eighty-three-year-old Brother Joseph Clark, who, it was ruled, could be removed from a respirator only on the basis of a court order.[35] "This," notes Jethro Lieberman, "seems more process than is due and the form unsuited to the problem." For, he continues, "[n]ot every inquiry needs to be adversary in nature, nor does every serious discussion need to be made in an adversary proceeding."[36]

It is well recognized, then, that above and beyond the problem of clogged calendars, there is a variety of cases that do not ordinarily lend themselves well to the litigiousness of the adversary system. But not even this effort to distinguish between cases suitable and cases not suitable for litigation is likely to be adequate to the size of the problem. For, the adversary system of the textbooks may yet wind up with no other forum in which to be viewed. Such seems to be the economics of the situation, at least in the opinion of Marvin E. Frankel:

> The scale and intensity of adversary legal proceedings, with their attendant risks and uncertainties, have brought us to a pass in which the "American way" in court survives at all by virtue of being used only in truncated and abbreviated forms. While Americans continue to litigate on a grand scale, full-scale lawsuits become increasingly impossible on economic grounds for all but the rich fighting over big stakes.[37]

Then, too, just to add to the drama of it all, there is some support for the idea that all these alternative approaches to case resolution may actually result in even worse clogging by diminishing the incentive to settle more complicated cases.[38]

What all of these expressions of concern about adversary justice have in common is an awareness that the system is clearly not working well under present circumstances and that, in fact, it may never work again. It takes only the slightest shift in perspective to arrive at the general proposition that it may not have worked any better in the past. Which in turn calls forth the thesis that it is, in the final analysis, a misconceived and misbegotten monster that ought never to have seen the light of day. This global condemnation, which found expression often enough in the past, has recently been articulated by Anne Strick, who is appalled by how little the adversary system has to do with the search for truth.[39]

Strick's disenchantment with the battlefield mentality that underlies standard courtroom strategy, especially in the fine art of cross-examination, is echoed by Priscilla Fox, who gave up her career in law because she did not choose to play by what she considers male rules. According to her:

> If women enter the courtroom, we must adopt existing (male) models of behavior, and play the game by men's rules. It is a game, and many people, men and women both, apparently enjoy it for that reason. The skills that one needs to win are what I think of as typically male ways of behaving: puffing and bluffing (overstating one's case), strutting around self-importantly, and finding ways to throw the other side off guard by subtle verbal put-downs.[40]

But for all her concerns about sex-specific behavior, Fox decides that the root of the problem is the "linear thinking," which she says is taught in law schools to the detriment of holistic thinking more appropriate to complex social problems.[41]

There is, I think, a significant grain of truth to Fox's thesis, but for reasons quite unrelated to her analysis. She is correct in her contention that a certain style of thinking is presupposed in the adversary system. The style in question, however, is not linear but dialectical. The dialectical model, which dates back at least as far as the ancient Greek philosophers, was depended upon by medieval and Renaissance thinkers to settle questions subject to uncertainty, and was elevated to the status of a metaphysical principle by the German philosopher Hegel, whose methodology Karl Marx applied to explain human progress in terms of economic conflict between opposing classes.[42]

Remaining constant throughout this long cumulative tradition was the assumption that positive benefits can be obtained from some sort of confrontation of opposites. From the time of Plato, through and including Hegel, the benefits were viewed as essentially epistemological, that is, a knowledge of truth superior to that of either of two competing opinions on a given subject. For idealists such as Plato and Hegel, the superior knowledge may be definitive truth. For realists of various persuasions, including Aristotle and Thomas Aquinas, truth attained dialectically is reliable only under conditions of endemic uncertainty because it is not methodologically tied to the unquestionable verities of demonstrative science. With Marx, however, the nature and purpose of the dialectic shifts from theory to practice and is understood not as a limited assault on debated questions but as a scientific instrument for transforming the world of one's experience. Nature itself, as revealed by Darwin's biology of competitive forces, is thought of as progressing dialectically, and culture is accordingly treated as being bipolar and as such susceptible to a deliberate manipulation of opposing interests.

Just how this dialectical view of nature and culture influenced the development of the adversary system in law has not, to my knowledge, been carefully studied. But it is clear that the pro and con logistics of a stylized debate can be traced directly to medieval scholastic disputation and its modified descendant, Renaissance rhetoric.[43] Moreover, there are rather close connections between social Darwinism, which is a kind of bourgeois response to Marx, and nineteenth-century reform of the British legal system under the aegis of utilitarian doctrine. Especially important to an assessment of the adversary system, however, is not so much its historical ideology as its historical consequences. And, as the preceding review of flaws in this system suggests, it is far from obvious that the system is any more productive of truth than any other actual or imagined system. Indeed, few contemporary analysts of the system think that it is; they tend to reject it as counterproductive or else defend it on nonepistemological grounds. Fairly common, for example, is the belief that the system helps participants work through their aggression and hostility in a comparatively civilized manner.

Yet another defense, articulated recently by Geoffrey C. Hazard, Jr., is that, unlike the inquisitorial system, ours keeps inter-party conflict resolution free of government control.[44] However accurate this explanation may be historically, yet another critic of the system, Marvin E. Frankel, views this independence of direct government control as a principal cause of its problems. He therefore proposes the establishment of a National Legal Service available to all citizens as a corrective. His reasoning:

> If a substantially larger proportion of the legal profession were comprised of public servants rather than private entrepreneurs, some of the incentives for all-out warfare would be lessened. . . . The interest in the system as social arrangement rather than manipulative occasion . . . would tend to be enhanced[45]

The views of Hazard and Frankel certainly seem to be diametrically opposed, hence good candidates for both dialectical treatment and adversarial litigation. But one's imagination is sorely taxed to come up with a workable synthesis that both would and would not involve direct government control. Except for the unbending ideologues, of whom there are indeed a few these days, few sensitive analysts of the issue would favor a pro or con decision based on an exclusive disjunction of the alternatives. What is called for here, as in most any other important issue before the public, is reasoned consideration of all important factors and the construction of an imperfect but broadly acceptable accommodation. The model for such a process of decision-making, however, will be found not in hostile confrontations but in sensitive conciliation of respectively legitimate but vulnerable claims. The institutional equivalent of this latter model will be found not so much in litigation as in negotiation and arbitration, with regard to both civil and criminal matters. This being the case, the only question that remains is whether the availability of litigation, like that of capital punishment, exercises some constraining influence on choices we make prior to and in lieu of that event. If not, then though the adversary system may yet be our adjudicative emperor, it truly has no clothes.

NOTES

1. Wigmore, *Evidence in Trials of Common Law,* vol. 3 (Boston: Little, Brown, 1923), p. 1367), as quoted by Jethro K. Liebermann, *The Litigious Society* (New York: Basic Books, 1981), p. 168.

2. Hazard, Jr., *Ethics in the Practice of Law* (New Haven, Conn., and London: Yale University Press, 1978), p. 133.

3. See ibid., p. 120.

4. See Joseph C. Gaulden, *The Beachwarmers: The Private World of the Powerful Federal Judges* (New York: Weybright and Talley, 1974); Bob Woodward and Scott Armstrong, *The Brethren: Inside the Supreme Court* (New York: Simon and Schuster, 1979); Jerold S. Auerbach, *Unequal Justice* (New York: Oxford University Press, 1975); John R. Schmidt, "Lawyers on Judges: Competence and Selection," in Ralph Nader and Mark Green, eds., *Verdicts on Lawyers* (New York: Thomas Y. Crowell, 1976), pp. 285–294; Jack Newfield, "The Ten Worst Judges," in Nader and Green, op cit., pp. 169–184.

5. As quoted by Margaret Gentry, Associated Press release, *Indianapolis Star* (December 6, 1979):43.

6. Janovsky, "The 'Big Case': A 'Big Burden' on Our Courts" *American Bar Association Journal* 66 (July 1980): 848, 850.

7. The wiles and craft of various attorneys are duly recorded in such works as Murray Teigh Bloom, *The Trouble with Lawyers* (New York: Pocket Books, 1970); Joseph C. Goulden, *The Superlawyers* (New York: David McKay, 1971). Burton Marks and Gerald Goldfarb, on the other hand, invite client exploitation of same in *Winning with Your Lawyer* (New York: McGraw-Hill, 1980).

8. See Ralph N. Kleps, "Transcripts by Minicomputer: A Solution for Court Delay" *American Bar Association Journal* 67 (February 1981): 224.

9. Leonard S. Janofsky, "A.B.A. Attacks Delay and the High Cost of Litigation" *American Bar Association Journal* 65 (September 1979):1323, 1324.

10. See Jethro K. Liebermann, op cit.

11. Ibid., pp. 17–18. See also Richard H. Field and Benjamin Kaplan, *Civil Procedure,* 3rd ed. (Mineola, N.Y.: Foundation Press, 1973), pp. 243–336.

12. Carl Person, "Justice, Inc." *Juris Doctor* (March 1978):32+.

13. Ibid., p. 32. See also Eugene Gressman, "Requiem for the Supreme Court's Obligatory Jurisdiction" 65 *American Bar Association Journal* (September 1979):1325. The latter argues, at 1327, that the comparatively small number of obligatory appeals "continued to clog the argument calendar and to force the Court to resolve the merits of many issues of less than national import."

14. Jack Anderson column, *The Indianapolis Star* (March 19, 1979):15.

15. For the history and rationale of Neighborhood Justice Centers, see U.S. House Judiciary Committee Report 96-492, pt. 2, 96th Cong., 1st session, October 23, 1979. With regard to LSC, as this is being written the future of legal services hangs in the balance before a budget-conscious Congress that will almost certainly reduce LSC's funding to no more than $241 million and possibly even to zero. Abundant documentation in support of LSC was compiled by the ABA Standing Committee on Legal Aid and Indigent Defendants and released August, 1981. For a balanced assessment of an LSO program see Samuel Jan Brakel, "Judicare in West Virginia" *American Bar Association Journal* 65 (September 1979):1346.

16. For an assessment of the future of pro bono legal work, see Ralph Nader, "Pro Bono: Going, Going, Gone?" *Barrister* (Summer 1981):4–8+. The screening function of an LSO can be discerned from even a casual glance at an annual report. In Indiana, for example, from 3/1/80 to 2/28/81 LSO rejected 19,118 cases and opened only 12,077. During the same period 11,626 cases were closed, and of that number 78% involved family, income maintenance, consumer/finance or housing.

17. "Mandatory Arbitration on Trial" *Business Week* (September 21, 1981):136, 141. This article is a report of Deborah R. Hensler's first-year study of the California program for the Rand

Corporation's Institute for Civil Justice. A comparable program has been mounted on the federal level: "Unclogging the Federal Courts," *Business Week* (March 27, 1978):77.

18. Person, op. cit., 34+.

19. "Jury Trials That Can Save Time and Money," *Business Week* (July 20, 1981):166.

20. Julius M. Title, "The Lawyer's Role in Settlement Conferences" *American Bar Association Journal* 67 (May 1981):593, 594.

21. Ibid.

22. "Business Saves Big Money with the 'Mini-trial'" *Business Week,* (October 13, 1980):168.

23. Byard G. Nilsson, "A Litigation Settling Experiment" *American Bar Association Journal* 65 (December 1979):1818.

24. Ibid.

25. Ibid.

26. Nilsson, op. cit., 1820. Just such an "atmosphere of settlement" prevailed in another patent mini-trial involving Shell Oil Corporation and InTel Corporation. Intel lost but its management was satisfied because, according to its corporate secretary and counsel, "even though we thought we were right, the case was disposed of rationally and in a fair way." *Business Week,* ibid., p. 169.

27. Ibid.

28. See "A Corporate Campaign to Slash Legal Costs" *Business Week* (May 24, 1981):9.

29. "The Need for Faster Action on Antitrust Suits" *Business Week* (October 4, 1976):78+.

30. Robert Wexler, "Consumer Arbitration: A Compromising Position" *Juris Doctor* (December 1977):38+.

31. Ibid., pp. 41–42.

32. Gillers, "Breaking Up Is Hard to Do," *Juris Doctor* (May 1978):8.

33. Ibid.

34. See Russell A. Smith et al., *Collective Bargaining and Labor Arbitration* (Indianapolis: Bobbs-Merrill, 1970), pp. 103–106, 205–240.

35. See Lieberman, op. cit., p. 170.

36. Ibid. See, in general, Lieberman's eloquent summary of all the bad effects of litigation, op. cit., p. 171. See also Marvin E. Frankel, *Partisan Justice* (New York: Hill and Wang, 1978), p. 86.

37. Frankel, op. cit., p. 19.

38. Lieberman, op. cit., pp. 174–175.

39. Strick, *Injustice for All* (New York: G. P. Putnam's Sons, 1977).

40. Fox, "Good-bye to Gameplaying" *Juris Doctor* (January 1978): 39.

41. Ibid., p. 40.

42. See in this regard Edmund F. Byrne, *Probability and Opinion* (The Hague: Martinus Nijhoff, 1968), pp. 139–187, 278–305.

43. See Neal W. Gilbert, *Renaissance Concepts of Method* (New York: Columbia University Press, 1960); Chaim Perelman and L. Olbrechts-Tyteca, *Rhétorique et Philosophie: Pour une Théorie de l'Argumentation en Philosophie* (Paris: PUF, 1952).

44. Hazard, Jr., op. cit., p. 129.

45. Frankel, op. cit., pp., 123–127.

William H. Simon

The Ideology of Advocacy: Procedural Justice and Professional Ethics

If you want to take dough from a murderer for helping him beat the rap you must be admitted to the bar . . . .

Rex Stout[1]

The system! I am told on all hands, it's the system. I mustn't look to individuals. It's the system. . . . I mustn't go to Mr. Tulkinghorn, the solicitor in Lincoln's Inn Fields, and say to him when he makes me furious by being so cool and satisfied—as they all do, for I know they gain by it while I lose, don't I?—I mustn't say to him, "I will have something out of someone for my ruin, by fair means or foul!" He is not responsible. It's the system. But, if I do no violence to any of them. . . . I will accuse the individual workers of that system against me, face to face, before the great eternal bar!

Charles Dickens[2]

Conventional morality frowns at the ethics of advocacy. Public opinion disapproves of what it considers the lawyer's most characteristic activities. Popular culture can reconcile itself to him only by pretending that all his clients are virtuous. The lawyer's response takes the form of a dialectic of cynicism and naiveté. On one hand, he sees his more degrading activities as licensed by a fundamental amorality lying beneath conventional morality. On the other hand, he sees his more heartening ones as serving an institutional justice higher than conventional morality. The two moods divide the profession as a whole, and the division can sometimes be seen in the professional lives of individual lawyers, as, for instance, when they turn from their paid efforts on behalf of what they admit to be private interests to their donated services on behalf of what they claim to be the public good.

The formal, articulate expression of the lawyer's response is the "Ideology of Advocacy." The purpose of the Ideology of Advocacy is to rationalize the most salient aspect of the lawyer's peculiar ethical orientation: his explicit refusal

From *Wisconsin Bar Review* 29 (1978):30–144. Reprinted in edited form by permission of the publisher and the author.

to be bound by personal and social norms which he considers binding on others. The most elaborate expressions of the Ideology of Advocacy occur in officially promulgated rules of ethics, in doctrinal writings on legal ethics, the attorney-client evidentiary privilege, and the constitutional right to counsel, and in writings on the legal profession.

Although this literature is voluminous, it is barren of any fundamental questioning of the ethical premises of legal professionalism. The profession has never been inclined to join issue on any but the most superficial level with the lay critique of these premises, and it presently seems less disposed toward reexamination of them than ever. The public disgust at the behavior of the lawyers in the Watergate affair has prompted an elaborate pretense of soul-searching on the part of the profession, but Watergate has in fact been an occasion for retrenchment and reindoctrination, rather than reexamination. The profession has viewed Watergate as revealing problems regarding the enforcement of professional norms, but has refused to see it as raising questions about the validity of those norms. In the profession's current view, what is needed is not criticism of legal ethics, but rather more zealous propagation of those ethics through greater emphasis on the professional catechism in law school curricula and bar examinations.

Of course, there is a growing body of writing addressed to the profession which is critical of the conduct of lawyers and professional organizations. Yet, most of these discussions take place within the framework of the Ideology of Advocacy and do not involve criticism of its premises.[3] The more prominent of these discussions have been of two types. First, doctrinal writings on legal ethics and judicial procedure often take the form of a debate between the partisans of a "battle" model and the partisans of a "truth" model of adjudication. A famous example of this debate will be discussed in the next section.[4] These writings criticize certain kinds of conduct by lawyers as inconsistent with one or the other of these models. Yet, almost all of the distinctive ethical views of lawyers can be rationalized in terms of one or the other of the models, and the differences between them are greatly exaggerated in the debate. Both models accept the basic principles of the Ideology of Advocacy and are primarily concerned with defending those principles.

Second, there is a substantial body of sociology and social criticism which focuses on the legal profession. Some of this literature argues that lawyers compromise their clients' interests in order to advance their own interests.[5] Other studies focus on an elite within the profession and argue that the elite has used professional ethics and organization to achieve prestige and economic privilege at the expense of the less powerful members of the profession and of the lower classes generally.[6] Studies which emphasize the exploitation of clients explicitly accept the Ideology of Advocacy and criticize lawyers for failing to live up to it. Although studies which emphasize elite domination purport to criticize legal ethics and professionalism, they do not deal with the basic principles expressed by the Ideology of Advocacy. Instead, they focus on principles such as restrictions on membership in the profession and prohibitions on advertising and solicitation. Such studies are concerned less with the nature of legal services than with their distribution.[7] In suggesting that the increased availability of legal services allegedly inhibited by professional ethics and organization would be desirable, these writings often rely on the Ideology of Advocacy. It is notable that writing from both perspectives often calls for reforms which would enlarge the size and power of the profession.

This essay attempts a critical examination of the Ideology of Advocacy. Section I outlines the basic principles of the Ideology. The following three sections are then devoted to a discussion and criticism of the jurisprudential doctrine with which these basic principles are defended. Each of these sections describes and criticizes one of the three most prominent versions of the Ideology. The descriptions of the three versions are not derived directly from officially promulgated doctrine or from the writings of any specific theorist. Rather, they are in the nature of denial types, heuristic constructions which are intended to be representative of the prevailing thought within the profession about the ethics of law practice. The use of this procedure involves the risk that the ideal types will be taken for "straw men." Yet, the procedure is necessary in view of the absence of any coherent, systematic defenses of legal ethics. . . .

The fifth section of the essay will attempt to formulate an overview of the subject matter from the critiques of the three versions of the Ideology of Advocacy and to describe the fundamental defects of all defenses of lawyers' ethics and legal professionalism. It will argue that the practices prescribed by the Ideology of Advocacy are inconsistent with the values invoked to justify those practices. At the base of each version of the Ideology of Advocacy is an appeal to an aspect of the fundamental value of individuality: autonomy, responsibility, dignity. Yet, in each instance, the practices and attitudes of professional advocacy subvert the norms of individuality in the interest of a repressive conception of social stability. The essay will argue that to take the value of individuality seriously would require the abandonment of the Ideology of Advocacy and of legal professionalism. Indeed, it will also suggest that respect for the value of law itself may require the repudiation of legal professionalism. The concluding section of the essay attempts to suggest an alternative approach to the problems of advocacy which might avoid the defects of the Ideology of Advocacy.

I. THE PRINCIPLES OF THE IDEOLOGY

Although certain issues of legal ethics are debated incessantly, the debates almost invariably take place within a framework of certain common, unquestioned principles. Consider the exchange between Monroe Freedman and John Noonan on what Freedman called "the three hardest questions" for the criminal defense lawyer. The questions concerned whether or not it is proper for a lawyer to attempt to discredit an adverse witness whom he knows to be telling the truth, to put a witness on the stand knowing he will commit perjury, or to advise a client in a manner likely to tempt him to commit perjury.

Freedman's answer to all three questions was affirmative.[8] The lawyer might argue with his client about the morality of such activities, but ultimately, he insisted, the lawyer must bow to his client's will. Freedman's argument focused on the notion of confidentiality. If the client thought that the lawyer would refuse to do anything which would mislead the trier, then the client would probably lie or withhold information in order to convince the lawyer that actions in his interest would not be misleading. But in order to present the best possible defense, the lawyer has to know all the facts. The client cannot know when it is in his interest to conceal or falsify information. Thus, the lawyer must have the confidence of the client. The only way to achieve this is to assure the client that he will not be prejudiced by telling his lawyer the facts. For the lawyer to refuse to follow the client's wishes after the facts had been revealed would betray the promise which had induced disclosure and would undermine the credibility of such promises in the future.

Freedman suggested that refusal to impeach accurate testimony would in some instances harm innocent defendants because evidence in itself accurate might still be misleading on the question of guilt. Yet, Freedman did not justify the conduct he advocated in terms of any contribution to the accurate determination of guilt or innocence. On the contrary, he relied on "policy considerations that at times justify frustrating the search for truth and the prosecution of a just claim" which are widely recognized in the legal system.[9] He pointed to the provisions in the Canons of Ethics that require adversary zeal and confidentiality. He noted that lawyers as eminent as Williston had recognized a professional duty to acquiesce in mendacity. And he emphasized the tacit sanction of mendacity in judicial procedures, such as the right of a defendant to plead not guilty regardless of his guilt.

Noonan congratulated Freedman on a candid and accurate portrayal of the working principles of a large segment of the profession, but he argued that these principles affront the dignity of the profession and the legal system by turning the lawyer into a "tool" of his client and the trial into an irrational battle.[10] Noonan criticized Freedman's reliance on the battle model of criminal procedure and advocated as more enlightened the truth model. In his view, the purpose of judicial proceedings is to produce wise and informed decisionmaking, and the lawyer's job is to assist the trier in this effort.[11] The lawyer's duty to advance his client's interests must be subordinated to the fundamental purpose of truth-seeking which brought the relationship into being. He must not therefore mislead the trier by introducing false testimony or discrediting accurate testimony. Moreover, this obligation applies even where the lawyer believes that by misleading the trier with respect to a particular piece of evidence he will promote a wiser and more informed decision on the ultimate issue. In addition to recognizing his duty to the goal of truth, the lawyer must recognize his auxiliary status in the quest for truth. The trial is structured as a whole to produce the

most accurate results possible, and it functions best when each participant adheres to his own role. The lawyer is sometimes expected to exclude evidence, but
his basic job is to introduce accurate evidence. The responsibility for assessing
the weight of the evidence on the ultimate issue rests with the trier. For the
lawyer to attempt to influence this asessment by deception on the basis of his
own judgment of the evidence would be to transgress the limit of his own role
and usurp the trier's function.

Freedman and Noonan differ less in their arguments than in the attitudes
they bring to the subject. They illustrate the modes of cynicism and naiveté in
which the Ideology of Advocacy is usually elaborated. In his article, Freedman
casually assumes that the legal system routinely convicts innocent people. He
shows no more indignation at this fact than he does discomfort at the fact that
the measures he advocates will result in the acquittal of guilty defendants. He
speaks of cases not in terms of justice or suffering, but in terms of probabilities
of acquittal.

On the other hand, Noonan assumes that the legal system produces justice
so dependably that the lawyer defending an innocent man need not even ask
himself whether following the usual rules might lead to a disastrous ultimate
result. He glosses over the aspects of the system which seem to institutionalize
aggression and dishonesty. He seems to think that lawyers could transform the
trial system from the battle model to the truth model simply by adopting a
different attitude toward it.

Despite their differing attitudes, Freedman and Noonan both clearly assume
four principles. These are the basic principles of the Ideology of Advocacy. Two
are principles of conduct which prescribe attitudes and behavior. They appear on
the surface of most discussions of advocacy. The other two are foundation
principles which have to do with the way the principles of conduct are derived
and applied. They rest below the surface of discourse on legal ethics, but they
are nevertheless pervasive and important.

The first principle of conduct is the principle of neutrality. This principle
prescribes that the lawyer remain detached from his client's ends. The lawyer is
expected to represent people who seek his help regardless of his opinion of the
justice of their ends.[12] In some cases, he may have a duty to do so; in others, he
may have the personal privilege to refuse.[13] But whenever he takes a case, he is
not considered responsible for his client's purposes. Even if the lawyer happens
to share these purposes, he must maintain his distance. In a judicial proceeding,
for instance, he may not express his personal belief in the justice of his client's
cause.[14]

The second principle of conduct is partisanship. This principle prescribes
that the lawyer work aggressively to advance his client's ends. The lawyer will
employ means on behalf of his client which he would not consider proper in a
non-professional context even to advance his own ends. These means may
involve deception, obfuscation, or delay. Unlike the principle of neutrality, the
principle of partisanship is qualified. A line separates the methods which a

lawyer should be willing to use on behalf of a client from those he should not use. Before the lawyer crosses the line, he calls himself a representative; after he crosses it, he calls himself an officer of the Court. Most debates within the Ideology of Advocacy concern the location of his line. Freedman and Noonan disagree on the location of the line, but they both take principle of partisanship for granted. Both men would probably agree that the lawyer should not reveal adverse evidence learned from the client even though it may be relevant and probative.[15] They would probably agree that he should exclude accurate, probative evidence at trial whenever the rules of evidence permit.[16] They would agree that he should not hesitate to plead his client not guilty even when he knows the client had committed the crime with which he is charged, and they would probably agree that he should invoke the statutes of frauds and limitations to defeat otherwise valid civil claims.[17] Also, Freedman thinks, though Noonan disagrees, that the lawyer should present perjured testimony and discredit accurate testimony. Others have thought that partisanship warrants the use of dilatory procedural tactics, lying under almost any circumstances in which discovery is unlikely, and the citation of false precedents to the judge.[18]

The principles of neutrality and partisanship describe the basic conduct and attitudes of professional advocacy. The two princples are often combined in the terms "adversary advocacy" or "partisan advocacy," and this essay will adopt that usage. However, it should be noted that the two principles are distinct in important respects. Many occupational roles, for instance the bureaucrat and the doctor, are expected to serve the general public without regard to the ends of those who seek their help. Yet, they are not expected to engage in the partisan pursuit of individual ends. On the other hand, political representatives are expected to be partisan, but they are not expected to serve all comers without regard to their ends.[19] Only the lawyer seems to insist on making a virtue of both neutrality and partisanship.

Two further principles, though less obvious, are also assumed by Freedman and Noonan. The first is the principle of procedural justice. In its most general usage, procedural justice holds that the legitimacy of a situation may reside in the way it was produced rather than its intrinsic properties.[20] Another aspect of the principle is that, given adequate procedures, one can act justly by conforming to them regardless of the consequences to which one's conduct contributes. In this essay, the term "procedural justice" is used more specifically to refer to the notion that there is an inherent value or legitimacy to the judicial proceeding (and to a more qualified extent, the entire legal system) which makes it possible for a lawyer to justify specific actions without reference to the consequences they are likely to promote. Freedman and Noonan tacitly embrace this principle. For both of them, the nature of the consequences to which the lawyer's actions may lead is irrelevant to the ethical decisions he must make. Freedman invokes procedural considerations which are explicitly indifferent to outcomes. Although Noonan refers to outcomes in his emphasis on truth-seeking, he clearly rejects the notion that any particular ethical decision can be made by determining which course of action is most likely to lead to the discovery of truth. Rather, Noonan insists that the lawyer must stay within the boundaries of his role regardless of whether doing so will promote the discovery of truth. For Noonan, the goal of truth legitimizes the entire system of procedures and informs its design, but it does not determine specific ethical decisions. Such decisions are determined by procedural requirements.

The second foundation principle of the Ideology of Advocacy is professionalism. In its most general usage, the term professionalism refers to the notion that social responsibility for the development and application of certain apolitical and specialized disciplines should be delegated to the practitioners of these disciplines.[21] In this paper, the term is used more specifically to describe the notion that the law is an apolitical and specialized discipline and that its proper development and application require that legal ethics be elaborated collectively by lawyers in accordance with criteria derived from their discipline. Freedman and Noonan both assume this principle. They never doubt that the "three hardest questions" are in fact questions of *professional* ethics. They assume that the questions are to be resolved in terms of legal doctrine and that they should be resolved by lawyers collectively in their occupational capacities and not by lawyers individually in terms of personal or social norms or by broad-based political institutions.

Most of this essay, Sections II through IV, will be concerned with criticizing the kind of advocacy defined by the principles of neutrality and partisanship. Yet, the foundation principles of procedural justice and professionalism will remain in the background, and in Sections V and VI, the essay will return to them directly in order to discuss their relationship to each other and to adversary advocacy.

II. THE LAWYER AS CHAMPION (THE WAR OF ALL AGAINST ALL)

> BOSWELL: *"But what do you think of supporting a cause which you know to be bad?"*
> JOHNSON: *"Sir, you do not know it to be good or bad till the Judge determines it."*
>
> James Boswell[22]

The fullest justification of the Ideology of Advocacy rests on Positivist legal theory. The term Positivist is used here to refer to the kind of theory which emphasizes the separation of law from personal and social norms, the connection of law with the authoritative application of force, and the systematic, objective character of law.[23] Positivism was the basis of the profession's conception of advocacy in the late nineteenth and early twentieth centuries, and it is still an important component of the professional self-image of some lawyers, despite its repudiation in most areas by the intellectual leaders of the bar. Even lawyers who reject

Positivism as a general jurisprudential theory are sometimes prone to fall back on it when justifying their professional roles.

*   *   *

The Tyranny of Advocacy

The dilemmas of enforcement and access undermine the Positivist notion of the role of the lawyer in the legal system as a whole. They suggest that lawyers as a group cannot safeguard the general social interest in the elimination or containment of uncertainty and oppression. The Positivist notion of the lawyer's role also involves another perspective, that of the individual lawyer and his client. From this perspective, Positivism envisions the lawyer as enhancing the client's autonomy, as enabling the client to make the fullest use of his freedom to pursue his own ends. This latter perspective is to some extent independent of the larger one. For even after acknowledging the failure of the legal system to check uncertainty and oppression, the Positivist can still argue that the lawyer enables individual clients to pursue their ends more effectively within the limits imposed by both the legal system and social disorder. Yet this second perspective involves difficulties as serious as those of the first. Positivism fails to show that the lawyer can enhance his client's autonomy. Rather, it appears from Positivism's own premises that the lawyer who adheres to the Positivist version of the Ideology of Advocacy must end by subverting his client's autonomy. The problem is that the lawyer's task of explaining the impact of the legal system on the client's personal ends cannot be accomplished without some direct understanding of these ends. Yet, Positivism forbids the lawyer to seek or rely on such an understanding.

The lawyer purports to assist his client by using his objective knowledge of the precise, regular, mechanical operation of the legal system to predict the consequences of alternative courses of action. The lawyer assumes specific courses of action as factual hypotheses and reasons from them in accordance with the rules of the legal system in order to determine the consequences in terms of state action which follow from them. Yet by itself, this type of assistance is of little use to the client. The client is not interested in the consequences of *any* course of action. Of the infinity of possible courses of action, he is interested in only those which might advance his ends. Moreover, the client is not interested in *all* the consequences of a course of action. Of the infinity of probable consequences, he is interested in only those that will affect his attainment of his ends.

The Positivist version of the Ideology of Advocacy focuses on the person for whom the law is a mystery. Such a person, even if conscious of and articulate about his ends, would not know which aspects of them the lawyer would need to understand in order to gauge the impact of the legal system on his life. In order to isolate these aspects, he would need the legal knowledge for which he relies on his lawyer. The lawyer, on the other hand, has no reliable way of learning the client's ends on his own. Because these ends are subjective, individual, and arbitrary, the lawyer has no access to them.[24] Because the lawyer's only direct experience of ends is his experience of his own ends, he cannot speculate on what the client's ends might be without referring to his own ends and thus biasing the neutral predictive analysis he is supposed to perform. Any attempt to frame inquiries to the client concerning his ends or to interpret the client's ambiguous replies will necessarily involve the intrusion of the lawyer's own ends. Thus, consciously or not, the Positivist lawyer is faced with a dilemma: On the one hand, he cannot give intelligible advice to his client without referring to ends; on the other hand, he cannot refer to ends without endangering the client's autonomy, and thus, undermining the basic purpose of his role.

Today, in most areas of law practice, lawyers have repudiated Positivism. Even at the turn of the century, when the prevailing jurisprudence was Positivist, many lawyers who purported to subscribe to this jurisprudence ignored some of its assumptions and prescriptions in practice. Yet, there are some areas of practice where lawyers do operate on Positivist premises. In these areas, the Positivist dilemma is a real problem. Thus, Positivism has developed a strategy for dealing with the dilemma. Sometimes the strategy is acknowledged; more often, it is implicit. It can be found in a variety of discussions which view the legal system from a Positivist viewpoint.

The strategy is to impute certain basic ends to the client at the outset and to work to advance these imputed ends. This strategy drastically compromises the Positivist premise of the individuality of ends, but it seems to be the Positivist's only choice. The Positivists seem to assume that, if the ends imputed are sufficiently simple and sufficiently widespread, the risk of interference in the client's autonomy can be minimized. By imputing ends to the client at the outset, the lawyer obviates dangerous inquiries into the particular ends of the particular client. On the other and, if most people actually do share the imputed ends to some degree, then the lawyer will usually advance the client's actual ends when he works to advance the imputed ends. The ends which Positivism imputes are derived from the basic Positivist premise of egoism, but they go beyond this initial premise to emphasize characteristics of extreme selfishness. The specific ends most often imputed are the maximization of freedom of movement and the accumulation of wealth.

The notion that the advocate should serve, not the individual ends of the client, but rather certain standard ends imputed to him is implicit in cases dealing with the effectiveness of advocacy. The law of procedure repeatedly recognizes that critical decisions are made by the lawyer without any participation by the client.[25] Occasionally, such a decision results in disaster to the client, and the issue arises whether he has been represented effectively. This issue is often seen to depend on whether the lawyer's decision was strategically reasonable under the circumstances in which it was made.[26] A strategically reasonable decision is one well calculated to advance certain ends. Yet, these discussions often proceed in total ignorance of the actual ends of the particular client. Rather, the strategic reasonableness is assessed with respect to the imputed ends of Positivism. The lawyer is not criticized for failing to ascertain his client's ends, but only for failing to advance the ends which have been imputed to him.

In the area of the criminal law, lawyers and laymen have recognized increasingly the extent to which the lawyer dominates the client in conducting the defense. Yet, this recognition has led them, not to a reexamination of the premises of adverse advocacy, but to a re-invigorated defense of it in terms of the imputed ends. Thus, critics deplore criminal defense lawyers who fail to exercise their broad discretion more vigorously in order to make it more difficult for the state to coerce the client.[27] The interest in escaping conviction in any circumstances is not something which these critics have discovered after examining the lives of any particular clients. Rather, it is an end which has been imputed to the clients *a priori.*

This Positivist strategy is a complete failure. It can only precipitate, rather than mitigate, the lawyer's subversion of the client's autonomy. The Positivist's vague, crudely drawn psychological assumptions cannot begin to do justice to the specific complexity of his client's actual ends. Unlike the hypothetical person assumed by the Positivist advocate, actual people have not just a few, discrete ends, but rather many ends which are interrelated in a complex fashion. Moreover, these ends are set in a social context in which the individual's fulfillment depends on his relations with others. Even assuming the basic Positivist psychology of egoism to be accurate, it would not follow that a person's ends could be reduced to a few crude presumptions. On the contrary, a person's fulfillment is likely to depend on a complex balance among many different satisfactions. Moreover, the attainment of individual satisfaction depends on the cooperation of others. Yet, Positivism is blind to all but the crudest ends, to the relations of ends among each other, and to the social relations on which personal fulfillment depends.

Thus, when the client comes to the Positivist seeking to protect the delicate rhythms of his private life from disruption by the mechanical operation of the state, the lawyer will implement the very result he was supposed to prevent. The lawyer explains to the client the probable impact of the state, not on the client's own life, but on the life of the hypothetical person assumed in the Positivist model whose simple, crude ends bear only the most problematical relation to those of the client. This advice is much worse than useless to the client. Though it will often be irrelevant to his ends, the client may not be in a position to reject it. The client of whom Positivism is most solicitous is the naive person, face to face with the alien force of the state, threatened with a massive disruption of his life. Confronted with the need to act in this strange situation, the client must make sense of it as best he can. The lawyer puts himself forth quite plausibly as the client's best hope of mastering his predicament. If he is to avoid being overwhelmed by chaos, he must acquiesce in his lawyer's definition of the situation. He must think in a manner which gives coherence to the advice he is given. He may begin to do this quite unconsciously. If he is at all aware of the change, he is likely to see it as a defensive posture forced on him by the hostile intentions of opposing parties, of whom his perception is mediated by the categories of his lawyer's framework of analysis.[28] His only strategy of survival requires that he see himself as the lawyers and the officials see him, as an abstraction, a hypothetical person with only a few crude, discrete ends.[29] He must assume that his subtler ends, his long-range plans, and his social relationships are irrelevant to the situation at hand. This is the profound and unintended meaning of Holmes's remark:

> If you want to know the law and nothing else, you must look at it as a bad man, who cares only for the material consequences which such knowledge enables him to predict, not as a good one, who finds his reasons for conduct, whether inside the law or outside of it, in the vaguer sanctions of conscience.[30]

The role of the bad man, conceived as an analytical device for the lawyer, becomes, under pressure of circumstances, a psychological reality for the client. . . .

Despite its complete irrationality, this Positivist strategy for dealing with the problem of inaccessibility of personal ends has become so widely accepted that many lawyers have come to equate the manipulation of the client in terms of imputed ends with neutral advice to the client on his rights. For instance, lawyers constantly express astonishment at the willingness of intelligent laymen, aware of their rights, to make inculpatory statements to the authorities. They can think of no other explanation for this phenomenon besides confusion or pressure from the interrogators, and they thus conclude that no one can be expected to make an "informed decision" on such matters without the assistance of counsel.[31] But the lawyer's assistance does not take the form of neutral information or the alleviation of pressure. Along with his knowledge of the law, the lawyer brings his own prejudices and his own psychological pressures. These derive from the conception of the roles of lawyer and client which is implicit in Positivism generally and in the strategy of imputed ends. As Justice Jackson put it, "[A]ny lawyer worth his salt will tell the suspect in no uncertain terms to make no statement to the police under any circumstances."[32] The Positivist lawyer is not an advisor, but a lobbyist for a peculiar theory of human nature.

Positivist lawyers fail to see that the kind of behavior they impose on their clients is meaningless when it originates in the lawyer's conception of his own role rather than in the will of the client. This is so even in the area of criminal defense, where the Positivist case for an imputed end is strongest, but nevertheless insufficient. It may be true that the desire to escape criminal punishment is basic and widespread. But the standard adversary defense cannot be justified by routinely imputing such a general desire to every client. The actual and specific ends of even a purely selfish individual may not be served by an adversary defense. For instance, such a defense may merely prolong and intensify an ordeal regarded as more terrible than the threatened punishment. Or it may make the punishment, if it should occur, more difficult to endure by forcing the client to struggle against it and to deny its legitimacy.[34]

The Positivist psychology either makes advocacy impossible or forces the lawyer into the strategy of imputed ends. Because the imputed ends ignore the most important dimensions of the client's personality,[35] the strategy leads to the manipulation of the client by the lawyer in terms of the lawyer's own moral and psychological prejudices. In this manner, the lawyer becomes the agent of the result he was supposed to prevent. He subverts his client's autonomy. . . .[36]

III. THE LAWYER AS PARA-BUREAUCRAT (THE HALF-HEARTED APPEAL TO TRUTH)

> *It's not [the trial lawyer's] job to pursue the truth, but [to] pursue the process from which the truth emerges.*
>
> Charles Haar[37]

The justification of partisan advocacy as instrumental to the attainment of concrete social ends was a secondary theme in the Ideology of Advocacy at the beginning of this century. The conservative, formalist attitudes which prevailed among lawyers at that time were not hospitable to this type of argument. In the nineteenth century, utilitarian political philosophers had considered legal institutions in instrumental terms, but their considerations had led them to condemn adversary advocacy.[38] However, an instrumental version of the Ideology of Advocacy became increasingly prominent throughout the present century. Its victory over the Positivist view was formally acknowledged by the replacement of the Canons of Ethics with the Code of Professional Responsibility.[39]

The instrumental approach was based on a jurisprudence which developed in opposition both to formalism and to the cynical, antijudicial attitude of the more extreme Realists. This jurisprudence, which had been elaborated in various ways in the writings of Pound, Brandeis, Fuller, Llewellyn, Freund, Hart and Sacks, and Hurst, among many others, was, at least until recently, the reigning philosophy in the law schools, and it continues to exert a powerful infuence on the judiciary and the bar.[40] It is not as precise or as coherent a theory as Positivism, and it can be treated as a single doctrine only by ignoring substantial differences among the theories in question. Yet, there is an important core of agreement among these theorists. This core, which can be called Purposivism, has a more ambiguous relationship to the Ideology of Advocacy than Positivism, and some Purposivists, have at least partially repudiated adversary advocacy.[41] However, most Purposivists, when faced with the question, have committed their doctrine to the defense of adversary advocacy, and a Purposivist version of the Ideology of Advocacy has emerged from their work.

* * *

The Purposivist answer to the general question of the compatibility of conflict and shared values was to insist that conflict was a result of short-sightedness and confusion rather than of divergent norms, and to recommend that it be resolved simply by showing individuals that their true interests converged with the public interest. The principal theoretical underpinnings of this view of advocacy were the Purposivist notions of the separation of functions and the long run. The separation of functions purported to explain the apparent difference in the levels of responsibility attributed to the lawyer and to other citizens. The principle of the long run purported to explain how norms could be integrated into a technical, predictive analysis and yet still be understood as binding moral imperatives.

The Technique of the Separation of Functions

The basic theory of the separation of functions is simple. Specialization into roles makes it possible to perform specific tasks more efficiently. This is so for two reasons: expertise and cognitive dissonance. First, there are limits to the amount of knowledge a person can absorb and the number of skills he can develop. Second, a person's understanding of a particular problem is limited by his tendency to develop preconceptions based on some aspects of the situation which distort his understanding of other aspects. The first factor limits the number of tasks a person can ever perform. The second factor limits the number of tasks a person can perform at the same time. Because of these factors, a person works most productively when he concentrates his efforts in a specific area. Yet, this specialization creates a new problem. Because a specialized role is designed to further only specific social values and needs, specialization creates the danger that the role occupants will pursue these values and needs at the expense of other values and needs outside the range of their role competences. This problem can be solved by coordinating the roles and functions so that each is confined to the sphere of operation where it is most effective and any deficiencies in the operation of one role can be remedied by the operation of the others. Thus, efficiency can be enhanced through specialization, while a proper balance among values and needs can be achieved by coordination.

The Purposivists saw the legal profession both as surrounded by coordinate, specialized roles and institutions and as itself divided into specialized roles. While the value of specialization for other institutions, such as agencies and legislatures, rested in large part on expertise, the value of role specialization within the profession rested for the most part on cognitive dissonance. The two most important legal roles were the counseling and advocacy roles, and the distinction between them was a central pillar of the Purposivist version of the Ideology of Advocacy. This distintion was emphasized by the early Purposivists whose demands for the reform of the profession were prompted by the out-of-court activities of the corporate bar.[42] One of their principal criticisms of the *Canons of Ethics* was that the *Canons* were exclusively addressed to the lawyer's function as courtroom advocate and ignored his function as counselor and private law-maker. As Purposivism evolved, it developed a complex intra-professional separation of functions, which included not only the counseling and advocacy roles but also two other roles for which Purposivism won recognition: the government lawyer, and the lawyer *pro bono publico*.[43]

The Purposivist theory of the separation of functions was well explained by Fuller and his collaborators in the Joint Conference of the American Bar Association and the American Association of Law Schools which worked on the revision of the *Canons*. In their view, the purpose of advocacy is to promote "a wise and informed decision of the case." The utility of adversary advocacy in promoting such a decision lies in the application of the principles of specialization and coordination within the judicial proceedings:

> In a very real sense it may be said that the integrity of the adjudicative process itself depends on the participation of the advocate. This becomes apparent when we contemplate the nature of the task assumed by any arbiter who attempts to decide a dispute without the aid of partisan advocacy.
>
> Such an arbiter must undertake, not only the role of judge, but that of representative for both of the litigants. Each of these roles must be played to the full without being muted by qualifications derived from the others. When he is developing for each side the most effective statement of its case, the arbiter must put aside his neutrality and permit himself to be moved by a sympathetic identification sufficiently intense to draw from his mind all that it is capable of giving—in analysis, patience and creative power. When he resumes his neutral position, he must be able to view with distrust the fruits of this identification and be ready to reject the products of his own best mental efforts. The difficulties of the undertaking are obvious.[44]

The practical consequence of such an undertaking is "that at some early point a familiar pattern will seem to emerge from the evidence; an accustomed label is waiting for the case and, without waiting for the proofs the label is promptly assigned." This results from the necessity of giving some pattern of coherence to the evidence, for "without some tentative theory of the case there is no standard of relevance by which testimony may be measured." Partisanship is seen as "the only effective means for combating the natural human tendency to judge too swiftly that which is not fully known." Thus, "[t]he arguments of counsel hold the case, as it were, in suspension between two opposing interpretations of it. While the proper classification of the case is thus kept unresolved, there is time to explore all of its peculiarities and nuances."[45]

Thus, the need for adversary advocacy arises not, as in Positivism, from divergent ends, but from the problem of cognitive dissonance. The separation of functions within the trial contributes to an informed decision by assuring that no aspect of either side's position will be overlooked. The advocate's partisanship is a psychological convention designed to enable him to achieve the benefits of specialization.

However, for the Purposivists, partisan advocacy was valuable only in certain situations, and the advocacy role was viable only as one of a number of specialized legal roles. A critical element of the Purposivist version of the Ideology of Advocacy was its emphasis on the residual nature of the function of advocacy. This emphasis follows from the Purposivist insistence that conflict is not the central element of social life. As Hart and Sacks put it, "The overwhelming proportion of the things which happen and do not happen in American society pass without any later question."[46] Adversary advocacy is needed only for that residuum of "trouble cases" as to which later question does arise. Adversary advocacy is not destructive in these situations because social relationships have already broken down, and private, voluntary efforts to restore them have failed.

In other situations, however, the Purposivists proposed to curb the principles of neutrality and partisanship and substitute new legal roles. The principle of specialization dictates a spectrum of ethical obligations to accord with different functions.

In the Purposivist view, the prototypical legal activity is counseling, rather than advocacy. The counselor most closely approaches the Purposivist ideal of the creator of mutually beneficial patterns of interaction. The counselor deals with individuals, but unlike the advocate's clients, they are not isolated individuals. Rather they are actual or potential participants in social relationships and institutions.

The fundamental ethical innovation which the Purposivists sought to establish was the counselor's affirmative duty to channel the client's egoistic impulses into socially desirable paths.[47] In this manner, they sought to find a middle way between the wholly public responsibilities of the civil servant and the aggressive partisanship of the adversary advocate. Unlike the civil servant, the counselor must be intimately concerned with, and sympathetic to, the special needs of particular people. Moreover, because the counselor does much of his work in the interstices of public policy, dealing with matters toward which public policy is indifferent, he has a greater range of discretion than the civil servant. Yet, unlike the advocate, the counselor does have an affirmative obligation to oppose his client's antisocial impulses. He can reconcile his obligations to his client and the public by focusing on the points of congruence between the particular interest of the client and the general welfare.

Yet the Positivists realized that the added but limited responsibilities of the counseling role were not sufficient to enable the legal profession to play the most effective role it could in the social order. Rather than raise the counselor's public obligations still higher, however, and thus sacrifice the benefits of specialization, the Purposivists attempted to integrate more public responsibility into the profession through the government and the pro bono roles.

The government lawyer is at the opposite pole of the spectrum of legal roles from the advocate.[48] He is concerned entirely with the general welfare, and his responsibilities are entirely public. His role is closest to that of the civil servant in that the government lawyer should not direct his sympathies or energies toward any particular individual or group. His primary task, the enforcement of statutes, can be most effectively performed with a non-partisan attitude.

The *pro bono* lawyer also has primary obligations to the public at large, but these obligations are more limited than those of the government lawyer because the pro bono function is residual.[49] The job of the *pro bono* lawyer is to serve people and interests which have been slighted by the law enforcement efforts of the government and who have not gained effective private legal representation. In this task, he needs to be more sensitive to the needs and aspirations of particular groups than does the government lawyer, but in order to decide which of the potentially infinite number of unrepresented or underrepresented interests he should serve, he needs to take a public viewpoint. (Of course, once the *pro bono* lawyer has committed himself to a particular group or interest, he will assume the counseling or adversary role.)

Though none of these roles is sufficient to guarantee a satisfactory legal order, all of them can be coordinated so as to remedy the deficiencies of each. Lawyers will adopt the role most suitable to the situation at hand and, when the situation changes, will defer to a coordinate role. The Purposivists did not overlook that through incompetence or ill-will lawyers might deviate from the prescriptions of the separation of functions. But they were confident that deviations on the part of any one role could be rectified by the operation of the other roles. The task of checking excesses on the part of the others is built into the functional competence of each role.

While the Purposivists had criticized the application of neutrality and partisanship in the counseling sphere, they were not troubled by its application in the adversary sphere because they felt that in the judicial proceeding excesses of adversary zeal could be checked by the judge and the opposing lawyer.[50] They did not fear that the antagonistic tendencies of adversary advocacy would damage viable social relationships because they counted on the counseling role to keep such relationships out of the adversary sphere. The counselor is charged with a higher standard of public duty than the advocate to reflect the fact that he is subject to less direct scrutiny by opposing interests and public officials. Nevertheless, this ethical prescription is supplemented by pressures exerted from coordinate roles. If the counselor should attempt to further his client's interests at the expense of the interests of others, other lawyers in the advocacy, pro bono, or government roles would bring things back into line, either by causing him to reconsider or by precipitating the situation into the adversary sphere.

From this perspective, the difference in the ethical obligations imposed on the attorney, judge, and client appears as an application of the principle of specialization. The advocate's distinctive ethical orientation enables him to pursue his special tasks more effectively and thus to serve better the social norms implicated in these tasks. His peculiar ethical orientation does not threaten other social norms because destructive tendencies on his part are checked by the operation of coordinate roles.

*   *   *

The Collapse of Functional Distinctions

The basic defect of the principle of separation of functions is the incompatibility of specialization and coordination. Purposivism insists on the efficiency of narrowing one's focus to a particular aspect of a situation. It also admits that the benefits of this specialization can be reaped only if the various limited perspectives can be coordinated from a broader point of view. Yet, the same reasons which make specialization efficient seem to make coordination impossible.

The rationalization of adversary advocacy in terms of the principle of specialization involves the Purposivists in the reverse of the difficulty which plagued the Positivist theory. Purposivism began with the important insight, ignored by Positivism, that in order to further his client's ends, the lawyer needs an intuitive grasp of them. But it begged an important question in reasoning from the premise that a single lawyer cannot fully discern the divergent views of two different people at the same time to the conclusion that partisan advocacy can effectively ascertain the truth. The argument fails to explain how the divergence of views is resolved. Purposivism never explains how the lawyer translates the insights achieved from a sympathetic consideration of his client's position into a form assimilable by the judge in an impartial consideration.[51]

It is true that the presence of advocates on each side may counterbalance any predisposition toward one side or the other which the judge might bring to the trial. In this way, advocacy makes for greater impartiality.[52] But this is not enough. The Purposivist must also show that the kind of impartiality enhanced by adversary advocacy is likely to lead to more accurate, socially efficient decisions. It is no virtue that adversary advocacy "hold[s] the case . . . in suspension between two opposing interpretations" while all the "peculiarities and nuances" are explored, unless it also increases the likelihood that the balance will ultimately be struck in favor of the correct interpretation.[53]

The Purposivist argument suggests no reason to believe that it does. In suggesting that partisan sympathy is necessary to fully understand a person's views, the Purposivist psychology of cognitive dissonance implies that no single person can ever simultaneously grasp the divergent views of different people. it would thus seem unlikely that a judge could ever fully understand both sides of the same case. If this is true, then Purposivist advocacy merely replaces prejudice with arbitrariness. The "familiar pattern" with which the trier begins may be subverted by the vigorous presentation of alternatives, but the pattern which ultimately emerges seems as likely to be the product of the distortions or obfuscations of one or both of the litigants as of anything else. In Purposivist terms, this displacement of the trier's initial prejudices by arbitrariness seems almost certain to be a loss in terms of the quest for truth. Prejudices, after all, are often very accurate, and in a world of shared values and common experiences, one expects "familiar patterns" to have a certain reliability.

Not only does Purposivism beg the question of the way the judge performs his job, but it misrepresents the way the lawyer performs his. The actual psychology of working lawyers does not conform to the model of partisan sympathy assumed by the Purposivist theory of cognitive dissonance. Practical discussions of litigation technique are full of warnings not to behave in precisely the manner that the Purposivist argument suggests the lawyer should act. They insist that a lawyer who accepts his client's version of the facts without being constantly sensitive to the possibility that he may be mistaken or lying, or who focuses on the arguments favorable to his client without making an equally vigorous attempt to anticipate those of his opponent, is likely to do a poor job regardless of the merits of the case.[54] For all its faults, the Positivist theory was a far more accurate description of the realities of adversary advocacy. Adversary advocacy tends more to encourage indifference toward the ends of the client than to encourage sympathy for them. The lawyer's analytical abilities are more compromised than enhanced by such sympathy.[55] The actual psychology of practicing lawyers in analyzing and preparing their clients' cases does not seem radically different from that of a judge trying to understand both sides with a view toward arriving at a decision. This psychology seems to contradict the contention that cognitive dissonance would compromise truth-seeking without adversary advocacy.

Yet even if it is assumed that the Purposivist psychology is accurate, the theory of the separation of functions is untenable both within the adversary sphere and within the legal system as a whole. The various roles in the system cannot be specified so as to permit their effective coordination with each other.

Purposivism suggests that roles are defined by lines. Within the lines, the role occupants are guided directly by social values, but when they reach the limits of the lines, they defer to other jurisdictions. But how are such lines to be drawn and understood? Two types of thought appear in Purposivism. First, there is the intuitive understanding of shared norms which all members of the society share. Second, there are a variety of technical skills possessed by various trained minorities which concern the use of institutional forms to advance the shared values. Neither of these types of thought can solve the problem of delineating the limits of role competences. Intuition cannot do the job because, in order to define the roles, one would need an understanding of the skills on which they were based. The roles are artificial; they are themselves instruments to social ends. Thus, technical knowledge is necessary to shape them. But one of the essential characteristics of technical knowledge is that it is specialized. Each particular skill is of no use in defining its relation to any other skill. The whole point of drawing the lines is to keep people within them, but it seems that they cannot be drawn unless people go beyond them.

One tempting solution to the dilemma is to delegate the task of line-drawing to some very generalized institutional competence, such as a philosopher-king, a constitutional convention, or a legislature. But this proposal only drives the Purposivist back toward the problem of formalism which he originally set out to escape. The lines will have to be expressed in a manner which can be understood by people who, because of the problem of specialization, have no direct, intuitive perception of their basis. The lines would take the form of rules. But the Purposivists have shown conclusively that rules are ineffective without some direct access to the understanding which lies behind them. When the Purposivists ignore their own insights and attempt to prescribe such lines, they fall into formalism and circularity.[56]

In the light of this dilemma, the Purposivist claim to rectify the inadequacies of the separate legal roles by coordinating them with one another is untenable. If cognitive dissonance limits the perspectives of the roles, then it also precludes the role occupants from perceiving the limits of their role competences. There is no way of confining the roles to the situations to which they are appropriate.

The counseling role is supposed to construct and maintain viable social relationships. It is supposed to do so by discouraging the client's short-sighted pursuit of his interests and channeling his energies along paths where these interests coincide with those of others. Yet, there is no reason to believe that the counselor will be able to recognize those short-sighted courses of action which are likely to bring his client into conflict with the interests of others. The counselor must seek an intimate and sympathetic understanding of his client's ends. The principle of cognitive dissonance suggests that this understanding must, at least to some extent, compromise his understanding of the interests of others. In constructing institutions and relationships, the counselor will thus interpret the interests of others in terms of his client's interest. He will be slow to see the point a which his client's short-term interests diverge from the interests of others. Failing to perceive such divergencies, he may devote his talents to maintaining relationships which have become exploitative or destructive. In doing so, he may retard or prevent the appropriate transition of the matter from the counseling to the government or adversary spheres, where corrective action could be taken. Thus, he may perpetuate a socially undesirable situation. On the other hand, if timely intervention by other roles does occur, the problem will be rectified only at the cost of the kind of friction the counselor was supposed to prevent.[57] The basic distinguishing feature of the counseling role is the lawyer's duty to divert short-sighted projects before they lead to the kind of behavior which requires litigation or government intervention. Yet, the counselor is un-likely to be able to perceive that projects which benefit his client immediately are short-sighted until litigation or government intervention is underway.

The advocate will not be able to insure that the destructive tendencies of his activities are confined to the area in which they are appropriate, that is, to situations in which beneficial relations have broken down irreparably. As the counselor will be slow to perceive divergencies of interests between his client and others, so the advocate will be slow to perceive opportunities for reconciliation between his client and others. Once he adopts the perspective of partisanship, cognitive dissonance will blind him to chances to alleviate the costs of an adversary battle and to rescue viable relationships.

The *pro bono* lawyer, in deciding where to allocate his services, will not be able to gauge what their impact will be once he has taken on a client and the relationship has assumed the form of counseling or advocacy. After he has taken on his client, particularly if he does so as an advocate, in order to represent the client's interests effectively he may be led to pursue a course which will jeopardize the public interest or the interests of other people who are not adequately represented. In attempting to decide how to remedy certain problems, he cannot be sure that he will ultimately not create worse ones.

Moreover, the semi-public orientation of the *pro bono* lawyer requires that he look at the world in terms of abstract notions of procedural fairness. Unlike the counselor, he cannot be expected to be sensitive to the more subtle ways in which social relationships serve the concrete needs of the participants. (If he undertakes representation as a counselor, he may ultimately achieve such sensitivity, but if, as more commonly happens, he undertakes representation as an advocate, his perspective will soon be biased by partisan sympathy.) Since the *pro bono* lawyer's primary job is to enhance access to the legal system, he will be prone to frame issues in terms susceptible to legal resolution and to seek whatever legal remedies are available. He will thus be likely to ignore dimensions of problems which are not susceptible to legal resolution and to present the problems to the courts outside of their relevant social context. He will encourage the courts to intervene with judicial remedies in situations with which the courts are not equipped to deal and where judicial remedies may aggravate aspects of the problems over which courts have no control. The specialized perspective of the *pro bono* lawyer is likely to lead him to damage viable social relationships.[58]

Similarly, the government lawyer, whose orientation is public, will be prone to view matters from a formal, legalistic, bureaucratic point of view. In exercising his prosecutorial or administrative discretion, he is likely to ignore the value and effectivensss of informal, spontaneous patterns of cooperation, and his efforts are likely to damage such patterns.[59]

To rely on other roles to discern where any particular role goes wrong merely reverses the problem. Each role will naturally tend to detect the considerations for which it is responsible and to ignore the considerations with which the other roles are charged. For instance, when examining the counselor's performance, the advocate will naturally tend to find conflict; the *pro bono* lawyer, procedural unfairness; and the government lawyer, inefficiency or illegality. Even to the extent that these perceptions are inaccurate, they are likely to ignore the possibility that intervention may damage spontaneous, informal patterns of cooperation worked out by the counselor and naturally overlooked by the other roles.

The phenomenon of cognitive dissonance which the Purposivists emphasize reflects a real problem which recurs in every area of law practice. Yet, the Purposivist scheme of separated functions merely institutionalizes the problem; it does not solve it. Purposivism fails because it treats what is really a moral and political problem as a psychological and technical one. The real source of the lawyer's dissonance is not his inherent mental limitations, but the weakness of the infrastructure of shared values on which Purposivism rests. The difficulty in coordinating the various specialized roles reflects the inability of the legal order Purposivism describes to reconcile private and public ends. Private individual ends are far more antagonistic than Purposivism allows. The public ends which actually are shared tend to be shallow, vague, and remote from the experience of individuals. This is the reason why in each of the roles and in the system as a whole, responsibility for private ends turns out to be incompatible with responsibility for public ends, or vice versa.

By treating the phenomenon of dissonance as a technical problem, Purposivism ignored the ethical and political issues raised by its proposal to integrate public responsibility into the lawyer's role. To accomplish this goal, it would have been necessary to work to establish a set of public norms of sufficient concreteness to serve as binding guides for private conduct. It would have been necessary to work to persuade people of the validity of these norms and to use power to institutionalize these norms and to block their frustration by purely private interests. Yet, to follow this route would have required a radical transformation of the role of the lawyer. Brandeis' career provides thrilling suggestions of what the Purposivist model could have been. Yet, the model which ultimately triumphed in Purposivism is best represented, not by Brandeis, but by those New Deal lawyers who left government practice to become servants of large corporations, helping the corporations to manipulate in their own interests the agencies the lawyers had helped to establish in the public interest.[60] They could rationalize abandonment of the public interest by associating it with a role they no longer occupied. The Purposivist scheme of the separation of functions proves to be merely a set of alibis. Each lawyer can rationalize his refusal to face the ethical and political contradictions of law practice by assigning a critical portion of responsibility to some other role. The contradictions persist, but it becomes easier to ignore them.

The tensions in the separation of functions approach are most severe in the counseling role. The counseling role was the focus of the purposivist claim to integrate responsibility to social norms into legal ethics. The most direct attempt to reconcile public and private ends was to be made in this sphere. Yet, by understanding the tension between private and public ends, by treating dissonance as a psychological problem, Purposivism usually ignored the difficult questions the counseling role raised. Much of the Purposivist literature was ambiguous as to whether the counselor might ever have a professional duty to actively oppose his client's antisocial projects. In the *Code of Professional Responsibility,* this ambiguity was resolved in a manner which confirms the bankruptcy of the separation of functions approach. The need to develop concrete guidelines for the counseling role squarely presented the draftsmen with the problem that any meaningful commitment to public norms would occasionally bring the lawyer into active opposition to his clients. The response was to reduce the distinction between advocacy and counseling to mere rhetoric.

Unlike the responsibility of the government lawyer, which is directly to public values,[61] the responsibility of the private lawyer under the *Code* is defined by "the bounds of the law."[62] But the *Code* emphasizes the fundamental Purposivist insight that the bounds of the law are uncertain and can be determined only by reference to social norms. This leads to the distinction between advocacy and counseling: "Where the bounds of the law are uncertain, the action of a lawyer may depend on whether he is serving as advocate or adviser. A lawyer may serve simultaneously as both advocate and adviser, but the two roles are essentially different."[63] But this distinction turns out to be of no practical significance. The ethical obligations imposed by the *Code* are generally consistent with the more Positivist approach attributed to the *Canons:*

> While serving as advocate, a lawyer should resolve in favor of his client doubts as to the bounds of the law. In serving a client as adviser, a lawyer in appropriate circumstances should give his professional opinion as to what the ultimate decisions of the courts would likely be as to the applicable law.[64]

As advocate, he will urge any position favorable to his client that is not "frivolous."[65] As advisor, he will continue to represent his client even if the client decides to ignore his advice as to what "would likely be the ultimate decisions of the courts."[66]

The *Code* refers to an "obligation to treat with consideration all persons involved in the legal process and to avoid the infliction of needless harm."[67] But no serious attempt is made to integrate this obligation into any specific prescriptions. The *Code* is quite clear on the priority of this obligation: "In the final analysis, however, the lawyer should always remember that the decision whether to forego legally available objectives or methods because of non-legal factors is ultimately for the client and not for himself."[68] Thus, in the final analysis, for all its rhetoric to the contrary, the *Code* abandons the attempt to distinguish advocacy from counseling and with it, the attempt to remedy the problems of the Ideology of Advocacy by integrating a responsibility to social norms into legal ethics. Ultimately, the *Code* falls back on a vision of the lawyer as the servant of private, individual will. In situations of conflict, where the critical decisions arise, it turns back to a notion of the "legal" defined in terms of the prediction of the authoritative application of force.

The *Code* does take one innovating step past the *Canons* in this area which reflects an approach typical of late Purposivism. The *Code* emphasizes the lawyer's discretion to dissociate himself from his client. Thus, it provides that the lawyer *may* "[r]efuse to aid or participate in conduct that he believes to be unlawful, even though there is some support for an argument that the conduct is legal."[69] This discretion is narrow in the area of advocacy, but broad in the area of counseling. But this is far from a significant step toward concretizing the counseling role. It does not solve any problems in terms of professional ethics, but rather simply withdraws certain problems from the area of professional ethics. The concern here is not to reconcile the client's proclivities with social norms, but to reconcile the client's proclivities with the lawyer's proclivities. The lawyer's perception of public values, which was once seen as the foundation of a new professional identity, is here given a purely private significance. To refuse to aid a client's anti-social plans, previously seen as a professional obligation, is here a mere personal privilege.

The *Code's* definition of the professional responsibilities of advocates and counselors almost entirely in terms of service to private ends reflects the ineffectuality of the Purposivist attempt to reconcile private ends and social responsibility in the separation of functions.

The Conflict of Morality and Efficiency

The morality of the long run fails to resolve the basic moral ambiguity of Purposivism. It cannot contain the doctrine's mutually subversive tendencies to view norms as values on the one hand and as facts on the other. In the Purposivist view, social norms, viewed as values, are ends in themselves. They are an important source of human satisfactions and the only source of the legitimacy of public institutions. But social norms, viewed as facts, are means. They are useful because people spontaneously conform to them and intuitively recognize their demands. They thus make it possible to have a social order which avoids the drawbacks of totalitarianism and a jurisprudence which avoids the embarrassments of Positivism. Yet, these two ways of looking at values undercut each other. To perceive norms intuitively as values leads to the inefficiencies of the short run. But to perceive norms instrumentally as facts destroys the sense of worth and obligation which made them important in the first place.[70]

This theoretical difficulty corresponds to a practical dilemma. The more directly and immediately the society concerns itself with shared values, the more it limits its technical options and causes its institutions to stagnate. On the other hand, the more it unleashes its technical dynamism, the more it attenuates the experience of the values which are the basis of its legitimacy. The majority of Purposivists have tended to pursue the instrumental logic of Purposivism at the expense of its moral infrastructure. For that reason, the history of Purposivism has been a history of technical triumph (and the triumph of technicians) and of normative disintegration. Under the Purposivist version of the Ideology of Advocacy, the advocate has risen to greatest power and prestige at a time when the values he is supposed to further have declined.

The critical power of the morality of the long run is its approval of deliberate injustice. In the Positivist system, all outcomes are just by definition. The Purposivists recognize that this kind of perfect justice is a lawyer's mirage. Yet, they do not merely recognize the inevitability of failure, they accommodate themselves to it. They support a legal system which in particular situations often prescribes that social norms intentionally be sacrificed.

These sacrifices are justified in terms of the more remote but greater implementation of social norms which they make possible. The validity of such justification depends on the scarely examined premise that the Purposivist technique includes some method of weighing effectively the relative values of present sacrifice and future benefit. The existence of such a method remains problematical. Yet, even if one could be demonstrated, it could not remedy the fundamental problem of the principle of the long run. In focusing on the relative value of the concrete *results* which follow from alternative decisions, the Purposivists ignore the impact of the *way* in which decisions are made on the experience of those involved. This impact is to diminish the sense of worth and obligation which attaches to the norms that provide the criteria of measurement. This impact cannot be assessed along with the other results in the weighing calculation because it arises in part from the calculation itself. It is inherent in the perspective of the long run.

In the judicial proceeding described by Purposivism, the litigant is brought to view social norms less as ends which he shares with others than as means to the advancement of interests which conflict with those of others. In the beginning, as the Purposivists assume, the litigant may feel that his personal concern implicates a generally shared norm. Thus, he may invoke a norm as a basis for the social recognition of his personal concern. Yet, he is soon disappointed. From the perspective of the long run, the court does not view his claim as a particular embodiment of a shared value, but rather as an opportunity for the general furtherance of a variety of social norms. The court does not recognize the litigant's personal concern in terms of a shared value, but rather manipulates the litigant in the interests of the larger society. A victory for the litigant does not mean the social vindication of his personal concern, but merely that allowing his claim has been found an adequate means for the advancement of social purposes (consider the exclusionary rule). Conversely, if the litigant loses, it is not because his claim is inconsistent with social norms, but merely because its denial is required in the interest of the long run (consider default procedures).

When social norms do not prove a vehicle for the social recognition of his personal concern, the litigant learns that social norms are neither shared, nor values. The failure to achieve recognition on the basis of norms emphasizes to the litigant his separateness. It teaches him that norms do not link his immediate personal concerns to those of the larger society. Yet, he also learns that the invocation of social norms produces somewhat predictable responses from social institutions. He discovers that he can use these norms to advance his personal concerns which he now feels to be separate and individual. He no longer perceives norms as ends or imperatives, but rather as facts and tools for the manipulation of society to serve his individual purposes.

Although the judicial decision plays an important role in this process, the process begins much earlier when the citizen is initiated into the proceeding. Purposivism expects and encourages the litigant to act not as an individual seeking justice but as a conduit for issues and arguments of public interest. The distinction is made clear in, for example, the case of *Federal Communications Commission v. Sanders Brothers Radio Station.*[71] Apparently motivated solely by the hope of preserving a private economic advantage, a radio station owner sought to challenge the granting of a license to a competitor. The Commission refused to hear the challenge because the station owner's concern implicated no relevant social norm. The applicable statutes were not intended to protect owners from competition. The Supreme Court did not dispute this premise, but it considered that the social norm of good broadcasting might be served by the denial of the license. Thus, it ordered that the challenger be given a hearing so that he might try to show the Commission that this public interest would be served by the advancement of his individual interest. Although the *Sanders* case has a special significance in the law of standing, it expresses with unusual directness the general Purposivist notion of the litigant. Litigants are expected to pursue immediate individual interests by invoking the public interest. Thus, the guilty criminal defendant is permitted to invoke the public interest in the protection of the innocent by excluding certain kinds of evidence of his crime. Thus, the welching doctor is permitted to invoke the public interest in the protection of those who pay their debts by pleading the Statute of Frauds. The problem is that in this process the public interest becomes something remote from, and contradicted by, the experience of individuals.

The conduct and attitudes of the lawyer, as prescribed by the Ideology of Advocacy, play a critical role in this experience. The principle of neutrality encourages the view of social norms as data. In the light of the lawyer's attitude of authoritative indifference, norms are stripped of their ethical significance. The principle of partisanship encourages the client to view norms as a means to individual concerns. From the perspective of partisanship, social norms merely define technical options to be weighed in accordance with individual concerns. The consequence of this psychological transformation is disastrous. At just the moments when the individual's sense of soldarity with the society is most at stake, the lawyer deprives him of confirmation of his social identity in terms of shared values and hence undermines his satisfaction from the implementation of social norms. At just the moments when the individual's disposition to conform to social norms is weakest, the lawyer releases him from the pressure of the expectations of his fellow citizens and hence aggravates his antisocial dispositions.

It is futile to hope that the litigant's tendency to view social norms as instruments to selfish ends can be redeemed by a simultaneous sense of the long-run coincidence of his private ends with social norms, or that his altered attitude toward social norms will be confined to the sphere of litigation and give way to a renewed sense of the binding quality of norms upon his return to private life. In the first place, the relation between the litigant's actions and the long-run social welfare is a technical matter which can be determined only with technical knowledge. It cannot be assumed that the litigant has the expertise necessary to understand how his course of conduct will, in the context of the specialized Purposivist institutional apparatus, affect social norms in the long run. Thus, he does not experience his pursuit of his individual ends as advancing social norms. In the second place, the experience of the judicial proceeding is not something which the litigant can step into and out of in the manner in which the lawyer dons and removes his professional role. The dispute which is the subject of the proceeding arises from the litigant's private life, and its resolution will affect his private life. It has developed naturally and unpredictably; it cannot be contained within the artificial confines of a formal role.

Moreover, the morally corrosive impact of the long run is not confined to those directly involved in the "trouble cases" which require resolution in the adversary sphere. Even assuming that the non-advocacy legal roles could be designed to preserve a more immediate experience of social norms, the corrosive experience of the adversary sphere extends beyond the direct participants. Purposivists themselves have emphasized the importance of indirect participation by the general public in the judicial proceeding. For instance, they have argued that adversary advocacy is "essential to a sound development of public opinion" because it facilitates the public resolution of controversies in a manner which provides full public exposure of the issues. Without adversary advocacy, it is argued, "a fear arises that perhaps more might have been said for the losing side and suspicion is cast on the decision reached."[72] Yet such arguments ignore the impact that the spectacle of a litigant reaping a private profit, or escaping his obligations, in the name of a remote public interest has on the citizens' experience of social norms. This impact is inevitably to weaken their sense of satisfaction in, and obligation to, the norms in question.

The principle of the long run undermines the moral infrastructure on which Purposivism depends. It makes the Purposivist calculation of present sacrifices and future benefits meaningless. Such calculation depends on the use of social norms both as data concerning the likelihood of future conduct for the prediction of results and as criteria by which the value of competing results can be measured. A change in norms resulting from the application of Purposivist technique between the time the calculation is made and the time the benefits are supposed to accrue vitiates the calculation in two respects. First, the predicted results may not occur because essential conduct predicted on the basis of the original norms may fail to occur. Second, even if the predicted results do occur, they may be no longer considered, when measured in terms of the altered social norms, worth the past sacrifices. On a more general level, the cumulative effect of the repeated application of Purposivist technique in various areas of public life is to attenuate the experience of social norms throughout the society and thus to destroy the principal basis Purposivism recognizes for social cooperation.

The basic problem of the morality of the long run has been most clearly perceived in relation to the Warren Court's reforms of criminal procedure. These reforms created myriad opportunities for defendants to manipulate judicial procedures so as to frustrate, in the immediate instance, the social norms protected by the substantive criminal law. These reforms were often defended as appropriate means to more effective long-run control of official discretion, and the commentary of both critics and defenders has often taken the form of attempts to weigh present sacrifices against long term benefits of this kind.[73] Yet, commentators also have discussed the impact of procedures designed with a view to the long run on people's experience of the substantive norms of the criminal law. For instance, Paul Bator has pointed out that the elaborate procedural apparatus created by the Warren Court tends to diminish the defendant's sense of the validity of substantive norms and to preclude a sense of the legitimacy of the final outcome of his case:

> A procedural system which permits an endless repetition of inquiry into facts and law in a vain search for ultimate certitude implies a lack of confidence about the possibilities of justice that cannot but war with the effectiveness of the underlying substantive commands. Furthermore, we should at least tentatively inquire whether an endless reopening of convictions, with its continuing underlying implication that perhaps the defendant can escape from corrective sanctions after all, can be consistent with the aim of rehabilitating offenders. The first step in achieving that aim may be a realization by the convict that he is justly subject to sanction, that he stands in need of rehabilitation; and a process of reeducation cannot, perhaps, even begin if we make sure that the cardinal moral predicate is missing, if society itself continuously tells the convict that he may not be justly subject to reeducation and treatment in the first place. The idea of just condemnation lies at the heart of the criminal law, and we should not lightly create processes which implicitly belie its possibility.[74]

Yet, having thus appeared to recognize the problem, Bator fails to perceive its implications. The solution he proposes resorts to the very institutional formalism which is the source of the problem. He argues for greater emphasis on the principle of finality and more specifically, for the limitation of post-conviction review. But the problem lies not in the quantity of procedures, but in their quality, specifically, in the fact that they fail to respect the defendant's immediate, subjective sense of the relation between his conduct and social norms. In arguing for a limitation of post-conviction review, Bator assumes that the sense of guilt which is the moral predicate of the criminal law arises not from the defendant's understanding of what he has done, but from his understanding of the operation of judicial procedure. If the defendant has violated the criminal law, there is no reason to believe that the effect of adversary advocacy in undermining his sense of responsibility for his criminal acts can be reversed merely by cutting off the formal procedures at some definite point. The damage will have begun once the client is introduced to the criminal process through his lawyer's attitude of authoritative indifference, once he comes to see himself as a private attorney general empowered to escape the consequences of his acts in the name of a remote public interest. On the other hand, if the defendant has not committed the crime for which he has been convicted, finality is equally irrelevant. The suggestion that the defendant who knows he has been erroneously convicted should cease regarding himself as a victim of injustice and submit to his condemnation merely because he has exhausted procedures for review is monstrous. It could be followed only by giving up any sense of the meaningfulness of substantive standards of guilt and innocence.

*   *   *

IV. THE LAWYER AS ACOLYTE (THE SANCTIFICATION OF CEREMONY)

[Thurman Arnold] put his finger on a matter too often overlooked: an impressive ceremonial has a value in making people feel that something is being done; this holds, whether the result is right or wrong; and there is some value in an institution which makes men content with fate, whatever that fate may be.

Karl Llewellyn[75]

The third version of the Ideology of Advocacy, which can be called Ritualism, has not achieved the preeminence of its predecessors. It is only one of several doctrinal responses to the decline of Purposivism. Yet, it is the most sensitive and ingenious response within the framework of the Ideology of Advocacy to the difficulties of both Positivism and Purposivism, and it comes closer than competing doctrines to resolving these difficulties. On the other hand, in creating new problems of its own, it shows the futility of attempting to reformulate the Ideology of Advocacy.

Ritualism responds to the critique of Positivism and Purposivism by changing the terms of the debate. It acknowledges the irrationality and inefficiency of the legal system, and then embraces it anyway. In a sense, it represents a synthesis of the two other versions, though only one of several possible syntheses. Ritualism refuses to follow Positivism in insisting that the legal system be viewed as independent of social ends; and it refuses to follow Purposivism in seeing the legal system as simply a means to such ends. The Ritualists suggest that judicial procedure be viewed as both means and end. Procedure can be seen as serving ends, but serving them less by producing them than by embodying them. This logical compromise is accompanied by similar compromises in politics and psychology. The Ritualists think the Positivists right in insisting on the presence of conflict in the social world. And they agree with the Purposivists that law is impossible without shared values. Thus, instead of strife on the one hand and harmony on the other, they propose to substitute the illusion of harmony. The Ritualists see with the Purposivists that men have other ends in common beside order, but they concede to the Positivists that it would be impractical to attempt to realize these ends. Thus, instead of retreat into private realism on the one hand and struggle for concrete social achievement on the other, they propose to substitute the performance of public ceremony.

*   *   *

The Jurisprudence of Resignation

For all their differences of mood, both the cynical and the naive versions of Ritualism share the basic defect of removing procedure from its context in the legal system and in society. Arnold adopts the stance of the objective social scientist so that he does not have to justify the irrational system from which he benefits as a lawyer. Fried takes the position of the abstract moral philosopher so that his justification can safely ignore the facts of suffering and bewilderment which the legal system produces. Arnold's thesis is founded on a sociological datum; Fried's on an aesthetic intuition. Yet, both foundations are weak. Arnold believes, without evidence and in defiance of fact, that people actually hold the views he would like them to hold. That is the naiveté of his cynicism. Fried implies that man's experience of shared values cannot go beyond ceremonial form, that result must be severed from the process in order to create public ritual. This is the cynicism of his naiveté.

For the Positivists, the law was a zero-sum game in which one could win only at someone else's expense. For the Purposivists, it was a "dynamic pie" from which everyone could have a slice.[76] For the Ritualists, the law neither inflicts losses nor produces rewards; it offers consolation in terms of a pleasing rhetoric and imagery detached from social reality.

Ritualism represents a policy of resignation. It is based on a strategy of avoiding disappointment by moderating expectations of success and putting the best possible face on failure. Ritualism acknowledges the irrationality of adversary advocacy just enough to establish credibility. It glamorizes adversary advocacy just enough to discourage criticism.[77] As Alvin Gouldner writes of Erving Goffman's "dramaturgical" sociology, "[i]t is an invitation to the *enjoyment* of appearances."[78]

*   *   *

The Finale: The Friendship Analogy

In a recent article, Charles Fried has defended legal ethics in terms of yet another analogy: friendship. Unlike drama, ritual, and game, friendship is an analogy, not for the legal system, but for the lawyer-client relation itself. It is interesting because it illustrates a tendency to think of the lawyer-client relation as having a value apart from and even antagonistic to the legal system as a whole.[79]

Perhaps surprisingly, in view of the unalloyed naiveté of his earlier rhetoric, the newer article is full of statements associated with the most primitive sort of Positivism. Fried emphasizes the preservation of the client's "autonomy" as a basic purpose of the lawyer's role. He speaks of lawyers' antisocial conduct in terms of pulling "legal levers" and of implementing the client's "rights." He explicitly recognizes and approves some of the lawyer's most unsavory activities such as helping the wealthy to exploit the poor or to avoid taxes.[80]

Yet, these points are peripheral to the basic thrust of Fried's new argument which is entirely foreign to Positivism. Fried's principal purpose is to defend lawyer-client relations as "good in themselves." As before, Fried is concerned with the embodiment of ideals such as "the ideal of personal relations of trust and care."[81] But how the relevant ideals are embodied, not in the legal system as a whole, but in the attorney-client relation itself. This relation is seen less as a component of a larger structure and more as an independent entity.

The defense of partisanship and neutrality as protecting an intrinsically worthwhile relationship is not new. In fact, it appears that the attorney-client evidentiary privilege was first rationalized in the seventeenth century precisely as safeguarding a valuable personal relationship. It was then argued that the rule of confidentiality followed from the more general principle that gentlemen do not reveal each other's confidences. However, in the following century the defense of confidentiality and legal ethics generally shifted to the claim that such principles are necessary to the proper functioning of the legal system as a whole.[82] Since that time, at least until recently, the Ideology of Advocacy has focused on the alleged requirements of the system. The notion that lawyer-client relationships were intrinsically valuable remained a background theme, but it played small part in the public defense of legal ethics.

By contrast, Fried now attempts to rationalize legal ethics by emphasizing the personal worth of the relations defined by the professional norms of partnership and neutrality. Fried suggests that partisanship is like friendship in that it involves "an authorization to take the interests of particular concrete persons more seriously and to give them priority over the interests of the wider collectivity." At the same time the lawyer's neutrality bespeaks a deference to the "concrete individuality" of the client which is similar to the deference one friend would show to another. The fact that the lawyer's concern is not reciprocated in kind by the client does not differentiate the relation from friendship. On the contrary, it exemplifies the lawyer's freedom to bestow and the client's "freedom to receive an extra measure of care" which also exists in friendship.[83] Fried argues that, after one has recognized in the lawyer-client relation the qualities generally valued in friendship, one should accept the lawyer-client relation as good in itself.

The friendship analogy represents a substantial development beyond Fried's earlier work, but it is a development which exacerbates rather than remedies the flaws of the earlier work. The first flaw, as discussed above, was that Fried's idealized model of the judicial process did not reflect the actual experience of litigants. Fried's recent article totally blurs the distinction between the ideal and the actual and tries to pre-empt the vocabulary needed to establish it.

Fried writes: "[L]ike a friend [the lawyer] acts in your interests, not his own; or rather he adopts your interests as his own. I would call that the classical definition of friendship."[84] Now this is clearly an error. The classical definition of friendship emphasizes, not the adoption by one person of another's ends, but rather the sharing by two people of common ends.[85] Moreover, the classical notion of friendship includes a number of other qualities foreign to the relation Fried describes. These missing qualities include affection, admiration, intimacy, and vulnerability.[86] On the other hand, if Fried's definition is amplified to reflect the qualification, which Fried repeatedly acknowledges, that the lawyer adopts the client's interests *for money,*[87] it becomes apparent that Fried has described the classical notion, not of friendship, but of prostitution.

The conflation of the ideas of friendship and prostitution is typical of the moral obfuscation which pervades the article. For Fried, the problem of a doctor who must decide what to do for "a severely deformed baby who can be kept alive only through extraordinarily expensive means" is "analogous" to the problem of a lawyer who must decide what to do for a client who wants "to avoid the effects of a tax or a form of regulation." The task of helping a "disagreeable dowager" tyrannize her relatives deserves the same intensity of commitment as the task of "defending the civil liberties case of the century."[88]

Fried's lawyer is a friend in the same sense that your Sunoco dealer is "very friendly" or that Canada Dry Ginger Ale "tastes like love." The friendship analogy is one of those "self-validating, analytical propositions" which Marcuse describes as typcial of "the closing of the universe of discourse":

> The unification of opposites which characterizes the commercial and political style is one of the many ways in which discourse and communication make themselves immune against the expression of protest and refusal. How can such protest and refusal find the right word when the organs of the established order admit and advertise that peace is really the brink of war, that the ultimate weapons carry their profitable price tags, and that the bomb shelter may spell coziness? In exhibiting its contradictions as the token of its truth, this universe of discourse closes itself against any other discourse which is not on its own terms.[89]

Marcuse's thesis that this style characterizes and rationalizes the flattening out of personality in contemporary society is amply confirmed by Fried's article. If Fried's earlier defense was a naive counterpart of Arnold's analysis, his recent one is a naive counterpart of Goffman's. Like Goffman, Fried celebrates the frankly exploitative alliances of convenience between desperate, selfish little men. Fried explicitly strives to infuse with pathos and dignity the financial problems of the tax chiseler and the "disagreeable dowager." By collapsing traditional moral categories, this rhetoric reflects the homogenization of previously distinct personal characteristics. Fried can assert that the lawyer affirms the client's individuality because, like Goffman's protagonists, Fried's clients have almost no individuality. Any pretense to the contrary is abandoned by the middle of the article when Fried insists that corporations as well as natural persons are entitled to "legal friendship." After all, Fried argues, corporations are "only formal arrangements of real persons pursuing their real interests."[90] Fried began his defense of the analogy by emphasizing that both friendship and the lawyer-client relation involve direct contact with a concrete individual. It now appears that these concrete individuals have so little individuality that a lawyer's relation to a "formal arrangement" can manifest the same qualities. Fried's final example of legal friendship involves friendship with a "finance company."[91]

The second major flaw in Fried's earlier work was its tendency to focus on judicial procedure to the exclusion of the consequences produced by the operation of the judicial system, that is, to collapse substance into process. The friendship analogy represents an even further narrowing of this focus. It focuses on the attorney-client relation to the exclusion, not only of substantive consequences, but of the other elements of the judicial proceeding as well. The most striking feature of Fried's position is that the "moral foundations of the lawyer-client relation" have so little to do with law of any kind.

For Fried, the legal system is a condition of the value of the lawyer-client relation, but it is not the source of this value. Legal friendship arises from the fact that the client has a special need for help in order to exercise the autonomy which the legal system guarantees. The fact that this autonomy is a moral value legitimates certain of the lawyer's antisocial conduct, but it does not give it the special pathos and dignity celebrated by the friendship analogy. These qualities arise, not from the specifically legal character of the client's need, but from the fact that the need is integrally related to the integrity of the person, that it is "implicated in crises going to one's concreteness and individuality."[92] Although Fried argues, somewhat half-heartedly, that the need is a special one which is different from needs for non-professional services,[93] he expressly indicates that the need for legal help is similar to the need for other professionals services, particularly, medical help.

Of course, the legal system defines the patterns and boundaries of the relation, but these patterns and boundaries seem to limit, more than to promote, the qualities emphasized by the friendship analogy. Fried does not contemplate that the lawyer do many things which friends might be expected to do for each other, such as to destroy evidence, lie to the court, or do anything else which would violate the law or the *Code of Professional Responsibility*. After first extolling friendship in glowing and unqualified terms, Fried breaks the bad news that the lawyer is only a "special-purpose friend."[94] Although the lawyer-client relation has value apart from considerations of fairness and efficiency, that value must yield in some situations to the need to maintain the integrity of the legal system.[95] The legal system thus appears as a threat to the lawyer-client friendship.

The game analogy expressed a sense of the meaninglessness of the operation of authoritative institutions. The friendship analogy acknowledges their legitimacy, but emphasizes their remoteness. In an earlier example of the friendship analogy Charles P. Curtis wrote, "Justice is a chilly virtue. It is of high importance that we be introduced into the inhospitable halls of justice by a friend."[96] Fried asserts the intrinsic value of legal friendship against the "cooler, more abstract" notions of justice and social welfare.[97] The judicial proceeding no longer appears, as it did in Ritualism, as a warm, comfortable setting in which the litigant's identity is affirmed. It is cold and inhospitable. Affirmation is possible within the lawyer-client relation, but this relation is no longer harmoniously integrated into the larger system. As with Goffman, the relation shelters the participants against the harsh operation of the system.

Social norms no longer provide any kind of satisfaction. Rather they pose an intolerable burden, and even their ceremonial enactment is threatening. Fried argues against the Purposivist notion of responsibility—which he portrays in a Utilitarian caricature—as a "monstrous conception."[98] Where the classical Purposivists saw social norms as energizing creative individual behavior, the friendship analogy sees them as frightening individuals into retreat. The autonomy Fried celebrates is much different from the aggressive egoism portrayed in the classic Positivist writings. It is defensive and passive.[99]

If the Ideology of Advocacy is a rationalization of the ethical orientation of lawyers, then the friendship analogy seems both its culmination and its finish. The lawyer's distinctive identity has emerged from behind the facade of the legal system and is now openly celebrated as an end in itself. The irony of this development is that at the same time that it celebrates the legal profession more openly than previous defenses, the friendship analogy also comes closer than previous defenses to acknowledging the failure of the legal profession to accomplish the task for which the lawyer's role was created in the first place, the reconciliation of public and private ends. Previously, the lawyer justified his role in terms of the resolution of individual differences through order, justice, welfare, or ceremony. Yet, in fact, to the extent that he was sensitive to outcomes at all, he experienced them not as resolutions, but as arbitrary concessions to one of two opposing spheres. In emphasizing the remoteness and coolness of public ends, the friendship analogy admits that the magic with which the lawyer once claimed he could resolve the clash of individual wills is a fraud.

Yet, the admission is only implicit. The friendship analogy diverts attention from failure by conflating the lawyer with a less problematical social role. The same effect occurs in the familiar comparison of the legal roll with that of doctors (also used by Fried) or clergymen,[100] Such comparisons emphasize the commitment of all three professionals to individual clients, patients, or penitents against the claims of the collectivity, as illustrated particularly by the norms of confidentiality to which all three adhere. Yet, they gloss over a critical difference. The insistence of the doctor and the clergyman on maintaining the confidence of those they serve represents a commitment to the values with which their professional activities are concerned above competing social values. On the other hand, the lawyer's insistence on confidentiality represents a compromise *among* the values with which he is professionally concerned, or perhaps even a sacrifice of these values to extrinsic values. The doctor and the clergyman insist that for them health and salvation must take precedence over justice. The lawyer asserts that his relationship with his client must take precedence over justice, but in doing so he forgets that his relationship was originally defined and rationalized in terms of justice.

In the friendship analogy, the plaintive tone of Ritualism reaches its highest pitch. The lawyer tacitly concedes his failure, but rather than apologize for it, urges the society to lower its expectations. Unable to justify his role in terms of public means and ends, he urges that it be accepted as an end in itself.[101]

V. PROCEDURAL FETISHISM

> [*T*]*he ubiquitous question asked, "Do you think the Rosenbergs were guilty?" is a wrong question and can only result in a wrong answer. The question should be "Do you think there was sufficient evidence warranting the jury, which sized up the witnesses, to decide that the Rosenbergs were guilty?"*
>
> Louis Nizer[102]

*　　*　　*

Discontinuity

The practices prescribed by all three versions of the Ideology of Advocacy alienate the individual from his own ends and actions at the moments when his individuality is most at stake. In this situation, autonomy, responsibility, and dignity—the very norms the Ideology of Advocacy invokes in its own defense—are frustrated. The fatal discontinuity is inherent in the notions of procedural justice and professionalism and is implemented in practice by the principles of neutrality and partisanship.

The problem is manifested in the most salient contradictions of the three versions. Positivism promises to safeguard the autonomy of the individual. Yet, when the individual's autonomy is threatened, it thrusts him into a situation where he cannot make rational choices and must submit to the will of his lawyer. Purposivism promises to enhance social welfare by encouraging individual responsibility. Yet, at points of stress, Purposivism exacerbates centrifugal tendencies by encouraging individuals to regard values in a manner which strips them of their meaning and force. Finally, Ritualism makes only the modest claim to ceremonially affirm individual dignity. Yet, the ceremonies it prescribes turn out to be a mockery of individual dignity.

The common defect of the three versions is that they require that disputes be resolved in a specialized setting discontinuous with the one in which they arose, and in specialized terms discontinuous with those in which they were originally framed. Disputes arise in the social world in terms of rules, values, and practices associated with the substantive law. Procedural considerations such as finality, self-incrimination, notice, hearing, confrontation, repose, and standing, play little part in this context. However, when disputes resist voluntary resolution, they must be precipitated into a distinct, specialized setting in which these procedural considerations become dominant and dispositive.

The first consequence of the shift from the social world to the procedural world is the alienation of the individual from his ends.[103] Each version of the Ideology of Advocacy describes a different form of this phenomenon. In Positivism, because his own ends are assumed to be unintelligible to others, the individual must adopt the more familiar and limited ends which the legal system imputes to him in order to be recognized by the others, and to make sense of the situation. In Purposivism, the individual may retain his own ends, but he is pressured to abstract them from his experience, to look at them from a perspective which weakens their ethical force. In Ritualism, the individual is forced to watch and participate in a formal affirmation of his abstract individuality at the same time that his particular ends are being frustrated.

A further consequence of this shift from the social world to the procedural world is the alienation of the individual from his actions.[104] In the social world, where individuals conduct disputes on their own behalf, they are conscious of creating and affecting the dispute through their own choices. The dispute appears to each disputant to proceed in accordance with actions which he and his adversary have taken, and the outcome of the dispute also appears to result from his and his adversary's actions. However, once lawyers move the dispute into the world of judicial procedure, this perspective changes. It seems to the disputants that the dispute has been taken out of their hands. Formal procedures seem to carry the dispute along with a momentum of their own. The client comes to see his actions as dictated by the requirements of procedures. He sees the lawyer's actions as representing, not the client's own choices, but rather features of an autonomous proceeding. The outcome of the dispute seems to have been determined, not by the client's actions, but by the autonomous operation of a system of rules, a mechanism of functional roles, or a ritual of ceremonial roles.

The Ideology of Advocacy cannot accommodate the autonomous, responsible, dignified individual. Such a person must be able to experience a set of ends as *his own* in the sense that they guide or explain his actions and constitute or contribute to his identity. Moreover, this experience must have some continuity over time. An individual does not make choices solely with regard to preferences of the moment, but rather with regard to ends which he has had and expects to have. This does not mean that a person's ends cannot change, but rather that when such change occurs a person's present ends are related to his past ends by a process of growth or development. Such change is continuous because it can be perceived, at least by the individual himself and often by others as well, as occurring within the framework of a single personality. A person who was merely the setting of a series of discrete transient desires would not be recognizable as an individual.[105]

In addition, an individual must be capable of conscious, deliberate action in furtherance of his ends. His actions can only be meaningfully related to his ends, and to him as an individual, if he has consciously and deliberately chosen to take the actions in the light of his ends.[106] Here too there must be continuity. A person's past choices will limit and influence his present choices, as his present choices will limit and influence his future choices. He must be capable of a continuous series of choices if he is not to blindly undo at night what he has purposefully accomplished by day.

The regime of procedural justice requires that this continuity be interrupted in situations of dispute. It radically abstracts the individual from the social context in which he created the dispute, and requires that he pursue it from a specialized, artificial perspective. It encourages him to forget what he has been and would like to be in the future, and to shape his concerns to the exigencies of the moment. It makes it impossible for him to relate the choices to be made in the procedural setting to the choices previously made, and expected to be made, in the social world. Underlying the disorienting experience of adversary advocacy is the client's sense of the autonomous, inherently legitimating force of procedure.[107] Because the judicial proceeding is designed to focus attention on its inherent norms, it subverts the participants' sense of their own ends. Because the pattern of the judicial proceeding is so formal and so alien to everyday social intercourse, it precludes active, coherent participation by the litigants.

The lawyer implements the discontinuity of procedural justice through the practice of neutrality and partisanship. Given the client's dependence on him, the lawyer, wittingly or not, will redefine the initial terms of the dispute in terms of his own procedural orientation. The fact that the lawyer presents himself (under the principle of partisanship) as sympathetic and committed to the client and yet (under the principle of neutrality) detached from and indifferent to his client's ends leads the client to view his own ends with detachment and indifference. The fact that (under the principle of partisanship) the lawyer is willing to take aggressive action on behalf of the client and yet (under the principle of neutrality) disclaims responsibility for the consequences of such action leads the client to see these consequences, not as results of his or his lawyer's choices, but as the products of autonomous forces.

Professionalism plays a critical part in this re-definition of the situation. The lawyer's formal and practical monopoly over access to the institutions of authoritative dispute resolution gives him a large measure of power over the client.[108] But the transformation of perspective can be accomplished only because the lawyer presents himself to the client, not as an individual with ends and responsibilities of his own, but as the embodiment of a neutral, specialized discipline. If the lawyer were merely an individual with personal ends, his definition of the situation would have no special priority. But because it is presented as standing above individual views, his professional view of the situation disarms defenses which might be raised to merely individual views, and lays claim to acceptance regardless of the client's personal views. Similarly, if the lawyer were an ordinary individual, he would be responsible for his actions, and his association with the client would not affect the client's responsibility for the client's own actions. But as an embodiment of a neutral, specialized discipline, the lawyer is a kind of filter through which the client's will is cleansed of responsibility. The client comes to see the lawyer not as an individual, but as a component in the procedural system. Thus, the consequences of the lawyer's actions on behalf of the client come to be seen as products of the system.[109] By creating this discontinuity whereby the client loses track of his own ends and his capacity to implement them, the Ideology of Advocacy precludes the most basic psychological prerequisites of individual autonomy, responsibility, and dignity.

It should be emphasized that the suggestion that legal experience should be continuous with other forms of social experience does not amount to a plea for a return to a pre-industrial communalism in which law is completely undifferentiated from other norms.[110] The values of individuality imply that law should be continuous with other social and moral experience, but not necessarily indistinguishable from it. Indeed, as I will emphasize below, liberal legal theory is correct in claiming that individuality and justice are best served by a distinctive form of law and legal experience which is differentiated from other categories of social norms and experience. The notion of continuity suggests only that people should be able to relate legal norms to other forms of understanding and experience in a coherent fashion. The critical point is that the law should be accessible to those who are governed by it. Thus, the notion of continuity is opposed, not to differentiation, but rather to specialization, that is, to the notion that the legal doctrine should or must be accessible only to a trained occupational minority, and that legal institutions should or must be dominated by such a minority.[111]

Far from being a repudiation of modernity, the appeal to continuity is a plea for the fulfillment of a principle which is acknowledged or assumed in most legal thought as fundamental to modern law: what Hegel calls the "right of giving recognition only to what my insight sees as rational."[112] Like contemporary legal theorists, Hegel considered that, to be seen as rational by the litigants, a judicial decision must be justified in a manner accessible to the litigants in terms of norms which they understand as binding on them. In addition, it must embody active, meaningful contributions by the litigants to the proceeding from which it emerges.[113] Yet, unlike most contemporary theorists, Hegel saw the danger posed by a specialized legal system to the principle of continuity.[114] When access to the courts is monopolized by an occupational group and legal discourse becomes isolated from social norms,

> the members of civil society, who depend for their livelihood on their industry, on their own knowledge and will, are kept strangers to the law, not only to those parts of it affecting their most intimate affairs, but also to its substantive and rational basis, the right itself, and the result is that they become the wards, or even in a sense the bondsmen, of the legal profession. They may indeed have the right to appear in court in person and 'to stand' there (*in judicio stare*), but their bodily presence is a trifle if their minds are not to be there also, if they are not to follow the proceedings with their own knowledge, and if the justice they receive remains in their eyes a doom pronounced *ab extra*.[115]

Not law, but rather the kind of law practice defined by the principles of professionalism and procedural justice engenders the discontinuity which subverts individual autonomy, responsibility, and dignity.

*   *   *

VI. CONCLUSION: NON-PROFESSIONAL ADVOCACY

Is the inside-dopester an enemy, with his sympathetic tolerance, but veiled lack of interest, and his inability to understand savage emotions? Are they enemies, those friends who stand by, not to block but to be amused, to understand and pardon everything? An autonomous person of today must work constantly to avoid shadowy entanglements with this top level of other-direction—so difficult to break with because its demands appear so reasonable, even trivial.

David Riesman[116]

Showing that the Ideology of Advocacy is incoherent in theory and destructive in practice is not the same thing as showing that it should be abandoned. It remains to be shown that there is a more satisfactory alternative. There is an alternative implicit in the critique of the Ideology of Advocacy. The alternative can be called "non-professional advocacy." Although this essay cannot show conclusively that non-professional advocacy would prove more satisfactory, it can suggest the issues involved in the decision whether or not to adopt it. The choice between the Ideology of Advocacy and non-professional advocacy rests on one's view of the relative priorities of individuality and stability, and of the prospects of reconciling the tension between them.[117]

Non-professional advocacy is difficult to describe with precision, but it is not at all mysterious. On the contrary, it relies on a style of thought and conduct with which everyone has at least some familiarity. The foundation principle of non-professional advocacy is that the problems of advocacy be treated as a matter of *personal* ethics. As the notion is generally understood, personal ethics presupposes two ideas diametrically opposed to the foundation principles of the Ideology of Advocacy. First, personal ethics apply to people merely by virtue of the fact that they are human individuals. The obligations involved may depend on particular circumstances or personalities, but they do not follow from social role or station. Personal ethics are at once more particular and more general than professional ethics. On the one hand, they require that every moral decision be made by the individual himself; no institution can define his obligations in advance. On the other hand, the individual may be called upon to answer for his decisions by any other individual who is affected by them. No specialized group has a monopoly which disqualifies outsiders from criticizing the behavior of its members. Second, personal ethics require that individuals take responsibility for the consequences of their decisions. They cannot defer to institutions with autonomous ethical momentum.

Personal ethics involve both a concern for one's own integrity and respect for the concrete individuality of others.[118] The non-professional advocate presents himself to a prospective client as someone with special talents and knowledge, but also with personal ends to which he is strongly committed. The client should expect someone generally disposed to help him advance his ends, but also prepared to oppose him when the ends of advocate and client conflict. If the two sets of ends coincide, then a strong alliance on behalf of these ends is possible. If the two sets of ends are irreconcilably opposed, then no relationship will be possible. It is essential that neither advocate nor client feel strong pressure to accept the other. Between the extremes of an alliance on behalf of entirely shared ends and a situation in which no relationship is possible, there is a broad category where one party will be able to win over the other to his position of where the parties will work out a compromise.

Non-professional advocacy does not preclude conflict. Conflict is possible both inside and outside of the relationship. Where their ends are opposed, the advocate may engage in conflict with the client (although obviously any large measure of conflict will end the relationship). Where their ends are shared, advocate and client may join together to engage outsiders in conflict. On the other hand, non-professional advocacy does not presuppose conflict any more than it presupposes the stylized aggression of the Ideology of Advocacy. The advocate may lead the client to modify or abandon a collision course so as to make voluntary, informal resolution possible. Indeed, one of the most important effects of non-professional advocacy should be to increase the client's concern for the impact of his conduct on others, and to enlarge the minimal role which norms such as reciprocity and community now play in attorney-client decisions.

If the major foundation principle of non-professional advocacy is that advocacy be deemed a matter of personal ethics, the major principle of conduct is this: advocate and client must each justify himself to the other. This justification need not embrace the person's entire life, but merely those aspects of it which bear on the dispute. Each must justify the goals he would pursue and the way he would pursue them. In this manner, the advocate-client relation is reconstructed in each instance by the participants themselves. It is not set in advance by formal roles. Such relationships will sometimes arise spontaneously, but they will often arise only after patient, step-by-step efforts. Advocate and client may become friends, not in Fried's sense, but in the more familiar sense of an intimacy made possible by shared ends and experience. Yet, friendshp is not necessary to the relationship. The basic requirement is that each have respect for the other as a concrete individual. In addition, some sharing of ends will be necessary, but this sharing need not approach a complete coincidence of ends.

Trust is an important value in non-professional advocacy.[119] But it is not a formal, definitional property of the advocate-client relation. It is a quality which the parties must create or fail to create in each instance. When confidentiality may be important to the client, advocate and client should arrive at some understanding at the outset concerning this issue. The scope of confidentiality need not be defined for the entire relation at the outset. It can be defined in stages as lawyer and client gain greater understanding of each other. The client's claim to assurances of confidentiality is a strong one, and once assurances have been made, his claim that they be honored is much stronger still. Yet, these claims must be viewed in the context of other, potentially conflicting values. They must be considered in the context of the specific ends which the client seeks to further. The claim of a client who seeks legal services to exploit or oppress another cannot have the same priority as the claim of one who seeks to escape exploitation and oppression. This approach to the problem of confidentiality means that the client must take a risk in seeking an advocate, and that the advocate-client relation will sometimes end in betrayal.[120] This element of risk is inherent in any effort by lawyer and client to come to terms with each other as concrete individuals. It is in part because of this risk that trust, when it is created, can be a vital and concrete psychological reality rather than an empty, formal claim.

The non-professional relation is quite different from the "helping" or "accepting" lawyer-client relation described by recent writing which draws on the concepts and jargon of existentialist psychotherapy.[121] This writing is valuable because it recognizes that the task of understanding the client's ends is a difficult one, and that the client's consciousness of his own ends is shaped in the lawyer-client relation. It also acknowledges, at least partially, that the lawyer's posture of detachment can threaten, rather than safeguard, the client's autonomy. Yet, the relation of relatively intimate, sympathetic, and personal involvement prescribed by the psychotherapists is unsatisfactory. Although these writers purport to be concerned with respecting the client's concrete individuality, the style of practice they propose will often be more of a threat to it than traditional advocacy. As they describe him, the lawyer claims to be dedicated to his client's concrete individuality, but he does not present *himself* to the client as a concrete individual. Individuals have ends about which they care deeply. Even the most tolerant individual cannot view everyone's ends with the same undifferentiated sympathy. Yet, the psychotherapists seem to contemplate that the same homogeneous acceptance be dispensed indiscriminately to the exploiters and the exploited, the creative and the destructive, the smug and the despairing. No individuality of any depth could be expressed through such an attitude.

A relation defined in advance in terms of acceptance is more likely to be a relation of bureaucratic impersonality than one of respect and understanding.[122] It is doubtful that either lawyer or client would achieve a heightened understanding of the client's ends in a relation of this kind. The fact that the lawyer withholds or denies his private ends, while he seeks to ascertain his client's, undermines the credibility of his claim of loyalty to the client. The lawyer's posture of selflessness often will seem either false and hypocritical, or a defensive retreat to the refuge of role. In either event, the client will be led, as Goffman suggests, to retreat himself rather than, as the psychotherapists predict, to open himself to understanding by the lawyer. Moreover, the psychotherapists ignore that tension and even conflict is often essential to the growth of both self-consciousness and mutual understanding. The flaccid, undifferentiated sympathy so extravagantly dispensed by the psychotherapists may discourage precisely the kind of doubt, questioning, and reflection which would best enhance the client's understanding of his own ends. Non-professional advocacy must recognize that a relation of respect and understanding between autonomous individuals can rarely be an entirely accepting relation.[123] Respect and understanding will often depend more on resistance than on acceptance.

One of the most important questions raised by non-professional advocacy concerns the bases for the establishment of a relationship in the absence of a coincidence of ends. The question is not as difficult as it initially appears. In the first place, in many situations in which ends are not shared, there will not be opposition, but merely indifference. In these situations, there will be a large range of courses of action on which the parties will be able to agree. In the second place, even in those situations in which ends are actually opposed, there are a variety of quite familiar bases for compromise. These are the formal values of liberal theory, such as reciprocity, promise keeping, the ideal of law, and the ideal of representative government. These values do not provide a precise, objective, neutral mechanism for the resolution of differing ends. Moreover, they can never be dispositive by themselves. However, as values, they will often provide a substantial basis for an alliance between people with differing concrete ends. Consider, for instance, the ideal of law. The ideal of law has taken a battering in recent years, but it is still alive. We do not always know what the law says, and we sometimes feel that what it says is unjust. But there are many situations in which we do know what the law says and have no reason to think it unjust. At least in these situations, many people still feel that the ideal of law does have independent moral authority, that it can still provide a reason for doing something even when it conflicts with many more concrete ends. Thus, where the lawyer is convinced that the claim against his client is unsupported by law, or that his client's claim against another is supported by law, the ideal of law will often provide a basis for association even in the absence of a sharing of more specific, concrete ends.

Although non-professional advocacy rejects the determinative role of procedural considerations in the Ideology of Advocacy, it does not ignore procedural values entirely. The non-professional advocate recognizes that the *way* in which a dispute is settled or a decision made can be a matter of importance. In particular, he recognizes the strong value of assuring the client an opportunity to attempt to explain or justify himself publicly. Moreover, the non-professional advocate may encounter situations in which he feels that he cannot effectively assess his client's position, and thinks that a judge or jury would be in a much better position to do so after an adversary hearing.

Such procedural considerations provide a further basis for accommodation between parties with opposing ends. The non-professional advocate should take them very seriously. He does not, however, regard them in the same manner as the Ideology of Advocacy does. First, he will never consider them independently of the substantive legal and moral values involved. Unlike Freedman and Noonan, the non-professional advocate cannot answer any of the "three hardest questions" without knowing the nature of the result to which his decision is likely to lead. Second, the non-professional advocate considers procedural considerations as they arise in each case. He refuses to assume that such considerations are necessarily present in every case, or that when present they will invariably be advanced by any particular mode of conducting the case. The value of enabling the client to explain and justify himself in public is implicated only when the client sincerely wants to explain or justify himself and proposes to do so. The utility of adversary advocacy in facilitating informed decisionmaking is relevant only when there is some reason to believe that the truth is not clear, and that the judge will be in a better position to decide after a trial than the advocate is now. Neither of these procedural considerations can ever justify attempts to exclude probative evidence, to discredit testimony which is not misleading, or to engage in any of the routine procedural tactics designed to obfuscate rather than clarify the issues. There may be other considerations which would justify such actions, but they must be identified and considered in each case along with the competing considerations which favor the exposure of truth.

So far in this essay, the terms procedural justice and procedural values have been used to refer to norms associated specifically with the judicial process. The terms can also be used to refer to a more general notion which is also relevant to non-professional advocacy. This is the notion of a legitimacy of fairness arising from equality of access and participation in the society as a whole. Where there is substantial inequality and the lawyer can assist the relatively powerless to a greater measure of access and participation, this general notion of procedural justice will often provide a basis for advocate-client relationships in the absence of shared substantive values. The general notion of procedural justice will have a particularly strong claim on the advocate where his prospective client has little or no prospect of finding another advocate. In such situations, given the drastic inequality of power between lawyer and client, it will be unusually difficult to work out a genuinely voluntary relationship, and there is a great danger that the lawyer's insistence on his substantive ends may force the client to compromise his own in order to secure some measure of access and participation. For this reason, many who reject the determinative role of the specific notion of procedural justice contend that the general notion should be the exclusive basis of the advocate-client relationship, at least where the client is among the relatively powerless. From this line of thought, a modified version of the Ideology of Advocacy has emerged in the field of public interest law.[124]

Yet, non-professional advocacy cannot regard general procedural considerations as exclusively determinative of the advocate's ethical obligations even within the area of representation of the powerless. The importance of substantive considerations is most apparent in situations where the oppressed client proposes a course of action which will injure others who are equally powerless. In such situations, the public interest lawyer's appeal to procedural justice as a basis for representation is self-contradictory. He first commits himself to his client on the basis of his belief that institutional processes do not operate fairly, and then rationalizes the harm he does to others by asserting that institutional processes should be relied upon to protect their interests. Moreover, even where the client's course of action does not implicate the interests of other oppressed people, the interests of the client's own autonomy, responsibility, and dignity will sometimes require that the advocate insist on his own substantive ends.[125]

Thus, non-professional advocacy rejects the foundation principles of professionalism and procedural justice entirely. Its response to the principles of conduct of the Ideology of Advocacy is more complex. The most important objections to the Ideology of Advocacy are addressed not to either of the principles individually, but to the stylized aggression which results from their combination. Non-professional advocacy rejects the notion that the advocate-client relation must invariably be characterized by both partisanship and neutrality, but it does not rule out the possibility that either principle might sometimes be relevant. There may be situations in which the non-professional advocate will find it appropriate to present to a tribunal a claim to which he is not willing to commit himself personally. And there may be situations in which he will find it appropriate to present a claim aggressively even to the point of engaging in obfuscation or deception. Yet, from the point of view of non-professional advocacy the two principles appear, not complementary, but antagonistic. Where the advocate is not committed to the cause of the client, aggresive methods will almost always seem improper. The non-professional advocate is likely to regard a strong commitment to a claim as a necessary condition to the use of such methods.

*   *   *

Yet, it seems unlikely that reform will ever completely abolish the problem of discontinuity. Ideally, everyone should be his own advocate, but this ideal does not seem capable of realization. The very existence of the occupation of the advocate presupposes some measure of alienation from law. Unlike the professional, the non-professional advocate can reduce, rather than aggravate, this alienation. Yet, except where advocate and client can develop a relation of genuine understanding and fraternity, he will not eliminate it. Except where the relation is based on shared substantive ends and experience, the client's dependence on the advocate will compromise his autonomy. It is important to recognize that, like the soldier's, the advocate's occupation arises from social imperfection. This imperfection may be inevitable, but it is important that the advocate not feel that he has a vested interest in it. If the non-professional advocate is to perform his job, he must be willing and even anxious to work to diminish the power and importance of his own role in order to enhance the client's autonomy. For this reason, it may be desirable for the non-professional to be a part-time advocate, one whose primary means of livelihood is in some activity other than advocacy.

The rejection of the Ideology of Advocacy in favor of non-professional advocacy would not guarantee progress toward the realization of the values of individuality in the legal system. Non-professional advocacy is a necessary, but not a sufficient, condition for the realization of these values. Progress toward this goal would depend on the particular ends which people brought to the judicial process, and on the extent to which the conflict unleashed by non-professional advocacy led to the enhanced sharing of concrete ends necessary to a social order in which individuality can flourish. The change would thus require a certain amount of optimism, but if lawyers were seriously committed to the values of individuality, they could do no better than to abandon their professionalism.

This brief suggestion of the nature of non-professional advocacy leaves many problems to be worked out in theory and in practice. For the present, it will be sufficient to anticipate two of the more prominent objections with which the basic proposal will be met.

First, it will be argued that non-professional advocacy will make it more difficult or impossible for many to secure an advocate. Lawyers will decline to represent at least some people whose values they do not share. Those with unpopular views may thus find themselves without representation. Moreover, people will be unwilling to consult lawyers or to confide in them for fear of oppression or betrayal. Contentions such as these are among the oldest and most common arguments on behalf of professional ethics. One answer to them is that they are beside the point. Since the principal thrust of the critique of the Ideology of Advocacy is to show the destructiveness of legal services as they are now rendered, the possibility that reform might diminish the availability of legal services is hardly a disadvantage. Even if it were a disadvantage, it would seem plausible that it would be outweighed by the qualitative improvement which non-professional advocacy would bring.

There is a further answer to these contentions. The parade of horribles which they put forth as the hypothetical outcome of hypothetical reform is in fact precisely the situation which obtains *now* and which has obtained for the past century under the hegemony of the Ideology of Advocacy. There is now a wealth of empirical studies which confirm what most laymen have always known: only a tiny minority, composed almost entirely of the wealthy and the powerful, is assured or ever has been assured substantial access to legal services. The majority of the public distrusts and dislikes lawyers and seeks their help, if at all, only in connection with a few types of routine transactions or in desperate situations as a last resort. This distrust is well grounded; lawyers commonly pursue self-interest at the expense of their clients' interests.[126] The history of the profession mocks the contention that there is any connection between the Ideology of Advocacy and the adequate provision of legal services. In this dismal situation, the risks of reform are slight. At best, the abandonment of professional ethics, by broadening the lawyer's ethical perspective, will lead to a more equitable distribution of services than now exists. At worst, it is difficult to see how it could produce a less satisfactory situation than now exists.

Second, it will be objected that non-professional advocacy puts an unrealistically large moral and psychological burden on the lawyer. The constant responsibility for the consequences of his efforts on behalf of so many others with varying ends will generate a "role strain" which will make non-professional advocacy intolerable for lawyers.[127] The often voiced premise of this criticism—that the lawyer's conditions of work involve greater responsibility or ethical pressure than others—seems wrong. Most occupations involve, directly or indirectly, constant, and often intimate and confidential, dealings with strangers which implicate moral responsibilities. The real difference between the position of the lawyer and that of, for instance, the corporate bureaucrat, lies not in the greater pressure on the lawyer, but in his greater freedom. The autonomy of the lawyer should not be exaggerated. Most lawyers work under conditions of bureaucratic routine. Nevertheless, compared with most other occupations, lawyers have achieved a remarkable measure of autonomy in their conditions of work. Not every lawyer has the opportunity to act like Brandeis, but some do, and many have more latitude in defining the nature of their work than the most powerful corporate executives. The strain which the lawyer feels results less from the weight of his responsibilities than from the weight of his freedom. The corporate executive sacrifices his personal values more easily because he perceives his choices as more limited. The lawyer must undertake more strenuous efforts to rationalize his compromises because the pressures on him to compromise are weaker. Non-professional advocacy merely asks the lawyer to make the most of the freedom he has.

The proposal to abolish legal professionalism will strike most lawyers as radical and unrealistic. But at least in some respects this impression is wrong. After all, it has become commonplace to speculate on the "death of law." It should not be surprising that such discussions rarely embrace the death of the legal profession; or indeed, that they often take place within the bastions of professional privilege and power.[128] For, legal professionalism thrives on contempt for the ideal of law. Yet, the ideal of law and the values of individuality have been a potent historical alliance, and they may well prove more tenacious than the most entrenched contemporary institutions. In this light, the death of the legal profession may be a more conservative and more practical alternative to the death of law.

NOTES

1. R. Stout, *In the Best Families* (1950), p. 199.
2. C. Dickens, *Bleak House* (Signet ed. 1964). p. 228, (emphasis in original).
3. Important exceptions, which do involve criticism of the basic premises, are Bellow & Kettleson, *The Mirror of Public Interest Ethics: Problems and Paradoxes* (1977) (unpublished manuscript on file with author) [hereinafter cited as Bellow & Kettleson]; Griffiths, "Ideology in Criminal Procedure or A Third 'Model' of the Criminal Process," *Yale Law Journal* 79 (1970): 359, [hereinafter cited as Griffiths]; Wasserstrom, "Lawyers as Professionals: Some Moral Issues," 5 *Human Rights* (1975):1 See this volume pp. 114-131.
4. See text accompanying notes 8-12 *infra*.
5. See,, e.g., D. Rosenthal, *Lawyer and Client: Who's in Charge?* (1974), pp. 106-116 [hereinafter cited as Rosenthal]; Blumberg, "The Practice of Law as a Confidence Game: Organizational Cooptation of a Profession," *Law & Society Review* 1 (1967):15 [hereinafter cited as Blumberg]; Skolnick, "Social Control in the Adversary System," *Journal of Conflict Resolution* 11 (1971):52, [hereinafter cited as Skolnick].
6. See J. Auerbach, *Unequal Justice: Lawyers and Social Change in Modern America* (1976) [hereinafter cited as Auerbach]; J. Carlin, *Lawyers' Ethics* (1966); Schuchman, "Ethics and Legal Ethics: The Propriety of the Canons as a Group Moral Code," *George Washington Law Review* 37 (1968):244.
7. More radical criticisms of conventional law practice are sometimes made by partisans of public interest law. See, e.g., Nader, "Law Schools and Law Firms, *Minnesota Law Review* 54 (1970):493; Comment, "The New Public Interest Lawyers," *Yale Law Review* 79 (1970):1069, 1119-1137 [hereinafter cited as Comment, "The New Public Interest Lawyers"]. However, such criticism is often ambiguous. Like the works cited in the preceding note, it tends to focus disapproval on the professional elite and on its service to the dominant social groups. On the other hand, it sometimes urges lawyers not only to make conventional legal services available to the less powerful but also to devote their efforts to specific substantive ends and interests. Such criticism seems to hesitate between a critique based on the distribution of legal services, which would be compatible with the Ideology of Advocacy, and a critique based on the nature of legal services, which would involve a repudiation of the Ideology of Advocacy.
8. Freedman, "Professional Responsibility of the Criminal Defense Lawyer: The Three Hardest Questions," *Michigan Law Review* 64 (1966):1469. See this volume pp. 328-339. [hereafter cited as Freedman].
9. *Id.* at p. 337.
10. Noonan, "The Purposes of Advocacy and the Limits of Confidentiality," *Michigan Law Review* 64 (1966):1485, 1491, [hereinafter cited as Noonan].
11. *Id.* at p. 1487.
12. See "Professional Responsibility: Report of the Joint Conference," *American Bar Association Journal* 44 (1958):1159, 1216-1217 [hereinafter cited as "Professional Responsibility"].
13. W. Forsyth, *Hortensius: An Historical Essay on the Office and Duties of the Advocate* (3rd ed. 1879) 387; A.B.A. Op. No. 281; *ABA Code of Professional Responsibility*, DR 7-101(b) (1976) [hereinafter cited as ABA Code].
14. ABA Code, *supra* note 13, at EC 7-24.
15. See *id.* EC 5-1 to 5-24.
16. Freedman, *supra* note 8, at pp. 331-333; Noonan, *supra* note 11, at pp. 1487-1488; see also ABA Code, *supra* note 13, at EC 7-20.
17. Freedman, *supra* note 8, at pp. 328-329; Noonan *supra* note 11, at pp. 1489-1490; see also H. Drinker, *Legal Ethics* (1953), p. 149 [hereinafter cited as Drinker]; Thode, "The Ethical Standard for the Advocate," *Texas Law Review* 39 (1961):575, 589, [hereinafter cited as Thode].
18. Drinker, *supra* note 18, at p. 83; *Le Droit de la Nature et des Nations* § XXI at pp. 195-198 (French trans. 1747); Curtis, "The Ethics of Advocacy," *Stanford Law Review* 4 (1951):3, 8; but see ABA Code of Professional Responsibility, EC 7-23 and DR 7-102(A)(1), (A)(5).

19. Similarly, an adjudicatory procedure can adopt one principle without the other. The principle of neutrality was not involved in the highly partisan adjudicatory procedure of trial by battle which was used during the Middle Ages. See generally 2 F. Pollock & F. Maitland, *The History of English Law* (1968 ed.), p. 633 n. 7. On the other hand, in the adjudicatory procedures of contemporary continental Europe, the principle of partisanship plays a muted role, while the principle of neutrality is enshrined. See D. Rueschmeyer, *Lawyers and their Society: A Comparative Study of the Legal Profession in the United States and Germany* (1973), pp. 85–87, 127–131, 143.

20. B. Barry, *Political Argument* (1965) pp. 97–98, 102–106 [hereinafter cited as Barry].

21. Carr-Saunders, "Professions," in *Encyclopedia of the Social Sciences* 12 (1934):476.

22. J. Boswell, *Life of Johnson,* quoted in *The World of Law* 2 (E. London ed. 1960), 765.

23. See, e.g., J. Austin, The Province of Jurisprudence Determined (Hart ed. 1954); H. Hart, *The Concept of Law* (1961) [hereinafter cited as Hart]; Holmes, "The Path of the Law," *Harvard Law Review* 10 (1897):457, [hereinafter cited as Holmes]; Kelsen, "The Pure Theory of Law: Its Methods and Fundamental Concepts," (pts. 1–2) *Law Quarterly Review* 50 (1934):474 and *Law Quarterly Review* 51 (1935): 517.

There is no general jurisprudential work representative of the version of Positivism which has had the greatest impact on American legal history. As Karl Llewellyn wrote, "The older Jurisprudence . . . is one which the profession did not have occasion to particularly study; a lawyer just absorbed it, largely through the fingers and the pores, as he went along." Llewellyn, "On Reading and Using the Newer Jurisprudence," *Columbia Law Review* 40 (1940): 581, 582-583. This jurisprudence, often called Legal Formalism, was the prevalent type of legal thought in the late nineteenth and early twentieth centuries. In the field of applied doctrine, it is well exemplified by the majority opinion in Lockner v. New York, 198 U.S. 45 (1905), and by J. Beale, *A Treatise on the Conflict of Laws* (1916). Since Formalism included some natural law elements, it may not be strictly accurate to designate it as Positivist. Nevertheless, the elements of the Formalist system which bear on the issues of advocacy are consistent with the Positivist doctrine sketched here. For an early treatment of legal ethics from a Formalist perspective, see the letters of David Dudley Field reprinted in A. Kauffman, *Problems in Professional Responsibility* pp. 249–266, especially at pp. 257-260 (1975) [hereinafter cited as Kauffman].

24. Cf. S. Wolin, *Politics and Vision: Continuity and Innovation in Westernd another").*

25. See, e.g., Restatement of Judgments §§ 126 (2)(e) & (f), 129 (a) (1942) (no relief from erroneous and inequitable judgment entered due to attorney negligence); see also Williams v. Beto, 354 F.2d 698, 706 (5th Cir. 1965) (The client "should know that in the course of a lawsuit there are many critical Rubicons at which the attorney must make finely balanced, often agonizing, decisions"). See generally Mazor, "Power and Responsibility in the Attorney-Client Relation," *Stanford Law Review* 20 (1968):1120; Cover & Aleinkoff, "Dialectical Federalism: Habeas Corpus and the Court," *Yale Law Journal* 86 (1977):1035, 1078-1086.

26. E.g., Estelle v. Williams, 425 U.S. 501, 514–515 (1976) (Powell, J. concurring); Henry v. Mississippi, 379 U.S. 443, 445-52 (1965); Finer, "Ineffective Assistance of Counsel," *Cornell Law Review* 58 (1973):1077, 1092-1116.

27. See generally Blumberg, *supra* note 5; Skolnick, *supra* note 5.

28. See, e.g., L. Auchincloss, *Powers of Attorney* (1963), pp. 184-186.

29. On the process by which an individual comes to accept the others' definition of his situation, see J. Sartre, *Being and Nothingness* (Barnes trans. 1952), pp. 55-56, 252-302, [hereinafter cited as Sartre]; Goffman, "The Moral Career of the Mental Patient," in *Asylums: Essays on the Social Situation of Mental Patients and Other Inmates* (1961), pp. 127-169, [hereinafter cited as Goffman]; Lukacs, "Reification and the Consciousness of the Proletariat," in *History and Class Consciousness* (Livingstone trans. 1971), pp. 83-110, [hereinafter cited as Lukacs].

30. Holmes, *supra* note 23, at p. 459.

31. E.g. Griffiths & Ayres, "A Postscript to the Miranda Project: Interrogation of Draft Protestors," *Yale Law Journal* 77 (1967):300. This article exemplifies the unconscious influence of ideological assumptions on empirical research. It is based on an actual, unstaged incident in which members of the Yale University community were interrogated individually on two occasions by agents of the FBI about their involvement in illegal draft protests. In the first series of interrogations, despite the fact that the agents gave *Miranda* warnings, all of those questioned discussed their involvement. After these sessions, those questioned attended a meeting at which they were then informed of their rights, this time in more detail and by a "friendly source," that is, three Yale law professors. At the subsequent interrogations, all refused to give any information to the agents. The authors attribute the change of mind to the "greater understanding" resulting from the meeting and suggest that the agents' *Miranda* warnings had been ineffective because they were mechanically and tersely given and because of psychological pressures inherent in the interrogation situation, stemming in part from middle-class habits of courtesy and cooperation and a natural fear of the alien, coercive force of the state. They conclude that mechanical recitals of the *Miranda* provisions by officials are not enough and that a person requires an "advocate" at interrogation proceedings.

The central thrust of the article is its portrayal of the psychological pressures involved in interrogation. It shows no awareness whatsoever of the possibility of pressure from a "friendly source" or an "advocate." Yet, from the authors' account of the incident, the following conclusions seem at least as plausible as theirs. First, the three friendly sources gave more than information; they also conveyed, tacitly or explicitly, the impression that cooperation with the FBI in an investigation into the political expression of students was contrary to the expected standards of behavior of members of a liberal university community. Second, the fact that the second interrogation was conducted under the indirect scrutiny of third parties, while the first was not, was a factor encouraging the students to refuse cooperation the second time when they had cooperated the first time. Cf. Darley & Latané "When Will People Help in an Emergency?" *Psychology Today* 2 (December 1968), (presence of third party observers inhibits willingness to take responsibility in an emergency). Third, put to the test, the students' middle-class instincts of cooperation proved stronger with respect to other students and faculty, members of the same upper-middle professional class to which the student subjects belonged, than with respect to the police, members of a lower social class and an occupational group held in low esteem by the upper-middle professional class.

32. Watts v. Indiana, 338 U.S. 49, 59 (1949); cf. Justice Jackson's remark on his experience of civil practice in Jamestown, N.Y., ". . . a lawyer there, if he was consulted on a matter, usually dominated the matter, no matter who the businessman was." E. Gerhart, *America's Advocate: Robert M. Jackson* (1958), p. 63.

33. See, e.g., F. Dostoevsky, *The Brothers Karamazov,* at pp. 552–553 (Magarshack trans. 1958). During the investigation by the examining magistrate and the public prosecutor, Dmitry Karamazov's fear and discomfort increase as the officials emphasize his procedural rights.:

> "You see, gentlemen," he said suddenly, restraining himself with difficulty, "you see—I listen to you and I seem to be haunted by a dream—you see, I sometimes have such a dream—a curious kind of dream—I often dream it—it keeps on recurring—that someone is chasing me—someone I'm terribly afraid of—chasing me in the dark at night—looking for me, and I hide somewhere from him behind a door or a cupboard—hide myself so humiliatingly—and the worst of it is that he knows perfectly well where I've hidden myself from him, but he seems to be pretending deliberately not to know where I am, so as to prolong my agony, to enjoy my terror to the full. . . . That's what you're doing now. It's just like that!"

34. See, e.g., A Speer, *Spandau: The Secret Diaries* (R. Winston & C. Winston, trans. 1977), p. 58: "Who could survive twenty years of imprisonment without accepting some form of guilt?"

35. If the imputed values of Positivism fail to approximate even purely selfish ends, *a fortiori,* they fail to take account of communitarian ends (e.g., the desire to be reconciled with one's fellows). It is possible, though not necessary, to interpret the Positivist emphasis on the

egoism of the individual as a denial of the existence of communitarian ends. See S. Lukes, *Individualism* (1973), pp. 99–106. Yet, such a denial would be unpersuasive. First, it would conflict with the fact that many people do experience such ends or at least profess to experience them and act as if they did. More fundamentally, it would conflict with the basic Positivist premise of the arbitrariness and individuality of ends. If ends are arbitrary, then there seems to be no logical reason for excluding any category of imaginable ends; and if ends are individual, then there seems to be no factual basis on which one individual could assert that another could not have a particular end. Yet, the imputed values of Positivist advocacy are completely inconsistent with communitarian ends, and Positivist advocacy is destructive of such ends. Cf. Griffiths, *supra* note 3, at pp. 371–417 (contrasting adversary advocacy with the "family model" of criminal procedure).

36. A Positivist might attempt to avoid the criticism made here by qualifying or retracting the principle of the subjectivity of ends. He might assert that ends are sufficiently shared, or at least understood, so that even strangers can achieve some understanding of each other's ends. This being so, the lawyer could respect his client's autonomy by making strong efforts to come to an understanding of his ends. The Positivist might assert that, although many lawyers do engage in the strategy of imputed ends, there is nothing in Positivism, so revised, which requires that they do so.

I doubt that Positivist Advocacy can be made more acceptable by such a revision. In the first place, to the extent that the revision avoids the problem of the inaccessibility of ends, it becomes less plausible ethically than the version stated above. There are severe limitations on the extent to which a person, particularly a stranger, can understand with any depth the ends of another without actually sharing those ends. The language in which we describe ends is often vague and indeterminate. To understand its meaning in a specific context, one must often share the moral outlook of the person who uses it. Thus, in order to suggest that the advocate can gain an understanding of his client's ends, the revision must assume a substantial degree of sharing of ends throughout the society. Yet, to the extent that such a sharing exists, the insistence that the advocate refrain from holding either himself or his client to personal or social norms becomes untenable. In the Positivist verison, the ethical validity of adversary advocacy depends heavily on the premise that values are subjective, arbitrary, and individual. If there were a substantial sharing of values in society, then the reference to such values by judges and lawyers would not be likely to cause uncertainty. If lawyer and client did share values, then the lawyer's adherence to such values would not constitute oppression of the client.

In the second place, the notion that ends are inaccessible accurately describes the experience of lawyers in some areas of practice. This is particularly true in criminal law, where the client is likely to be from a different social background than the lawyer. Albert Alschuler has written, "Most criminal defendants do not understand our [sic] system of criminal justice and cannot be made to understand." "The Defense Attorney's Role in Plea Bargaining," *Yale Law Review* 84(1975):1179, at p. 1310. In this situation, Alschuler suggests, no meaningful choice by the client as to the exercise of certain procedural rights is possible. *Id.* If this is true, then it can only be because most defense lawyers do not understand their clients and cannot be made to understand. If the lawyer understood his client, he would be able to give him the information about the criminal justice system which the client would need in order to make an autonomous choice. The strategy of imputed ends is not merely a theoretical ploy. It is a response to the experience of the inaccessibility of client ends in actual practice. It seems unlikely that the problem can be solved merely by telling lawyers to try to learn their clients' ends.

37. Professor Charles Haar, Harvard Law School, quoted in *The Boston Phoenix,* January 15, 1974 at p. 20 (commenting on James St. Clair's decision to represent President Nixon in the Watergate investigations).

38. See e.g., *The Works of Jeremy Bentham* Vol 7 (Bowring ed. 1962 reprint).

39. The Code was promulgated in 1969, but it embodied ideas which had been considered and studied by the American Bar Association for decades. A particularly influential document from this long period of gestation is a report by a joint conference of the ABA and the Associa-

tion of American Law Schools. See *Professional Responsibility, supra* note 12.

40. See, e.g., L. Brandeis, "Business—A Profession, The Opportunity in the Law, The Living Law," in *Business: A Profession* (1914), pp. 1–12, 313–327, 344–363 [hereinafter cited as Brandeis]; P. Freud, *The Supreme Court of the United States* (1961) [hereinafter cited as Freud, *Supreme Court*]; L. Fuller, *The Anatomy of the Law* (1968); Hurst, *supra* note 35; K. Llewellyn, *The Common Law Tradition: Deciding Appeals* (1960); R. Pound, *The Spirit of the Common Law* (1921), chs. 7–8; Freud, "The Legal Profession," *Daedalus* 92 (December 1963):689; Pound, "The Lawyer as a Social Engineer," *Journal of Public Law* 3 (1954):292.

41. See Frankel, "The Search for Truth: An Umpireal View," *University of Pennsylvania Law Review* 123 (1975):1031; Pound, "The Causes of Popular Dissatisfaction with the Administration of Justice," *American Bar Association Report* 29 (1906):395, 404.

42. See, eg., Brandeis, "The Opportunity in the Law," in *Business: A Profession, supra* note 40, at pp. 339–341.

43. See *ABA Code of Professional Responsibility*, EC 2–25, 7–13, 7–14, 8–1, 8–6, 8–9.

44. *Professional Responsibility, supra* note 13, at p. 1160. (Fuller was co-chairman of the group which produced the report.) See also *ABA Code of Professional Responsibility*, EC 7–19; Fuller, "The Adversary System," in *Talks on American Law* (Berman ed. 1971), pp. 43–44.

45. *Professional Responsibility, supra* note 12, at p. 1160.

46. H. Hart and A. Sacks, *The Legal Process: Basic Problems in the Making and Application of Law* chap. II (1958) (unbound edition prepared for classroom use) [hereinafter cited as Hart and Sacks], at p. 312.

47. See, e.g., *ABA Code of Professional Responsibility*, EC 7–3 to 7–5; Patterson & Cheatham, *supra* note 44, at 134–138; Thode, *supra* note 17, at pp. 578–579.

48. See *ABA Code of Professional Responsibility*, EC 7–13 to 7–14.

49. See *ABA Code of Professional Responsibility*, EC 2–25, 8–1 to 8–6, 8–9.

50. See, e.g., Patterson & Cheatham, *supra* note 44, at p. 181; Brandels, "The Opportunity in the Law," in *Business: A Profession, supra* note 76, at pp. 339–341; Thode, *supra* note 17, at pp. 576–579.

51. It should be noted that the problem of advocacy in Purposivism is in some ways distinct from the problem of rule interpretation. Purposivists sometimes suggest that the latter problem can be solved by a compromise method in which both rules and norms are taken into account. While such a method might justify the judge's role in resolving disputes, it does not justify the ethical and methodological division of labor between lawyer and judge. In order to explain this, two separate methods must be elaborated, and their congruence must then be shown.

52. See Thibaut, Walker & Lind, "Adversary Presentation and Bias in Legal Decision-making," *Harvard Law Review* 86 (1972):386.

53. *Professional Responsibility, supra* note 12, at p. 1161.

54. See, e.g., Keeton, *Trial Tactics and Methods* §§ 9–10 (1954).

55. C. Curtis, *It's Your Law* (1954), p. 26 [hereinafter cited as Curtis].

56. This is most dramatically evident in Purposivist critiques of the Warren Court. For instance, Philip B. Kurland introduces one such critique as follows: "I suggest that we ask whether, as the Warren Court has moved toward the legislative mode and away from the judicial mode of carrying on its business, it has endangered the capacity to perform its peculiar function." Kurland, "Toward a Political Supreme Court," *University of Chicago Law Review* 37 (1969):19, 20 [hereinafter cited as Kurland]. Of course, since any "peculiar function" of the Supreme Court must be defined in terms of the "judicial mode," the reader is not surprised that the answer is that the departure from the latter endangers the former.

57. Brandeis, the first theorist of the counseling role, is also the source of striking examples of the problems which the principle of specialization poses for the notion of the counselor. In 1906, Brandeis acted on behalf of the United Shoe Machinery Company in successfully opposing a bill before the Massachusetts legislature which would have outlawed the tying clause in United's leases to shoe manufacturers. Brandeis argued that the clauses were in the interests of the public and the shoe manufacturers. In fact, as Brandeis later acknowledged, the tying clauses were an oppressive

exercise of United's monopoly power. Brandeis's biographer suggests persuasively that in 1906 his perception of the public interest and the interests of the shoe manufacturers was distorted by his close relation to United. His successful representation had the effect of preserving an exploitative relation by retarding intervention by the government.

Another example is the Lennox case in which Brandeis agreed with the insolent Lennox that a member of the Brandeis firm would become trustee of his property for the benefit of creditors. Disputes later developed between Lennox and the trustee over how much Lennox would be paid for managing the property and over his father's obligation to turn over hidden assets. Ultimately, the trustee put Lennox into bankruptcy. Lennox and others alleged that Brandeis had accepted him as a client and then acted contrary to his interests in the administration of the assignment. However, the record indicates that Brandeis did not undertake to act on behalf of Lennox but rather on behalf of the creditors. Nevertheless, it seems fair to criticize Brandeis for failing to perceive the significance of the conflict between Lennox's interests and those of the creditors and for failing to emphasize to Lennox that he was not his lawyer and that the trustee might have to act contrary to his interest. Brandeis's identification with the creditors colored his perception of the interests of others involved in the situation. See Frank, "The Legal Ethics of Louis D. Brandeis," *Stanford Law Review* 17 (1965):683; see also Kauffman, *supra* note 23, 15 at p. 109 n.3.

If one were to accept the Purposivist psychology of specialization upon which the counseling role and the separation of functions are based, one would have to regard situations of this sort as inevitable and typical.

58. A familiar example, which for present purposes can be taken as hypothetical, is the argument that the pro bono lawyer who brings lawsuits on behalf of poor tenants against landlords to compel compliance with housing codes worsens the plight of low-income tenants by compelling the landlords to raise the rent, or if the rents are already as high as the market will bear, to abandon the buildings. The court can compel compliance with the code, but the housing situation of the poor depends on other factors which it cannot control, such as the income of the poor and the level of investment in low-income housing. See, e.g., Blum & Dunham, "Slumlordism as a Tort—A Dissenting View," *Michigan Law Review* 66 (1968):451, 460-461.

59. Cf. Jaffe, "The Effective Limits of the Administrative Proces: A Reevaluation," *Harvard Law Review* 67 (1954):1105, 1113-1119 (the administrator develops a presumption in favor of regulation).

60. See, e.g., J. Goulden, *The Superlawyers* (1972), pp. 110-173.

61. *ABA Code of Professional Responsibility*, EC 7-13 to 7-14.

62. *Id.* at EC 7-1.

63. *Id.* at EC 7-3.

64. *Id.*

65. *Id.* at EC 7-4.

66. *Id.* at EC 7-5.

67. *Id.* at EC 7-10.

68. *Id.* at EC 7-8.

69. *Id.* at DR 7-101 (B) (2).

70. The following discussion concerning the conflict of morality and efficiency draws on E. Durkheim, *Moral Education* (Wilson and Schnurer trans. 1961); Williams, "A Critique of Utilitarianism," in J. Smart & B. Williams, *Utilitarianism: For and Against* (1973), pp. 77-150, [hereinafter cited as Williams]; Tribe, "Technology Assessment and the Fourth Discontinuity: The Limits of Instrumental Rationality," *Southern California Law Review* 46 (1973):617, 630-633, [hereinafter cited as Tribe]. See also D. Wigdor, *Roscoe Pound: Philosopher of Law* (1974), pp. 207-232, (discussing tension between "organicism" and "instrumentalism" in Pound's writings).

71. 309 U.S. 470 (1940).

72. *Professional Responsibility, supra* note 12, at p. 1216; see Kaplan, "The Limits of the Exclusionary Rule," *Stanford Law Review* 26 (1974):1027, 1035-1036 [hereinafter cited as Kaplan].

73. See, e.g., Oaks, "Studying the Exclusionary Rule in Search and Seizure," *University of Chicago Law Review* 37 (1970):665.

74. Bator, "Finality in Criminal Law and Federal Habeus Corpus for State Prisoners," *Harvard Law Review* 76 (1963):441, 452.

75. Llewelyn, "On Reading and Using the Newer Jurisprudence," *Columbia Law Review* 40 (1940): 581, 610 (emphasis in original).

76. Hart & Sacks, *supra* note 46, at p. 111.

77. This is the Ritualist kiss-off: "Things are not as bad as you think."

78. A. Gouldner, *The Coming Crisis of Western Sociology* (1970), p. 384 (emphasis in original) [hereinafter cited as Gouldner]; see generally *id.* at pp. 378-390.

79. See Redmount, "Humanistic Law Through Legal Counseling," *Connecticut Law Review* 2 (1969):98; Shafer, "Christian Theories of Professional Responsibility," *Southern California Law Review* 48 (1975):721 [hereinafter cited as Shafer].

80. Fried, "The Lawyer as Friend: The Moral Foundations of the Lawyer-Client Relation," *Yale Law Journal* 85 (1976):1060, 1074, 1077, 1085, see this volume Part 2, pp. 132-157 [hereinafter cited as Fried, *The Lawyer as Friend*]. For an excellent critique of this article, see Dauer & Leff, "Correspondence: The Lawyer as Friend," *Yale Law Journal* 86 (1977):573.

81. Fried, *The Lawyer as Friend, supra* note 78, at p. 142.

82. J. Wigmore, *Evidence* 8 (McNaughton ed. 1961) §§ 2286-90.

83. Fried, *The Lawyer as Friend, supra* note 78, at pp. 135, 138, 141.

84. *Id.* at p. 139.

85. See Aristotle, *Nicomachean Ethics*, bk. 8, especially at pp. 218-223, 231 (Ostwald ed. 1962).

86. *Id;* see also F. Nietzsche, "Thus Spoke Zarathustra" in *The Portable Nietzsche*, pp. 167-169 (Kaufmann ed. 1954) [hereinafter cited as Nietzsche]; W. Shakespeare, *The Merchant of Venice*, especially I:iii, Il. 131-138; IV:i, Il. pp. 265-288.

87. 'It is undeniable that money usually cements the lawyer-client relationship," Fried, *The Lawyer as Friend, supra* note 78, at p. 142.

Fried adds, "But the content of the relation is determined by the client's needs. . . . So the fact that the lawyer works for pay does not seriously undermine the friendship analogy." *Id.* at p. 142. This is unconvincing. The content of any commercial relation is determined by the buyer's needs. Of course, the lawyer's customers get "personalized" service, but so do the customers of tailors and insurance salesmen, if they can pay for it. Fried's suggestion that the lawyer is different because he feels obliged to continue to represent a client even when he becomes unable to pay is wrong. The profession recognizes no such obligation. *See ABA Code of Professional Responsibility*, DR 2-110 (C) (1) (f) (lawyer may withdraw if client deliberately fails to pay fees); see also *id.* at DR 4-101 (C) (4) (lawyer may reveal client's confidences when necessary to collect a fee).

88. Fried, *The Lawyer as Friend, supra* note 78, at pp. 133-139. The nadir in the use of "Orwellian" discourse to defend legal ethics occurs, not in Fried's article, but in Shafer's. See *Shafer, supra* note 77, at pp. 738, 753, where the Code is analogized to "St. Matthew's Gospel" and the lawyer's attitude of neutrality to the "human experience Jesus identified as the source of his salvation."

89. H. Marcuse, *One-Dimensional Man: Studies In the Ideology of Advanced Industrial Society* (1964), pp. 88, 90.

90. Fried, *The Lawyer as Friend, supra* note 78, at p. 143.

91. *Id.* at p. 151.

92. *Id.* at p. 139-140.

93. Fried needs to make this argument to distinguish the lawyer from the friendly Sunoco dealer or the friendly insurance salesman, but the distinction is untenable. In the first place, while some clients, particularly the criminal defendant, can plausibly be viewed as involved in a "critical assault on one's person" or at least in a situation implicating their "concreteness and individuality," others cannot be so viewed. If a finance company's attempt to foreclose on a poor widow or a wealthy person's attempt to evade taxes—both examples used by Fried—can be viewed as implicating concreteness and individuality, then it is difficult to think of any effort to satisfy any desire which could not be so viewed. Moreover, Fried ignores the fact that for people who do not

have secure employment or independent wealth it is precisely in the material dealings with landlords, employers, and bureaucrats that their individuality is most at stake. For most people individuality is jeopardized not by an ignorance of the law, but by an economic dependence which is largely sanctioned and complemented by the law. For them, concreteness and individuality would be better served by a friendly landlord than by a friendly lawyer.

94. Fried, *The Lawyer as Friend, supra* note 78, at pp. 138-139, 146-151.

95. Fried's article seems particularly incoherent at this point. At the beginning, the basic characteristic of friendship was portrayed as "an authorization to take the interests of particular concrete persons more seriously and to give them priority over the interests of the wider collectivity." *Id.* at p. 136. Yet, in recognizing an obligation not to violate the law or the *Code of Profesional Responsibility* on behalf of the client, the lawyer refuses precisely to give priority to his client's interests over "the interests of the wider collectivity." This obligation to the system seems incompatible with friendships as Fried himself has described it.

It is no answer to this objection to say that the legal system gives meaning to the client's autonomy by defining the rights which protect it and that, therefore, the lawyer respects his client's autonomy by respecting the law. For the law gives meaning to autonomy only in a very abstract and general sense, and it is precisely such abstract and general notions which Fried rejects in favor of the commitment to the concrete interests of the particular client.

96. Curtis, *supra* note 54, at p. 1.

97. Fried, *The Lawyer as Friend, supra* note 28, at p. 138.

98. *Id.* at p. 144.

99. Fried also relies on the familiar distinction between wrongs "of the system" and the lawyer's "personal wrongs." The reasons why this type of rationalization is untenable have been discussed in the criticism of Positivism. But Fried's version deserves further comment. He attempts to distinguish between the lawyer's putting the client on the stand to lie ("exploiting the system") and the lawyer's telling the lie himself ("engaging his own person in doing personal harm to another"). Putting the client on to perjure himself is all right because in doing so the lawyer is "like the letter carrier who delivers the falsehood." On the other hand, a direct lie is unethical because "every speech act invites belief." Fried, *The Lawyer as Friend, supra* note 78; at pp. 149-151.

Here are Fried's characteristic mistakes in striking form. First, the treason to actual experience: the competent trial lawyer must invite the trier's belief with his appearance and gestures just as much as with his speech, with the questions he asks and the way he asks them just as much as with the statements he makes. As Freedman writes, "[e]ffective trial advocacy requires that the attorney's every word, action, and attitude be consistent with the conclusion that his client is innocent." Freedman, *supra* note 9, at p. 330. The ABA-ALI's *Civil Trial Manual* suggests that the trial lawyer "practice before a mirror on his mannerisms" and it observes that the advocate acquires his skills by "hard work and self-reformation." R. Figg, R. Macullough, & J. Underwood, *Civil Trial Manual* (1974), p. 358. The distinction between speech and conduct is meaningless; personality is engaged in both, and in both it intentionally misleads. (On a more practical level, Fried ignores that the lawyer will have to argue explicitly to the jury that the client's lie is credible in his summation.)

Second, the suppression of consequences: Fried ignores that the client's lie—directed and affirmed by the lawyer—will, if successful, probably lead to an unjust result. The letter carrier analogy would be more truthful if the letter contained a bomb likely to blow up in the face of the recipient.

100. Fried, *The Lawyer as Friend, supra* note 78, at pp. 151-156; see also S. Williston, *Life and Law* (1940), p. 272.

101. Cf. Sartre's critique of Nietzsche's ethic of recurrence as a strategy of self-consolation for the philosopher's failure to change an intolerable situation: "[T]his man who is drowning demands that the instant of his choking last forever." J. Sartre, *Saint Genet* (Frechtman trans. 1963), p. 349.

102. L. Nizer, *The Implosion Conspiracy* (1973), p. 9.

103. See generally Williams, *supra* note 123, at pp. 77-150.

104. See generally Lukacs, *supra* note 29, at pp. 83-110.

105. See T. Nagel, *The Possibility of Altruism* (1970), ch. VIII; Sartre, *supra* note 29, at pp. 462-467; Williams, *supra* note 69, at pp. 93-118.

106. See H. Hart, *Punishment and Responsibility: Essays in the Philosophy of Law* (1968), ch. 4.

107. This psychology has been acknowledged insofar as it affects the lawyer, but its impact on the client has been generally ignored. See, e.g., Parsons, "A Sociologist Looks at the Legal Profession," in *Essays in Sociological Theory: Pure and Applied* (rev. ed. 1957), p. 380 [hereinafter cited as Parsons]:

> The fact that the case can be tried by a standard procedure relieves . . . [the lawyer] of some of the pressure of commitment to the case of his client. He can feel that, if he does his best, then having assured his client a fair trial, he is relieved of responsibility for an unfavorable verdict if it comes. He may even take a case with considerable reservations about its soundness, counting on procedural fairness to protect the interests of the opponent.

108. It should be recalled that I am speaking of the relatively powerless and unsophisticated client. Of course, powerful, sophisticated clients are less likely to be dominated by their lawyers. But the arguments of the Ideology of Advocacy become inapplicable, or at least more implausible, to the extent that the client is powerful and sophisticated. The Ideology of Advocacy focuses on the relatively naive and unsophisticated client, and the validity of its prescriptions must stand or fall on their impact on that kind of client.

109. See, e.g., Rosenthal, *supra* note 5:

> If I had not had a lawyer here I would probably have settled for about $2,000 to cover my out-of-pocket expenses. But the lawyer is a reassuring presence who takes away our guilt feelings. He says, "Hey, this is the way the game is played; you take as much as you can get; it's what they expect; it's the way it is done." He takes upon his own shoulders the burden of your guilt—he's the professional. I hadn't thought of this before but it occurs to me now as what's [sic] involved.

Id. at p. 171 (quoting a plaintiff interviewed during a survey of personal injury litigation in New York City).

110. *Contra,* Diamond, "The Rule of Law Versus The Order of Custom" in *The Rule of Law* (Wolff ed. 1971). Neither does it amount to a plea for revolutionary socialist communalism. But see Pashukanis, "The Soviet State and the Revolution in Law," in *Soviet Legal Philosophy* (Babb trans. 1951).

111. Sociological writing on law often obscures the tension between the notion that modern law is specialized and the notion that it serves as a legitimating function by controlling the exercise of state power in a manner which citizens can perceive as rational. Some writers emphasize that modern law is specialized and discontinuous with social experience without considering the claims of modern legal systems to legitimate the actions of the state. See, e.g., L. Rudolph & S. Rudolph, *The Modernity of Tradition* (1967), pp. 254-259; Nader, "Styles of Court Procedure: To Make the Balance," in *Law in Culture and Society* (L. Nader ed. 1969). On the other hand, other writers emphasize that the legitimating function of law in modern society requires continuity between legal and other social experience, but ignore the extent to which modern legal systems engender discontinuity. See, e.g., Fuller, "Human Interaction and the Law," in *The Rule of a Law* (Wolff ed. 1971) [hereinafter cited as Fuller, "Human Interaction and the Law"]. For a discussion of legitimation which addresses the problem of discontinuity, see Tushnet, "Perspectives on the History of American Law: A Critical Review of Friedman's 'A History of American Law,'" *Wisconsin Law Review* 81 (1977): 100-102 [hereinafter cited as Tushnet].

112. G. Hegel, *Philosophy of Right* (Knox trans. 1952), p. 87 [hereinafter cited as Hegel].

113. *Id.* at pp. 140-145.

114. The contradiction between the notion that the law serves democracy by enabling citizens to perceive as rational the exercise of state power, and the notion of law as specialized, is evident in late Purposivism. The later Purposivists often emphasized that the legitimation of the exercise of judicial power requires that courts establish the rationality of their decisions. They base this requirement on the nature of democracy and the right of citizens not to be subject to arbitrary power. They distinguished "law" from "fiat" on the ground that the former is used to "gain reasoned acceptance." Bickel & Wellington, "Legislative Purpose and the Judicial Process: The Lincoln Mills Case," *Harvard Law Review* 71 (1957):1, 5. Yet, in applying their theories, these writers were never less satisfied than when judicial decisions were most accessible to ordinary citizens. The criteria by which they tested the rationality of judicial decisions were drawn not from ordinary moral and political discourse but from the technical discourse of lawyers. See generally Arnold, "Professor Hart's Theology," *Harvard Law Review* 73 (1960):1298, 1306-1309 [hereinafter cited as Arnold]. In practice, the only audience from whom they insisted that decisions gain reasoned acceptance was the legal profession. The need for reasoned acceptance was said to stem from the moral and social imperatives of democracy; yet the test of reasoned acceptance was the satisfaction of a small elite.

115. Hegel, *supra* note 109, at p. 145. Hegel's theory of the civil service as a "universal class," *id.* at pp. 188-193, has flaws analogous to those he criticized in the theory of legal professionalism. See K. Marx, *Early Writings* (Vintage ed. 1975), pp. 100-116 .

116. See generally D. Reisman, *The Lonely Crowd* (1950) [hereinafter cited as Riesman] at pp. 256-257.

117. The principal thrust of the present argument is that adversary advocacy is incompatible with the norms of individuality to which it appeals. An alternative critique of the Ideology of Advocacy could be constructed on the basis of norms of community. See Griffiths, *supra* note 3. Such a critique would not necessarily be inconsistent with the present argument.

Individuality and community are best viewed, not as opposing norms, but rather as interdependent aspects of what Unger calls the Paradox of Sociability. The notion of individuality depends on the norms of community because individuality is a social phenomenon. Because an individual's sense of self depends on recognition by others, individuality can flourish only in a community committed to the autonomy, responsibility, and dignity of each of its members. At the same time, the notion of community depends on the norms of individuality because it implies voluntary commitment to the values which are the basis of the community, and voluntary acceptance of membership in the community. For the members to exercise the voluntary choice necessary to form a genuine community, their capacities as individuals must be developed.

Thus, the notion of individuality discussed here implies a complementary rather than an antagonistic notion of community. For instance, I will suggest below that a style of advocacy which seriously respected individuality would be more likely to promote mutuality and altruism in the judicial process than partisan advocacy. This is because people actually do hold communitarian values which partisan advocacy represses. To the extent that individuals do hold communitarian values, a style of advocacy which respected the litigant's own values and permitted him to act on them would promote both individuality and community. Moreover, even where they do not hold such values, a style of advocacy which respected the individual's capacity for personal growth would make possible the development of such values.

It may be objected that the notion of individuality discussed here is not the same one assumed by the Ideology of Advocacy. The objection is possible because the writing on partisan advocacy contains no analysis of the norms of individuality which it constantly invokes. But to be persuasive, the objection would have to elaborate an alternative notion of individuality which would be a plausible basis for an ethical or legal theory, and which would be consistent with the prescriptions of the Ideology of Advocacy. It seems unlikely that this can be done.

118. The concern for both one's own integrity and the integrity of others makes personal ethics somewhat problematical. It raises difficult questions in situations where one's own ends and the ends of others conflict. As I will suggest below, one of the ways in which personal ethics deal with such situations is by referring to social norms and institutions such as those associated with

law. Conceived in this way, personal ethics differ from two other alternatives to professional ethics; radical individualist ethics and radical politicization.

Radical individualist ethics hold that moral decisions should be a matter of entirely autonomous, independent, and self-conscious choice by the individual decision-maker. See, e.g., Sartre, *supra* note 29; J. Sartre, *Saint Genet* (Frenchtman trans. 1963). From this point of view, social norms and institutions, and even the concrete ends of other people, are at best irrelevant and at worst oppressive constraints on the moral freedom of the individual. The radical individualist approach is unsatisfactory because it fails to take adequate account of the social dimension of individuality. Because the individual's sense of self depends on recognition by others, individuality depends on social relations. To a significant extent, individuality can only be expressed in terms which are meaningful to others. A person whose ethical choices were entirely independent of social norms and the ends of others could not have a coherent moral personality. See R. Jacoby, *Social Amnesia: A Critique of Conformist Psychology from Adler to Laing* (1965), chs. 3, 5, 7 [hereinafter cited as Jacoby].

The approach of radical politicization holds that moral decisions should be entirely instrumental to the establishment of a new social order. See generally Lukacs, "Legality and Illegality," in *History and Class Consciousness* (Livingstone trans. 1971). From this point of view, existing social norms and institutions and the concrete ends of individuals are merely reflections of the injustice and repressiveness of the existing order. Moral decision on the basis of personal ethics must await the establishment of the new order. This view suffers from the defects of moralities of the long run. See text accompanying notes 37-40 *supra*. It treats existing norms, institutions, and personal ends as means to future ones, and hence collapses process into result. The problems of justice and freedom must be confronted in the course of social change; they cannot be deferred to an idealized future order. Moreover, the radical politicization approach ignores the extent to which the ideals for which it strives are themselves rooted in existing social norms and institutions and the concrete present concerns of individuals. To a significant extent, the realization of these ideals may require the resolution of problems and contradictions within the existing order. In relying solely on a vague idealized negation of the existing order, radical politicization begs the questions presented by these problems and contradictions.

119. The goal of trust does not arise, as Freedman and Noonan suggest, from the requirements of the legal system. Nonprofessional advocacy cannot justify confidentiality as protecting the client's capacity to invoke formal procedural rights. Nor can it accept the premise that confidentiality will enhance the capacity of the legal system to produce substantively desirable results. However, as Fried comes close to suggesting, the value of trust is implicated in any situation in which a dependent person seeks the help of another. The priority of confidentiality does not arise from the specifically legal character of the client's need, but simply from the facts that he has a need, and that he seeks the advocate's help. Legal norms will probably weigh against confidentiality more often than they will support it.

120. Since this statement is likely to outrage the pious professional more than any other, two points should be made to put it in perspective. First, even hard-line professional defenses of confidentiality contemplate some situations in which the lawyer will betray his client. *ABA Code of Professional Responsibility*, DR 4-101(C)(3) (when client intends to commit crime); *id.* at DR 4-101(C)(4) (when client fails to pay fee). Second, most professional defenses of confidentiality rest on a moral formalism and absolutism which most people, including even most lawyers, reject in other areas of moral decision. The contradiction is strikingly evident in Freedman's work. See M. Freedman, *Lawyers' Ethics in an Adversary System* (1975). Freedman fully appreciates the defects of formalist, absolutist moralities when it suits his purposes. He rails at length against "legalist-anti-utilitarian" moral views, which he associates with Kant, in arguing against people like Chief Justice Burger who assert that lawyers should never participate in the deception of the trier. *Id.* at pp. 46-47. Yet, Freedman's own defense of confidentiality is quintessentially legalistic, anti-utilitarian, and Kantian in precisely the sense he rejects in Burger's argument. See *id.* at pp. 1-5.

121. Goodpaster, "The Human Arts of Lawyering: Interviewing and Counseling," *Journal of Legal Education* 27 (1975):5; Redmount, "Humanistic Law Through Legal Counseling," *Con-*

necticut Law Review 2 (1969):98; see also Shaffer, "Christian Theories of Professional Responsibility," *Southern California Law Review* 48 (1975):721. For a critique of the psychological literature on which these articles draw, see Jacoby, *supra* note 114, at chs. 2-3.

122. Cf. Riesman, *supra* note 116, at pp. 307-325 (on "false personalization").

123. Although the advocate-client relation will rarely assume the intimacy of friendship, Nietzsche's remarks about friendship are pertinent to it:

> If one wants to have a friend one must also wage war for him: and to wage war, one must be *capable* of being an enemy.
>
> In a friend one should still honor the enemy. Can you go close to your friend without going over to him?
>
> In a friend one should have one's best enemy. You should be closest to him with your heart when you resist him.

Nietzsche, *supra* note 84, at p. 168.

124. See Comment, *The New Public Interest Lawyers, supra* note 7, at pp. 1110-1137.

125. Although public interest lawyers are generally more sophisticated than conventional lawyers about client autonomy, they tend to commit the error of the Ideology of Advocacy in assuming that the lawyer's detachment from the client is the best guarantee of his autonomy. Thus, public interest lawyers warn their colleagues not to become politically involved with their clients. *Id.* at p. 1124 (citing to the California Rural Legal Assistance guidelines). They exhort lawyers to leave their "middle-class values" at home and to submit to their clients' decisions and values. They insist that for the lawyer to introduce his own substantive ends with any force into the relationship would be elitist or paternalistic. These views are fundamentally mistaken.

In the first place, the attitudes expressed toward "middle-class vlaues" are inconsistent. Although the public interest theorists rarely specify these values, they often appear to have in mind conventional views on topics such as sex, honesty, and private property. Yet, the value of procedural justice is as middle class as any other value. See C. B. MacPherson, *The Political Theory of Possessive Individualism* (1962), p. 186. Moreover, the attitude of diffidence toward one's own values, and of reluctance toward personal commitment, is also distinctively middle class. See generally Riesman, *supra* note 116, at chs. 5, 9. The public interest proponents do not hestitate to insist that this middle-class value and this middle-class attitude be incorporated into the advocate's role. They do not hestitate because they do not see this value and this attitude as impositions on the client. But, as this essay has tried to show, the lawyer's procedural values and his attitude of detachment do affect the way the client sees his situation, and thus can limit his practical options and subvert his autonomy.

In the second place, the public interest proponents fail to see that, far from guarding against elitism, their insistence on the lawyer's independence reflects an elitism of its own. The public interest lawyer assumes that the client should remain mired in the limitations of self-interest or class-interest while he himself is struggling to reach a higher moral plane which transcends egoistic and class orientations. Cf. F. Nietzsche, "Twilight of the Idols," in *The Portable Nietzsche* (Kaufmann ed. 1954), p. 523 (arguing that the detached person is more exploitative than the political manipulator: "Perhaps he even wants a worse advantage: to feel superior to other human beings, to be able to look down on them, and no longer to mistake himself for one of them.")

In the actual practice of public interest law, the principle of procedural justice may be less destructive than it could be because it is frequently ignored. One suspects that public interest lawyers allow substantive considerations to enter into their practical decisions much more than they acknowledge in their theoretical discussions.

126. See Auerbach, *supra* note 6; Rosenthal, *supra* note 5; Carlin & Howard, "Legal Representation and Class Justice," *U.C.L.A. Law Review* 12 (1965):381.

127. See Parsons, *supra* note 104, at p. 380.

128. See, e.g., *Is Law Dead?* (E. Rostow ed. 1971).

PROBLEMS

A DELAY THAT MAY KILL

Your clients are the parents of a child critically injured in an accident two days ago. The child needs an operation to live and blood transfusions to survive the operation. Your clients refused to authorize the transfusions because, according to their religion, taking the blood of another for any purpose is a grave sin. To receive the blood of another is, they believe, to be damned. They refused the transfusions at the risk of their child's "earthly life" in order to save his "eternal life." That, anyway, is what they belive they are doing.

When you took the case yesterday, the child was in stable condition. The hospital had already filed a neglect petition. You had only to appear in court, ask for the statutory three-day delay, and set about preparing your case. The decision to give the transfusions or let the child die was to be the judge's, not yours. He would have the time he needed to make it. Your only responsibility was to present your clients' side. Everything was just as it should be.

Then, about half past four this afternoon, you received a call from opposing counsel. The child's condition was no longer stable. The doctors now believed the child would be dead by tomorrow morning if he could not have the operation tonight. The child still could not be operated on without a blood transfusion. In two days there would be nothing for the hearing to decide. Opposing counsel wanted to know whether you would agree to move up the hearing to five o'clock this afternoon. He had found a judge who was willing to stay late.

You know the judge to be fair. You have just finished your preparations (except for a bit of double-checking) and so are just about as ready as you will ever be. Should you agree to move up the hearing date? Should you consult your clients or at least inform them of your intentions? If you do inform them, they may very well refuse the change of day. After all, if they refuse it, their child will die but go to heaven. If they agree, he may survive and be damned. What should you do? Why?

You are now and always have been in favor of freedom of religion. You consider the present case to raise important questions and you believe your clients to have a good case, though you expect them to lose. You took the case because you thought they deserved to have their day in court.

THE SEX JACKET

It is your third year in practice as well as your third year working for the respected criminal-defense firm of Backpeddle, Backslyde, and Skemer. You are assisting Skemer in preparing an armed-robbery case for trial. The facts make it appear that the defense will have a hard time of it at trial:

Two females were involved in the robbery of a grocery story: your client,

Jennifer McKinney, and Denise Tannery who is not your client. One of the females waited in the car while the other entered the store (wearing a bright yellow jacket with "sex" emblazoned in large black letters on the back); held up the grocer; ran back to the car, which was parked just down the street from the store (its motor running); and jumped in. The grocer followed the robber far enough to see the car, noted that there were two people in it, took down its license plate number, and immediately reported all he knew to the police. The two occupants of the car were arrested on Jackson Boulevard about five minutes later "while fleeing south at about fifteen miles above the speed limit." The police found in the car both a gun like that used in the robbery and the stolen money.

At the time of arrest, Jennifer was sitting in the passenger's seat wearing the yellow jacket. Denise was in the driver's seat wearing a dark blue jacket. Jennifer, eighteen years old, was charged with armed robbery (an offence carrying a sentence of up to thirty years imprisonment). Denise, seventeen years old, was charged as an accomplice (an offence carrying a much lighter sentence). Jennifer was chargd as an adult; Denise, as a juvenile. And, for that reason, Jennifer is to be tried alone.

Jennifer and Denise look enough alike to fool friends and relatives. And, as teenage girls often do, they regularly wear each other's clothing. Neither has been arrested before.

During preparation for trial, this exchange occurred between Jennifer and attorney Skemer in his office with only the three of you present:

> S: You claim you didn't do the job. You just went along for the ride. But the robber wore a "sex" jacket. Weren't you wearing such a jacket at the time of the arrest?
>
> J: Yah. But I didn't wear it during the robbery. Denise did. We swopped jackets in the car as we drove down Jackson Boulevard.
>
> S: No jury is going to believe that you managed to take off your jacket; that Denise managed to take off hers; and that you exchanged jackets—Denise put on your jacket and you put on hers—all that with her driving down Jackson at fifty miles an hour! Now, if you had exchanged jackets before you pulled away from the curb, or while you waited at a stop light, or after the police pulled you over—then you might have a chance.
>
> J: Oh, that's right. We swopped when Denise got into the car. She tore off her jacket as she got in, and said "Here, give me yours," which I did. It was her jacket anyway.

Is Skemer doing anything unethical? What would you do if he were? What part in your decision would be played by the *Model Rules,* by your general conception of professional responsibility, by moral considerations, and by prudence?

THE HELPLESS WITNESS

What should I do? I am a legal-aid attorney. My client, Bernie, was holding a gun when it went off and killed Alfie. There was just one witness, Carl. Both Bernie and Carl are juveniles. Bernie has not told the police anything about Carl and does not want Carl to get into trouble. Bernie has not yet been charged with any offense but is likely to be charged with delinquency (for having the gun) or homicide (manslaughter). Bernie admitted to the police that he was holding the gun when it went off but claimed the discharge was accidental. Bernie's statement may or may not be admissible in evidence against him. Carl could confirm Bernie's story or, by telling quite a different story, he could make it possible to prosecute Bernie successfully. I believe 1) that I need to talk to Carl to prepare the case properly, 2) that my connection with legal-aid would lead Carl and his parents to want to cooperate fully (unless I give full warning of the possible consequences), and 3) that, if what Bernie tells me is true, Carl could be charged in Juvenile court once he has testified on Bernie's behalf. (Just to put him at the scene would, under the circumstances, probably constitute delinquency.)

Suggested Readings

For other works on issues raised here, see Bibliography, Part 3, especially Curtis (1951), Frankel (1975), Freedman (1975), and Luban (1984).

Part IV

Conflict of Interest

Introduction

The lawyer's role has built into it certain enduring tensions. The lawyer, is, for example, supposed to be both "a zealous advocate" and "an officer of the court," to perform a public service and to serve a private client, to be relatively neutral concerning the client's ends and yet scrupulously moral concerning the means employed to achieve those ends. *The Model Rules of Professional Conduct* are certainly right to observe in their Preamble that "virtually all difficult ethical problems arise from conflict between a lawyer's responsibilities to clients, to the legal system, and to the lawyer's own interest in remaining an upright person while earning a satisfactory living." The first three sections of this book have provided a framework for discussion of legal ethics. This section begins our discussion of particular problems.

We may be tempted to think of *all* the enduring tensions built into the lawyer's role as "conflicts of interest." Like most temptations, this one is better resisted. The more use a term has, the less useful it is. "Conflict of interest" can be a very useful term but only if its use is limited to circumstances over which lawyers have some control. For lawyers, one has conflict of interest when the circumstances in which one is called upon to exercise professional judgment tend to undermine the ability to exercise that judgment properly on behalf of the clients. One's judgment, though still competent, is no longer "independent." A conflict of interest is a tension within the lawyer's role that is not supposed to be there. A conflict of interest is a threat to the ordinary lawyer-client relation.

Lawyers usually try to avoid conflict of interest. Sometimes they fail. When a lawyer finds herself with a conflict, she may have two options. Some conflicts can be resolved simply by informing the client and giving him the opportunity to change lawyers or to change the terms of employment. This sort of resolution is often described as "consent after full disclosure." But some conflicts can be resolved only by withdrawing from the representation in question. Disclosure is just not enough.

A few conflicts cannot be resolved at all. The lawyer may be unable to resolve the conflict by disclosure because the disclosure itself would require doing something she should not: for example, revealing the confidences of another client. The lawyer may also be unable to withdraw without producing an adverse effect on the client's interests. Such a conflict of interest can present a dreadful dilemma.

279

Lawyers do not view all potential conflicts of interest with equal trepidation. A lawyer who is asked to represent codefendants in a criminal case will usually refuse unless there is some special reason for the joint representation (for example, the informed desire of all defendants to coordinate a political defense). When asked to advise a couple in an amicable divorce involving little property and no children, a lawyer often accepts, thinking that saving the couple money outweighs any potential conflict of interest. The lawyer is willing to risk the further breakdown in the couple's relationship that would make them adversaries and leave him unable to serve either. But an attorney who has been invited to serve on the board of directors of a client corporation will ordinarily jump at the chance even though board membership means that he will have to be both an active participant in deciding corporation policy and a detached judge of related legal matters.

Kenneth Kipnis is concerned to know what makes conflicts of interest "ethically interesting." He distinguishes two sorts of conflicts of interest: a) "conflict of obligation" and b) "conflict of interest" proper. A conflict of obligation occurs when someone cannot satisfy one obligation without failing to satisfy another. The lawyer who is asked to represent codefendants in a criminal case may, for example, find that he cannot win acquittal for one defendant without implicating another. Unable to be a zealous advocate for both, he must give up representation of at least one. In contrast, a conflict of interest (proper) occurs when someone has an interest that he cannot satisfy without failing to satisfy his obligations to those he is supposed to serve. His interest conflicts with his role. Thus, a lawyer who is asked to draft a will naming himself chief beneficiary suddenly has a pecuniary interest in drafting the will, an interest that is not consistent with, for example, reminding the client of various alternative distributions. This second sort of conflict of interest might better be called a "a conflicting interest."

Morally, this distinction between conflicts of obligations and conflicting interest does not seem important. Both are objectionable for much the same reason. For Kipnis, what is wrong with a conflict of obligation is that the lawyer involved is put in circumstances where he must betray the justified trust of some client, or at least appear to betray it. What is wrong with having a conflicting interest is that loyalty to one's client includes both exercising independent professional judgment on the client's behalf *and* giving the client no reason to believe the lawyer will do otherwise. A conflicting interest gives the appearance of undermining independent judgment even if it does not. All conflicts of interest, whether conflicts of obligation or conflicting interests, are (unless resolved) betrayals of trust.

Kipnis's analysis seems to explain why certain conflicts can be resolved by disclosure while others must be resolved by withdrawal from representation. Under some circumstances, informed consent after disclosure redefines the lawyer-client relationship so that there is no longer a risk of betrayal (or the appearance of any). Under other circumstances, however, informed consent after disclosure is not enough to resolve the conflict because even informed consent cannot change the lawyer's obligations enough to eliminate risk of betrayal (or, at least, the appearance of it). A lawyer who is asked to advise a couple on their amicable divorce can, for example, define his relationship with them so they understand that he can help them only so long as they remain agreed and must withdraw as soon as there is a serious disagreement between them. He can arrange the relation so that, in effect, they are a single client and thus avoid even the appearance of betrayal. But the lawyer who is asked to draft a will in which he is chief beneficiary cannot escape the appearance of betrayal unless another lawyer drafts the will. However cautious his advice, the relation between lawyer and client is too intimate for any consent upon full disclosure to assure that the lawyer would not exercise undue influence upon the terms of the will. Even the lawyer himself is in no position to know that he has not gone too far.

Geoffrey Hazard connects Kipnis's discussion of conflicts of interest with preceding discussions of the adversarial style. Hazard's concern is that "lawyer for a situation" be a recognized role that lawyers can assume when necessary. A "lawyer for a situation" is a mediator or go-between, a common helper of parties who wish to cooperate even though they have (as people always do) at least potentially conflicting interests. Though laywers commonly call all that they do for a client "representing," being a lawyer for a situation does not look like representing. The lawyer does not "act for" either party, nor does he make either party "present" to the other. What the lawyer actually does is let the parties to the situation share his knowledge, skill, and judgment. For lawyers who are used to thinking in terms of "representing," "total loyalty," and "warm zeal" in defense of one client's interests against the rest of the world, lawyering for a situation looks strikingly like any other conflict of interest.

But, as Hazard points out, it looks that way only while we think of lawyering in adversarial terms. Once we stop looking at it that way, we can see that even the best American lawyers have in fact been doing such things for a century even though the bar's official policy seemed to condemn it. Why then should lawyers not officially permit themselves to be lawyers for a situation? Why indeed?

Linda Silberman's paper may suggest one explanation. Her focus is quite narrow: certain experiments with divorce mediation. Her concern is also quite technical: a comparison of how the old *Code* and the final draft of the new *Model Rules* handle the ethical problems inherent in such mediation. Her conclusion is that, though the *Rules* constitute an advance over the *Code,* the advance is surprisingly small. The technical detail constantly points to a problem of conceptualizing the lawyer's role in a "nonadversarial" context. For example, does the lawyer "represent" both parties or neither? Does he exercise "professional judgment" or just provide "information"? Her criticism of the *Model Rules* suggests that more than good will and intelligence will be necessary to make an official place in American legal ethics for the role of "lawyer for the situation." (Hazard, whose good will and intelligence no one doubts, was the chief drafter of the *Model Rules.*) Only the first part of Silberman's paper is included here because the technical detail of the second half only provides further evidence for the conclusion.

Kenneth Kipnis

Conflict of Interest and Conflict of Obligation

The term "conflict of interest" is not very well understood outside the legal profession and inside of the legal profession it is probably not understood well enough. Part of the problem is that the term itself is ambiguous, denoting at least two very different types of circumstance. Moreover, problems pertaining to conflicts of interest are most easily understood in formal types of relationship, like that which obtains between lawyer and client. These have few counterparts in ordinary day-to-day life. Our purpose here will be twofold. In the first place, we shall endeavor to distinguish among the different kinds of conflicts of interest. It is not only important for lawyers but for others as well—doctors, journalists, social workers, etc.—to be sensitive to the possibility that they may be involved in a conflict of interest. For this reason, where possible our discussion in what follows will take examples, not only from law, but from other areas as well. In the second place, we shall attempt with respect to each of these types of conflict to isolate what it is exactly that makes the circumstance ethically interesting. Why should the ethically competent attorney be wary of conflict of interest? It is not enough to say, as many discussions of conflict of interest seem to, that you or your client may be caused to suffer for such inattention. That may be so, but the question still must be faced whether such penalties ought to be paid.

The two situations denoted by the term "conflict of interest" have very different ethical characteristics. Henceforth, we will use the term "conflict of obligation" to refer to the first type of situation and will reserve the term "conflict of interest" exclusively for the second type.

CONFLICTS OF OBLIGATION: ACTUAL AND POTENTIAL

Dexter, who used to box as a boy, has just started teaching his son and some of the youngsters from the neighborhood the basic elements of the sport. Working with heavily padded gloves, the boys have done well during several practice

From Kenneth Kipnis, *Legal Ethics,* © 1986, pp. 40-53. Reprinted by permission of the author and Prentice-Hall, Englewood, Cliffs, New Jersey.

sessions and seem ready for their first matches. With Dexter serving as referee, the second bout begins with Dexter's son contending in the ring. Dexter tries to be fair as the two boys land punches on each other but nonetheless feels uncomfortable struggling to suppress any suggestion of favoritism for his son. The match is a close one and he wonders how the other boy will feel if he gives the bout to his son. He wonders how his son will feel if he gives the bout to the other boy.

At the core of Dexter's uneasiness is an insoluble ethical dilemma that he has unwittingly brought upon himself. For Dexter is a father and, arguably, fathers have obligations to be partisan supporters of their young sons. But Dexter is also the referee in a boxing match. As such his obligation is to be even-handed and fair. Clearly, there is nothing wrong with being a father and nothing is wrong with being a referee. But there does seem to be something morally perilous about refereeing a match in which one's son is a contestant. With respect to one and the same youngster, Dexter must be both a partisan supporter and disinterested judge. Clearly, it is impossible to meet either obligation without compromising one's ability to fulfill the other. It is of little solace that there may be a right or a best answer to the dilemma. "If you have to decide between being a bad referee and a bad father, always choose. . . ." Regardless of the answer, Dexter is in the unenviable position of having to decide what kind of creep he is going to be. The situation Dexter has brought upon himself is one in which his obligations conflict with one another. Although the dilemma is probably unresolvable once it has arisen, had he been sufficiently attentive to the ethical implications of the roles he had assumed (father and referee), Dexter could have prevented the problem from arising in the first place. He could have, for example, put off the boxing matches until he had found someone else to referee them. But conflicts of obligation are not always that simple.

Flynn is driving along in her car with her two friends, Chang and Ripley, and, out of nowhere, a bus collides with her vehicle. Chang and Ripley are injured and have to receive medical attention. While Flynn is not hurt, her car is damaged. A few weeks later the three meet with attorney Parker to discuss suing the bus company for damages. The evidence supports the bus driver's being at fault and Parker agrees to take the case. Chang's medical bills total $14,000 and Ripley's $3,000. Flynn's car requires $1,500 worth of repairs. Taking into account other costs to his clients, Parker files suit against the bus company for $25,000. As Parker anticipated it would, the bus company files a countersuit against Flynn, claiming that the accident was her fault. At trial, each side has the chance to present its case and the jury is asked to decide who is at fault and how much they have to pay to whom. Horrified, Parker listens as the jury finds Flynn and the bus company equally at fault and equally liable for $17,000 in medical bills.[1]

Just why is Parker horrified? If Flynn, the driver of the car, had been Parker's sole client, Parker would have been obligated to discuss with her the option of filing an appeal. There is a chance that Flynn could escape the $8,500 judgment against her and perhaps even recover the costs of repairing the car. Filing an appeal might have been a very good idea. But if Chang and Ripley had been Parker's only clients, suggesting an appeal would have been absurd. They have essentially won their case. Merely to mention the word "appeal" to Flynn could be to betray Chang and Ripley. If Flynn decides to appeal, their award could be delayed for years. Conceivably, they might never receive payment. The authors of Canon 6 of the old American Bar Association *Canons of Professional Ethics* (superseded in 1970) had this situation in mind when they wrote that "a lawyer represents conflicting interests when, in behalf of one client, it is his duty to contend for that which duty to another client requires him to oppose." Parker has an obligation, to Flynn, to discuss with her the advisability of an appeal. And simultaneously he has an obligation to Chang and Ripley not to discuss with Flynn the advisability of an appeal. Parker is caught in a classic conflict of obligations.

But where was it exactly that Parker went wrong? We can appreciate, perhaps, that fathers should not referee in boxing matches where their sons are contenders. But what practical rule can attorneys adhere to that will serve to protect against having to decide which client they are going to betray?

Without doubt, the most commonly given reply to our question is the injunction to be found in Matthew: "No man can serve two masters: For either he will hate the one and love the other; or else he will hold to the one and despise the other." While there may be wisdom in this New Testament language, it seems unlikely that Matthew's words can helpfully illuminate professional responsibility in law. In the first place, lawyers do not serve their clients as servants do their masters. (We suppose that attorneys are not to be compared to slaves serving their masters.) For masters are owed obedience by those who serve them. Lawyers only rarely have obligations to obey their clients. For the most part, their service is autonomous. In the second place and more importantly, most practicing attorneys have no ethical problems in providing legal services for more than one client. If the rule in Matthew is taken to be applicable to legal practice, it entails the preposterous conclusion that no lawyer can have more than one client! While this would clearly reduce the incidence of conflicts of obligation in legal practice, it is hardly a suggestion that any attorney would take seriously. On this account, Parker could not even decide to represent Chang and Ripley simultaneously. And indeed because Parker, like every attorney, is an "officer of the court," he is as beholden to the judicial system as he is to his client. He is in the service of both. A strict application of the Matthew Rule would thus preclude anyone from ever serving as anybody else's attorney.

A second more promising approach would require Parker to foresee that conflicting obligations are a possibility and to withdraw from such situations at once. When Flynn, Ripley, and Chang sit down to tell their problem to Parker (who has not yet agreed to be their attorney), Parker must anticipate that, given the occurrence of certain events, he will be faced with an actual conflict of obligation if he agrees to represent all three clients. The bus company may file a countersuit against Flynn and the jury may find Flynn liable for the injuries sustained by the two passengers. If those events occur—there is no way effectively to prevent them from occurring—Parker will be required to betray one or two of his clients. For that reason he may agree to represent Flynn or he may agree to represent Chang and Ripley. He may not agree to represent all three. The bare possibility that a conflict of obligation may arise would require the conscientious attorney, under this rule, to decline simultaneous representation of potentially conflicting interests. A responsible attorney must therefore be sensitive to the potential for conflict and be ready to step aside should a conflict of obligation be a possibility. On this account, the Matthew Rule should be modified to prohibit an attorney from agreeing to serve more than one client where there is any reason to believe that meeting professional obligations to one of the clients might require the lawyer to forbear meeting professional obligations to the other.

Like the original Matthew Rule, this version will effectively prevent the occurrence of actual conflicts of obligation. But also like the Matthew Rule, it may be a far more draconian measure than is justified by the problem it seeks to prevent. For one thing, it will mean that the general public will have to support many more attorneys than it would otherwise need. If cases are not dropped, new lawyers will have to be employed whenever a potential conflict of obligation arises. While this may be financially beneficial for those in the legal profession, it may be that trust in lawyers will be eroded, especially if less drastic measures can do the job.[2]

The presence of multiple attorneys may also promote more litigiousness than there needs to be. Where Chang and Ripley might be able to reach agreement with Flynn in an informal setting, it may be that such agreement will be difficult where both sides are represented by attorneys *before* an actual conflict has arisen. Geoffrey C. Hazard has been helpful in illuminating this point:

> In respect to these broader terms in which conflict of interest is defined, the culture of law itself is a contributing determinant. The point can be made more clearly by considering cultures that sharply contrast in this regard. In this country, the ideals of due process, private property, and formal equality (that is equality in legal status) lead to the definition of human relationships in legal terms. They also imply that adjudication is a normal and in some sense an ideal form of resolving disputed relationships. A derivative of this premise is that the role of partisan advocate and counselor is a normal, primary, and perhaps idealized one for a lawyer to play. By way of sharp contrast, in Japanese culture the ideals of concord and deference to traditional authority predominate. The definition of human relationships in legal terms is regarded as the exhibition of something like anti-social tendencies. A derivative of this premise is that in Japan it is uncommon to resort to legal assistance and more uncommon still for lawyers to assume the role of partisan rather than neutral expositor of the law. Within both countries, certainly this one, the degree of "legalism" in definition of relationships varies with specific context, as already suggested. But when an American lawyer is consulted, the client's orientation to the problem is usually adversarial, precisely because the lawyer's normal or expected role is that of partisan. Hence the fact

that a client contemplates a legally assertive course of action and itself is a step in the direction of defining a divergency of interest as a conflict of interest.[3]

If the potential for conflict of interest is understood well enough by the attorney and the prospective clients, it may be that agreement can be reached as to the attorney's obligations if events occur that would ordinarily give rise to an actual conflict of obligations. The obligations that Parker has to his clients, he has because they delegated responsibilities to him. If the clients explicitly forbear delegating to Parker responsibilities that may give rise to a conflict of obligations, then, since Parker cannot then find himself in an actual conflict, he will have no reason to decline representation of all three. Let us see how this might work.

The scene is once again Parker's initial interview with Flynn, Chang, and Ripley. The subject of the conversation is whether Parker will agree to represent any or all of them in their proposed lawsuit against the bus company. The three potential clients have just completed recounting to Parker their story of the mishap and its consequences. Parker speaks:

> Based on what all of you tell me, the three of you appear to have a solid case against the bus company. You are all in agreement that the accident was caused by the bus driver. If the rest of the evidence holds up, I would expect that we would have a very good chance of prevailing at trial. But the bus company will not take this lying down. We can expect that they will file a countersuit against you, Ms. Flynn, and try to prove that the accident was your fault. From what all of you tell me, it doesn't look like they will succeed. But they might. No one can be certain which way the jury will go. If the jury finds Ms. Flynn to be at fault, she will be held liable for the injuries that the rest of you have sustained. That will be a problem for you, Ms. Flynn, and it may be a problem for your two friends. But it will also be a problem for me.
>
> As Ms. Flynn's attorney, it would ordinarily be my responsibility to advise her on whether she should file an appeal in the hope of getting a new trial and overturning the jury's judgment against her. The bus company will have won its lawsuit against you, Ms. Flynn, but there may be something we can do about it on appeal. If there is, while that will be a good thing for you, it may not be such a good thing for your two friends. An appeal and a new trial will take a great deal of time and, during that period, you will not have received money to pay your medical bills. The remaining two of you will essentially have won your case and yet, because of my responsibilities to Ms. Flynn, I will be working both to delay your payments and to subject you to the difficulties of an appeal. If we are "successful" on appeal, there could be a second trial that will probably not net you one extra penny. Just as I would ordinarily have an obligation to advise and represent Ms. Flynn in connection with her appeal, I would ordinarily have an obligation not to work to overturn any judgment in your favor. In short, I think that any responsible attorney would have some reservations about taking on all three of you as clients.
>
> There may be, however, something that we can do now that will prevent such

a conflict from arising later on. For example, if you, Ms. Flynn, were to stipulate now in our agreement that I am to have no responsibility to advise you and no responsibility to represent you concerning any matter that may arise subsequent to the jury's verdict in this case, then I believe that that would take care of my reservations. I will advise you now that if the jury should return a judgment against you it would be wise immediately to seek legal counsel on the question of appeal. I will be happy to suggest the names of several attorneys who would be able to help you to make your decisions, should the need arise. On the other hand, if you two gentlemen were to stipulate now in our agreement that I am being retained, not merely to press the claims that you three have against the bus company, but equally to defend Ms. Flynn against any countersuit the company might file against her, at trial, on appeal, and, if necessary, at retrial, then it may be that we can reach agreement in that way. Perhaps we will want to discuss the responsibility for fees in the event it becomes necessary to file for an appeal. In any case, if we decide to go this second route, I would want to have it clearly stated in our agreement that the appeals process may delay and even jeopardize any payment to you that the courts may find owing.

There is possibly a third option that the three of you may wish to consider. We could agree that in the event that the jury returns a judgment against Ms. Flynn, I will neither have the responsibility to advise her nor the authority to represent her on appeal and thereafter unless the two of you explicitly consent to my doing so in full understanding of what the consequences might be.

I think that I can live quite comfortably with any of these three options. It will probably be less expensive and there will be less duplication of effort if the three of you proceed, for now, with one attorney. But you should consider carefully that your interests might diverge, now or later on, and that it may be better to bring in a second attorney or to accept that it may be costly to some of you if I work to meet all the responsibilities you have delegated to me. Why don't you talk these arrangements over among yourselves and if one of them seems suitable, I will be happy to draw up the appropriate agreement. On the other hand, if you feel it is better to go with separate attorneys, I will be happy to recommend several who can do the work.

Here, attorney Parker is treating a potential conflict of obligation, not as a flashing red signal to stop, but, rather, as a problem that perhaps can be resolved to the advantage of his clients. When a potential conflict of obligation becomes apparent, it is clear that the first step ought to be disclosure. The lawyer-client relationship tends to be an unfamiliar one to many laypersons and the exercise of explaining the problem can serve to clarify the nature of an attorney's obligation to a client. The second step, on this analysis, would be to set out the ways in which the dilemma can be prevented from arising. Is it possible for clients to specify and limit the attorney's responsibility and authority so that the conflict cannot arise? Can clients explicitly waive certain rights or disavow expectations in order to consent to multiparty representation that would otherwise be ethically questionable? Is it possible adequately to advise clients in advance of those circumstances under which independent counsel should be sought? At the very minimum—and this may not be enough—the attorney should tell clients precisely what he or she will do in the event that a conflict of obligations arises and should secure from each client a consent that is informed by adequate knowledge of the consequences. What is suggested here is not so much a rule as a set of strategies. To be sure, there will be many occasions in which a conscientious attorney, committed to doing the best for clients, can do nothing better than decline simultaneous representation. But it is often possible for an ethically competent lawyer to fashion a framework for cooperation that will serve all of the clients well.[4]

Our discussion of conflict of obligation has focused thus far on problems arising in simultaneous representation of divergent interests. But similar problems arise out of successive representations. While most of an attorney's obligations to a client end when the lawyer-client relationship is dissolved, there is one that does not. It is the obligation of confidentiality. It is typically involved in conflicts involving the former client.

For several years Mr. Gould refers legal questions arising in the course of his business to Mr. Kimura, an attorney. Eventually Gould's business grows and he begins to take his legal matters to another firm. Several years afterwards, Mrs. Gould shows up in Kimura's office to talk with him about getting a divorce from her husband. Because of Kimura's earlier relationship with Mr. Gould, Kimura knows a fair amount about the businessman's assets. He may have information that could be very useful to Mrs. Gould if there is litigation regarding a property settlement. But at the same time, Kimura is under an obligation not to disclose the information to anyone unless Mr. Gould's permission is obtained. If Kimura agrees to serve as Mrs. Gould's attorney in the divorce proceedings against the former client, he will have the obligation to serve as her "zealous advocate," using all means at his disposal to prevail in the courts. If there is something Kimura has learned from his former client that is crucial or even helpful to his current client, Kimura will be caught in a second type of conflict of obligation. He must advise and represent his current client to the best of his ability and yet, at the same time, there may be information that he has that is essential to her welfare and that he is not at liberty to utilize or divulge. Once the actual conflict of obligations becomes apparent to Kimura, it becomes patently clear that he must withdraw immediately as Mrs. Gould's attorney. He must abandon her. Indeed, he is not even permitted to explain in any detail the reasons for his withdrawal: To do so may be to violate the confidences he is obligated to preserve.

Conflicts of obligations arising out of successive representation are not manageable in the same way as those arising out of simultaneous representation. There is no longer a continuing relationship with one of the parties and not always an opportunity to hammer out agreements to the advantage of all. It is also frequently a nice question whether, before exploring in detail the nuances of a new client's case, there is a potential conflict of obligation arising out of confidential communications from a prior client. Suppose Kimura only handled one or two minor matters twelve years ago. Suppose most of what Kimura learned while serving as Mr. Gould's attorney has since become generally known. Since it may be difficult if not impossible to know in advance whether one has confidential information from a prior client that could be helpful or even critical to a potential client whom one is interviewing for the first time, attorneys should probably err on the side of caution and decline representation when there is a possibility that zealous advocacy may be incompatible with the preservation of a former client's confidences.

One possible solution is to get the former client's consent. Waiving confidentiality, Mr. Gould can explicitly permit Kimura to represent his wife in the divorce action. But it might also be suggested that the representation would be permissible provided that the new client was put on notice that the attorney might withdraw at any moment without explanation. Perhaps there are some clients who would accept representation under such conditions. But the attorney may have obligations to the court not to abandon clients in the midst of litigation. More to the point, the sudden decision to abandon a client can itself compromise the former client's confidences. Mr. Gould's wife can infer that the attorney knows something that would be useful to her but that he cannot tell her. For this reason, unless there is consent from the former client, an attorney should disqualify himself or herself for representing any client where the matters under consideration are substantially related to matters considered in representing a former client.[5] Good judgment is called for in making this decision.

An attorney's good judgment is also a requirement where vicarious disqualification is a possibility. Suppose it wasn't Kimura who represented Gould but Kimura's law partner. Must Kimura then decline representation of Mrs. Gould? Or suppose it was Mr. Kimura's wife who represented Mr. Gould in his business transactions. Or suppose it was merely the attorney with whom Kimura shares office space. Kimura may know that he knows nothing whatever about Mr. Gould's financial status, past or present. From Kimura's perspective, we no longer have a potential conflict of obligations. But from Mr. Gould's perspective, however, we may have a towering appearance of impropriety. It may look for all the world as if Kimura is relying upon confidential information gained from an earlier slender or indirect relationship with Mr. Gould; information that is now being used to further the cause of one who has it in for Mr. Gould. Moreover, Mr. Gould may not be able to elaborate upon his suspicions and Kimura may not be able to defend himself against the charges without disseminating the very information that is intended to be confidential. In terms of its effect upon clients' willingness to trust lawyers, the appearance of betrayal is every bit as damaging as the real thing. Clients may refrain from sharing their confidences with their attorneys because they fear that the information may someday be used against them. This will mean that attorneys may be less able to give clients good advice. Hence, conflict of obligation in successive client representations, as an ethical problem for the practitioner, merges gradually into a concern that the profession has to prevent flagrant appearances of impropriety among its members. We will return to this issue in the next section.

It is in this context that we are brought to our final point in our discussion of conflicts of obligation. For if the evidence that a court is permitted to examine supports the conclusion that an attorney may have relied upon confidential information entrusted to him (or to his partner) by his present adversary; if it appears that there was an opportunity for him to be entrusted with such information and that the information could have been utilized on behalf of his present client against the former client, then a court may well be inclined to disqualify him as the client's attorney and to vacate a judgment he may have gained on his client's behalf. As one court put it: "An attorney must avoid not only the fact, but even the appearance, of representing conflicting interests."[6] The trial may have been defective because one of the parties may have had improper or inadequate representation. Indeed, in *Jedwabney* v. *Philadelphia Transportation Co.* (upon which we loosely based our saga of Parker, Flynn, Chang, and Ripley), the attorney, whom we presume *was* horrified, stood by as the company won a new trial because the driver of the automobile was inadequately informed of his attorney's potentially conflicting obligations. The judge felt that the driver had not been "given the chance to make an informed choice." In his dissenting opinion in the case, Justice Musmanno laments that the two injured passengers who had won their verdict must once again "be subjected to the turmoil, the expense, the loss of time, the worry and the agony which accompany a trial—with the possibility of drowning in a river they have already crossed."[7] Clients may indeed be ill-served if attorneys neglect conflicts. While this is not the whole reason for lawyer attention to the potential for conflict, it is certainly part of it.

CONFLICTS OF INTEREST: PERSONAL AND STRUCTURAL

In the preceding section we have seen how attorneys can get into ethical trouble if an obligation they have to one client is in potential or actual conflict with an obligation they have to another client. A more frequent type of conflict occurs where attorneys themselves have interests that may incline them away from fulfillment of their obligations to clients. Problems of this general type can arise whenever there are clear obligations associated with a social position. Consider the following:

1. The Anodyne Pharmaceutical Corporation is introducing a new drug for the treatment of diabetes. In its effort to promote sales as the drug enters the market, physicians are offered expensive premiums if they prescribe sufficient quantities before a certain date. Physicians who succeed in this can receive a home stereo system, an all-expenses-paid vacation for two in Hawaii, or a self-propelled lawnmower. Dr. Brisby switches a number of his patients over to the new drug and opts for the Hawaiian vacation.

2. For the past nine years, the 400 to 600 students who take Professor Darnay's introductory-level political science course each semester have been required to read *An Introduction to Politics,* written by Professor Darnay himself. The book costs $30 and Professor Darnay collects $4 in royalties from the publisher for every copy sold. Professor Darnay is the only professor who teaches this course and student advisors regularly recommend it for pre-law undergraduates. Because new editions of the text are published regularly and specifically assigned by the instructor, used books are seldom available for purchase.

3. Wiggins is the purchasing agent for a small municipality. He has responsibility for the final decision on all significant purchases made by the city government. For the past seven years, the city has purchased all of its automobiles from Ray's Motors. Ray, the owner and general manager of the company, is Wiggins's brother-in-law.

Now let us examine some similar cases in legal settings.

4. Big Jake, a reputed underworld leader, has a reputation for distributing extravagant gifts whenever things go well. After prevailing in a criminal case against him, Jake sends expensive presents to the prosecuting attorney, to the judge, and to all twelve of the jurors.

5. Mullens, who has been struck by an automobile and is recovering from injuries, contacts Taney, an attorney, about suing the driver of the car. Taney declines to take the case but recommends that Mullens see Hargitty, a specialist in personal injury cases. Mullens seems agreeable and, while still in Taney's office, Taney gets Hargitty on the telephone. A time for an initial interview is scheduled. Taney and Hargitty have a standing agreement that whenever Taney refers a case to her she will give him a small amount of work in connection with the case and one-third of whatever fees she obtains. Mullens is not aware of the arrangement.

6. Three years ago, Scribner did some estate planning and drafted a Will for Whipple who was then seventy-eight years old. Now Whipple has died and his Last Will and Testament are in probate. The will that Scribner earlier prepared for his client provides that one-third of the deceased's substantial estate is to go to his "good friend and faithful attorney, Scribner."

To begin, let us note that in the first three situations above, we are not looking at conflicting obligations. Each actor can be said to have a personal interest in the outcome of the transaction but not an obligation to pursue that interest. Dr. Brisby clearly has no obligation to accept the Hawaiian vacation. While Professor Darney, one assumes, is not completely disinterested as regards the $4,000 he collects annually from students he requires to purchase his book, he has no obligation to collect these funds. Wiggins, one supposes, is not displeased that some of the city's business has gone to a member of his family. Still, it would not have been wrong for him to have stepped aside and allowed someone else to select the most competitive bid and issue the contract. There is certainly no obligation to take every opportunity to enrich oneself (and one's relatives), especially when one occupies a social position in virtue of which one is beholden to others, as the doctor is to his patients, as the teacher is to his students, and as the purchasing agent is to the citizens of his community.

Nor are we necessarily looking at a series of betrayals. Dr. Brisby's patients, let us suppose, will not suffer for having been switched to the new medication. Other conscientious professors use Darnay's *An Introduction to Politics.* And Wiggins's municipality is not being made to pay exorbitant prices for second-rate automobiles. We will suppose then that Dr. Brisby's patients, Professor Darnay's students, and the citizens of Wiggins's municipality are not the victims of deliberate efforts to shortchange them. Under different circumstances, another doctor, professor, or purchasing agent could reasonably have made the same choice without the extra incentive.

Let us suppose, then, that, despite their expectation that they might receive expensive gifts from the overjoyed Jake, the prosecutor, the judge, and the jurors do their very best not to let possible benefits for themselves affect either their effort or their judgment. Even without Jake's reputation of largesse, the outcome might have been the same. Suppose further that Taney has the highest regard for Hargitty's legal abilities and might well choose to go to her himself if the need arose. Finally, let us accept that Scribner did not twist Whipple's arm in order to get him to sign the will. It was Whipple's own idea to give a portion of the estate to Scribner and, while Scribner did not object, other attorneys might well have found the bequest to Scribner to be unexceptional had they been drafting the will. Our concern here is not with the reasonableness or unreasonableness of the actions undertaken in behalf of the clients. It is rather with the acceptances of the gift, the referral fee, and with the drafting of the will, each enriching fiduciaries who are otherwise beholden to clients.

It might be plausibly suggested that what is ethically perilous in these cases is the possibility that judgment might be affected despite the care taken to avoid influence. Subconsciously, the expectation that one has something to gain may play a hidden role in one's deliberations. To the extent that this is so (*ex hypothesi,* one cannot know it is not so), one may not be doing the most responsible work that can be done under the circumstances. While we might suppose in setting up our examples that other attorneys, judges, and officers of the court might have acted similarly even without a comparable personal interest in the outcome, it may not be possible for one who is subject to a conflicting personal interest to be equally confident about what a disinterested judgment would look like. Without the attorney knowing about it, a personal interest in the matter may compromise an attorney's ability to exercise independent professional judgment on behalf of a client. Standing to benefit from specific advice or representation, the attorney also has an interest in underestimating the degree to which advantage to self may interfere with the fulfillment of obligations to the client. And so for many—perhaps for all—it may be ethically imprudent to trust one's own opinion that professional judgment will be unaffected by personal interest.

Still, an attorney might be confident—let us suppose, reasonably so—that her independent judgment will not be compromised by a personal interest. Is there reason still for the responsible attorney to be concerned about conflict of interest? Does "reasonable" confidence that independent judgment will not be affected suffice to satisfy an attorney's doubts about the propriety of proceeding in the face of a conflicting personal interest?

In a professionalized legal system such as ours, people are not expected to understand their legal situation without professional counsel, nor are they expected to be able to secure that to which they are legally entitled unless they have access to professional services available only through a licensed attorney. Clients are thus sitting ducks for unscrupulous attorneys and, in general, they know it. Legal advice may further the attorney's cause more than the client's and legal action can benefit the attorney at the client's expense. For this reason, loyalty to the client must be an overriding obligation of attorneys if the general public is to trust the members of the legal profession. To the extent that laypersons believe that people generally pursue their own interests, attorneys must make a special effort to try to get across to clients that it is the client's interests that are determinative of lawyer advice and representation and that the lawyer's personal interests will not compromise loyalty to the client. It is clearly part of the profession's responsibility that this be done. It is also in the profession's considered interests.

The duty of loyalty thus has two parts. There is a guarantee that the profession makes to clients on behalf of the attorney that he or she will exercise independent judgment on the client's behalf and will be a zealous advocate in representing the client's interests within the judicial system. That part is satisfied when the attorney is confident that significant personal interests will not interfere with independent judgment or zeal. But, additionally, there is a second guarantee: it is that the attorney will not give reason to believe that that loyalty has been compromised. A lawyer may be confident that potentially compromising influences are not having an effect. We may suppose that such confidence is reasonable in light of the attorney's experience. But it is not possible to be equally confident that others, who may believe that attorneys are as self-interested as anyone else, will be ready to accept the attorney's own assurances that personal interests played no role in professional judgment. In each of the six cases above, the existence of the conflicting personal interest *calls into question* the propriety of an action that might otherwise be unexceptional. Should it come out that physicians participate in Anodyne's sales promotion plan, patients may be less willing to accept the advice of doctors. One will not know whether a prescription is being written because the patient needs a new medication or because the physician wants a self-propelled lawnmower. Likewise, the students in Professor Darnay's class may underestimate the significance of his book on the grounds that it is being assigned, not because of some independent judgment as to its quality and appropriateness, but rather because Darnay needs the supplement to his income. His action may be construed as exploitative of his students. Thirdly, Wiggins's award of the contract to his brother-in-law can call into doubt the integrity of the governmental process. Suspicions will be aroused and confirmed that government offices do not exist to serve the community but, rather, the officeholders.

It is not difficult to appreciate how the fairness of Big Jake's trial is called into question by his distribution of expensive gifts. By way of comparison, suppose that the losing quarterback in an important professional football game were to receive from the owner of the winning team the sum of $100,000 in a brown paper bag. Suppose it was widely publicized that this transfer had taken place only a few hours after the conclusion of the game, a game in which the quarterback, normally a star player, had appeared to play rather badly. Consider how the bare fact that the money changed hands can compromise the integrity of the game. Apart from whether or not the quarterback deliberately shaved points or threw the game; apart from whether or not the payments were made in satisfaction of some agreement made earlier; in the light of the payment we have good reason to be uncertain whether what took place in the stadium was a genuine football game or an elaborate charade engineered to create the appearance of a fair test. Under the circumstances, the outcome of the game gives us scant reason to believe that the winners were the better football players. Likewise, if a trial is to serve as a social procedure for settling disputed questions, it is crucial that key participants in the transaction keep themselves above reproach. As with the role of quarterback, the positions of judge, prosecutor, and juror can create golden opportunities for self-enrichment at the expense of the integrity of the judicial process. The social positions themselves would lack point in the absence of a commitment not to benefit oneself in ways that *can be construed* as abusive of the privileges attaching to the roles. Thus, with only a few minor exceptions, the American Bar Association *Code of Judicial Conduct* (adopted in 1972) provides that "[n]either a judge nor a member of his family residing in his household should accept a gift, bequest, favor, or loan from anyone. . . ." Specifically barred is the acceptance of gifts from donors whose interests have come or are likely to come before the judge. Comparable constraints are applicable to the roles of jurors and prosecutor.

Taney's referral of the Mullens case to Hargitty raises questions that are similar to those in the Dr. Brisby example. The existence of the referral fee calls into question the purpose of Taney's advice: Is it being given for the client's benefit or the attorney's? Even though it may be true that the attorney's recommendation is sound and that the client is not being charged an unreasonable amount, most laypeople, unschooled in the intricacy of the legal process, are probably not likely to believe Taney when he says, with a straight face, that the kickback had no influence whatever upon his professional judgment. To the extent that such referral fees are customary, the profession runs the risk that the general public will become aware of the practice and will look upon such recommendations with cynicism.[8]

Scribner's decision to draft the Whipple will, making himself a beneficiary, raises a different problem. Since Whipple is dead and since Scribner was carrying out Whipple's instructions, there is no occasion here for a client to lose trust. If eyebrows are raised at all, they will be those of the disinherited friends and relatives. Instead of decisively settling Whipple's intentions regarding the disposition of his estate, Scribner's document raises questions of undue influence and overreaching on the attorney's part; perhaps even questions of fraud arising out of the fiduciary relationship. Roman law would not permit the individual drawing a will to receive a legacy under it and, today, the laws of some states provide that such a circumstance gives rise either to a presumption or an inference of undue influence.[9] Not only is it the case that Scribner may not receive the portion of the estate that Whipple wanted him to have, his interest as a beneficiary of the will he was drafting can suffice to void the entire document. As a beneficiary, Scribner's own testimony regarding the validity of the will can be called into question. Clearly, if Scribner wanted to do his best work for his client, he would have suggested, without recommending names, that Whipple retain some other attorney of his own choosing and ask that attorney to draft a codicil providing for the bequest.[10] In part, this is a matter of prudence and competence. To do any less is to do less than one's best work for one's client. But, in this case, the expected outcome of the shoddy legal workmanship involves a substantial benefit for the attorney. The conflict of interest could hardly be more glaring.

The conflicts of interest that are of most concern to the legal profession are those in which the attorney reaps a substantial financial benefit quite apart from payment for work done on the case. But as all of us value things other than money, the possibilities for conflicts of interest are perhaps as far-ranging as human desire itself. Service to a client can suffer if an attorney is uncomfortable unless he has control of the client, or, alternatively, uncomfortable unless the client is involved in the making of all decisions; if the attorney is worried about being too aggressive or not aggressive enough; or if the attorney is insufficiently concerned or excessively concerned about competency to handle a client's problem. Conflicts can arise as a consequence of assuming too many responsibilities. Which client's affairs can be put on a back burner? Which pressing problem am I going to neglect?[11] The process of becoming a responsible attorney is in large measure a matter of coming to understand the personal tensions here and learning to manage and to avert the problems. Adaptation of one's self to the constraints of the professional role is rarely an easy matter.

There are some conflicts of interest, however, that are neither personal in the sense just discussed nor the product of some special financial interest of the attorney. These cannot be averted merely by referring the case to another attorney. They are rooted in the very structure of the role of the professional. Attorneys are paid for their work and, under the hourly fee arrangements governing much attorney income, there is an ineradicable conflict of interest every time a lawyer advises a client to get legal help with a problem and that he or she is available to do the job. The conflict comes to the fore whenever a professional advises a client to purchase more professional services. The lawyer has a clear financial interest in the advice. Some might think that the problem can be ameliorated if attorneys were paid flat salaries in prepaid legal services plans, rather than on an hourly rate or a fee-for-service basis. But, instead of solving the problem, this arrangement merely changes its effect. The employee on a flat salary can be supposed to have an interest in working less for the same amount of money. Thus the incentive for a salaried attorney might be to say to prospective clients, not that they need professional services when they do not but, rather, that they do not need professional services when in fact they do.

The problem is well understood in the medical context: The fee-for-service system has for years been criticized for encouraging unnecessary medical treatment. Conversely, health maintenance organizations (HMO's) that pay doctors on a salary basis have been criticized for not providing patients with needed medical services. The patient belonging to an HMO may spend less time in the hospital than a similar patient whose medical bills are paid for on a fee-for-service basis. But it is difficult to tell in practice whether the HMO patient is being deprived of needed medical care or whether the fee-for-service patient is being given unnecessary medical care. Conflicts of interest at this level require very careful specification of the concept of a need, medical or legal, and consideration of alternative incentive systems that can suffice to provide for those needs. The trick is to specify the details of a social structure that will make it reasonable for clients (or patients) to believe that the services they are denied are services they don't need. This is perhaps the most difficult question arising in the area of conflict of interest. At this writing, it cannot be said that there is a favored answer.

NOTES

1. The facts here are adapted from Jedwabny v. Philadelphia Transportation Company, 390 PA 231, 135 A.2d 252, (1957).

2. See Thomas D. Morgan, "The Evolving Concept of Professional Responsibility," *Harvard Law Review* 90 (1977):702, 727.

3. Geoffrey C. Hazard, *Ethics in the Practice of Law* (New Haven, Conn.: Yale University Press, 1978), pp. 79–80.

4. One option that Parker does not discuss is the possibility of Chang and Ripley suing the bus company *and Flynn* for their injuries. Has a conflict of obligations prevented Parker from giving his best advice to two of his clients? Nor does Parker discuss with Flynn the possibility that Chang and Ripley may have caused the accident—and their own injuries—by interferring with Flynn's driving. Perhaps Ripley, but not Chang, interfered.

5. This is essentially the standard applied in T. C. Theater Corp. v. Warner Bros. Pictures,

113 F. Sup. 265 (S.D.N.Y. 1953) and specified in the *Model Rules of Professional Conduct.*

6. Edelman v. Levy. 346 N.Y.S. 2d 347 (1973).

7. Jedwabney v. Philadelphia Transportation Co., see note 1 above. It is a nice question, but one we will table, whether the company ought to have had the standing to complain to the court and to win an appeal on the basis of the conflict of obligation in the other side's attorney. The injured party—the driver of the car—never saw fit to protest that he had been unfairly treated. On the other hand, since the driver's attorney also represented the passengers, is it reasonable to expect that the court would hear of the driver's complaint through his attorney? How might a judge decide if a new trial is required because one of the parties was possibly not properly represented?

8. Though there are differences in the way they approach the problem, the *Canons of Professional Ethics* (Canon 34, Division of Fees), the *Code of Professional Responsibility* (DR 2-107, Division of Fees Among Lawyers), and the *Model Rules of Professional Conduct* (Rule 1.5, Fees) each prohibit the financial arrangement contemplated by Taney and Hargitty. Nothing, however, would prohibit Taney from charging Mullens a reasonable fee for his advice to retain Hargitty.

9. State v. Horan, 21 Wis. 2d 66, 123 N.W. 2d 488 (1963).

10. This is the advice given by Henry Drinker, *Legal Ethics* (New York: Columbia University Press, 1953), p. 94.

11. A useful source here is Andrew S. Watson, "A Psychological Taxonomy of Lawyer Conflicts" in his *The Lawyer in the Interviewing and Counselling Process* (Indianapolis: The Bobbs-Merrill Company, Inc., 1976), pp. 94–100.

Geoffrey C. Hazard, Jr.

Lawyer for the Situation

The problem of deciding who is the client arises when a lawyer supposes that a conflict of interest prevents him from acting for all the people involved in a situation. That is, if the interests of the potential clients were in harmony, or could be harmonized, no choice would have to be made between them and the lawyer could act for all. When the lawyer feels that he can act for all, it can be said simply that he has several clients at the same time. When the clients are all involved in a single transaction, however, the lawyer's responsibility is rather different from what it is when he represents several clients in transactions that have nothing to do with each other. This difference is suggested by the proposition that a lawyer serving more than one client in a single transaction represents "the situation."

The term is the invention of Louis D. Brandeis, justice of the United States Supreme Court and before that practitioner of law in Boston. It emerged in a hearing in which Brandeis's professional ethics as a lawyer had been questioned.[1]

Brandeis seems to have been the only first class American lawyer whose professional ethics have been the subject of a formal investigation. The occasion was the 1916 Senate hearings on his nomination as justice of the Supreme Court. Brandeis's nomination to the Court by President Wilson was bitterly opposed, chiefly by the conservative establishment within the legal profession. The opposition appears actually to have been based on the fact that Brandeis was an intellectually powerful liberal and a Jew, but ostensibly it was based on alleged improprieties in his professional conduct. One charge, which did not hold up, was that Brandeis represented some clients too resolutely. The other charge was that his representation of some clients was not resolute enough in that he had simultaneously acted for clients who had conflicts of interest. The attack ultimately failed, but out of it came the notion of "lawyer for the situation."

From Geoffrey C. Hazard, Jr., *Ethics in the Practice of Law* (New Haven, Conn.: Yale University Press, 1978), pp. 58-68. Copyright © 1978 Seven Springs Farm Center. Reprinted by permission of the author and the publisher.

*   *   *

The transactions complained of included the following. First, Brandeis had at one time represented one party in a transaction, later represented someone else in a way that impinged on that transaction. Second, he had acted in situations where those he served had conflicting interests, for example, by putting together the bargain between parties to a business deal. Third, he had acted for a family business and continued so to act after a falling out among the family required reorganization of the business arrangement. Fourth, over a course of several years he had mediated and adjusted interests of the owners and creditors of a business in such a way as to keep the business from foundering.

The objections to Brandeis's conduct in all these situations were twofold. One was that his conduct was unethical per se because he represented conflicting interests. The other was that he had not adequately made clear to the clients that their interests were in conflict. On the second point, Brandeis acknowledged that at least in some instances he may not have adequately explained the situation to the clients and adequately defined his role as he saw it. Having acknowledged this, he defended his conduct not only on the ground of its being common practice but also on the ground that it was right. In instances questioned, he said, he did not regard himself as being lawyer for one of the parties to the exclusion of the others, but as "lawyer for the situation." Eventually, the charge did not so much collapse as become submerged in concessions from other reputable lawyers that they had often done exactly as Brandeis.

Brandeis's term was mentioned by the Seven Springs participants as descriptive of many settings in which they had found themselves, among them:

—Acting for a partnership or corporation, not only as legal adviser but also as mediator, go-between, and balance wheel among the principals in the business.
—Acting as an informal trustee for second-and third-generation members of a family having various active and passive interests in inherited property holdings.
—Acting as counsel, board member, and business affairs advisor for charitable organizations such as hospitals, libraries, and foundations.
—Acting as intermediary between a business and its creditors in a period of financial difficulties.
—Acting as intermediary between a corporate chief executive and his board of directors in the face of fundamental differences of policy.
—Acting as something like a marriage broker between clients wanting to settle a complex contract arrangement on terms that would be "fair to everyone."

Similar functions are performed by lawyers on corporate legal staffs regarding differences between divisions and levels in the corporation, and by lawyers for government agencies that become enmeshed in conflicts of policy. It is safe to say that "ordinary" practitioners do the same sorts of things all the time for small businesses, families, public bodies such as school boards, and local civic and political organizations.

The *Code of Professional Responsibility* recognizes only a fragment of this kind of lawyering, and with some reluctance at that. It observes that a lawyer may "serve as an impartial arbitrator or mediator" between clients. It is not clear what this is supposed to mean. It may mean "impartial arbitrator" as one thing and "mediator" as another; it may mean "impartial arbitrator" and "impartial mediator." Although the difference in interpretation may be only a quibble, more is involved that may be at first apparent.

The term "impartial arbitrator" refers to a quite definite legal function, in which one person acts as a judge and decides a legal controversy that has broken out between two other persons. The term "impartial mediator" is approximately as definite, and means a person who assumes a role of neutral go-between in a dispute that the parties are trying to resolve by negotiation. Both roles presuppose the existence of a ripened dispute. They also presuppose that each party is speaking for himself, with the third person hearing both and responding accordingly. If this is what the Code is referring to, it falls far short of what Brandeis had in mind and far short also of the situations described by the Seven Springs lawyers.

On the other hand, if the Code means to say "mediator," as well as "impartial arbitrator," a much broader connotation might be suggested. It can imply a role in which the lawyer becomes involved when the difference between the parties is still only a future contingency. It can imply that the lawyer is a spokesman for the position of each of the parties, as well as one who listens to the parties express their positions for themselves. It can imply that the lawyer is actively involved, indeed aggressively involved, in exploring alternative arrangements by which the positions of the parties can be accommodated in a comprehensive resolution of the matter at hand.

Lawyers do indeed find themselves in the roles contemplated by the narrower definitions of "impartial arbitrator and mediator." However, being an arbitrator between clients is not a function that a lawyer likes to perform. An arbitrator has to be impartial, not only detached in judgment but willing to decide the case adversely to the party who is wrong according to law. An arbitrator's verdict necessarily condemns the loser as it vindicates the winner. For both financial and moral reasons, a lawyer does not want to get into the position of having to condemn someone who has been a client.

"Mediation" does not necessarily involve so polarized a relationship. It can entail adjustment and de-escalation of defined positions, which is what the Code apparently contemplates. But it may mean various kinds of more fluid and positive intercession before the point has been reached where positions are defined. If the latter connotation is accepted, the role is essentially that of "lawyer for the situation."

"Situations" can arise in different ways. Two or more people who have not been clients may bring a "situation" to a lawyer. Sometimes a client who has a lawyer will become involved in a transaction with a third party who does not, and the transaction is one that ought to be handled as a "situation." Most commonly, perhaps, a lawyer may find himself in a "situation" involving clients whom he has previously served in separate transactions or relationships. In this circumstance the lawyer, if he properly can, will intercede before the transaction between his clients reaches counterposed positions. Doing so is in his interest, because that way he can retain both clients.

Having a lawyer act for the situation is also in the clients' interests, if adjustment on fair terms is possible, because head-on controversy is expensive and aggravating. A lawyer who failed to avoid a head-on controversy, given reasonable opportunity to do so, will have failed in what his clients generally regard as one of his chief functions—"preventive" legal assistance.

If Brandeis was wrong, then "lawyering for the situation" is marginally illicit professional conduct because it violates the principle of unqualified loyalty to client. But if Brandeis was right, and the record of good practitioners testifies to that conclusion, then what is required is not interdiction of "lawyering for the situation" but reexamination of what is meant by loyalty to client. That is, loyalty to client, like loyalty to country, may take different forms.

It is not easy to say exactly what a "lawyer for the situation" does. Clearly, his functions vary with specific circumstances. But there are common threads. The beginning point is that no other lawyer is immediately involved. Hence, the lawyer is no one's partisan and, at least up to a point, everyone's confidant. He can be the only person who knows the whole situation. He is an analyst of the relationship between the clients, in that he undertakes to discern the needs, fears, and expectations of each and to discover the concordances among them. He is an interpreter, translating inarticulate or exaggerated claims and forewarnings into temperate and mutually intelligible terms of communication. He can contribute historical perspective, objectivity, and foresight to the parties' assessment of the situation. He can discourage escalation of conflict and recruitment of outside allies. He can articulate general principles and common custom as standards by which the parties can examine their respective claims. He is advocate, mediator, entrepreneur, and judge, all in one. He could be said to be playing God.

Playing God is a tricky business. It requires skill, nerve, detachment, compassion, ingenuity, and the capacity to sustain confidence. When mishandled, it generates the bitterness and recrimination that results when a deep trust has been betrayed. Perhaps above all, it requires good judgment as to when such intercession can be carried off without unfairly subordinating the interests of one of the parties or having later to abort the mission.

When a relationship between the clients is amenable to "situation" treatment, giving it that treatment is perhaps the best service a lawyer can render to anyone. It approximates the ideal forms of intercession suggested by the models of wise parent or village elder. It provides adjustment of difference upon a wholistic view of the situation rather than bilaterally opposing ones. It rests on implicit principles of decision that express commonly shared ideals in behavior rather than strict legal right. The basis of decision is mutual assent and not external compulsion. The orientation in time tends to be a hopeful view of the future rather than an angry view of the past. It avoids the loss of personal autonomy that results when each side commits his cause to his own advocate. It is the opposite of "going to law."

One would think that the role of "lawyer for the situation" would have been idealized by the bar in parity with the roles of partisan advocate and confidential advisor. The fact that it has not been may itself be worth exploring.

It is clear that a "lawyer for the situation" has to identify clearly his role as such, a requirement that Brandeis conceded he might not always have fulfilled. But beyond saying that he will undertake to represent the best interests of all, a lawyer cannot say specifically what he will do or what each of the clients should do in the situation. (If the outcome of the situation were clearly foreseeable, presumably the lawyer's intercession would be unnecessary.) Moreover, he cannot define his role in the terms of the direction of his effort, for his effort will not be vectored outward toward third persons but will aim at an interaction among the clients. Hence, unlike advocacy or legal counselling involving a single client, lawyering for a situation is not provided with a structure of goals and constraints imposed from outside. The lawyer and the clients must create that structure for themselves, with the lawyer being an active participant. And like the other participants he cannot reveal all that is on his mind or all that he suspects the others may have on their minds, except as doing so aids movement of the situation along lines that seem productive.

A lawyer can proceed in this role only if the clients trust him and, equally important, he trusts himself. Trust is by definition ineffable. It is an acceptance of another's act without demanding that it bona fide be objectively provable; to demand its proof is to confess it does not exist. It is a relationship that is uncomfortable for the client but perhaps even more so for the lawyer. Experienced as he is with the meanness that people can display to each other, why should the lawyer not doubt his own susceptibility to the same failing? But trust is involved also in the role of the confidential advisor and advocate. Why should lawyers regard their own trustworthiness as more vulnerable in those roles than in the role of "lawyer for the situation"?

Perhaps it is because the legal profession has succeeded in defining the roles of confidential advisor and advocate in ways that substantially reduce the burden of being trustworthy in these roles. The confidential advisor is told that he may not act to disclose anything about the client, except an announced intention to commit a crime. Short of this extremity, the rules of the role have it that the counsellor has no choices to make between the interests of his client and the interests of others. His commitment is to the client alone. Correlatively, the advocate is told that he may assert any claim on behalf of a client except one based on fabricated evidence or one empty of substance at all. Short of this extremity, the advocate also has no choices to make.

The "lawyer for the situation," on the other hand, has choices to make that obviously can go against the interest of one client or another, as the latter perceives it. A lawyer who assumes to act as intercessor has to evoke complete confidence that he will act justly in the circumstances. This is to perform the role of the administered justice itself, but without the constraints inherent in that process (such as the fact that the rules are written down, that they are administered by independent judges, and that outcomes have to be justified by references to reason and precedent). The role of lawyer for the situation therefore may be too prone to abuse to be explictly sanctioned. A person may be entrusted with it only if he knows that in the event of miscarriage he will have no protection from the law. In this respect, acting as lawyer for the situation can be thought of as similar to a doctor's "authority" to terminate the life of a hopeless patient: It can properly be undertaken only if it will not be questioned afterwards. To this extent Bradeis's critics may have been right.

Yet it seems possible to define the role of intercessor, just as it has been possible to define the role of the trustee or guardian. The role could be defined by contrast with those of confidential counsellor and advocate, perhaps to the advantage of clarity in defining all three.[2] At minimum, a recognition of the role of lawyer for the situation could result in a clearer perception by both clients and lawyers of one very important and socially estimable function that lawyers can perform and do perform.[3]

NOTES

1. For an account of the Brandeis case, see Frank, "The Legal Ethics of Louis D. Brandeis," *Stanford Law Review* 17 (1965):683.

2. The "securities bar" (lawyers handling stock issues sold publicly) has been deeply embroiled in the question of the nature and extent of the obligation of the lawyer for a securities issuer concerning the veracity of statements made by the issuer. One analysis of the problem is that there is conflict over whether the lawyer should be regarded as representing the issuer or as representing the situation of an issuance of stock. See Sommer, "The Emerging Responsibilities of the Securities Lawyer," 1974-75 *Federal Securities Law Report* par. 79, p. 631.

3. See Paul, "A New Role for Lawyers in Contract Negotiations," *American Bar Association Journal* 62 (1976):93.

Linda J. Silberman

Professional Responsibility Problems of Divorce Mediation

INTRODUCTION

Divorce mediation is a growing trend in the United States as couples seek alternatives to the traditional adversary model for rearranging their personal and financial affairs.[1] Various types of "family mediation" have been undertaken by lawyers, mental health professionals, and others as part of this new wave. Though individual programs include any number of differing arrangements, mediation contemplates a neutral third party who will guide the parties toward resolution of their marital disputes, outside of, or preliminary to litigation. In the usual situation, the parties will not be individually represented in the mediation; rather the mediator attempts to gain the trust of both parties and helps them to reach agreements on matters of property, support, and custody of children.[2] Likewise, in most mediation programs, the mediator does not act as the arbitrator or decisionmaker for the parties, although several mediation centers add an arbitration component if the mediation itself is unsuccessful.

Proponents of mediation claim it avoids the adversarial relationship and concomitant hostility that often characterizes the traditional divorce process.[3] Also, returning responsibility and autonomy to the parties in reaching their own settlement of marital disputes will likely mean that agreements will be adhered to.[4] Finally, it is generally thought that mediation will be more expeditious and less expensive than traditional adversarial negotiations or litigation.[5]

The future of divorce mediation is still unclear. Programs are in an early stage, and research efforts and evaluations are only just the beginning.[6] What is dismaying, however, is that mediation efforts may be stymied before they have even begun. A variety of restrictive professional responsibility rulings have come from bar associations, which have impeded experimentation with divorce mediation programs. That is not to say that there are not serious ethical issues

Reproduced by permission from *Family Law Quarterly* vol. 16, no. 2 (1982), American Bar Association.

that must be addressed by the law—and indeed the mental health—professions. But perhaps what is needed more is serious reflection on how those ethical responsibilities can be met within the structure of individual mediation programs.[7]

Mediation which is conducted or referred under the auspices of the court or its auxiliary services does not seem subject to ethics challenges.[8] However, mediation which is not court-referred and which takes place independently and preliminary to any traditional legal processes has been the subject of several ethics opinions and the object of some controversy. The professional responsibility issues implicated by these latter divorce mediation projects depend in part on the type of program used. . . .

THE SINGLE LAWYER MEDIATOR

A lawyer who wishes to undertake divorce mediation as part of his legal practice faces the prohibition of Canon 5, preventing representation of conflicting or potentially differing interests.[9] In nonmatrimonial contexts there are exceptions to this prohibition. Dual representation is permitted "in matters not involving litigation,"[10] where the lawyer has "explained fully to each client the implications of the common representation . . . and the clients . . . consent."[11] However, representation of both spouses in a matrimonial action has traditionally been viewed as being so inherently prejudicial that dual representation is always prohibited.[12] This classic stance has been taken by most bar associations. With the advent of no-fault divorce, however, several bar committees have departed from it.

Recently, the Ohio State Bar Ethics Committee[13] ruled that although dual "representation" would not adequately protect the parties' rights, a single lawyer could draft a separation agreement as long as (A) the lawyer represented one of the parties and the second party (1) was fully aware that (s)he was not being represented and (2) was given full opportunity to get independent counsel, and (B) both parties gave written consent to the arrangement—which consent was contained in or attached to the separation agreement. Indeed, the Arizona State Bar Ethics Committee[14] has gone a step further and approved of dual representation in divorce cases when there are few assets and no children, and the divorce is uncontested. Although emphasizing that dual representation would still be the exception rather than the rule, the Arizona committee took a significant step in giving couples an option to traditional adversarial divorce. Similarly, a recent case in California[15] permitted dual representation in limited circumstances. The California court, responding to a separating couple's writ of mandamus to compel the court to permit them to be jointly represented in their uncontested dissolution proceeding, stated: "Attorneys who undertake to represent parties with divergent interests owe the highest duty to each to make sure that there is full disclosure of all facts and circumstances that are necessary to enable the parties to make a fully informed choice regarding the subject matter of litigation, including the areas of potential conflict and the possibility and desirability of seeking independent legal advice."[16]

Another Virginia ethics opinion permitted an attorney to give non-partisan advice to a husband and wife concerning the transfer of property and to draft the property of settlement for both parties.[17] The circumstances indicated that the husband and wife had reached a decision to divorce, apparently without animosity, and had determined how they desired to divide their property. Because the relationship was not one in which the attorney "was obligated to argue for one party that which he was obligated to defend for another," the attorney was permitted to advise the parties on tax consequences and to represent one of the parties in securing a no-fault divorce.

In a divorce mediation, the question is somewhat different from the usual dual representation because, in one sense, the mediator represents neither of the parties. Indeed, a New York State Bar opinion[18] outlawing dual representation referred to Ethical Consideration 5-20[19] which permits lawyers to mediate in matters involving former or present clients and stated in dicta: "a lawyer approached by a husband and wife in a matrimonial matter and asked to represent both may, however, properly undertake to serve as a mediator or arbitrator."[20]

In one of the first ethics opinions on the subject, the Boston Bar Ethics Committee[21] considered the actions of a lawyer who proposed to offer services as a mediator to a married couple considering divorce and to draft a separation agreement and related documents setting forth agreed-upon terms arrived at in mediation. As mediator, the lawyer agreed to refrain from representing either of the parties in any proceeding between them. Although stating that it did not "enthusiastically endorse" mediation, the Boston Bar approved the mediation service so long as the attorney did not represent either party and the parties were advised of the possible conflict and of the various alternatives open to them (e.g., appearing pro se or obtaining separate representation) The Boston Bar opinion pointed to some of the drawbacks of an attorney serving as a mediator: unequal bargaining power where commitments are made without the benefit of the advice and assistance of counsel, concern by the clients about the mediator's possible bias in giving advice, and the reopening of negotiations if independent lawyers are later consulted. On the other hand, it chose to permit a lawyer to render mediation services for clients who wished to experiment since the committee found that the usual alternatives—resort to the adversarial process and to pro se divorce—had their own disadvantages.

The Oregon State Bar Association adopted the reasoning of the Boston Bar in an informal opinion[22] on the propriety of divorce mediation. Although the opinion was the result of an unauthorized practice investigation into the Portland-based Family Mediation Center, which used lawyer-therapist teams to mediate separation agreements, the opinion initially discussed the propriety of a solo lawyer-mediator. Accepting the Boston Bar position, the Oregon Bar Committee emphasized that the lawyer did not represent either party. It also imposed four conditions that must be satisfied before mediation by an attorney is appropriate: The lawyer (1) must clearly inform the parties that (s)he represents neither and they must both consent; (2) can give legal advice only to both parties in the presence of each other; (3) can draft the proposed agreement but must advise and encourage the parties to seek independent legal counsel; and (4) must not represent either or both parties in a later legal proceeding.

Disciplinary Rule 5-105, which requires a lawyer to decline employment if the interests of another client may impair the independent professional judgment of the lawyer,[23] has been relied upon by several bar ethics committees in ruling that it would be unethical for a lawyer to offer services as a divorce mediator. A 1980 Washington State Bar Committee[24] found that a lawyer who proposed to offer a mediation service to resolve property, custody, and support issues could not adequately represent the interests of each party as required by section (c) of Rule 5-105.[25]

A 1982 opinion of the New Hampshire Ethics Committee[26] refused to approve a lawyer's proposal to provide mediation for a husband and wife, who were former clients, prior to either party filing for divorce. In this context, the Committee ruled that mediation was not an adequate safeguard against a potential violation of DR 5-105, the Committee also expressed doubt that the mediator could invoke the attorney-client privilege to prevent disclosure of confidences divulged in mediation, and to that extent, suggested that divorce mediation might conflict with Canon 4, which requires a lawyer to preserve the confidences of a client.[27] Given the particular background of this inquiry— where the attorney had previously represented both clients—the New Hampshire Committee ruled that the lawyer should not undertake divorce mediation and thus avoid even the appearance of professional impropriety, as commanded by Canon 9.[28]

Despite its negative decision on this mediation inquiry, the New Hampshire Committee indicated that other mediation plans for divorce might contain adequate safeguards. In addition to advising that the mediator should clearly delineate the "mediating" as contrasted with "advocating" role, the Committee added that "judicial recognition of mediators as quasi judicial officers would greatly aid the Canon 4 problem." Moreover, the acknowledgment that divorce mediation might be appropriate in some circumstances was to some degree a reversal of the Committee's earlier position. A prior draft opinion by the New Hampshire Committee had revealed a more generally negative view of mediation.[29] Even its more moderate opinion, however, may have rested on a questionable premise. It is not clear that confidentiality is a value that need be maintained at all costs, particularly when the process is not the traditionally adversarial one.

A more relevant concern—and one echoed by other bar ethics committees—relates to the lawyer's ability to maintain impartiality in the divorce mediation context.

The Wisconsin State Bar Committee[30] refused to permit a lawyer to offer a mediation service, in which he proposed to educate the parties as to their legal rights, mediate disputes arising in the negotiations, draft a separation agreement for the parties, and process the divorce through the courts. The Wisconsin committee found that the lawyer's responsibilities under the proposed arrangement went beyond those contemplated by Ethical Consideration 5-20.[31] And although the step of representing the parties in a divorce litigation seems outside the scope of a mediative role, the Wisconsin committee did not limit its concern to whether or not the lawyer processed the divorce. The committee thought that even the task of educating the parties about their legal rights was suspect because the lawyer would be perceived in the role of advice-giving and any "advice" would necessarily be contrary to the interests of one of the parties. Moreover, the committee speculated that mediated agreements might not endure and that future litigation would result: "Neither the public's interest or [sic] the parties' is best served by the creation of future litigation."[32]

The Wisconsin ruling appears to be rooted in an assumption that a lawyer cannot step out of the traditional role of legal advisor whose obligation is to pursue the best interest of his client, and that the public will perceive the lawyer only in that posture. Two other bar committees, in thoughtful, lengthy opinions, have explored that question in detail in attempting to ascertain whether a lawyer can function impartially in the divorce mediating setting.

The Maryland State Bar Association was asked to rule on the propriety of a lawyer's participation as an impartial advisory attorney in a "family mediation center."[33] The lawyer in this role is not the mediator, but the "impartial" legal advisor for the parties. In this capacity as well, the Maryland Bar detected Canon 5 difficulties for the lawyer. It referred to an earlier Maryland opinion where the bar expressed the view that it was virtually impossible, given the wide range of potential disputes in a marital separation, for an attorney representing both husband and wife to come within the scope of Disciplinary Rule 5-105(c). That provision states that a lawyer can properly represent multiple clients if it is obvious that he can adequately represent the interest of each and if each consents to the representation after full disclosure of the possible effect of such representation on the exercise of his independent professional judgment on behalf of each. In the mediation context, the Maryland Bar felt that the parties' consent to mediation did not eliminate the conflicting interests upon which the lawyer would be re-uired to offer an independent professional judgment. Indeed, the Maryland Bar suggested that at least one object of the clients' concern might be whether they have made intelligent and proper compromises during the mediation.

The Maryland opinion also indicated that the responsibility placed on the lawyer to draw up the settlement for the parties and the mediator was troublesome. It said:

> If the preparation of a Property Settlement Agreement in mediation can be equated to filling in blanks on forms, then the services of an attorney are probably not necessary. If the preparation of such an Agreement requires the independent judgment of an attorney—to choose what language best expresses the intent of

the parties, to allocate the burdens of performance and the risks of non-performance, and to advise whether the Agreement as a whole promotes the best interests of both clients and not just some interests of the other—then such preparation is likely to place the attorney in a position where he senses a conflict of interest. In any case, where such a conflict exists, the attorney must comply with the requirements of DR 5-105(c).

An inquiry to the Committee on Professional and Judicial Ethics of the New York City Bar Association[35] involved a mediation program undertaken by a nonprofit mental health facility in which mental health professionals consulted with divorcing couples to work out various aspects of their separation or divorce, including economic and custody issues. In determining whether a lawyer could, (a) become part of the mediating service, (b) give impartial legal advice to the parties, and (c) draft an agreement for the parties once terms had been generally approved by the parties, the New York committee addressed the question of a lawyer's nonadversarial role in dispute resolution. The committee acknowledged competing policies reflected in the Code of Professional Responsibility and prior ethics rulings: that conflicts inherent in a matrimonial proceeding preclude a lawyer from "representing" both parties but that a lawyer may serve as an "impartial arbitrator of mediator."

Resolving the tension was difficult, observed the committee, because the code did not explain what activities constituted mediation and what responsibilities a lawyer has when acting as a mediator. The New York panel recognized that parties might rely on the professional judgment of the lawyer to recognize the significance of legal issues and the impact on their individual interests, even when the lawyer-mediator disclaims a representative role. However, the committee also indicated that in some situations a lawyer's professional judgment would not be called upon and (s)he could perform in a way that (s)he did not represent either party. Attempting to distinguish the two situations, the committee imposed an initial condition on the participation of a lawyer in divorce mediation: a lawyer may not participate in the divorce mediation process where it appears that the issues between the parties are of such complexity or difficulty that the parties cannot prudently reach a resolution without the advice of separate and independent legal counsel.[36]

In addition, the New York ruling established seven guidelines for lawyers participating in mediation:

1. the lawyer must clearly advise the parties that the mediating role was a limited one and that they should not look to the lawyer to protect individual interests or to keep confidences from one another;
2. the lawyer must clearly explain the risks of proceeding without separate counsel;
3. lawyer mediation is limited to those activities permissible to lay mediators and must not require the exercise of professional legal judgment;
4. impartial legal advice may be given and an agreement may be reduced to writing only when the lawyer outlines the pertinent considerations and con-

sequences of choosing the agreed-upon resolution;
5. legal advice may be given only to both parties in the presence of others;
6. the lawyer must advise the parties of seeking independent legal counsel before executing any agreement; and
7. the lawyer may not represent either of the parties in a subsequent legal proceeding.[37]

In spelling out the responsibilities of a lawyer who acts in a mediating capacity, the New York committee has helped to shape an alternative model for dispute resolution. Such clarification is critical for it is inevitable that lawyer-mediators will be exposed to charges of impropriety by unhappy clients. In *Lange* v. *Marshall*,[38] one of the first reported malpractice cases brought against a lawyer-mediator, the wife claimed that the mediated settlement was inadequate. She based her contention on the fact that she later sought independent legal counsel and obtained a more favorable settlement from her husband. The Missouri court ruled that even if the lawyer had been derelect in his responsibilities, the plaintiff could not show that she had suffered any damage since there was no proof that the husand would have settled the case without litigation at the higher figure. However, it is interesting to probe the basis of the plaintiff's charges. She argued that the lawyer-mediator failed to: (1) inquire into the financial state of the husband and advise her; (2) negotiate a better settlement for her; (3) advise her that she would get a more favorable settlement if she litigated the matter; and (4) fully and fairly advise her regarding her rights to marital property, maintenance, and custody. The lawyer conceded that he had not performed these tasks but maintained that they were not appropriate functions for a mediator. Although the court did not reach the question of the appropriate responsibilities of a lawyer-mediator in that it ruled that plaintiff suffered no damages in any event, the case emphasizes the need for more precise standards and guidance from the bar in developing alternative dispute resolution processes.

A recent draft opinion by the Connecticut Bar Association[38] indicates the need for a consensus about the proper tasks that may be undertaken by a lawyer-mediator. Although the New York City Bar opinion expressly permitted a lawyer-mediator to draft a separation agreement for the parties, the Connecticut opinion indicated that a lawyer who acts as a mediator may not draft the agreement for the parties or advise clients with respect to the consequences of such an agreement. Although the need for the independent review by an outside attorney might be advisable, the Connecticut opinion does seem to place an artificial restriction on mediation by its ruling.

The Connecticut Ethics Committee might want to rethink its position in light of its reliance on a New York appellate division case, *Levine* v. *Levine*[40] which was recently overruled by the New York Court of Appeals a few days after the Connecticut opinion was released. In *Levine,* the husband and wife had entered into a separation agreement prepared by a single attorney. In fact, the parties had previously agreed to the essential terms of the agreement and had asked the lawyer to prepare the agreement for them. Although advised to seek independent counsel, the wife failed to do so. Later, the wife tried to have the agreement set aside, claiming that the agreement was inequitable and unconscionable because she had not been independently represented by counsel and had been unduly influenced by her husband. The trial court rejected the wife's application, finding that the agreement was fair and that the attorney had "remained neutral throughout his involvement with the parties." That decision was reversed by the appellate division[41] which held that the joint representation evinced a sufficient degree of overreaching to require the agreement to be set aside. The Court of Appeals,[42] in overturning that decision and upholding the separation agreement, stressed the parties' "absolute right" to be represented by the same attorney provided there was full disclosure. It pointed to an express acknowledgment by the wife in the separation agreement that through this representation she was entering into a better agreement than if she had consulted with independent counsel who tried to bargain on her behalf. And in its acceptance of the trial court's finding that the attorney who had drafted the agreement for the parties remained neutral, the New York Court of Appeals seemed to recognize something other than a strictly adversarial role for a lawyer who drafts a separation agreement. In that sense, the *Levine* case may have important reverberations for mediation.

Kutak View

The proposed American Bar Association Model Rules of Professional Conduct (Kutak Commission)[43] address the issue of the lawyer as intermediary, but leave an unfortunate gap in delineating the difference between mediation and representation. And nowhere in the rules or comments does the ABA recognize or endorse the variety of alternative dispute resolution mechanisms embraced in the concept of mediation.

Rule 2.2,[44] entitled Intermediary, prescribes the circumstances in which a lawyer acting as an intermediary meets ethical standards. Rule 2.2(a) sets forth the following conditions: (1) The lawyer must disclose to each client the implications of the common representation, including the advantages and risks involved, and must obtain each client's consent to the common representation; (2) the lawyer must reasonably believe that the matter can be resolved on terms compatible with the clients' best interests, that each client can make informed decisions in the matter, and that there is little risk of prejudice to the interest of any client if the contemplated resolution is unsuccessful; and (3) the lawyer can act impartially and without improper effect on other responsibilities the lawyer has to any of the clients.[45] Rule 2.2(b) also requires the lawyer acting as intermediary to explain fully to each client the decisions to be made and the considerations relevant to making them,[46] and Rule 2.2(c) mandates that a lawyer shall withdraw from an intermediary role if any client so requests, if the conditions under section (a) cannot be met, or if in light of subsequent events the lawyer should reasonably know that a mutually advantageous resolution cannot be achieved.[47]

The comment to rule 2.2 states that a lawyer acts as an intermediary in seeking to establish or adjust a relationship between clients on an amicable and mutually advantageous basis.[48] Its list of examples includes "mediating a dispute between clients," but the other examples—helping to organize a business in which two or more clients are entrepreneurs, working out the financial reorganization of an enterprise in which two or more clients have an interest—are closer to a practice of "common" representation. This confusion in the new code between "common representation" and "mediation," particularly divorce mediation, is troublesome because the lawyers' tasks in each are widely divergent.[49] Moreover, in describing situations where the risk of failure is so great that "intermediation is plainly impossible,"[50] the commentary points to "clients between whom litigation is imminent or who contemplate contentious negotiations" and "where the relationship between the parties has already assumed definite antagonism."[51] These characterizations easily fit potential divorce mediations, and thus the Kutak Commission's failure to specifically address the subject is distressing. Curiously, commentary in earlier Kutak drafts specifically stated that "under some circumstances a lawyer may act as an intermediary between spouses in arranging the terms of an uncontested separation or divorce settlement,"[52] but that language was deleted in the final draft. In light of the continuing proliferation of mediation programs and conflicting state ethics committee rulings on the subject, a direct and specific response on the subject of divorce mediation should have been forthcoming from the framers of the new code of professional responsibility.

Assuming that divorce mediators do fall within the "intermediary" rubric of the Kutak rule, its conception of the "Intermediary" differs from that of other bar committees that have confronted the issue. The commentary states that a lawyer acts as intermediary under the rule when the lawyer represents all parties.[53] In contrast, the Boston, Portland, and New York opinions characterized the lawyer-mediator as representing "neither of the parties," thus marking a clearer shift in the lawyer's role.

The difference between the Model Code's requirement of "representation of all parties" and the view that the lawyer "represents neither party" may be only a semantic one or may indicate that the ramifications of the concepts have not been fully explored. Alternatively, the different formulations may signify important assumptions about the role of the lawyer in mediation and about the tasks and responsibilities that may be undertaken. For example, the Maryland opinion suggested that unlike a traditional representation, the attorney-client relationship did not necessarily exist in mediation and "while honesty would remain a fundamental duty of the lawyer regardless of the role, loyalty would not."[54] Likewise, the New York opinion indicated that clients in a mediation should not look to the lawyer-mediator to protect their individual interests. But if the lawyer can be said to "represent both parties," the obligation may be to act in a representative capacity toward both parties and move back and forth between the parties in an effort to protect the interests of each.

Additionally, if a lawyer "represents" the parties in mediation, it would seem to follow that the traditional tasks of the lawyer would appropriately be part of the mediation. The concept of representation would seem to include giving legal advice, draftng the separation agreement, and perhaps even filing the necessary papers to process the divorce through the courts. However, when the lawyer is said to "represent neither party," a different and more limited set of functions is suggested. Indeed, the New York opinion which presumes that the lawyer can give impartial legal advice and can draw up the separation agreement for the parties but not represent them in subsequent proceedings is a useful start in shaping the identity of the lawyer-mediator. Hopefully, interpretations under the new code will also address these difficult questions.[55]

Other Variations and Additional Problems

Within the lawyer-mediator context, various adaptations to the model are possible, some of them alleviating in part the professional responsibility concerns. There is a hint in the Boston opinion that the lawyer-mediator might advise the parties to seek independent counsel, thus implying that the mediator emerges "in addition to" rather than "instead of" the lawyers. Obviously, such a practice provides the parties with maximum protection if the lawyers exercise truly independent judgment. On the other hand, invoking independent lawyers on each side might undermine negotiations and agreements that were reached with the mediator. Also, the mediator begins to look like an additional tier in the traditional adversarial process that merely increases the expense of the divorce. Most importantly, some couples seek mediation as an alternative to the adversarial process which they envision as inevitably hostile.

However, the prospect of a mediation client seeking limited independent legal advice about or review of the mediated agreement is likely. This option raises its own separate ethical issue: What is the obligation of the lawyer who reviews such an agreement? Is the lawyer's responsibility only to assure that the client had appropriate information and considered various issues in the mediation process? Or must the lawyer review underlying financial documents and make independent decisions about questions like the valuation of assets, perhaps reopening the process already concluded by mediation? The most important concern in this context should be the needs and demands of the individual client, and a lawyer serving in this review capacity should be clear in understanding what the client is seeking and be precise in communicating to the client what the lawyer is giving. . . .

NOTES

1. See generally   O. J. Coogler, *Structured Mediation in Divorce Settlement* (1978); J. Haynes, *Divorce Mediation* (1981), Spencer & Zammitt, "Mediation-Arbitration: A Proposal for Private Resolution of Disputes Between Divorced or Separated Parents," *Duke Law Journal* 911 (1976); Winks, "Divorce Mediation: A Nonadversary Procedure for the No-Fault Divorce,"

Journal of Family Law 19 (1980): 615; Note, "Non-Judicial Resolution of Custody and Visitation Disputes."

2. See Gaughan, "Taking a Fresh Look at Divorce Mediation," *Trial* 17(April 1981):39; Haynes, "Divorce Mediator: A New Role," *Journal of Social Work* (January 1978):5; Pearson, "Child Custody: Why Let the Parents Decide?" *Judges Journal* 20 (1981):5; Pickrell & Bendheim, "Family Disputes Mediation—A New Service for Lawyers and Their Clients," *Arizona Bar Journal* 15 (1979):33. See generally Fuller, "Mediation—Its Forms and Functions," Southern California Law Review 44 (1963):305.

3. See Coogler, Weber, and McKenry, "Divorce Mediation: A Means of Facilitating Divorce Adjustment," *Family Coordinator* 28 (1979):255; Pearson, *supra* note 2, at p. 6; Note, "Non-Judicial Resolution of Custody and Visitation Disputes," *supra* note 1, at pp. 584-591 (1979). For discussion of the negative effects that the traditional adversary divorce has had on the family, see J. Wallerstein and J. Kelly, *Surviving the Breakup* (1980).

4. See Druckman and Rhodes, "Family Impact Analysis: Application to Child Custody Determination," *Family Coordinator* 26 (1977):451, 456-457; Pearson, *supra* note 1, at pp. 593-597 (1979).

5. See Fiske, "Divorce Mediation As a Less Painful Path," *Massachusetts Law Weekly* 8 (1979); Harris, "Divorce's Friendly Persuaders," *Money* (April 1980):85; Haskett, "Arbitration Ends the Torture of Divorce," *Moneysworth* (January 1981):16; Pearson, *supra* note 2, at p. 10.

6. Interesting date appears in Bahr, *Divorce Mediation: An Evaluation of an Alternative Divorce Policy,* Bush Institute for Child and Family Policy, University of North Carolina at Chapel Hill (1980); Bahr, "Mediation Is the Answer," *Family Advocate* 3 (Spring 1981):32; Kressel, Jaffee, Tuchman, Watson, and Deutsch, "A Typology of Divorcing Couples: Implications for Mediation and the Divorce Process," *Family Process* 19 (1980):101; Pearson, *supra* note 2, at pp. 8-10; Pearson and Thoennes, "Mediation and Divorce, The Benefits Outweigh the Costs," *Family Advocate* 4 (1982):26.

7. Some of the difficulties are noted in Crouch, "Mediation and Divorce: The Dark Side Is Still Unexplored," *Family Advocate* 4 (1982):27. Others argue that what is needed is a rethinking of the lawyering role. See Coogler, "Changing the Lawyer's Role in Matrimonial Practice," *Conciliation Courts Review* 15 (1977):1.

8. Court-supervised or court-reffered mediation has been undertaken in several states. See, e.g., Family Conciliation Unit, Ft. Lauderdale, Florida; Probate and Family Court (Norfolk and Middlesex County), Massachusetts; Domestic Relations Division, St. Paul, Minnesota; Family Court Counseling Service, Dane County, Wisconsin. In California, mediation of custody issues has become a mandatory part of the divorce process. See Jenkins, "Divorce California Style," *Student Law* 9 (1981):3.

8. Court-approved mediation usually operates within the traditional context where clients are represented by their lawyers. The ethical issues involved in private mediation thus do not usually arise in this type of mediation.

9. *The Code of Professional Responsibility* consists of Canons, Ethical Considerations, and Disciplinary Rules. The canons, nine in number, are statements of "axiomatic norms," expressed in general terms. The ethical considerations are "aspirational in character": and constitute a body of principles upon which the lawyer relies for guidance. The disciplinary rules are mandatory in character and disciplinary action can be taken for violation of such rules. Preliminary Statement, *Code of Professional Responsibility.*

Canon 5 states: "A Lawyer Should Exercise Independent Professional Judgment on Behalf of a Client." Ethical Consideration 5-1 reads: "The professional judgment of a lawyer should be exercised, within the bounds of law, solely for the benefit of his client and free of compromising influences and loyalties." All references are to the American Bar Foundation, *Annotated Code of Professional Responsibility* (1979).

10. Ethical Consideration 5-15 provides, in part, that "there are many instances in which a lawyer may properly serve multiple clients having potentially differing interest in matters not involving litigation."

11. Ethical Consideration 5-16.

12. See Bedford, "Possible Effect on Conflict of Interests in a Divorce Action Arising from One Attorney Framing the Decree," *Alabama Law Review* 15 (1963):502; American Bar Association Committee on Professional Ethics, Opinions, No. 58 (1931); Michigan State Bar Association Committee on Professional Ethics, *Michigan State Bar Journal* 38 (opinion 85, January 1945): 112; New York City Law Association Committee on Professional Opinions, No. 265 (1928) ; West Virginia State Bar Association Committee on Legal Ethics, Opinions, Case 1169 (April 13, 1963). These state bar ethics opinions have been digested in Maru and Clough, *Digest of Bar Association Ethics Opinions* (1970) ; Maru, *1970 Supplement to the Digest of Bar Association Ethics Opinions* (1972) ; Maru, *1975 Supplement to the Digest of Bar Opinions* (1977).

13. Ohio State Bar Association Ethics Committee, Ohio State Bar Association Report pp. 780, 783-384 (opinion 30, May 1975) ; ". . . of course you can't represent both parties. The most you can do for agreed spouses is to be scrivener in the separation agreement process."

14. Arizona State Bar Association Committee on Legal Ethics, Opinions, No. 76-25 (November 25, 1976), stating that in exceptional cases, dual representation is not improper, and approving the practice of the lawyer for one spouse filing for both if the second party is appearing in propria persona or has no other counsel. See also Coogler, "Changing the Lawyer's Role in Matrimonial Practice," *Conciliation Courts Review* 15 (1977).

15. Klemm v. Superior Court of Fresno County, 75 Cal. App. 3d 893, 142. 509 (1977).

16. *Id.* at p. 901, 142 Cal. Rptr. at p. 514.

17. Virginia State Bar Association Committee on Legal Ethics, Informal Opinions, No. 296 (1977).

18. New York State Bar Association Committee on Professional Ethics, *New York State Bar Association Journal* 45 (Opinion 258, September 15, 1972):556-557. The same view was adopted by the West Virginia State Bar Association in Legal Ethics Opinion 77-7 in Fall, 1977. See also Gibson, "ABA Canon 5 Professional Judgement," *Texas Law Review* 48 (1970):351.

19. Ethical Consideration 5-20 provides: A lawyer is often asked to serve as an impartial arbitrator or mediator in matters which involve present or former clients. He may serve in either capacity if he first discloses such present or former relationships. After a lawyer has undertaken to act as an impartial arbitrator or mediator, he should not thereafter represent in the dispute any of the parties involved.

20. New York State Bar Association Committee on Professional Ethics, *New York State Bar Journal* 45 (Opinion 258, September 15, 1972):556-557.

21. Boston Bar Association Committee on Ethics, Opinions No. 78-1 (1978).

22. Oregon Bar Association Committee on Legal Ethics, Proposed Opinion, No. 70-46 (April 2, 1980).

23. DR 5-105 (A) and (B) state that it is improper for a lawyer to engage in representation if the lawyer's "independent professional judgment . . . will be or is likely to be adversely affected" or if representation is "likely" to involve representation of interests that will adversely affect the lawyer's "judgment" or loyalty to a client.

24. Washington State Bar Association Code of Professional Responsibility Committee, Informal Opinions, Item 385 (Feb. 20, 1980).

25. D.R. 5-105 (c) provides:
In the situations covered by DR 5-105 (A) and (B), a lawyer may represent multiple clients if it is obvious that he can adequately represent the interest of each and if each consents to the representation after such disclosure of the possible effect of such representation on the exercise of this independent professional judgment on behalf of each. These problems are explored further in Note, "Family Law—Attorney Mediation of Marital Disputes and Conflicts of Interest Considerations," *North Carolina Law Review* 60 (1981):171.

26. New Hampshire State Bar Association Ethics Committee (March 16, 1982), *New Hampshire Law Weekly* 8 (1982):385.

27. Canon 4 provides: "A Lawyer Should Preserve the Confidences and Secrets of a Client."

28. Canon 9 provides: "A Lawyer Should Avoid Even the Appearance of Professional Impropriety."

29. New Hampshire State Bar Association Ethics Committee (April 21, 1981) (Proposed Opinion).

30. Wisconsin State Bar Association Committee on Professional Ethics, Opinions E-79-2 (January 1980).

31. *Id.*

32. *Id.*

33. Maryland State Bar Association Committee on Ethics, No. 80-55A (August 20, 1980).

34. *Id.* at pp. 8-9.

35. New York City Bar Association Committee on Professional and Judicial Ethics, No. 80-23 (February 27, 1981).

36. *Id.* at p. 11.

37. *Id.* at pp. 11-12. A related prophylactic rule was enunciated in a recent Illinois State Bar Association opinion, which prohibited an attorney from establishing a separate marriage counseling, arbitration, and mediation service in connection with and operated out of his law office. By prohibiting the lawyer from later representing either party and by admonishing that any "related" mediation business would have to be kept separate, the Committee indicated intent to guard against unlawful solicitations of business as prohibited by Disciplinary Rules 2-102(c) and 2-104. See Illinois State Bar Association Committee on Professional Ethics, Opinions, No. 745 (March 26, 1982).

38. *Family Law Reporter* 7 (Mo. Ct. App. 1981) :2583.

39. Connecticut State Bar Association Committee on Ethics (May 1982).

40. 83 App. Div. 2d 606, 441 N.Y.S. 2d 299 (1981), rev'd *New York Law Journal,* May 26, 1982 at p. 1.

41. *Id.*

42. *New York Law Journal* (May 26, 1982) at p. 1.

43. See American Bar Association Commission on Evaluation of Professional Standards, Proposed Final Draft, *Model Rules of Professional Conduct,* (May 30, 1981).

44. *Id.* at pp. 112-113. An alternative draft by the American Bar Association Commission on Evaluation of Professional Standards presents the recommendations in the format of the current Professional Responsibility Code. In the Alternative Draft, the provision on the lawyer as intermediary appears as Disciplinary Rule 5-105. See American Bar Association Commission on Evaluation of Professional Standards. Alternative Draft, *Model Rules of Professional Conduct* (May 30, 1981).

45. American Bar Association Commission on Evaluation of Professional Standards, Proposed Final Draft, *Model Rules of Professional Conduct* (May 30, 1981), at p. 112.

46. *Id.*

47. *Id.* at pp. 112-113.

48. *Id.* at p.113.

49. Part of the difficulty lies in defining the role and activities of the mediator. On the one hand, the mediator might be in the position of giving neutral advice—"representing the situation" rather than either of the parties. Alternatively, the lawyer might be the spokesman for the position of each of the parties. See Hazard, *Ethics in the Practice of Law* (1978), pp. 58-68. Nonetheless, it seems clear that these tasks are substantially different from the situation where a lawyer represents parties with common, yet potentially conflicting interests.

50. American Bar Association Commission on Evaluation of Professional Standards, Proposed Final Draft, *Model Rules of Professional Conduct,* Comment (May 30, 1981), at p. 113.

51. *Id.*

52. American Bar Association Commission on Evaluation of Professional Standards, Discussion Draft, Rule 5.1 (January 30, 1980), at p. 94.

53. American Bar Association Commission on Evaluation of Professional Standards, Proposed Final Draft, *Model Rules of Professional Conduct,* Comment (May 30, 1981), at p. 113.

54. Maryland State Bar Association Committee on Ethics, Opinions, No. 80-55A (August 20, 1980), at p. 6.

55. Prospects for an amendment to proposed Rule 2.2 are favorable. One present proposal is to broaden the scope of Rule 2.2 to cover intermediation, dual representation, mediation, and arbitration and to address each of the distinct concepts separately.

PROBLEMS

MAINTAINING A LAWSUIT

Tam Wallach suffered whiplash when his 1961 Valiant was hit from behind by a city bus. He came to you, and you brought suit. The case has dragged on for a year (as such cases regularly do). Wallach has exhausted his unemployment benefits and savings; times are hard, and he has been unable to find work he can do given his injuries (which are substantial). He has been refused welfare. His medical expenses are covered by insurance he had before the accident, but his living expenses are not. He has no family, lives alone, and (while a pleasant enough person) has no close friends.

You believe his injuries to be worth between $50,000 and $100,000 (supposing no good or bad surprises). You have taken the case on a contingency basis (and so, if you settle now, you will receive 15 percent of the settlement, but if you go to trial, your share will be 33⅓ percent). The bus company is offering $3,000 (about what you expected at this point in negotiations). Wallach has come to your office today to tell you that he can't afford to wait any longer. You point out that $3,000 won't last him very long, to which he responds that it will last longer than nothing. You wonder whether you couldn't just write him a check for $500 and ask him to hold out at least till that's gone. You would consider the $500 a loan. You recognize, of course, that you may have to write him several more such checks before the case is over. Such cases usually take several years. And you recognize as well that the more you loan him, the more you may want to settle just to get back what you invested in the case. What should you do?

SUING A FORMER CLIENT

You are an attorney for an automobile dealer who wants to bring suit against his manufacturer and an associated real estate corporation for breach of the dealership lease. You were once an associate with a firm employing eighty attorneys, which represented the manufacturer during the period when the firm prepared the lease now in controversy. You have since joined another law firm. Your part in preparing that lease was limited to preparing briefs, informal discussions on procedural matters, and research into specific points of law. While much that you learned by such participation will be helpful now, you were not entrusted with any confidences that could be used against the manufacturer in this case. Would there be anything unethical about you representing the dealer in this case? Would there be anything unethical if some other member of your new firm represented the dealer instead?

THE BEST IN TOWN

Evelyn Grand, a senior partner in a major law firm, has informed her firm that she purchased stock in a certain company two years ago based upon what the Securities and Exchange Commission has now declared to be a fraudulent prospectus. Grand has decided to file a class action suit against the company on her own behalf and on behalf of all other stockholders similarly situated. The case might well produce a judgment exceeding $25,000,000. She is willing to bear the "costs of litigation" herself but wants to employ the firm "because you're the best in town." The costs of litigation include the cost of notifying other members of the class (amounting to perhaps $3000), filing fees (amounting at most to a few hundred dollars), and certain other minor expenses, but *not* the cost of the firm's time. The firm would be retained on contingency, as is customary in such cases. If the case were won, the firm would get between 10 and 25 percent of the judgment (depending on how long the case dragged on); the partner would get back whatever she paid in costs; and the remainder would be divided up among the members of the class in proportion to their original investment in the stock (the partner taking her share just as the rest would). If the case were lost, the partner would be out her costs and the firm would be out its time. Is there anything unethical in the firm taking such employment? Would the answer be different if the partner proposed to resign from the firm?

Suggested Readings

For other works on issues raised here, see Bibliography, Part 4, especially Aronson (1977), Davis (1982), Furrow (1979), Moore (1982), and Rotunda (1977).

Part V

Perjury and Confidentiality

Introduction

What should a lawyer do when he or she is surprised by a client who knowingly gives false testimony before a tribunal? What should be done when a client merely announces an intention to give such testimony? What part, if any, may a lawyer have in the fabrication or presentation of false evidence?

Laypeople (and law students) are often surprised at the extent of the duties lawyers suppose themselves to owe "the court." A lawyer should not (it is agreed) knowingly make a false statement of law or fact, fail to inform the court of controlling precedent even if to do so is adverse to the client's position, or offer evidence that the lawyer knows to be false. Indeed, lawyers are, in general to avoid "all fraud and chicane" in their dealings with the court (and with one another).

Were these all the duties of a lawyer, the questions posed above would not be *problems* of legal ethics. The duty of a lawyer (as lawyer) would be clear. It would be unprofessional to participate in the fabrication or presentation of false evidence. An attorney would have to dissuade his client from perjury or withdraw from the case. He would have to withdraw even if the client were already on the stand testifying. The only *ethical* problem the lawyer would have would be whether to honor his professional obligations or allow other considerations to decide what he would do. The lawyer's professional concern would be for the court, not the client.

Such "duties of candor" are, however, not all there is to the lawyer's role. Lawyers also suppose themselves to have extensive duties to their clients. Among these are "warm zeal" in the pursuit of a client's cause and keeping confidential what is learned from the client (or about him) during the course of representation. Part four of this volume was concerned with how far lawyers should go to preserve their "zeal" against threats from conflicting obligations and interests external to their role as lawyer for a particular client. This section addresses a conflict of obligations *internal* to the lawyer's role, that is, with how far a lawyer should go to preserve the confidences entrusted to him when preserving them threatens (as Fuller and Randall put it) to "muddy the headwaters of decision."

The duty of confidentiality is, of course, not absolute. A lawyer may, for example, reveal to the police that a client has announced an intention to commit a violent crime if it seems probably that the client will do what he says. In this respect, lawyers are much like other professionals having a duty of confidentiality.

For example, doctors may have a legal duty to report a patient's bullet wound to the police, or an outbreak of measles to public health officials.

Even so, the limits of the lawyer's duty of confidentiality seem to be a subject of special controversy. There is no agreement even about whether a lawyer may reveal a client's intention to commit a serious but nonviolent crime (for example, tax fraud or pollution). Much remains to be decided. The questions discussed in this section belong to that controversy. The problem is how to define the lawyer's role. Proposed solutions involve decisions about what considerations are relevant to deciding what lawyers should do (and how much weight those considerations should have). Though the discussion has some analogy with the wider discussion of "whistleblowing," it is different in that confidentiality seems to be more important to lawyering than to the work of most other professions, that is, those in which the information the client provides is less important.

Monroe H. Freedman began the discussion almost two decades ago in the now classic paper included here. His conclusions are strikingly client-centered but, he believes, as much a consequence of any justice-centered conception of lawyering. The duty of confidentiality does not allow a lawyer to use information learned from the client to do anything that would harm that client. That duty is, for Freedman, the glue holding the lawyer-client relationship together. The lawyer cannot provide effective advocacy or useful advice if the client will not share all that he knows. The client will not be candid if he believes the lawyer will turn what is learned *against* him. Without a strict duty of confidentiality, the client cannot justifiably look upon the lawyer as (in Fried's phrase) a "legal friend."

The lawyer need not, however, be neutral with respect to the client's perjury. Recognizing perjury as a threat to justice, Freedman agrees that the lawyer has a duty to try to dissuade the client from giving false testimony. Freedman contends that breaches of confidentiality are *more* threatening to justice. Hence, if the client persists in his intention to commit perjury, the lawyer should not withdraw. To withdraw under such circumstances would mean that the client would find another lawyer to whom he would probably not tell as much, given his previous experience with truth-telling. Withdrawal would most likely not prevent the perjury in question, but it would tend to undermine the integrity of the lawyer-client relation. Thus the lawyer, surprised to hear the client testifying falsely, must proceed in public as if she did not know the truth. She cannot use information received from the client against him, however much her participation in his acts seems to lead the tribunal from a just result.

Since Freedman wrote his classic paper, the ABA replaced the *Canons of Ethics* with the *Code of Professional Responsibility* and then replaced the *Code* with the *Model Rules.* Debate over disclosure of confidences has taken up a surprisingly large part of the deliberation that preceded adoption of both the *Code* and the *Rules;* and both times amendments from the floor substantially reduced permissible (or required) disclosure. The problem Freedman raised seems much the same today as it did in 1966. It is not the result of any lack of imagination in the development of alternatives. The two responses to Freedman included in this section will give some idea of the variety of practical alternatives offered in the last two decades. But none has won the bar's wholehearted support. Many lawyers still find Freedman's argument appealing even if they find the conclusion embarrassing. Many more find the argument itself troubling, in much the same way one is troubled when a position one accepts is made to look absurd by being carried to its "logical" exteme. One wants to say, "Stop!" but it is not easy to justify stopping anywhere short of the extreme. Criticism of Freedman has therefore generally taken the form of trying to provide some defensible criterion for stopping short of Freedman's extreme. The two responses to Freedman included here are, in that respect at least, typical.

The first response, by Norman Lefstein appeared before the ABA began drafting the *Model Rules*. Clients have, Lefstein argues, a right to tell their story but they have no right to tell lies. A lawyer will seldom have the problem Freedman puts forth, but when he does, the client can have no right to the lawyer's help in committing perjury, because clients have no right to commit perjury. Freedman's problem exists only when a client implicitly relies upon a misunderstanding of what lawyers are supposed to do. Only when the client acts on the mistaken assumption that lawyers can help him present perjured testimony does a lawyer face the choice of betraying his client's (misplaced) trust or betraying the trust the court (justifiably) places in him. There is no happy solution once things have gotten that far. Lawyers should therefore be required not to let things get that far. Lefstein suggests avoiding Freedman's problem altogether by requiring that lawyers tell their clients in the initial interview what happens if a client tries to commit perjury. Such a warning may (as Freedman argued) make some clients hesitate to reveal all the information the lawyer needs to know to do the best possible job. But such clients are, Lefstein thinks, just those who would reveal their guilt and then insist on committing perjury. What, Lefstein wonders, is troubling about such a client hurting his own case by withholding information from his lawyer?

Both Freedman and Lefstein treat lawyer-client confidentiality as if it had little connection with the moral problems of confidentiality in nonprofessional life. There is no attempt to understand professional rules as a special case of a more general phenomenon. Bruce M. Landesman makes just such an attempt. The result is a seemingly telling criticism of Freedman's position. The client cannot reasonably believe that lawyer-client confidentiality is absolute; and a lawyer certainly should not try to get his client to believe that it is.

According to Landesman, Freedman has relied on a "spread argument," one that forces us to appeal to *general* considerations to spread protection to cases which cannot be justified on their own particular merits. Client confidentiality is to be protected no matter what a client tells a lawyer, because the client cannot know what information is relevant and what is not and we want to be sure clients in general tell all they know. If the client does not feel free to tell all, the lawyer may not get all the information he needs to present the best case.

That, according to Landesman, is the heart of Freedman's argument and there is nothing wrong with it—except that Freedman treats it as a decisive consideration whereas it is properly just one reason among many.

In other contexts in which confidentiality is a factor, there are reasons sufficient to override the obligation of confidentiality. For example, it may be morally permissible to reveal the confidence that a friend has imparted if to do so results in little or no harm to the friend, while keeping the confidence would do others great harm. The friend should understand. Freedman's appeal to the need for "zealous advocacy" is, according to Landesman, "ideological" because it unjustifiably simplifies the moral complexity of the situation.

It may be useful to compare the *Model Rules* provision for confidentiality with that in the final draft. The differences are substantial.

Rule 1.6 "Confidentiality of Information" as adopted reads:

> (a) A lawyer shall not reveal information relating to representation of a client unless the client consents after consultation, except for disclosures that are impliedly authorized in order to carry out the representation, and except as stated in paragraph (b).
>
> (b) A lawyer may reveal such information to the extent the lawyer reasonably believes necessary:
>
>> (1) to prevent the client from committing a criminal act that the lawyer believes is likely to result in imminent death or substantial bodily harm; or
>>
>> (2) to establish a claim or defense on behalf of the lawyer in a controversy between the lawyer and the client, to establish a defense to a criminal charge or civil claim against the lawyer based upon conduct in which the client was involved, or to respond to allegations in any proceeding concerning the lawyer's representation of the client.

But the final *draft,* allowed much more disclosure:

> (a) A lawyer shall not reveal information relating to represension of a client except as stated in paragraph (b), unless the client consents after disclosure.
>
> (b) A lawyer may reveal such information to the extent the lawyer believes necessary:
>
>> (1) to serve the client's interests, unless it is information the client specifically requested not to be disclosed;
>>
>> (2) to prevent the client from committing a criminal or fraudulent act that the lawyer believes is likely to result in death or substantial bodily harm, or substantial injury to the financial interests or property of another;
>>
>> (3) to rectify the consequences of a client's criminal or fraudulent act in the commission of which the lawyer's services had been used;

(4) to establish a claim or defense on behalf of the lawyer in a controversy between the lawyer and the client, or to establish a defense to a criminal charge or civil claim against the lawyer based upon conduct in which the client was involved; or

(5) to comply with the rules of professional conduct or other law.

Is Rule 1.6 as adopted an improvement over that contained in the final draft? What explains the changes?

Monroe H. Freedman

Professional Responsibility of the Criminal Defense Lawyer: The Three Hardest Questions

In almost any area of legal counseling and advocacy, the lawyer may be faced with the dilemma of either betraying the confidential communications of his client or participating to some extent in the purposeful deception of the court. This problem is nowhere more acute than in the the practice of criminal law, particularly in the representation of the indigent accused. The purpose of this article is to analyze and attempt to resolve three of the most difficult issues in this general area:

1. Is it proper to cross-examine for the purpose of discrediting the reliability or credibility of an adverse witness whom you know to be telling the truth?

2. Is it proper to put a witness on the stand when you know he will commit perjury?

3. Is it proper to give your client legal advice when you have reason to believe that the knowledge you give him will tempt him to commit perjury?

These questions present serious difficulties with respect to a lawyer's ethical responsibilities. Moreover, if one admits the possibility of an affirmative answer, it is difficult even to discuss them without appearing to some to be unethical.[1] It is not surprising, therefore, that reasonable, rational discussion of these issues has been uncommon and that the problems have for so long remained unresolved. In this regard it should be recognized that the Canons of Ethics, which were promulgated in 1908 "as a general guide,"[2] are both inadequate and self-contradictory.

THE ADVERSARY SYSTEM AND THE NECESSITY FOR CONFIDENTIALITY

At the outset, we should dispose of some common question-begging responses.

From *Michigan Law Review* 64 (June 1966):1469-1484. Reprinted by permission of the publisher and the author. Professor Freedman has expanded on his views and modified them somewhat in *Lawyers' Ethics in an Adversary System* (1975) (ABA Gavel Award Certificate of Merit, 1976), and in "Personal Responsibility in a Professional System," *Catholic University Law Review* 27 (1976): 191.

The attorney is indeed an officer of the court, and he does participate in a search for the truth. These two propositions, however, merely serve to state the problem in different words: As an officer of the court, participating in a search for truth, what is the attorney's special responsibility, and how does that responsibility affect his resolution of the questions posed above?

The attorney functions in an adversary system based upon the presupposition that the most effective means of determining truth is to present a judge and jury a clash between proponents of conflicting views. It is essential to the effective function of this system that each adversary have, in the words of Canon 15, "entire devotion to the interest of the client, warm zeal in the maintenance and defense of his rights and the exertion of his utmost learning and ability." It is also essential to maintain the fullest uninhibited communication between the client and his attorney, so that the attorney can most effectively counsel his client and advocate the latter's cause. This policy is safeguarded by the requirement that the lawyer must, in the words of Canon 37, "preserve his client's confidences." Canon 15 does, of course, qualify these obligations by stating that "the office of attorney does not permit, much less does it demand of him for any client, violations of the law or any manner of fraud or chicane." In addition, Canon 22 requires candor toward the court.

The problem presented by these salutary generalities of the Canons in the context of particular litigation is illustrated by the personal experience of Samuel Williston, which was related in his autobiography.[3] Because of his examination of a client's correspondence file, Williston learned of a fact extremely damaging to his client's case. When the judge announced his decision, it was apparent that a critical factor in the favorable judgment for Williston's client was the judge's ignorance of this fact. Williston remained silent and did not thereafter inform the judge of what he knew. He was convinced, and Charles Curtis[4] agrees with him, that it was his duty to remain silent.

In an opinion by the American Bar Association Committee on Professional Ethics and Grievances, an eminent panel headed by Henry Drinker held that a lawyer should remain silent when his client lies to the judge by saying that he has no prior record, despite the attorney's knowledge to the contrary.[5] The majority of the panel distinguished the situation in which the attorney has learned of the client's prior record from a source other than the client himself. William B. Jones, a distinguished trial lawyer and now a judge in the United States District Court for the District of Columbia, wrote a separate opinion in which he asserted that in neither event should the lawyer expose his client's lie. If these two cases do not constitute "fraud or chicane" or lack of candor within the meaning of the Canons (and I agree with the authorities cited that they do not), it is clear that the meaning of the Canons is ambiguous.

The adversary system has further ramifications in a criminal case. The defendant is presumed to be innocent. The burden is on the prosecution to prove beyond a reasonable doubt that the defendant is guilty. The plea of not guilty does not necessarily mean "not guilty in fact," for the defendant may mean "not legally guilty." Even the accused who knows that he committed the crime is entitled to put the government to its proof. Indeed, the accused who knows that he is guilty has an absolute constitutional right to remain silent.[6] The moralist might quite reasonably understand this to mean that, under these circumstances, the defendant and his lawyer are privileged to "lie" to the court in pleading not guilty. In my judgment, the moralist is right. However, our adversary system and related notions of the proper administration of criminal justice sanction the lie.

Some derive solace from the sophistry of calling the lie a "legal fiction," but this is hardly an adequate answer to the moralist. Moreover, this answer has no particular appeal for the practicing attorney, who knows that the plea of not guilty commits him to the most effective advocacy of which he is capable. Criminal defense lawyers do not win their cases by arguing reasonable doubt. Effective trial advocacy requires that the attorney's every word, action, and attitude be consistent with the conclusion that his client is innocent. As every trial lawyer knows, the jury is certain that the defense attorney knows whether his client is guilty. The jury is therefore alert to and will be enormously affected by, any indication by the attorney that he believes the defendant to be guilty. Thus, the plea of not guilty commits the advocate to a trial, including a closing argument, in which he must argue that "not guilty" means "not guilty in fact."[7]

There is, of course, a simple way to evade the dilemma raised by the not guilty plea. Some attorneys rationalize the problem by insisting that a lawyer never knows for sure whether his client is guilty. The client who insists upon his guilt may in fact be protecting his wife, or may know that he pulled the trigger and that the victim was killed, but not that his gun was loaded with blanks and that the fatal shot was fired from across the street. For anyone who finds this reasoning satisfactory, there is, of course, no need to think further about the issue.

It is also argued that a defense attorney can remain selectively ignorant. He can insist in his first interview with his client that, if his client is guilty, he simply does not want to know. It is inconceivable, however, that an attorney could give adequate counsel under such circumstances. How is the client to know, for example, precisely which relevant circumstances his lawyer does not want to be told? The lawyer might ask whether his client has a prior record. The client, assuming that his is the kind of knowledge that might present ethical problems for his lawyer, might respond that he has no record. The lawyer would then put the defendant on the stand and, on cross-examination, be appalled to learn that his client has two prior convictions for offenses identical to that for which he is being tried.

Of course, an attorney can guard against this specific problem by telling his client that he must know about the client's past record. However, a lawyer can never anticipate all of the innumerable and potentially critical factors that his client, once cautioned, may decide not to reveal. In one instance, for example, the defendant assumed that his lawyer would prefer to be ignorant of the fact that the client had been having sexual relations with the chief defense witness.

The client was innocent of the robbery with which he was charged, but was found guilty by the jury—probably because he was guilty of fornication, a far less serious offense for which he had not even been charged.

The problem is compounded by the practice of plea bargaining. It is considered improper for a defendant to plead guilty to a lesser offense unless he is in fact guilty. Nevertheless, it is common knowledge that plea bargaining frequently results in improper guilty pleas by innocent people. For example, a defendant falsely accused of robbery may plead guilty to simple assault, rather than risk a robbery conviction and a substantial prison term. If an attorney is to be scrupulous in bargaining pleas, however, he must know in advance that his client is guilty, since the guilty plea is improper if the defendant is innocent. Of course, if the attempt to bargain for a lesser offense should fail, the lawyer would know the truth and thereafter be unable to rationalize that he was uncertain of his client's guilt.

If one recognizes that professional responsibility requires that an advocate have full knowledge of every pertinent fact, it follows that he must seek the truth from his client, not shun it.[8] This means that he will have to dig and pry and cajole, and, even then, he will not be successful unless he can convince the client that full and confidential disclosure to his lawyer will never result in prejudice to the client by any word or action of the lawyer. This is, perhaps, particularly true in the case of the indigent defendant, who meets his lawyer for the first time in the cell block or the rotunda. He did not choose the lawyer, nor does he know him. The lawyer has been sent by the judge and is part of the system that is attempting to punish the defendant. It is no easy task to persuade this client that he can talk freely without fear of prejudice. However, the inclination to mislead one's lawyer is not restricted to the indigent or even to the criminal defendant. Randolph Paul has observed a similar phenomenon among a wealthier class in a far more congenial atmosphere:

> The tax adviser will sometimes have to dynamite the facts of his case out of the unwilling witnesses on his own side—witnesses who are nervous, witnesses who are confused about their own interest, witnesses who try to be too smart for their own good, and witnesses who subconsciously do not want to understand what has happened despite the fact that they must if they are to testify coherently.[9]

Paul goes on to explain that the truth can be obtained only by persuading the client that it would be a violation of a sacred obligation for the lawyer ever to reveal a client's confidence. Beyond any question, once a lawyer has persuaded his client of the obligation of confidentiality, he must respect that obligation scrupulously.

THE SPECIFIC QUESTIONS

The first of the difficult problems posed above will now be considered: Is it proper to cross-examine for the purpose of discrediting the reliability or the credibility of a witness whom you know to be telling the truth? Assume the following situation. Your client has been falsely accused of a robbery committed at 16th and P Streets at 11:00 p.m. He tells you at first that at no time on the evening of the crime was he within six blocks of that location. However, you are able to persuade him that he must tell you the truth and that he was at 15th and P Streets at 10:55 that evening, but that he was walking east, away from the scene of the crime, and that, by 11:00 p.m., he was six blocks away. At the trial, there are two prosecution witnesses. The first mistakenly, but with some degree of persuasion identifies your client as the criminal. At that point, the prosecution's case depends on this single witness, who might or might not be believed. Since your client has a prior record, you do not want to put him on the stand, but you feel that there is at least a chance for acquittal. The second prosecution witness is an elderly woman who is somewhat nervous and who wears glasses. She testifies truthfully and accurately that she saw your client at 15th and P Streets at 10:55 p.m. She has corroborated the erroneous testimony of the first witness and made conviction virtually certain. However, if you destroy her reliability through cross-examination designed to show that she is easily confused and has poor eyesight, you may not only eliminate the corroboration, but also cast doubt in the jury's mind on the prosecution's entire case. On the other hand, if you should refuse to cross-examine her because she is telling the truth, your client may well feel betrayed, since you knew of the witness's veracity only because your client confided in you, under your assurance that his truthfulness would not prejudice him.

The client would be right. Viewed strictly, the attorney's failure to cross-examine would not be violative of the client's confidence because it would not constitute a disclosure. However, the same policy that supports the obligation of confidentiality precludes the attorney from prejudicing his client's interest in any other way because of knowledge gained in his professional capacity. When a lawyer fails to cross-examine only because his client, placing confidence in the lawyer, has been candid with him, the basis for such confidence and candor collapses. Our legal system cannot tolerate such a result.

> The purposes and necessities of the relation between a client and his attorney require, in many cases, on the part of the client, the fullest and freest disclosures to the attorney of the client's objectives, motives and acts. . . . To permit the attorney to reveal to others what is so disclosed, would be not only a gross violation of a sacred trust upon his part, but it would utterly destroy and prevent the usefulness and benefits to be derived from professional assistance.[10]

The client's confidences must "upon all occasions be inviolable," to avoid the "greater mischiefs" that would probably result if a client could not feel free "to repose [confidence] in the attorney to whom he resorts for legal advice and assistance."[11] Destroy that confidence, and "a man who would not venture to consult any skillful person, or would only dare to tell his counsellor half his case."[12]

Therefore, one must conclude that the attorney is obligated to attack, if he can, the reliability or credibility of an opposing witness whom he knows to be truthful. The contrary result would inevitably impair the "perfect freedom of consultation by client with attorney," which is "essential to the administration of justice."[13]

The second question is generally considered to be the hardest of all: Is it proper to put a witness on the stand when you know he will commit perjury? Assume, for example, that the witness in question is the accused himself, and that he has admitted to you, in response to your assurances of confidentiality, that he is guilty. However, he insists upon taking the stand to protest his innocence. There is a clear consensus among prosecutors and defense attorneys that the likelihood of conviction is increased enormously when the defendant does not take the stand. Consequently, the attorney who prevents his client from testifying only because the client has confided his guilt to him is violating that confidence by acting upon the information in a way that will seriously prejudice his client's interests.

Perhaps the most common method for avoiding the ethical problem just posed is for the lawyer to withdraw from the case, at least if there is sufficient time before trial for the client to retain another attorney.[14] The client will then go to the nearest law office, realizing that the obligation of confidentiality is not what it has been represented to be, and withhold incriminating information or the fact of his guilt from his new attorney. On ethical grounds, the practice of withdrawing from a case under such circumstances is indefensible, since the identical perjured testimony will ultimately be presented. More important, perhaps, is the practical consideration that the new attorney will be ignorant of the perjury and therefore will be in no position to attempt to discourage the client from presenting it. Only the original attorney, who knows the truth, has the opportunity, but he loses it in the very act of evading the ethical problem.

The problem is all the more difficult when the client is indigent. He cannot retain other counsel, and in many jurisdictions, including the District of Columbia, it is impossible for appointed counsel to withdraw from a case except for extraordinary reasons. Thus, appointed counsel, unless he lies to the judge, can successfully withdraw only by revealing to the judge that the attorney has received knowledge of his client's guilt. Such a revelation in itself would seem to be a sufficiently serious violation of the obligation of confidentiality to merit severe condemnation. In fact, however, the situation is far worse, since it is entirely possible that the same judge who permits the attorney to withdraw will subsequently hear the case and sentence the defendant. When he does so, of course, he will have had personal knowledge of the defendant's guilt before the trial began.[15] Moreover, this will be knowledge of which the newly appointed counsel for the defendant will probably be ignorant.

The difficulty is further aggravated when the client informs the lawyer for the first time during trial that he intends to take the stand and commit perjury. The perjury in question may not necessarily be a protestation of innocence by a guilty man. Referring to the earlier hypothetical of the defendant wrongly accused of a robbery at 16th and P, the only perjury may be his denial of the truthful, but highly damaging, testimony of the corroborating witness who placed him one block away from the intersection five minutes prior to the crime. Of course, if he tells the truth and thus verifies the corroborating witness, the jury will be far more inclined to accept the inaccurate testimony of the principal witness, who specifically identified him as the criminal.[16]

If a lawyer has discovered his client's intent to perjure himself, one possible solution to this problem is for the lawyer to approach the bench, explain his ethical difficulty to the judge, and ask to be relieved, thereby causing a mistrial. This request is certain to be denied, if only because it would empower the defendant to cause a series of mistrials in the same fashion. At this point, some feel that the lawyer has avoided the ethical problem and can put the defendant on the stand. However, one objection to this solution, apart from the violation of confidentiality, is that the lawyer's ethical problem has not been solved, but has only been transferred to the judge. Moreover, the client in such a case might well have grounds for appeal on the basis of deprivation of due process and denial of the right to counsel, since he will have been tried before, and sentenced by, a judge who has been informed of the client's guilt by his own attorney.

A solution even less satisfactory than informing the judge of the defendant's guilt would be to let the client take the stand without the attorney's participation and to omit reference to the client's testimony in closing argument. The latter solution, of course, would be as damaging as to fail entirely to argue the case to the jury, and failing to argue the case is "as improper as though the attorney had told the jury that his client has uttered a falsehood in making the statement."[17]

Therefore, the obligation of confidentiality, in the context of our adversary system, apparently allows the attorney no alternative to putting a perjurious witness on the stand without explicit or implicit disclosure of the attorney's knowedge to either the judge or the jury. Canon 37 does not proscribe this conclusion; the canon recognizes only two exemptions to the obligation of confidentiality. The first relates to the lawyer who is accused by his client and may disclose the truth to defend himself. The other exception relates to "the announced intention of a client to commit a crime." On the basis of the ethical and practical considerations discussed above, the Canon's exception to the obligation of confidentiality cannot logically be understood to include the crime of perjury committed during the specific case in which the lawyer is serving. Moreover, even when the intention is to commit a crime in the future, Canon 37 does not require disclosure, but only permits it. Furthermore, Canon 15, which does proscribe "violation of law" by the attorney for his client, does not apply to the lawyer who unwillingly puts a perjurious client on the stand after having made every effort to dissuade him from committing perjury. Such an act by the attorney cannot properly be found to be subornation—corrupt inducement—of perjury. Canon 29 requires counsel to inform the prosecuting authorities of perjury committed in the case in which he has been involved, but this can only refer to perjury by opposing witnesses. For an attorney to disclose his client's perjury "would involve a direct violation of Canon 37."[18] Despite Canon 29, therefore, the attorney should not reveal his client's perjury "to the court or to the authorities."[19]

Of course, before the client testifies perjuriously, the lawyer has a duty to attempt to dissuade him on grounds of both law and morality. In addition, the client should be impressed with the fact that his untruthful alibi is tactically dangerous. There is always a strong possibility that the prosecutor will expose the perjury on cross-examination. However, for the reasons already given, the final decision must necessarily be the client's. The lawyer's best course thereafter would be to avoid any further professional relationship with a client whom he knew to have perjured himself.

The third question is whether it is proper to give your client legal advice when you have reason to believe that the knowledge you give him will tempt him to commit perjury. This may indeed be the most difficult problem of all, because giving such advice creates the appearance that the attorney is encouraging and condoning perjury.

If the lawyer is not certain what the facts are when he gives the advice, the problem is substantially minimized, if not eliminated. It is not the lawyer's function to prejudge his client as a perjurer. He cannot presume that the client will make unlawful use of his advice. Apart from this, there is a natural predisposition in most people to recollect facts, entirely honestly, in a way most favorable to their own interest. As Randolph Paul has observed, some witnesses are nervous, some are confused about their interests, some try to be too smart for their own good, and some subconsciously do not want to understand what has happened to them.[20] Before he begins to remember essential facts, the client is entitled to know what his interests are.

The above argument does not apply merely to factual questions such as whether a particular event occurred at 10:15 or at 10:45.[21] One of the most critical problems in a criminal case, as in many others, is intention. A German writer, considering the question of intention as a test of legal consequences, suggests the following situation.[22] A young man and a young woman decide to get married. Each has a thousand dollars. They decide to begin a business with these funds, and the young lady gives her money to the young man for this purpose. Was the intention to form a joint venture or a partnership? Did they intend that the young man be an agent or a trustee? Was the transaction a gift or a loan? If the couple should subsequently visit a tax attorney and discover that it is in their interest that the transaction be viewed as a gift, it is submitted that they could, with complete honesty, so remember it. On the other hand, should their engagement be broken and the young woman consult an attorney for the purpose of recovering her money, she could with equal honesty remember that her intention was to make a loan.

Assume that your client, on trial for his life in a first-degree murder case, has killed another man with a penknife but insists that the killing was in self-defense. You ask him, "Do you customarily carry the penknife in your pocket, do you carry it frequently or infrequently, or did you take it with you only on this occasion? He replies, "Why do you ask me a question like that?" It is entirely appropriate to inform him that his carrying the knife only on this occasion, or infrequently, supports an inference of premeditation, while if he carried the knife constantly, or frequently, the inference of premeditation would be negated. Thus, your client's life may depend on his recollection as to whether he carried the knife frequently or infrequently. Despite the possibility that the client or a third party might infer that the lawyer was prompting the client to lie, the lawyer must apprise the defendant of the significance of his answer. There is no conceivable ethical requirement that the lawyer trap his client into a hasty and ill-considered answer before telling him the significance of the question.

A similar problem is created if the client has given the lawyer incriminating information before being fully aware of its significance. For example, assume that a man consults a tax lawyer and says, "I am fifty years old. Nobody in my immediate family has lived past fifty. Therefore, I would like to put my affairs in order. Specifically, I understand that I can avoid substantial estate taxes by setting up a trust. Can I do it?" The lawyer informs the client that he can successfully avoid the estate taxes only if he lives at least three years after establishing the trust or, should he die within three years, if the trust is not found to have been created in contemplation of death. The client then might ask who decides whether the trust is in contemplation of death. After learning that the determination is made by the court, the client might inquire about the factors on which such a decision would be based.

At this point, the lawyer can do one of two things. He can refuse to answer the question, or he can inform the client that the court will consider the wording of the trust instrument and will hear evidence about any conversations which he may have or any letters he may write expressing motives other than avoidance of estate taxes. It is likely that virtually every tax attorney in the country would answer the client's question, and that no one would consider the answer unethical. However, the lawyer might well appear to have prompted his client to deceive the Internal Revenue Service and the courts, and this appearance would remain regardless of the lawyer's explicit disclaimer to the client of any intent so to prompt him. Nevertheless, it should not be unethical for the lawyer to give the advice.

In a criminal case, a lawyer may be representing a client who protests his innocence, and whom the lawyer believes to be innocent. Assume, for example, that the charge is assault with intent to kill, that the prosecution has erroneous but credible eyewitness testimony against the defendant, and that the defendant's truthful alibi witness is impeachable on the basis of several felony convictions. The prosecutor, perhaps having doubts about the case, offers to permit the defendant to plead guilty to simple assault. If the defendant should go to trial and be convicted, he might well be sent to jail for fifteen years; on a plea of simple of assault, the maximum penalty would be one year, and the sentence might well be suspended.

The common practice of conveying the prosecutor's offer to the defendant should not be considered unethical, even if the defense lawyer is convinced of his client's innocence. Yet the lawyer is clearly in the position of prompting his client to lie, since the defendant cannot make the plea without saying to the judge that he is pleading guilty because he is guilty. Furthermore, if the client does decide to plead guilty, it would be improper for the lawyer to inform the court that his client is innocent, thereby compelling the defendant to stand trial and take the substantial risk of fifteen years' imprisonment.[23]

Essentially no different from the problem discussed above, but apparently more difficult, is the so-called *Anatomy of a Murder* situation.[24] The lawyer, who has received from his client an incriminating story of murder in the first degree, says, "If the facts are as you have stated them so far, you have no defense, and you will probably be electrocuted. On the other hand, if you acted in a blind rage, there is a possibility of saving your life. Think it over, and we will talk about it tomorrow." As in the tax case, and as in the case of the plea of guilty to a lesser offense, the lawyer has given his client a legal opinion that might induce the client to lie. This is information which the lawyer himself would have, without advice, were he in the client's position. It is submitted that the client is entitled to have this information about the law and to make his own decision as to whether to act upon it. To decide otherwise would not only penalize the less-educated defendant, but would also prejudice the client because of his initial truthfulness in telling his story in confidence to the attorney.

CONCLUSION

The lawyer is an officer of the court, participating in a search for the truth. Yet no lawyer would consider that he had acted unethically in pleading the statute of frauds or the statute of limitations as a bar to a just claim. Similarly, no lawyer would consider it unethical to prevent introduction of evidence such as a murder weapon seized in violation of the fourth amendment or a truthful but involuntary confession, or to defend a guilty man on grounds of denial of a speedy trial.[25] Such actions are permissible because there are policy considerations that at times justify frustrating the search for the truth and the prosecution of a just claim. Similarly, there are policies that justify an affirmative answer to the three questions that have been posed in this article. These policies include the maintenance of an adversary system, the presumption of innocence, the prosecution's burden to prove guilt beyond a reasonable doubt, the right to counsel, and the obligation of confidentiality between lawyer and client.

NOTES

1. The substance of this paper was recently presented to a Criminal Trial Institute attended by forty-five members of the District of Columbia Bar. As a consequence, several judges (none of whom had either heard the lecture or read it) complained to the Committee on Admissions and Grievances of the District Court for the District of Columbia, urging the author's disbarment or suspension. Only after four months of proceedings, including a hearing, two meetings, and a *de novo* review by eleven federal district court judges, did the Committee announce its decision to "proceed no further in the matter."

2. *American Bar Association, Canons of Professional Ethics,* Preamble (1908).

3. Williston, *Life and Law* (1940), p. 271.

4. Curtis, *It's Your Law* (1954), pp. 17-21. See also Curtis, "The Ethics of Advocacy," *Stanford Law Review* 4(1951):3, 9-10; Drinker, "Some Remarks on Mr. Curtis' 'The Ethics of Advocacy,'" *Stanford Law Review* 4(1952):349, 350-351.

5. Opinion 287, Committee on Professional Ethics and Grievances of the American Bar Association (1953).

6. Esobedo v. Illinois, 378, 485, 491 (1964).

7. "The failure to argue the case before the jury, while ordinarily only a trial tactic not subject to review, manifestly enters the field of incompetency when the reason assigned is the attorney's conscience. It is as improper as though the attorney had told the jury that his client had uttered a falsehood in making the statement. The right to an attorney embraces effective representation throughout all stages of the trial, and where the representation is of such low caliber as to amount to no representation, the guarantee of due process has been violated." Johns v. Smyth, 176 F. Supp. 949, 953 (E.D. Va. 1959); Schwartz, *Cases on Professional Responsibility and the Administration of Criminal Justice* (1962), p. 79.

8. "[C]ounsel cannot properly perform their duties without knowing the truth." Opinion 23, Committee on Professional Ethics and Grievances of the American Bar Association (1930).

9. Paul, "The Responsibilities of the Tax Adviser," *Harvard Law Review* 63 (1950):337, 383.

10. 2 Mechem, *Agency* § 2297 (2d ed. 1914).

11. Opinion 150, Committee on Professional Ethics and Grievances of the American Bar Association (1936), quoting Thornton, *Attorneys at Law* § 94 (1914). See also Opinion 23, *supra* note 8.

12. Greenough v. Gaskell, 1 Myl, & K. 98, 103, 39 Eng. Rep. 618, 621 (Ch. 1833) (Lord Chancellor Brougham).

13. Opinion 91, Committee on Professional Ethics and Grievances of the American Bar Association (1933).

14. See Orkin, "Defense of One Known To Be Guilty," *Criminal Law Quarterly* 1 (1958):170, 174. Unless the lawyer has told the client at the outset that he will withdrawn if he learns that the client is guilty, "it is plain enough as a matter of good morals and professional ethics" that the lawyer should not withdraw on this ground. Opinion 90, Committee on Professional Ethics and Grievances of the American Bar Association (1932). As to the difficulties inherent in the lawyer's telling the client that he wants to remain ignorant of the facts, see note 8 *supra* and accompanying text.

15. The judge may infer that the situation is worse than it is in fact. In the case related in note 23 *infra,* the attorney's actual difficulty was that he did not want to permit a plea of guilty by a client who was maintaining his innocence. However, as is commonly done, he told the judge only that he had to withdraw because of an ethical problem." The judge reasonably inferred that the defendant had admitted his guilt and wanted to offer a perjured alibi.

16. One lawyer who considers it clearly unethical for the attorney to present the alibi in this hypothetical case, found no ethical difficulty himself in the following case. His client was prosecuted for robbery. The prosecution witness testified that the robbery had taken place at 10:15, and identified the defendant as the criminal. However, the defendant had a convincing alibi for 10:00 to 10:30. The attorney presented the alibi, and the client was acquitted. The alibi was

truthful, but the attorney knew that the prosecution witness had been confused about the time, and that his client had in fact committed the crime at 10:45.

17. See note 7 *supra.*

18. Opinion 287, Committee on Professional Ethics and Grievances of the American Bar Association (1953).

19. *Ibid.*

20. See Paul, *supra* note 9.

21. Even this kind of "objective fact" is subject to honest error. See note 16 *supra.*

22. Wurzel, *Das Juristische Denken* (1904), p. 82 translated in Fuller, *Basic Contract Law* (1964), p. 67.

23. In a recent case, the defendant was accused of unauthorized use of an automobile, for which the maximum penalty is five years. He told his court-appointed attorney that he had borrowed the car from a man known to him only as "Junior," that he had not known the car was stolen, and that he had an alibi for the time of the theft. The defendant had three prior convictions for larceny, and the alibi was weak. The prosecutor offered to accept a guilty plea to two misdemeanors (taking property without right and petty larceny) carrying a combined maximum sentence of eighteen months. The defendant was willing to plead guilty to the lesser offenses, but the attorney felt that, because of his client's alibi, he could not permit him to do so. The lawyer therefore informed the judge that he had an ethical problem and asked to be relieved. The attorney who was appointed in his place permitted the client to plead guilty to the two lesser offenses, and the defendant was sentenced to nine months. The alternative would have been five or six months in jail while the defendant waited for jury trial, and a very substantial risk of conviction and a much heavier sentence. Neither the client nor justice would have been well served by compelling the defendant to go to trial against his will under these circumstances.

24. See Traver, *Anatomy of a Murder* (1958).

25. Cf. Kamisar, "Equal Justice in the Gatehouses and Mansions of American Criminal Procedure," in *Criminal Justice in Our Time* (Howard-ed. 1965), pp. 77-78:

Yes, the presence of counsel in the police station may result in the suppression of truth, just as the presence of counsel at the trial may, when a client is advised not to take the stand, or when an objection is made to the admissibility of trustworthy, but illegally seized, "real" evidence.

If the subject of police interrogation not only cannot be "coerced" into making a statement, but need not volunteer one, why shouldn't he be so advised? And why shouldn't court-appointed counsel, as well as retained counsel, so advise him?

Norman Lefstein

The Criminal Defendant
Who Proposes Perjury

In a 1966 lecture, Professor Monroe H. Freedman was the first to advance the unorthodox view for which he has become well-known: A criminal defense lawyer must put his client on the stand to testify even though he knows that the client will commit perjury.[1] Subsequently, Professor Freedman defended his views in an oft-quoted law review article[2] and more recently refined his presentation in a book.[3]

The time is now ripe to reexamine the defense lawyer's dilemma when faced with a client who insists on testifying falsely. Recently, the American Bar Association began to update and revise its criminal justice standards, including its defense function standards (ABA Defense Function Standards).[4] ABA Defense Function Standards § 7.7 proposes a solution for the defense lawyer's handling of a client bent on perjury: The attorney should seek to withdraw; if that fails, the defendant should be asked to make a statement to the trier of fact, but his false testimony should not be argued to the jury.[5] The ABA approach obviously differs from that of Professor Freedman and it, too, has been criticized.[6]

Indeed, while a lively debate on the client-perjury issue has developed in the literature during the past decade, and while the number of court decisions on the problem has increased during this time, no single view has emerged predominant. Appellate divisions are in disagreement, and often fail to analyze the problem fully. In the course of this article, the various approaches for handling the defendant's proposed perjury are discussed. Subsequently, I offer my own suggestions for the defense lawyer's resolution of the perjury issue—suggestions which differ from Professor Freedman's and the ABA Defense Function Standards.

DEFINING THE ISSUE

To understand the role of the defense attorney, it is helpful first to define the

From *Hofstra Law Review* 6 (1978):665-692. Reprinted by permission of the publisher and the author.

nature of the perjury issue. We are *not* concerned with the lawyer who learns *after* his client has testified that perjury was committed. Although the duty of the lawyer when this occurs has not always been clear, recent developments have greatly clarified the attorney's obligation. Most importantly, the *ABA Code of Professional Responsibility* (the Code) was amended to provide that an attorney cannot reveal a fraud perpetrated by his client upon the court, when the source of the attorney's information of the fraud "is protected as a privileged communication."[7] This provision of the Code, with a recent Formal Opinion of the ABA Committee on Professional Ethics, makes clear that when knowledge of the client's past perjury derives from a "confidence" or "secret," as it almost always will, the attorney may not divulge his client's crime.[8] In this situation, the policy favoring maintenance of attorney-client privileges takes precedence, particularly since the wrong already has been committed and the attorney played no role in it.[9]

We also are not concerned with the criminal case where the defense attorney strongly believes that his client is not being truthful and thus will probably commit perjury if he testifies during the trial. Defense attorneys will attest to the frequency of cases where there is substantial evidence that the client is lying, yet the client adamantly, although unconvincingly, insists that he is innocent. Sometimes the client will even alter the facts each time he tells the attorney what happened, suggesting thereby that truth will have little or nothing to do with his testimony at trial. Yet, in this situation, the attorney may allow the client to testify without fear of suborning perjury, for one is guilty of that crime only if he induces another to commit perjury.[10] The ABA Defense Function Standards, moreover, adopt the position that the client may be permitted to testify as long as he insists upon his innocence.[11] Such a rule is essential; otherwise, defense attorneys would constantly be judging the innocence of their clients, and then deciding whether to allow them to testify. If this occurred, the adversary system of criminal justice would no longer function as we now know it.[12]

The focus of this title, then, is on the defendant who tells his lawyer, unequivocally, that he is guilty, but who proposes that during the trial he deny his guilt and offer testimony which is fictitious. It is further assumed that the defense attorney has independent knowledge of the client's guilt that corroborates what the client has told the attorney.[13] Some years ago, when I was actively engaged in criminal defense work, I had just such a case. I was appointed by the court to represent a defendant, whom I shall call Mr. X, charged with the nighttime burglary of a barbershop. During my first interview with Mr. X, I explained the nature of the attorney-client privilege, assuring him that I could not be compelled to divulge what he told me. Almost immediately the defendant confessed that he had broken into the barbershop, that he was accustomed to having his hair cut there, and that he was arrested near the scene of the break-in hiding in some bushes. The defendant explained that he took cover in the bushes when he heard police sirens. I advised the defendant that I would "check out" the Government's case against him and would be back in touch.

From the police officer who arrested the defendant, I learned that an eyewitness saw the defendant both enter and leave the barbershop; the witness then called the police and led them to the defendant hidden in the bushes. According to the eyewitness, who made an on-the-scene identification, there was no doubt that the defendant was the person who entered the barbershop. I also learned that the barbershop owner knew the defendant as a frequent patron of his establishment. In short, my investigation fully corroborated my client's admission of guilt; though I had no reason to doubt my client during our first interview, I was positive of his guilt upon completing my investigation.

When I met with the client for our second interview, I explained that the case against him was strong and that a successful challenge to the eyewitness identification would be quite difficult. I noted, however, that since no fruits of the crime were discovered on his person and since his fingerprints were not found inside the barbershop, there were at least some arguments we could make. As I was about to explain that I thought it advisable to conduct plea negotiations with the prosecutor, the client interrupted to state that he would testify at the trial that he was with his girl friend during the evening of the burglary, and that he was walking home when he heard police sirens and hid in the bushes out of fear. He further told me that he would explain to the jury that because he had a prior record, which would be brought out on cross-examination, he believed it likely that the police would blame him for any criminal activity that might have occurred in the area. As the finishing touch to his story, the client handed me a sheet of paper with the name and telephone number of his girl friend, who was prepared to corroborate his alibi for the period just prior to the burglary.

Perhaps because of my relative youth and lack of experience in criminal defense, I was shocked by what my client proposed. Instinctively, I advised the client that I could not permit him to testify, since his testimony would be perjury, and that I would not call his girl friend as a witness for the same reason. Shortly thereafter, I left what had become an increasingly unpleasant interview, telling the defendant to think over what I had said. The defendant obviously did so; within a few days, I received a call from another attorney, who advised me that he had been retained by my client's father to provide representation in the case.[14] Out of curiosity, I later attended part of the trial and listened to what I knew to be perjured testimony presented by my former client and his girl friend. "Justice" triumphed, however; the defendant was convicted.

PROFESSOR FREEDMAN'S VIEW

At the time I represented Mr. X, Professor Freedman had not yet written about what a lawyer should do when presented with a client who wishes to commit perjury. Had I known about and followed the course which Professor Freedman was later to urge, I might have continued to represent Mr. X and presented his perjured testimony.[15] Faced with Mr. X's desire to commit perjury, my "obligation," according to Professor Freedman, was "to advise the client that the proposed testimony [was] unlawful, but to proceed in the normal fashion in presenting the testimony and arguing the case to the jury if the client [made] the decision to go forward."[16] Primarily, this conclusion derives from what Professor Freedman calls the lawyer's trilemma.[17] In criminal defense representation, the attorney must learn all the facts from his client, he must keep them in strictest confidence,[18] and he must always be candid in his dealings with the court.[19] After examining these obligations and the alternatives to presenting perjured testimony, Professor Freedman concludes that the attorney cannot forego knowing all of the facts, and that between confidentiality and candor to the court, the former is significantly more important.

The problem with Professor Freedman's trilemma is that it rests on the false premise that the confidentiality requirement applies to a client's statement that he intends to commit the crime of perjury. Historically, however, the attorney-client privilege has never extended to the client who seeks legal assistance in the commission of a future crime.[20] The law is succinctly stated in a leading evidence treatise:

> Since the policy of the privilege is that of promoting the administration of justice, it would be a perversion of the privilege to extend it to the client who seeks advice to aid him in carrying out an illegal or fraudulent scheme. Advice given for those purposes would not be a professional service but participation in a conspiracy. Accordingly, it is settled under modern authority that the privilege does not extend to communciations between attorney and client where the client's purpose is the furtherance of a future intended crime or fraud.[21]

Thus, for example, in *Sawyer v. Barczak,*[22] where a prospective state's witness told an attorney that he was prepared to commit perjury if it would lead to dismissal of criminal charges pending against him, the court held that the client's statements were not privileged and that the attorney should have been allowed to testify to what the client had said. The Code, moreover, states that a lawyer *may* reveal the "intention of his client to commit a crime and the information necessary to prevent the crime."[23] A client's statements which reflect an intent to commit a crime are not characterized by the Code as either "confidences or secrets.[24] The Code's drafters must have recognized that no privilege attaches to the client's statements concerning commission of future crime. Conseqently, if a lawyer reveals the client's intent to commit perjury, he is not revealing protected information; the attorney-client privilege never covered the client's statements. This, of course, does not answer the question whether the client's intent to commit perjury *should* be disclosed. It does suggest, however, that Professor Freedman is inaccurate in claiming that *all* disclosures of the client *must* be held in strictest confidence.[25]

As a guide to the practicing attorney, there is another major difficulty in Professor Freedman's analysis. The Code provides that "a lawyer shall not . . . [k]nowingly use perjured testimony or false evidence."[26] To do so subjects the attorney to disciplinary sanction.[27] In the case of Mr. X, for example, had I called my client to testify I would have "knowingly" used perjured testimony.[28] Although Professor Freedman concedes the presence of the Code's perjury prohibition, he offers no effective defense for an attorney accused of ignoring it. Essentially, he argues that because the attorney's trilemma is not addressed in the Code, its clear admonitions against using perjury are not a problem. Therefore, the only satisfactory course is for an attorney to preserve his client's confidences.[29]

Aside from the law of confidentiality and the provisions of the Code, there is another important reason that Professor Freedman's position should be resisted. Ultimately, what Professor Freedman advocates is a significant extension and corruption of the defense attorney's role. In his view, the criminally accused is not only entitled to effective counsel, he is entitled to counsel who will provide active assistance in presenting perjured testimony to the jury. This is surely the antithesis of what the lawyer's role ideally should be.[30]

To avoid assisting a client in presenting false testimony, it is sometimes suggested that the attorney should seek to withdraw from the case.[31] Professor Freedman criticizes this alternative, arguing that if the motion is granted, the identical perjured testimony will be presented anyway, because the client will acquire a new attorney with whom he will not be candid; the new attorney will then present the perjured testimony without knowing that it is false.[32] Although this scenario may be troublesome, it is preferable to permitting the original attorney knowingly to present the perjured evidence. While a fraud may be practiced on the court, at least the responsibility for the fraud will rest solely with the defendant. No attorney will have sacrificed his integrity by serving as an agent for a client by knowingly presenting false testimony. In contrast, Professor Freedman does not concede that avoiding participation of attorneys in the client's crime is an objective worth achieving.

No court decisions have been discovered which endorse Professor Freedman's view, but this absence of decisions might exist because no attorney who has followed Professor Freedman's recommendation has been discovered.[33] In the mid-1960s, two writers did suggest that it would be permissible to allow the defendant to present perjured testimony, athough one urged that the lawyer first seek to withdraw from the case,[34] and the other suggested that the lawyer not argue the perjured testimony to the jury.[35] The strongest endorsement of Professor Freedman's position has been made by the Supreme Judicial Court of Massachusetts Rules Committee, which recommended that the state's defense representation standards provide that, where a client rejects an attorney's advice not to commit perjury, "an attorney may examine him in the usual way, and may argue the validity of his testimony to the jury."[36] This position, clearly influenced by Professor Freedman's writings, was urged upon the Rules Committee by both the Massachusetts and Boston Bar Associations.[37] A final decision on the issue has not yet been rendered by the Supreme Judicial Court of Massachusetts.[38]

THE ABA APPROACH

The ABA position concerning the defendant who wishes to commit perjury is articulated in section 7.7 of the ABA Defense Functions Standards.[39] First, the defense lawyer must seek to dissuade the client from testifying falsely. If this fails, the attorney must attempt to withdraw from the case, but the reason for seeking to withdraw should not be revealed to the court.[40] If withdrawal is either unfeasible or not permitted by the court, the attorney should confine direct examination of his client to permitting the defendant to make a statement to the judge or jury. The lawyer, however, should not rely upon the false testimony in his closing argument. Section 7.7 also recommends that the lawyer record that the client is testifying against counsel's advice.[41]

For the attorney who cannot avoid the perjury problem by withdrawing, the ABA position is a compromise. The defendant is permitted to testify, yet the lawyer avoids offering his personal support of the client's lies. Accordingly, the ABA position is regarded as a means of circumventing the prohibitions in the Code pertaining to the use of "perjured testimony or false evidence"[42] and "conduct that the lawyer knows to be illegal or fraudulent."[43] The ABA recommendation, which was adopted in 1971, is consistent with views Chief Justice (then Judge) Burger expressed in 1966.[44]

In discussing the ABA approach, Professor Freedman offers an intensely practical criticism: Suppose the prosecutor objects to the defendant delivering a narrative on the grounds that it will not be possible to know in advance if the defendant will make inadmissible statements.[45] Trial lawyers ordinarily object when a witness is asked to tell all he knows about a case, because such a broad question fails "to provide an orderly means by which objections to improper evidence can be raised and ruled upon before the evidence is heard by the jury."[46] Thus, a trial judge might sustain the prosecutor's objection to defense counsel's general question to his client.[47] Yet, neither section 7.7 nor the accompanying Commentary offers any solution for what the defense lawyer should then do. Presumably, the attorney could either examine the witness in the normal fashion or advise the court of the client's proposed perjury, a solution which is examined later.[48]

There appear to be only two reported decisions in which appellate courts have discussed the ABA's approach to the perjury problem,[49] and they both illustrate the difficulty with section 7.7's recommendation that lawyers attempt to withdraw from a case under these circumstances. In *State v. Lowery*,[50] counsel moved to withdraw during the direct examination of his client, apparently because the client, much to counsel's surprise, began to testify falsely. When the trial court asked counsel his reason for seeking to withdraw and counsel replied that he could not state the reason, the motion was denied.[51] In *Thornton v. United States*,[52] the defense attorney moved to withdraw prior to the start of trial "for moral ethical reasons."[53] The trial court however, pressed the attorney for greater specificity and the attorney, contrary to the ABA's recommendation, then revealed that the client had changed his "story" and was planning to give false testimony.[54] The trial court, apparently believing that he might now be prejudiced against the defendant at sentencing, certified the case to a second judge. Defense counsel again moved to withdraw, but this time gave no reason for seeking to do so; accordingly, the second judge denied the motion.[55] In affirming the defendant's conviction, the appellate court ruled that the conduct of the second judge was reasonable, because the specific grounds for counsel's motion to withdraw were never disclosed.[56]

TELLING THE COURT OF THE PROPOSED PERJURY

A third possible approach to the client-perjury problem is simply to disclose the defendant's intention to the court. Although section 7.7 does not suggest that a lawyer should reveal the client's proposed perjury, the Commentary to the section implies that it may be proper to do so:

> On one hand, some lawyers hold that the lawyer's general obligation to protect the court from fraud in its processes and the exception to the attorney-client privilege for statements of intention to commit a crime may place the lawyer in the position of being required to disclose the fact of perjury.[57]

The ABA Committee on Ethics and Professional Responsibility expresses important support for this position. In an Informal Opinion issued in 1975, the committee was asked to decide the duty of an attorney "where a defendant in a criminal case, whether it be in a traffic case or a felony case, insists upon taking the stand and giving perjured testimony."[58] The committee replied that the lawyer has only two alternatives: He must either withdraw from the case before the client commits perjury or report the proposed perjury to the court. According to the committee, "the right of a client to effective counsel in any case (criminal or civil) does not include the right to compel counsel to knowingly assist or participate in the commission of perjury or the creation or presentation of false evidence."[59] Remarkably, section 7.7 of the ABA Defense Functions Standards approved four years earlier by the ABA, is not even mentioned.

In two state appellate decisions, State v. Henderson[60] and State v. Robinson,[61] defense counsel requested leave to withdraw and, in doing so, advised the trial court that the defendant was planning to present perjured testimony. In both cases, the appellate courts commended defense counsel for having acted in a professionally responsible manner;[62] the defendants, however, declined to testify after counsel advised the court that the testimony would be untrue.[63]

Suppose that the defendants in Henderson and Robinson requested to testify despite what their attorneys had told the trial courts. The question whether a criminal defendant who proposes to commit perjury has an absolute right to testify remains. In Henderson and Robinson the appellate courts apparently assumed that the trial judges were required to allow false testimony to be given by the defendants. In *Henderson* the appellate court stated that "defendant was fully informed by counsel, as well as the court, of his right to take the stand and 'tell his story,' but defendant declined to do so."[64] Similarly, in *Robinson* the appellate court noted that the trial judge inquired of the defendant "if he desired to take the witness stand."[65]

Neither Professor Freedman nor the ABA Defense Function Standards discusses in detail whether a defendant has a right to testify falsely. Professor Freedman says only that "there is a point of view, which has been expressed to me by a number of experienced attorneys, that the criminal defendant has a 'right to tell his story.'"[66] In the ABA's Defense Function Standards, the Commentary to section 7.7 refers, without citation of authority, to the "defendant's absolute right . . . to testify in his own behalf. . . ."[67] Further Commentary to section 7.7, however, speaks somewhat less certainly of the defendant's right to testify. Referring to the views of "experienced defense counsel," the Commentary states: "Our legal system, permitting the defendant to testify under oath, has not, in their view, completely foreclosed to him the opportunity to speak to the jury. . . ."[68] Again, no citation of authority is provided.

As a general rule, the defendant in a criminal case is entitled to testify in his own behalf.[69] When a defendant reveals to his lawyer his intention to give perjured testimony, however, he arguably may be precluded from testifying. Courts have held that when a defendant misbehaves on the witness stand, the right to testify may be deemed waived. Thus, in *United States v. Ives,*[70] where the defendant's first trial ended in mistrial because of his misconduct and he insisted that he be allowed to testify in the second trial, the judge ruled that he could not do so because of his prior disruptive conduct.[71] Twice the defendant took the stand. The first time he refused to confine his testimony to the issues and cursed the defense counsel and the judge; on the second occasion, the defendant again verbally abused the court and his counsel and gave unresponsive answers. The Court of Appeals for the Ninth Circuit affirmed the trial court's actions, noting that the conduct of the defendant was sufficient to waive his opportunity to testify.[72] The court of appeals analogized the right to testify with the right of the accused to attend the trial, which may also be waived due to misconduct.[73]

Arguably, there is a basic difference between denying a defendant the right to testify because of proposed perjury and denial because of disruptive activity. In the latter situation, the defendant has unequovically demonstrated that he must be controlled in the courtroom; otherwise, the trial cannot proceed in orderly fashion. Where proposed perjury is involved, the defendant has not yet misbehaved, and the court has only defense counsel's report of his client's intention. Even assuming that defense counsel's assessment of the client's intent is completely accurate, if the defendant were to change his mind on the way to the witness stand, the prediction of the client's proposed perjury would not be realized.

Nevertheless, decisions of the Supreme Court support the proposition that a defendant lacks the constitutional right to present perjured testimony; however, the decisions do not address the manner in which a defendant may be prevented from doing so. In *Harris v. New York*,[74] the Court held that defendants could be impeached with statements obtained in violation of *Miranda v. Arizona.*[75] In reaching this decision, the Court in dictum offered the following view of defendants who testify: "Every criminal defendant is privileged to testify in his own defense, or to refuse to do so. But that privilege cannot be construed to include the right to commit perjury. . . . Having voluntarily taken the stand, petitioner was under an obligation to speak truthfully and accurately . . . . "[76]

More recently, in *United States v. Wong*,[77] the Supreme Court reaffirmed that when authorities mistakenly fail to warn a person of the privilege against self-incrimination, the suspect is not justified in offering perjured testimony. In *Wong* the defendant was summoned before a grand jury and told of her fifth amendment rights.[78] Due to her limited command of English, however, she did not understand the prosecutor's warning and believed that she had to answer all questions. Not wishing to incriminate herself, she lied and was subsequently indicted for perjury.[79] At a suppression hearing, the district court ordered the testimony suppressed. On appeal to the Supreme Court, after affirmance by the Ninth Circuit, the Government conceded that defendant had not understood her fifth amendment rights and hence, in legal effect, was unwarned of her privilege against self-incrimination. The defendant argued that since she was in effect forced by the Government to answer all questions, her choice was confined either to incriminating herself or lying under oath. The Supreme Court disagreed, stating that "the Fifth Amendment privilege does not condone perjury. It grants a privilege to remain silent without risking contempt, but it 'does not endow the person who testifies with a license to commit perjury.'"[80] It would seem to follow from *Wong,* and from the cases on which it is based,[81] that if a suspect unwarned of the privilege against self-incrimination has no right to present perjured testimony, such a right is similarly unavailable to the criminal defendant who is aware of his privilege to remain silent.

VIOLATING THE ATTORNEY-CLIENT PRIVILEGE CONCERNING THE CRIME CHARGED

Even if the defendant does not have an absolute right to present perjured testimony, there is a substantial problem with permitting the defense lawyer to tell the court of the client's proposed perjury. Assume the defense attorney says to the judge: "My client proposes to present perjurious testimony; I will not, therefore, call him to the witness stand to testify." The trial judge will almost certainly assume that the client has confessed his guilt to the attorney and is contemplating false testimony to conceal it. Such an assumption by the trial court will mean that, as a practical matter, the defense lawyer will have breached his confidentiality obligation. Unlike the attorney's duty when his client intends to commit a crime, his duty to keep his client's confessions of past crimes confidential is absolute.[82] The same problem inheres in the ABA's solution to a client's proposed perjury, as specified in section 7.7 of the ABA Defense Function Standards. If a lawyer unsuccessfully seeks to withdraw from his client's case, puts the client on the witness stand, and asks him to make a statement, and then does not argue the defendant's version to the jury, the trial judge will almost surely recognize that the defense attorney is implementing section 7.7 and that the defendant's testimony is false.[83] Further, the judge will reason that the defendant has confessed guilt of the crime charged to his attorney, which is why the attorney is following section 7.7 of the ABA Defense Function Standards.

It can be argued that the lawyer who tells the court of his client's proposed perjury or who follows the ABA's formula has revealed neither a client's confidence nor his guilt. Technically, this is true. The court has simply made assumptions which may in fact be unjustified. Conceivably, the client wishes to commit perjury to conceal embarrassing information. Indeed, the client may have insisted to his lawyer that he is totally innocent of the offense charged, but he does not feel that he can publicly admit where he was when the crime occurred.[84] Experience suggests, however, that it is much more likely that the client's perjury—as as in the case of Mr. X described earlier—will be aimed at concealing the client's guilt. Accordingly, the trial court's assumption that the client has fully confessed to the lawyer is apt to be accurate. Perhaps worse, the court will assume the client's guilt even if he is innocent of the crime charged and has never admitted his guilt to the lawyer.

Another problem may arise if the attorney informs the court of the client's proposed perjury, and the court then asks the lawyer how the intended testimony differs from the attorney's knowledge of the truth.[85] If the client has confessed his guilt to the attorney, the attorney would have to tell the court that the question is not one which he should be required to answer. Should this occur, the court would almost certainly conclude that the client has confessed his guilt to the attorney, and counsel's duty to protect the client's confidences concerning past crimes will have been effectively breached.[86]

Finally, suppose that the trial court does assume that the client has admitted his guilt to the lawyer. Besides having a complaint about a violation of the attorney-client privilege, the issue whether a defendant has a right to insist that a different judge try his case is unresolved. Although the question has never been litigated, in all likelihood he does not. While it may be preferable that a different judge try the case, a court in pretrial proceedings will often receive *specific* information about past offenses committed by a defendant without being disqualified from presiding at the defendant's trial.[87] Moreover, where a court suspects that the defendant has committed perjury, it has no specific information, but rather is merely assuming that the defendant has admitted the offense to counsel. In fact, even where a judge learns of a defendant's express admissions of the crime charged, the judge often is permitted to preside at a subsequent bench trial. In *People v. Britt*,[88] the judge in a bench trial was advised in a pretrial hearing of admissions the defendant had made to police; however, it was agreed that these statements would not be introduced by the prosecution. Thus, the defendant was held not to be entitled to a new trial.[89] Similarly, federal courts have sometimes held that a judge is not disqualified from presiding at a defendant's trial even though presentence materials on the defendant are examined in advance.[90]

AN ALTERNATIVE APPROACH: WARN THE CLIENT OF THE SCOPE OF THE ATTORNEY-CLIENT PRIVILEGE

The preceding analysis suggests that none of the three principal approaches to handling the client's proposed perjury is entirely satisfactory. Professor Freedman's suggestion of treating the perjurious client like any other witness means that the attorney assists the client in breaking the law. In addition, Professor Freedman's view requires that the lawyer violate the clear admonitions of DR 7-102(A)(4) and DR 7-102)(A)(7) which prohibit the lawyer from using his client's perjured testimony and from assisting him in illegal conduct.[91] The ABA's approach, as outlined in section 7.7 of the ABA Defense Function Standards, is also imperfect.[92] Permission to withdraw from a criminal case is frequently denied,[93] and the defendant may not be allowed by the court, over the prosecutor's objection, to make the suggested narrative statement.[94] In addition, under both the ABA's approach and the third alternative—revealing the client's proposed perjury to the court—the lawyer's conduct is tantamount to revealing privileged information, because the court invariably will assume that the client has confessed guilt of the crime charged to his attorney.[95]

Because of the difficulties inherent in these proposals, I believe a different approach is justified—one which will simultaneously reduce the likelihood of the problem arising and also clarify the lawyer's appropriate conduct if his client nevertheless proposes perjury. Accordingly, I suggest that at the beginning of their relationship, the defense attorney advise his client of the scope of the attorney-client privilege. For example, the attorney might inform his client:

> Anything you tell me is privileged. That is, I cannot reveal what you tell me to anyone, including the judge. However, I can reveal information about a crime you are planning to commit, including the crime of perjury. Thus, if you were planning to lie on the witness stand in your forthcoming trial, I could reveal this fact to the court. Now, of course, I am not assumng that you are planning to do this, but I did think that, in fairness, I ought to explain to you how the attorney-client privilege works.

Such an approach is consistent with the recommendation of the Canadian Bar Association which provides in its Code of Professional Conduct: "Admissions made by the accused to his lawyer may impose strict limitations on the conduct of the defense, *and the accused should be made aware of this.*"[96] In other words, the lawyer who seeks candor from the client should be candid in return; there are limits on what is included within the attorney-client privilege, and the client should be told what these limits are.

This proposed admonition is not intended as an invitation to clients to lie to their lawyers or to conceal information. Nor is there any reason to believe that it would have that effect, except in the few cases where clients are intending to commit perjury *and* are prepared to admit that this was their intent prior to speaking to their attorneys. If the client was planning to lie to the lawyer prior to receiving the attorney's admonition concerning proposed perjury, he will proceed to do so. On the other hand, if the client was planning to be truthful with the lawyer, there is no reason to believe that the proposed admonition will discourage his honesty. Accordingly, I believe that attorneys should continue to impress upon their clients that the entire truth is needed if an effective defense is to be prepared.[97]

In contrast, the ABA Defense Function Standards state: "The lawyer should explain the necessity of full disclosure of all facts known to the client for an effective defense, and he should explain the obligation of confidentiality which makes privileged the accused's disclosures relating to the case."[98] The standards do not suggest that the client should be made aware of any of the limitations attached to the attorney-client privilege.[99] Thus, under the ABA approach, if the client admits inculpatory facts to the attorney and then insists upon testifying falsely, the attorney is obliged to follow the commands of section 7.7, thereby revealing to the court, for all practical purposes, that the accused is guilty of the offense charged. The defendant at this point is likely to feel deceived, since his attorney failed to keep his promise of confidentiality.

Alternatively, assume that the attorney seeks leave to withdraw pursuant to the ABA Defense Function Standards, and his motion is granted. Then, if the client still wishes to present perjured testimony, he will simply fail to be honest with his second attorney. The client will tell the lawyer his proposed testimony, but he will not admit that it is false. As noted earlier, the client will be able to present false testimony, and no member of the bar will knowingly provide assistance to the criminal enterprise.[100] The ABA's approach, therefore, is not really aimed at prohibiting perjured testimony, but is instead directed toward the laudable objective of disengaging lawyers from involvement with it. Essentially, then, the ABA's approach recognizes that prevention of perjury by the client is impossible. Warning the client in advance that his intent to commit perjury is not privileged is predicated on the same premise, except that it is far more straightforward. The client who is adamant about presenting perjury will know the rules at the outset and, if he desires to be dishonest, his dishonesty presumably will be practiced on the first lawyer, thereby avoiding the difficulties incident to withdrawal and retention or assignment of new counsel.[101]

Professor Freedman rejects the proposal of the Canadian Bar Association, because he believes that the proposal may require the attorney to sacrifice obtaining complete knowledge from the client.[102] The cases where complete knowledge will be sacrificed, however, are precisely those where the client otherwise would have conceded his guilt to the lawyer and then would have insisted upon testifying falsely. Where this occurs, as we already have seen, the lawyer is thrust into an impossible dilemma. Rather than aiding in the client's defense, the complete knowledge furnished to the lawyer greatly complicates the client's continued representation. Indeed, the difficulty for the lawyer is so substantial that Professor Freedman argues that the only appropriate action is for counsel knowingly to aid the client in presenting perjured evidence. Ironically, where the client insists on perjury and Professor Freedman's view is followed, the truth acquired from the client will no doubt enable counsel to be more effective in presenting and arguing the defendant's false evidence. Fortified with precise knowledge of what really happened, counsel should be better able to cross-examine the prosecutor's truthful witnesses. Conversely, under the approach recommended here, counsel who unwittingly presents the perjured testimony of a defendant may be less effective. Since the defendant's testimony is completely false, however, there should be no great concern that defense counsel might have been a more compelling advocate had he known of his client's lies.[103]

CHOOSING PROFESSOR FREEDMAN'S VIEW, THE ABA APPROACH, OR REVEALING PROPOSED PERJURY TO THE COURT

Suppose that the attorney advises the client that a plan to commit perjury is not protected as a confidential communication. Assume further that despite what the lawyer has told the client, the client admits that he is guilty of the offense but still insists that he wishes to present perjured testimony. If the client cannot be dissuaded from doing so, counsel must decide upon his actions.

My preference would be either to follow the ABA approach or to reveal the client's proposed perjury, depending upon which course I thought would be the least advantageous to the client. For example, if the client's proposed perjury was so incredible that I felt certain the jury would never believe it and the judge would become angry upon hearing it, I probably would tell the court about the client's proposed perjury. Conceivably, the court would then either discourage the client from testifying or deny him the opportunity to do so. As discussed previously, however, regardless of which approach is used, the court will assume that the client has admitted his guilt to the attorney.[104] Nevertheless, I believe either of these approaches is justified because the client will have been warned from the very beginning that his intent to commit perjury was unprotected by the attorney-client privilege. If the client is prejudiced by the attorney's conduct, the client has only himself to blame; the attorney should not have to assume responsibility for the client's criminal designs.

Ultimately, in deciding which of the three principal alternatives to follow, the attorney must decide whether it is preferable to violate the client's confidence, by implicity signaling to the court the client's guilt of the crime charged, or explicit ethical standards, by knowingly using the client's perjured testimony. The decision obviously involves difficult value judgments which remain unresolved under the Code of Professional Responsibility. The Code, like the law of evidence relating to attorney-client privileges, states both that there is no exception for revealing past crimes which the client has confided in the lawyer and that perjured testimony may not knowingly be used.[105]

CONCLUSION

The recommendation of this article—that the attorney advise the defendant at the beginning of their relationship that the intent to testify falsely is not a privileged communication—anticipates the client-perjury problem before it arises. In contrast, neither Professor Freedman's approach nor that of the ABA Defense Function Standards attempts to deal with the client's proposed perjury until it is too late. When a client tells the lawyer that he intends to commit perjury after a lawyer has assured the client that all of his communications are confidential, or after the client believes that they are confidential, it is difficult to justify action which is tantamount to revealing to the court the client's acknowledgment of guilt. While Professor Freedman's approach preserves the client's communications beyond that required by the law of evidence or the Code of Professional Responsibility, it also requires that the defense attorney serve as the client's active agent in presenting perjured testimony. Therefore, it is preferable simply to inform the client, at the outset, of the specific scope of the attorney-client privilege. If subsequently the defense attorney, either implicitly or explicitly, reveals the defendant's proposed perjury, at least the client will not have been deceived into thinking that everything told to the lawyer was confidential.

NOTES

1. Lecture by Monroe H. Freedman, Criminal Trial Institute, Washington, D.C. (1966).

2. Freedman, "Professional Responsibility of the Criminal Defense Lawyer: The Three Hardest Questions," *Michigan Law Review* 64 (1966):1469. See this volume pp. 328-339.

3. M. Freedman, *Lawyers Ethics in an Adversary System* (1975), pp. 27-42 [hereinafter cited as Freedman]. Substantially the same material from Professor Freedman's book is reprinted in Freedman, "Perjury: The Lawyer's Trilemma," *Litigation* 1 (1975):26.

4. For the ABA's defense function standards, see ABA, *Standards Relating to the Defense Function* (Approved Draft 1971) [hereinafter cited as *ABA Defense Function Standards*]. The ABA has received approximately $160,000 from the Law Enforcement Assistance Administration to review its 18 volumes of criminal justice standards. ABA Press Release (July 2, 1977) (on file at the office of the *Hofstra Law Review*.). The project is under the auspices of the ABA's Special Committee on the Administration of Criminal Justice. *Id.*

5. *ABA Defense Function Standards, supra* note 4. § 7.7. For the text of § 7.7, see note 39 *infra.*

6. See Sevilla, "Between Scylla and Charybdis: The Ethical Perils of the Criminal Defense Lawyer," *National Journal of Criminal Defense* 2 (1976): 237, 262.

7. *ABA Code of Professional Responsibility* DR 7-102(B)(1) (1976) [hereinafter cited as ABA Code]. More fully, DR 7-102(B)(1) states:

A lawyer who receives information clearly establishing that:

His client has, in the course of the representation, perpetrted a fraud upon a person or tribunal shall promptly call upon his client to rectify the same, and if his client refuses or is unable to do so, he shall reveal the fraud to the affected person or tribunal, except when the information is protected as a privileged communication.

Id. (footnotes omitted). *Id.* DR 4-101(C) (footnotes omitted) specifies privileged information which a lawyer "may reveal":

(1) Confidences or secrets with the consent of the client or clients affected, but only after a full disclosure to them.

(2) Confidences or secrets when permitted under Disciplinary Rules or required by law or court order.

(3) The intention of his client to commit a crime and the information necessary to prevent the crime.

(4) Confidences or secrets necessary to establish or collect his fee or to defend himself or his employees or associates against an accusation of wrongful conduct.

For a discussion of DR 4-101(C)(3), see text accompanying notes 23 & 24 *infra.*

8. See ABA Committee on Ethics and Professional Responsibility, *Formal Opinions No. 341* (1975) [hereinafter cited as Formal Opinions]. The definition of "confidences" and "secrets" is contained in ABA Code, *supra* note 7, DR 4-101(A): "'Confidence' refers to information protected by the attorney-client privilege under applicable law, and 'secret' refers to other information gained in the professional relationship that the client has requested be held inviolate or the disclosure of which would be embarrassing or would be likely to be detrimental to the client." The amendment to DR 7-102(B)(1), *ABA Formal Opinions No. 341,* and the duty generally of attorneys to preserve confidences of clients relating to past crimes is discussed in Callan & David, "Professional Responsibility and the Duty of Confidentiality: Disclosure of Client Misconduct in an Adversary System," *Rutgers Law Review* 29 (1976):332, 356-365. Counsel's duty to protect confidences related to past crimes also has been stated in ABA Committee on Ethics and Professional Responsibility, *Informal Opinons No. 1314* (1975) (emphasis added) [hereinafter cited as Informal Opinions]:

[*The attorney*], *pursuant to the provisions of DR 7-102(B), has the primary duty to protect the confidentiality of any privileged communication from his client.* Subject, however, to affording the client proper protection on the basis of any privileged communication, the lawyer does have the obligation to call upon his client to rectify the fraud; and if the client refuses or is unable to do so, the lawyer may withdraw at that point from further representation of the client. See DR 2-110(C). *In other words, the confidential privilege, in our opinion, must be upheld over any obligation of the lawyer to betray the client's confidence in seeking rectification of any fraud that may have been perpetrated by his client upon a person or tribunal.*

9. The analysis in this article is based on the assumption that a lawyer confronted with a client's intent to commit perjury is bound by the *ABA Code of Professional Responsibility* (the Code). However, in 1977 a special committee of the ABA was appointed to evaluate the professional standards and to make recommendations concerning a new Code of Professional Responsibility. If a new code were to authorize a lawyer to reveal the past frauds of his client, contrary to ABA Code, *supra* note 7, DR 7-102(B)(1), a different approach would be available to

lawyers for handling the client-perjury problem. For a discussion of the desirability of permitting attorneys to preserve the confidences of clients related to past and continuing wrongs, see Callan & David, *supra* note 8.

10. Federal law provides: "Whoever procures another to commit any perjury is guilty of subornation of perjury . . . ." 18 U.S.C. § 1622 (1976). Similarly, the definitions of subornation of perjury contained in *Corpus Juris Secundum* states:

[S]ubornation of perjury consists in procuring or instigating another to commit the crime of perjury . . . . .

. . . . .

It is essential to subornation of perjury that the suborner should have known or believed or have good reason to believe that the testimony given would be false; that he should have known or believed that the witness would testify willfully and corruptly and with knowledge of the falsity; *and that he should have knowingly and willfully induced or procured the witness to give such false testimony.* 70 C.J.S. *Perjury* § 79 (1951) (emphasis added) (footnotes omitted). For decisions consistent with this definition, see Petite v. United States, 262 F.2d 788, 796 (4th Cir. 1959), *rev'd on other grounds,* 361 U.S. 529 (1960); People v. Jones, 254 Cal. App. 2d 200, 217, 62 Cal. Rptr. 304, 316 (4th Dist. 1967), *cert. denied,* 390 U.S. 980 (1968); State v. Lucas, 244 N.C. 53, 54, 92 S.E.2d 401, 403 (1956). The defense attorney who strongly believes that the client is lying obviously cannot be said to have "procured" or "instigated" the false testimony. Similarly, the crime of subornation of perjury is not committed even when the defendant testifies falsely and the attorney is aware of the false testimony, particularly if the attorney sought to dissuade the client from lying on the witness stand.

11. *ABA Defense Function Standards, supra* note 4, § 7.7, Commentary: "The existence of this dilemma [where the client proposes to commit perjury] is predicated upon the defendant's admitting inculpatory facts to his lawyer which are corroborated by the lawyer's own investigation. So long as the defendant maintains his innocence, the lawyer's realistic appraisal that he is in fact guilty does not preclude a vigorous defense."

12. ABA Code, *supra* note, DR 7-102(A)(4) (footnote omitted), provides that "a lawyer shall not . . . [k]nowingly use perjured testimony or false evidence." A definition of "knowingly" is not contained in the Code; however, in criminal statutes the word is normally defined as including both actual knowledge and a belief in the "high probability" of the existence of certain facts. Thus, Model Penal Code § 2.02(7) (Proposed Official Draft 1962) provides: "When knowledge of the existence of a particular fact is an element of an offense, such knowledge is established if a person is aware of a high probability of its existence, unless he actually believes that it does not exist." For criminal cases which interpret "knowingly" similarly, see Leary v. United States, 395 U.S. 6, 46 (1969); United States v. Jewell, 532 F.2d 697, 702 (9th Cir.), *cert. denied,* 426 U.S. 951 (1976); United States v. Sarantos, 455 F.2d 877, 881 (2d Cir. 1972). While it could therefore be argued that an attorney violates DR 7-102(A)(4) when he uses the defendant's testimony with strong reason to believe that it is false, such an interpretation would seriously disrupt attorney-client relations and the practice of criminal law. Probably for these reasons, there is apparently no specific authority for the proposition that the Code is, in fact, violated when counsel permits the defendent to testify to matters *believed* to be false.

13. *See ABA Defense Function Standards, supra* note 4, § 7.7(a). This article also discusses the closely related problem of the defendant who wishes to commit perjury but who does not admit that he is guilty, see note 84 *infra* and accompanying text. See also Annotation 64 A.L.R. 3d 385 (1975).

14. I did not divulge to the new attorney what the client had told me. This was consistent with Formal Opinions, *supra* note 8, No. 268 (1945):

It is not infrequently the case that a lawyer who has been retained by a client accused of crime, having been told by the client facts which make it certain that the client is guilty, declines to represent the defendant, insomuch as a successful defense cannot be hoped for without suborning perjury under such circumstances. In such case, the lawyer is bound by the Canon not to disclose the information received from the client in confidence, though he ascertains that the client, having subsequently retained another lawyer, has, in his defense, stated the facts to be otherwise.

15. It would not have been proper, under any circumstances, to have allowed the girl friend to present perjured testimony. The duty of the criminal defense lawyer to to use false testimony of persons other than the defendant is well-established. See, e.g., Herbert v. United States, 340 A.2d 802, 804 (D.C. 1975); People v. Pike, 58 Cal. 2d 70, 96, 372 P.2d 656, 672, 22 Cal. Rptr. 664, 680 (1962). Although Professor Freedman concedes that there is an "important distinction" between collateral witnesses and the defendant when it comes to perjury, he appears to suggest that defense counsel should use the perjured testimony of members of the defendant's immediate family:

> Certainly a spouse or parent [who sought to commit perjury] would be acting under the same human compulsion as a defendant, and I find it difficult to imagine myself denouncing my client's spouse or parent as a perjurer and, thereby, denouncing my client as well. I do not know, however, how much wider the circle of close identity might be drawn.

Freedman, *supra* note 3, at p. 32.

16. Freedman, *supra* note 3, at p. 31.

17. *Id.* at pp. 27-28.

18. *Id.* Professor Freedman refers, for example, to the "'sacred trust' of confidentiality [which] must 'upon all occasions be inviolable.'" *Id.* at p. 5 (citing Address by Chief Justice Burger, Opening Session, American Law Institute [May 18, 1971], reprinted in 52 F.R.D. 211, 212-214 (1971). Elsewhere, Professor Freedman claims that the "lawyer must hold in strictest confidence the disclosures made by the client in the course of the professional relationship." *Id.* at p. 27.

19. *Id.*

20. It has been agreed from the beginning that the attorney-client privilege cannot avail to protect the client in concerting with the attorney a *crime* or other evil enterprise. This is for the logically sufficient reason that no such enterprise falls within the just scope of the relation between legal adviser and client. J. Wigmore, *Evidence* 8 (McNaughton rev. 1961), § 2298 at p. 572.

21. C. McCormick, *Evidence* § 95 (2d ed. 1972), at p. 199 (footnote omitted).

22. 229 F.2d 805 (7th Cir. 1956).

23. ABA Code, *supra* note 7, DR 4-101(C)(3) (footnotes omitted).

24. Compare ABA Code, *supra* note 7, DR 4-101(C)(3) with *id.* DR 4-101(C)(1)-(2),(4).

25. Professor Freedman recognizes that there is a "major exception to the strict rule of confidentiality" for the client's intent to commit a crime. Freedman, *supra* note 3, at p. 6. Elsewhere, however, Professor Freedman describes the duty of confidentiality in such broad terms as to suggest that a client's intent to commit perjury is fully entitled to protection. See note 18 *supra* and accompanying text. For criticism of Professor Freedman's view of the attorney-client privilege as overly broad, see Rotunda, Book Review, *Harvard Law Review* 89 (1976):622. Professor Freedman also argues that for counsel to seek to withdraw from the case is tantamount to informing the court that the client has admitted his guilt to the lawyer. Freedman, *supra* note 3, at p. 34. For a discussion of this argument, see notes 82-86 *infra* and accompanying text.

26. ABA Code, *supra* note 7, DR 7-102(A)(4) (footnote omitted). The Code also declares that a lawyer shall not "[p]articipate in the creation or preservation of evidence when he knows or it is obvious that the evidence is false," *id.* DR 7-102(A)(6), and shall not "[c]ounsel or assist his client in conduct that the lawyer knows to be illegal or fradulent," *id.* DR 7-102(A)(7). The Code has been substantially adopted in all states except California. See Callan & David, *supra* note 8, at p. 352.

27. See e.g., *In re* Carroll, 244 S.W.2d 474 (Ky. 1951) (per curiam) (attorney disciplined for knowingly allowing client to testify falsely). The disciplinary rules of the Code are "mandatory in

character" and "state the minimum level of conduct below which no lawyer can fall without being subject to disciplinary action." ABA Code, *supra* note 7, Preliminary Statement.

28. For a discussion of the meaning of "knowingly," see note 12 *supra.*

29. Professor Freedman's only specific response to the Code's prohibition against the use of perjury is contained in four sentences. Referring to what he concedes to be, "at first reading," the apparently "unambiguous" obligation not to use perjured testimony, Professor Freedman replies:

> The difficulty, however, is that the Code does not indicate how the lawyer is to go about fulfilling that obligation. What if the lawyer advises the client that perjury is unlawful and, perhaps, bad tactics as well, but the client nevertheless insists upon taking the stand and committing perjury in his or her own defense? What steps, specifically, should the lawyer take? Just how difficult it is to answer that question becomes apparent if we review the relationship between lawyer and client as it develops, and consider the contexts in which the decision to commit perjury that may arise.

Freedman, *supra* note 3, at p. 29.

30. Consider the strong language in "Introduction" to *ABA Defense Function Standards, supra* note 4, at p. 142:

> It has even been suggested, but universally rejected by the legal profession, that a lawyer may be excused for acquiescing in the use of known perjured testimony on the transparently spurious thesis that the principle of confidentiality requires this. While no honorable lawyer would accept this notion and every experienced advocate can see its basic fallacy as a matter of tactics apart from morality and law, the mere advocacy of such fraud demeans the profession and tends to drag it to the level of gangsters and their "mouth-piece" lawyers in the public eye. That this concept is universally repudiated by ethical lawyers does not fully repair the gross disservice done by the few unscrupulous enough to practice it.

See also Dash, "The Emerging Role and Function of the Criminal Defense Lawyer," *North Carolina Law Review* 47 (1969):598, 630-632.

31. See *ABA Defense Function Standards, supra* note 4, § 7.7(b). For the text of this provision, see note 39 *infra.*

32. Freedman, *supra* note 3, at p. 33. The first attorney, morever, is not authorized to reveal the client's proposed perjury to the second attorney. See Formal Opinions, supra note 8, No. 268 (1945).

33. There is some evidence that practicing attorneys favor Professor Freedman's approach. In 1972, a second-year Georgetown University law student sent questionnaires to 135 lawyers in Washington, D.C., in which he asked questions about ethics. One question was what the attorney would do if, during a criminal trial, the client whom the lawyer knew was going to perjure himself insisted upon taking the witness stand. Ninety-five percent said they would call the defendant; three percent said they would not; and two percent said that they would seek leave to withdraw. A majority of the attorneys also said that they would elicit the testimony from the defendant in a normal fashion and argue the defendant's perjured testimony to the jury. See Friedman, "Professional Responsibility in D.C.: A Survey," *Res Ipsa Loquitur* 25 (1972):60. A somewhat similar questionnaire was sent to attorneys in Chicago several years earlier. There, 58 percent of the lawyers surveyed disapproved of the attorney in a criminal case allowing the defendant to present perjured testimony. However, of the attorneys from small firms, 52 percent approved of permitting the defendant to perjure himself, whereas only 12 percent of the attorneys from large firms approved of the practice. See Reichstein, "The Criminal Law Practitioner's Dilemma: What Should the Lawyer Do When His Client Intends to Testify Falsely?" *Journal of Criminal Law, Criminology & Political Science* 61 (1970):1, 7 n. 74.

34. Bowman, "Standards of Conduct for Prosecution and Defense Personnel: An Attorney's Viewpoint," *American Criminal Law Quarterly* 5 (1966):28, 30.

35. Gold, "Split Loyalty: An Ethical Problem for the Criminal Defense Lawyer," *Cleveland-Marshall Law Review* 14 (1965):65, 71. Two recent articles also have discussed the client-perjury

dilemma. See Polster, "The Dilemma of the Perjurious Defendant: Resolution, Not Avoidance," *Case Western Reserve Law Review* 28 (1977):3. Wolfram, "Client Perjury," *Southern California Law Review* 50 (1977):809. In the first of these articles, the author suggests that the client's proposed perjury be handled in much the same manner urged in this discussion. Compare Polster, *supra* at pp. 34-37 with text accompanying notes 92-104 *infra*. The second article suggests that counsel inform the court of the client's perjury. Wolfram, *supra* at p. 853.

36. Levine, "Struggling with Ethical Standards in Massachusetts," *Litigation* 3 (1976):43, 50.

37. See *Id.*

38. Telephone conversation with Levine (July 13, 1977) (author of article cited note 36 *supra*).

39. *ABA Defense Function Standards, supra* note 4, § 7.7 provides:

(a) If the defendant has admitted to his lawyer facts which establish guilt and the lawyer's independent investigation establishes that the admissions are true but the defendant insists on his right to trial, the lawyer must advise his client against taking the witness stand to testify falsely.

(b) If, before trial, the defendant insists that he will take the stand to testify falsely, the lawyer must withdraw from the case, if that is feasible, seeking leave of the court if necessary.

(c) If withdrawal from the case is not feasible or is not permitted by the court, or if the situation arises during the trial and the defendant insists upon testifying falsely in his own behalf, the lawyer may not lend his aid to the perjury. Before the defendant takes the stand in these circumstances, the lawyer should make a record of the fact that the defendant is taking the stand against the advice of counsel in some appropriate manner without reavealing the fact to the court. The lawyer must confine his examination to the identifying witness as the defendant and permitting him to make his statement to the trier or the triers of the facts; the lawyer may engage in direct examination of the defendant as a witness in the conventional manner and may not later argue the defendant's known false version of facts to the jury as worthy of belief and he may not recite or rely upon the false testimony in his closing argument.

40. Paragraph (b) of § 7.7, which deals with the duty of a lawyer to withdraw, is silent on whether the attorney should tell the court his reason for seeking to do so. *Id.* § 7.7(b). However, paragraph (c), which pertains to the lawyer's duty if the motion to withdraw is denied, states that the defendant should be allowed to take the stand, but that a record of the circumstances should be made by counsel without the court being advised. *Id* § 7.7(c). It follows, therefore, that counsel is not to tell the court his reason for wishing to withdraw; otherwise, there would be no point in stating that the court is not to be advised of the circumstances relating to the defendant's taking the stand. For the text f § 7.7 see note 39 *supra*.

41. The court is not to be advised of the record which is made by counsel. See note 40 *supra*. For the text of § 7.7(c), see note 39 *supra*. The Commentary to § 7.7(c) suggests that the "record" may be made, "for example, by having the defendant subscribe to a file notation, witnessed, if possible, by another lawyer," *ABA Defense Function Standards, supra* note 4, § 7.7, Commentary.

42. ABA Code, *supra* note 7, DR 7-102(A)(4) (footnote omitted).

43. *Id.* DR 7-102(A)(7).

44. Burger, "Standards of Conduct for Prosecution and Defense Personnel: A Judge's Viewpoint," *American Criminal Law Quarterly* 5 (1966):11, 13.

45. Freedman, *supra* note 3 at p. 37.

46. R. Keeton, *Trial Tactics and Methods* 185 (2d ed. 1973).

47. Normally, the decision to permit testimony in narrative form rather than by question and answer is said to be committed to the sound direction of the trial court. Compare Faust v. State, 319 N.E.2d 146 (Ind. Ct. App. 1st Dist. 1974) (trial court held not to have committed error in allowing complaining witness to testify in narrative form) with Deams v. State, 265 S.W.2d 96 (Tex. Crim. App. 1953) (trial court held not to have committed error in denying defendant opportunity to testify in narrative form.)

48. See text accomanying notes 57-81 *infra.*
49. For cases in which § 7.7 of the *ABA Defense Function Standards* is mentioned, but in which proposed perjury of the client was not clearly at issue, see People v. McCalvin, 55 Ill, 2d 161, 302 N.E.2d 342 (1973); People v. Brown, 54 Ill. 2d 21, 294 N.E.2d 285 (1973).
50. Ill Ariz. 26, 523 P.2d 54 (1974).
51. *Id.* Technically, State v. Lowery, *id.,* did not involve a situation where counsel should have sought to withdraw pursuant to § 7.7. Defense counsel in *Lowery* appears to have been unaware that the client intended to testify falsely, learning of the false testimony only while the client was speaking from the witness stand. Hence, the client already had committed the crime of perjury, without advance knowledge of counsel, and counsel therefore would seem to have been duty-bound to preseve the client's confidence regarding the crime just committed. See ABA Code, *supra* note 7, DR 7-102(B)(1). Moreover, the *ABA Defense Function Standards* do not envision counsel's withdrawal from the case "if the situation arises during the trial and the defendant insists upon testifying falsely in his own behalf . . . ." *ABA Defense Function Standards, supra* note 4, § 7.7(c).
52. 357 A.2d 429 (D.C.), *cert. denied,* 429 U.S. 1024 (1976).
53. *Id.* at p. 432 (footnote omitted).
54. *Id.*
55. *Id.* at p. 435.
56. *Id.* at p. 435 n.9. The appellate court explained the propriety of the second court's denial of counsel's motion to withdraw, stating:

> Having been given no explanation for trial counsel's request to withdraw, the second trial judge saw no justification for granting it. Defense counsel indicated his lengthy association with the case and his extensive contact with appellant. He also informed the court that he was retained, rather than appointed, counsel. Forced to decide defense counsel's motion on less than an adequate basis, the court's denial of the motion was reasonable.

Id. The second trial court's approach, affirmed by the appellate court in *Thorton,* indicates that the recommendation of § 7.7 that counsel seek to withdraw when the client wishes to present perjury is totally unworkable; the reason for counsel's motion to withdraw is not supposed to be revealed to the court, see note 40 *supra.*
57. *ABA Defense Function Standards, supra* note 4, § 7.7, Commentary.
58. Informal Opinions, *supra* note 8, No. 1314 (1975).
59. *Id.* The few opinions of state bar ethics committees on client-perjury are consistent with the ABA ruling. Thus, the Florida bar grievance department has stated that an attorney must seek to dissuade the defendant from committing perjury and, if this fails, withdraw from the case. See Quiz, "What is Your Ethics Rating?" *Florida Bar Journal* 50 (1976):157, 158. Further, the grievance department suggests that the attorney "must take steps to prevent [the perjury] or to inform the court of its occurrence." *Id.* For criticism of the grievance department's position, see Glazer, "What Are Limits of Lawyer's Professional Conduct in Defending a Client?" *Florida Bar Journal* 50 (1976):332. See also New Jersey Asvisory Committee on professional Ethics, "Opinions, No. 116," *New Jersey Law Journal* 90 (1976):688.
60. 205 Kan. 231, 468 P.2d 136 (1970).
61. 290 N.C. 56, 224 S.E.2d 174 (1976).
62. State v. Henderson, 205 Kan. 231, 238, 468 P.2d 136, 140-141 (1970); State v. Robinson, 290 N.C. 56, 66, 224 S.E.2d 174, 180 (1976).
63. State v. Henderson, 205 Kan. 231, 238, 468 P.2d 136, 140 (1970); State v. Robinson, 290 N.C. 56, 62, 224 S.E.2d 174, 177 (1976).
64. State v. Henderson, 205 Kan. 231, 238, 468 P.2d 136, 142 (1970).
65. State v. Robinson, 290 N.C. 56, 62, 224 S.E.2d 174, 177 (1976).
66. Freedman, *supra* note 3 at p. 31.
67. *ABA Defense Function Standards, supra* note 4 § 7.7, Commentary.
68. *Id.* (emphasis added).

69. Although courts recognize that a defendant should be allowed to testify in his own defense, disagreement exists as to whether there is a "right" or "privilege" to do so. Compare, e.g., United Stated v. Bentvena, 319 F.2d 916, 943 (2d Cir.),*cert. denied,* 375 U.S. 940 (1963) (defendant has "privilege" to testify in his own behalf) with Poe v. United States, 233 F. Supp. 173, 176 (D.D.C 1964), *aff'd,* 352 F.2d 639 (D.C. Cir. 1965) (defendant has "right" to testify on his own behalf). However, for a recent case holding that a defendant has a "right" to testify, see Wilcox v. Johnson, 555 F.2d 115 (3d Cir. 1977). Courts sometimes fail to make clear whether the source of the defendant's entitlement to testify rests on the due process clause, the right to counsel, the self-incrimination privilege, or the compulsory process clause. See Westen, "The Compulsory Process Clause," *Michigan Law Review* 73 (1974):71, 119. Regardless of the source of the defendant's "right" or "privilege" to testify, it is clear that the right is personal to the defendant. Thus, defense counsel cannot require that the defendant forego the opportunity to testify. See e.g., People v. Robles, 2 Cal. 3d 205, 214-215, 466 P.2d 710, 716, 85 Cal Reptr. 166, 172 (1970); Ingle v. State, 546 P.2d 598, 599 (Nev. 1976). This is consistent with the *ABA Defense Function Standards,* which provide that the decision whether to testify should be made by the accused. *ABA Defense Function Standards, supra* note 4, § 5.2(a).

70. 504 F.2d 935 (9th Cir. 1974).

71. *Id.* at p. 938.

72. *Id.* at pp. 943-944.

73. *Id.* at p. 941. See Illinois v. Allen, 397 U.S. 337 (1970). Similarly, the accused may be denied the right to conduct his own defense because of misconduct, Faretta v. California, 422 U.S. 806, 834 (1975). In announcing the constitutional right to self-representation, the Court stated:

> We are told that many criminal defendants representing themselves may use the courtroom for deliberate disruption of their trials. But the right of self-representation has been recognized from our beginnings by federal law and by most of the States, and no such result has thereby occurred. Moreover, the trial judge may terminate self-representation by a defendant who deliberately engages in serious and obstructionist misconduct.

Id. at p. 834 n.46 (citing Illinois v. Allen, 397 U.S. 337 (1970)). See also United States v. Dougherty, 473 F.2d 1113, 1124 (D.C. Cir. 1972).

74. 401 U.S. 222 (1971).

75. 384 U.S. 436 (1966).

76. Harris v. New York, 401 U.S. 222, 225 (1971) (citations omitted).

77. 431 U.S. 174 (1974).

78. See *id.* at p. 175.

79. See *id.* at pp. 175-176.

80. *Id.* (quoting Glickstein v. United States, 222 U.S. 139, 142 (1911)).

81. E.g., United States v. Knox, 396 U.S. 77 (1969) (perjurous information furnished on federal wagering tax return not justified even though return required to be filed and truthful answers would have incriminated defendant). See generally United States v. Mandujano, 425 U.S. 564 (1976).

82. Thus, in People v. Belge, 83 Misc. 2d 186, 372 N.Y.S. 2d 798 (Onondaga County Ct. 1975), where the client told his lawyers of the location of the bodies of two women the client had murdered, and attorneys personally verified the accuracy of the client's information, the attorneys still "were bound to . . . maintain what has been called a sacred trust of confidentiality." *Id.* at p. 190, 372 N.Y.S.2d at p. 802. No exception is contained in ABA Code, *supra* note 7, DR 4-101(C), for an attorney revealing a client's confidence or secret relating to a past crime. For the text of DR 4-101(C), see not 7 *supra.*

83. The recommendation contained in § 7.7 of the *ABA Defense Function Standards* may have been so new following its approval by the ABA in 1971 that the trial judges might not have recognized the procedure. Now that the ABA's suggestion is more than six years old, however, it seems likely that trial courts everywhere are familiar with it. Indeed, when an attorney moves to

withdraw from a criminal case without giving his reasons, the assumption usually is that he has withdrawn because the defendant wishes to commit perjury. For example, in Lessenberry v. Adkisson, 255 Ark. 285, 297, 499 S.W.2d 835, 841-842 (1973), the court observed:

> It is apparent from the full record before us, that . . . Mr. Lessenberry [, defense counsel,] had learned from the defendant matters fe was unwilling to reveal to the trial judge . . . . If Mr. Lessenberry was convinced of the defendant's guilt . . . , and if she was insisting that he prepare a fictitious defense in her behalf, he of course was correct in requesting that he be relieved as attorney of record . . . .

Similarly, in State v. Lowery, 111 Ariz. 26, 28, 523 P.2d 54, 56 (1974), the court stated:

> The defendant contends on appeal that by moving to withdraw . . . the attorney was indicating that to the court that the defendant was lying . . . .
> The record does not reflect the reason's why the defendant's attorney wished to withdraw, but we can surmise that he did not wish to assist the defendant in perjuring herself on the witness stand as the evidence strongly suggested she was doing when she denied that she shot the victim.

84. In writing about the client-perjury problem, Professor Freedman has advanced the hypothetical of the defendant charged with robbery who, though innocent of the offense, was accurately identified as being a block from the robbery five minutes before it occurred. The defendant, according to the hypothetical, wishes to commit perjury because he fears the jury will convict him if he admits he was in the vicinity of the robbery so near the time that it transpired. See Freedman, *supra* note 3, at pp. 30-31.

85. A similar development occurred in Thorton v. United States, 357 A.2d 429 (D.C.), *cert. denied*, 429 U.S. 1024 (1976). In *Thorton* the attorney moved to withdraw without disclosing his reasons. The trial court urged the attorney to be explicit about his reason for wanting to get out of the case. For further discussion of *Thorton*, see text accompanying notes 52-56 *supra*.

86. When the court asks a lawyer whether certain information is correct, and the lawyer's knowledge of the information is privileged, it has been suggested that counsel "ask the court to excuse him from answering the question . . . though this would doubtless put the court on further inquiry as to the truth." Formal Opinions, *supra* note 8, No. 287 (1953). This issue in Formal Opinion 287 was *inter alia*, whether an attorney is obligated to tell the court that his client has a prior criminal record when, at sentencing, the court asks defense counsel about the existence of a record and counsel's knowledge of the record is protected by the attorney-client privilege. *Id.*

87. There are numerous instances in which a district judge will be informed of the past deeds of a defendant before the trial. Facts can come to a judge's attention in pre-trial proceedings such as motions to suppress, reduction of bail, or for discovery. There is no rule that a trial judge must disqualify himself after presiding at these proceedings.

United States v. Montecalvo, 533 F.2d 1110, 1113-1114 (9th Cir. 1976) (Real, J., dissenting) (footnote omitted), *vacated on rehearing,* 545 F.2d 684 (9th Cir. 1976). The issue in *Montecalvo* was whether the trial judge was disqualified from presiding at the defendant's jury trial for bank robbery. Prior to the trial, at the request of the defense which contemplated that a guilty plea would be entered, the judge examined presentence materials concerning the defendant's background. The plea was never entered, however, and a trial ensued. On rehearing, the Ninth Circuit Court of Appeals held that it had been proper for the trial court to have read the presentence materials, particularly since defense counsel had invited the court to do so. United States v. Montecalvo, 545 F.2d 684 (9th Cir. 1976). For a discussion of disqualification of judges for reading presentence materials prior to trial, see note 90 *infra*.

88. 37 Mich. App. 175, 194 N.W.2d 528 (Ct. App. 1971).

89. *Id.* Obviously, if a judge is not disqualified from acting as factfinder in a bench trial, he would not be precluded from presiding at a jury trial, where the jury serves as the trier of fact. For a discussion of cases similar to *Britt*, see Note, "Improper Evidence in Nonjury Trials: Basis for Reversal?" *Harvard Law Review* 79 (1965):407. Contrary to *Britt* and similar holdings, Chief

Justice Burger has stated: "In a nonjury case the prior record of the accused should not be made known to the trier of fact except by way of traditional impeachment." Argersinger v. Hamlin, 407 U.S. 25, 42 n.* (1972) (Burger, C.J., concurring). See also People v. Ramsey, 385 Mich. 221, 187 N.W.2d 887 (1971) (conviction reversed where, during bench trial, judge "glanced" at transcript of preliminary hearing).

90. See United States v. Duhart, 496 F.2d 941, 945-946 (9th Cir. 1974); United States v. Small, 472 F.2d 818, 820-822 (3d Cir. 1972) (dictum); Webster v. United States, 330 F. Supp. 1080, 1086 (E.D. Va. 1971). *Contra,* United States v. Pruitt, 341 F.2d 700, 702 (4th Cir. 1965) (dictum). In Gregg v. United States, 394 U.S. 489 (1969), the Supreme Court in dictum suggested that district court judges should never examine a presentence report prior to presiding at a defendant's jury trial. *Id.* at p. 491. The Court explained that the purpose of rule 32 of the Federal Rules of Criminal Procedure, which then provided that the "report shall not be submitted to the court . . . unless the defendant has pleaded guilty . . . or has been found guilty," Fed. R. Crim. P. 32(c)(1) (amended 1974), was designed to prevent possible prejudice of the judge by exposing him to unfavorable information about the defendant. Gregg v. United States, 394 U.S. 489, 491-492 (1969). However, rule 32 was amended effective December 31, 1975, Federal Rules of Criminal Procedure Amendments Act of 1975, Pub. L. No. 94-64, § 32-33, 89 Stat. 370, to provide that a presentence report may be submitted to the court at any time with the written consent of the defendant. The foregoing cases indicate that lower federal courts have carved exceptions to the broad prohibition suggested in *Gregg.* For example in *Duhart,* the court held that the trial judge did not err when, prior to sentencing, he familiarized himself with a prison report relating to the defendant, since the document technically was not prepared as a presentence report pursuant to rule 32. See United States v. Duhart, 496 F.2d 941 (9th Cir. 1974).

91. See note 26 *supra* and accompanying text.

92. For text of § 7.7, see note 39 *supra.*

93. See text accompanying notes 50-56 *supra.*

94. See text accompanying notes 45-47 *supra.*

95. See text accompanying notes 82-86 *supra.*

96. Canadian Bar Association Code of Professional Conduct, (1974), ch.VIII, "Commentary," p. 9, (emphasis added).

97. See 1 A. Amsterdam, B. Segal, & M. Miller, *Trial Manual for the Defense of Criminal Cases* § 79, (1969), pp. 2-48.

> The client must be told very explicitly that cousel exects him to tell counsel the truth, the whole truth, and the exact truth; that failure to do so will hamstring presentation of the defense. If the client has done this thing, counsel has to know it. He will represent the client anyway (and should tell the client this), but he must know the truth. Admonition that counsel will learn the truth in court, together with the judge and jury, and that he cannot be prepared to meet it unless he knows it in advance, is helpful. Reminding a client that he, the defendant, will suffer the consequences of any wrong information helps to convince him of the necessity to be truthful.

98. *ABA Defense Function Standards, supra* note 4, § 3.1(a).

99. See Commentary to § 3.1, dealing with the desirability of the attorney-client privilege:

> Nothing is more fundamental to the lawyer-client relationship than the establishment of trust and confidence. Without it, the client may withhold essential information from the lawyer. The result may be that the case is prepared by counsel without important evidence that might have been obtained, that valuable defenses are neglected and, perhaps most significantly, that the lawyer is not forewarned of evidence which will be presented by the prosecution. It is to encourage candor and full disclosure that the obligation of confidentiality which surrounds the lawyer-client relation has been erected. The Canons of the American Bar Association reflect the ancient doctrine that a lawyer must preserve all confidences which relate to the representation of the accused.

ABA Defense Function Standards, supra note 4, § 3.1, Commentary.

100. See text accompanying notes 31 & 32 *supra.*

101. See text accompanying notes 50-56 *supra*.

102. Freedman, *supra* note 3, at p. 38.

103. There is one undeniable drawback to warning the accused that his proposed perjury is not protected by the attorney-client privilege. Counsel may lose the opportunity to dissuade some defendants from testifying falsely, because they will not have admitted to counsel that they are guilty. I regard this as a minimal problem, however, compared with the vexing dilemma confronted by counsel where the client admits his guilt, wants to commit perjury, and cannot be dissuaded from doing so. Moreover, it seems likely, though scarcely subject to proof, that the defendant who acknowledges his guilt to counsel and then proposes to commit perjury has given the matter considerable thought. Therefore, it may be exceedingly difficult to dissuade him from committing perjury. Certainly this was true in the case of Mr. X discussed earlier. See text accompanying notes 13 & 14 *supra*.

104. See text accompanying notes 82-86 *supra*.

105. See notes 7-9, *supra* and accompanying text.

Bruce M. Landesman

Confidentiality and the Lawyer-Client Relationship

The Model Rules of Professional Conduct proposed by the American Bar Association[1] differ from the presently enforced Code of Professional Responsibility[2] in a number of ways. This essay focuses on the differences with regard to the scope and limits of confidentiality in the lawyer-client relationship. In general, the Model Rules permit or require more disclosure of information learned by the lawyer in the course of the lawyer-client relationship than does the Code. In Section I, I describe the differences between the Rules and the Code in the area of confidentiality. Then in Sections II and III, I make some suggestions about the moral basis, complexity and limits of confidentiality. I focus in these sections on ordinary, nonprofessional contexts and consider not only confidentiality but the more general question of the moral appropriateness of passing on information about other people, whether it has been given in confidence or not. In Section IV, I look at various accounts of the scope of lawyer-client confidentiality and criticize some of the typical arguments given for the view that very little, if anything, should be disclosed by the lawyer. I therefore favor the greater disclosure provisions of the Model Rules, although not enough is said to allow me to deserve that conclusion. My tentativeness and the fact that much here is exploratory are calculated. The discussions of lawyer-client confidentiality of which I am aware do not go very deep.[3] In the hard cases in dispute there are valid competing interests at stake: those of the client, the court, the public, the truth, *etc.* Those who discuss this issue tend simply to weigh these interests differently, backing their weightings with arguments that do not meet each other.[4] I intend to avoid this pattern and to suggest some possible ways to move beyond it.

From *Utah Law Review* (1980):765-786. Reprinted by permission of the author.

I. CONFIDENTIALITY—THE MODEL RULES VS. THE CODE

This section considers the major differences between the Code and the Model Rules about confidentiality. These can be divided into four groups: (a) crimes and other misdeeds, (b) perjury, (c) misapprehensions and (d) corporate misconduct.

A. Crimes and Other Wrongful Acts

The Code says that a lawyer *may* reveal a client's intention to commit a crime, and the information necessary to prevent it.[5] According to the Model Rules, a lawyer *must* disclose information when necessary to prevent a client from causing death or serious bodily harm to another person.[6] The Model Rules, therefore, make disclosure of potential violent acts mandatory, while the Code only brings it within the scope of a lawyer's discretion. The Model Rules also permit (but do not require) a lawyer to reveal information necessary to prevent other deliberate wrongful acts,[7] where a "wrongful act" is defined as one that violates a civil or penal standard "in which knowledge of the circumstances is an element of the violation."[8] This broadens the area of discretion laid down by the Code, for the Code permits lawyers to reveal only crimes, while the Model Rules permit the disclosure of nonpenal violations as well. Depending upon how the Model Rules are interpreted, however, the discretion of the Rules may be in some ways more limited than that of the Code. The Model Rules restrict discretion to acts that involve knowledge on the part of the agent, and so exclude revealing strict liability offenses and possibly offenses involving negligence.[9]

No provisions of the Code even discuss disclosure of past crimes and wrongful acts—that is, acts other than the ones for which the lawyer is representing the client in the current case. Such disclosure is therefore prohibited by the general rule that a lawyer shall not knowingly reveal a confidence or secret of a client.[10] The Model Rules, by contrast, are presently unclear about disclosure of past acts. They do not address the issue explicitly, either in the rules or in the explanations. Yet, Rule 1.7(c)(2) provides that a lawyer may disclose information "to the extent it appears necessary to prevent or *rectify* the consequences of a deliberately wrongful act by the client."[11] If such an act has been done in the past, it might be rectified were the lawyer to notify the police or the injured parties that his client was the perpetrator. Accordingly, the Model Rules seem to permit disclosure of past misdeeds. It may be that drafters did not intend this interpretation, but meant the rule to apply only to the rectification of wrongs yet undone. If so, however, rule 1.7(c)(2) needs to be clarified; and if not, an explicit discussion of what the rule is meant to cover would be helpful.

B. Perjury

The Code is notoriously ambiguous about whether a lawyer should reveal client perjury. Disciplinary Rule 4-101(b) says that a lawyer shall not knowing reveal a client's secret or confidence, but the exceptions include revealing confidences or secrets "when permitted under Disciplinary Rules."[12] Disciplinary Rule 7-102(B)(10) provides that a lawyer receiving information clearly establishing that his client has perpetrated a fraud upon a person or tribunal must try to get the client to rectify it and must reveal the fraud himself "except when the information is protected as a priviledged communication." It is unclear whether the fraud rule is to be qualified in light of the confidence rule or vice versa. In other words, the Code leaves open whether confidences should not be revealed except when a fraud has been perpetrated, or whether a fraud may be revealed, but only when it does not reveal any confidences.[13] The latter interpretation seems more likely, but its effect is to nullify any serious duty to reveal perjury.[14] The Model Rules, on the other hand, unambiguously require a lawyer to reveal client perjury, not only in civil cases, but in criminal cases as well. The only exception is in criminal cases when applicable law requires the lawyer to comply with the client's demand to offer evidence, regardless of the lawyer's belief that the evidence is false.[15]

C. Misapprehensions

The Model Rules require a lawyer in an adversary proceeding to disclose a fact adverse to his client when necessary to correct a manifest misapprehension that resulted from the lawyer's previous representations to the court.[16] The exception to this parallels the exception regarding perjury: such disclosure may not be made in a criminal trial where applicable law prohibits it.[17] An example of such misapprehension is found in the well-known case of In re A,[18] where the client's testimony that his mother was "in Salem" was taken to imply that she was alive (therefore affecting the monetary aspects of a divorce settlement) when in fact she was buried in Salem cemetery. The Model Rules also require the disclosure of adverse facts during the negotiation in order to correct a misapprenhension resulting from the lawyer's or client's remarks.[19] Again, the exception is that disclosure of a misrepresentation made by the defendant is "not required" in negotiations relating to criminal cases.[20] No duty to correct misapprehensions in either adversary proceedings or negotiations appears in the Code and thus would seem to be ruled out, at least whenever correction would disclose confidences or secrets.[21] The duty in the Code to rectify a fraud upon a person or tribunal[22] could be interpreted to require correcting misapprehensions, but doing so stretches the term "fraud," and, in any case, is allowed only in limited circumstances.[23]

D. Corporate Misconduct

Both the Code and the Model Rules assert that lawyer representing an organization or corporation has as client the organization and not its officers or directors.[24] The Model Rules add that when the lawyer knows that a member of an organization or corporation is engaged in or intends to engage in an act that is illegal and likely to result in significant harm to the organization, the lawyer must take steps *within* the organization to prevent the harm.[25] Further, if the highest authority within the corporation refuses to act, and the action is a clear violation of law and likely to substantially injure the organization, the lawyer may take remedial action outside the organization. Such a step is likely to involve the disclosure of information gained from corporate officers and employees.[26] The Code says nothing explicit about these matters. Nevertheless, the clause in the Code that permits a lawyer to reveal his client's intention to commit a crime[27] would seem to imply a discretion to reveal corporate crimes as well. Nothing in the Code, however, mandates efforts internal to the corporation to prevent or stop the crime. So the Model Rules do go beyond the Code: the requirement of internal action is new and the explicit discretion to reveal a crime outside the corporation gives more solid support than the Code now provides to the lawyer who does so.[28]

In sum, with respect to future crimes and other wrongful conduct, perjury, misapprehensions, corporate misconduct and perhaps with respect to past misdeeds, the Model Rules permit or require more disclosure of otherwise confidential information on legal evaluations prepared for third parties provided the client has agreed to the disclosure of facts that are necessary for fair, accurate evaluation,[29] while the Code simply does not consider this matter. There may be other differences, but these are the major ones.

II. THE USE AND MISUSE OF PERSONAL INFORMATION

What should we think about these liberalized disclosure provisions of the Model Rules? Are they reasonable, in accord with sound moral requirements and consistent with the necessities of an adversary system of justice? Do they express a fair balance among a lawyer's duties to his clients, to other persons and to the demands of his own moral personality? Or do they go too far, requiring or permitting conduct of the lawyer that is either unethical or destructive to the system of justice or both? It has been recently asserted that the Model Rules would "erode basic constitutional protection by making the lawyer an agent of the state"[30] and would deprive troubled individuals of a needed confessional by making the lawyer's office "a listening post for the state."[31] Furthermore, it might be charged that the Model Rules are based on the view that the end of finding out the truth in a case justifies the means. Can such charges be supported or refuted?

In order to progress toward answering these questions, it is helpful to understand confidentiality more fully, independent of professional contexts. We want to understand the moral grounds for not disclosing confidential information and the moral limits to such disclosure. To this end, I will often consider the situation in which a person discloses to a second person information about himself. We shall call the first person the *speaker*, the second person the *hearer* and the sort of information conveyed *personal information*. Should the hearer disclose the information to a third person, that person is termed a *listener*. When is it and when is it not morally acceptable for a hearer to convey personal information learned from a speaker to a listener? In general, how morally free is the hearer to make use of that information by disclosure?[32]

To answer these questions, it is helpful to draw a basic distinction between those contexts in which the speaker conveys the information with an understanding that it will be kept confidential and those in which there is no such understanding. Surely this difference strongly affects the moral freedom to disclose the information. This difference, however, is not as strong as might initially appear. Within the context in which the information is understood to be confidential, there are two kinds of cases. In one case, confidentiality is explicit because the speaker has asked for and received a promise from the hearer that the information will not be passed on. In the second case, confidentiality is implicit; no express promise of confidentiality is given, but because of the nature of the information or the relationship between the parties, there is an unspoken understanding that the information is not to be transferred. The basic distinction between contexts in which information is explicitly or implicitly understood to be confidential and those in which it is not is an important one, although it must realized that the difference is not a sharp difference in kind, with quite different moral implications, but a matter of degree.

To see that the difference is not sharp, we might note first that information conveyed by a speaker could be used by a hearer to harm or embarrass the speaker, interfere with the speaker's interests, thwart the speaker's and others' plans, and upset or disturb or even harm other parties. There will often, therefore, be strong moral reasons for not disclosing information even if it has not been delivered with an explicit promise of confidentiality. Second, the revelation of damaging personal information frequently carries with it an implicit understanding that the hearer keep the information confidential, unless the speaker in some way cancels or rejects this understanding. Such information is not to be passed on unless the speaker releases the hearer from an obligation not to pass it on.[33] The reason for this has to do with the underlying moral basis for confidentiality, discussed in more detail below: roughly, because the basis for confidentiality is that speakers need to express damaging information without losing control over its use, such information is typically given out with a tacit understanding that it will not be further disclosed. We respect confidentiality because of a moral requirement to respect both this understanding and the needs that underlie it. Any explicit promise to keep information confidential provides an additional moral consideration reinforcing the obligation of confidentiality, but promise-keeping of this sort is not the basic reason for the obligation. Indeed, in many cases, the request for a promise to keep something confidential is simply a way for the speaker to make sure that the tacit understanding really exists, to produce it in ambiguous contexts, or to remind the hearer of its presence.[34] Some of these claims need refinement and qualification but their plausibility is enough to support the main point: that confidentiality is not the only reason for being careful with personal information, but a reason that appears somewhat ubiquitously in many kinds of cases involving the communication of damaging or "negative" personal information.

For these reasons, the distinction between contexts in which information is understood implicitly or explicitly to be confidential and contexts in which it is not will give us only part of the basis for knowing how to use and treat personal information. In fact, I suggest that we all accept and are more or less governed by a fairly subtle, complex and imprecise set of principles concerning what we may and may not do, by way of disclosure, with personal information conveyed to us by others. How we should use such information will be a function of a variety of factors such as the nature of the information revealed, the speaker's expectations concerning confidentiality, the consequences of disclosure, the hearer's relationship to the speaker and the potential listener, the speaker's relationship to the listener, and the likelihood that the listener will or will not in turn keep the information confidential or restrict its use in appropriate ways. As an illustration, consider a case in which a speaker imparts to a hearer some embarrassing personal information without explicitly asking that the information be kept secret. To whom might the hearer reveal the information? It would surely be incorrect to give as a general answer for every case that it might be revealed to anyone or to no one. Much will depend on the factors just listed. Very likely, it would be wrong for the hearer to disclose the information to a listener who would use it to embarrass or harm the speaker. Even if the information is not used detrimentally, or in any way at all, telling others might constitute an unjustified invasion of the speaker's privacy simply because others know the embarrassing fact.

Consider now imparting the information to a hearer who is a friend of and cares for the speaker, and one who could use the information in a way helpful to him. The appropriateness of disclosure to such a listener will depend on a number of factors: whether the friend really can help, whether the speaker would welcome the help, whether the speaker really wants (without admitting it) the information to be spread around, whether the information is as embarrassing as the speaker perceives it to be, whether the listener can be trusted to use the information appropriately, *etc.* What the hearer does will raise difficult questions about when and how to help others, when to respect their autonomy and privacy, and when to intervene paternalistically—that is, for another's good, independent of or against his wishes.

Suppose, however, that the information is really not as embarrassing as the speaker supposes; his friends are not surprised to hear of it and perhaps even cherish it as interesting foibles or character traits. Would it be wrong for the hearer to reveal it, even gossip about it, at a gathering of some of the speaker's friends? Revelation is at least a minor indiscretion, perhaps a hint of betrayal. But clearly we are all quite interested in other people and gossip in this way; people seem too easily embarrassed, and no real harm is done, *etc.* And what about the propriety of a hearer revealing even genuinely embarrassing information to his spouse or the person with whom he shares his life? I suspect that people are not expected to keep certain sorts of information from the person with whom they are accustomed to sharing both their lives and all sorts of information. So it may be acceptable to tell certain things to one's mate that may not be told to anyone else, unless one's mate cannot keep a secret.

Let me mention one final pair of cases. Suppose the speaker reveals genuinely embarrassing personal information and extracts a promise of secrecy from the hearer. Suppose further that the speaker is the sort of person who rarely reveals such personal information and the hearer knows this. In many such cases, it may seem seriously wrong to tell even a spouse and friends, although there are obviously cases in which it would be justified. Contrast this situation, however, with a case in which the speaker is the sort of person who characteristically informs one and all of personal information others tend to guard more carefully. Then an obligation to keep the information secret or confidential may be lessened or disappear, even if a promise of confidentiality is extracted.

How one may treat personal information conveyed by another is thus a complex matter to which many different considerations are relevant. I make this point in order to put confidentiality in a broader context. The obligation of confidentiality grows out of the ordinary communication of personal information; questions concerning it are part of questions concerning the use in general of information imparted by others. Setting confidentiality against a broader background will give us a better chance of understanding the obligation, a task to which I now turn.

III. CONFIDENTIALITY IN GENERAL

Confidentiality—the speaker's revelation of information with the explicit or implicit understanding that it will not be disclosed further—can be "attached" to many different sorts of information. I have restricted the discussion to personal information, that is, information about one's self. Other sorts of information might be kept confidential, but I am not dealing here with the questions these raise. I would now like to distinguish several different categories of confidential information and then turn to the basic reasons for confidentiality.

The first sort of information I shall call *embarrassing* information: by this I mean information that simply embarrasses or shames the speaker. Embarrassing information need not involve wrongful or illegal acts. From this, we can distinguish what I shall call *guilty* information: the information that the speaker has done something wrong which, if imparted to the appropriate listener, would cause the speaker to be sanctioned by formal punishment or by informal blame, disapproval, chastisement, *etc.* Information about a speaker's crime, a speaker's betrayal, or a child's mischievousness would all come within this category. Next, there is what could be called *dangerous* information. This is information that the speaker intends to commit some harm, injury or other damage to the interests of a third party. A fourth category I shall call *detrimental* information, which is information that could be used by a listener to bring harm to the speaker. Information that is embarrassing, guilty or dangerous might fall into this class, but information that is none of these may also be included: *e.g.,* the whereabouts of a rich man's child conveyed to a would-be kidnapper. A fifth category of information I shall call *planning* information—information about a speaker's plans, intentions, projects or purposes. The key reason for confidentiality here would be that revealing such information might cause the speaker's plans to be thwarted (or helped) by others. The sixth and last category of information I call simply *positive* information, which is information involving good or indifferent facts about a person. Such information could not be embarrassing, guilty or dangerous, but it could be detrimental or planning.

These categories are not meant to be exhaustive or exclusive, but only a good rough classification for the purposes of understanding the limits of confidentiality. I shall argue that the moral force of the obligation of confidentiality will differ with respect to these different types of information, after making clearer a certain conflict which I take to be inherent in confidentiality.

A person may reveal embarrassing, guilty or dangerous information to another person for a number of reasons. He may wish advice, seek sympathy, desire the human response of another person, need to express what is on his mind, to confess or admit or just to share his knowledge and feelings. Of course, there are other possible motivations, such as enlisting the hearer as a confederate, but the main point is that the speaker wishes both to retain the privacy of the information and at the same time to express it to someone else. Confidentiality is the device for doing this.

This dual nature of confidentiality can be understood in a somewhat metaphorical way: when a speaker delivers information in confidence, the speaker attempts to make the hearer a part of his own self, his "extended self," with respect to the information revealed. He needs the hearer to be another person, another "ear" and mind who can register his information and respond to it; "revealing" a confidence to a wall or a dog is no substitute for telling a person. At the same time, he needs the hearer not to be another person, but to be a part of his own self so that the information will not be used except as he chooses. Dropping the metaphorical notion of an extended self, the idea is that with respect to the piece of information revealed, the hearer is not free to use it as an autonomous moral agent. The information, in effect, still "belongs" to the speaker who would not have "lent" it unless he knew he could retain control of it. I suggest that both the speaker and hearer in a situation in which information is imparted in confidence perceive the situation this way, or at least realize that this is how it is supposed to be perceived.[35]

The situation of the hearer just presented is morally difficult, characterized by inevitable moral conflict. On the one hand, the hearer has given up moral autonomy with respect to a certain piece of information. On the other hand, the hearer still remains an autonomous moral agent with the capacity for moral deliberation and choice. Morally speaking, his autonomy with respect to the information received cannot be given up, or be fully given up. He remains a moral being and thus free to deliberate about what to do with the information once he has received it. The fact that it has been revealed in confidence is a powerful reason for keeping it secret, but cannot settle the issue. The hearer cannot remain a moral agent without retaining his right to consider the information in light of other factors which may, all things considered, provide even stronger reasons for revealing it.

We all implicitly realize this about confidentiality. On the one hand, we need the confidential transfer of information and the consequent inclusion of the hearer into the speaker's wider self. Yet, the presuppositions of this relationship cannot be legalized simultaneously; the hearer cannot be expected to give up his autonomy. Revealing information to another is a dangerous act, involving both trust that the hearer will keep the information secret, and fear not only that he will not but that he justifiably will not, that he will perceive the situation as one in which other moral demands rightly overcome the demand to keep the information secret.[36] Of course, we fear also the hearer's moral weakness, temptations to reveal gossip to others for frivolous or self-serving reasons and betrayal out of neglect or malevolence. Yet, these are not the only concerns involved when we reveal information.

An hegelian might sum up by saying that confidentiality is a concept that involves a "contradiction": the giving up of something, moral autonomy, which cannot be given up. It has two sides or "moments," surrendering and retaining independent moral choice. These are in both unity and dialectical opposition because they pull in different directions. The tension of the hearer's situation, of course, will be resolved in many cases, but that it may remain unsolved in hard cases is fully appropriate.

Let me summarize in different langauge by saying that there is a "prima facie obligation"[37] to keep information given in confidence secret, which is based on two things: the promise to keep it secret, whether explicit or implicit; and the need of the speaker, which underlies the promise, to express but retain control of the information. One ought, other things being equal, to honor not only the promise but the need that gives rise to it. A further reason reinforcing the prima facie obligation is the fact that in many cases, revealing the information will bring disadvantage upon the speaker and/or other parties. Such potential disadvantage provides a moral reason for guarding information. These remarks about confidentiality are not only meant to bring out the reasons underlying the prima facie obligation but also to emphasize that, as strong as these reasons may be—and in many cases they are very strong—they cannot be strong enough to remove the hearer's own moral autonomy, his right and duty to act on strong countervailing reasons.

The difficult question that now must be confronted is the strength of the reasons on both sides. To shed some light on this, I want to compare some of the types of information mentioned earlier. With respect to dangerous information—*i.e.,* information that the speaker intends to harm another—the need will often be less compelling. Further, the hearer's disclosure of dangerous information will often have very good consequences, which the consequences of hearer disclosure of guilty information, though good, will be less important to society and less certain to occur. These generalizations are almost certainly too strong, even if only roughly true; however, they show that the obligation to guard guilty information is often stronger than the obligation to guard dangerous information.

On what fact are these generalizations based? Quite often the motive to reveal guilty information is the speaker's need to confess, to share the knowledge and the burden of his guilt, to express what is on his mind and to receive sympathetic advice about what to do. These are important needs and much can be gained by permitting wrongdoers this opportunity to express themselves. On the other hand, a speaker might reveal dangerous information from boastfulness, the expression of revenge (against the potential victim) or the desire to enlist the hearer as a confederate or keep him quiet. Such disclosure may surely come from better motives, such as seeking advice or hoping to be talked out of the wrongful act; conversely, confiding guilty information could result from boastfulness, revenge, or less admirable motives. I am inclined, nevertheless, to think that there is a difference with respect to consequences. Revealing dangerous information can often, with near certainty, have very good consequences: the prevention of injury and harm. The consequence of disclosing guilty information is usually the sanctioning of the offender. In many cases, the sanction is less important to society than the prevention of impending harm. One reason for this is that the punishment of any particular offender may not matter so much if the general system of punishment is maintained. Further, the punishment may do no good if the offender is not inclined to commit other wrongs. And the offender, if allowed the opportunity to confess, may sooner or later reveal publicly his own wrong-doing and thus undergo sanctions without disclosure by the hearer. I admit that these claims are controversial and hold at best in a general way, but if correct they underlie the intuition that there are often stronger reasons for not disclosing guilty information than for not disclosing dangerous information. This intuition may well be at the basis of the fact that the Code and the Model Rules treat differently the disclosure of future and of past crimes or wrongful acts.[38]

With respect to embarrassing information, if we focus just on consequences it may seem that the obligation of confidentiality is weakened by the fact that the consequences of disclosure will often not be very bad. On the other hand, disclosure by the hearer is unlikely to attain good consequences or prevent bad consequences, so there is little compelling reason for revelation. Consequences do not play a very important role here. What are important are the needs for self-expression and understanding, which move people to reveal embarrassing information that is not at the same time also guilty or dangerous. These needs deserve respect and thus many strengthen the obligation to keep such information confidential. Here we might also recall our earlier discussion of cases in which disclosure may help the speaker. In such cases, there will be reasons for disclosure, although these raise the complex issue of paternalism. Planning and positive information are difficult to generalize about since there are probably no typical needs or consequences which characterize imparting it. Finally, with regard to detrimental information, the potential harm to the speaker stands out as a strong reason against disclosure, which may be nullified if the information is also dangerous.

The point implicit in this rough survey is that it does matter what needs give rise to imparting information and what consequences will follow disclosure. The obligation of confidentiality varies in strength with these features. Keeping these needs and consequences in mind will help us make reasonable distinctions between cases.

IV. CONFIDENTIALITY IN LEGAL CONTEXTS

Turning from the ordinary contexts to the legal context, we need to tackle a cluster of issues concerning the scope of confidentiality. How much and what kinds of information revealed by the client or otherwise learned in the course of the lawyer-client relationship should come within the domain of confidentiality? We might include within confidentiality all the information revealed in the relationship. Another possibility would be to include all information the disclosure of which would be embarrassing or detrimental to the client, as the Code provides.[39] A further possibility would be to include all and and only information that is relevant to the legal matter for which the client has sought the lawyer's aid. We might of course, have to explore additional responsibilities.

To answer these questions, we must begin by examining two ways of understanding the permissibility of disclosure in legal contexts. First, information that is permissible to disclose might be entirely outside the domain of confidentiality and be completely unprotected. Second, information that is permissible to disclose might be prima facie[40] confidential under the rules of professional ethics; disclosure provisions would then specify the contexts in which the confidentiality provisions may or must be overcome. On the latter understanding, the information comes within the scope of confidentiality: revealing it involves a prima facie wrong even though disclosure is justified, *all* things considered. It may seem that the distinction between these two ways of understanding disclosure is unimportant since in ether case the information may be disclosed. It makes a difference, however, in the way we understand what we and others are doing. On the former understanding, there is no reason for confidentiality since the information is unprotected; disclosure does no harm and no apologies are required. On the latter view, there is a moral reason for keeping information confidential, which is quite likely strong but nevertheless is overcome. In such cases, regret, apologies and concern that one has judged properly are appropriate. The moral situation and dilemmas presented by these contrasting understandings are quite different.

It might be thought obvious that information that lawyers may disclose should be considered in the first way, as simply unprotected. This seems plausible as an account of disclosure of such information as the intention to commit a future crime or wrongful act, but consider the information on the basis of which a lawyer may be required to disclose perjury or correct misapprehensions. This information will be quite ordinary information about the case which will have been learned from the client or through the lawyer's research. The lawyer would have not occasion to disclose it, absent perjury. This information, therefore, is best understood as falling within the scope of confidentiality, but losing this status in certain contexts. This analysis is also necessary for the information a lawyer may not reveal to collect his fee or to defend against charges of wrongful conduct.[41] Where the reporting of the intention to commit a crime is discretionary rather than mandatory, it too is perhaps best construed as laying down an exception to a prima facie rule.

When I say that information falls within the domain of confidentiality, I shall therefore mean that it is prima facie confidential, to be held confidential unless there are overriding reasons for disclosure. I argued in Section III[42] that whenever information is given in confidence there is a prima facie obligation not to disclose it. This background obligation will exist for information in the legal context, even with respect to information the disclosure of which is completely forbidden by whatever professional standards are in force. This obligation of confidentiality is not absolute or exceptionless since it is still possible that, morally speaking, a circumstance may obtain in which the lawyer should reveal information that is required to be kept confidential by professional standards. Of course, he may be disciplined, but his moral, as distinct from his legal or professional, obligations cannot be confirmed to those articulated by existing codes of professional ethics. Having said this, however, we should distinguish between information in regard to which professional standards lay down conditions in which the prima facie obligation of confidentiality may be overcome and information for which they do not. We have, then, three categories into which pieces of information may fall: (1) unprotected by professional standards, (2) prima facie protected by professional standards, but the standards lay down circumstances in which it may be revealed, and (3) absolutely protected by professional standards, though morally the possibility of exceptions must be admitted. Keeping these categories in mind, let us now turn to the question of what information should be placed within the domain of confidentiality, that is, should fall into either categories (2) or (3).

A very simple and natural view is that the information to be absolutely protected is all and and only information which is *about* the matter on which the client has sought legal aid, that is, information relevant to the case for which the lawyer is representing the client.[43] We might call this the "particular case" view. Many find this view too weak and believe that more information should be included. But, in some ways, the particular case view may be found too strong, at least if perjury and misapprehensions are to be corrected and lawyers are to be allowed to defend themselves against charges of wrongful conduct. These circumstances involve disclosing information and thus require the inclusions of exceptions to the rule that such information may not be revealed; such information will then be prima facie protected by professional standards. But before looking at this way of weakening the particular case view, we now turn to some of the reasons for thinking that the domain of confidentiality should be much broader than the simple theory suggests.

There is a social or psychological reason why we think the scope of confidentiality should be larger than the particular case view suggests. When a client receives the services of a professional there will be occasion for them to discuss many things that are not relevant to the professional matter. They may chat about family affairs or the client's work simply as a means of warming up to each other or because they are people, not just clients and lawyers in the abstract, they have developed a friendship or have come to take an interest in each other. Or their chat may just be typical small talk. The client may disclose information that the professional should not reveal to others, whether it is explicitly given in confidence or not. But this obligation of confidentiality will not result from the professional-client relationship but from the ordinary relationships of conveying information and confidentiality that become easily established between persons. Part of the reason why the scope of lawyer-client confidentiality seems to be wider than the particular case view admits is the inclusion of this added dimension of ordinary confidentiality in the relationship. In a relationship characterized by confidentiality in some areas, there is also likely to be a tendency to extend the habit of confidentiality to other areas. This extension may be sought by the client who, having found an advisor on one issue, seeks to extend this relationship to other issues. It may be acquiesced in by the lawyer because it enhances the smooth functioning of the relationship, because the lawyer enjoys the role, or for other reasons. Most likely, the extension is unconscious and undeliberate for either party. In any case, the broader confidentiality that arises in this way cannot be defended on the basis of its necessity for the working of the lawyer-client relationship. It does mean, however, that we should realize how the ways in which the lawyer-client relation is embedded in ordinary life tend to extend confidentiality.

I now return to the particular case view and the two main areas of disclosure treated by the Code and the Model Rules: the intention to commit future crimes and the disclosure of facts needed to rectify perjury or misapprehensions. Many would want to strengthen the particular case view and there are several ways in which they might do so. The most protectionist view would require absolute protection for all information learned by the lawyer in the course of the lawyer-client relationship. A somewhat more complex view would recommend absolute protection for information concerning past and future crimes in addition to information concerning the particular case at issue and reject an exception allowing for disclosure of perjury or misapprehensions.[44]

There is an argument typically given for protectionist views which I shall refer to as the "spread" argument and which I shall now examine. I will first state it in a way that gives it the most protectionist conclusion, that all information be protected. I shall then modify it so that it has a narrower and more plausible conclusion. The spread argument begins with the plausible premise that for the lawyer to present the best possible case for the client he needs to know everything of relevance. From this premise it infers, also plausibly, that the client must be able to tell the lawyer, in confidence, anything he knows that is relevant to the case. The next crucial premise has two versions. One version, as put by Monroe Freedman, is that the "client is not ordinarily competent to evaluate the relevance or significance of particular facts. What may seem incriminating to the client may actually be exculpatory."[45] Alternatively, it might be held not that the client lacks competence, but that whether any particular facts are relevant to the case cannot be determined in isolation. Thus, all the facts the client has in mind need to be brought out before he or the lawyer can determine which are genuinely relevant. Whichever premise is used, it follows that the client must be free to say in confidence anything that is on his mind, leaving assessments of relevance up to the lawyer after all the facts are brought out. If certain areas were exempted from the scope of confidentiality, the client would want to ensure that he does not reveal damaging information that falls in these areas. Since either the client is unable to assess relevance or his assessment cannot be made in isolation from all the possible evidence, the client may omit facts that are relevant for fear that they will be unprotected. Confidentiality must, therefore, apply to *all* information if the lawyer is to be able to represent the client effectively.

The crucial premise of the spread argument, however, is too strong. There are facts that anyone can see are either totally irrelevant or clearly germane to the case. All the facts—whatever these are—do not need to be revealed in order to assess the relevance of any of them. As a general claim about client capacities or the interrelations of evidence, therefore, the premise is implausible. The spread argument is not a persuasive defense of the very strong conclusion that all information should be protected absolutely.

A more plausible version of the spread argument is that the premise holds with respect to information about past and future crimes and perjurious intentions.[46] Such information, it is said, is often relevant to the case at hand, and where it is not relevant, the client is often unable to tell this correctly. If the information is not protected, clients will be careful not to convey it, relevant communication will not be communicated to the lawyer and he will be unable to present the best case. The information, then, must come within the domain of confidentiality and needs to be absolutely protected by professional standards.

While more plausible, this version of the spread argument also fails with respect to the intention to commit crimes or wrongful acts. What are clearly relevant to presenting the best defense for a client are what he did, what his motives were, what the circumstances were, and so forth. It is unlikely that his future intentions will, logically, bear on these matters. There may be a client who, for psychological reasons, is unable to discuss the instant case without revealing future plans, but this is not very common. If there are compelling reasons for officially saying that lawyers have discretion to report future crimes and wrongful acts, these rare possibilities do not overcome them. The strength of the spread argument is, therefore, limited. Where the spread argument holds, the permissibility of disclosure in some cases may have a "chilling effect" on the client's frankness.[47] But if other, stronger reasons support disclosure, the chilling effect may simply be a reasonable price to pay. To conclude that a certain sort of information should not be disclosed, it is not enough to show that permitting its disclosure will have a chilling effect. The chilling effect may be insignificant or rare and the arguments for disclosure may be strong and compelling. The spread argument is, at best, half an argument.

The spread argument is most plausible with respect to past crimes and wrongful acts. Such information may shed light on the circumstances of the client, his motives and aims, and may enable the lawyer to understand his actions. I have already suggested that the distinction between past and future crimes is an important one and the spread argument offers some additional support for this view.

With respect to perjury and the correction of misapprehensions, the spread argument has cogency: if a client wishes to lie or mislead, he must conceal some facts from the lawyer, and in doing so may conceal not only incriminating but exculpatory facts as well. The unambiguous treatment in the Model Rules, requiring the lawyer to report perjury and correct misapprehensions, will definitely do some chilling. But here, the ultimate resolution of the issue depends on how great the chilling effect is and on the strength of the positive arguments that can be marshalled in favor of disclosure. I am inclined to think that the positive arguments are strong and that the chilling effect may be little, especially since it can be avoided if the client gives up the intention to perjure himself, something he is not legally entitled to do in any case. I shall, however, avoid this difficult issue here. The point to be emphasized is the indecisiveness of the spread argument by itself. The limits of the spread argument need not have been emphasized if others had not written as if it were sufficient.[48]

I have thus given reasons to think that the arguments underlying strengthening the particular case view can be resisted. I have also noted how the scope of confidentiality inherent in the lawyer-client relationship can be extended to other areas through confidential relations. For this reason, a lawyer needs to think about the particulars of his relationship with a client when he considers disclosing something professional standards permit him to disclose. He may violate no professional obligation by such disclosure, but he might well violate a personal obligation that has grown out of the professional relationship, even though he may, on balance, be justified. I have also suggested that the particular case view may plausibly be weakened to allow revealing perjury and the correcting of misapprehensions in the manner expressed by the Model Rules. But a great deal more needs to be said. The problem of perjury raises the question of what the lawyer may do for the client. Clearly, he may and should present the strongest case. But what is the strongest case? Although a case involving perjured testimony and manufactured evidence may be very strong, neither the lawyer nor the client is entitled to present *this* case, despite its strength. On the other hand, they need not be confined to what they really believe, based on the evidence, is the strongest case—for this case might be quite weak. Uncounterfeit evidence may be treated with flexibility, welcome facts may be stressed, unwelcome facts may be played down and the whole may be interpreted in the most favorable light.[49] There may or may not be something arbitrary in the distinction between evidence that is perjured or manufactured and evidence that is given greater emphasis than the client or lawyer believes it deserves. Both cases involve a kind of deception. However, the line drawn at perjury is drawn in the right place, for while permitting perjury would place an impossible burden on the trier of fact, forbidding any stretching of evidence would negate a person's day in court.

CONCLUSION

I said at the beginning that I would not reach a solid conclusion, and I have not. We have, however, made some progress. Let me return briefly to the charges made against the Rules that they make the lawyer an agent of the state.[50] From what has been said, we can conclude that these charges oversimplify; the motive that gives rise to greater disclosure is not "big brotherhood." It is, rather, the clear recognition of obligations to third parties and, more importantly, of something that lies at the foundation of such obligations—the lawyer's own moral autonomy.[51] The stress on confidentiality and on an exclusive obligation to the client leads to an unjustifiable surrender of moral autonomy and gives rise to the amorality and impersonality of the lawyer's role which has often been noticed.[52] It is in combating this surrender that the Model Rules are a large improvement. Perhaps the improvement has unforeseen bad consequences. The discussion of the underlying grounds of confidentiality, however, shows that "ideological" appeals either to zealous advocacy of the client's cause, on the one hand, or to the truth, on the other, are only likely to simplify the moral complexity of the issue.

NOTES

1. ABA Committee on Evaluation of Professional Standards, *Model Rules of Professional Conduct* (Discussion Draft, January, 1980) [hereinafter cited as *Model Rules*].

2. *ABA Code of Professional Responsibility* (1977) [hereinafter cited as *Code*].

3. Among the standard essays on this subject are: M. Freedman, *Lawyer's Ethics in an Adversary System* (1975) (especially chs. 1-6); Curtis, "The Ethics of Advocacy," *Stanford Law Review* 4 (1951):3; Drinker, "Some Remarks on Mr. Curtis' 'The Ethics of Advocacy,'" *Stanford Law Review* 4 (1952):349; Frankel, "The Search for Truth: An Umpireal View,"*University of Pennsylvania Law Review* 123 (1975):1031; Freedman, "Professional Responsibility and the Criminal Defense Lawyer: The Three Hardest Questions," *Michigan Law Review* 64 (1966):1469 [see this volume pp. 328-339]. See also Luban, "Professional Ethics: A New Code for Lawyers?" *Hastings Center Reports* 10 (1980):11; Morgan, "The Evolving Concept of Professional Responsibility," *Harvard Law Review* 90 (1977):702; Schwartz, "The Professionalism and Accountability of Lawyers," *California Law Review* 66 (1978):669; Note, "Client Fraud and the Lawyer—An Ethical Analysis," *Minnisota Law Review* 62 (1977):89.

4. E.g., M. Freedman, *supra* note 3; Frankel, *supra* note 3.

5. *Code, supra* note 2, DR 4-101(C)(3).

6. *Model Rules, supra* note 1, Rule 1.7(b).

7. *Id.*, Rule 1.7(c)(2).

8. *Id.* at p. 6.

9. The drafters of the Model Rules do not comment on how the Rules' definition of "wrongful act" as violations "in which knowledge of the circumstances is an element," *id.*, is to be interpreted. Luban argues that this definition excludes all but a "small and rather arbitrary" list of torts, since although the tortfeasor may have knowledge, knowledge is not an element of the wrong. Luban, *supra* note 3, at p. 14.

10. *Code, supra* note 2, DR 4-101(B)(1).

11. *Model Rules, supra* note 1, Rule 1.7(c)(2) (emphasis added).

12. *Code, supra* note 2, DR 4-101(C)(2).

13. See Note, *supra* note 3.

14. *Id.* at pp. 103-104.

15. *Model Rules, supra* note 1, Rule 3.1(b)(3).

16. *Id.*, Rule 3.1(d)(2).

17. *Id.*, Rule 3.1(f)(2).

18. 276 Or. 225, 554 P.2d 479 (1976).

19. *Model Rules, supra* note 1, Rule 4.2(b)(2).

20. *Id.*

21. *Code, supra* note 2, DR 4-101(B)(1).

22. *Id.*, DR 7-102(B).

23. *Id.*, DR 4-101(C)(1)-(4).

24. *Id.*, EC 58; *Model Rules, supra* note 1, Rule 1.13(a).

25. *Model Rules, supra* note 1, Rule 1.13(b).

26. *Id.*, Rule 1.13(c).

27. *Code, supra* note 2, DR 4-101(C)(3).

28. See generally Solomon, "The Corporate Lawyer's Dilemma," *Fortune* (November 4, 1979), at p. 138.

29. *Model Rules, supra* note 1, Rule 6.2.

30. Koskoff, "Introduction" to The Roscoe Pound-American Lawyers Foundation Committee on Professional Responsibility, "The American Lawyer's Code of Conduct" (Public Discussion Draft, June, 1980), reprinted in *Trial,* (August, 1980):46. But see Luban, *supra* note 3, at p. 15.

31. Koskoff, *supra* note 30, at pp. 46-47.

32. I omit discussion of other possible uses of the information, such as for blackmail.

33. By contrast, positive, nondamaging information is typically nonconfidential unless confidentiality is requested.

34. To be asked by a speaker to keep something confidential can be irritatingly expressive of a lack of trust, particularly when confidentiality is implicit in the context.

35. The general obligation of loyalty and the obligation to fill the demands of the roles one

plays can perhaps also be understood along these lines. To have obligations based on loyalty to someone or to some entity, or to have an obligation because one fills a role, is to consider oneself unfree to act in certain respects as an autonomous moral agent, because one is under the control of the person or agent and must act according to their wishes or choices. I cannot pursue this more general issue here. For a provocative discussion of how this may characterize the lawyer's role, see Wasserstrom, "Lawyers as Professionals: Some Moral Issues," *Human Rights* 5 (1975):1 (see this volume pp. 114-131).

36. These other demands, incidentally, might involve not only obligations to third parties but to the speaker himself, when revealing the information would be for the speaker's own good.

37. As moral philosophers tend to use the term, to say that one has a prima facie obligation to do an act of kind X is to say that one has a moral reason for doing X such that one should in fact do X, unless there are stronger and weightier moral reasons against doing X. Such counter reasons are often said to override or ovecome the prima facie obligation. A prima facie obligation needs to be contrasted with an "absolute" or "exceptionless" obligation, which may not be overridden. The talk of prima facie obligations often goes along with the view that there are a plurality of cogent moral obligations which may conflict in particular situations; in such cases, some judgment must be made as to which are weightier.

38. See pp. 766-767 *supra.*

39. *Code supra* note 2, DR 4-101(A).

40. That is, confidential unless there are strong reasons overriding confidentiality. See note 37 *supra.*

41. *Code supra* note 2, DR 4-101(C)(4).

42. See pp. 775-777 *supra.*

43. I owe this way of putting the matter to Don Scheid.

44. The code of conduct proposed by the American Trial Lawyers Foundation contains two alternative proposals that are somewhat similar to this view. Alternative A allows disclosure only when required by law (after a good faith effort to test the validity of the law), when the lawyer reasonably believes disclosure will prevent imminent danger to human life, when the lawyer knows of the corruption of a judge or juror or when disclosure is necessary for the lawyer to defend himself or his associates against formal criminal charges. The Roscoe Pound-American Trial Lawyers Foundation Committee on Professional Responsibility, "The American Lawyer's Code of Conduct" §. I, Alternative A (Public Discussion Draft, June, 1980) (reprinted in *Trial,* 1980, at p. 50). The more limited Alternative B allows disclosure only when required by law (after a good faith effort to test the validity of the law) or when necessary for the lawyer to defend himself or his associates against formal criminal charges. *Id.,* Alternative B.

45. M. Freedman, *supra* note 3, at p. 4.

46. I am sure this is the version that Monroe Freedman intends. *Id.*

47. But see Schwartz, *supra* note 3, at pp. 683-684.

48. See generally M. Freedman, *supra* note 3.

49. Criminal cases, civil cases and negotiations will obviously need relatively different treatment in these respects.

50. See p. 770 and note 30 *supra.*

51. See generally Flynn, "Professional Ethics and the Lawyer's Duty to Self," *Washington University Law Quarterly* 19 (1976):429.

52. Wasserstrom, *supra* note 35.

PROBLEMS

GUARDING THE GUARDIAN

A court-appointed guardian of the person and property of a minor has informed you, his attorney, that he (the guardian) has misappropriated a considerable amount of his ward's estate. The information was more or less unintended, although it was the obvious conclusion from what he had to tell you to receive legal advice. Upon hearing of the misappropriation, you immediately arrange to deny the guardian further access to the deposited funds in the ward's estate. The guardian is not a lawyer. You were employed by him rather than imposed by the court, but the guardianship is your only connection with him. The guardian is bonded; so it is the bonding company and not the ward who will suffer the ultimate loss. So far as you know, the guardian has not yet had to file any accounting of the estate's assets either with the court or the bonding company. But he will have to file such an accounting eventually. So, while there has been no perjury yet, it may be in the offing. Should you report the misappropriation to the court? Should you seek removal of the guardian? Should you resign as his attorney if he does not agree to make restitution? Or should you do something else? Indeed, should you have arranged to deny your client further access to his ward's estate in the first place?

LOOKING OUT FOR NUMBER ONE

As an oil business expert, you were employed as attorney to help company X, a corporation organized to engage in wildcat drilling, to obtain leases for drilling on certain federal lands. Your fee was to include part of the proceeds from oil discovered on the land. Company X obtained the leases by acting as you advised, found oil, and has now tendered you $130,000 as your fee for all services rendered under the agreement. Based on information you received from X in the course of your employment, you have good reason to believe that your fee should be at least $150,000 and that X has on deposit in the state funds sufficient to pay everything owed to you. May you use this information obtained from X to support your suit to compel payment of the full sum owed to you, and use the information to attach (that is, have a court seize and hold) the funds X has in the state until the suit is tried? If you do not attach X's assets in the state, you may have trouble collecting on the judgment even if you win. X is a foreign corporation that would be hard and expensive to collect from but for its deposits in this state. Would it be professionally proper to do these things? There is no doubt that the suit will cost X a good deal of money, that attaching X's funds will be a substantial inconvenience for X, and that you may not prevail in court.

DOING JUSTICE AGAINST THE CLIENT'S WISHES

You are an attorney for C, who was convicted of rape. His case is now on appeal. One day during the trial you had lunch with attorney L, a member of your firm. The conversation naturally turned to the trial. When you described the rape in question, he remarked that he had a client two years ago who had been accused of three similar rapes. That client had been convicted largely on the identification of several witnesses (and even though he had taken the stand to deny the charges and had continued to deny them even when to admit the rapes might have helped him get a lower sentence). More discussion revealed that L's client looked very much like yours. After the trial you ask C about the other rapes. He admitted committing all of them, giving details only the actual rapist could have known. But he refused to admit them to anyone else: "One rape conviction is enough for me. I want to get out while I'm still young enough to have some fun."

You could take your information to the district attorney. You could tell him what you know without revealing your client's name. The district attorney might take you at your word, investigate on his own, and perhaps do something to get lawyer L's client out of prison. But would he agree to leave your client alone if the trail of evidence led back to him? You believe he would. Your client will be in prison for a long time no matter what.

May you—against your client's wishes and without his knowledge—reveal your information (minus your client's name) to the district attorney (a) if the D.A. agrees not to prosecute your client for the three rapes in question or (b) even if he refuses to agree? *Should* you reveal that information under either condition?

Suggested Readings

For other works on issues raised here, see Bibliography, Part 5, especially Chamberlan (1975), Kramer (1979), Note (1980), and Wolfram (1977).

Part VI

Providing Legal Services

Introduction

Lawyers have organized as a profession, they tell us, in part to make competent legal help available to those who need it. But having so organized does not itself mean that any particular lawyer has a duty to do anything, much less that he has a duty to help prospective clients in any general or specific way. Someone needs to decide what part each lawyer is to have in providing legal services. The options are many: The profession could, for example, decide that providing legal services to whomever one chooses is all a lawyer need do to contribute to the goal of making such services available to all who need it. The marketplace (and government money) can do the rest. Charles Fried seems to take such a view in "The Lawyer as Friend." Or, instead, the profession could decide that a lawyer must accept any person who seeks help, whether or not the prospective client is able to pay. In some states, lawyers still take an oath in which (among other things) they undertake "never to reject the cause of the defenseless."

The essays in this section are concerned with defining the lawyer's duty to help make legal services available. The first essay, by Steven B. Rosenfeld, concerns a novel proposal to require lawyers personally to engage in a certain amount of unpaid legal service each year. The second and third essays, by Michael D. Bayles and Michael Davis, respectively, concern a traditional reason for *refusing* to provide legal services. All serve once again to reaffirm the importance that the idea of "profession" has in determining what lawyers demand of one another.

Lawyers have long believed themselves to have a duty to do some work *pro bono (publico)*, that is, "for the public good." Steven Rosenfeld explains and defends a proposal to codify and enforce that duty. The proposal is similar to a provision of the first draft of the *Model Rules*. But as finally adopted, the rule (Rule 6.1) states the duty with a hortatory "should" rather than its original "shall." That "should" is unique in the "blackletter" provisions of the *Rules*. Why might the ABA have been unwilling to adopt the mandatory rule Rosenfeld defends? Why did it adopt the hortatory rule rather than none? Does not such a "rule" belong in the Preamble or Comments of the ABA document?

Rosenfeld explains the rule in part by reviewing certain important objections made against it. The proposal does not, he says, conscript lawyers to perform poverty litigation. Any sort of public interest legal work would satisfy the requirement. The requirement would not flood the courts with new litigation (but might well shift somewhat the balance between kinds of litigation). Most legal service would probably not require any litigation. Rosenfeld's mandatory rule would not introduce into a code consisting of mandatory minimum standards an affirmative obligation of a different order. Public service is a minimum standard, and the code already includes affirmative requirements. The proposal would not invade the attorney-client privilege or threaten first amendment rights. The *amount* of public interest work can be determined without deep probing of what goes on between attorney and client or judging the value of what is done. What is proposed is not involuntary servitude to be enacted suddenly by government fiat. The profession itself would impose whatever additional burden is involved. The burden itself seems to be no different in kind from burdens the profession of law already imposes on its members.

Having disposed of these objections, Rosenfeld makes his positive case. The mandatory obligation of public service is as old as the profession. The novelty of the proposal is primarily in defining what shall count as public service outside the courtroom and in setting minimum standards for time to be spent. The courts have always had the power to appoint an attorney for an indigent party in a criminal or civil case, the attorney having to serve without compensation. That is as it should be. Law is a profession, but times change; law is no longer primarily litigation. Most lawyers seldom see a trial any more. The attorney's office has replaced the courtroom as the center of activity. Furthermore, the courts are no longer the best channel for making legal help available to those who need it or to make sure that all members of the profession do their fair share. Even the bar associations cannot do that directly. Would-be clients seldom go to the bar association for help finding an attorney. For precisely this reason, lawyers need to make themselves available. The bar associations can do no more than keep records and check them. The proposed mandatory requirement would assure that lawyers do what they should. There are problems of administration but, according to Rosenfeld, they can be solved.

Lawyers sometimes refuse a case for "moral reasons." One can, for example, easily imagine the response of the lawyer asked to sue "Happy Sam" in the problem posed in Part Two: "George, I'm sorry, but I can't take the case. Happy Sam treated you fairly and all you want to do is kick him in the teeth for it. Though technically legal, what you want to do is terribly unjust. I don't think lawyers should be instruments of injustice, and I certainly don't intend to let myself be used in that way. I'm not saying that no decent lawyer would take the case. I think some would and I'm prepared to refer you to one. All I'm saying is that the moral wrong you want to do is reason enough to refuse the case. For me, the moral considerations are decisive. For someone else, they may not be." Traditionally, the lawyer in this example would feel himself under a greater duty to accept the case if, say, he were the only lawyer in town (besides the one who would defend Happy Sam) or if no other lawyer would take the case.

For Michael Bayles, all of this is simply confused. If the lawyer sincerely believes that morality says he should not help George sue Happy Sam, then, Bayles argues, he should also believe (a) that he should not help George find another lawyer and (b) that he would have even more reason to refuse

George if no one else would take the case. Bayles claims to derive these conclusions from an "uncontroversial consequentialism," including such principles as: that it is better for wrongful conduct not to occur, that one ought not to assist in such conduct, and that one should use appropriate moral techniques to prevent it. This consequentialism is, according to Bayles, uncontroversial because all reasonable moral systems must aim at preventing wrongful conduct (however "wrongful conduct" is defined).

Bayles's claim belongs to a larger discussion in ethics. It is an application of what has come to be known as "the no-difference argument." The argument allows one to conclude from the fact that a certain act does not add to the amount of the wrong in the world that the act itself is not wrong. Many philosophers have found the argument troubling because, on the one hand, it is hard to see the *point* of calling an act morally wrong if it does not make the world a morally worse place; while, on the other hand, the argument leads to conclusions that seem to be morally outrageous. Consider, for example, whether it would be morally wrong to murder someone if you know others will murder him if you do not. What "moral point" could there be to your not murdering him? (He will be murdered whatever *you* do.) Yet, surely you should not murder him whatever others would do instead.

Bayles's claim has wider application within legal ethics than may at first appear. Many lawyers seem to appeal to the no-difference argument to justify questionable conduct. A lawyer might, for example, excuse bribing a public official to expedite a contract by noting, "If I don't do it, some other attorney will." Bayles's use of the argument differs from such uses only in being concerned with an act that even the refusing lawyer admits is neither illegal nor professionally improper. He contends that the only appropriate means to prevent conduct that is morally objectionable yet lawful and professionally proper is to try to change the law or the rules of professional conduct. However, he does not argue that one has a moral obligation to take a case even if one has moral reasons to refuse it, only that one has no moral reason to refuse it if others will not. But, given the lawyer's general obligation to make legal services available, it seems that Bayles's argument would put lawyers under a professional (and perhaps moral) obligation to accept such a case, whatever their scruples, if other lawyers would.

Responding to Bayles, Michael Davis begins by considering the traditional defense of the lawyer's right to refuse a case for moral reasons. That right seems to be a compromise serving as much as possible both the lawyer's liberty and the client's need for legal help. The obligation to refer and the greater obligation to take a case if no else will are part of that compromise. Davis draws on the language of the old *Code of Professional Responsibility* for the terms of that compromise. The new *Model Rules* have far less to say on the subject. Why?

Having presented the traditional defense of the lawyer's right to refuse a case, Davis confronts Bayles's argument. As it turns out, the argument has a number of unstated assumptions, some of which are both controversial and far from inescapable. Davis lays special stress on Bayles's seeming failure to distinguish between the *right* and the *good* (a distinction having its counterpart in the Code's division of rules into "mandatory" and "aspirational." Davis agrees that lawyers should not assist in wrongdoing, but that "should" indicates only that assistance in wrongdoing is what weighs against performing an act, not that such assistance is in general wrong. The lawyer with moral reasons to refuse a client may balance these considerations against others, for example, the client's need or the likelihood that he will find someone else to help him. The lawyer does not necessarily do wrong just because he *assists* in wrongdoing.

Bayles would, of course, agree with that conclusion, but only where the assistance "makes no difference." Davis needs to show that whether assisting in wrongdoing is morally wrong or not is (sometimes) independent of the moral difference such assistance makes (in Bayles's sense). And that is what Davis tries to do. The point of a moral *rule* may be to prevent wrongdoing (that is, certain sorts of undesirable acts) just as Bayles says. But that does not mean, according to Davis, that individual acts are right insofar as they prevent such acts and wrong insofar as they do not. The acts may be judged by the rules and the rules may themselves be stated without reference to their "point." A lawyer can do wrong even if his act "makes no difference" because he can disobey a moral rule even if the act in fact makes no difference in the amount of wrong being done. Davis's response to Bayles therefore rests upon a distinction, now common in moral philosophy, between "justifying rules" and "justifying an act under a rule."

This distinction is, however, not itself enough to dispose of Bayles's argument. Bayles might question what moral point there could be to following a rule when doing so would not in fact prevent what the rule is supposed to prevent. Bayles might object that following the rule in such circumstances seems to be a pointless fetish rather than a rational regard. Davis seems to recognize the seriousness of this objection when he argues that rules, if justified, have a special status in our reasoning because our fallibility makes relying on rules (rather than on particular judgments of particular acts alone) safer in the long run. We are better able to gauge the general effect of following a particular rule than we are the particular effect of this or that act. In this way, Davis also explains the usefulness of elaborating a code of ethics rather than leaving each professional to do right as he sees it.

Bayles's response to Davis's epilogue suggests that much remains to be said on the topic of refusing services and about the relation of moral theory to moral practice generally.

Steven B. Rosenfeld

Mandatory *Pro Bono*

Serious controversy was of course expected when a Special Committee of the Association of the Bar of the City of New York proposed in January 1980 that the legal profession move in the direction of public service practice as a mandatory obligation of each lawyer.[1] Although that proposal matched, in broad outlines, one of the proposed "Model Rules of Professional Conduct" circulated by the American Bar Association's Commission on Evaluation of Professional Standards,[2] the City Bar's Special Committee recognized that the concept was "innovative."[3] For that reason, the Committee acknowledged that a mandatory *pro bono* obligation should be adopted only after "the necessary discussion and ferment within the Bar" resulted in the development of "an informed consensus of the Bar that the mandatory obligation is both necessary and workable."[4]

Informed debate in the wake of the Special Committee's Report was not only expected, but expressly invited. The Report, published along with four dissenting opinions[5] and a summary of the contrasting views of other Committees of the Association,[6] sharply defined for further discussion such issues as these: whether there exists a demonstrable need for public interest legal services sufficient to justify added burdens on the profession; the appropriate definition and scope of the lawyer's *pro bono* obligation; the enforceability of any such mandatory obligation; whether certain categories of lawyers ought to be exempt; and whether any such obligation might be discharged by monetary contributions and/or collective efforts.

Opponents of the Report, however, have gone beyond these issues: they have questioned the historical antecedents of the proposed mandatory obligation and its constitutionality. Although the Committee majority founded its determination "not on the basis of history, but upon pressing current need, and the ethical responsibility of the legal profession to act in response,"[7] it nevertheless examined briefly the historical antecedents of the lawyer's *pro bono* obligation.[8] That examination led to the realization that the proposal to move one step beyond the express ethical obligations in the current *Code of Professional*

From Cardozo Law Review 2(1981):255-297. Copyright © 1981 Cardozo Law Review. Reprinted by permission.

Responsibility[9] to a mandatory duty was "not revolutionary" but rather, in fact, a call to reaffirm the highest and finest traditions of our profession."[10] But critics attacked the mandatory obligation as a "radical change"[11] lacking any historical precedent.[12] Beyond that, they have insisted that institution of such an obligation would be unconstitutional under the "involuntary servitude" prohibition of the thirteenth amendment, the "just compensation" requirement of the fifth amendment and the equal protection clause of the fourteenth amendment.[13]

It is not the purpose of this article to repeat and analyze all of the arguments for and against the mandatory *pro bono* proposal.[14] Such arguments can be dealt with in the course of the brief review of what the Report proposed, which comprises Part I of this article. Part II will consider the historical antecedents which demonstrate that the proposal is a step forward, but hardly a radical change. Part III of the Article will then examine the asserted constitutional impediments, which upon analysis are seen to be no obstacles to adoption by the bar of a mandatory *pro bono* obligation as part of the ethical code by which all American lawyers have long agreed to practice their profession.[15]

I. ORIGINS AND SUBSTANCE OF THE SPECIAL COMMITTEE'S PROPOSAL

A. The Evolving Code of Professional Responsibility

The Special Committee's conclusion that its proposal was "innovative but not revolutionary" stems from the recognition that *pro bono* services as a duty of every practicing lawyer has been part of American lawyers' code of conduct for many years. Even the original Canons of Professional Ethics, adopted in 1908, enunciated the principles that every lawyer had a duty to accept assignment as counsel for an "indigent prisoner" and to "exert his best efforts on his behalf,"[16] and that each lawyer "should strive at all times . . . to improve not only the law but the administration of justice."[17] In the middle part of this century, the American Bar Association took the lead in expanding upon that formulation, establishing the principle that meeting the *many* legal needs of the poor was part of each lawyer's professional responsibility.[18] The current *Code of Professional Responsibility,* adopted in August 1969, perpetuated these emerging principles. Thus, Canon 2 significantly broadened the 1908 concept of representing "indigent prisoners" by its decree that "a lawyer should assist the legal profession in fulfilling its duty to make legal counsel available,"[19] while Canon 8 preserved the exhortation that "a lawyer should assist in improving the legal system."[20]

In the 1969 Code, the Canons were intended to enunciate "axiomatic norms, expressing in general terms the standards of professional conduct expected of lawyers in their relationships with the public, with the legal system and with the legal profession."[21] Both Canons 2 and 8 were accompanied by "Ethical Considerations"[22] giving specific meaning to these two established duties of every lawyer. Thus, Ethical Consideration 2-25, recognizing that the *pro bono* obligation was not new, provides, in part:

The basic responsibility for providing legal services for those unable to pay ultimately rests upon the individual lawyer. . . . Every lawyer, regardless of professional prominence or professional workload, should find time to participate in serving the disadvantaged. The rendition of free legal services to those unable to pay reasonable fees *continues to be* an obligation of each lawyer. . . .[23]

Likewise, several Ethical Considerations under Canon 8 elaborate upon the equally important duty of each lawyer to assist in improving the legal system:

By reason of education and experience, lawyers are especially qualified to recognize deficiencies in the legal system and to initiate corrective measures therein. Thus they should participate in proposing and supporting legislation and programs to improve the system, without regard to the general interests or desires of clients or former clients.[24]

. . . [Each lawyer] should encourage the simplification of laws and the repeal or amendment of laws that are outmoded. Likewise, legal procedures should be improved whenever experience indicates a change is needed.[25]

. . . The fair administration of justice requires the availability of competent lawyers. . . . Those persons unable to pay for legal services should be provided needed services.[26]

Six years after adoption of the present Code, the ABA House of Delegates passed a resolution giving further content and meaning to the Ethical Considerations under Canons 2 and 8.[27] That resolution recognized that "it is a *basic professional responsibility* of each lawyer engaged in the practice of law to provide public interest legal services" and that "it is incumbent upon the organized bar to assist each lawyer in fulfilling his professional responsibility to provide such services."[28] The term "public interest legal service" was defined in that resolution as constituting "service provided without fee or at a substantially reduced fee" and which falls into one or more of five defined areas: Poverty Law, Civil Rights Law, Public Rights Law, Charitable Organization Representation, and Administration of Justice.[29]

The following year, the ABA took still another step toward the objectives outlined in the Ethical Considerations under Canons 2 and 8. The House of Delegates requested that the ABA Special Committee on Public Interest Practice study and report on specific means for implementing the 1975 resolution. In June of 1977, that Committee published its Report, which recommended that each state and local bar association be encouraged (1) to adopt specific guidelines quantifying the level of each lawyer's expected public interest practice, and (2) to give guidance to members of the bar on such issues as whether the responsibility could be met collectively through a law firm or by financial contributions in lieu of providing time, whether the obligation applied to government lawyers and corporate house counsel, and the appropriate role of state and local bar associations in meeting their responsibility to "assist each lawyer in fulfilling" his or her individual duty.[30]

It was in response to that call of the ABA's Special Committee on Public
Interest Practice that the City Bar Association's Special Committee on the
Lawyer's Pro Bono Obligations was appointed in December 1978. Concurrently,
the ABA's Commission on Evaluation of Professional Standards, known as the
"Kutak Commission,"[31] was at work on an overall revision of the 1969 Code.
Two features of the Kutak Commission's 1980 draft "Model Rules of Professional Conduct" are of interest here. First, the Commission proposed elimination
of the distinction between "Disciplinary Rules"[32] and "Ethical Considerations,"
and their replacement by a series of "black letter rules," enforceable by disciplinary proceedings, but followed by explanatory and definitional commentary.[33]
Second, under such a revised structure, the 1980 Model Rules contained a
mandatory *pro bono* requirement in the following "black letter rule":

> A LAWYER SHALL RENDER UNPAID PUBLIC INTEREST LEGAL
> SERVICE. A LAWYER MAY DISCHARGE THIS RESPONSIBILITY BY
> SERVICE IN ACTIVITIES FOR IMPROVING THE LAW, THE LEGAL
> SYSTEM, OR THE LEGAL PROFESSION, OR BY PROVIDING PROFES-
> SIONAL SERVICES TO PERSONS OF LIMITED MEANS OR TO PUBLIC
> SERVICE GROUPS OR ORGANIZATIONS. A LAWYER SHALL MAKE
> AN ANNUAL REPORT CONCERNING SUCH SERVICE TO APPRO-
> PRIATE REGULATORY AUTHORITY.[34]

B. What the Special Committee Proposed

Like the Kutak Commission, the City Bar's Special Committee recommended
that the Ethical Considerations now appearing under Canons 2 and 8 of the present Code be combined into a single, simple mandatory rule, reading as follows:

> Every lawyer shall devote a significant portion of his or her professional time
> each year to public service practice.[35]

In the revised structure of the proposed Model Rules of Professional Conduct,
as envisioned by the City Bar's Special Committee, that black letter rule would
be followed by explanatory text defining the scope of "public service practice,"
establishing minimum standards for quantifying the obligation—initially thirty
to fifty hours per year, with the expectation that the minimum would be gradually increased—and providing for certain "hardship exemptions" and other
elements of flexibility.[36]

Recognizing that a mandatory obligation would apply to thousands of
lawyers in every conceivable type of practice, the Special Committee opted for a
considerable expansion of the definition of "public service practice" beyond the
five-part definition of "public interest legal service" in the ABA's 1975 resolution.
Thus, the Special Committee would adopt, with minor modifications, the ABA's
categories of "Poverty Law," "Civil Rights," "Public Rights Law," and "Charitable Organization Representation," but would considerably expand the scope of

the category labelled "Administration of Justice" to include any professional activity designed to carry out or improve the administration of justice, to simplify the legal process or increase access to that process for all, or to increase the availability and quality of legal services.[37] Thus, for example, professional services of any nature (even if not, strictly speaking, legal representation) to an organization whose purpose it is to provide legal services to the poor or to work for improvements in the administration of justice, would satisfy the obligation under the Special Committee's definition.[38]

The Special Committee gave much consideration to issues involving the coverage of the public service obligation, regardless of whether or not it is to be mandatory. Although recognizing the possible need for *ad hoc* exemptions in individual hardship cases, the Committee concluded that the obligation should be universal—applicable to any lawyer, regardless of age, specialty, or nature of employment, who is actively engaged in the practice of law.[39] Likewise, the majority of the Committee, after much debate, concluded that the requirement should remain the individual obligation of each lawyer, and that satisfaction on a collective or firm-wide basis, or by a monetary contribution in lieu of services, should not be permitted.[40] The Committee also concluded that the initial standard quantifying the meaning of "significant portion of his or her professional time each year" should remain at thirty to fifty hours per year.[41] Nevertheless, the Committee recognized that the established professional obligation to complete any assignment once undertaken, regardless of the number of hours entailed, required that there be the ability to "carry forward" to future years any substantial excess time over the minimum standard expended in a particular year.[42] Finally, the Committee recommended that time expended in education or training for participation in *pro bono* services should be counted toward the requirement to render service, provided that such training is followed by utilization of the skills acquired in providing public service legal representation.[43]

No elaborate mechanism would be created for the enforcement of such a mandatory obligation. Rather, each lawyer would be required, as an additional part of his or her biennal registration with New York State's Office of Court Administration,[44] to attest to the number of hours spent in the past two years on public service practice.[45] Beyond that simple self-enforcement system, the proposed new obligation would be enforced in the same way as the Disciplinary Rules have always been enforced; the established grievance machinery would deal with cases of total and long-standing disregard of the obligation, reserving the most serious sanctions for the most egregious violations.[46]

C. What the Special Committee Did Not Propose

All of the foregoing recommendations by the Special Committee are, of course, fair ground for informed debate within the bar, and, for that matter, the public at large. Without such debate, adoption of a mandatory obligation would be unthinkable. Much of the criticism of the mandatory proposal, however, has taken issue with alleged features which were never part of the Committee's recommendation. Any informed discussion of the proposal, as well as the historical and constitutional questions it raises, should begin with elimination of these criticisms. Here, then, is what the Special Committee is often accused of having proposed, but did not:

1. Universal Conscription for Poverty Litigation

Many of the specific criticisms of the proposal have been based on the assumption that, at its heart, the Committee's recommendation is that every practicing lawyer, regardless of age, stature or specialty, be conscripted to represent poor clients in landlord-tenant, welfare and matrimonial cases in the lower courts. One need look no further than the dissents by Committee members for evidence that the proposal envisioned "an army of lawyers . . . to champion the cause of the poor," which, the dissenter concluded, would be an army "with no conviction, no motivation, no incentive (other than meeting the obligation to work the required 50 hours), and no skills or training to wage the war on poverty into which it was being drafted.[47] Or, as another dissenter stated:

> A tax lawyer, a patent attorney, a securities lawyer, a bond lawyer will not know how to restore denied welfare benefits to a poor person. It would take days to learn how; and even then the effort will be bumbling. Society will have been denied the skilled tax, patent, securities, and bond services of these lawyers and, instead, will have received their patchwork services as temporary welfare lawyers.[48]

But the Special Committee's proposal was by not means limited in the way that these criticisms imply. True, the perceived compelling need for additional lawyers to represent individuals unable to pay for necessary legal counsel was one of the factors motivating the Committee's proposal.[49] The majority harbored the reasonable expectation that, if each and every lawyer is required to perform some kind of public service, many would elect (out of "conviction") to satisfy the obligation by representing those unable to pay and would obtain the necessary skills. That would, in turn, make a substantial contribution to the legal needs of the disadvantaged.

But the Committee never suggested, nor would it expect, that every lawyer would choose poverty law as the means of satisfying the obligation. Lawyers who have done nothing but bond work for decades need not fear that they must suddenly learn how "to restore denied welfare benefits." Rather, the Committee believed, there is some kind of public service function which every lawyer can competently perform, even without the additional training which, under the Committee's proposal, would also count toward satisfying the obligation. As the Committee's report stated:

> In using the term "legal functions," we intend to include representation, counsel, advice, drafting and other services of the kind which people and organizations have traditionally expected lawyers to provide because of their special training

and experience or because of their central role in and responsibility for the functioning of our legal system.[50]

In light of that definition, and within the very expansive definition of "public service practice" adopted by the Committee (including the "Administration of Justice" category), the Committee cncluded that "few specialists have such limited skills or narrow interests that they could not, under any circumstances, be of value in assisting a recognized public service practice activity."[51]

It would, of course, be an illuminating and instructive experience to see distinguished senior members of the bar appearing in landlord-tenant court on occasion—and it might have the added effect of upgrading the quality of justice dispensed to litigants in such courts—but that is not the typical scenario envisioned by the Special Committee's proposal.

2. Flooding the Courts with New Litigation

A related, but equally unfounded, criticism has been that, by insuring the availability of thousands of additional lawyers without fee, the Special Committee's proposal would foster a host of new (and, it is implied, meritless) litigations in areas where nonlitigated solutions should be sought, thereby taxing the court system beyond its already overstrained limits.[52]

Putting aside the implication that denying lawyers to the disadvantaged is an appropriate means of curbing new litigation, while those who can afford lawyers are free to litigate at will, the Special Committee's proposal would not engender new litigation. As the definition of "legal functions" makes clear,[53] there is no requirement that the obligation be satisfied by representing clients in litigation any more than there is a requirement that each lawyer represent the poor. If it is true that most lawyers are not litigation specialists and cannot be expected to satisfy the obligation competently by performing services outside their own area of expertise, it must be expected that the majority of lawyers will choose to discharge their mandatory obligation by rendering services which do not involve litigation. Indeed, considering the broad scope of the "Administration of Justice" category, it would seem that the objectives of relieving the strains upon the court system and developing nonlitigated solutions to legal controversies ought to be furthered by adoption of the Committee's proposal, since many lawyers would begin giving their time, talents and attention to projects designed to improve, simplify and streamline the legal system.[54]

3. Doing Violence to the Structure of the Code

Critics have also suggested that an affirmative mandatory requirement that every lawyer perform services is foreign to the *Code of Professional Responsibility* and thus ought to be rejected. The Code, they argue, at least in its Disciplinary Rules, is made up of "thou shalt nots" which enunciate "the minimum level of conduct below which no lawyer can fall." But, they argue, affirmative obligations such as mandatory *pro bono* cannot be accommodated to the concept of Disciplinary Rules.[55]

Such an argument is largely one of semantics: many of the current Disciplinary Rules could just as easily be phrased in terms of exhortatory commands, rather than prohibitions. And, indeed, there are many instances in which the present Code does impose affirmative obligations upon lawyers through Disciplinary Rules.[56] Especially in the context of the Model Rules of Professional Conduct proposed by the Kutak Commission, an affirmative mandatory *pro bono* obligation is by no means foreign to the *Code of Professional Responsibility.*

4. Invading Attorney-Client and First Amendment Privileges

Critics have argued that any enforceable—and actually enforced—mandatory obligation would necessarily involve inquiry by an enforcement body into the nature of attorney-client relationships, and provide at least a "chilling effect" upon the exercise of first amendment freedoms by both lawyers and their clients.[57] Although this may have been a fair criticism of the Special Committee's earlier discussion draft, which proposed a much more elaborate system of enforcement involving detailed reports on the *nature* of the services rendered and the identity of clients, it is not a feature of the Special Committee's final report. Indeed, these criticisms were the principal reason why the Special Committee withdrew its more elaborate enforcement mechanism, substituted the simple biennial affirmation of compliance, and relied upon the normal disciplinary mechanism to weed out serious violations. Most lawyers would file the biennial affirmation and would not lightly swear in such an officially-filed form that they have discharged an obligation when they have not. Only in cases of persistent and egregious defiance of the rule would there be any need for disciplinary proceedings. It seems clear, then, that the question of an individual lawyer's compliance with the obligation can be resolved without the need to probe impermissibly into confidential attorney-client relationships: representation of a client without fee can easily be established without such probing, and a lawyer's participation in charitable or court reform enterprises can also be confirmed without the need to make value judgments as to the particular "public interest" furthered by such participation.

5. Imposition of the Obligation by Government Fiat

A final theme of many critics, and the foundation of the "involuntary servitude" argument, is the assumption that the Committee envisions imposition of the mandatory obligation upon an unwilling profession by government fiat—either court rule or legislative enactment.[58] But that was not the Committee's objective. Like all of the features of the *Code of Professional Responsibility,* the mandatory *pro bono* obligation should be imposed only after it is accepted by a consensus of the members of the profession. Indeed, the Committee specifically recognized "the need to move gradually, rather than all at once, in the direction of a mandatory obligation. The profession must be convinced to take on the obligation before it can be enforceable."[59]

To be sure, once "an informed consensus of the Bar" adopts a mandatory obligation, it will fall to the legislatures and/or the courts to implement that obligation and, ultimately, to enforce it.[60] But an analysis of the proposal, and especially the asserted constitutional objections, should keep in mind the Committee's realization that there must first be a voluntary acceptance of the obligation by a consensus of the profession. In submitting its proposal, the Committee shared Chief Justice Burger's conviction that "the dynamics of the profession have a way of rising to the burdens placed on it."[61]

D. The Dynamic Code

The Special Committee's proposal is "innovative" because it recommends that the duties recognized in Ethical Considerations be upgraded to the nature of Disciplinary Rules.[62] Such a change would be "revolutionary" only if the Code is viewed, contrary to its history, as an immutable standard, in which the nature of obligations and the distinctions between what is mandatory and what is aspirational are incapable of evolution.

Is it fair to view the Code as such a static document? It seems unlikely. As noted, the narrow duty of the 1908 Canons to represent "indigent prisoners" had evolved by 1969 into a recognized obligation of every lawyer to render "free legal services"—civil and criminal—to those unable to pay.[63] Moreover, the very definitions of Disciplinary Rules and Ethical Considerations in the 1969 Code are further illustrative of the Code's dynamism. Disciplinary Rules are intended to "state the minimum level of conduct below which no lawyer can fall without being subject to disciplinary action."[64] Can it seriously be argued that lawyers, of all professionals, do not constantly seek to change and upgrade "minimum levels of conduct"?[65] Likewise, Ethical Considerations under the 1969 Code were intended to "represent the *objectives toward which every member of the profession should strive.*"[66] Were the objectives set in the mid-1960s when Ethical Consideration 2-25 was written simply unattainable and EC 2-25 simply hypocritical? Or was it anticipated that the profession would "strive" to reach the point where the *pro bono* obligation, like other affirmative obligations in the Code, would become part of "the minimum level of conduct below which no lawyer can fall"?

The decade since the 1969 Code went into effect has been one in which many individual lawyers and segments of the organized bar have indeed striven in the direction of the *pro bono* objectives set forth in Ethical Considerations 2-25 and 8-1 through 8-3. *Pro bono* programs of all kinds have been established in which thousands of private lawyers have contributed a full array of legal services.[67] Lawyers were instrumental in the creation and expansion of the Legal

Services Corporation, which channels federal funds to support legal services programs,[68] and which has itself supported the establishment and development of *pro bono* programs throughout the country.[69] And the American Bar Association, rather than accepting the provisions of the 1969 Code as a final standard, has been very active in the process of "striving" to meet the *pro bono* objectives stated in the Ethical Considerations. This activity is evidenced by the 1975 House of Delegates resolution,[70] the 1977 Report of the Special Comittee on Public Interest Practice,[71] and the Kutak Commission's Model Rules of Professional Conduct.[72]

It is against this background of development of the Code of Professional Responsibility, by which the profession has by consensus agreed to be bound, that the proposal of the City Bar Association's Special Committee should be considered, before any determination is made as to whether it is "revolutionary."

II. HISTORICAL ANTECEDENTS OF A MANDATORY OBLIGATION

Opponents of the proposal are of course correct when they point out that the legal profession has never been subject to a universal requirement that every lawyer devote time every year to uncompensated public interest services. Were it otherwise, the idea would not even be "innovative." But history does provide some guidance, and some indication of the direction in which the "dynamics of the profession"[73] are heading. Indeed, many of the judicial decisions cited by opponents to show a lack of historical and constitutional underpinnings for the mandatory requirement are in fact evidence of the rising expectations that lawyers do have enforceable obligations which now extend beyond the 1908 concept of representing "indigent prisoners." And the very concerns cited in those decisions as reasons for not requiring individual lawyers to render uncompensated services in individual cases would be in large measure alleviated if every lawyer were required to devote an average of thirty to fifty hours each year to the broad spectrum of public service practice.

A. The Litigant's Right to Counsel: The Criminal-Civil Dichotomy

When opponents of the proposal consider the historical record, they are quick to note that most judicial decisions recognizing the obligation of lawyers to serve without fee have been individual *criminal* cases, where the accused has a constitutional right to the assistance of counsel.[74] They argue that the rationale for imposing such an obligation in individual criminal cases—assertedly that the lawyer "is performing a duty to the state by helping carry out one of the state's obligations"[75]—is not present in civil litigation (or in nonlitigated matters) and, therefore, that the history of court appointments of counsel in criminal cases must be rejected as affording any basis for moving toward a broad mandatory obligation of every lawyer.[76] It is therefore assumed that the litigant's right to counsel and the lawyer's duty to serve go hand in hand.

It has already been seen how the ABA Code has evolved from the 1908 "indigent prisoner" formulation to the 1969 recognition of a duty to render "free legal services to those unable to pay"—without reference to the accused's right to counsel in criminal cases, or even litigated cases at all.[77] Likewise, the origins and development of the attorney's obligation to accept court appointments in particular cases—as opposed to the litigant's right to demand an appointed lawyer—afford no basis for limiting the obligation to criminal cases. For the lawyer's obligation has not been historically tied to the indigent's right to counsel at public expense or to the notion that the lawyer is helping carry out that obligation of the state. Rather, it has been based on the concept that the attorney has a duty to assist in the administration of justice as a condition of the license to practice and/or as an officer of the court, and that accepting court appointments is part of that duty.

An excellent review of the origins and history of the attorney's obligation to accept court appointment without compensation appears in *United States* v. *Dillon.*[78] There, the Ninth Circuit rejected an appointed attorney's claimed right to compensation for representing an indigent plaintiff in a civil action to set aside a sentence under 28 U.S.C. § 2255.[79] Without distinguishing between civil and criminal cases, the court concluded from examining historical precedents that the obligation "to represent indigents upon court order, without compensation" was well established in "the traditions of the profession."[80]

As the *Dillon* court noted, the practice of representing indigents upon judicial order with little or not compensation dates from as far back as fifteenth-century England, where "serjeants-at-law" could be required by the courts before which they practiced "to plead for a poor man."[81] In his 1923 article, *Poverty and Civil Litigation,* Professor Maguire quoted pleadings from a fifteenth-century *in forma pauperis* case in the Court of Requests which showed an impoverished litigant having been assigned serjeants and an attorney "to geue hym Councell without payng eny Feez For the same."[82]

The duty of lawyers to serve when judicially assigned was articulated unequivocally in the seventeenth century by Chief Justice Hale, who stated that "if the Court should assign [a serjeant] to be counsel, he ought to attend," and "if he refuse . . . we would not hear him, nay, we would make bold to commit him. . . ."[83] As the old English cases cited in *Dillon* make clear, this common law tradition of appointed counsel was not at all confined to criminal cases.[84]

In America, it was the criminal sphere that saw pronounced development of a tradition of court-appointed counsel. That is not remarkable, since many state constitutions, as well as the United States Constitution, have long provided for the right to counsel in criminal cases, thus presenting the most frequent occasions for such appointments.[85] The litigant's right to counsel in civil actions was never as fully developed in America as it was in England after Henry VII. That was in part because, in the nineteenth century, the high average wealth and low court fees and costs in this country rendered legal aid for the poor a relatively low priority,[86] and in part because the explosion in civil rights and remedies for indigents has been a product of the growth of modern cities and the expansion of public welfare programs in the past four decades. Nevertheless, several states have enacted statutes empowering, although not requiring the courts to assign counsel to indigents in civil litigation.[87] In recent years, some courts have gone further, finding that certain civil litigants have a right to appointment of counsel—usually on the theory that the case involves government action adversely affecting fundamental rights.[88]

The fact that the litigant's right to counsel has developed mainly in criminal cases in this country does not mean that the courts only have the power to appoint counsel—and attorneys a duty to accept appointment—in criminal cases. Rather, what emerges clearly from the history of appointed counsel in particular litigations is that three separate and distinct questions are involved: the right of the litigant to assignment of counsel; the power of the court to appoint counsel; and the obligation of the attorney to accept court appointment.[89] It is only the first of these that has largely been limited, at least until now, to criminal cases. But, as will be seen, the *power* of the courts to appoint counsel where necessary, and the corresponding *duty* of members of the bar to accept such appointments, are not confined to criminal prosecutions.

B. Judicial Power and the Lawyer's Duty

Although the courts have usually been reluctant to grant litigants a *right* to counsel in civil litigations,[90] they have repeatedly reaffirmed their own power to appoint counsel in civil cases where, in the exercise of judicial discretion, such assignment is deemed warranted.[91] Appointments have been made of attorneys to represent both plaintiffs and defendants,[92] and the courts have routinely assumed the appointed lawyer's duty to accept such assignment without guaranteed compensation.[93] Such a professional obligation of each lawyer to accept appointment without compensation is widely recognized in almost every state,[94] and has been codified by statute in more than half the states and in the federal system.[95] Indeed, courts have frequently pointed out that, while retaining the power to appoint counsel, they lack the power to order use of public funds to compensate counsel.[96]

The Eighth Circuit's opinion in *Peterson* v. *Nadler*[97] is instructive. In that civil tort case, the plaintiff was none other than an "indigent prisoner" suing his former attorney for fraudulent conversion of the plaintiff's automobile.[98] The court of appeals reversed the district court's ruling that it had no power to appoint counsel for indigents in civil cases, distinguishing that power from the litigant's right:

> This ruling overlooks the express authority given it in 28 U.S.C. § 1915 to appoint counsel in civil cases. This court and other courts of appeals regularly

make these appointments in habeas corpus and civil rights cases; district courts throughout the country do the same. It is true that there exists no statutory or constitutional *right* for an indigent to counsel appointed in a civil case. We have affirmed this principle many times. Still, federal courts do possess the statutory power to make this appointment, if within the court's discretion the circumstances are such that would properly justify it. This right has long been recognized.[99]

The court went on to consider whether the power should have been exercised in that particular case. It quickly concluded that the circumstances (principally, the fact of plaintiff's incarceration preventing him from investigating the case or obtaining evidence) "fully justif[ied] the appointment of counsel" and that "failure to do so here would amount to an abuse of discretion."[100] Finally, it considered the question of lawyers' duty to accept such an appointment:

> Lawyers have long served in state and federal practice as appointed counsel for indigents in both criminal and civil cases. The vast majority of the bar have viewed such appointments to be integrally within their professional duty to provide public service. Only rarely are lawyers asked to serve in civil matters. We have the utmost confidence that lawyers will always be found who will fully cooperate in rendering the indigent equal justice at the bar.[101]

The Eighth Circuit's decision, then, was based not on any right of the indigent prisoner to assistance of a lawyer to redress the wrong of his stolen car, but on the court's conviction that it had the power to appoint counsel and that it could reasonably expect that appointed counsel would serve as part of his professional responsibility.

The distinction between the litigant's right and lawyer's duty is nowhere more evident than in the majority and dissenting opinions of the New York Court of Appeals in the *Smiley* case.[102] There, the court split four-three against granting indigent litigants an absolute right to appointed counsel in civil actions. But both sides agreed that the courts have the inherent discretionary power to make such appointments and that members of the bar have a concomitant duty to accept such appointments. Thus, writing for the majority, Chief Judge Breitel said:

> Inherent in the courts and historically associated with the duty of the Bar to provide uncompensated services for the indigent has been the discretionary power of the courts to assign counsel in a proper case to represent private indigent litigants. Such counsel serve without compensation. Statutes codify the inherent power of the courts (CPLR 1102, subd. [a] . . .).
>
> . . . .
>
> . . . As for the Bar they follow, *as they are obliged to do,* the canons of their profession in performing obligations to the indigent and duties imposed by assignment of the courts.[103]

Although urging in dissent that civil litigants ought to have a right to counsel, at least in divorce cases, Judge Fuchsberg echoed the view that "the courts may nevertheless assign counsl and, in view of the *obligation of all lawyers* under EC 2-25 to represent the poor, such assignment does not constitutionally require compensation."[104]

The lower courts have not ignored the message of *Smiley*. Thus in *Farrell* v. *Farrell*,[105] a year later, the appellate division reversed a refusal to appoint counsel in a divorce case "in the interest of justice and exercise of discretion. . . ."[106] It's per curian opinion noted that:

> [D]efendant has established indigency beyond doubt, and, "in the circumstances, counsel should have been assigned in accordance with the Bar's traditional responsibility 'to willingly accept assignments . . . to help those who cannot afford financially to help themselves.' *Jacox* v. *Jacox,* 43 A.D.2d 716, 717, 350 N.Y.S.2d 435, 437." (*Yearwood* v. *Yearwood,* 54 A.D.2d 626, 387 N.Y.S.2d 433, First Dept.). The Legal Aid Society, which represents defendant-appellant on this appeal, is not able in the current financial stringency, to accept assignment of an unlimited number of cases of this kind without compensation, and it becomes necessary for the Bar, as of old, to fulfill its longtime duty.[107]

Thus, at least in New york, even if the civil litigant's right to appointed counsel continues to be a matter of discretion, the lawyer's *duty* to accept appointment is not.

C. Rationale for the Lawyer's Duty Today

If the lawyer's duty to accept uncompensated court appointment does not depend on the litigant's right to counsel, what has been its rational and what should be its rationale today? American courts have answered the first question either by finding the obligation to be inherent in the attorney's position as an "officer of the court" or by imposing such an obligation as an implied condition of the attorney's license to practice law,[108] which may really be two ways of saying the same thing.

As Chief Justice Weintraub of the New Jersey Supreme Court Stated in *State* v. *Rush:*[109]

> The duty to defend the indigent without charge is not a personal duty in the conventional sense of an obligation owed by one man to another, for the breach or nonperformance of which that other is entitled to dollar or other relief. A lawyer does not owe free representation to any and every indigent who chooses to demand it of him. Rather the duty is owed to the Court, and it is the Court's call that he is obliged to answer. The duty is to assist the Court in the business before it. The duty thus is an incident of the license to practice law. . . .

Likewise, the Ninth Circuit in *United States* v. *Dillon* reasoned as follows:[110]

> [R]epresentation of indigents under court order, without a fee, is a condition under which lawyers are licensed to practice as officers of the court, and . . . the

obligation of the legal profession to serve without compensation has been modified only by statute. An applicant for admission to practice law may justly be deemed to be aware of the traditions of the profession which he is joining, and to know that one of these traditions is that a lawyer is an officer of the court obligated to represent indigents for little or no compensation upon court order.

And, in *People* v. *Randolph,* The Supreme Court of Illinois reiterated that "[a]n attorney is an officer of the court and his license to practice carries with it the *steadfast obligation* to serve the court whenever called upon to do so."[111]

This consistent recognition of the attorney's "steadfast obligation" to accept uncompensated appointment as an officer of the court and/or as a condition of the license to practice has become even more essential in today's expanded and increasingly complex system of law and government regulation. Such recognition of the lawyer's unique obligation must be strengthened and broadened, not limited to the cases in which it was first enunciated. For today, as never before, citizens unable to afford even the most modest legal fees are nonetheless confronted by a myriad of laws and administrative regulations touching many parts of their daily lives and livelihood. This "explosion of laws"[112] has affected not only the poor, but the middle class and the rich as well, making everyone increasingly dependent upon the services of lawyers and the workings of the legal system. Moreover, it has been largely the legal profession which has supplied the combustible material, constructed the explosive devise, and ignited the fuse. As described in a 1978 *Time* magazine cover story:

> [L]egislative bodies of every size across America have been spewing forth new laws at a prodigious rate, more than 10,000 in some years; as it happens, more than half of the members of Congress and one-fifth of the state legislators are lawyers. Federal agencies, meantime, are generating an additional 35,000 or more new regulations every year. These developments have brought about a virtual revolution in American society: an all-pervasive invasion by courts, law and administrative agencies into areas that had previously been ruled by custom, practice or plain old-fashioned private accommodation.[113]

Nor has the "revolution" been restricted to the burgeoning of statutes and regulations. In the past fifteen years, the courts, at the urging of pioneering lawyers representing the disadvantaged, have created a host of new substantive rights and procedural remedies for the benefit and protection of the poor.[114] But those advances become empty promises without lawyers to vindicate the rights and pursue the remedies. As Justice Brennan wrote in an article published more than a decade ago:

> The complexities of modern society are not confined to the technological and scientific spheres; they infect all phases of social organization. The intricacy and pervasiveness of the webbing of statutes, regulations and common law rules in this country which surrounds ever contemporary social endeavor of consequence give lawyers a peculiar advantage in coming to grips with our social problems.[115]

The same point was made by Judge Seiler of the Missouri Supreme Court in 1971:

> The judge and the lawyers together are necessary for the courts to function. The lawyers cannot escape being officers of the court and cannot escape a certain amount of pro bono publico work, which inevitably go with the special and exclusive privilege of being allowed to represent others in the court. Despite the increasing (and I think regrettable) trend toward commercialization of the law profession, these obligations remain a part of the practice of law and I believe that thoughtful lawyers would not want it otherwise.
>
> . . . It would be a sad day for the courts and the profession if we get to the point where there is no obligation for a lawyer to serve as an officer of the court unless he is first assured of a fee.[116]

Thus, if it was true in 1872 that the duty of uncompensated services was, in the words of the Georgia Supreme Court, "not only the admitted *obligation* but the pride and glory of the profession from time immemorial,"[117] how much more important is it that the profession recognize an even greater obligation in the 1980s? On that basis, the Special Committee concluded that

> [l]awyers are the only key giving access to that bewildering, enveloping governmental-legal system which increasingly touches so many aspects of the life of individuals. If we regard the law as a unique profession, and recognize that the powers that accompany a license to practice law are equally unique, then we should be willing to accept a unique obligation in order to permit our profession to fulfill our own high perceptions of its role.[118]

D. The Judicial Backlash and Mandatory *Pro Bono*

Not all courts in recent years have responded to the "legal explosion" by reaffirming and broadening the "pride and glory of the profession" to accept uncompensated appointments. Rather, some recent decisions have dealt with the expanding need and rising expectations for legal assistance and the prospect of ever-increasing burdens on the profession by refusing to' appoint counsel to serve without compensation.[119] This judicial backlash reflects, more than anything else, the concern of some judges that it is unfair to single out the legal profession, and more particularly the relatively few litigating lawyers qualified and willing to accept court appointments, to bear a burden that should be more widely shared.

The concerns expressed in these few decisions, far from proving that the mandatory obligation must be rejected—as urged by opponents of the proposal[120]—would in fact be largely ameliorated if the profession as a whole embraced the kind of mandatory rule proposed by the Special Committee.

To begin with, several of the recent backlash opinions were written by courts in states which, as of those writings, relied exclusively on the tradition of uncompensated appointed counsel to discharge the state's constitutional duty to provide counsel to indigent criminal defendants.[121] These courts thus expressed understandable sympathy for the plight of a litigating bar which—especially in view of the increasing length and complexity of criminal prosecutions—was asked to bear that mounting burden alone.[122] But the Special Committee's proposal does not contemplate imposing upon the profession the entire burden of providing counsel for indigent litigants. Nor, as already noted,[123] does it require that every lawyer satisfy the mandatory obligation by accepting such court appointments. Rather, the proposal presupposes a state, like New York, in which full-time legal aid or public defender lawyers, paid from public funds, are the principal source of indigent representation. Those private lawyers who elect to satisfy their thirty-to-fifty hour annual obligation through acceptance of court appointments would be expected only to supplement, not replace, publicly-funded legal services programs.[124] Thus, the Special Committee's Report emphasized at the outset that

> lawyers as a group cannot alone do the whole job of providing for adequate *pro bono* representation and reform of the system of justice. Government has a major, till now scanted, role to play in funding and organizing these efforts, and other elements of society must contribute as well. What we have sought to identify is the special contribution the Bar can—and as a unique profession ought to— make toward these goals.[125]

The decisions declining to make particular appointments contain no suggestion of opposition to such a broadly defined and universally applied mandatory obligation.

Beyond the perceived unfairness of imposing the entire burden of indigent criminal defense work on the legal profession as a whole, the backlash opinions have even more frequently expressed judicial concern over the inequitable burden which court appointments place upon those individual lawyers—the relatively small segment of the total bar qualified and available for criminal defense work—who are typically tapped to serve as assigned counsel. Thus, a Georgia court, while "fully cognizant that an undue burden is placed on the legal profession as a matter of custom," also noted that "this burden is itself borne unequally by members of the profession in practice."[126] Likewise, a Kentucky decision observed that "an intolerable burden has been thrust particularly upon the younger members of the legal profession."[127] And another opinion, by the Chief Justice of Missouri, quoted the finding of an American Bar Association Project on Standards for Criminal Justice that "many individual lawyers have suffered personal hardship because of their loyalty to the tradition that no one should lack counsel because of indigency."[128] Finally, the Illinois Supreme Court distinguished between the acceptable burden imposed on the profession as a whole,

> where an appointed attorney can continue to accommodate his regular practice and business and is not compelled to assume a staggering burden and sacrifice that no reasonable person could expect of any member of the bar

and the "extraordinary" case in which

> appointed counsel cannot continue to serve because they are suffering extreme, if
> not ruinous, loss of practice and income and must expend large out-of-pocket
> sums in the course of the trial.[129]

It was only the latter case, not the former, in which the Illinois court was willing
to grant compensation.

The Special Committee's proposal of a thirty-to-fifty hour annual obligation
would not force any attorney to suffer "an extreme, if not ruinous, loss of
practice and income."[130] But it would help in at least three respects to alleviate
the concerns of unequal burdens expressed in the foregoing decisions. First, by
requiring every practicing lawyer to undertake some form of "public service
practice" each year, it would necessarily increase the number of lawyers who
would elect to discharge that duty by making themselves available and qualified
to accept court appointments, thus spreading the total burden among a greater
number of lawyers, young and old. Second, by increasing the number of relatively simple cases which can be assigned to private attorneys devoting thirty to
fifty hours annually, the mandatory system would enable full-time paid legal
services attorneys to handle more of the complex cases which might indeed
impose "extreme, if not ruinous" burdens upon any assigned counsel. Finally, by
assuring that every practicing lawyer is devoting the same minimum number of
hours annually to some form of public service practice, the proposal would
remove any basis for concern that an inordinate degree of personal hardship
would be visited upon those individual lawyers who exhibit "loyalty to the
tradition" of *pro bono* service. In these respects, then, a proposal that the
profession move in the direction of a universal mandatory obligation of all
lawyers does not fly in the face of these recent decisions, as suggested by some
critics,[131] but is in fact responsive to concerns expressed by those courts.

III. THE ASSERTED CONSTITUTIONAL IMPEDIMENTS

Some of the decisions discussed in the preceding section, motivated by the
courts' perceptions of undue and unequal burdens, have declared—often in
dicta—that the appointment of counsel for indigents without compensation is
unconstitutional.[132] Armed with this handful of decisions over the past fifteen
years, opponents of the mandatory *pro bono* proposal have now mounted a
full-scale constitutional attack grounded on three separate theories. They contend
that the Special Committee's plan would transgress constitutional bounds by:
(1) taking lawyers' services without just compensation in violation of the due
process clauses of the fifth and fourteenth amendments (and most state constitutions); (2) compelling involuntary servitude in violation of the thirteenth amendment; and (3) discriminating against lawyers as a class in violation of the equal

protection clause of the fourteenth amendment. Each such challenge, however, has been rejected by the vast majority of the courts that have addressed these issues. Numerous judicial decisions affirm that the appointment of individual counsel without compensation is a firmly established and constitutionally sanctioned practice. The imposition of a universal obligation on all lawyers would, if anything, fall more comfortably within established constitutional doctrine.

A. Public Taking Without Just Compensation

The constitutional argument most frequently advanced is that mandating *pro bono* service constitutes a taking of property without just compensation, in violation of the fifth and fourteenth amendments.[133] Of course, the fifth amendment's specific command that "private property [shall not] be taken for public use, without just compensation"[134] was long ago held to be one of the provisions of the Bill of Rights made applicable to the states through the fourteenth amendment.[135] Under that clause of the fifth amendment, the attorney's services are said by proponents of this argument to constitute "private property" and the court-ordered appointment to be a "taking for public use." In adopting that rationale in *Menin* v. *Menin,*[136] New York State Supreme Court Justice Joseph F. Gagliardi acknowledged that he was clearly in the minority, but reasoned as follows:

> It has often been said that an attorney is an officer of the court and his position is a matter of privilege, subject to certain burdens. . . . However, the right to conduct a business and enter a profession is considered a property right within the meaning of various constitutional provisions. . . . It has been said that the right to practice in any profession is "a valuable property right, in which, under the Constitution and laws of the State, one is entitled to be protected and secured" (*Matter of Bender* v. *Board of Regents of Univ. of State of N.Y.,* 262 App. Div. 627, 631 [30 N.Y.S.2d 779, 784]; Ann. 6 L. ed. 2d 1328, Professional License— Due Process). Whether an attorney's right to practice is regarded as a property or privilege . . ., such right is protected by the Federal Constitution . . . since "lawyers also enjoy first-class citizenship" (*Spevack* v. *Klein,* 385 U.S. 511, 516). Admission to the Bar is not a matter of grace. . . . Membership in the Bar with its attendant stringent requirements is a device designed to protect the public and assure them of competent advice. . . .[137]

But as Justice Gagliardi himself recognized,[138] the "overwhelming majority" of courts that have rejected the "taking of property" rationale have not done so because they disagreed with the notion that legal services are valuable property.[139] Rather, they have concluded that court appointments of counsel do not constitute a compensable "taking" of that property for "public use."[140] That conclusion follows from the established rule that enforcement of an obligation already owed to the public cannot constitute a taking for public use within the fifth amendment's strictures.[141]

Thus, the Ninth Circuit's decision in *United States* v. *Dillon*[142] squarely adopted the rational that court appointments of counsel are not an unconstitutional taking because the attorney owes a preexisting public duty to serve the court without compensation. The *Dillon* court first found, based on the analysis discussed earlier,[143] that "the obligation of the legal profession to serve indigents on court order is an ancient and established tradition."[144] It then reasoned that because an applicant for admission to the bar must be deemed to be aware of the traditions of his profession, his application indicates his consent to traditional legal obligations. By thus enlisting in his trade, an attorney undertakes to owe these duties to the government when called upon by the court. The court thus concluded that by an attorney's application to the bar, he "has consented to, and assumed, this obligation and when he is called upon to fulfill it, he cannot contend that it is a 'taking of his services.' "[145]

Dillon was cited with approval by the Supreme Court in *Hurtado* v. *United States*[146] in support of its conclusion that detaining a material witness at compensation of only one dollar per day was not an unconstitutional taking because "the Fifth Amendment does not require that the Government pay for the performance of a public duty it is already owed."[147] The *Dillon* rationale was also cited with approval by the Georgia Court of Appeals in *Weiner* v. *Fulton County,* as a prelude to the following conclusion:

> We incline to the proposition that lawyers undertake certain professional obligations over and above those demanded of some of the other professions, among them being never to reject, for a consideration personal to themselves, the cause of the defenseless. We also incline to believe that a lawyer, except in unusual circumstances, has no right and will make no effort to refuse a case which he is requested to take by a judge of the court before whom he regularly appears, and that such request is tantamount to a demand.[148]

Numerous other decisions have also rejected the "just compensation" argument on similar reasoning.[149] And even the minority of courts that have expressed sympathy for the argument includes some that have done so only as to those "extraordinary" assignments that cause unreasonable hardship for the unlucky attorney asked to take on an unusually heavy burden.[150]

The universal requirement of thirty to fifty hours per year, if adopted by the profession as part of its accepted code of conduct, would clearly pass muster under the *Dillon* rationale. The broadly-defined obligation proposed by the Special Committee would be one in the words of the *Dillon* court, "imposed upon [the lawyer] by the ancient traditions of his profession and as an officer assisting the courts in the administration of justice."[151] As an integral part of the Code, it would become a continuing duty to which every practicing lawyer must be deemed to have given his assent—as fully as the time-honored obligations to refrain from conflicts of interest[152] or to preserve client confidences.[153] Since the obligation would be one "already owed," lawyers called upon to fulfill that obligation could not, under *Dillon* and similar cases, be heard to argue that their property was being taken "for public use." Moreover, the Special Committee's proposal would also be upheld under the rationale of those courts that have expressed sympathy with the fifth amendment argument in cases involving "extraordinary circumstances" that impose undue hardship. A universal commitment of thirty to fifty hours annually—especially with the Committee's recommendations for a carry-forward provision and hardship exemptions—cannot possibly meet the "undue sacrifice or hardship" test of these cases.[154]

B. Involuntary Servitude

A second constitutional impediment frequently asserted[155] is the thirteenth amendment's decree that "[n]either slavery nor involuntary servitude . . . shall exist within the United States, or any place subject to their jurisdiction."[156] But few of the critics or courts that have advanced this argument have based it on any historical analysis of that Civil War enactment, or of the numerous decisions interpreting it over the course of a century.[157] Rather, the argument that mandatory *pro bono* constitutes involuntary servitude is typically couched in emotional terms, quite often including the following quote from the 1964 district court opinion in *United States v. Leser:*

> [The court] has no more power to compel a member of the Bar . . . to do the tremendous amount of work and put in the tremendous amount of time it would require to conscientiously examine the files and records in this case, and represent the defendants on appeal, and thus compel involuntary servitude by a lawyer to convicted criminals, than [it has] to make an order compelling these defendants, had they not been convicted, to pick cotton for a private individual.[158]

That quotation from *Leser* was featured prominently in District Judge Guin's recent opinion in *In re Nine Applications*,[159] which nevertheless remains the only decision that attempts to marshall any analytical support for the involuntary servitude thesis. There, the plaintiffs in Title VII civil rights actions applied for the appointment of uncompensated counsel under section 2000e-5(f)(I) of the Civil Rights Acts of 1964.[160] Judge Guin rejected the application, finding it to be "plain" that "inasmuch as Section 2000e-5(f)(I) allows for the creation of an involuntary servitude between attorney and complainant, it is unconstitutional and void."[161]

Judge Guin's conclusion proceeds from the unassailable proposition that the thirteenth amendment was intended by its framers to do more than abolish Negro slavery. Thus, as Judge Guin noted, the Supreme Court long ago held that the amendment "was a charter of universal civil freedom for all persons, of whatever race, color, or estate, under the flag" and therefore acted "to make labor free, by prohibiting that control by which the personal service of one man is disposed of or coerced for another's benefit, which is the essence of involuntary servitude."[162]

But Judge Guin's thirteenth amendment analysis not only begins there, it ends there as well. After adding the foregoing quotation from *Leser,* the opinion simply concludes that uncompensated appointment of counsel in civil cases would be "utterly in disregard of the constitutional protection afforded all to labor in freedom."[163] The remainder of the opinion concentrates on reaching the conclusion that civil litigants have no constitutional right to counsel, and thus distinguishing on *that* basis the established tradition of appointing uncompensated counsel in criminal cases. The opinion thus confuses, as noted earlier,[164] the litigant's right to counsel and the attorney's duty to serve. Moreover, it never explains why coerced service to indigents in criminal cases does not offend the perceived right under the thirteenth amendment of "all to labor in freedom," while in civil cases the violation of that provision is "clear."

In relying solely on such high-sounding phrases and the proposition that the thirteenth amendment did more than abolish slavery, *Nine Applications,* and those who rely upon it, overlook a venerable line of decisions in which the thirteenth amendment has been held inapplicable to "a call for service made by one's government according to the law to meet a public need."[165] As long ago as 1916, in *Butler* v. *Perry,*[166] the Supreme Court upheld against a thirteenth amendment challenge a Florida statute requiring "every able bodied male person" between the ages of twenty-one and forty-five to work without pay "on the roads and bridges of the several counties" for six ten-hour days each year. Such forced labor by every male was not involuntary servitude, the Court held, because it was "part of the duty which he owes to the public."[167]

Since *Butler,* the courts have recognized in numerous contexts that mandated service to meet a public need does not offend the thirteenth amendment. Most obvious, of course, has been the consistent rejection of thirteenth amendment challenges to both military conscription[168] and alternative civilian service by conscientious objectors.[169] But the courts have likewise rejected claims of involuntary servitude by citizens required to testify in criminal cases[170] or to prepare and file tax returns,[171] by a company required to perform involuntary labor to collect and submit data on toxic emissions,[172] and by students obligated to serve on cafeteria duty in public schools.[173]

The school lunch case, *Bobilin* v. *Board of Education,*[174] is most instructive in the present context. There, an extensive review of the leading thirteenth amendment cases persuaded the court that a balancing test was appropriate— "weighing the duties and impositions mandated by law against the public need [to be] served."[175] Noting that the mandatory cafeteria duty at issue required students to work no more than three hours per day, seven days a year, the court concluded that "the imposition is more than outweighed by the conceded public benefit involved."[176]

Such a balancing test ought clearly to result in rejection of the thirteenth amendment challenge to the proposed *pro bono* obligation of thirty to fifty hours per year. Because the mandatory provision of legal services is a reasonable step toward meeting recognized public needs, it would not be foreclosed by the thirteenth amendment under a consistent and unemotional application of the established precedents. To begin with, meeting the legal needs of the poor and improving the administration of justice for all are certainly as compelling public purposes as constructing highways or serving school lunches. Moreover, they are needs that lawyers alone are particularly suited to fill: almost anyone can serve in the military, work on a road or serve a lunch, but only lawyers can practice law. And thirty to fifty hours per year is a burden fairly comparable to sixty hours of road and bridge work upheld in *Butler* or the twenty-one hours of cafeteria duty upheld in *Bobilin.* Finally, of course, the proposal would not mandate that any lawyer render any particular service for any particular employer—which is the hallmark of "involuntary servitude."

The courts have also recognized that the thirteenth amendment does not prevent the imposition of *some* involuntary duties attendant to the right to pursue certain forms of employment, especially where the complainant is free to pursue some other calling. Thus, in *Pollock v. Williams,*[177] the Supreme Court said that, under the thirteenth amendment, the "defense against oppressive hours, pay, working conditions or treatment is the *right to change employers.*"[178] It was on that basis that, in the Curt Flood suit against professional baseball, the Second Circuit rejected the thirteenth amendment challenge to the baseball reserve clause, pointing out that no one is compelled to be a baseball player.[179]

If the courts tell a baseball star who has devoted many years of training and play to achieving excellence in his chosen profession that his only constitutional alternative to being forced to remain with a single team is simply to quit baseball, on what basis may lawyers be heard to demand less harsh treatment? No one compels us to enter the profession or to remain there. Presumably, we do so because we are induced by the material and intangible rewards that flow from the practice of law. Lawyers have long accepted the burdens that accompany such rewards—including the ethical obligation to continue a representation until formally relieved[180] and the obligation to accept court appointments—without complaining that those burdens are akin to slavery. Undoubtedly, a thirty-to-fifty hour annual *pro bono* obligation, if adopted by a consensus of the profession, will prompt some lawyers to conclude that the burdens of law practice have become too heavy and to change their calling rather than comply. But—unless we are to have one standard for ball players and another for ourselves—the thirteenth amendment cannot be held to prohibit the mandatory *pro bono* proposal.

C. Equal Protection

The last of the asserted constitutional objections, under the equal protection clause of the fourteenth amendment, is based largely on intuitive appeal; it has never been upheld or even seriously considered in any reported decision. The attorney's equal protection rights would be violated, the argument runs, if he is singled out from among all citizens or all other professions and alone required to donate services free of charge.[181]

The argument fails most noticeably from its fallacious assumption that attorneys would alone be burdened by the mandatory performance of uncompensated services. Tasks must be performed pursuant to public duties by a host of professional and business people. Governmental regulations of all sorts require individuals to conform their actions to legal standards without compensation for time thereby expended.[182] Indeed, the very practice of licensing professionals imposes upon them numerous obligations demanded by their professions as the *quid pro quo* of retaining the license.

The courts have consistently upheld against equal protection challenges laws imposing both affirmative obligations[183] and restrictions[184] upon particular professions as an incident to licensing. The state's power to impose duties as an incident to licensing is limited only by the "rational relation" test, since a particular trade or profession is not a "suspect class." So long as the regulation imposed on the profession is rationally related to a legitimate public purpose, it will withstand an equal protection challenge.[185] As the Supreme Court wrote in *Semler* v. *Oregon State Board of Dental Examiners,* there is no

> ground for objection because the particular regulation is limited to dentists and is not extended to other professional classes. The State was not bound to deal alike with all these classes, or to strike at all evils at the same time or in the same way. It could deal with the different professions according to the needs of the public in relation to each.[186]

This rationale for upholding particular impositions upon individual trades or professions dates back to the Supreme Court's opinion in *Seaboard Air Line Railway* v. *Seegers.*[187] That decision upheld not a duty placed upon a particular profession, but rather a law requiring common carriers—alone among business enterprises—to settle damage claims within forty days. The Supreme Court rejected the argument that common carriers were unfairly singled out for a special burden, in terms which could as well apply to lawyers:

> It may be stated as a general rule that an act which puts in one class all engaged in business of a special and public character, requires of them the performance of a duty which they can do better and more quickly than others, and imposes a not exhorbitant penalty for a failure to perform that duty within a reasonable time, cannot be adjudged unconstitutional as a purely arbitrary classification.[188]

In sum, so long as all members of the group being regulated are treated in a similar manner, any professional regulation rationally related to a valid public purpose may pass constitutional muster under the equal protection clause. The valid public purpose has been explained herein at length; that lawyers can perform services to further that purpose "better and more quickly than others" is beyond dispute. Accordingly under the Supreme Court's "rational relation" test, the mandatory *pro bono* obligation would not deny equal protection of the laws to lawyers as a group.

CONCLUSION

The Special Committee's mandatory *pro bono* proposal is of course controversial. The idea deserves serious and widespread controversy, not only in the journals and conclaves of the profession, but also among the concerned public, which supposedly benefits by legal services and is most directly affected by the problems plaguing our system of justice. The issues worthy of informed debate were noted at the outset of this article. It is hoped that the foregoing pages have helped lay to rest tangential and unmerited historical and constitutional arguments which only cloud the issues. For the proposal while innovative, is not without firm roots in history and tradition, and does not offend the Constitution of the United States.

Informed debate should continue, notwithstanding the apparent rejection of mandatory *pro bono*, for now at least, by the ABA,[189] and it adoption only in form, but without "teeth," by the Executive Committee of the City Bar Association.[190] Acceptance of innovative proposals takes time; only revolutionary change is accomplished quickly.

NOTES

1. Association of the Bar of the City of New York, *Toward A Mandatory Contribution of Public Service Practice by Every Lawyer* (January 1980) [hereinafter cited as *Special Committee Report*]. The other members of the Special Committee were Ronald B. Alexander, Hon. George D. Covington, Jack David, Alexander D. Forger, Stephen L. Kass, Edmund H. Kerr, Gail Koff, Daniel L. Kurtz, Bevis Longstreth, Norman Redlich, Martin F. Richman, Hon. Leonard B. Sand, Asa D. Sokolow, Saul Sorkin and Joseph L. Torres. Mr. Torres is the coauthor of a forthcoming article in the *Emory Law Review* on the ABA's proposed Model Rule 8.1. See note 2 *infra*.

The Special Committee recognized the need to move gradually toward a mandatory obligation. A "break-in" period before the final implementation of the plan was believed necessary in part to stimulate discussion among members of the bar and the public and to refine further extent of the obligation. *Special Committee Report, supra,* at p. 11. See text accompanying notes 4 & 59 *infra*.

2. ABA Commission on Evaluation of Professional Standards, *Model Rules of Professional Conduct* 8.1 (1980) (Discussion Draft) [hereinafter cited as *Model Rules*].

3. *Special Committee Report, supra* note 1, at p. 9.

4. *Id.* at p. 11. See note 59 *infra*. The "discussion and ferment" during the ensuing months resulted in a "Statement of Position" on behalf of the Association, issued by its Executive Committee on December 17, 1980. That position adopts mandatory *pro bono* as a rule of professional conduct, but considerably broadens the scope of activities that would qualify as "public interest legal services," permits financial contributions as an alternative, and would enforce the affirmative duty "through self-evaluation" rather than through reporting and disciplinary sanctions. See Association of the Bar of the City of New York, *Statement of Position Concerning Proposed Revisions to the Code of Professional Conduct* (December 17, 1980) [hereinafter cited as *Statement of Position*].

5. *Special Committee Report, supra* note 1, at pp. 37-49. The published Report also contains the separate individual views of committee member Alexander D. Forger, current president of the New York State Bar Association. *Id.* at pp. 35-37. The author considers Mr. Forger's stated views to be very much in the nature of a concurrence, rather than a dissent, since

he strongly supports institution of a mandatory obligation, albeit more broadly defned and justified by a somewhat different rationale than the proposal advanced by the Committee majority.

6. *Id.* at pp. 53-63.

7. *Id.* at p. 7.

8. *Id.* at pp. 9-11.

9. *ABA Code of Professional Responsibility* EC 2-25, EC 8-1, EC 8-2, EC 8-3 (1969) (as amended) [hereinafter cited as 1969 *Code*].

10. *Special Committee Report, supra* note 1, at p. 9.

11. *Id.* at p. 38 (Jack David).

12. See, e.g., *id.* at pp. 37-41 (Jack David), pp. 42-44 (Ronald B. Alexander).

13. *Id.* at pp. 38-39 (Jack David), p. 42 (Ronald B. Alexander), pp. 48-49 (Saul Sorkin), pp. 56-58 (Association's Committee on Corporate Law Departments).

14. These arguments are fully set forth in the majority report, the dissents, and the synopses of the views of other Association Committees. See generally id., *supra* note 1.

For discussions in favor of a mandatory *pro bono* obligation, see *The Oganized Bar: Self-serving or Serving the Public?, Hearings Before the Subcommittee on Representation of Citizen Interests of the Senate Committee on the Judiciary,* 93d Cong., 2d Sess. 64-83 (1974) (statement of Orville H. Schell, President, Association of the Bar of the City of New York) reprinted in T. Morgan & R. Rotunda, *Problems and Materials on Professional Responsibility* (1976), p. 82-85; Rosenfeld, "Legal Services for the Poor", *New York Law Journal* (December 13, 1975):1, col. 1. See also Elliot, "The Proposed Model Rules of Professional Conduct: Invention Not Mothered by Necessity," *Connecticut Bar Journal* 54 (1980):265, 284; Silkenat, "Lawyers' *Pro Bono* Duty," *New York Times* (February 6, 1979):17, col. 1; Tisher, "The Sad State of *Pro Bono* Activity," *Trial* 13 (1977):43. See generally Castillo, "New York Bar Group Rejects Overhaul of Ethics Code," *New York Times* (November 2, 1980):45, col. 5; Goldstein, "Lawyers Debate a Public 'Tithe,' " *New York Times* (October 21, 1979):§ 4, at p. 8e, col. 3; Margolick, "Ethics Panel Tempers Disputed *Pro Bono* Plan," National Law Journal (October 29, 1979):2, col. 3; Winer," Ethics Draft Ignites Uproar,"*National Law Journal* (August 27, 1979):1, col. 1.

15. That ethical code has undergone several permutations in this century. What is now the *Code of Professional Responsibility,* adopted by the ABA in 1969, began as the 32 Canons of Professional Ethics, adopted by the ABA in 1908. The Canons were supplemented and amended from time to time thereafter. See *Preface* to 1969 *Code, supra* note 9, at p. i. See also R. Wise, *Preface* to *Legal Ethics* at p. v (2d ed. 1970). The 1908 Canons were ultimately adopted in almost every state, *id.* at p. ix, and the 1969 Code is currently in effect in whole or in part in 49 states and in the District of Columbia. Wolfram, "Barriers to Effective Public Participation in Regulation of the Legal Profession," *Minnesota Law Review* 63 (1978):619, 632 nn. 51 & 52. For a comparison of the 1969 *Code, supra* note 9, as passed by the ABA House of Delegates with the code as adopted by each state, see ABA Committee on Ethics and Professional Responsibility, *Code of Professional Responsibility by State* (1977). The Model Rules currently under discussion by the ABA would, in turn, supplant the Code.

16. *ABA Canons of Professional Ethics* No. 4, reprinted in R. Wise, *supra* note 15, at p. 422.

17. *Id.* No. 29, reprinted in R. Wise, *supra* note 15, at p. 433.

18. See Legal Services Corporation, *Volunteer Lawyers for the Poor: A Guide to Model Action Programs* (April 1980):3, [hereinafter cited as *Volunteer Lawyers*].

19. 1969 *Code, supra* note 9, Canon 2.

20. *Id.* Canon 8.

21. *Id.* at Preamble.

22. For the definition of "Ethical Considerations," see text accompanying note 66 *infra*.

23. 1969 *Code, supra* note 9, EC 2-25 (emphasis added).

24. *Id.* EC 8-1 (footnotes omitted).

25. *Id.* EC 8-2 (footnotes omitted).

26. *Id.* EC 8-3.

27. ABA House of Delegates Resolution on Public Interest Legal Services (August 1975), reprinted in ABA Special Commission on Public Interest Practice, *Implementing the Lawyer's Public Interest Practice Obligation* (June 1977), pp. 19-20 app. [hereinafter cited as *Public Interest Practice*]. The House of Delegates is the policymaking body of the ABA and has the power to approve, disapprove or amend any resolution presented to it by any committee of the ABA. ABA Constitution art. 5, § 5.2, art. 6, § 6.1, reprinted in 101 ABA Report 1234 (1976).

28. See *Public Interest Practice, supra* note 27, at pp. 19-20 app. (emphasis added).

29. The full resolution, adopted by the House of Delegates in Montreal in August 1975, read as follows:

RESOLVED, That it is a basic professional responsibility of each lawyer engaged in the practice of law to provide public interest legal services;

FURTHER RESOLVED, That public interest legal service is legal service provided without fee or at a substantially reduced fee, which falls into one or more of the following areas:

1. Poverty Law: Legal services in civil and criminal matters of importance to a client who does not have the financial resources to compensate counsel.

2. Civl Rights Law: Legal representation involving the right of an individual which society has a special interest in protecting.

3. Public Rights Law: Legal representation involving an important right belonging to a significant segment of the public.

4. Charitable Organization Representation: Legal service to charitable, religious, civic, governmental and educational institutions in matters in furtherance of their organizational purpose, where the payment of customary legal fees would significantly deplete the organization's economic resources or would be otherwise inappropriate.

5. Administration of Justice: Activity, whether under bar association auspices, or otherwise, which is designed to increase the availability of legal services, or otherwise improve the administration of justice.

FURTHER RESOLVED, That public interest legal services shall at all times by provided in a manner consistent with the Code of Professional Responsibility and the Code of Judicial Conduct;

FURTHER RESOLVED, That so long as there is a need for public interest legal services, it is incumbent upon the organized bar to assist each lawyer in fulfilling his professional responsibility to provide such services as well as to assist, foster and encourage governmental, charitable and other sources to provide public interest legal services.

FURTHER RESOLVED, That the appropriate officials, committees or sections of the American Bar Association are instructed to proceed with the development of proposals to carry out the interest and purpose of the foregoing resolutions.

Id.

30. *Id.* at pp. 3-7.

31. Robert J. Kutak is chairman of the Commission.

32. For the definition of "Disciplinary Rules," see text accompanying note 64 *infra.*

33. *Model Rules, supra* note 2, at Scope and Definitions.

34. *Id.* 8.1. Due to the controversy engendered by rule 8.1, the revised draft of the Model Rules, to be published in May 1981, is expected to replace that rule with one which would *not* make the *pro bono* obligation mandatory. See "Proposed New Ethics Code Ready for Release in May," *New York Law Journal* (December 10, 1980):1, col. 2.

35. *Special Committee Report, supra* note 1, at p. 11. The Executive Committee's December 1980 Statement of Position advocates a longer black letter rule defining the scope of "public interest services" and permitting satisfaction of the obligation by financial contributions and/or through law firm programs. See *Statement of Position, supra* note 4 at p. 1.

36. *Special Committee Report, supra* note 1, at 5. The *Statement of Position* concludes that thirty to fifty hours annually "may be reasonable even under our broader definition" of public

service practice, but suggests an alternative rule of five percent of "professional time." See *supra* note 4, at p. 6.

37. *Special Committee Report, supra* note 1, at p. 13; see generally *id.* at pp. 11-16. The *Statement of Position* would expand the definition even further to include all "activities on behalf of the public for improving the law, the legal system or the legal profession, by providing legal services to persons unable to afford adequate legal representation or to public service groups or organizations by financial support for such activities or legal services." *Supra* note 4, at p. 1.

38. *Special Committee Report, supra* note 1, at pp. 11-16. Indeed, about the only activities excluded under the Committee's formulation are (1) those which do not involve use of the lawyer's "special training and experience," *id.* at p. 12; (2) bar association work and continuing legal education "unless exclusively directed to support of other parts of the public service practice definition," *id.* at p. 13; activities for which a normal fee is paid, *id.* at p. 12.

39. *Id.* at p. 16.

40. *Id.* at pp. 18-20. Although these were issues on which the Committee was closely divided, they were not critical to the majority's support for the basic concept of a mandatory obligation. And, as noted, the Executive Committee's *Statement of Position* endorsed *both* the financial and collective alternatives, *supra* note 4, at pp. 4-5.

41. *Special Committee Report, supra* note 1, at pp. 17-18.

42. *Id.* at pp. 20-21. The Committee believed that the carry-forward provision should be limited, and recommended that excess service be credited for more than four years beyond the year in which the excess service was performed.

43. *Id.* at p. 21.

44. See, eg., 22 N.Y.C.R.R. § 609.1 (1979) (App. Div. 1st Dep't):

Section 609.1 Filing Requirement. (a) Every attorney admitted to practice in New York State before April 1, 1979, who resides or maintains his or her office in this department, shall file a registration statement with the Office of Court Administration no later than June 1, 1979, and every two calendar years thereafter within 30 days after said attorney's birthday. Within 30 days of closing his or her office, opening any new office or changing a place of residence, said attorney shall file a new registration statement containing such information. An attorney whose office and place of residence are located in different departments need file only one registration statement every two calendar years.

. . .

(c) Such registration statement shall be on a form to be provided by the Office of Court Administration, and shall include the following information:

(1) name of attorney;

(2) date of birth;

(3) name when admitted to the bar;

(4) year admitted to the bar;

(5) judicial department admission to the bar;

(6) office addresses (including department);

(7) home address;

(8) business telephone number;

(9) social security number (may be provided voluntarily); and

(10) areas of concentration of practice (may be provided voluntarily).

The form shall contain an affirmation.

(d) Every attorney newly admitted to practice after April 1, 1979, who resides, or whose office for the practice of law is located, within this department, shall file registration statement within 30 days of the date of such admission, and every two calendar years thereafter within 30 days aftr the attorney's birthday.

. . . .

(f) Failure by any attorney to comply with the provisions of this section shall constitute grounds for appropriate disciplinary action by this court.

An identical rule is in effect in each of the four judicial departments in New York State. See *id.* §§ 696.1 (2d Dep't), 805.5 (ed Dep't), 1022.29 (4th Dep't) (1979).

45. Inclusion of such an attestation in the biennial registration would seem to be less onerous than the "annual report concerning such service to appropriate regulatory authority," which was contemplated by the 1980 draft of the Kutak Commission. *Model Rules, supra* note 2, 8.1. However, the City Bar's Executive Committee rejected *any* means of sanction or enforcement beyond "Self-evaluation"—thus rendering the obligation "affirmative" or "mandatory" in wording only. See *Statement of Position, supra* note 4, at pp. 1-3.

46. See 1969 *Code, supra* note 9, DR 1-101 to 1-103; 22 N.Y.C.R.R. §§ 603.1, .2, .4, .9, .14 (1980)

47. *Special Committee Report, supra* note 1, at p. 40 (Jack David).

48. *Id.* at p. 43 (Ronald B. Alexander). See also id. at pp. 60-61 (Committee on Professional and Judicial Ethics).

49. *Id.* at pp. 7-8.

50. *Id.* at p. 12.

51. *Id.* at p. 16.

52. The view that the mandatory obligation would breed a wave of new litigation in areas where nonlitigated solutions should be sought was expressed by one of the Committee's dissenters, see *id.* at 41 (Edmund H. Kerr), and by several of the other Committees of the Association that commented on the Report, see, e.g., *id.* at pp. 58-59.

53. See text accompanying note 50 *supra.*

54. Thus, services within the broad category of "Administration of Justice" would include many aspects of bar and civic association work, court reform studies, writing, teaching, service as an arbitrator, special master or referee—indeed, any uncompensated or nominally compensated activity related to improving the system of justice. *Special Committee Report, supra* note 1, at pp. 13-14.

55. This argument was raised by various commentators during the drafting of the Special Committee Report. See also Elliot, *supra* note 14, at p. 285.

56. The Committee noted the following examples:
E.g., DR 1-103 (duty to disclose certain Code violations); DR 2-110 (duty to withdraw from representation under certain circumstances and to continue representation under certain circumstances); DR 4-101(D) (duty to take reasonable care to ensure that employees keep client confidences); DR 7-102(B) (duty to reveal client's fraud); DR 7-106(B) (duty to disclose to a court directly adverse precedents); DR 9-102 (requirement of maintaining client funds in separate accounts).

In addition, the Canon 6 obligation to act with competence and proper care, though expressed in DR 6-101 as a "shall not," is in effect an affirmative conduct requirement.
Special Committee Report, supra note 1, at p. 51 n.8.

57. See, e.g., *id.* at pp. 40-41 (Jack David), 60 (Committee on Professional and Judicial Ethics).

58. This argument was raised by various commentators during the drafting of the Special Committee Report. See also Elliot, *supra* note 14, at p. 285.

59. *Special Committee Report, supra* note 1, at p. 11. Upon publication of the discussion draft of the Model Rules in January 1980, see note 2 *supra,* the ABA Commission on Evaluation of Professional Standards solicited comments from all segments of the legal profession and the public at large, and, in addition, held formal hearings throughout the country.

Of course, adoption of the Model Rules, which would supplant the current Code, see note 9 *supra,* requires the approval of the ABA House of Delegates. See note 27 *supra.* The House of Delegates is designed to represent the various segments of the legal profession: its membership includes, for the most part, one delegate from each state appointed by the ABA members from that state as well as delegates from state and local bar associations. ABA Constitution art. 6, § 603.2, reprinted in 101 ABA Rep. 1235 (1976).

60. If the House of Delegates approves a mandatory *pro bono* obligation, it will *then* fall to the local code-enacting authorities to give legal effect to that obligation. In New York, for instance, a mandatory *pro bono* obligation would be given legal effect upon adoption by the

several appellate devisions of the obligation as a rule of court. See, e.g., 22 N.Y.C.R.R. § 603.2 (1977) (adopting as rules of court the Disciplinary Rules of the Code of Professional Responsibility). See *Special Committee Report, supra* note 1, at pp. 22-23. Every state except Texas recognizes the inherent power of the courts to regulate the admission to the bar and the discipline of attorneys. Note, "Disbarment in the United States: Who Shall Do the Noisome Work?" *Journal of Law and Social Problems* 12 (1975):1, 8. See, e.g., Maryland State Bar Association, Inc. v. Agnew, 271 Md. 543, 549, 318 A.2d 811, 814 (1974) ("A court has the duty, since attorneys are its officers, to insist upon the maintenance of the integrity of the bar and to prevent the transgressions of an individual lawyer from bringing its image into disrepute."); Smith v. Kates, 46 Ohio 2d 263, 265-66, 348 N.E. 2d 320, 322 (1976) (per curiam) (authority of supreme court over discipline of attorneys is absolute); Note, "The Inherent Power of the Judiciary to Regulate the Practice of Law—A Proposed Delineation," *Minnesota Law Review* 60 (1976):783, 784-787.

61. Argersinger v. Hamlin, 407 U.S. 25, 44 (1972).

62. *Special Committee Report, supra* note 1, at p. 23.

63. See text accompanying notes 19 & 20 *supra*.

64. 1969 *Code, supra* note 9, at Preamble.

65. See, e.g., Tarasoff v. Regents of Univ. of Cal., 17 Cal. 3d 425, 551 P.2d 334, 131 Cal. Rptr. 14 (1976). *See generally* W. Prosser, *The Law of Torts* § 3, (4th ed. 1971) at pp. 14-16.

66. 1969 *Code, supra* note 9, at Preamble (emphasis added).

67. In New York City, the Community Law Offices (founded in 1968 and now the Volunteer Division of the Legal Aid Society), Volunteer Lawyers for the Arts (founded in 1969) and New York Lawyers for the Public Interest (a joint project of the Council of New York Law Associates and the Association of the Bar of the City of New York established in 1977) are but a few examples of organizations that enable private lawyers to fulfill their professional obligations under Ethical Considerations 2-25, 8-1 to 8-3.

68. See Legal Services Corporation Act of 1974, 42 U.S.C. §§ 2971e, 2996-2996*l* (Supp. V 1975), *as amended by* Legal Services Corporation Amendments of 1977, 42 U.S.C. § 2701 (Supp. II 1976).

Some of the activities of the Legal Services Corporation include "demonstration projects" designed to increase the *pro bono* involvement of private lawyers. There are also approximately 75 staff-attorney programs in which private attorneys serve as co-counsel, consultants or as legal counsel in conflict of interest cases. Legal Services Corp., News 1 (Mar.-Apr. 1979).

The Volunteer Lawyers Project of the Boston Bar Association consists of "a seven-person staff coordinating the work of approximately 650 private attorneys . . . involved in direct client services as co-counsel services with the staff. Each attorney agrees to accept five cases during the course of a year." *Id.* at p. 8. A similar program exists in San Francisco. *Id.* Finally, the Quality Improvement Project was recently established "to tap private bar resources, including paralegals, law librarians, office managers, and others. . . ." *Id.*

In spite of these and other *pro bono* programs by the Legal Services Corporation, former Corporation President Thomas Ehrlich noted in January 1979 that "the Corporation [would] be unable to fulfill its Congressional mandate" of providing high quality legal services to those unable to pay "unless the private bar substantially increase[d] its pro bono work." *Id.* at p. 1. See 42 U.S.C. § 2996 (1976).

69. See generally *Volunteer Lawyers, supra* note 18.

70. See note 29 & text accompanying notes 27-29 *supra*.

71. See note 30 *supra* & accompanying text.

72. See notes 2, 32 & 34 *supra* and text accompanying notes 30 & 31 *supra*.

73. See note 61 *supra* & accompanying text.

74. See, e.g., *Special Committee Report, supra* note 1, at p. 38 (Jack David), 56-57 (Committee on Corporate Law Departments).

75. Id. at p. 57 (Committee on Corporate Law Departments).

76. See *id.* at p. 38 (Jack David), 57 (Committee on Corporate Law Departments).

77. See text accompanying notes 16-23 *supra*.

78. 346 F.2d 633, 636 app. (9th Cir.), *cert. denied,* 382 U.S. 978 (1965). For a more detailed historical review, reaching the same conclusion in a criminal case, see Runckenbrod v. Mullins, 102 Utah 2d 548, 133 P.2d 325 (1943).

79. (1976). The court specifically recognized that the proceeding was not a criminal case and that Dillon's right to an appointed counsel rested not on the sixth amendment's guarantee for criminal defendants, but on due process. 346 F.2d at 635 n.1.

80. *Id.* at p. 635.

81. *Id.* at p. 636 (quoting 2 W.M. Holdsworth, *A History of English Law* 491 (3d ed. 1923). Holdsworth identifies one request by plaintiffs that the court "grant them a serjeant . . . for that they are poor folk" made as early as 1292. *Id.* at p. 491 n.3.

82. Maguire, "Poverty and Civil Litigation," *Harvard Law Review* 36 (1923):361, 370 (quoting Selby v. Mulsho, 215 Seld. Soc. 319 (1910)). Professor Maguire also noted that ecclesiastical lawyers, although formally forbidden by church canons to practice in the temporal courts, were permitted to do so if assisting or representing poor persons. *Id.* at p. 365. See also Note, "The Right to Counsel in Civil Litigation," *Columbia Law Review* 66 (1966):1322, 1325-1327. Both Maguire, *Harvard Law Review*:36 at pp. 376-377, and the Note, *Columbia Law Review* 66 at p. 1327, report that these early procedures did not survive in England.

83. Scroggs, 1 Freeman 390, 89 Eng. Rep. 289 (K.B. 1674).

84. See, e.g., Trevanion v. Anon., 12 Mod. 583, 88 Eng. Rep. 1535 (K.B. 1702) (Counsel was appointed for the plaintiff in a civil case "for none would voluntarily appear for him. . . ."). *Id.* at p. 583, 88 Eng. Rep. at p. 1535. See also Maguire, *supra* note 82, at pp. 363-369 (1923).

85. See W. Beaney, *The Right to Counsel in American Courts* (1955), pp. 18-24.

86. See Maguire, *supra* note 82, at p. 382.

87. See, e.g., *New York Civil and Practical Law* § 1102(a) (McKinney 1976) ("The court in its order permitting a person to proceed as a poor person *may* assign an attorney.") (emphasis added).

88. See, e.g., Cleaver v. Wilcox, 499 F.2d 940 (9th Cir. 1974) (child dependency hearing); Danforth v. State Department of Health & Welfare, 303 A.2d 794 (Me. 1973) (child custody); Farrell v. Farrell, 55 A.D.2d 586, 390 N.Y.S.2d 87 (1976) (defense of divorce action); Madeline G. v. David R., 95 Misc. 2d 273, 407 N.Y.S.2d 414 (Fam. Ct. 1978) (paternity suit). But see *In re* Smiley, 36 N.Y.2d 433, 330 N.E.2d 53, 369 N.Y.S.2d 87 (1975) (4-3 decision).

89. Even the courts have occasionally been guided by the nature of litigants' rights in concluding that they could not appoint counsel without fee. See, e.g., *In re* Nine Applications, 475 F. Supp. 87 (N.D. Ala. 1979), *appeal docketed sub nom. In re* Five Applicants, No. 79-3863 (5th Cir. Nov. 29, 1979), in which the court denied its own power to appoint uncompensated counsel in Title VII employment discrimination cases—despite a specific provision in the 1964 Civil Rights Act permitting such appointments, 42 U.S.C. § 2000e-5(f)(1) (1976). Judge Guin, who held that provision unconstitutional, was largely influenced by his view that "the property interest of a claimant under Title VII does not rise to the level of interest in safeguarding the liberty of the criminal defendant." 475 F. Supp. at p. 90.

90. See, e.g., Caston v. Sears, Roebuck & Co., 556 F.2d 1305, 1309 (5th Cir. 1977); SEC v. Alan F. Hughes, Inc., 481 F.2d 401, 403 (2d Cir.), *cert. denied,* 414 U.S. 1092 (1973); Peterson v. Nadler, 452 F.2d 754, 757 (8th Cir. 1971); *In re* Smiley, 36 N.Y.2d-433, 438-39, 330 N.E. 2d 53, 55-56. 369 N.Y.S.2d 87, 90-92 (1975). But see Note, *supra* note 82 (arguing that such right should be recognized); Note, "The Indigent's Right to Counsel in Civil Cases," *Yale Law Journal* 76 (1967):545 (same).

91. See, e.g., Peterson v. Nadler, 452 F.2d 754, 757 (8th Cir. 1971) (conversion action); Massengale v. Commission of Internal Revenue, 408 F.2d 1373 (4th Cir.), *cert. denied,* 396 U.S. 923 (1969) (civil tax case); Whelan v. Manhattan Ry., 86 F. 219 (C.C.S.D.N.Y. 1898) (personal injury action); Lee v. Crouse, 284 F. Supp. 541 (D. Kan. 1967), *aff'd,* 396 F.2d 952 (10th Cir. 1968) (civil rights case). See also *In re* Smiley, 36 N.Y.2d 433, 438, 454, 330 N.E.2d 53, 55, 66, 369 N.Y.S.2d 87, 91, 105 (1975), in which both the majority and the dissent agreed that the courts have power in civil cases.

92. E.g., Peterson v. Nadler, 452 F.2d 754 (8th Cir. 1971) (plaintiff); Farrell v. Farrell, 55 A.D.2d 586, 390 N.Y.S.2d 87 (1976) (defendant). See also Note, "The Indigent's Right to Counsel in Civil Cases," *supra* note 90, at pp. 555-556.

93. E.g., Whelan v. Manhattan Ry., 86 F. 219, 220-21 (C.C.S.D.N.Y. 1898) ("The attorney assigned by the court, in the event of nonsuccess, will, of course, receive nothing. . . ."); see Note, "The Indigent's 'Right' to Counsel in Civil Cases," *Fordham Law Review* 43 (1975):989, 1004.

94. Only Indiana, Iowa, Kentucky, Missouri, New Jersey, Utah and Wisconsin dissent from the otherwise unanimous view that in performing court assignments attorneys have no enforceable right to compensation. See State *ex rel.* Grecco v. Allen Circuit Court, 238 Ind. 571, 153 N.E.2d 914 (1958): Ferguson v. Pottawattamie County, 224 Iowa 516, 278 N.W. 223 (1938); Bradshaw v. Ball, 487 SW.2d. 294 (Ky. 1972); State v. Green, 470 S.W.2d 571 (Mo. 1971); State v. Rush, 46 N.J. 399, 407-409, 217 A.2d 441, 446-447 (1966); Bedford v. Salt Lake County, 22 Utah 2d 12, 447 P.2d 193 (1968); Dane County v. Smith, 13 Wis. 585 (1861). Of these, only the Indiana, Iowa, Kentucky and Wisconsin positions rest on constitutional grounds. The Missouri and New Jersey holdings were based on policy arguments of fairness to the legal profession. The Utah court objected only to legislative directions to appoint counsel without compensation, while reaffirming the power of the court to make similar appointments on its own initiative.

95. Note, "Indigent's Right to Appointed Counsel in Civil Litigation," *Georgia Law Journal* 66 (1977):113, 115-116 & nn.16 & 21; see, e.g., 28 U.S.C. § 1915(d) *New York Civil and Practical Law* § 1102(a) (McKinney 1976). One recent decision has construed the phrase "[t]he court may *request* an attorney" in 28 U.S.C. § 1915(d) (1976) (emphasis added), as indicative of the absence of any judicial power to compel such service. *In re* Nine Applications, 475 F. Supp. 87, 90 (N.D. Ala. 1979), *appeal docketed sub nom. In re* Five Applicants, No. 79-3863 (5th Cir. Nov. 29, 1979). The consensus of judicial decisions, however, has been that service in response to a court appointment is a mandatory obligation of each member of the bar—even enforceable by contempt. See, e.g., Schoolfield v. Darwin, 182 Tenn. 192, 185 S.W.2d 509 (1945); State v. Frankel, 119 N.J. Super. 579, 293 A.2d 196 (App. Div.), *cert. denied,* 409 U.S. 1125 (1973).

96. Moss v. ITT Continental Baking Co., 83 F.R.D. 624, 625-27 (E.D. Va. 1979); Haymes v. Smith, 73 F.R.D. 572, 574 (W.D.N.Y. 1976) (citing Tyler v. Lark, 472 F.2d 1077, 1078-79 (8th Cir. 1973); Payne v. Superior Court, 17 Cal. 3d 908, 920 n.6, 924, 553 P.2d 565, 574 n.6, 576, 132 Cal. Rptr. 405, 414 n.6, 416 (1976); *In re* Smiley, 36 N.Y.2d 433, 439, 330 N.E.2d 53, 56, 369 N.Y.S.2d 87, 92 (1975). But see People v. Randolph, 35 Ill. 2d 24, 29, 219 N.E.2d 337, 340 (1966) (in extraordinary case of extreme financial hardship for appointed attorney, court's inherent power of appointment necessarily includes power to ensure that counsel not suffer intolerable sacrifice).

97. 452 F.2d 754 (8th Cir. 1971).

98. The court did not say whether it was the conversion of that asset which rendered plaintiff an indigent.

99. 452 F.2d at p. 757 (citations and footnotes omitted).

100. *Id.* at p. 758.

101. *Id.*

102. *In re* Smiley, 36 N.Y.2d 433, 330 N.E.2d 53, 369 N.Y.S.2d 87 (1975).

103. *Id.* at pp. 438, 441, 330 N.E.2d at 55, 58, 369 N.Y.S.2d at pp. 91, 94 (emphasis added). Between the two quoted passages, Judge Breitel expressed concern over the "intolerable burden" on particular lawyers which might result from recognition of a *right* to assignment under N.Y. Civ. Prac. Law § 1102 (McKinney 1976) and the unfairness to certain segments of the bar of recognizing such a right in all matrimonial cases. 36 N.Y.2d at 441, 330 N.E.2d at 57-58, 369 N.Y.S.2d at 93-94. Such concerns are discussed in Part II-D *infra.*

104. 36 N.Y.2d at pp. 454, 330 N.E.2d at pp. 66, 369 N.Y.S.2d at p. 105 (citations omitted) (emphasis added). Judge Fuchsberg also note that, except for lawyers "who are only marginally able to maintain their practices, the private Bar can be expected to meet its service obligations to a substantially greater extent than it is doing at the present time." *Id.* at pp. 454, 330 N.E. at pp. 66, 369 N.Y.S. 2d at p. 106.

105. 55 A.D.2d 586, 390 N.Y.S.2d 87 (1976).

106. *Id.*, 390 N.Y.S.2d at p. 88.

107. *Id.*

108. See, e.g., Dolan v. United States, 351 F.2d 671, 672 (5th Cir. 1965); United States v. Dillon, 346 F.2d 633, 635 (9th Cir.), *cert. denied,* 382 U.S. 978 (1965); Jackson v. State, 413 P.2d 488, 490 (Alaska 1966); Rowe v. Yuba County, 17 Cal. 62, 63 (1860); Weiner v. Fulton County, 113 Ga. App. 343, 348, 148 S.E.2d 143, 146, *cert. denied,* 385 U.S. 958 (1966); People v. Randolph, 35 Ill. 2d 24, 28-29, 219 N.E.2d 337, 340 (1966); Warner V. Commonwealth, 400 S.W.2d 209, 211 (Ky.), *cert. denied,* 385 U.S. 858 (1966); State v. Rush, 46 N.J. 399, 410, 217 A.2d 441, 447 (1966); Ruckenbrod v. Mullins, 102 Utah 548, 561-62, 133 P.2d 325, 331 (1943); cf. Powell v. Alabama, 287 U.S. 45, 73 (1932) (dictum) ("Attorneys are officers of the court, and are bound to render service when required by such an appointment.")

One commentator has suggested that a "social contract [exists] between the legal profession and the general public, in which the bar receives monopoly power over the legal services delivery system in return for undertaking to deliver those services in an efficient and affordable manner." Brickman, "Of Arterial Passageways Through the Legal Process: The Right of Universal Access to Courts and Lawyering Services," *New York University Law Review* 48 (1973):595, 626.

109. 46 N.J. 399, 410, 217 A.2d 441, 447 (1966).

110. 346 F.2d 633, 635 (9th Cir.), *cert. denied,* 382 U.S. 978 (1965).

111. 35 Ill. 2d 24, 28, 219 N.E.2d 337, 340 (1966) (emphasis added).

112. *Special Committee Report, supra* note 1, at p. 8.

113. *Time,* (April 10, 1978) at p. 56. See Manning, "Hyperlexis: Our National Disease," *Northwestern University Law Review* 71 (1977):767.

114. E.g., Boddie v. Connecticut, 401 U.S. 371 (1971) (waiver of court fees in divorce action); Goldberg v. Kelly, 397 U.S. 254 (1970) (termination of welfare benefits subject to procedural due process requirements); Martinez v. Richardson, 472 F.2d 1121 (10th Cir. 1973) (same regarding medicare benefits); Escalera v. New York City Housing Authority, 425 F.2d 853 (2d Cir.), *cert. denied,* 400 U.S. 853 (1970) (same regarding public housing tenancy); Javins v. First National Realty Corp., 428 F.2d 1071 (D.C. Cir. 1970) (implied warranty of habitability for residential leases).

115. Address by Justice William J. Brennan, Jr., Harvard Law School Sesquicentennial Convocation (September 23, 1967), printed in *The Path of Law From 1967* (A. Sutherland ed. 1968) at p. 89.

116. State v. Green, 470 S.W.2d 571, 574 (Mo. 1971) (Seiler, J., concurring) (footnote omitted).

117. Elam v. Johnson, 48 Ga. 348, 350 (1873) (emphasis in original).

118. *Special Committee Report, supra* note 1, at p. 9. While the legal profession is unique for the reasons here discussed, it is not alone in recognizing a professional obligation to serve society without regard to compensation. Doctors are required to provide attending hospital services to poor patients as a condition of admitting privileges for private patients. Moreover, the new code of medical ethics adopted this year by the American Medical Association provides that "[a] physician shall recognize a responsibility to participate in activities contributing to an improved community." *New York Times,* (July 23, 1980):A12, col. 2.

119. E.g., *In re* Nine Applications, 475 F. Supp. 87, 91 (N.D. Ala. 1979), *appeal docketed sub nom. In re* Five Applicants, No. 79-3863 (5th Cir. Nov. 29, 1979); Bradshaw v. Ball, 487 S.W.2d 294, 299-300 (Ky. 1972); State v. Green, 470 S.W. 2d 571, 573 (Mo. 1971); Menin v. Menin, 79 Misc. 2d 285, 293, 359 N.Y.S.2d 721, 730 (Sup. Ct. 1974), *aff'd,* 48 A.D.2d 904, 372 N.Y.S.2d 985 (1975). See also Weimer v. Fulton County, 113 Ga. App. 343, 348-49, 148 S. E.2d 143, 147, *cert. denied,* 385 U.S. 958 (1966) (affirming denial of compensation to appointed counsel, but expressing strong concerns about unfair burden).

120. *Special Committee Report, supra* note 1, at pp. 38-39 (Jack David), 56-58 (Committee on Corporate Law Departments).

121. E.g., Bradshaw v. Ball, 487 S.W.2d 294 (Ky. 1972); State v. Green, 470 S.W.2d 571 (Mo. 1971); State v. Rush, 46 N.J. 399, 217 A.2d 441 (1966) (state law allowed compensation only in murder cases).

122. See Bradshaw v. Ball, 487, S.W.2d at 297 (quoting *State v. Rush* and adding emphasis on the word "alone"); State v. Green, 470 S.W.2d at 576 ("Society cannot justly impose this heavy demand on one segment of the population."); State v. Rush, 46 N.J. at 412, 217 A.2d at 448 ("We are satisfied the burden is more than *the profession alone* should shoulder. . . .") (emphasis added).

123. See text accompanying notes 49-51 *supra.*

124. A universal mandatory obligation would require, of course, a change in the current rule that every lawyer is bound to accept court appointments when asked, see notes 90-107 *supra* and accompanying text. Those lawyers who elected to satisfy the obligation by *pro bono* service of a nonlitigated nature, or in litigation representation accepted directly from clients, rather than through court appointments, ought in all fairness to be excused from any obligation to accept court appointments in addition. The problem could easily be solved by creating rosters of attorneys who signify their willingness to accept court appointments as their means of satisfying the obligation and limiting the courts to selecting by random rotation from such rosters. To ensure that enough lawyers choose that option to meet the courts' needs, it might be prudent to provide that simply listing one's name on such a roster satisfies the obligation, even if, in a particular year, actual court appointments do not generate thirty to fifty hours of work.

125. *Special Committee Report, supra* note 1, at p. 6.

126. Weiner v. Fulton County, 113 Ga. App. 343, 349, 148 S.E.2d 143, 147, *cert. denied,* 385 U.S. 958 (1966).

127. Bradshaw v. Ball, 487 S.W.2d 294, 297 (Ky. 1972).

128. State v. Green, 470 S.W.2d 571, 576 (Mo. 1971) (Finch, C.J., dissenting).

129. People v. Randolph, 35 Ill. 2d 24, 30, 219 N.E.2d 337, 341 (1966) (citation omitted). Cf. State v. Rush, 46 N.J. 399, 217 A.2d 441 (1966), in which the Supreme Court of New Jersey rejected an equal protection challenge to the appointed counsel system, finding no evidence that New Jersey's "sytem of assignment casts an unequal burden as among members of the profession" and concluding that the system "seeks to assure such equality of treatment as the subject will permit." *Id.* at 409, 217 A.2d at 446. See also SEC v. Tellco Information Serv., Inc., [Current] Fed. Sec. L. Rep. (CCH) ¶ 97,733. at 98.850 (S.D.N.Y. Dec. 16, 1980) (Judge Height found the full defense and trial of an SEC enforcement action to be "a burden far beyond that which I am willing to impose upon uncompensated counsel."); Brown v. Board of County Comm'rs, 85 Nev. 149, 153, 451 P.2d 708, 711 (1969) (The court, denying compensation to appointed counsel beyond the statutory limit, noted that "[i]t is to be presumed that courts charged with the appointment of counsel will never so burden one, or a few, members of the bar to the exclusion of others.")

130. Undoubtedly, as dissenters have noted, lawyers accepting court appointments will frequently find themselves forced to devote more than the mandatory minimum number of hours in order fully to discharge their professional obligations to their clients. It was precisely to meet that problem that the proposal contemplates a "carry-forward" of excess hours into future years. See *Special Committee Report, supra* note 1, at pp. 20-21.

131. *Id.* at pp. 38-39 (Jack David), pp. 56-58 (Committee on Corporate Law Departments).

132. See *In re Nine Applications,* 475 F. Supp. 87. 89. 91-92 (N.D. Ala. 1979), *appeal docketed sub nom. In re Five Applicants,* No. 79-3863 (5th Cir. Nov. 29, 1979) (involuntary servitude); United States v. Leser, 233 F. Supp. 535, 537 (S.D. Cal. 1964) (same, but dictum); Weiner v. Fulton County, 113 Ga. App. 343, 346, 148 S.E.2d 143, 145, *cert. denied,* 385 U.S. 958 (1966) (taking of property without just compensation, but dictum); Bradshaw v. Ball, 487 S.W.2d 294, 298 (Ky. 1972) (holding the same); State v. Green, 470 S.W.2d 571, 573 (Mo. 1971) (constitutional ground unclear, but apparently based primarily on Missouri state constitution); Menin v. Menin, 79 Misc. 2d 285, 293, 359 N.Y.S.2d 721 729-30 (Sup. Ct. 1974) Gagliardi, J.) (due process, but dictum because attorney's right to compensation was not before the court); Bedford v. Salt Lake County, 220 Utah 2d 12, 14-15, 447 P.2d 193, 194-95 (1968) (one-sentence conclusion of uncompensated taking an involuntary servitude). But see State v. Rush, 46 N.J. 399, 407-09, 217 A.2d 441, 445-46 (1966), in which the New Jersey Supreme Court, while declining prospectively to order further uncompensated appointments on policy grounds, rejected constitutional challenges on due process, involuntary servitude and equal protection grounds.

133. See, e.g., *Special Committee Report, supra* note 1, at p. 39 (Jack David), p. 42 (Ronald B. Alexander), p. 56 (Committee on Corporate Law Departments).

134. U.S. Const. amend. V.

135. Chicago, Burlington & Quincy R.R. v. Chicago, 166 U.S. 226 (1897).

136. 79 Misc. 2d 285, 359 N.Y.S.2d 721 (Sup. Ct. 1974), *aff'd mem.,* 48 A.D.2d 904, 372 N.Y.S.2d 985 (1975).

137. *Id.* at pp. 292, 359 N.Y.S.2d at 728-29 (some citations omitted), *aff'd mem.,* 48 A.D.2d 904, 372 N.Y.S.2d 985 (1975).

138. *Id.* at pp. 289, 359 N.Y.S.2d at 726, *aff'd mem.,* 48 A.D.2d 985 (1975).

139. See Comment, "The Uncompensated Appointed Counsel System: A Constitutional and Social Transgression," *Kentucky Law Journal* 60 (1972):710, 714-715 [hereinafter cited as "Uncompensated Appointed Counsel"]. Indeed, in the leading case of United States v. Dillon, 346 F.2d 633, 636 (9th Cir.), *cert. denied,* 382 U.S. 978 (1965), the Ninth Circuit Found it unnecessary to consider that issue because it held that there was no "taking."

140. A lengthy catalog of the many decisions in the "overwhelming majority" that reject the fifth/fourteenth amendment argument may be found in Weiner v. Fulton County, 113 Ga. App. 343, 347-18, 148 S.E.2d 143, 146, *cert. denied,* 385 U.S.958 (1966).

141. Hurtado v. United States, 410 U.S. 578, 588 (1973); see Kunhardt & Co. v. United States, 266 U.S. 537, 540 (1925); Monongahela Bridge Co. v. United States, 216 U.S. 177, 193-94 (1910).

142. 346 F.2d 633 (9th Cir.), *cert. denied,* 382 U.S. 978 (1965).

143. See notes 78-84 *supra* & accompanying text.

144. 346 F.2d at p. 635 *cert. denied,* 382 U.S. 978 (1965).

145. 346 F.2d at p. 635. The Ninth Circuit also cited the following language in Powell v. Alabama, 287 U.S. 45, 73 (1932), in support of its position: "Attorneys are officers of the court, and are bound to render service when required by such an appointment." 346 F.2d at p. 635.

146. 410 U.S. 578, 589 (1973).

147. *Id.* at p. 588.

148. 113 Ga. App. 343, 348, 148 S.E.2d 143, 147, *cert. denied,* 385 U.S. 958 (1966).

149. See, e.g., Dolan v. United States, 351 F.2d 671, 672 (5th Cir. 1965); Jackson v. State, 413 P.2d 488, 490 (Alaska 1966); Warner v. Commonwealth, 400 S.W.2d 209, 211 (Ky.), *cert. denied,* 385 U.S. 858 (1966).

150. E.g., People v. Randolph, 35 Ill. 2d 24, 30, 219 N.E.2d 337, 340-41 (1966); Brown v. Board of County Comm'rs, 85 Nev. 149, 152-53, 451 P.2d 708, 710-11 (1969).

151. 346 F.2d at 636.

152. See 1969 *Code, supra* note 9, Canon 5.

153. *Id.* Canon 4.

154. Compare People v. Randolph, 35 Ill. 2d at pp. 29-30, 219 N.E.2d at 340 (lengthy pretrial proceedings and a murder trial at a courthouse 150 miles from the attorney's residence, consuming several months, including nine weeks just to pick a jury) with Brown v. Board of County Comm'rs, 85 Nev. at 152-53, 451 P.2d at 710-11 (single practitioner engaged in criminal trial for over two months at cost of allegedly losing several regular clients did *not* meet the "extraordinary circumstances" test of *Randolph*). See also SEC v. Tellco Information Serv., Inc., [Current] Fed. Sec. L. Rep. (CCH) ¶ 97,733, at 98,850 (S.D.N.Y. Dec. 16, 1980), an SEC civil enforcement action in which the court had appointed *pro bono* counsel "for the limited purpose of making an initial review of the case and furnishing [an indigent defendant] with some preliminary advice." However, when that review indicated that the case was complex and "substantial efforts" would be required to try it, the court found that to be "a burden far beyond that which I am willing to impose upon uncompensated counsel."

155. See, e.g., *Special Committee Report, supra* note 1, at p. 38 (Jack David), p. 42 (Ronald B. Alexander), pp. 56-58 (Committee on Corporate Law Departments). See also *In re* Nine Applications, 475 F. Supp. 87 (N.D. Ala. 1979); *appeal docketed sub nom. In re* Five Applicants, No. 79-3863 (5th Cir. Nov. 29, 1979) United States v. Leser, 233 F. Supp. 535, 538 (S.D. Cal.),

remanded on other grounds, 335 F.2d 832 (9th Cir. 1964), *cert. denied,* 379 U.S. 983 (1965); Bedford v. Salt Lake County, 22 Utah 2d 12, 14-15, 447 P.2d 193, 194-95 (1968); *Uncompensated Appointed Counsel, supra* note 139, at pp. 716-717.

156. U.S. Const. amend. XIII, § 1.

157. Thus, for example, the Utah Supreme Court took but a half-sentence to conclude that uncompensated mandatory appointments would "impose a form of involuntary servitude upon" the lawyer appointed. Bedford v. Salt Lake County, 22 Utah 2d 12, 14, 447 P.2d 193, 195 (1968).

158. 233 F. Supp. 535, 538 (S.D. Cal.), *remanded on other grounds,* 335 F.2d 832 (9th Cir. 1964), *cert. denied,* 379 U.S. 983 (1965).

159. *In re* Nine Applications, 475 F. Supp. 87 (N.D. Ala. 1979), *appeal docketed sub nom. In re* Five Applicants, No. 79-3863 (5th Cir. Nov. 29, 1979).

160. 42 U.S.C. § 2000e-5(f)(1) (1976) provides in pertinent part: "Upon application by the complainant and in such circumstances as the court may deem just, the court may appoint an attorney for such complainant and may authorize the commencement of the action without the payment of fees, costs, or security."

161. 475 F. Supp. at p. 88.

162. *Id.* at p. 89 (quoting Bailey v. Alabama, 219 U.S. 219, 241 (1911)). *Accord,* Pollock v. Williams, 322 U.S. 4, 17 (1944) (purpose of thirteenth amendment "was not merely to end slavery but to maintain a system of completely free and voluntary labor throughout the United States"). In both *Bailey* and *Pollock* the Court struck down state statutes that punished a mere breach of a labor countract as violative of the thirteenth amendment.

163. 475 F. Supp. at p. 90.

164. See notes 74-89 *supra* & accompanying text.

165. Heflin v. Sanford, 142 F.2d 798, 799 (5th Cir. 1944); *accord,* Pollock v. Williams, 322 U.S. 4, 17-18 (1944); Butler v. Perry, 240 U.S. 328 (1916); United States v. Tivian Labs., Inc. 589 F.2d 49, 54 (1st Cir. 1978).

166. 240 U.S. 328 (1916).

167. *Id.* at p. 330.

168. See, e.g., The Selective Draft Cases, 245 U.S. 366 (1918); United States v. Gidmark, 440 F.2d 773 (9th Cir.), *cert. denied,* 404 U.S. 868 (1971); United States v. Crocker, 420 F.2d 307 (8th Cir.), *cert. denied,* 397 U.S. 1011 (1970); United States v. Fallon, 407 F.2d 621 (7th Cir.), *cert. denied,* 395 U.S. 908 (1969); Bertelsen v. Cooney, 213 F.2d 275(5th Cir.), *cert. denied,* 348 U.S. 856 (1954) (doctor's draft). Nor are these decisions distinguishable on the ground that conscripted soldiers receive a salary, since "the mere payment of a compensation . . . cannot serve to justify forced labor." Jobson v. Henne, 355 F.2d, 129, 132 n.3 (2d Cir. 1966) (dictum) (forced labor in a state mental institution).

169. See, e.g., O'Connor v. United States, 415 F.2d 1110 (9th Cir. 1969), *cert. denied,* 397 U.S. 968 (1970); United States v. Holmes, 387 F.2d 781 (7th Cir. 1967), *cert. denied,* 391 U.S. 936 (1968); Heflin v. Sanford, 142 F.2d 798 (5th Cir. 1944).

170. Hurtado v. United States, 410 U.S. 578 (1973).

171. Kasey v. Commissioner, 457 F.2d 369 (9th Cir.), *cert. denied,* 409 U.S. 869 (1972).

172. United States v. Tivian Labs., Inc. 589 F.2d 49 (1st Cir. 1978), *cert. denied,* 442 U.S. 942 (1979).

173. Bobilin v. Board of Educ., 403 F. Supp. 1095 (D. Hawaii 1975).

174. *Id.*

175. *Id.* at p. 1104.

176. *Id.*

177. 332 U.S. 4 (1944).

178. *Id.* at p. 18 (emphasis added).

179. Flood v. Kuhn, 443 F.2d 264 (2d Cir. 1971), *aff'd,* 407 U.S. 258 (1972). See also Powell v. National Distillers Prods. Co., 22 Empl. Prac. Dec. ¶ 30,630 (S.D. Ohio 1980) (plaintiff's thirteenth amendment cause of action dismissed absent evidence of compulsion to work); Beltran v. Cohen, 303 F. Supp. 889, 893 (N.D. cal. 1969) ("Plaintiff is not being compelled to work against her will for the benefit of the government. She may choose not to work.").

180. 1969 *Code, supra* note 9, DR 2-110.

181. See, e.g., Cheatham, "Availability of Legal Services: The Responsibility of the Individual Lawyer and of the Organized Bar," *U.C.L.A. Law Review* 12 (1965):438, 444; *Uncompensated Appointed Counsel, supra* note 139, at p. 715.

182. Similar fallacies plague the argument rasied in Webb v. Baird, 6 Ind. 13, 17 (1854), that requiring gratuitous services from lawyers in effect imposes a special tax on them in violation of the requirement of a uniform and equal rate of taxation for all citizens.

183. E.g., Hackin v. Lockwood, 361 F.2d 499, 502-04 (9th Cir. 1966), *cert. denied,* 385 U.S. 961 (1966) (minimum education requirement for admission to state bar); Golden v. State Bd. of Law Examiners, 452 F. Supp. 1082, 1085-93 (D. Md. 1978) (residency requirement for state bar admission); Tucson v. Stewart, 45 Ariz. 36, 51-54, 40 P.2d 72, 77-79 (1935) (electricians required to post bond); Robinson v. Hamilton, 50 Iowa 134, 135-36, 14 N.W. 202, 203 (1882) (periodic reports required of doctors). See generally 58 Am. Jur. 2d *Occupations, Trades, and Professions* §§ 6-11 (1979); 16 Am. Jur. 2d *Constitutional Law* § 322 (1971).

184. E.g., Williamson v. Lee Optical, Inc., 348 U.S. 483, 488-89 (1955) (opticians prohibited from fitting eyeglasses without ophthalmologist's prescription); Daniel v. Family Sec. Life Ins. Co., 336 U.S. 220, 220-25 (1949) (undertakers prohibited from selling life insurance); Semler v. Oregon State Bd. of Dental Examiners, 294 U.S. 608, 610 (1935) (dentists prohibited from advertising in an unprofessional manner). See generally Barsky v. Board of Regents, 347 U.S. 442, 449 (1954) (doctors subject to license revocation or suspension if convicted of a crime).

185. Williamson v. Lee Optical, Inc., 483, 489, 491 (1955).

186. Semler v. Oregon State Bd. of Dental Examiners, 294 U.S. 608, 610 (1935).

187. 207 U.S. 73 (1907).

188. *Id.* at p. 78.

189. *See* note 34 *supra.*

190. *See* notes 4, 35-37, 40 & 45 *supra.*

Michael D. Bayles

A Problem of Clean Hands

Consider the following situations. A gynecologist's five-month pregnant client requests an abortion because she is carrying a female fetus. The gynecologist, however, believes that abortions for such a reason are morally wrong. Should the gynecologist refuse to perform the abortion? If so, should he advise her where she can obtain one? Were no other physician available to perform the abortion, would he still be justified in refusing to perform it?

A prospective client asks a lawyer to defend him in a suit for breach of contract. The prospective client orally agreed to pay an elderly couple two thousand dollars if they would manage the rental of his house while he was out of the country for two years. The elderly couple has completely fulfilled their part of the agreement and due to recent illnesses and financial losses needs the money for rent and other necessities. However, the quite wealthy prospective client wants to defend on the statute of frauds barring the enforcement of oral contracts which cannot be completed within a year. The attorney believes the perspective client would be morally wrong not to live up to his bargain even though it is not legally enforceable. Should the lawyer refuse to take the case?[1] Should he refer the prospective client to another lawyer who will take the case on the client's terms? Suppose the prospective client says all the other lawyers in the community have refused to take his case? Should the attorney still refuse?

In both of these situations, a professional is asked to provide services to a prospective client whose proposed conduct, while lawful, the professional believes to be morally wrong. There is a standard view in the United States as to the answers to these questions of professional ethics.[2] It holds (1) that the professional has good reason to refuse his services if the thinks a prospective client's proposed course of conduct is immoral, but (2) he has an obligation to refer him to a professional who will provide the services. Finally, (3) if no other available professional will provide the services, it is more difficult to justify the refusal of services. There is less agreement about the form of this last point than the other two. Some people hold that the professional should provide the services; others that

From Michael D. Bayles, "A Problem of Clean Hands: Refusal to Provide Professional Services," *Social Theory and Practice*, vol 5, no. 2 (Spring 1979):165-181. Copyright 1979 Social Theory and Practice, Tallahassee, Florida. Reprinted by permission of the publisher and the author.

he should sometimes but not always do so; and others merely claim that it is more difficult (takes stronger reasons) to justify refusing to provide the services.

This paper challenges this standard view. The first section considers the claim that a professional who refuses to provide services on ethical grounds should refer a prospective client to one who will provide them. It argues that this claim rests upon a confusion between moral and personal norms and that by such referrals the professional aids the commission of moral wrong. The second section considers the principal claim that the professional has a good ethical reason to refuse to provide the services even though the prospective client will receive them elsewhere. The commonly dismissed argument that "if I do not do it somebody else will" is in fact a good one. Nor is there any advantage of personal integrity or responsibility which supports refusal. The third section argues against the claim that if no other professional is available, it is more difficult to justify refusal than were another available. Instead, it is claimed, only in such cases does a professional have a good moral reason for refusal. The standard view on this point rests upon either an assumption which supports performing the services regardless of the availability of others or an assumption of an individual relativism.

I

One difference between moral and personal norms is that the former apply to all persons. One's personal norms, such as returning student exams at the next class meeting or never dating clients, are not thought to bind everyone. Moral norms, however, do bind everyone. If one believes it is morally wrong to lie, steal, and cheat, one believes it is wrong for anyone to do so in relevantly similar circumstances.

If a person sincerely believes conduct is immoral, then he is willing to use the appropriate techniques of morality to prevent it. This point is part of what is meant by saying that a person sincerely thinks conduct is immoral. If a person will not use the techniques of morality to prevent immoral conduct, a good reason exists to doubt he sincerely thinks the conduct is wrong. People may dispute which techniques are appropriate for preventing immoral conduct. The minimum techniques are dissuading people from engaging in it and expressing blame of them if they do. One need not always attempt dissuasion or express blame; other considerations may militate against doing so. Yet, other things being equal, if a person sincerely believes conduct is wrongful, he is inclined to dissuade others from it and to express blame of them for it.

As it is appropriate to use moral techniques to prevent wrongful conduct, it is inappropriate to assist others in it. If a physician sincerely believes abortion in a particular case is morally wrong, he cannot consistently advise a patient where she may obtain one. To do so would be to assist someone in immoral conduct by knowingly providing a means to it. The physician would bear some responsibility for the wrongful deed. Believing the abortion to be morally wrong, he believes that it is wrong for anyone to perform it and for the woman to obtain it. If he directs her to a physician who will perform it, then he assists both of them in acting wrongfully.

It may be objected that as the abortion results from the free and voluntary actions of the woman and other physician who do not believe it is wrong, the referring physician is not responsible for the wrong. However, that someone does not believe conduct is wrongful does not make it permissible for them. The fact that neither the woman nor the other physician believes the abortion is wrong provides the referring physician with no reason to believe it is permissible for them. That they act freely and voluntarily does not absolve him of responsibility. Were the conduct illegal, whatever his legal responsibility might be, his moral responsibility would not be doubtful. Suppose Stevens asks accountant Thomas to falsify his financial statement on a stock issue to be filed with the Securities and Exchange Commission. Thomas would not be completely free of moral responsibility were he to refuse to falsify the statement but knowingly to refer Stevens to Ulrich who would do so.

Someone might suggest that the difference between conduct which is merely immoral and that which is also illegal is significant. If people were agreed that the client's proposed conduct is seriously immoral, then it would be illegal. As it is not illegal, public doubt about its immorality must exist. Given the doubtful moral status of the action, the professional should assist the client in acting autonomously and refer him to another.

There are two points about this argument. First, it assumes a doubtful account of the relation between law and morality. Some immoral conduct is not so bad that its prevention would outweigh the bad in exercising coercion. Nor may one assume that all conduct which would justify coercion is in fact illegal. Second, and more importantly, to the extent the professional has doubts about the immorality of the conduct, he has less reason for refusing to provide the services. Henceforth, I assume the professional is quite certain of the conduct's immorality.

The argument against referring prospective clients to other professionals appears consequential. It assumes that the rightness of one's actions partly depends on their effect in reducing morality. The aim is to avoid increasing the incidence of wrongful conduct. However, it does not assume that the correct morality is pure consequentialism. The professional may well have nonconsequentialist grounds for believing a prospective client's proposed conduct is immoral. Indeed, few antiabortionists are consequentialists. The consequentialism involved is inescapable in morality, for it is the "consequentialism" of claiming that it is better that wrongful conduct not occur, that one ought not assist in it, and that one ought to use appropriate moral techniques to prevent it. While this "consequentialism" is assumed in the rest of the paper, no assumption is made about the correctness of standard consequentialist or deontological approaches to ethics. The arguments are drawn from the inescapable consequentialism of having moral principles. The arguments thus apply to both consequentialists and deontologists.

II

Suppose a professional accepts the previous argument. He decides that if he refuses to accept clients because their proposed conduct is immoral, he will not refer them to other professionals. He must still decide whether he should refuse to provide such requested services. This question needs to be made more precise. In this section, it is assumed that if a professional refuses, the prospective client can obtain the services elsewhere. The next section considers the situation when the prospective client cannot obtain services elsewhere.

Charles Fried has discussed whether a lawyer may refuse to accept a client who asks him to do do something personally distasteful or immoral. He argues that to require a lawyer to provide services would limit his freedom and autonomy. Thus, he concludes, a lawyer is free to refuse a morally repugnant case if another lawyer can be found.[3]

This issue is not the one to be considered here. Rather, the one here is whether a professional has a good ethical reason for refusing to provide services to a prospective client whose proposed conduct he deems immoral. This question is more basic than Fried's. It may not even be capable of being raised on his view, for he holds that in a reasonably just society "the individual lawyer does a morally worthy thing whomever he serves. . . .[4] The lawyer intends to assist the client in exercising his legal rights, and has no part in the ultimate harm the client may produce by so doing. The lawyer's role insulates him from responsibility for the ultimate effect of the client's exercise of rights.[5] Even if one accepts this argument for lawyers, it will not serve for physicians. The Constitutional right to an abortion is a protection from state prohibition of it, not a guarantee that one will be provided. Yet, many people think that a professional has a good reason not to provide services for clients whose conduct he deems immmoral. Federal funding of hospitals permits them and medical personnel to refuse to participate in abortions on grounds of conscience. But would a professional be performing a wrong act in providing services to a client engaged in morally wrong conduct when another professional would provide them if he did not? Does he have a good ethical reason to refuse?

The basic argument for claiming a professional would not act wrongly is as follows: Refusal to perform the services will not prevent the wrongful conduct. As the wrong will occur anyway, there is no moral gain from refusing to perform the services. Assuming the professional does not have a special relation with the prospective client, the world is not morally worse if he rather some other professional performs the services. In short, it makes no difference whether or not he does it, because if he does not someone else will. The conclusion is not that he has an obligation to perform the services, only that it is not morally wrong to do so.

Previous philosophical dicussion of this "no difference" argument has usually been in the context of the acceptability of a purely consequentialist or utilitarian theory.[6] As the argument is the revese of that in the previous section, it shares its "consequentialism." The previous argument was that one should not refer the prospective client to another professional, because that would increase the chances of wrongful conduct occurring. This argument is that as wrongful conduct cannot be prevented by moral techniques, no reason supports not providing the services. This argument does not assume a pure consequentialism in ethics any more than the previous one. The basis for believing the proposed conduct to be immoral need not be consequentialist. All that need be assumed is that if an act makes no difference to the occurrence of moral wrong, it is not morally wrong. To deny this premise would be irrational, for it would be to claim that doing A is wrong but refraining from doing A is not wrong although there is no difference in the moral wrong that results. Because the "no difference" argument does not assume consequentialism, one must distinguish between criticisms which are directed to consequentialism and those which apply to the "no difference" argument.

It is crucial to get the structure of the "no difference" argument correct. M. J. Scott-Taggart claims it has the following form: "If X does A then X does something wrong, while if I[Y] do A then I[Y] shall not do something wrong."[7] He objects that it is nonsense unless one can point to a morally relevant difference between X and Y. But the situations are different. Y would not do A if X would not. But X would do A even if Y would not. The difference is in the behavior of others. Clearly, the behavior of others is sometimes morally relevant. Anyone who would deny its relevance here must show
why it is irrelevant in this type of situation but relevant in others.

Scott-Taggart's formulation of the structure of the argument is inadequate, because it does not properly show the relevance of others' conduct. The structure is as follows: "(P1) It is morally better that no one do A than that someone do A. (P2) Someone will do A if Y does not. (P3) It will not be better if Y refrains from doing A, because A will be done anyway. (C1) Hence, it makes no difference whether Y does A. (P4) If an act makes no difference to the occurrence of moral wrong, it is not morally wrong. (C2) Therefore, Y's doing A is not morally wrong." This structure shows the difference between X and Y because in X's case P2 is not true.

This argument is not self-contradictory. One might think that P1 contradicts C2, that Y's doing A is not wrong. If P1 stated that it is wrong for anyone to do A, a contradiction would result. P1 does not make that absolute claim; instead, it is comparative. It states that no one's doing A is morally preferable to someone's doing A. It does not follow from this comparative statement that Y's doing A is wrong.

One line of attack on the argument is to challenge P3. It is ambiguous between P3′, "it will not be better with respect to A's occurring if Y refrains from doing it," and P3″, "it will not be better, everything considered, if Y refrains from doing it." P3″ is needed for the argument to be valid. It may be claimed (as utilitarians often do) that P3″ is rarely true because of side effects.[8]

The side effects arguments are not terribly compelling for professionals. (a) Y might do something very good instead, for example, save a life or defend an innocent, indigent client. But X might also do something very good instead. Moreover, this alleged side effect assumes Y has clients banging on his door, which is often untrue of lawyers in solo practice. (b) Y's refusal might significantly influence others not to perform such services. But as professional-client discussions are confidential, refusal in the particular case will not be widely known. Nor may one plausibly contend confidentiality should not obtain when professionals refuse a case, because such a practice would discourage clients from explaining their cases before professionals agree to help them. (c) Y might slither down a slippery slope and engage in immoral conduct in other situations. Like any other slippery slope argument, this one requires supporting evidence. Situations in which the "no difference" argument applies are conceptually distinct from others, so one needs evidence that professionals would either not make or not conform to the conceptual distinction.

For most people inclined to reject the "no difference" argument, side effects arguments are crucially defective because they are contingent. Perhaps in most cases side effects are sufficient to show that Y should refuse, but they may not be so. Indeed, they may indicate that, everything considered, it would be better that Y rather than X perform the services. For example, without knowing what the case was, Y may have promised a friend that he would take the prospective client's case.

Another objection to the "no difference" argument rests upon knowledge. If Y refuses to perform the services, he cannot be sure the wrongful conduct will occur, but if he undertakes to perform them, then he is sure it will occur. Consequently, in refusing, Y chooses a possibility of wrong rather than certainty. There are two responses to this objection. First, it is not always less certain that the wrongful conduct will occur if Y refuses. Even if Y refrains from referring the prospective client, he may know that other professionals will perform the services and that the client will retain one of them. The client may simply say, "I know attorney X will do it, but I would rather retain you because I think you are more capable." Second, the other professionals may not think the conduct wrong and so not attempt to dissuade the client. If Y accepts the client himself, he may be able to dissuade him or at least mitigate the wrong done. The more adamant the client, the less likely he will be dissuaded, but the more likely he will retain another professional.

Another usual objection is that the "no difference" argument would justify Germans cooperating with the Nazi Gestapo or concentration camps. A frequent claim of Nazi collaborators was, "Had I not done it, someone else would have." If one accepts the "no difference" argument, one must exonerate those who collaborated with the Nazi brutalities.

This objection fails to consider sufficiently the underlying principle of argument. The general aim is to prevent wrong occurring. It has been tacitly assumed that the professional would not be justified in coercively preventing the client from his course of conduct. One can imagine an obstetrician kidnapping his patient and, to prevent self-abortion, keeping her bound until she delivers. If the wrong is bad enough, coercion may be justified to prevent it. Lawyers are obligated by the *Code of Professional Responsibility* to inform authorities if they know beyond a reasonable doubt that their client intends to commit a crime.[9] Similarly, Germans were justified in active resistance to the Nazis. The evils being perpetrated by the Nazis justified coercion to prevent them.

Moreover, one must distinguish between particular acts and a whole course of conduct. At most it justifies particular acts, such as making a particular run with a Nazi military supply train. It does not justify complete submission to Naziism, because the resistance of one more person does make a difference. A German might have both worked for the Nazis and participated in the resistance, but then he would not use the "no difference" argument. Instead, his justification would be that he could make the greatest contribution to resistance (prevention of wrongful conduct) by doing so.

A parallel point applies to professionals. The "no difference" argument does not imply that a professional should refrain from trying to prevent future immoral conduct of that type. Indeed, he should probably actively campaign to get all professionals to cease providing services in such cases. Such activity would also help prevent situations in which X does it because he thinks Y will if he does not, and Y does it because he thinks X will if he does not. By campaigning to get all professionals to cease providing services in such cases, they are likely to learn of each other's views and overcome the ignorance.

If the usual side effects do not pertain and one still wishes to argue that professional Y ought not provide the services merly because X will, then one must show something intrinsic to Y which makes it morally worse for him to perform the services than for X to do so. Someone will do A, so the world will be morally worse than if no one did A. The issue is whether it is any worse if Y rather than X does it. Numerical difference alone is morally irrelevant. Nor can one simply appeal to agency, as both X and Y will be agents. One must show some difference in the agency of X and Y. Another and more difficult objection attacks at just this point. The "no difference" argument, it contends, misses the element of personal integrity. If Y performs the services, he will be a morally worse person. The evil may occur, but if he does not do it, his hands will be clean; he will preserve his moral integrity.[10]

To some people this objection appears to involve a moral egoism, being concerned only with the cleanliness of one's own hands. "It is excessively self-regarding," Jonathan Glover remarks, "placing considerations of either my own feelings or purity of character far too high on the scale of factors to be considered."[11] This reply will not be pursued because a more serious difficulty affects the objection. Performing services cannot make a professional a morally worse person unless it is wrong for *him* to perform them. Yet the "no difference" argument's conclusion is that it would not be wrong for him to perform the services. While it would be better that the client not do what he proposes to do, the issue is whether it is any worse if Y aids him than if X does. The objection either assumes that it is or ignores the issue. Consequently, this objection begs the question. For example, the Socratic argument that it is better to suffer a wrong (even death) than to commit a wrong begs the question. It assumes the act is wrong which is precisely the point the "no difference" argument disputes. If correct, this reply is conclusive. As many persons will think that this reply is too easy and that the objection was not sufficiently or properly developed, this issue deserves further exploration.

Perhaps the crux of the standard view is a particular thesis about a person's responsibility. On this view, if Y provides the services, he is responsible for the wrong done, but he does not provide them, although he may foresee that wrong will result despite his refusal, he is not responsible for it—his hands are clean. It distinguishes causing or allowing an evil from doing something which will fore-seeably be followed by a wrong action. Alan Donagan specifies these distinctions as follows:

> A human being causes an event . . . either by directly making it happen or by directly making something else happen, which, as an intervention in the course of nature, is among a set of nonredundant conditions jointly sufficient for the event's occurrence. He allows an event to happen when he abstains from intervening in some way open to him, while being aware that, apart from interventions by others, the event both will happen if he does not intervene in that way and will not happen if he does. . . . What an agent causes or allows to happen follows in the course of nature from his intervention or abstention. But he can foresee is not confined to what follows in the course of nature. A man can often foresee (not infallibly) how others will react to what he does. And his foresight does not affect the causal status of their actions. What they do, even though he foresees it, is neither caused nor allowed to happen by him.[12]

Donagan recognizes that it may be wrong for a person to perform an action when he foresees it will be met by a wrongful reaction, for example, when he has an alternative which would not be so met. Yet, Donagan notes, traditional morality forbids one to perform certain actions, such as treason, even if refusal will be foreseeably followed by the murder of an innocent hostage, although it is (with few exceptions) also forbidden to cause the death of an innocent person.

Donagan is correct about traditional morality, and the traditional morality is reflected in the standard view that a professional has a good reason to refuse to assist a client in wrongful conduct. However, the issue is whether the traditional and standard views have a rational basis. Although one cannot conclusively establish that they have no reasonable basis, one can show that the most plausible reasons which might be advanced are unsatisfactory and that another account will plausibly cover usual cases.

The distinction between causing or allowing an event to happen and per-forming an action which will foreseeably result in a wrongful reaction is not itself the decisive factor in the usual cases. Consider cases in which it is wrong to perform an action which will be met by a wrong reaction, namely, when an alternative action would not be so met. For example, suppose a criminal defense attorney learns that his client's best friend has offered to testify against him. If the attorney informs his client that his friend will testify against him, the client will beat up his friend. If the attorney breaks down the friend's testimony at trial (as he believes he can), then his client will not beat the man up. In this situation, it would be wrong for the attorney to inform his client that his friend will testify against him. The most obvious reason for the action being wrong is that he could prevent wrongful conduct. If that is so, then when the wrong will occur whether or not one performs an action, there is no reason not to perform it. That is, if his client will beat up his friend in any case, there is not reason to delay telling him.

Next, consider cases in which it is appropriate to perform an action which will foreseeably be followed by a wrongful reaction in order to avoid performing one which causes or allows wrong. The decisive factors may be the comparable seriousness of the wrongs and the certainty of their occurrence. In Donagan's treason example, it might be judged that the wrong of treason is more serious than the wrong of the murder of an innocent person. Or, it might be judged that while the wrongs are equally serious, the treason is certain to occur whereas the murder is not; the other person may not carry out his threat.

An example of Bernard Williams suggest that it is the seriousness or certainty of the wrong which is decisive.[13] A man in a South American town finds twenty bound Indians against a wall about to be executed. The captain in charge of the execution offers to let the other nineteen go free if the man kills one. Williams does not claim that it would be wrong to kill the single Indian, only that it is not *obviously* the right thing to do. But if killing an Indian in his case may be right, it is because fewer innocent lives will be lost.

In discussing this example, Donagan claims that a reasonable person in the situation "would on no account agree to kill anybody."[14] His reason is the uncertainty of a refusal resulting in all the Indians being killed. He objects to the suggestion that the death of all twenty Indians must be the result of a refusal to kill one. However, if the reason for not killing one Indian is uncertainty, then the difference between causing or allowing an event to happen and foreseeing that one's action will be met by a wrongful reaction is not decisive.

Donagan's claim about uncertainty is surely too strong. if one considers the difference in the likelihood of events occurring, one must also consider the seriousness of the harm or wrong. Since the seriousness of the wrongs in Williams's example is 20 to 1, then to reasonably refuse to kill one Indian one should believe there is only a five percent chance of all Indians being killed if one refuses. Nevertheless, the difference in certainty could account for Williams's hestitation about it being obviously right to kill one Indian.

Thus far the discussion of Williams's example has concerned whether actions would be wrong. Williams presents it as concerned with responsibility. He suggests that if one refuses to kill an Indian one is not responsible for the deaths of twenty. However, Donagan's cases of performing actions foreseeably followed by wrongful reactions when one could have performed others not so followed, show that one may be morally responsible for such conduct. If one is morally responsible for some actions which foreseeably will be met by wrongful reactions, then one is always morally responsible unless factors such as insanity specifically negative responsibility. That other alternatives result in as serious a wrong does not negative responsibility; it justifies the conduct. That is, one is responsible when one does permissible acts as well as wrong ones.

One may claim that if a person kills an Indian, he is morally tainted because he participates in an evil project. Yet, a person need not adopt the captain's evil end. His end throughout may be good—to prevent as many innocent deaths as possible.[15] Killing an Indian need not reflect adversely upon his character. He need not evidence an evil disposition, and he may be consumed with regret that he faced a situation in which some innocent person would die no matter what he did. Nor can he be tainted for getting into the situation, for it was not by any fault of his own he was there.

Finally, Barrie Paskins has argued that in some cases one ought to refuse in order to avoid what he calls "the trap." If one does not refuse, one may be led to a state of complete moral impotence in which all moral agency is lost. It is unclear from Paskins' account that the professional would fall into "the trap." This might occur to a professional who accepts a client hoping to mitigate the wrong done but cannot, or hoping to dissuade the client and cannot,[16] or loses his moral sense, or develops a loyalty to the client and becomes morally unable to avert the evil he set out to avoid.[17] He will have lost moral agency because there will no longer be anything he can do to prevent the wrong.

If I understand Paskins' argument, either it is too late for the professional to avoid the trap, or it depends on his reason for accepting the client. If the side effects are evenly balanced, the professional cannot prevent the wrong occurring since it will happen whatever he does. If he accepts the client hoping to dissuade him or mitigate the wrong done, then he may later be trapped. However, if he claims "it makes no difference," then he will not lose any moral agency he meant to exert, so he will not have lost any agency he thought he had. He will have recognized that he was already in the trap so far as this client was concerned. Of course, he retains moral agency to campaign to get all professionals to refuse to provide services in such cases.

To sum up this examination. The professional can foresee that a wrongful action will occur should he refuse to accept the prospective client. The fact that he merely foresees it rather than causes or allows it to happen does not, in itself, make any difference to the rightness of his action. Side effects may not provide any reason for his not providing the services; indeed, they may indicate that it is better he rather than another provide them. Since the same action will occur in either event, no difference exists in the seriousness of the wrong done depending on whether he or another performs the services. The wrong need not be less certain to occur should he refuse. Consequently, no reason exists to believe that refusing to perform the services is right while performing them is wrong. Nor does any reason exist to think the professional is responsible for the wrong if he performs the services but not if he refuses. One is responsible for foreseeing wrongful reactions to one's actions. (The degree of responsibility may vary depending on the certainty of the reaction and the degree to which the action contributes to the reaction.)[18] Even if the professional performs the services, he does not make the client's end his own and thus become a morally worse person. Consequently, when a professional has good reason to believe that a prospective client may secure another professional to perform services needed in a wrongful but lawful course of conduct, he has no moral basis to refuse his services.

III

The standard view's third claim is that it is more difficult to justify refusing professional services for a wrongful course of conduct if the prospective client cannot obtain them elsewhere than if he can. The arguments in the previous sections imply the contradictory of this claim Their basic premise is that one should use morally appropriate means to prevent the occurrence of wrongful conduct. If a prospective client cannot obtain the services of another professional, then refusal of services will usually decrease the chances of the wrongful conduct occurring. If a lawyer refuses to accept a case and plead the statute of frauds, then the client is less likely to successfully interpose that defense. Similarly, if a woman cannot obtain an abortion elsewhere, then a physician's refusal to perform one will decrease the chances of a wrongful abortion.

The basic premise of the standard view is a generally accepted obligation of professions to provide services for all. This obligation is one of a profession collectively. Refusal by one professional when another will serve does not result in denial of services to those who need them. But if no other professional will provide services, then refusal by the only available professional results in denial of services.

A morally conscientious and clear thinking professional cannot use this obligation as a basis for providing services if others will not, yet refusing to do so if others will provide them. Suppose, as some people argue, people who "need" medical treatment or legal representation have a right to the services by some professional or other. Then even though, independently of such a right the conduct would be wrong, everything considered, the client ought to receive the services. If so, then a professional has no moral basis, only one of personal taste, for refusing to provide them—regardless of the availability of other professionals. Suppose the client does not have a right to services. Then it is wrong for them to be provided as doing so will assist him in his wrongful conduct.

There are two possible ways of escaping this dilemma. The professional may believe the prospective client has a right to services and that, because he believes the client's conduct would be immoral, he would provide ineffective services.[19] This ineffectiveness argument is most plausible for an attorney engaged in advocacy; it is not very plausible that an attorney could not effectively draft a simple will or an answer asserting the statute of frauds as a defense. Physicians who believe abortions or sterilizations to be immoral should, except for lack of experience, be able to do them as well as others. In any case, the professional's reason is not the immorality of the prospective client's conduct but the effectiveness of professional services. A professional who maintained that the conduct was wrong, everything considered, would have to believe that it is wrong to assist ineffectively in the commission of a wrong when another person might more effectively assist in its commission. Such a view certainly improperly elevates professional technique over substance.

The other and even less plausible escape is to hold that conduct is not wrong if those engaging in it do not think it is, or at least that it is less wrong than if they think it is. Such a radical, individual relativism—asserting that actions are right or wrong if the actor thinks they are—is implausible. If a professional did hold this view, he could never have a reason for thinking that what a prospective client sincerely believes is permissible is not permissible for him. He could still think it wrong for him to provide services. Only he could not have any reason for so thinking; his thinking it to be so would be a sufficient and the only possible reason for it being so.

Consequently, if a prospective client wishes to engage in a wrongful course of action and cannot obtain services elsewhere, a professional should refuse to provide them. As the point is to prevent wrong, he should consider whether the action the client will take in reaction to his refusal (for example, self-abortion) would be a more serious wrong. If it would, then, everything considered, he ought to perform the services. The obligation to provide professional services to all does not detract from this point. If for some reason a prospective client has a right to the services, then, everything considered, it is not wrong to provide them and refusal is based on mere personal distaste. If the prospective client does not have such a right, then a refusal to provide services will likely prevent wrongful conduct.

In conclusion, one caveat must be made. The whole discussion has been based on the consistency of thought of a professional who believes a prospective client's course of conduct is morally wrong. A professional may be mistaken about the wrongness of a prospective client's proposed conduct. A professional's conduct is objectively justified only if he is correct about the morality of what the client proposes to do. A recognition of his fallibility in this regard may reasonably lead a professional to provide services even if he is the only available professional and he thinks the client's proposed course of conduct is probably wrong. As noted in section 1, on the standard view such skepticism of one's infallibility might make a professional reluctant to refuse services on ethical grounds. While a recognition of fallibility will affect practice on either the

standard view or that proposed herein, it does not provide a reason for preferring one view to the other.

NOTES

1. Some lawyers object that it would be negligence not to plead the statute of frauds, and,
therefore, the lawyer would do no moral wrong to do so. This point, however, applies to the
lawyer's conduct if he accepts the case, whereas the issue raised here is whether the case should be
accepted. Anyway, one could vary the example: suppose the client had promised to include the
elderly couple in his will and had done so, but now, with only a few weeks to live, wants to make
a new will which does not provide for them.

2. Although I have heard the standard view expressed in public meetings and discussions by
a large number of lawyers and physicians, I have been unable to find a clear written statement of
it. Perhaps because it is so widely accepted, it is rarely set down.

3. "The Lawyer as Friend: The Moral Foundations of the Lawyer-Client Relation," in *1977
National Conference on Teaching Professional Responsibility: Pre-Conference Materials,* ed.
Stuart C. Goldberg (Detroit: University of Detroit School of Law, 1977), p. 152.

4. Ibid., p. 147.

5. Charles Fried, *Right and Wrong* (Cambridge, Mass.: Harvard University Press, 1978), p.
183.

6. See the articles by Jonathan Glover and M. J. Scott-Taggart, "It Makes No Difference
Whether or Not I Do It," *Aristotelian Society, Supplementary Volume* 49 (1975):171-209.

7. Scott-Taggart, "It Makes No Difference," pp. 200, 206.

8. For a more detailed discussion of side effects, see Glover, "It Makes No Difference," pp.
177-188. His discussion of "spirals" is a subclass of my (b).

9. *Code of Professional Responsibility* (Chicago, Ill.: American Bar Association, 1976),
Disciplinary Rule 4-101(C)(3), and *ABA Opinion* 314 (1965).

10. Glover dubs this the Solzhenitsyn principle, due to the latter's remark: "And the simple
step of a simple courageous man is not to take part in the lie, not to support deceit. Let the lie
come into the world, even dominate the world, but not through me." Quoted in Glover, "It
Makes No Difference," p. 184. Scott-Taggart challenges Glover's interpretation of Solzhenitsyn,
"It Makes No Difference," pp. 208-208. I do not wish to dispute the exegetical point. I merely
take it as a possible statement of the view that it would be morally worse for Y than X to provide
the services because Y would lose his moral integrity.

11. Glover, "It Makes No Difference," p. 185.

12. Alan Donagan, *The Theory of Morality* (Chicago, Ill.: University of Chicago Press,
1977), pp. 50-51.

13. J. J. C. Smart and Bernard Williams, *Utilitarianism: For and Against* (Cambridge: At
the University Press, 1973), pp. 98-99.

14. Donagan, *Theory of Morality,* 208.

15. Barrie Paskins, "Some Victims of Morality," *Proceedings of the Aristotelian Society* 76
(1975-76):97.

16. If after having accepted a client a professional becomes convinced the client cannot be
dissuaded, then he is nearly equally certain the wrongful conduct will occur should he withdraw
his services. Withdrawal of services would also be an inappropriate breaking of a bilateral
promise; one cannot avoid keeping one's promise on the ground that when one made it one did
not expect the promisee to hold one to it.

17. Paskins, "Some Victims of Morality," pp. 98-99.

18. Donagan, *Theory of Morality,* p. 51.

19. "A lawyer should decline employment if the intensity of his personal feeling as distinguished from a community attitude may impair his effective representation of a prospective
client." *Code of Professional Responsibility,* Ethical Consideration 2-30.

Michael Davis

The Right to Refuse a Case

May a lawyer refuse a case for moral reasons if he believes other lawyers will take it if he does not? May a lawyer refer a client whose case she has refused for moral reasons to a lawyer she believes will take it? If a lawyer would ordinarily refuse a case for moral reasons, does his believing no other lawyer will take it give him more reason to accept than he would otherwise have?

These are not usually considered to be among the harder questions of professional ethics. The standard answer to each is yes. A philosopher, Michael Bayles, has, however, argued that the right answer to each is no.[1] His argument is supposed to rest on a few uncontroversial assumptions. To lawyers, Bayles's paper may seem the work of the devil's advocate. His argument is certainly devilishly clever. Yet, close examination will, I think, reveal it to rest upon a controversial consequentialism. That close examination will also reveal the huge difference a fundamental difference in moral theory can make in our conception of the lawyer's role.

I. THE STANDARD DEFENSE OF THE STANDARD ANSWERS

Let us begin with the standard defense of the standard answer to our three questions. Beginning there will help us to see both the importance of Bayles's argument (were it sound) and the importance of refuting it (because it is not sound). Having seen that, we shall be ready to examine Bayles's argument.

The standard defense of the lawyer's right to refuse a case for moral reasons, if he believes others will take it, may be put this way. A lawyer is under no obligation to act as an advisor or advocate for every person who may wish to become his client.[2] He is entitled to pick his clients just as any of us are entitled to pick those upon whom we bestow charity, friendship, or patronage (provided perhaps that the criteria of selection are themselves not morally improper). But, as the ABA's *Code of Professional Responsibility* puts it, "in furtherance of the objectives of the bar to make legal services fully available, a lawyer should not lightly decline proffered employment."[3] A lawyer should (all else equal) accept proffered employment.

Declining a case for moral reasons is not necessarily declining it "lightly." Some moral reasons are certainly weighty enough. Thus the Code expressly approves of some moral reasons for declining a case. A lawyer should not accept employment "when he knows or it is obvious that a person seeking to employ him desires to institute or maintain an action merely for the purpose of harassing or maliciously injuring another or to present a claim or defense in litigation that is not warranted under existing law (unless it can be supported by good faith arguments for an extension, modification, or reversal of existing law)."[4] Lawyers are also not supposed to accept a case requiring them to engage in illegal conduct involving moral turpitude, conduct (whether legal or not) involving them in dishonesty, fraud, deceit, or misrepresentation, conduct prejudicial to the administration of justice, or any other conduct reflecting on their fitness to practice law.[5] In *general,* a lawyer must reject any prospective client who wishes to achieve an unlawful objective or wishes to achieve his objective by immoral means. The lawyer's role seems to have been constructed (more or less successfully) to assure that his means will be morally permissible. There is, for example, nothing immoral about pleading the statute of frauds as such even if there is something immoral about pleading it to defeat a just debt.

Most moral reasons for rejecting a case are, then, professionally mandated. They are reasons every lawyer should treat the same (though some may not). Our three questions are usually thought to concern only a small class of cases, those in which the would-be client's objective is morally wrong (or bad) but lawful and the means of pursuing it professionally proper. Would declining a case for such reasons be declining it too lightly?

Some reasons certainly are (on the standard view) too light. For example, the Code expressly declares that a lawyer "should not decline representation because a client or a cause is unpopular or community reaction is adverse."[6] When a lawyer is appointed by a court or requested by a bar association to represent a person otherwise unable to obtain a lawyer, the lawyer may not decline even because of "the repugnance of the subject matter of the proceeding, the identity or position of a person involved in the case, the belief of the lawyer that the defendant in a criminal proceeding is guilty, or the belief of the lawyer regarding the merits of a civil case."[7] The Code clearly treats making legal services available to those who need them as a professional duty capable of overriding important moral considerations.

The Code is, however, silent about whether the mere immorality of a client's objective (or of the professionally proper means necessary to carry it out) could be sufficient reason to justify refusing an otherwise good case (where neither a court nor a bar association has asked the lawyer to take the case). The closest the Code comes to the question is to *permit* a lawyer (a) to ask her client to forego an action she believes to be unjust and (b) to withdraw from employment if a client in a non-adjudicatory matter insists upon a course of conduct contrary to her judgment or advice but not prohibited by the Code.[8]

The few legal writers who have urged that lawyers decline employment if they do not approve of their clients' objectives have presented their views as if a departure from common practice. For example, Mark Green concludes his argument for greater selectivity in accepting corporate clients by quoting with approval a Washington lawyer's statement that "I think we are going to have to start making moral judgments on our clients."[9] The departure seems, however, not to be in making moral judgments on clients but in the range of judgments allowed. During the nineteenth century, some writers on legal ethics argued that an attorney should never plead the statute of frauds to defeat a just debt. Today the decision clearly falls within the discretion of the individual lawyer. If a lawyer takes the case, she must plead the statute (or get permission from her client to forego that defense); but she is free to reject the case if she does not want to defeat a just debt by such a plea (provided she is not appointed by a court or requested by a bar association to take the case). So long as there are other lawyers who might take the case instead, leaving such discretion to the individual lawyer seems to strike a reasonable balance between the liberty of individual lawyers and the legal needs of would-be clients.

The standard answer to the second and third questions follows almost immediately from what has already been said. Because a lawyer has a professional duty to help make legal services available, he should help someone with a legal problem find a competent lawyer and also accept a "share of tendered employment which may be unattractive both to him and to the bar generally."[10] A lawyer who would like to decline a case for moral reasons thus has a professional obligation to recommend a competent lawyer who will not decline the case. He also has a professional obligation to take some cases he would not otherwise take, whether he is inclined to reject them for moral or other reasons, if other lawyers are similarly inclined. The standard view thus seems to be that your becoming a lawyer gives would-be clients a claim on you they would not otherwise have, a claim capable of overcoming moral reasons for not helping them that might otherwise be conclusive.

These three answers, subject to local variation, together constitute a proud tradition among lawyers throughout much of the world. That tradition (it is said) assures that even the guilty will have an attorney to make the state prove its case, that controversial moral opinion of particular lawyers (or even of the profession generally) will not decide civil cases without a public hearing, that laymen will have the legal knowledge to get what the law has set aside for them.[11] The tradition seems to recognize that while most moral questions are closed (hence the mandated reasons for refusing a case), some are not (hence the Code's silence on the propriety of rejecting a case for certain reasons).

II. BAYLES'S "BASIC ARGUMENT"

It is this tradition that Bayles challenges. Bayles claims: (1) that a lawyer can (justiably) refuse a case for moral reasons only if no other lawyer will take the case; (2) that a lawyer cannot consistently believe both that he is rejecting a case for moral reasons and that he is morally obligated to help the would-be client find a lawyer who will not reject it; and (3) that if a lawyer has moral reasons to reject a case, the fact that other lawyers would reject it too *reduces* any obligation the lawyer might otherwise have to take it. So, for example, a lawyer who believes it morally wrong to plead the statute of frauds to defeat a just debt, has a moral reason to refuse the case if, but only if, all other lawyers would refuse the case too. If other lawyers would take the case, he has (according to Bayles) no *moral* reason to reject it (his reasons being "personal," not moral, that is, reasons he cannot view as applying to everyone).

Bayles claims to derive these conclusions from three assumptions constituting "the inescapable consequentialism of having moral principles." These assumptions are, he believes, the common ground between "consequentialists" and "deontologists." They are: (1) that it is better (all else equal) that wrongful conduct not occur, (2) that one ought not (all else equal) to assist in wrongful conduct, and (3) that one ought (all else equal) to use appropriate moral techniques to prevent wrongful conduct.[12]

Bayles states these assumptions without the parenthetical phrase "all else equal." I have nevertheless stated them with it. I did so for two reasons. First, Bayles's argument seems to assume the clause throughout. Now and then he even takes the trouble expressly to rule out "side effects," special circumstances, and so on. Second, without the "all else equal," Bayles's three assumptions would be open to obvious objection. For example, it surely would *not* be better that wrongful conduct not occur if the means of preventing it were the extinction of all life. Such an objection cannot be eliminated merely by inserting "morally" before "better" (as Bayles seems to intend). At least some moral theories would hold that the world would not be morally better were the amount of wrongful conduct reduced in that way.

Bayles also states his assumptions without explaining their relation to one another. They do not seem to be independent. In particular, assumption 2 seems to be a special case of assumption 3. Not assisting in wrongful conduct seems to be an appropriate moral technique to prevent wrongful conduct. Having both assumptions 2 and 3 suggests there may be a reason (all else equal) not to assist wrongful conduct even if not assisting would not prevent it. That nonsequentialist suggestion is, of course, unfortunate. Bayles's argument depends on recognizing no independent duty not to assist such conduct. That one assists in wrongdoing is *not,* according to Bayles, morally wrong, provided one cannot prevent the wrong by refusing to assist. Assumption 2 thus seems both unnecessary and misleading. I assume Bayles included it to save himself a step or two in some arguments.

Most of Bayles's paper is taken up defending his answer to our first question ("May a lawyer refuse a case for moral reasons if he believes other lawyers will take the case if he does not?"). Once we have understood that defense (including what is wrong with it), everything else should fall into place. So, let us begin with it.

Bayles first gives his "basic argument" in this way:

> Refusal to perform the service will not prevent the wrongful conduct. As the wrong will occur anyway, there is no moral gain from refusing to perform the service. Assuming the professional does not have some special relation with the prospective client [that is, all else is equal], the world is not morally worse if he rather than some other professional performs the service. In short, it makes no difference whether or not he does it, because if he does not someone else will. The conclusion is not that he has an obligation to perform the service, only that it is not morally wrong to do so.[13]

Following recent literature, Bayles calls this "the no-difference argument." Much of his discussion is, however, concerned with a formalized restatement. Because that restatement makes precise criticism easier, I shall concentrate on it. I quote the informal statement because, as so often happens, the informal statement conveys the intuitive appeal of the argument much better than the formal restatement does. Having the two formulations side by side should foreclose any suspicion that they are not the same argument.

Bayles restates the no-difference argument this way:

P1: It is morally better that no one do A than that someone do A.

P2: Some will do A if Y does not.

P3: It will not be morally better if Y refrains from doing A, because A will be done anyway.

C1: So, it will make no difference whether Y does A.

P4: If an act makes no difference to the occurrence of moral wrong, it is not morally wrong.

C2: So, Y's doing A is not morally wrong.[14]

The no-difference argument should come as something of a surprise in Bayles's paper. There is nothing in the argument about morally appropriate means of preventing wrongful conduct or about not assisting in such conduct. Of Bayles's three initial assumptions, only one seems to have a part in the argument. And even it is not expressly used. Premise P4 assumes, as we shall see, (something like) Bayles's assumption that it is better that wrongful conduct not occur. We must look at this argument more carefully. If the no-difference argument does not rest on Bayles's initial assumptions, on what does it rest?

Premises P1 and P2 simply state the conditions of our problem. There is an act we think it morally better that no one do and someone will do it if lawyer Y does not. Premise P3 is, however, more troublesome. That "because" conceals an inference. One cannot get "it will not be (morally) better if Y refrains from doing A" from "A will be done anyway"—a variant of P2—without another premise, something like:

P2½: If A will be done anyway (that is, whether Y refrains from doing it or not), it is not (morally) better if Y refrains from doing A (all else equal).

P2½: seems to be a special case of the *principle of moral equality* (that is, that—all else equal—who does an act does not change the act's moral status). That principle is common ground between consequentialists and deontologists (at least while they are concerned with evaluating acts rather than with choosing them). So, premise P3 is consistent with Bayles's claim to rest his argument on an "inescapable consequentialism" (though it would have been better had he listed the principle of moral equality among his initial assumptions).

Premise P4 is, however, different for two reasons. First, P4 is concerned with "moral wrong." Up till now, the no-difference argument has been concerned with what is "morally better." There must be a missing premise, bridging the gap between "morally better" and "morally wrong." I suggest:

P3½: If it is not morally better that no one do A than that someone do A, A is not morally wrong.

This premise does not follow from any of Bayles's initial assumptions. It is, in fact, the converse of Bayles's assumption that it is better (all else equal) that wrongful conduct not occur. P3½ is also controversial. Such an identification of the right and the good is characteristic of utilitarians. Deontologists generally believe that acts can be morally worse than the alternatives without being morally wrong. For example, many deontologists would be willing to say that, though it is morally better to do public interest law than to help the rich sue each other for libel, it is nevertheless not morally wrong to help the rich in that way instead of doing public interest law. As we shall see in section IV, this distinction between the right and the good is important to understanding much about the lawyer's role. But my purpose now is simply to throw premise P3½ into question.

Bayles probably missed P3½ because he drew that initial conclusion C1. C1 is ambiguous. Given what comes before it, C1 must mean that Y's doing A will make no difference in what is morally better. Given what comes after it, C1 must mean that Y's doing A will make no difference in the occurrence of wrongful conduct.

That is, I think, enough to show Bayles's argument to rest on an equivocation. But that is not all that is wrong with it. There is premise P4 itself. P4 states what we might call "the no-difference principle" (because it is the crucial step in the no-difference argument). The no-difference principle ties an act's wrongful-ness to the amount of wrongful conduct that will occur if it is done compared to the amount of wrongful conduct that will occur if it is not done. The act's wrongfulness is understood as a function of certain consequences, not just of whether it is in accord with what one should do. In effect, the no-difference principle tells each moral agent to put himself in a neutral position when deciding what to do. He is to consider whether it makes any difference to the amount of wrong done if he or someone else does the act. If it makes "no difference" who does it, he may do the act. A moral agent cannot, the principle seems to say, be responsible for the wrong he does since it will be done whether he does it or not. Who does the act is a matter of moral indifference. That another will do an act if I do not is, according to the no-difference principle, enough to make it morally permissible to do the act even if acts of that kind are prohibited by a moral rule.

Bayles seems to think that the no-difference principle is self-evident. "To deny this premise would be," he says, "irrational, for it would be to claim that doing A is wrong but refraining from doing A is not wrong although there is no difference in the moral wrong that results."[15] Nevertheless, underlying much of what Bayles says while responding to various criticisms of the no-difference principle, there is, I think, an argument for the principle—though not a good argument. An examination of that underlying argument will show why denying the no-difference principle can be quite rational.

The point of morality is, Bayles seems to think, to prevent certain undesir-able acts from occurring (and perhaps to encourage others). Moral agents do right insofar as they serve that end and wrong insofar as they disserve it. If an undesirable act will occur whether I commit it or not, there can be no moral point to my not committing it. My abstinence will not (according to Bayles) serve the ends of morality. What morally relevant difference might there be between me and someone who refrains? I am not like someone who would do the act even if no one else would do it. I am not someone willing to add to the amount of wrongful conduct in the world. My concern that I not be the one to do the wrong under such circumstances can be nothing more than squeamishness, pietism, or misplaced conscience, reasons not to do the act perhaps, but reasons of "personal taste" rather than of morality. What I do cannot be morally wrong if there is no moral point ("no moral gain") from my not doing it.

If this is Bayles's argument for the no-difference principle, the principle is plainly "act-consequentialist." An act's rightness is to be determined (when the principle applies) by the actual consequences of that act in particular (but taking into account what others would have done instead). The no-difference principle is, however, no ordinary act-consequentialist principle. It is supposed to be compatible with any form of consequential or deontological moral theory, part of that "inescapable consequentialism" upon which Bayles promised to rest his argument. Bayles therefore expressly allows "morally wrong" (or, at least, "morally better") to be defined according to any moral theory we may prefer, deontological or consequentialist.[16]

III. REFUTING THE NO-DIFFERENCE PRINCIPLE

That is Bayles's defense of the claim that a lawyer cannot have a moral reason to refuse a case if another lawyer will take it if she does not. That defense has, I think, two flaws—besides the problem with P3½ already noted. One is that the consequentialism upon which it rests is far from inescapable. Many deontologists (and rule utilitarians!) would, I think, reject premise P4 because it ignores the place rules have in the evaluation of acts. The second flaw is that the no-difference principle seems systematically to confuse the perspective of moral agent with that of moral legislator. For Bayles, I am no more responsible for what I do than for what others do in response. I am to look only to the consequences as a legislator would. The two flaws are not independent. Deontologists (and rule utilitarians) tend to take the distinction between moral agent and moral legislator seriously while act utilitarians (and other similar act consequentialists) generally do not. So, I shall not be able to explain the first flaw without (tacitly) explaining the second as well.

A typical deontologist would, I think, respond to the no-difference argument that Bayles has forgotten that the primary concern of a moral agent *as moral agent* is to act morally, that acting morally means following the appropriate rules (or giving due weight to the appropriate moral considerations), and that the amount of wrongdoing resulting from what a moral agent does is (all else equal) not his concern (even though, for any particular wrong, it really is better that it not occur). For example, the lawyer confronted by a would-be client wishing to do something morally wrong with the lawyer's help, may have good moral reason to refuse to take the case even though the would-be client will have no trouble finding a lawyer who will not refuse. Taking the case would mean assisting in wrongdoing. One should not (all else equal) assist in wrongdoing. So (the typical deontologist would say) the lawyer should not take the case. That other lawyers will take the case if he does not would seem to be irrelevant. One should not assist in wrongdoing even if one's refusal does not in fact prevent the wrong. The question for a moral agent choosing a particular act is not ordinarily whether the world will be morally worse or better if he does the act, but whether he will do what he should. And what he should do is, for a deontologist, determined by duty, not directly by the consequences of the act.[17]

The deontological or duty-based response is suggestive. But it does not quite dispose of Bayles's argument. If the point of morality is to prevent certain actions (as perhaps everyone would agree it is), we must wonder why even deontologists would not be concerned that their acts not add to the amount of wrongful conduct. And, indeed, I think most deontologists are concerned about that. The typical deontologist (or, at least, the typical rule deontologist) would, however, want to distinguish sharply between the end of morality (for example, preventing certain conduct) and the means by which that end is pursued. For act consequentialists (our typical deontologist would point out), the means and ends of morality are closely related. One achieves the ends by aiming to achieve them in each act. One is to reduce wrongful conduct by choosing those acts that seem to do just that. But, for most deontologists (and rule utilitarians), the relation between means and ends is not so close. For most duty-based moral theory, the means of achieving the ends of morality will be doing one's duty whatever (within limits) the consequences of one's particular act. One can do one's duty without making any difference in the amount of wrongful conduct in the world. One achieves the ends of morality without aiming at them in each act.

If that is the difference between Bayles's act consequentialism and typical deontological theories, why (it might be asked) would anyone prefer a duty-based moral theory over some form of act consequentialism? How can it be rational to let rules guide one's conduct whatever the consequences? To answer that question, let us imagine a duty-based morality in which the duties are stated in relatively precise rules (perhaps with certain "exception clauses" or principles for adjudicating between rules when they conflict). Imagining a duty-based morality in this way will make it easy to explain why rational persons might prefer a duty-based morality over the directness of act consequentialism. But this choice of example is not meant to suggest that duty-based moralities must have such a structure. There may be other ways to construct a satisfactory theory of morality (though, I must admit, I prefer this one).

Defending a duty-based morality requires that we (a) defend its rules (or principles) and then (b) defend acting under them even when the no-difference principle applies. Defending the rules is relatively simple. We simply show that everyone in fact wants everyone else to act in accordance with each rule, or that one could not consistently will any alternative, or that the rules in some other way serve the ends of morality as deontologists might define them. The rules so defended need not be stated in terms of the ends of morality. For example, the rule "Don't (all else equal) assist in wrongful conduct" could be understood to prohibit assisting in wrongful conduct whether or not assisting in a particular instance seemed to serve the ends of morality. Indeed, the rules of a duty-based morality will seldom make reference to the ends of morality (e.g., preventing bad acts or guaranteeing to each a minimum of what he wants).

Defending acts under the moral rules so defended is somewhat more complicated. Making a general practice of following the rules would, of course, be defended by pointing out that, given the defense of the rule itself, following the rule in general will in general serve the ends of morality. The complications begin when it is pointed out (correctly) that sometimes following the rules seems not to serve the ends of morality. For example, one lawyer's refusing to assist a would-be client in wrongdoing may not prevent the client's doing the wrong or some other lawyer's assisting him in doing it.

Arguments for following a rule even when following it seems not to serve the ends of morality are almost as diverse as deontological theories. I will give one, "the argument from fallibility." I give just one because I want to keep this paper a reasonable length and because even one such argument is enough to dispose of Bayles's no-difference principle. I give the argument from fallibility because I find it especially congenial and also because even consequentialists are likely to admit its force.

The argument goes like this. Humans can come to false conclusions even under the best conditions, but they are more likely to come to such conclusions the less information they have, the less time they have to ponder what they know, the more their own interests are directly involved, the more emotionally involved they are, and the more their reasoning is shielded from the criticism of others. An individual trying to achieve the ends of morality by aiming at them in each act is therefore less likely to serve morality than if he followed rules designed to serve those ends. Moral rules are, after all, worked out over many years, after wide discussion and experiment. Information tends to be better. Passions have a chance to cool. One can take seriously the possibility that others may follow the rule too. And so on. Following moral rules will always be the less risky way to achieve the ends of morality, except in circumstances fundamentally different from those envisaged by the rule-makers.

Consider, for example, our lawyer asked to take a case requiring him to plead the statute of frauds to defeat a just debt. However certain he may be that others will take the case, it is possible that he is wrong. His belief may be founded on what other lawyers have *said* when they wished to sound "professional" rather than on what they *did*. He may have thought this or that particular debt was just when the attorney for the other side thought it was not. He may simply be so blinded by the fee the client is offering that he is lying to himself. But, even if, in fact, he is right this time and some other lawyer will take the case if he does not, he would still run the risk of being wrong, the risk of assisting in a wrong no one else would have assisted in. Given human fallibility, that risk must be substantial. We also have good reason not to want lawyers to run such risks. Even if each lawyer assisted in wrongdoing only when he was certain that some other lawyer would if he did not, lawyers would sometimes assist in wrongdoing when others would not. If the ends of morality are not served by wrongdoers having assistance, then there is good reason to have a strict rule against assisting in wrongdoing that does not permit lawyers to make an exception merely because they *believe* others would assist if they do not.[18] Such a rule would reduce the assistance in wrongdoing people received.

The argument from fallibility undermines Bayles's no-difference principle by throwing premise P4 into doubt. The argument suggests that it is rational to claim that a person's act can be morally wrong even if, taking into account what others would do instead, the act does not increase the amount of wrongful conduct. The act can be wrong because while the act may not in fact increase wrongful conduct, it nevertheless risks doing so and that risk disserves the ends of morality. Letting people run such risks will, in the long run, assure that there will be more wrongful conduct than there would otherwise be. There will be more wrongful conduct because people cannot make such judgments infallibly and following the appropriate rule reduces the bad effects of their fallibility. So, an act can be morally wrong even if it does not itself make the world a morally worse place.

Bayles cannot, I think, absorb this argument into his. Premise (P4) can, it is true, be read so that "wrongful conduct" includes prohibited risk-taking as well as such consequences as unjust loss of property. (P4) might, for example, be rewritten:

> P4': If an act makes no difference in either the occurrence of moral wrong *or in the risk of it,* the act is not morally wrong.

But even rewritten in this way, the premise would make morally permissible taking a risk if another would take it if one did not. So, a P4' permitting such risk-taking would be open to the same argument from fallibility as P4 is. Fallibility provides an argument for treating moral rules as foreclosing consideration of certain consequences. And, for our purposes, risks are consequences. No nonarbitrary definition of consequences can, I think, change that.[191]

IV. REFERRING AND RECONSIDERING

Bayles's answer to our second and third questions does not assume his answer to our first (though, as we shall see, it does share one of its faults). "A morally conscientious and clear thinking professional" cannot, Bayles claims, use the obligation to help make legal services available as a basis for referring a would-be client bent on wrongdoing if others will provide the service, or providing the service himself if others will not, yet refusing to provide them if others will.[20] Consistency, he argues, rules that out. His answer to our second and third questions is of interest whatever our opinion of his answer to our first.

Bayles's argument is relatively straightforward. His only (important) premises are (a) that "it is [all else equal] morally wrong . . . to assist . . . in . . . wrongful conduct," (b) that taking a case or helping a would-be client find another lawyer is assisting in wrongful conduct if the client is bent on wrongful conduct, and (c) that one ought (all else equal) to use appropriate moral techniques to prevent wrongful conduct.[21] The argument has the form of a dilemma. Either a would-be client has a right to the lawyer's help or he does not. If he has such a right, all else is *not* equal and it would be morally wrong ("all things considered") for the lawyer not to take the case. The right would be decisive. If, however, the would-be client has no right to the lawyer's help, all else *is* equal and it would be morally wrong for the lawyer to assist in the wrongful conduct, whether assisting is done by taking the case or merely by helping the client find someone who will. The duty not to assist in wrongful conduct is decisive. The lawyer with moral reasons to reject a would-be client is, then, never in a position requiring her to refer the client to someone who will take the case. She is always in a position requiring her to do something else.

Such a lawyer also cannot (Bayles continues) have a greater obligation to accept a case if no one else will take it. The argument so far establishes either that the lawyer has no obligation to take the case (whether other lawyers will take the case or not) or that the lawyer is required to take the case (whether other lawyers will or not). The client cannot (it seems) have a moral right to a service it would be morally wrong to perform. If, however, "the point is" (as Bayles says) "to prevent wrong,"[22] the lawyer could have a greater obligation to refuse a case if no one else will take it than if someone else will. If a would-be client bent on wrongdoing cannot find help elsewhere, the lawyer's refusal will prevent the wrong. That would seem to be a decisive consideration if nothing else is.

That's Bayles argument. Is there anything wrong with it? For most deontologists, the answer is that there certainly is. Bayles has again confused the right and the good (or, at least, the wrong and the bad). His premise (a) is that it is (all else equal) morally *wrong* to assist in wrongdoing. He apparently takes that premise to be equivalent to his initial assumption that one ought not (all else equal) to assist in wrongdoing. That seems to be a mistake. Claims about what is morally bad are (as noted before) not in general equivalent to claims about what is morally wrong. For example, a lawyer who makes it her practice to turn away any would-be client who cannot afford her fee, is (all else equal) doing something morally bad. A lawyer should take a fair share of clients who cannot pay. But she is not therefore doing anything morally wrong. Doing something morally bad is not necessarily doing something morally wrong. To do wrong, she would have to do more than fail to do what she should.

This is not the place to lay out in detail the variety of norms morality seems to include, much less to trace their interconnections. But I must say something more about such things if what I have said so far is not to be misunderstood. Space allows me to do no more than call attention to the more important norms, suggest some important differences, and hope that will be enough to make clear how far wrong I think Bayles has gone.

Morality is in part "shall" and "shall not" (or "Do" and "Don't"), that is, acts required or prohibited. To do what is morally required (or permitted) is morally right; to do what is prohibited is morally wrong. We may call this part of morality "basic" because its rules constitute *minimum* standards of conduct. The rules of basic morality are either obeyed or disobeyed. There is no in-between. If one act is more right than another, one of the two is wrong. The all-else-equal in a rule of basic morality holds place for an "except clause." Moral wrongs differ in seriousness, but one rule of basic morality does not outweigh another. In principle, all can be obeyed. Those who frequently disobey such rules are evil, immoral, or unjust; those who (almost) never disobey are moral, just, or upright.

Beyond basic morality, there are "should" and "should not" (or "ought" and "ought not"). It is morally good to do what one morally should; morally bad to do what one morally should not. We might call this part of morality "extended" (though it is often called "ethics" as distinguished from "morals"). Extended morality can be stated in rules just as basic morality can be. Such rules may appear to differ from those of basic morality only in having "should" in place of "shall." But they always differ in more than that. I do not *disobey* a rule of extended morality just because I do not do as it says I should. I should, for example, help the sick, but if I eat dinner instead of going to the hospital to help strangers, I do not disobey the rule. The rules of extended morality state considerations to be taken into account, values to have some weight in a good person's deliberations. An all-else-equal clause in such a rule does not hold place for an exception. (I really should help the sick even if I am hungry.) Instead, such a clause indicates that other considerations may be weighed against the good the rule itself recommends. Such considerations may include nonmoral considerations (for example, my own comfort). One is a better person the more the rules of extended morality have weight in one's deliberations, a worse person the less they do. One can, however, be a good person even though nonmoral considerations often win out in one's deliberations. Even saints have trouble doing all they should. One is a bad person only insofar as considerations have positive weight in one's deliberations that morality says should have negative weight (or none at all). The requirements of *basic* morality can*not* be outweighed by considerations of extended morality. To be a good person one must give due weight to basic morality. To do good by doing wrong is bad as well as unjust. One should not do wrong.

So, to assume (as Bayles does initially) that a lawyer *should* (all else equal) not assist in wrongdoing is not necessarily to assume as well (as Bayles seems to) that it would be wrong for a lawyer to assist in such conduct. Bayles's argument must be amended in one of two ways. Bayles either must show that assisting in wrongdoing is morally wrong as well as morally bad or he must recast his argument in terms of his initial assumption that one ought not to assist in such conduct.

To show that assisting in wrongdoing is (all else equal) not morally wrong seems difficult. The all-else-equal makes it hard to provide a *clear* counter example to the claim that nonassistance is required. But it is possible to give reasons to suppose there is no such rule. There are so many degrees of assistance and so many degrees of wrongdoing that the rule would either demand far too much (for example, that one not sell a postage stamp to a lawyer who will use it to mail a pleading repudiating a just debt) or include so many exceptions that it would be better stated as a simpler rule against certain forms of assistance.

Recasting Bayles's argument in terms of what one *should* do would, on the other hand, deny him his conclusion in another way. The lawyer who wishes to turn away a client bent on wrongdoing must balance (at least) two moral considerations: that it is good to provide legal services to those who need them and that it is bad to assist in wrongdoing. If the would-be client can find another lawyer, the good of providing this client with legal services will not weigh heavily in the balance against the bad of assisting in wrongdoing by providing such services. (Such considerations can, of course, be balanced without taking into account the ends of morality as such.) If we refuse the would-be client because the balance of moral considerations is against taking the case, we may nonetheless (and indeed should) refer him to another lawyer. The good of assisting him by helping him find a suitable lawyer may (and indeed probably does) outweigh the small assistance we give him in wrongdoing. (The wrong he will do with another's help need not weigh heavily in *our* deliberations.) If, however, he comes back to us because no other lawyer will take the case, the good of providing legal services will weigh much more heavily. The effect of refusal now would be to deny the would-be client not only *our* legal services but (we are supposing) *all* legal help.[23]

This reasoning will, I think, seem mere common sense. It differs from Bayles's consequentialism in being concerned with weighing particular considerations rather than with serving "the ends of morality" as such. By now, that difference should seem an advantage. We have, then, escaped Bayles's "inescapable consequentialism" and have resolved as well as his "problem of clean hands."

V. CONCLUSION

The above analysis presupposes that providing legal help is morally good (all else equal), good enough at least sometimes to outweigh the bad inherent in assisting in wrongdoing. I see no problem with that presupposition. It is easy to imagine cases satisfying it. For example, imagine that the would-be client who wants to defeat a just debt by pleading the statute of frauds is a poor old man; his creditor, a large corporation; and the debt, small in the corporation's budget but big in his. Surely, helping such a client defeat such a debt is not, on balance, morally bad (though the client would still be doing something morally wrong).

That providing legal services is morally good itself presupposes that the services are performed within a legal system that is itself relatively just. I see no more problem with this presupposition than with the last (so long as our concern is a typical jurisdiction in the United States, Western Europe, or the like). Whatever our objections to the statute of frauds, for example, we must admit that the law has a good purpose, that it was in force when debts such as that in the example above were contracted, and so that invoking it to defeat a debt is not arbitrarily redefining people's rights. Under such circumstances, the moral wrong a client does by defeating a just debt cannot be great. (Pleading the statute of frauds is, then, quite different from performing an abortion—if one believes abortion to be murder.)

The conclusion I draw from this is not, however, that a lawyer within a relatively just legal system can do anything professionally permitted and still be a good person. My conclusion is stricter than that. To be a good person, a lawyer must do good as well as do right. The lawyer who, for example, devotes all his efforts to defeating the just debts of the poor, would not be doing what he should even if his methods were professionally proper. Providing legal services in even a relatively just legal system is not an activity so morally good in itself that it can outweigh all the bad a lawyer's profession permits him to do.[24] One certainly can be a good lawyer and a bad person.

One can, however, also be a good person. It is, I think, a useful exercise to try to understand each profession as an organization to assure (as far as humanly possible) that its members will never have to choose between refusing to exercise their special skills as their peers expect and doing something morally wrong. It is even more useful, though more frustrating, to try that substituting "morally bad" for "morally wrong." Each profession provides a certain good at the expense of others. A good code of ethics can reduce that expense somewhat.[25] But no code can eliminate it. The rules of extended morality compete in a way the rules of basic morality do not.

Lawyers provide help with the law, including advice, preparation of legal documents, and representation. Because helping someone with the law often means helping him *against* someone else, lawyering is an adversary calling in a way such professions as medicine or engineering, teaching or the ministry, are not. In this respect, lawyering is more like soldiering than any other profession. Most of legal ethics is concerned with the moral problems an adversary calling generates. For lawyers, the good moral character of other lawyers is as much a guarantee that one's peers will not push one too far as it is a means of protecting the client from fraud. Conflict of interest must be avoided as much as possible because the lawyer's ability to help his client depends in large part on his not being the client's adversary. And so on. But the central problems of legal ethics are concerned with how to act in an adversary proceeding. Should a lawyer stand by while her client commits perjury? Should a lawyer be rough on a witness if that is necessary to get the truth? May a lawyer fail to reveal some fact necessary to do justice? And so on. The conflict is plainly between the legal good of the client and the good of others (sometimes even of society as a whole).

Though one can be a good person and a good lawyer, it is probably not possible to be both a good lawyer and a saint. An adversary calling is not the stuff of sainthood. Bayles's paper will be worth all the trouble we have taken with it if it helps us to understand why that is so.

NOTES

1. Michael Bayles, "A Problem of Clean Hands: Refusal to Provide Professional Services" *Social Theory and Practice* 5 (1976):165-181. See this volume pp. 428-440.

2. American Bar Association, *Code of Professional Responsibility* (Chicago: National Center for Professional Responsibility, 1980), EC 2-26. For a full defense of the view, see Charles Fried, "The Lawyer as Friend: The Moral Foundations of the Lawyer-Client Relation" *Yale Law Review* 85 (1976): 1060–1089. See this volume pp. 132-157.

3. Ibid.

4. Ibid., EC 2-20 and DR 2-109.

5. Ibid., DR 1-102(A), EC 7-4, and EC 7-6.

6. Ibid., EC 2-27.

7. Ibid., EC 2-29.

8. Ibid., EC 7-8 and EC 7-9.

9. Mark J. Green, *The Other Government: The Unseen Power of Washington Lawyers* (New York: Grossman Publishers, 1975), p. 288.

10. *Code,* EC 2-1 and EC 2-26.

11. Cf. Murray Seasongood, "What Employment Must a Lawyer Accept?" *The Practical Lawyer* 2 (1956):43-49.

12. Bayles, p. 430.

13. Ibid., p. 431.

14. Ibid., p. 432.

15. Ibid.

16. Ibid.

17. One line of reasoning for this refusal appeals explicitly to the threat accepting such a case would pose for a lawyer's "integrity." If by "integrity" is meant "good character" (a tendency to act in certain ways hereafter), the reasoning would be consequentialist, loss of integrity being a bad consequence (and one certainly worth considering—provided the psychological claim can be established). The argument I shall make below is not supposed to rely on considerations of integrity in this sense. There is, however, another sense of integrity upon which the argument below does rely (if only trivially). This is the sense in which every wrongful act, just because it is wrongful, violates the agent's integrity, whatever its effects on his later action may be. This sense of "integrity" is related to "guilt" rather than "good character." Cf. Hans Oberiek, "Clean Hands and Professional Responsibility: A Rejoinder to Michael Bayles," in *Moral Responsibility and the Professions,* Bernard Baumrin and Benjamin Freedman, eds., (New York: Haven Publications, 1983), pp. 151-155.

18. For more detailed discussion of such appeal to risk, see my "Racial Quotas, Weights, and Real Possibilities: A Moral for Moral Theory" *Social Theory and Practice* 7 (1981):49-84; and "Smith, Gert, and Obligation to Obey the Law" *Southern Journal of Philosophy* 20 (1982): 139-152.

19. Cf. Bayles, pp. 436-437. I think Bayles missed the point of Donagan's comments on William's South American example. Alan Donagan, *The Theory of Morality* (Chicago: University of Chicago Press, 1977), pp. 207-209. Bayles responds to Donagan's perceptive listing of "uncertainties" in the situation by making equally perceptive comments about the "probabilities" as if Donagan's concern were what to do *in the absence* of a moral rule forbidding killing one Indian to save twenty. But Donagan's discussion is clearly a defense of a rule not allowing consideration of such probabilities. I cannot read Donagan's discussion without feeling that we would all be better off if, when people supposed themselves to be in such a situation, they did not take it upon themselves to save lives by committing murder. Apparently, Bayles can. Theory can help us see, but it can also make us blind.

20. Bayles, p. 438.

21. Ibid., pp. 438-439.

22. Ibid., p. 439.

23. The intervention of a court or bar association would, of course, transform the situation. The court order or bar request would impose a professional duty to accept the case. That duty would, it seems, be a moral requirement as well because the lawyer's express oath (or the tacit consent he gives by remaining in a profession the code of which imposes such a duty) would involve the rule of basic morality about doing (all else equal) what one has undertaken to do.

24. But see Thomas L. Shaffer, "Guilty Clients and Lunch with Tax Collectors" *The Jurist* 37 (1977):89-111, or "Christian Theories of Professional Responsibility" *Southern California Law Review* 48 (1975):721-759. Shaffer seems to hold that, so long as a lawyer does not do anything professionally improper, he is a good person whatever he helps his client do.

25. Most writers on professional ethics see this, but some interpret it as a suspension of "ordinary" (that is, basic) morality. See, for example, Benjamin Freedman, "A Meta-Ethics of Professional Morality" *Ethics* 88 (1978):1-19, or Robert M. Veatch, "Professional Ethics and Role-Specific Duties" *Journal of Medicine and Philosophy* 4 (1979):1-19 The view defended here is closer to Fried's. Lawyers are not exempt from any requirement of basic morality. They simply undertake to pursue one good at the expense of others, something we may all do (within limits). The lawyer has special responsibilities ("professional ethics") because of that undertaking, but no

more right to do wrong than anyone else. For a curiously mixed view, see Alan Goldman, *The Moral Foundations of Professional Ethics* (Totowa, N.J.: Littlefield Adams, 1980), who seems to think that some professionals (for example, lawyers) are *not* exempt from the requirements of basic morality while others (for example, judges) are to some extent.

Michael D. Bayles

Reply to Davis

A number of years ago I published a paper that argued for views of professional ethics counter to the received ones. The paper evolved from extended discussions concerning the role of personal integrity in professional ethics; until now the criticism of my views have based on personal integrity. Michael Davis critisizes them on seemingly different grounds, but paradoxical as my arguments and conclusions seem, I am not yet persuaded that they are incorrect. As Davis has well summarized my original arguments, I need not repeat them.

However, Davis has misstated one of my conclusions. He attributes to me the view that a lawyer can justifiably refuse a case for moral reasons only if no other lawyer will take it. Instead, I contend that a lawyer has a good moral reason to refuse a case only if doing so is likely to decrease the chances of the potential client's moral wrongdoing (which may be legal, for example, disinscriting a loving daughter for marrying outside a religious sect). There are various reasons why a refusal might deter a potential client. Although other lawyers might be available, the potential client might respect the lawyer and be swayed by the lawyer's emphatic moral conviction.

Esentially, Davis makes two objections to my original "no-difference" argument: (1) that it rests on an equivocarion in C1, and (2) that P4 is false. The first objection can, I think, be obviated by restating the argument in a simpler way which also avoids the need for the additional premises Davis supplies. Although Davis is correct that all the premises have *ceteris paribus* clauses, for simplicity of statement I will continue to omit them.

> P1: The occurrence of conduct A(x)[pleading the statute of frauds in this case] would be wrong.

> P2: Wrongful conduct A(x) will occur whether or not Y does it [whether or not a(y) occurs].

> C1: Hence, it makes no difference to the occurrence of wrongful conduct A(x) whether or not Y does it [if not A(y), then A(i)].

P3: [originally P4]: If an act makes no difference to the occurrence of wrongful conduct, it is not morally wrong.

C2: Therefore, Y's doing A(y) is not morally wrong.

Two comments about the argument are appropriate. First, I originally wrote of the argument assuming an "inescapable consequentialism." That was probably misleading; it has mislead Davis in some of his criticisms. P3 [P4] is not concerned only with the causal consequences of an act but also its occurrence—the instantiation of A(x). If A(x) occurs, then there is more wrongful conduct than if it does not; that is a logical, not a causal, consequence of A(x). Second, the paradoxical nature of the argument—that A(y) is not wrong while A(x) is wrong—stems from the assumption for (condition on) C2. In effect, C2 is "if the conduct A(x) will occur, then Y doing it rather than someone else is not wrong." It is wrong that the statute of frauds be pleaded, but it is not worse that it be pleaded by Y rather than someone else. Thus, Y's doing it does not add to the moral wrong in the world.

Has Davis shown that P3 above (originally P4) is false? His criticism rests on the difference between rule and act theories, not that between rule and act *consequentialist* ones. Davis's argument from fallibility does not show that P3 is false; at most, it shows that one would never be justified in acting as though it were true and applicable. The general version of what Davis calls the fallibility argument has, I think, been conclusively refuted.[1] However, the fallibility argument seems plausible in the context Davis uses it, because all the error costs seem to be on one side. That is, all the morally undesirable mistakes would be accepting clients and performing wrongful acts that would not occur were the case refused. There would be no moral disadvantages from mistakenly refusing clients.

Unfortunately, there are moral disadvantages in mistakenly refusing clients. There are the costs of morally restricting lawyers' liberty to act as well as the trouble and expense to which clients are put. Moreover, while my original argument eschewed side effects, they are relevant to Davis's argument, because he is considering the overall effects of the adoption of a rule. Some side effects can be moral costs in mistakenly refusing clients. A lawyer might be more likely than another to dissuade the client from the wrongful conduct. The lawyer might be mistaken about the wrongness of the client's conduct; if the lawyer is mistaken about that, then refusing the client is undesirable. Consequently, as there are moral costs in mistakenly refusing as well as accepting, there is no reason to adopt a rule of always refusing such clients. The only question is how certain a lawyer should be of the wrongfulness of the conduct and that others will accept the case.

In any case, I do not think P3 can be false. Indeed, Davis's conclusion is paradoxical if not contradictory. He suggests that an act is wrong even though there is no more wrongful conduct if it occurs than if it does not. In light of my explanation above, he must maintain that A(y) is wrong for reasons other than, or in addition to, it being an instantiation of A(x). This leads back to considerations of personal integrity, that A(y) would be morally worse than some A(i) because it would violate Y's personal integrity but there is some other person, *i,* whose integrity would not be violated. Davis has not presented an argument for this claim, and in the original paper I criticized all those that I knew.

Finally, Davis criticizes my arguments (1) that it would be wrong to refer a client that one rejects on moral grounds, because that would be assisting in wrongdoing; and (2) that one should refuse a client bent on wrongdoing if that is likely to prevent the client's wrongful conduct. Davis contends that I have confused an act being morally wrong with act being one that ought not be done. Part of his argument rests on confusing my arguments for (1) and (2). So far as I can tell, I never said that referral would be wrong, only that one would be partly responsible for the wrong that occurred. In any case, I did not distinguish 'ought not' and 'wrong' but used them synonomously. I do think, *pace* Davis, that, in ethics as in criminal law, one can formulate a rule about when it is wrong to assist in wrongdoing, rather than it being something one merely ought not to do. For example, "It is morally wrong knowingly to provide material assistance in wrongdoing."

Yet, I would be reasonably satisfied with the conclusions that lawyers ought not to accept such clients or to refer them to others. Davis thinks that a potential client's claim for legal assistance varies depending on whether other lawyers will provide services. This is ambiguous between a general claim to assistance and a particular claim to the assistance of a specific lawyer. The general claim does not vary. If the right to (good of) legal assistance is greater than the wrong (bad) of the wrongdoing, then providing assistance is justifiable. Thus, other things being equal, a lawyer cannot have moral reasons, only personal ones, for refusing such a case. The particular claim can vary in strength depending on the availability of lawyers. If other lawyers are unlikely to provide assistance, then if a lawyer does not take the case, the net good of assistance will not be achieved. Consequently, it would be good for the lawyer to accept the case; the lawyer ought to accept it, although it would not be wrong not to. If other lawyers are likely to take the case, then a lawyer's refusal will probably not prevent the good being achieved, so the claim on the lawyer is less. If the wrong (bad) of the wrongdoing outweighs the right (good of) assistance, then the client ought not to be assisted, either by taking the case or by referring the client. It cannot become good for the client to be assisted simply because the chances of this happening have decreased.

NOTE

1. See Barry Hoffmaster, "The Reliable Criterion Argument and Social Policy," *Social Theory and Practice* 5 (1978):75-93.

Michael Davis

Rejoinder to Bayles

Bayles raises many issues in his response. Space allows me to take up only a few. I should therefore like to focus on his reformulation of the no-difference argument, what I take to be the centerpiece of his response. Agreeing that his original formulation is unsatisfactory, Bayles offers this alternative:

P1: The occurrence of conduct A(x) would be wrong.

P2: Wrongful conduct A(x) will occur whether or not Y does it.

C1: Hence, it makes no difference to the occurrence of wrongful conduct A(x) whether or not Y does it.

P3: If an act makes not difference to the occurrence of wrongful conduct, it is not morally wrong.

C2: Therefore, Y's doing A(y) is not morally wrong.

How helpful is this alternative formulation? Is it any more convincing than the original? Is it a good argument? To answer such questions, let us try to restate the argument in different terms.

One way to restate the argument is to eliminate all "consequentialist" terms. This would not be unfair since Bayles now considers his original claim of "inescapable consequentialism" to have been misleading. If we substitute "morally irrelevant" for "makes no difference to the occurrence of wrongful conduct" and "doing acts" for "occurrence of conduct," we get the following argument, valid only with the addition of premise P2½':

P1': Anyone's doing A is morally wrong.

P2': Act A will be done whether or not a certain person Y does A.

P2½': If an act A will be done whether a certain person Y does A or not, whether Y does A is morally irrelevant to the evaluation of A (and so, of Y's doing A).

C1': Hence, whether Y does A is morally irrelevant to the evaluation of A (and so, Y's doing A).

P3': If whether Y does A is morally irrelevant to the evaluation of A, it is not morally wrong for Y to do A.

C2': Hence, Y's doing A is not morally wrong.

Now, if this is a fair restatement of Bayles's argument, there are at least two flaws in his argument. First, premise P1' has no role in the deduction. The fact that A is morally wrong is irrelevant to the conclusion of the argument. This is troubling but, by itself, merely inelegant. The second flaw is more serious. Premise P3' (the no-difference principle) is plainly false. The moral irrelevance of who does an act cannot make a wrong act right (or a right act wrong). Indeed, it is exactly the moral *ir*relevlance of who does the act that assures that, whoever does it, the act will be just as wrong as premise P1' says it is. So, this cannot be a fair restatement of Bayles's argument.

We might then try to restate the argument in language that is explicitly consequentialist, for example, by connecting "moral wrong" with "harm." The result is an argument using *all* of his original premises (premises P1″ and P1½″ being implicit in his P1):

P1″: Anyone doing A will do harm H.

P1½″: Doing harm H is (all else equal) morally wrong.

P2': (Therefore) the wrongful conduct (doing harm H) will occur whether X does A or Y does A.

C1″: Hence, it makes no difference (all else equal) to the occurrence of wrongful conduct (doing harm H) whether X does A or Y does A.

P3″: If it makes no difference to the occurrence of the wrongful conduct (doing harm H) whether X does A or Y does A, it is (all else equal) not morally wrong to do A.

C2″: Therefore, Y's doing A is not morally wrong.

This restatement seems much closer to Bayles's original. But it is almost as troubling as the last. Premise P1″ and P1½″ together yield the conclusion:

C3″: Anyone's doing A is morally wrong.

C3″ and Bayles's C2″ cannot both be true. If *anyone*'s doing A is morally wrong, then Y's doing A must be morally wrong too. There must, it seems, be some inconsistency in the premises. But where P1″ and P1½″ seem impeccable and P2″ seems to follow from them. That leaves only one premise to be the object of suspicion, P3″, the no-difference principle itself.

What might we do about P3″ to free it of suspicion? We might try to clarify it, for example, by reading it to mean, "If someone's doing A will not do harm H, it is (all else equal) not wrong to do A." Such a reading would make P3″ true, but only by making the deduction of C2″ impossible. For according to P1″, doing A *will* do harm H (and, according to P1½″, doing harm H is what makes doing A morally wrong). So, it seems rereading P3″ will not be enough to save the argument.

Bayles can, of course, point out that (according to P1½″) doing harm H is morally wrong *only if* all else is equal and then claim that all else is not equal *because* X will do A if Y does not. (Indeed, Bayles's switch from premises in which he talks of Y doing A(x) to an ultimate conclusion in which he talks of Y doing A(y) strongly suggests just such an implicit claim.) But there is trouble here too. To rest his defense of the no-difference principle on that claim alone would rest it on just what he set out to prove, that is, that A done by Y is morally different from A done by X (even though either act will do harm H). So, this second attempt to give a fair restatement of Bayles's argument seems no more successful than the first. The argument seems to contain an irremediable flaw.

These comments may suggest that Bayles has been careless. Since philosophers of Bayles's reputation are rarely careless, that is probably not the correct conclusion. A more likely conclusion, one I would suggest, is that a fundamental difference in moral theory has affected in detail how Bayles and I approach the problem before us. I should like to conclude this rejoinder by saying a little more about that.

Every situation is already understood in a certain way the moment we begin to think about it. "The facts" are often no more than the shadows cast by theories. Bayles provides a good illustration of this when he responds to my comment about the difficulty of formulating a rule for determining responsibility. His response is to provide a rule ("It is morally wrong knowingly to provide material assistance in wrongdoing"). He seems to consider this rule unproblematic. I do not. The help I give another is never just a "causal factor" in what he succeeds in doing. If what he is doing is morally wrong *and* I am *not* supposed to provide the help I do provide, my help may be "material assistance" and I will be in part responsible for the wrong he does. If, however, I *am* supposed to provide the help, I will not be responsible even in part for the wrong he does. I will not be responsible though he could not have done the wrong without me and though I knew that when I helped him. For example, the lawyer who gets an innocent man off by her unequaled brilliance is not responsible even in part for the tax fraud the man then commits even if the man told her of his plans and could not have carried them out had he been imprisoned for the crime he did not commit. "Material assistance" is the conclusion of a moral argument, not a neutral premise.

It is, then, a mistake to distinguish too sharply between fact and value, "theory" and "practice." Often, it seems, we must at least implicitly appeal to moral theory to settle "the facts" in a difficult case. When different moral theories yield different "facts" (as sometimes happens), it may be hard to know what to do until the issues are sorted out, the source of trouble identified, and a procedure for disposing of the trouble discovered (and accepted). The dispute between Bayles and me seems in large part to be of this difficult kind.

I draw two conclusions from this: (1) legal ethics should not be done in isolation from moral theory, and (2) being a good lawyer may now and then require doing some philosophy.

PROBLEMS

HELPING MURDERERS GO FREE

You are an attorney in a small city, one of only twenty who do criminal trials on a regular basis. Mr. Debachnik has sought your services. He turned to you only after every other attorney turned him down. Although not an indigent, Mr. Debachnik cannot afford your usual fee.

Based on what he has already admitted to you, Mr. Debachnik is guilty of the charges against him. However, he has a good chance of getting off on a technicality. The police force, while honest and good at catching criminals, suffers from small-town nonchalance: The police did not exactly read Mr. Debachnik his rights before questioning him. They just asked him whether he knew his rights and, when he responded that he had watched a lot of TV, they started their questioning. Mr. Debachnik gave them a good deal of damaging information without asking for an attorney (though he offered nothing that resembled a confession). The state will not have much of a case if all the evidence resulting from these damaging statements is thrown out, and a good attorney would certainly have a good chance of doing it.

Mr. Debachnik is accused of raping, torturing, and then killing six children during the last year. The oldest child was fifteen; the youngest, ten. Mr. Debachnik is not, as far as you can tell, legally insane. May you refuse to take the case? Should you refuse? If you refuse, the court will appoint an attorney fresh out of law school who will most likely not be equipped to make the full defense Mr. Debachnik needs to get off. Is the fact that the court will probably appoint an inexperienced attorney reason enough not to refuse the case? Is it a reason to refuse?

SPREADING DEVASTATION

Your client, a large coal company, owns the mineral rights to tens of thousands of acres of Illinois farmland. The company bought these rights during the Great Depression for a few cents an acre. The deeds permit the company to do whatever is necessary (and legal) to mine the minerals under the land (in this case, coal). The mining will be done by stripping off the buildings, topsoil, and anything else lying on the surface; digging down until there is no coal left; and then filling the huge hole with whatever fill is available. When the company is done with the land, even grass will have trouble growing there. No one knows how to make such strip-mined land good for much of anything.

Since the oil embargo, the price of coal has risen sharply. Your client can now make a substantial profit mining the coal it bought during the 1930s. The company has also become concerned that if it sits on the coal too long, the state will make strip-mining of good farmland too expensive or impossible. Thus, your client has asked you to begin eviction proceedings against one hundred families to make room for a huge mining operation. Even given the recent changes in state law, your client will probably prevail if the evictions are contested in court. If you proceed as planned one hundred wealthy Illinois farming families will suddenly be transformed into paupers. Farms worth almost a million dollars each will be reduced to worthless desert. Society will lose but your client stands to make a good profit.

May you refuse to do as your client has asked? Should you? If you were to decline, some attorney would, you am sure, do what you have refused to do, and he would do it citing the duty of attorneys to make legal counsel available.

HELPING THE ALMOST POOR

Uchettle Omoz has an eight-unit apartment building about two blocks from his home. He is an aging factory worker who invested his savings in "income-producing property." The neighborhood in which the building is located, while not "changing," is a rough mixture of hardworking Puerto Ricans, heavy-drinking Irish, and the poor residue of several Eastern European nationalities who once dominated the neighborhood. Omoz belongs to one of those nationalities and does not trust the Irish or the Puerto Rican residents. His building, unfortunately, is filled entirely with those he generally distrusts. "I can't rent to nobody else," he says. Most of his tenants are "exceptions" about whom he has no complaints. But he has had trouble now and then with nonpayment of rent, belligerence, and noise. "I try to run a good building. I keep the building good and don't want no trouble."

Until now he has rented without leases, since he thought he could just throw out anyone he wanted evicted. But recently he read in a consumer newsletter that a tenant could hold out, even without a lease, for at least ninety days and maybe not even have to pay the rent for that period. The possibility made him look for a new way to avoid trouble, a new tactic to protect his property. His idea is to make each tenant sign a lease that says in effect, "If you don't pay the rent or if you cause trouble, you have to leave the day I tell you to, no delay, no courts, no nothing." He wants the eviction provision in "bold print, simple English, so that I can show it in their faces when I want them out." He wants a lease prepared with blanks he can fill in for the particular tenant at the time he rents an apartment. He would have copies run off at the local print shop and use the lease for years to come.

Omoz has (quite rightly) a suspicion that the lease he wants would not stand up in court: "They don't care about the little property anymore." But he is not worried by this fact. He does not believe his tenants would go to court: "They are working people, like myself. They have too much money, too much pride, to go to legal aid. But they don't have enough money to feel they can go to attorneys, not when the lease says plain 'You lose.' Ah, even I can barely afford an attorney." The lease is to be a shortcut to save both money and trouble.

Should you prepare the lease? If not, what should you do instead?

Suggested Readings

For other works on issues raised here, see Bibliography, Part 6, especially Abel (1981), Cann (1981), Comment (1974), Devine (1982), Fallow (1980), Weckstein (1978), and Wolfram (1984).

ADDITIONAL PROBLEMS

IS HONESTY THE BEST POLICY?

You recently advised J. J. Cantilever concerning his nonresidential $130,000 mortgage with the Minimal Mortgage Company, which was threatening foreclosure. You informed him as gently as you could that there was no legal way to prevent the foreclosure, and you explained why. Cantilever said, "I see" and left.

Two days later he kidnapped Mr. Heindricks, the president of Minimal Mortgage, and hid Heindricks in his apartment. According to police, Cantilever claims to have wired the apartment so that it will explode if anyone opens the front door. Cantilever is known to have received extensive demolition training in the Army and is believed to be technically capable of carrying out his threat. The police are afraid to storm the building for just that reason.

Cantilever also strapped a shotgun to Heindrick's neck and threatened to kill him if the mortgage company did not cancel the obligation and apologize publicly for the terrible way he had been treated. Minimal Mortgage met both demands quickly.

You had followed these events with considerable interest but as no more than an interested bystander. Now you are no longer a bystander. Cantilever also demanded total immunity from criminal or civil prosecution or psychiatric confinement arising out of his acts during the last two days. He demanded that the immunity be in writing and signed by the county prosecutor. The county prosecutor has provided such a guarantee and publicly said he intended to honor it. But Cantilever was not satisfied. He thought there might be some legal trick. So, he has asked you to review the grant of immunity and give him your professional opinion on its completeness and effectiveness. The police transmitted his request to you.

Though you had previously advised Cantilever on business matters only, you are qualified to answer the questions he is asking. Your research has convinced you that the prosecutor is probably not legally bound by his grant of immunity, especially under the circumstances. You therefore wonder what to tell Cantilever. You have every reason to believe that he will kill Heindricks if he believes the prosecutor's offer is not good. Should you advise Cantilever at all in this matter? If so, how should you advise him?

HONESTY CONTINUED

Suppose again the facts of the previous problem, except that you are now the prosecutor rather than Cantilever's adviser. You know you cannot make an effective offer of immunity under these extraordinary circumstances. But you are morally certain that if you do not appear to make such an offer, Cantilever will kill his hostage. You cannot appear to make such an offer without publicly making false or misleading statements. Should you, as an attorney and a public prosecutor, make such statements?

YOUR CLIENT WANTS TO BLAB

Your client is one of four persons indicted in a narcotics conspiracy case. Each of those indicted has his own attorney. To avoid having the government play them off one against the other, you all agreed to meet in your conference room to coordinate strategy.

During the meeting, the defendants discussed their roles in the conspiracy, each making damaging admissions. The conspiracy was a complex affair. As it turned out, your client had no idea how complex it really was. He had thought himself a crucial figure linked to the others in a single chain. He was both disappointed and relieved to find out that he was only an expendable part of a series of interlocking wheels.

Before the meeting, your client wanted to fight the case every inch of the way. But now he wants to go to the district attorney and tell everything he knows. Most of what he knows, it turns out, is what he picked up at the meeting. There is no doubt that the D.A. would be willing to drop most or all of the charges against your client in return for his information *provided* the information includes admissions made in your conference room.

What should you do if your client persists in his plan to tell all? May you continue to represent him? Or must you withdraw? Should you do everything you can to assist him? May you—must you—inform counsel for the co-defendants of what your client is about to do? What do you owe those who trusted your client and you? What do you owe your client now?

FINDING A WAY TO HELP YOUR CLIENT

An attorney in a sensational robbery case entered into an agreement with his client taking as his fee (a) a lien on the defendant's home, (b) assignment of the defendant's right to money seized by police (not all of which may be *provably* part of the loot), and (c) all publication rights to the story of the defendant's life. The agreement was entered into before the case was tried. Did the attorney do anything unethical? Does the answer to this question depend upon how much the attorney told his client about the legal consequences of his agreement? Does it matter that the client could not otherwise have paid the attorney anything approaching his usual fee?

WHAT IF ERNEST ISN'T EARNEST

You are an assistant district attorney in a big city. Most of the cases you deal with are simple misdemeanors (for example, shoplifting or carrying a concealed weapon), and most are settled by plea-bargaining between you and the accused's attorney after the usual give-and-take. Most attorneys with whom you deal are long-time members of the "lower" criminal bar, plodding but hard-nosed, businesslike, and skilled in making a deal. Most days there is nothing memorable about what you do or whom you talk to.

Today, however, is different. You have before you one Frank Lee Ernest, Esq., a recent graduate of a local law school and an even more recent admittee to the bar. A solo practitioner, he has come to you to plea-bargain for a client accused of shoplifting. In the course of a three-minute conversation with you, he has revealed (quite unintentionally, of course) that all he knows of his client's record is what he learned from his client (an experienced shoplifter and confidence man for whom, it seems, most of his past is a closed book). He has also made it pretty clear that he does not have a firm grasp of the law of shoplifting and is depending on you to tell him what he needs to know to make a good deal. Because you are a decent sort, you tell him (and otherwise help him to make a fair deal for his client).

But you find the whole experience troubling. At best, Ernest has been gullible and lazy. He has believed his client without checking the public record and has not bothered to learn the law relevant to the case because he assumed you would be fair with him. At worst, he is an incompetent attorney, whom his client, however unsavory himself, has relied on to present his case in the best light possible so that he can make the best deal. The deal you have made with Ernest, though fair, probably is not the deal an experienced attorney would have wrung from you.

Has Earnest done anything ethically wrong? Should he be disciplined in some way? How and why? Do you have a professional obligation to say anything to him about what he has done? Do you have a professional obligation to report him to the local Grievance Committee?

USING WHAT ONE LEARNED IN GOVERNMENT SERVICE

An attorney worked for the federal government in the antitrust division for six years during which he spent almost one year helping to prepare a case against a certain company for conspiring to fix prices for police radios. Although never in charge of the case, he did much to give it its final shape. The case was settled by a consent decree in 1976, three years after the attorney left government service. Suppose the attorney, now in private practice in Chicago, were to be offered employment by the City of Chicago to sue the very same company for recovery of monies the city paid in excess of the fair market value of the police radios it purchased. Chicago intends to bring a class action on behalf of all cities similarly situated and proposes to retain the attorney on a contingency basis. Would it be unethical for the attorney to accept the proferred employment? Would your answer be any different if the city had (a) offered to pay the attorney on an hourly basis instead of on a contingency basis or (b) if it asked the attorney to join the city's legal office part-time for the duration of the case?

USING YOUR WITS

An attorney in Idaho has been retained to file suit against a California company for unfair business practices and violation of trademark rights. It would be more convenient for the client if the suit could be filed in a federal court in Idaho rather than in a federal court in California. If the California company does substantial business in Idaho, it can be sued there. Otherwise it cannot be. Information will be needed to establish such substantial business before the attorney can make use of discovery and other means of forcing the California company to reveal the extent of its business dealings in Idaho. The information can be obtained simply by phoning the company's main office and asking for the names of its outlets in Idaho. Is there anything unethical about an attorney getting the information in this way? You may suppose (1) that the person giving the information will be a low-level clerk, (2) that any person wishing to buy the company's product could do the same thing, (3) that the reason the clerk will give out the information is that he supposes the person requesting such information to be a potential customer, (4) that the California company has permanent counsel the name of which the company would happily reveal if the attorney were to ask for it, and (5) that the company's counsel would not reveal the information in question unless a court ordered it.

Jane van Schaick

Selected Topical Bibliography

PART ONE: THE PROFESSION OF LAW

A. Historical View

Armstrong, Walter P. "Century of Legal Ethics." *American Bar Association Journal* 64 (July 1978):1063-1072.

Bloomfield, Maxwell. *American Lawyers in a Changing Society, 1776-1876.* Cambridge, Mass.: Harvard University Press, 1976.

Chroust, Anton-Hermann. "The American Legal Profession: Its Agony and Ecstasy (1776-1840)." *Notre Dame Lawyer* 46 (1971):487-525.

———. *The Rise of the Legal Professional in America.* (2 vols.). Norman: University of Oklahoma Press, 1965.

Cohen, Herman. "The Origins of the English Bar." *Law Quarterly Review* 30 (1914):464-480.

Fetner, Gerald. "Public Power and Professional Responsibility; Julius Henry Cohen and the Origins of the Public Authority." *American Journal of Legal History* 21 (1977):15-39.

Frank, John P. "The Legal Ethics of Louis D. Brandeis." *Stanford Law Review,* 17 (1965):683-709.

Hazard, Geoffrey C. "An Historical Perspective on the Attorney-Client Privilege." *California Law Review* 66 (1978):1061-1091.

Holmes, Oliver W. "The Path of the Law." *Harvard Law Review* 10 (1897): 457-478.

Horwitz, Morton J. "The Conservative Tradition in the Writing of American Legal History." *American Journal of Legal History* 17 (1973):275-294.

Hurst, James W. *The Growth of the American Law: The Lawmakers.* New York: Little, Brown and Co., 1950.

Kalish, S. E. "David Hoffman's Essay on Professional Deportment and the Current Legal Ethics Debate." *Nebraska Law Review* 61 (1982):54-73.

Kirk, Harry. *Portrait of a Profession: A History of the Solicitors' Profession, 1100 to the Present Day.* London: Oyez, 1976.

Kogan, Herman. *The First Century: The Chicago Bar Association 1874-1974*. Chicago: Rand McNally, 1974.

Pound, Roscoe. *The Lawyer from Antiquity to Modern Times*. St. Paul, Minn.: West Publishing Co., 1953.

———. "Mechanical Jurisprudence." *Columbia Law Journal* 8 (1908):605-623.

Schudson, Michael. "Public, Private, and Professional Lives: The Correspondence of David Dudley Field and Samuel Bowles." *American Journal of Legal History* 3 (1977):191-211.

Sharswood, George. *An Essay on Professional Ethics*. 5th ed. (Reprint of 1844 ed.). Philadelphia, Penn.: T. & J. W. Johnson & Co., 1930.

Stone, Harlan. "The Public Influence of the Bar." *Harvard Law Review* 48 (1934):1-14.

Warren, Charles. *A History of the American Bar*. New York: Howard Fertig, 1966.

Wilkin, Robert N. *The Spirit of the Legal Profession*. New Haven: Conn.: Yale University Press, 1938.

B. Moral Fitness

Black, R. C. "Attorney Discipline for 'Offensive Personality' in California." *Hastings Law Journal* 31 (1980):1097-1138.

Bradway, John S. "Moral Turpitude as the Criterion of Offenses that Justify Disbarment." *California Law Review* 24 (1935):9-27.

Carothers, C. Graham. "Character and Fitness: A Need for Increased Perception." *The Bar Examiner* 51 (August 1982):25-34.

Comment. "The Concept of Attorney-Fitness in New York: New Perspectives." *Buffalo Law Review* 24 (1975):553-566.

Comment. "Florida Bar Admission Rule Requiring Good Moral Character Does Not Defeat the Purpose of the Federal Bankruptcy Act in Violation of the Supremacy Clause of the United States Constitution." *Florida State University Law Review* 7 (1979):587-592.

Comment. "Good Moral Character and Admission to the Bar." *Cincinnati University Law Review* 48 (1979):876-885.

Comment. "Good Moral Character and Homosexuality." *Journal of the Legal Profession* 5 (1980):139-149.

Comment. "The Good Moral Character Requirement for Admission to the Bar." *University of San Fernando Valley Law Review* 4 (1975):317-331.

Comment. "Homosexuality and the Good Moral Character Requirement." *University of Detroit Journal of Urban Law* 56 (1978):123-139.

Custer, Lawrence B. "Georgia's Board to Determine Fitness of Bar Applicants." *The Bar Examiner* 51:3 (August 1982):17-21.

Elliston, Frederick A. "Character and Fitness Tests: An Ethical Perspective." *The Bar Examiner* 51:3 (August 1982):8-16.

Herman, James E. "Screening for Character and Fitness." *The Bar Examiner*

51:3 (August 1982):23-25.

Hill, Harold N., Jr. "Appellate Review of Moral Character and Fitness Determinations." *The Bar Examiner* 51:3 (August 1982):22-24.

Kaslow, Florence W. "Moral, Emotional and Physical Fitness for the Bar: Pondering (seeming) Imponderables." *The Bar Examiner* 51:3 (August 1982):38-47.

Krohn, Lauren. "Two-Lawyer Marriages: The Ethics." *Barrister* 10 (Winter 1983):20(6).

Manson, A. S. "Observations from an Ethical Perspective on Fitness, Insanity, and Confidentiality." *McGill Law Journal* 27 (1982):196-249.

McChrystal, Michael K. "A Structural Analysis of the Good Moral Character Requirement for Bar Admission." *Notre Dame Law Review* 60 (Winter 1984):67-101.

Schwartz, Arthur H. "What Is a Character and Fitness Committee?" *New York State Bar Journal* 49 (1977):302-306, 398-401, 440-442, 494-499.

Smith, Len Young. "Abraham Lincoln as a Bar Examiner." *The Bar Examiner* 51:3 (August 1982):35-37.

Starrs, John R. "Considerations in Determination of Good Moral Character." *Catholic Lawyer* 2 (1956):161-171.

Weckstein, Donald T. "Maintaining the Integrity and Competence of the Legal Profession." *Texas Law Review* 48 (1970):267-284.

C. Discipline

Albert, Edward. "How 42 Lawyers Were Disbarred in New York as an Indirect Result of the Grisly David Berkowitz Murder Case." *Barrister* 7 (Summer 1980):6-8.

American Bar Association. National Center For Professional Responsibility. *The Rules File.* Chicago: American Bar Association, 1981. (microfiche cards).

Brown, Barry. "Reinstatement Dilemma: The Hiss Decision and Its Effect Upon Disciplinary Enforcement," in *Lawyers' Ethics,* Allen Gerson, ed. New Brunswick, N.J.: Transaction Books, 1980. pp. 225-235.

Brunelli, Richard. "Court Refuses to Reinstate Lawyer." (Irving Louis Gottlieb) *Chicago Daily Law Bulletin* 131 (November 21, 1985):3, col. 2.

Carpenter, Edmund N. "Negligent Attorney Embezzler: Delaware's Solution." *American Bar Association Journal* 61 (1975):338-341.

Comment. "Controlling Lawyers by Bar Associations and Courts." *Harvard Civil Rights and Civil Liberty Law Review* 5 (1970):301-392.

Comment. "Discipline of Attorneys for Non-Professional Misconduct." *Arkansas Law Review* 5(1951):411-419.

"The Disability Defense: How It Serves to Mitigate Changes of Professional Misconduct by Attorneys." *William Mitchell Law Review* 12 (Winter 1986): 119-141.

Divine, J. R. "Lawyers Discipline in Missouri: Is a New Ethics Code Necessary?"

Missouri Law Review 46 (1981): 709-763.

Dreibelbis, Ellen. "Ain't Misbehavin'" *California State Bar Journal* 55 (July 1980):304-306.

Finman, T. and T. Schneyer. "Role of Bar Association Ethics Opinions in Regulating Lawyer Conduct: A Critique of the Work of the ABA Committee on Ethics and Professional Responsibility." *UCLA Law Review* 29 (1981): 67-167.

Garbus, Martin and J. Seligman. "Sanctions and Disbarment: They Sit in Judgment," in *Verdicts on Lawyers.* Ralph Nader and Mark Green, eds., New York: Thomas Y. Crowell, 1976. pp. 47-62.

Gray, Jeanne and Mark I. Harrison. "Standards for Lawyer Discipline and Disability Proceedings and the Evaluation of Lawyer Discipline Systems." *Capital University Law Review* 11:3 (1982):529-576.

Kidney, James. "Lawyers: Can They Police Themselves?" in *Readings in Criminal Justice* 1978-1979 annual editions by Donald E. J. MacNamara. Guilford, Conn.: Dushkin Publishing Group, Inc., 1978.

Levey, J. M. "Judges' Role in the Enforcement of Ethics—Fear and Learning in the Profession." *Santa Clara Law Review* 22 (1982):95-116.

McGoff, Kevin P. "Disciplining Attorneys: Correcting No-No's." *Res Gestae* 25 (1981):478-483.

McPike, Timothy. "Disciplining the Errant Lawyer: Judges Can and Should—Make Better Use of Conduct Probes." *Los Angeles Daily Journal* 98 (July 23, 1985):4, col. 3.

Murphy, Francis T., Jr. "Grievance Counsel for the Public." *New York Law School Law Review* 26 (1981):221-236.

Note. "Discipline of Attorneys in Maryland." *Maryland Law Review* 35 (1975): 236-269.

Raven, Robert D. "President's Message." *California State Board Journal* 56 (1981):268-269.

Roberts, Charley. "Bills Will Propose Agency to Oversee Attorney Discipline: Non-Lawyer Control?" (California) *Los Angeles Daily Journal* 98 (December 27, 1985):1, col. 2.

Rosenthal, Douglas. *A Model Peer Review System.* Philadelphia, Penn: ALI-ABA Committee on Professional Competence and Responsibility, 1980.

Schwartz, Alan. "Automatic Discipline: A Concept Whose Time Has Arrived." *Detroit College of Law Review* (Spring 1981):1-28.

Smith, Mark P. and Robert H. Davis. "I Say 'Yes' and You Say 'No': The Proper Role of the Bar Spokesman in Disciplinary Matters." *Bar Leader* 11 (November-December 1985):19-20.

Steele, Eric H. and Raymond T. Wimmer. "Lawyers, Clients, and Professional Regulation." *American Bar Association Research Journal* (1976):917-1019.

Stewart, David O. "Are Lawyers Free to Speak Out About the Courts?" *American Bar Association Journal* 71 (May 1985):81-84.

Todd, John J. "The Role of State Appellate Court in the Professional Disciplinary Process." *Capital University Law Review* 11 (1982):577-584.

PART TWO: THE MORAL CRITIQUE OF PROFESSIONALISM

A. Ethics (General)

Baier, Kurt. *The Moral Point of View.* New York: Random House, 1965.
Donagan, Alan. *The Theory of Morality.* Chicago: University of Chicago Press, 1977.
Frankena, William K. *Ethics.* Englewood Cliffs, N.J.: Prentice Hall, 1963.
Fried, Charles. *Right and Wrong.* Cambridge, Mass.: Harvard University Press, 1978.
Gert, Bernard. *The Moral Rules.* New York: Harper and Row Publishers, 1970.
Hare, R. M. *The Language of Morals.* Oxford: The Clarendon Press, 1952.
Harman, Gilbert. *The Nature of Morality.* New York: Oxford University Press, 1977.
Mackie, J. L. *Ethics.* New York: Penguin Books, 1978.
MacIntyre, Alasdair. *After Virtue.* Notre Dame, Ind.: University of Notre Dame Press. 1981.
Sartorius, Rolf. *Individual Conduct and Social Norms.* Encino, Calif.: Dickenson Publishing Company, Inc., 1975.
Smart, J. J. C. "Utilitarianism," in *Encyclopedia of Philosophy,* vol. 8, pp. 206-212.
Stevenson, C. L. *Ethics & Language.* New Haven, Conn.: Yale University Press, 1946.

B. Professional Ethics

Baumrin, Bernard and Benjamin Freedman, eds. Moral Responsibility and the Professions. New York: Haven Publications, 1983.
Bayles, Michael D. *Professional Ethics.* Belmont, Calif.: Wadsworth Publishing Co., 1981.
Bennion, F. A. R. *Professional Ethics: The Consultant Professions and Their Code.* London: Charles Knight & Co., 1969.
Camenisch, Paul. *Grounding Professional Ethics in a Pluralistic Society.* New York: Haven Publications, 1983.
Dansereau, H. R. "Unethical Behavior: Professional Deviance," in *Deviance in Business and the Professions,* John M. Johnson and Jack D. Douglas, eds. Philadelphia: J. B. Lippincott, 1978.
Davis, Michael. "The Moral Authority of a Professional Code," in *Nomos XXIX: Authority Revisited,* J. Roland Pennock and John W. Chapman, eds., New York: New York University Press, 1986 (forthcoming).
Elliston, Frederick A. "Professionalism and Professional Ethics." Paper presented at the American Society of Public Administrators in Honolulu, Hawaii, March 25, 1982.

"Ethics in America: Norms and Deviations." *Annals of the American Academy of Political and Social Science* 363 (January 1966), entire.

Freedman, Benjamin. "A Meta-Ethics for Professional Morality." *Ethics* 89 (October 1978):1-19.

————. "What Really Makes Professional Morality Different: Response to Martin." *Ethics* 91 (1981):626-630.

Goldman, Alan H. *The Moral Foundations of Professional Ethics.* Totowa, N.J.: Rowman and Littlefield, 1980.

Kipnis, Kenneth. "Professional Responsibility and the Responsibility of Professions," in *Profits and Professions,* Wade L. Robison, Michael S. Pritchard and Joseph Ellin, eds. New York: Humana Press, 1983, pp. 9-22.

Larson, M. S. *The Rise of Professionalism: A Sociological Analysis.* Berkeley: University of California Press, 1977.

C. Lawyers' Ethics

American Bar Association. Consortium for Professional Education. *Dilemmas in Legal Ethics.* Chicago: American Bar Foundation. (videotapes)

Archer, Gleason L. *Ethical Obligations of the Laywer.* (Reprint of 1910 ed.) Littleton, Colo.: Rothman and Co., 1981.

Aronson, Robert and Donald Weckstein. *Aronson and Weckstein's Professional Responsibility in a Nutshell.* St. Paul, Minn.: West Publishing Co., 1980.

Aronson, Robert H. *Problems in Professional Responsibility.* St. Paul, Minn.: West Publishing Co., 1978.

Auerbach, Jerold S. *Unequal Justice.* New York: Oxford University Press, 1976.

Bloom, Murray Teigh, ed. *Lawyers, Clients and Ethics.* New York: Council on Legal Education for Professional Responsibility, Inc., 1979.

Carlin, Jerome E. *Lawyers' Ethics: A Survey of the New York City Bar.* New York: Russell Sage Foundation, 1966.

Carrington, Paul. "The Ethical Crisis of American Lawyers." *University of Pittsburgh Law Review* 36 (1974):35-54.

Cohen, Lucy Kramer, ed. *The Legal Conscience: Selected Papers of Felix S. Cohen.* New Haven, Conn.: Yale University Press, 1960.

Costigan, George P., Jr. *Cases and Other Authorities on Legal Ethics.* St. Paul, Minn.: West Publishing Co., 1917.

Dauer, Edward A. and Arthur A. Leff. "Correspondence: The Lawyer as a Friend." *Yale Law Review* 86 (1981):573-587.

Drinker, Henry S. *Legal Ethics.* New York: Columbia University Press, 1953.

Elkins, J. R. "Moral Discourse and Legalism in Legal Education." *Journal of Legal Education* 32 (1982):11-52.

Freedman, Monroe H. "Personal Responsibility in a Professional System." *Catholic University Law Review* 27 (1975):191-206.

Gerson, Allen, ed. *Lawyer's Ethics.* New Brunswick, N.J.: Transaction Books 1980.

Gewirth, Alan. "Professional Ethics: The Separatist Thesis." *Ethics* 96 (January 1986):282-300.

Glenn, Peter G. "Alternative Approaches to Legal Ethics." (Review of *Ethics in the Practice of Law,* by Geoffrey C. Hazard and *Crisis At the Bar: Laywers' Unethical Ethics and What To Do About It* by Jethro K. Lieberman) *Texas Law Review* 57 (1979):307-320.

Greenebaum, Edwin H. "Attorneys' Problems in Making Ethical Decisions." *Indiana Law Journal* 52 (1979):627-635.

Hazard, Geoffrey C. "The Lawyer's Obligation to be Trustworthy When Dealing with Opposing Parties." *South Carolina Review* 33 (1981):181-195.

———. "Legal Ethics: Legal Rules and Professional Aspirations." *Cleveland State Law Review* 30 (1981):571-576.

———. *Ethics in the Practice of Law.* New Haven, Conn.: Yale University Press, 1980.

Held, Virginia. "The Division of Moral Labor and the Role of the Lawyer," in *The Good Lawyer: Lawyers' Roles and Lawyers' Ethics.* David Luban, ed. Totowa, N.J.: Roman and Allanheld, 1984 pp. 60-79.

Hoover, Michael J. "What a Lawyer May Say to the Media." *Bench and Bar* 42 (February 1985):31-52.

Imwinkelried, E. J. "Sociological Approach to Legal Ethics." *American University Law Review* 30 (1981): 349-373.

Kaberon, Seth. "Daley Hits Judges: Lawyers on Ethics." *Chicago Daily Law Bulletin* 132 (March 4, 1986):1, col. 2.

Kaufmann, Andrew. *Problems in Professional Responsibility.* Boston, Mass.: Little, Brown & Co., 1976.

Kipnis, Kenneth. *Legal Ethics.* Englewood Cliffs, N.J.: Prentice-Hall, 1986.

Knight, Richard F. "Professional Responsibility." *Louisiana Law Review* 40 (Spring 1980):728-741.

Leventhal, Harold. "Professional Responsibility: Keynote Address of the Second Annual Baron De Hirsch Meyer Lecture Series." *University of Miami Law Review* 30 (1976):789-802.

Lieberman, Jethro K. *Crisis at the Bar: Lawyers' Unethical Ethics and What to Do About It.* New York: W. W. Norton, 1978.

Luban, David, ed. *The Good Lawyer: Lawyers' Roles and Lawyers' Ethics.* Totowa, N.J.: Rowman and Allanheld, 1984.

———. "Calming the Hearse Horse: A Philosophical Research Program for Legal Ethics." *Maryland Law Review* 40 (1981):451-476.

Marks, F. Raymond. *The Lawyer, The Public and Professional Responsibility.* Chicago, Ill.: American Bar Foundation, 1972.

Maru, Olavi. *Bar Association Ethics Opinions.* Chicago: American Bar Foundation, 1985.

McDaniel, Ann. "Symposium: Legal Ethics in the Age of Marketing." (transcript) *Legal Times* 8 (July 22, 1985):32, col. 1.

McKay, R. B. "Beyond Professional Responsibility." *Capital University Law*

Review 10 (1981):709-719.

Mellinkoff, David. *The Conscience of a Lawyer*. St. Paul, Minn.: West Publishing Co., 1977.

Morgan, Thomas D. "Evolving Concept of Professional Responsibility," in *Teaching Professional Responsibility: Materials and Proceedings from the National Conference*. Patrick A. Keenan et al. eds., Detroit, Mich.: University of Detroit School of Law, 1979, pp. 742-743.

Morgan, Thomas. "The Fall and Rise of Professionalism." *University of Richmond Law Review* 19 (Spring 1985):451-466.

Patterson, L. Ray. *Legal Ethics: The Law of Professional Responsibility*. New York: Bender, 1982.

Petrowitz, Harold C. "Some Thoughts about Current Problems in Legal Ethics and Professional Responsibility." *Duke Law Journal* 1979 (1979):1275-1290.

Pirsig, Maynard E. and Kenneth F. Kirwin. *Cases and Materials on Professional Responsibility*. 3rd ed. St. Paul, Minn.: West Publishing Co., 1976.

Redlich, Norman. *Professional Responsibility: A Problem Approach*. Boston, Mass.: Little, Brown and Co., 1976.

Redmount, Robert S. "New Dimensions of Professional Responsibility." *Journal of the Legal Profession* 13 (1978):43-56.

Rhode, Deborah L. and Murray L. Schwartz. "Ethical Perspectives on Legal Practice." (Symposium on the Law Firm as a Social Institution, Stanford Law School, February 1984) *Stanford Law Review* 37 (January 1985):589-659.

Rubin, James H. "Should a Lawyer Reveal When a Client is Lying?" *Chicago Daily Law Bulletin* 131 (November 11, 1985):1, col. 2.

Schwartz, Murray L. *Lawyers and the Legal Profession: Cases and Materials*. New York: Bobbs-Merrill, 1979.

———. "Professionalism and Accountability of Lawyers." *California Law Review* 66 (1978):669-697.

Shaffer, Thomas L. *On Being a Christian and a Lawyer: Law for the Innocent*. Provo, Utah: Brigham Young University Press, 1980.

———. "The Practice of Law as Moral Discourse." *Notre Dame Lawyer* 55 (1979):231-253.

Simon, William H. "Homo Psychologicous: Notes on a New Legal Formalism." *Stanford Law Review* 32 (1980):487-559.

Slovak, J. S. "Ethics of Corporate Lawyers: A Sociological Approach." *American Bar Foundation Research Journal* (1981):753-794.

Stephens, William T. "The Alabama Ethics Cases." *Cumberland-Samford Law Review,* 10 (1979):317-357.

Stern, Duke N. Review of "Crisis at the Bar Lawyers' Unethical Ethics and What to Do About It," by Jethro Lieberman. *American Bar Association Journal* 64 (September 1978):1403-1404.

Stewart, Potter. "Professional Ethics for the Business Lawyer: The Morals of the Market Place." *Business Lawyer* 31 (1975):463-468.

Sturm, Douglas. "American Legal Realism and the Covenantal Myth: World Views in the Practice of Law." *Mercer Law Review* 31 (1980):487-508.

Trumbull, William M. *Materials on the Lawyer's Professional Responsibility.* Englewood Cliffs, N.J.: Prentice-Hall, 1957.

Wallingford, Whitney. "Professional Responsibility." *Kentucky Law Journal* 67 (1978-1979):757-774.

Warvelle, George W. *Essays in Legal Ethics,* 2nd ed. Chicago: Callaghan & Co., 1920.

Wolf, Susan. "Ethics, Legal Ethics, and the Ethics of Law," in *The Good Lawyer: Lawyers' Roles and Lawyers' Ethics.* David Luban, ed. Totowa, N.J.: Rowman & Allanheld, 1984, pp. 38-59.

PART THREE: THE ADVERSARY SYSTEM

Cohen, Elliot D. "Pure Legal Advocates and Moral Agents: Two Concepts of a Lawyer in an Adversary System." *Criminal Justice Ethics* 4 (Winter-Spring 1985):38-59.

Curtis, Charles P. "The Ethics of Advocacy." *Stanford Law Review* 4 (1951): 3-23.

Donagan, Alan. "Justifying Legal Practice in the Adversary System," in *The Good Lawyer: Lawyers' Roles and Lawyers' Ethics.* David Luban, ed. Totowa, N.J.: Rowman & Allanheld, 1984, pp. 123-149.

Dorsen, Norman. "*Lawyers' Ethics in an Adversary System:* Freedman, M. H." *Harvard Civil Rights and Civil Liberties Law Review* 11 (1976):764-769.

Douglass, John J. Review of "*Lawyers' Ethics in an Adversary System:* Freedman, M. H." *Houston Law Review* 14 (1977):519-526.

Drinker, Henry S. "Some Remarks on Mr. Curtis's 'The Ethics of Advocacy.' " *Stanford Law Review* 4 (1952):349-357.

Frankel, Marvin E. "From Private Fights Toward Public Justice." *New York University Law Review* 51 (1976):516-537.

———. "The Search for Truth: An Umpireal View." *University of Pennsylvania Law Review* 123 (1975):1031-1059.

Freedman, Monroe H. "Are There Public Interest Limits in Lawyers' Advocacy?" *Journal of the Legal Profession* 2 (1977):47-54.

———. *Lawyers' Ethics in an Adversary System.* Indianapolis, Ind.: Bobbs-Merrill, 1975.

Gilmore, Hon. Horace W. "Professional Responsibility Problems and Contempt in Advocacy." *San Diego Law Review* 12 (1975):288-305.

Hegland, Kenney. "Moral Dilemmas in Teaching Trial Advocacy." *Journal of Legal Education* 32 (1982):69-86.

Kaufman, Irving R. "In Defense of the Advocate." *University of California Los Angeles Law Review* 12 (1965):351-360.

Landsman, S. "Decline of the Adversary System and the Changing Role of the

Advocate in that System." *San Diego Law Review* 18 (1981):251-261.

Lehman, Warren. "The Pursuit of a Client's Interest." *Michigan Law Review* 77 (1979):1078-1097.

Luban, David. "The Adversary System Excuse," in *The Good Lawyer: Lawyers' Roles and Lawyers' Ethics.* David Luban, ed., Totowa, N.J.: Rowman & Allanheld, 1984, pp. 83-122.

Miller, D. L. "Advocate's Duty to Justice: Where Does it Belong?" *Law Quarterly Review* 97 (1981):127-142.

Miller, Henry G. "Ethics: The Ten Most Common Transgressions Against Manners and Morals of Advocates." *New York Law Journal* 194 (October 18, 1985):1, col. 1.

Morgan, Charles, Jr. "In Defense of the 'Hired Gun'." *Los Angeles Daily Journal* 98 (October 18, 1985):4, col. 3.

Noonan, John T. "Professional Ethics or Personal Responsibility?" Review of *Lawyers' Ethics in an Adversary System,* by Monroe H. Freedman. *Stanford Law Review* 29 (1977):363-370.

Noonan, John T. Jr. "The Purposes of Advocacy and the Limits of Confidentiality." *Michigan Law Review* 64 (1966):1485-1482.

Rich, William. "The Role of Lawyers: Beyond Advocacy." *Brigham Young University Law Review* 1980 (1980):767-784.

Rogers, Showell. "The Ethics of Advocacy." *Law Quarterly Review* 5 (1899): 259-280.

Scardilli, Frank J. "Law, Lawyers and the Tyranny of Illusion." *Humanist* 41 (September-October 1981):20-26.

Schwartz, Murray. *The Zeal of the Civil Advocate.* College Park, Md.: Center for Philosophy and Public Policy of the University of Maryland, 1982.

Shaffer, Thomas L. "Advocacy as Moral Discourse." *North Carolina Law Review* 57 (1979):647-670.

Simon, William H. "The Ideology of Advocacy: Procedural Justice and Professional Ethics." *Wisconsin Law Review* 1978 (1978):29-144.

Singley, Carl E. Review of *Lawyers' Ethics in an Adversary System,* by Monroe Freedman. *University of Pittsburgh Law Review* 38 (1976):135-143.

Taylor, Allen. "The Adversary System of Justice: An Ethical Jungle." *Journal of Critical Analysis* 3 (April 1971):23-28.

Thurman, Samuel D. "Limits to the Adversary System: Interests That Outweigh Confidentiality." *Journal of the Legal Profession* 5 (1980):5-19.

Underwood, R. H. "Curbing Litigation Abuses: Judicial Control of Adversary Ethics." *St. John's Law Review* 56 (1982):625-668.

PART FOUR: CONFLICT OF INTEREST

Aronson, Robert H. "Conflict of Interest." *Washington Law Review* 52 (1977): 807-858.

Bayne, D. C. "Lawyer and Corporate Governance Conflict of Interest." *St. Louis University Law Journal* 26 (1982):400-425.

Comment. "A Dilemma in Professional Responsibility: The Subsequent Representation Problem" *Journal of Missouri-Kansas City Law Review* 50 (1982):165-181.

Comment. "Ethical Concerns of Lawyers Who Are Related by Kinship or Marriage." *Oregon Law Review* 60 (1981):399-411.

Davis, Michael. "Conflict of Interest." *Business and Professional Ethics Journal* 1:4 (1982):17-27.

"Developments in the Law—Conflicts of Interest in the Legal Profession." *Harvard Law Review* 94 (April 1981):1244-1503.

Furrow, Brian D. "The Corporate Law Department: Counsel to the Entity." *Business Lawyer* 34 (1979):1797-1830.

Geer, J. S. "Representation of Multiple Criminal Defendants: Conflicts of Interest and the Professional Responsibilities of the Defense Attorney." *Minnesota Law Review* 62:2 (1978):119-162.

Kindregan, Charles P. "Conflict of Interest and the Lawyer in Civil Practice." *Valparaiso University Law Review* 10 (1976):423-452.

Kizer, John O. "Legal Ethics and the Prosecuting Attorney." *West Virginia Law Review* 79 (1977):367-380.

Merrick, G. W. "Government Service and the Chinese Wall: An Accommodation Founded on Practicality." *University of Colorado Law Review* 52 (1981):499-510.

Midonick, Millard L. "Attorney-Client Conflicts and Confidences in Trusts and Estates." *Record of New York City Bar Association* 35 (April 1980):215-226.

Moore, Nancy J. "Conflict of Interest in the Simultaneous Representation of Multiple Clients: A Proposed Solution to the Current Confusion and Controversy." *Texas Law Review* 61 (1982):211-288.

Note. "Unchanging Rules in Changing Times. The Canons of Ethics and Intrafirm Conflicts of Interest." *Yale Law Journal* 73 (1964):1058-1079.

Rotunda, Ronald D. "Law, Lawyers, and Managers," in *The Ethics of Corporate Conduct*. Clarence Walton, ed., Englewood Cliffs, N.J.: Prentice-Hall, 1977, pp. 127-141.

Stern, Jeffrey. "Dilemmas For Insurance Counsel—Coping With Conflicts of Interest." *Massachusetts Law Review* 65 (1980):127-132.

Tague, Peter W. "Multiple Representation of Targets and Witnesses During a Grand Jury Investigation." *American Criminal Law Review* 17 (1980):638-709.

Underwood, R. H. "Doctor and His Lawyer: Conflicts of Interest." *Kansas Law Review* (1982):385-407.

Wice, Brian William. "Representation of Multiple Criminal Defendants: Conflicts of Interest and the Responsibility of the Defense Lawyer." *Texas Bar Journal,* 44 (July 1981):729-736.

PART FIVE: PERJURY AND CONFIDENTIALITY

American Business Law Association. *Recent Developments in the Law of Confidentiality.* Atlanta, Ga.: American Business Law Association, 1976. (microfiche) 10p.

Armani, Frank H. "The Obligation of Confidentiality." *Juris* (March 1975):3-5.

"Attorney-Client Privilege—Fixed Rules, Balancing, and Constitutional Entitlement." *Harvard Law Review* 91 (December 1977):464-487.

Burke, M. M. "Duty of Confidentiality and Disclosing Corporate Misconduct." *Business Law* 36 (1981):239-295.

Callan, J. Michael, and Harris David. "Professional Responsibility and the Duty of Confidentiality: Disclosure of Client Misconduct in an Adversary System." *Rutgers Law Review* 29 (1976):332-396.

Chamberlain, Jeffrey F. "Legal Ethics: Confidentiality and the Case of Garrow's Lawyers." *Buffalo Law Review* 25:1 (1975):211-239.

"Client Fraud and the Lawyer—An Ethical Analysis." *Minnesota Law Review* 62:1 (1977):89-118.

Comment. "Responding to the Criminal Defense Client Who Insists on the Presentation of Perjuring Nonparty Witnesses: The Schultheis Solution." *Iowa Law Review* 68 (1983):359-378.

Comment. "'Secrets' on the Public Record?" *Journal of Legal Profession* 6 (1981):357-365.

Denecke, Arno H. "The Dilemma of the Virtuous Lawyer, or When Do You Have to Blow the Whistle on Your Client?" *Arizona State Law Journal* (1979):245-252.

"Discovery of 'Privileged' Communications." *Defense Law Journal* 22 (1973): 399-413.

Fedders, John M. and Lauryn H. Guttenplan. "Document Retention and Destruction—Practical, Legal and Ethical Considerations." *Notre Dame Lawyer* 56:1 (1980):5-64.

Freedman, Monroe H. "'Major Deficiencies' Mar Roles in Lawyer-Client Confidences." *Legal Times Washington* 4 (August 10, 1981):23, col. 1.

Gordon, Michael D. "The Invention of a Common Law Crime: Perjury and The Elizabethan Courts." *American Journal of Legal History* 24 (April 1980): 145-170.

Grace, Roger M. "Invading the Privacy of the Attorney-Client Relationship." *Case and Comment* 81 (July-August 1976):46-49.

Hipler, Harry M. "Turning Point Between Lawyers and Accomplice." *Trial* 12:5 (1976):48-50, 61.

Hunter, Muir. *False Witness—The Problem of Perjury—A Report by Justice.* London: Stevens and Sons, 1973.

Jacobs, Myra R. "Ethical Quandary—The Extension of Attorney-Client Privilege to Communication of Past Crimes." *Case and Comment* 81:4 (July-August 1976):24-28, 30, 3233, 36-39.

Kramer, Victor H. "Clients' Frauds and Their Lawyers' Objections: A Study in Professional Irresponsibility." *Georgetown Law Journal* 67 (1979):991-1006.

Lawry, Robert P. "Lying, Confidentiality, and the Adversary System of Justice." *Utah Law Review* 1977 (1977):653-695.

"Legal Ethics and the Destruction of Evidence." *Yale Law Journal* 88:8 (July 1979):1665-1688.

Note. "Disclosure of Incriminating Physical Evidence Received from a Client: The Defense Attorney's Dilemma." *University of Colorado Law Review* 52 (1981):419-463.

Note. "Ethics, Law, and Loyalty: The Attorney's Duty to Turn Over Incriminating Physical Evidence." *Stanford Law Review* 32 (1980):977-999.

O'Neal, F. Hodge and Stephen R. Thompson. "Vulnerability of Professional Client Privilege in Shareholder Litigation." *Business Lawyer* 31 (1976):1775-1797.

Ostergaard, Joni H. "The Failure of Situation Oriented Professional Rules to Guide Conduct: Conflicting Responsibilities of the Criminal Defense Attorney Whose Client Commits or Intends to Commit Perjury." *Washington Law Review* 55 (1979):211-242.

Plescia, Joseph. *The Oath and Perjury in Ancient Greece.* Tallahassee, Fla.: State University Press, 1970.

"Perjury—The Forgotten Offense." *Journal of Criminal Law and Criminology* 65:3 (September 1974):361-372.

Polster, Dan Aaron. "Dilemma of the Perjurious Defendant—Resolution, Not Avoidance." *Case Western Reserve Law Review* 28 (Fall 1977):3-40.

Pye, A. Kenneth. "Role of Counsel in the Suppression of Truth." *Duke Law Journal* 4 (October 1978):921-959.

Sampson, R. "Client Perjury: Truth Autonomy, and the Criminal Defense Lawyer." *American Journal of Criminal Law* 9 (1981):387-403.

Wolfram, Charles W. "Client Perjury." *Southern California Law Review* 50 (1977):809-870.

PART SIX: PROVIDING LEGAL SERVICES

Abel, Richard L. "Toward a Political Economy of Lawyers." *Wisconsin Law Review* 1981 (1981):1117-1187.

Abel, Richard I. "Socializing the Legal Profession: Can Re-Distributing Lawyers' Services Achieve Social Justice?" *Law and Policy Quarterly* 1:1 (January 1979):5-51.

Armstrong, Walter P. "Ethical Problems in Connection With the Delivery of Legal Servies." *San Diego Law Review* 12 (1975):336-358.

Bodle, George E. "Group Legal Services: The Case for *BRT.*" *University of California Los Angeles Law Review* 12 (1965):306-326.

Brownell, Emery A. *Legal Aid in the United States.* Rochester, N.Y.: Lawyers

Cooperative Publishing Co., 1951.

Cann, W. A. "Frivolous Lawsuits—the Lawyer's Duty to Say 'No'." *University of Colorado Law Review* 52 (1981):367-391.

Christensen, Barlow F. "Toward Improved Legal Service Delivery: A Look at Four Mechanisms." *American Bar Foundation Research Journal* 2 (1979):277-293.

Comment. "Group Legal Services, The Ethical Evolution." *Baylor Law Review,* 27 (1975):525-543.

Comment. "Legal Services—Past and Present." *Cornell Law Review* 59 (1974):960-988.

Curran, Barbara A. *The Legal Needs of the Public: The Final Report of a National Survey.* Chicago: American Bar Foundation, 1977.

Devine, J. R. "Lawyer Advertising and the Kutak Commission: A Refreshing Return to the Past." *Wake Forest Law Review* 18 (1982):503-522.

Fallows, James. "Sheepskins Are for Sheep." *Washington Monthly* (1980):9-17.

Galanter, Marc. "The Duty *Not* to Deliver Legal Services." *University of Miami Law Review* 30 (1976):929-951.

Kettleson, Jeanne. "Ethical Outlook—Revising the Code of Professional Responsibility." *NLADA Briefcase* 35 (March 1978):40-43.

Marks, F. Raymond. "A Lawyer's Duty to Take All Comers and Many Who Do Not Come." *University of Miami Law Review* 30 (1976):915-927.

National Resource Center for Consumers of Legal Services. *Group Legal Service Plans: Organization, Operation, and Management.* New York: Law & Business, 1981.

Schwartz, Murry L. "Foreword: Group Legal Services in Perspective." *University of California Los Angeles Law Review* 12 (1965):279-305.

Smith, Chesterfield H. "A Mandatory *Pro Bono* Service Standard—Its Time Has Come." *University of Miami Law Review* 35 (1981):727-737.

Staton, Robert H. "Access to Legal Servies Through Advertising and Specialization." *Indiana Law Journal* 53 (1977-1978):247-276.

Simpson, Frank. "Group Legal Services: The Case For Caution." *University of California Los Angeles Law Review* 12 (1965):327-340.

Stewart, Potter. "Professional Ethics for the Business Lawyer-Morals of the Market Place." *Business Lawyer* 31:1 (1975):463-468.

Waid, B. J. "Ethical Problems of the Class Action Practitioner: Continued Neglect by the Drafters of the Proposed Model Rules of Professional Conduct." *Loyola Law Review* 27 (1981):1047-1078,

Weckstein, Donald T. "Limitations on the Right to Counsel: The Unauthorized Practice of Law." *Utah Law Review* 1978 (1978):649-680.

Zander, Michael. "How to Explain the Unmet Need for Legal Services?" *American Bar Association Journal* 64 (November 1978):1676-1679.

PART SEVEN: THE PHILOSOPHY OF LAW

Albrecht, Adalbert. trans. *Philosophy of Law* by Josef Kohler. New York: Augustus M. Kelley, 1969.

Bingham, Joseph Walter, et al. *My Philosophy of Law: Credos of Sixteen American Scholars.* Boston, Mass.: Boston Law Book, 1941.

Bishin, William R. and C. D. Stone. *Law, Language and Ethics.* Mineola, N.Y.: Foundation Press, 1972.

Burns, Jeremy H., gen. ed. *The Collected Works of Jeremy Bentham.* London: Athline Press, 1970.

Cairns, Huntington. *Legal Philosophy from Plato to Hegel.* Baltimore: John Hopkins Press, 1949.

Davis, Philip E., ed. *Moral Duty and Legal Responsibility: A Philosophical-Legal Casebook.* Reprint of 1966 edition. New York: Meredith Publishing Co., 1981.

Dworkin, Ronald. *Taking Rights Seriously.* Cambridge, Mass.: Harvard University Press, 1977.

De Gregorio, Cosimo. *Treatise on Ethics at Law.* Boston, Mass.: Meador, 1948.

Feinberg, Joel and Hyman Gross, eds. *Philosophy of Law.* Belmont, Calif.: Wadsworth Publishing Co., 1975.

Friedrich, Carl J. *The Philosophy of Law in Historical Perspective.* 2nd ed. Chicago: University of Chicago Press, 1963.

Fuller, Lon L. *The Morality of Law.* New Haven, Conn.: Yale University Press, 1964.

―――. "Positivism and Fidelity to Law—A Reply to Professor Hart." *Harvard Law Review* 71 (1958):630-672.

Golding, Martin P. *Philosophy of Law.* Englewod Cliffs, N.J.: Prentice-Hall, 1975.

―――. *Legal Reasoning.* New York: Alfred A. Knopf, 1984.

Grey, Thomas. *The Legal Enforcement of Morality.* New York: Random House, 1980.

Hacker, P. M. S. "Definition in Jurisprudence." *Philadelphia Quarterly* 19 (October 1969):343-347.

Harding, Arthur L., ed. *Origins of the Natural Law Tradition.* Dallas: Southern Methodist University, 1954.

Hart, H. L. A. *Concept of Law.* Oxford, Oxford University Press, 1976.

―――. *Essays in Jurisprudence and Philosophy* Oxford: Oxford University Press, 1984.

―――. "Positivism and the Separation of Law and Morals." *Harvard Law Review* 71 (1958):593-629.

Kipnis, Kenneth, *Philosophical Issues in Law: Cases and Materials.* Englewood Cliffs, N.J.: Prentice Hall, 1977.

King, J. Charles and James A. McGilvray, eds. *Political and Social Philosophy.* New York: McGraw Hill, 1973.

Leff, Arthur Allen. "Unspeakable Ethics, Unnatural Law." *Duke Law Journal* 1979 (1979):1229-1249.

Martin, Michael. "Roscoe Pound's Philosophy of Law." Archives of the Philosophy of Law and Social Philosophy 51 (1965):37-55.

Morawetz, Thomas A. *The Philosophy of Law: An Introduction.* New York: Macmillan, 1980.

Morris, Clarence, ed. *The Great Legal Philosophers.* Philadelphia: University of Pennsylvania Press, 1959.

Richards, David A. J. *The Moral Criticism of Law.* Encino, Calif.: Dickinson Publishing, 1977.

Sawer, Geoffrey. *Law in Society.* Oxford: Clarendon Press, 1965.

Sayre, Paul. *Philosophy of Law.* Iowa City: State University of Iowa, 1954.

Stumpf, Samuel Enoch. *Morality and the Law.* Nashville, Tenn.: Vanderbilt University Press, 1966.

Summers, Robert S. ed. *Essays in Legal Philosophy.* Berkeley: University of California Press, 1968.

———. ed. *More Essays in Legal Philosophy: General Assessments of Legal Philosophies.* Berkeley: University of California Press, 1971.

Unger, Roberto M. *Law in Modern Society.* New York: Free Press, 1977.

Wasserstrom, Richard A. *The Judicial Decision.* Stanford, Calif.: Stanford University Press, 1961.

Weinreb, Lloyd L. "Law as Order." *Harvard Law Review* 95 (1978):909-959.

PART EIGHT: BIBLIOGRAPHIC MATERIALS

Abel, Richard I. "The Sociology of American Lawyers: A Bibliographic Guide." *Law and Policy Quarterly* 2:3 (July 1980):335-392.

Arnesen, Nancy., ed. *Plea Negotiation: A Selected Bibliography.* Washington, D.C.: U.S. Government Printing Office, May, 1980.

Auerbach, Jerold S. *Unequal Justice: Lawyers and Social Change in Modern America.* New York: Oxford University Press, 1976, pp. 368-380.

Bayles, Michael D. *Professional Ethics.* Belmont, Calif.: Wadsworth Publishing Co., 1981, pp. 152-156.

Blumberg, Abraham S., ed. *The Scales of Justice,* Newark, N.J.: Transaction Books, 1970, pp. 177-188.

Bowie, Norman E. and Frederick A. Elliston, eds. *Ethics: Public Policy and Criminal Justice.* Cambridge. Mass.: Oelgeschlager, Gunn and Hain, Inc., 1982, pp. 472-475.

Bowman, James S., Frederick A. Elliston, and Paula Lockhart. *Professional Dissent: An Annotated Bibliography.* New York: Garland Publishing Co., 1983.

Cain, A. A., J. Fisher, N. Arneson, and T. Schrinel. *Plea Negotiation—A Selected Bibliography.* Rockville, Md.: National Criminal Justice Reference Service, 1980, 109 pages.

Elliston, Frederick A. and Jane van Schaick. *Legal Ethics: An Annotated Bibliography and Resource Guide.* Littleton, Colo.: Fred B. Rothman and Co., 1984.

Fuchs, A. E. *Ethics and the Law: Final Narrative Report,* College of William and Mary, Department of Philosophy. Williamsburg, Va: Grant EN-31843 78-0864.

Gorovitz, Samuel and Bruce Miller. *Professional Responsibility in the Law.* A Curriculum Report from the Institute on Law and Ethics. Williamstown, Mass.: Council for Philosophical Studies, Summer 1977, 42-46.

Kelly, Michael J. *Legal Ethics and Legal Education.* Hastings-on-theHudson, N.Y.: The Institute of Society, Ethics and Life Sciences, 1980, pp. 55-69.

Lefcourt, Robert, ed. *Law Against the People.* New York: Random House, 1971, pp. 348-371.

Klein, Fannie J. *National Conference on the Judiciary: An Annotated Bibliography.* New York: New York University Institute of Judicial Administration, 1971.

Maru, Olavi. *Research on the Legal Profession: A Review of Work Done.* Chicago: American Bar Foundation, 1985.

Mathews, Robert E. *Problems Illustrative of the Responsibilities of Members of the Legal Profession.* 2nd rev. ed. New York: Council For Legal Education and Professional Responsibility, 1968, pp. xii-xiv.

Mellinkoff, David. *The Conscience of a Lawyer.* St. Paul, Minn.: West Publishing Co., 1977, pp. 275-293.

Van Schaick, Jane and Katherine M. Sampson. *Selected Literature on Judicial Conduct and Disability: An Annotated Bibliography.* Chicago: American Judicature Society, 1983.

Wasserstrom, Richard A. *The Judicial Decision.* Stanford University Press, 1961, pp. 191-194.

Weckstein, Donald T., ed. *Education in the Professional Responsibilities of the Lawyer.* The Proceedings of the National Conference, Boulder, Colo.: University of Colorado, June 10-13 1968, pp. 359-401.

Zemans, Frances K. and Victor G. Rosenblum. *The Making of a Public Profession.* Chicago: American Bar Foundation, 1981, pp. 235-247.

About the Editors

MICHAEL DAVIS received his Ph.D. in philosophy from the University of Michigan (1972) and thereafter taught at Case Western Reserve University, Illinois State University, and the University of Illinois at Chicago (formerly "Chicago Circle"). He is now Senior Research Associate at the Center for the Study of Ethics in the Professions, Illinois Institute of Technology. He has published more than two dozen articles on topics in philosophy of law, political philosophy, and ethics; prepared (with Paula Wells and Hardy Jones) a teaching module on conflict of interest in engineering; and taught legal ethics both to senior law students (at Case Western Reserve University) and to advanced undergraduates (at Illinois State University). He held a research fellowship from the National Endowment for the Humanities during the 1984-1985 academic year.

FREDERICK A. ELLISTON received his Ph.D. in philosophy from the University of Toronto (1974). He has held positions at York University (Toronto), Union College, State University of New York at Albany, Illinois Institute of Technology, and is currently teaching at the University of Hawaii at Manoa. He has edited four books on phenomenology (*Husserl: Expositions and Appraisals* [1977], *Husserl: Shorter Works* [1981]) and existentialism (*Sartre* [1980] and *Heidegger's Existential Analytic* [1978]). His work in applied philosophy and professional ethics covers sex (*Philosophy and Sex* [1975, 1984]), crime (*Ethics, Public Policy and Criminal Justice* [1982], women (*Feminism and Philosophy* [1977]), and whistleblowing (*Professional Dissent* [1983], *Whistleblowing,* and *Whistleblowing Research* [1984]) as well as medicine (*Humanities, Health Care and the Elderly* [1984]), law (*Legal Ethics* [1984]), and the police (*Moral Issues in Police Work* [1985] and *Teaching Police Ethics* [1985]). His current research deals with the professional responsibilities of teachers and governmental officials.

Notes on the Contributors

MICHAEL D. BAYLES, Ph.D., is Professor in the Center for Applied Philosophy and Ethics in the Professions, and Senior Research Associate in the Center for Studies in Criminology and Law, both at the University of Florida. He is the author of four books, editor or coeditor of five others, and the author of over sixty articles. Among his publications are *Reproductive Ethics* (1984); *Justice, Rights, and Tort Law* (1983); and *Professional Ethics* (1981). He is also Co-Managing Editor of the Law and Philosophy Library (D. Reidel).

EDMUND F. BYRNE, J.D., Ph.D., is Professor and Chair of the Department of Philosophy, Indiana University-Purdue University at Indianapolis. Since writing *Probability and Opinion* in 1968 and *Human Being and Being Human* in 1969, Dr. Byrne has been focusing on public policy issues concerning the impact of technology on society. He is currently writing a book on technology and work. His articles have appeared in such journals as *Philosophy and Technology* and the *Journal of Business Ethics*.

MONROE H. FREEDMAN, LL.B. (1954), LL.M. (1956), is Professor of Law at Hofstra University School of Law and has served as Chairman of three professional committees on lawyers' ethics, including The Legal Ethics Committee of the District of Columbia Bar. His publications include: *Lawyer's Ethics in an Adversary System* (1975, for which he received the ABA Gavel Award Certificate of Merit in 1976) and "Personal Responsibility in a Professional System," *Catholic University Law Review* (1978).

CHARLES FRIED, J.D., is Solicitor General of the United States and Carter Professor of Jurisprudence at the Harvard Law School. He is the author of *Contract as Promise: A Theory of Contractual Obligation* (1981), *Right and Wrong* (1978), *Medical Experimentation: Personal Integrity and Social Policy* (1974), and *An Anatomy of Values* (1970).

LON L. FULLER (1902-1978), J.D., until his retirement in 1972, was for many years Carter Professor of General Jurisprudence at the Harvard Law School. He authored six books including: *Legal Fictions* (1967), *The Morality of Law* (1962), *Basic Contract Law* (1947), and *The Law in Quest for Itself* (1940). Fuller also authored more than fifty articles. During the early 1940s, he practiced law in the prominent firm of Ropes, Gray, Best, Coolidge, and Rugg. Fuller is perhaps the most important American legal theorist of the period between 1945 and the 1970s.

GEOFFREY C. HAZARD, JR., LL.B., (1954), is Nathan Baker Professor of Law at Yale University Law School, where he also serves as Director of the American Law Institute. Hazard served as executive director of the American Bar Foundation (1964-1970) and as reporter for the American Bar Association's Special Commission on Evaluation of Professional Standards (1978-1983). His publications include: *The Law of Lawyering: A Handbook on the Model Rules of Professional Conduct* (1985, with William Hodes), *Civil Procedure* (3d ed. 1985, with Flemming James, Jr.), *Managing Complex Litigation: A Practical Guide to the Use of Special Masters* (1983, with Wayne Brazil and Paul Rice), *Pleading & Procedure, State and Federal* (5th ed. 1983, with D. W. Louisell and Colin Tait), and *Ethics in the Practice of Law* (1978).

KENNETH KIPNIS, Ph.D., is Associate Professor of Philosophy at the University of Hawaii at Manoa. He is the author of *Legal Ethics* (1986); *Philosophical Issues in Law: Cases and Materials* (1977); and the editor of three volumes on legal, political and social philosophy.

BRUCE M. LANDESMAN, Ph.D., is Associate Professor of Philosophy at the University of Utah. His major interests are political philosophy and professional ethics. He has published several papers in these areas, including "Egalitarianism," *Canadian Journal of Philosophy* (1983).

NORMAN LEFSTEIN, LL.B. (1961), LL.M. (1964), is Professor of Law at the University of North Carolina School of Law. His work appears in such journals as *North Carolina Law Review, Criminal Law Review, Temple Law Quarterly, Loyola of Los Angeles Law Review, New York University Review of Law and Social Change,* and *Criminal Justice.* He is the author of *Criminal Defense Services for the Poor: Methods and Programs for Providing Legal Representation and the Need for Adequate Financing* (1982).

DAVID R. PAPKE, J.D. (1973), Ph.D. (1984), is Assistant Professor of Law and American Studies at the Indiana University School of Law at Indianapolis. His articles have appeared in *Legal Studies Forum* and the *American Bar Foundation Research Journal.* Papke is the author of *Framing the Criminal: Crime, Cultural Work and Loss of Critical Perspective, 1830-1900* (1986). His scholarly interests include American legal history, the role of law in American literature and culture, and assorted law school doctrinal areas (Constitutional Law, Local Government Law, and Debtor-Creditor Relations).

GERALD J. POSTEMA, Ph.D., is Associate Professor of Philosophy at the University of North Carolina at Chapel Hill. His publications include: *Bentham and the Common Law Tradition* (1986); "The Normativity of Law," in *Issues in Contemporary Legal Philosophy: The Influence of H. L. A. Hart,* edited by Ruth Gavison (1986); "Self-Image, Integrity, and Professional Responsibility," in *The Good Lawyer,* edited by David Luban (1983); and "Coordination and Convention at the Foundations of Law," *Journal of Legal Studies* (1982).

STEVEN B. ROSENFELD, LL.B. (1967), is a partner in the law firm of Paul, Weiss, Rifkind, Wharton & Garrison in New York City. He is Vice President and Director of the Legal Aid Society and Chair of the Council on Criminal Justice of the Association of the Bar of the City of New York. The views expressed in Mr. Rosenfeld's article printed in this volume are solely his own.

LINDA J. SILBERMAN, J.D. (1968), is Professor of Law at New York University. She is author of *Non-Attorney Justice in the United States* (1979) and *Family Law: Cases and Materials* (1977, with Foster and Freed).

WILLIAM H. SIMON, J.D. (1969), is Professor of Law at Stanford University School of Law. He is the author of such recent articles as "Rights and Redistribution of the Welfare System," *Stanford Law Review* (1986); "The Invention of and Reinvention of Welfare Rights," *Maryland Law Review* (1985); "Babbitt v. Brandeis: The Decline of the Professional Ideal," *Stanford Law Review* (1985); and "Legal Informality and Redistributive Politics," *Clearinghouse Review* (1985).

JANE VAN SCHAICK, MBA, is on the faculty of Hawaii Pacific College and is the Executive Director of the Honolulu chapter of the Alzheimer's Disease and Related Disorders Association. She has coauthored four books, three with Frederick A. Elliston: *Legal Ethics: An Annotated Bibliography and Resource Guide* (1984), *Whistleblowing* (1984), and *Whistleblowing Research* (1984); and *Selected Literature on Judicial Conduct and Disability* (1983, with K. M. Sampsom). She has conducted community-based workshops in bioethics.

RICHARD WASSERSTROM, Ph.D. LL.B., (1960), is Professor and Chairman of the Philosophy Board of the University of California, Santa Cruz. He holds an honorary LL.D. from Amherst College, and has been a Woodrow Wilson Fellow (1957-1958), a University of Michigan Fellow (1958-1959), a Guggenheim Fellow (1970-1971), and a Visiting Fellow at All Souls College in Oxford (1970-1971). He has published over two dozen articles on philosophical and legal subjects and his books include: *Philosophy and Social Issues: Five Studies* (1980), *Today's Moral Problems* (1975, 1979), *Morality and the Law* (1971, edited), *War and Morality* (1970, edited), and *The Judicial Decision* (1961).

Additional contributors include DARLENE CATHCART, F. RAYMOND MARKS, and JOHN D. RANDALL, for whom current biographical information was not available.